AFRICAN DOMINION

African Dominion

A NEW HISTORY OF EMPIRE IN EARLY AND MEDIEVAL WEST AFRICA

Michael A. Gomez

PRINCETON UNIVERSITY PRESS
PRINCETON & OXFORD

Published by Princeton University Press,
41 William Street, Princeton, New Jersey 08540

In the United Kingdom: Princeton University Press,
6 Oxford Street, Woodstock, Oxfordshire OX20 1TR

press.princeton.edu

Cover photo: Great Mud Mosque, Djenné, Mali. Courtesy of Ruud Zwart

First paperback printing, 2019

Paperback ISBN 9780691196824

The Library of Congress has cataloged the cloth edition as follows:

Names: Gomez, Michael A., 1955- author.
Title: African dominion : a new history of empire in early and medieval West Africa / Michael A. Gomez.
Description: Princeton : Princeton University Press, 2017. | Includes bibliographical references and index.
Identifiers: LCCN 2017029692 | ISBN 9780691177427 (hardcover : alk. paper)
Subjects: LCSH: Islam—Africa, West—History. | Slavery—Africa, West—History. | Africa, West—History—To 1884.
Classification: LCC DT476 .G66 2017 | DDC 966.02—dc23 LC record available at https://lccn.loc.gov/2017029692

British Library Cataloging-in-Publication Data is available

This book has been composed in Miller

Printed on acid-free paper. ∞

Printed in the United States of America

CONTENTS

PREFACE

WHAT FOLLOWS FULFILLS A QUEST that began at the University of Chicago, where, as an undergraduate transfer from Amherst College, I enrolled in the Islamic Civilization sequence and wrote a paper on Islam in early West Africa. Graded a "C-" by a graduate assistant who found the very concept "dubious," the paper was for reasons unknown to me subsequently reviewed by the course professor, John E. Woods, who, in changing the grade to an "A-," counseled me that, if serious, I would need to learn Arabic. It was a fateful intervention.

Immersed in other projects since graduate study, I only returned to focus on this subject around 2007, traveling to Mali to canvass and explore the manuscript collections in Timbuktu and Jenne. The early 2012 outbreak of war in northern Mali proved disruptive, but I have proceeded with materials already in hand that, as will be demonstrated, have not been fully exploited. It was also my finding that the vast majority of manuscript materials in Mali concern the eighteenth century and thereafter, but there are collections I have yet to see, and more may be uncovered. I therefore look forward to the opportunity to revise my findings in light of new documentation. I extend heartfelt thanks to all who assisted and extended their hospitality to me, especially Abdel Kader Haïdara, director of the Mama Haïdara Library in Timbuktu.

What is before the reader is only sixty percent of its original submission (as a two-volume work), addressing the most critical areas of inquiry. In underscoring the actors and issues themselves, my approach is not at all meant to slight the secondary scholarship; my debt to many will be obvious, especially the pioneering efforts of the late John Hunwick who, with Ralph Austen and Fred Donner, were my advisors, many moons ago. I would also mention the work and mentorship of Boubacar Barry and Lansiné Kaba—principal sources of encouragement over the years.

Parts 1 and 2 of the book cover the period through medieval Mali, and given the universal acceptance of the *Corpus of Early Arabic Sources for West African History* by Nehemia Levtzion and J.F.P. Hopkins, I adopt their rendering and forego haggling over minor disagreements in translation. I reference Joseph M. Cuoq's *Recueil des sources arabes concernant l'Afrique occidentale du XIIIe au XVIe siècle (Bilad al-Sudan)* where it provides additional insight, or where appears a pertinent source not included in Levtzion and Hopkins. Finally, I follow Franz Rosenthal's classic translation of Ibn Khaldūn's *Muqaddimah*. I provide my own translations in parts 3 and 4 of the book; some materials are not available in European languages, while in those for which such translations exist, nuances in the Arabic are important to underscore, with divergences substantive on occasion. I dispense with diacriticals for place names, retaining them in Arabic designations for either individuals or groups.

Finally, I employ a dual dating system in which the Islamic or Hijri date appears first, followed by the Gregorian equivalent, as the former better corresponds to how historical actors actually understood time. In using the terms "early" (third century CE to the seventh/thirteenth) and "medieval" (seventh/thirteenth to the end of the tenth/sixteenth century), I do not mean to suggest West African history conforms to European or Asian periodizations (though there is some correspondence). Rather, "early" and "medieval" effectively represent watershed developments in the conjoined region itself.

AFRICAN DOMINION

PROLOGUE

MALI'S *MANSĀ* SULAYMĀN could hardly have anticipated the consequences. The mid-eighth/fourteenth-century Muslim ruler of what may have been the most extensive realm Africa has ever known had deposed and imprisoned his chief wife Qāsā, but developments following her release offer critical vistas into the unfolding of Malian society. Supported by a faction of royal women, Qāsā openly defied Sulaymān, daily riding before an entourage of servants to the very gates of the Malian council. Inquiry would uncover intrigue and the early stages of insurgency, with Qāsā mobilizing disaffected royals while guaranteeing the army's support. Found in neither oral traditions nor external records, the episode is known only because Ibn Baṭṭūṭa happened to be in Mali at the time. A direct threat to Sulaymān's authority, Qāsā's rebellion was apparently put down, her ultimate fate unknown. Tantalizingly, Ibn Khaldūn records that with Sulaymān's death in 761/1360, he was succeeded by a son . . . one Qāsā.

More than tangential, Qāsā's rebellion is central to the history of early and medieval West Africa. The rise of Islam, the relationship of women to political power, the growth and influence of the domestically enslaved, and the invention and evolution of empire were all unfolding. In contrast to notions of an early Africa timeless and unchanging in its social and cultural categories and conventions, here was a western Savannah and Sahel that from the third/ninth through the tenth/sixteenth centuries witnessed *political innovation* as well as the evolution of such mutually constitutive categories as *race, slavery, ethnicity, caste*, and *gendered notions of power*. By the period's end, these categories assume significations not unlike their more contemporary connotations.

As indigenous responses to Islam and the trans-Saharan slave trade, these developments serve not only as a corrective to a popularized African past, but also as commentary on interpretations of modernity concerned with the transformation of global markets. Specifically, arguments that the transatlantic slave trade resulted in novel productive capacities (including industrialization) and labor relations, in turn generating new hierarchies of class, race, and gender, are of particular relevance. Here is an opportunity to observe the impact of parallel, anterior processes.

In pursuit of this anterior history, the present study mirrors as it uncovers its unfolding, providing substantive analyses where the evidence is sustaining. As such, successive chapters feature an approach to *race* informed by multiple rather than singular registers, with local, cultural signification in dialogue with translocal, discursive ideas. *Caste*—those endogamous groups with differentiated social and productive roles—is treated as processual and unsettled well into the medieval period, at which point begins a discussion of *empire* as well as *gendered notions of power*, threading throughout until *empire* forms the focus. *Ethnicity* also takes concrete shape, assuming juridical status in the effort to determine enslavement eligibility, and is commensurate with *slavery*'s expansion under imperial Songhay, for which an equation of reciprocating slaveholder-enslaved interests substitutes for theorizations of proprietary, kinship, and social death.

All of these transformations were engaged with the apparatus of the state and its progression from the city-state to the empire. The transition consistently featured minimalist notions of governance replicated by successive dynasties, providing a continuity of structure as a mechanism of legitimization. Replication had its limits, however, and would ultimately prove inadequate in addressing unforeseen challenges.

To be sure, many aspects of the West African past have little to do with empire, as the region is diverse and complex, with histories often escaping unifying narratives. But as variability is not the focus here, no apology is offered. The small state and the village each have a place at the table, as does empire.

The history of the early and medieval Savannah and Sahel was of a piece with kings and queens and rulers of the earth consolidating lands and resources. Empires expanded and contracted in response to the vagaries of location, in tandem with combinations of creed and greed. The Chinese had long been in imperial formation, transitioning from the Yuan to the Ming dynasties in the eighth/fourteenth century, while Europe was nearing the end of internal transformations that would have global consequences. Bridging the polarities of "Old" and "New" Worlds were the Mongols of the sixth/twelfth and seventh/thirteenth centuries (with the Golden Horde continuing to the tenth/sixteenth), part of whose vast expansion (and fracturing) included integration into states and societies all responding, one way or another, to the call of Islam. Ethnically, racially, and culturally myriad, a Muslim world whose political unity had long ended stretched from Iberia to China to Indonesia. Muslim innovation, largely responsible for linking European and Asian lands and all points in between, served as the conduit through which European medieval thought reconnected with that of ancient predecessors, and as the technological basis for Europe's "discovery" of Mesoamerican Aztecs and Andean Incas. The eighth/fourteenth century was therefore on the cusp of developments so far-reaching that within a few hundred years the collective human condition would be dramatically (and perchance irrevocably) altered.

It was precisely at this moment that a handsome, precocious, ambitious young ruler pondered the night sky in search of answers. *Mansā* Mūsā, Sulaymān's predecessor, had decisions to make. At the head of Mali's sprawling empire, he was aware of developments elsewhere. He knew of Berber success in engineering a kingdom that, beginning with the late fifth/eleventh century's religious militancy of the Almoravids, reached from the fringes of West Africa through North Africa into Europe. He may have understood that feats alleged to have been accomplished by the seventh/thirteenth-century founder of the Malian empire, Sunjata, were partially informed by political upheaval to the northwest (al-Maghrib), reconfiguring commerce and travel through the Sahara. As trade with the northeast was also of considerable vintage, Mūsā would have known that the formerly servile Mamluks, just decades following Sunjata's ascension, had wrested control of Egypt (Miṣr) from the Ayyubids (who ascended under Ṣalāḥ al-Dīn, or Saladin, in 569/1174), occupying the center of the Muslim world with the fall of Baghdad to the Mongols in 655/1258.

Whether in response to these developments, or as an expression of aspirations largely internal, Mali attempted to connect with the outside world, to touch that world directly, without the mediation of Saharan middlemen. Mali was itself in an expansive, transcontinental frame of mind.

The very claim that toward the beginning of the eighth/fourteenth century *Mansā* Muḥammad b. Qū, grandson or great-grandson of Sunjata, prepared the launch of hundreds of vessels into the Atlantic world, inaugurating West Africa's own large-scale seafaring venture into the deep, is indicative of the prevailing mood. The labor, material, and organization for the expedition, if it indeed took place, would have been enormous, suggesting a level of ambition on a breathtaking scale, an attempt to reverse patterns of transregional engagement dominant since the Garamantes of Graeco-Roman antiquity, reinforced and intensified by their descendants, the Berber and Tuareg. Organized and financed for the most part in North Africa, such trans-Saharan commerce resulted in accruing transregional expertise and advantage. Even if entirely mythical, the account of Muḥammad b. Qū 's gambit reflects recognition of Mali's landlocked status, the unknown western sea beckoning resolution. Rather than accounts of new treasure and trading prospects, however, there returned reports of failure at sea and massive loss of life, followed by the disappearance of Muḥammad b. Qū himself who, commanding a second fleet, is never heard from again.

The source attesting to Muḥammad b. Qū 's Atlantic project was none other than *Mansā* Mūsā, underscoring that its very "imagining" is far more critical to the question of the *mansā*'s state of mind than its verifiability; that he would tell such a story more than suggests a desire to transfigure his relationship to the wider world. Whatever his actual ambition, he would settle upon a course that had no parallel elsewhere, though in scope and scale hardly less ambitious than his predecessor's purported western watery trajectory (and indeed quite consistent with it). For within twelve years of his coming to power, *Mansā* Mūsā would bring together the considerable resources of the realm to make an unprecedented Pilgrimage to Egypt and Arabia, the known fonts of political and spiritual power, where he would make his case for the recognition of Mali as a peer. Traveling with a retinue of thousands across some 2,700 miles, its effect was nothing less than scintillating, leaving an impression in Europe as well as Egypt. If only brilliant theater, the voyage nonetheless became iconic, emblematic of West Africa's wealth and potential. In bringing Mali to the world, the *mansā* succeeded in elevating its global stature while attracting both greater commercial attention and cultural investment. It is Mali's and, by extension, West Africa's most illustrious moment.

In undertaking such an extraordinary venture, neither *Mansā* Mūsā's precise objectives nor his plans to achieve them are transparent. Maybe he simply wanted to elevate Mali's profile on the world stage, leveraging influence relative to North Africa by effecting closer relations with the central Islamic lands. Or, he may have been in search of foreign assistance to maximize Mali's potential, his over-the-top display of wealth designed to persuade needed expertise to relocate to West Africa. It is even conceivable that, reaching the limits of the desert to the north and the forest and savannah to the south, he envisioned a transregional empire by which he could project power into North Africa itself.

For all of the splendor and sizzle of one of the world's most famous pilgrimages, the fundamental dynamics of transregional commercial relations would not change: financing and routes outside of West Africa remained under the control of trading partners, and this would only intensify over the next several centuries, at the end of which West Africa (and the rest of the continent) would be subject to nations steeped in the knowledge of seafaring.

Furthermore, *Mansā* Mūsā's Pilgrimage, in relation to subsequent events, may have taken place from twenty-five to 125 years too soon. He would selectively borrow what he observed, initiating a series of cultural projects in Mali modeled after central Islamic features. However, as weaponry would later prove rather decisive in West Africa's history, in that moment there were no profound differences between the Mamluks and the Malians, as both relied on archery, cavalry, and lances (though tactics differed). Gunpowder weapons, a technological revolution, had yet to fully develop. As *Mansā* Mūsā possessed the resources to pay for such technology, their adoption might have better prepared the region for the challenges to come.

Songhay's *Askia* al-ḥājj Muḥammad of Songhay would subsequently appropriate Mūsā's vision of West Africa as an international peer among other great powers. But if he and his successors were aware of gunpowder weapons, there is no evidence they sought to acquire them. This is a puzzle, as firearms had been adopted by Sahelian neighbors farther east in Kanem-Bornu, their advantage over conventional implements perhaps far from apparent in the west.

The ninth/fifteenth-century shift in the political center of gravity from Mali to Songhay would usher in a new era of international relations, its dynamics characterized by intellectual vibrancy as well as social transformation. Imperial Songhay represents a height of West African cultural efflorescence and political imagination, its success characterized by novel policies of political integration. Its pursuit of erudition is unprecedented in West Africa's history, underscoring much that is distinctive about the realm. With its elite's avid embrace of Islam, Songhay became better integrated into the Muslim world, but it would not be afforded sufficient time to realize further advances.

What follows is both an account and a critique of West African empire and attendant social and cultural transformations, a tale of immense potential undermined by regrettable decisions and the inflexibility of critical conventions. It is an analysis for which the aperture is widened to include multiple social registers, representing a history from both above and below, exploiting sources that ostensibly reflect the interests of the former, but which actually expose intimacies between polarities of advantage and disadvantage, revealing interdependencies of power and debility.

If Songhay represents the height of medieval West African statecraft, it was preceded by experimentation in imperial Mali, from which it borrowed heavily. Polity in the early West African Savannah and Sahel often rested in the city-state, in the singular urban collection of communities usually connected to inter/intraregional commerce. This was certainly true of early Gao and Ghana (though the latter may have extended power over satellite settlements and outposts). In contrast, the seventh/thirteenth-century establishment of Mali in the full Savannah saw a projection of authority from the center to outlying areas, in many but not all instances culturally aligned with that center, having previously boasted a political independence of longue durée. A critical threshold was crossed when such states no longer simply paid tribute to the center, but assumed its political identity and embraced a subordinate position within an emerging superstructure. The evolving center would regulate not only relations with external powers, but also relations between what were now provinces, so that the rise of imperialism was an ordered process of horizontal linkages between distinct communities and vertical alignments among elites. Songhay would go beyond its predecessor in incorporating disparate and culturally dissimilar ethnic groups not only into the polity, but into the very fabric of the ruling family itself, knitting the empire together in a conscious strategy of political pluralism.

Directly connected to empire's formulation in West Africa was the emergence of both Islam and domestic slavery, and it is impossible to understand imperial Mali and Songhay without appreciating the close if not inextricable relationship between these two forces. As Islam and empire became tightly intertwined, slavery became increasingly insinuated within both. In turn, religion and labor were highly gendered, and in ways deeply woven into the fabric of society and its collective consciousness.

Songhay's rise and ensuing control of the middle Niger valley help to explain Mali's decline, while epidemics and civil war precipitated exigency in Songhay, contributing to its ultimate demise. But if Songhay, with all of its achievements, yet fell short of its full potential, domestic slavery's expansion may have been an important factor, as it destabilized subject societies and redirected their potential. Widespread latifundia and large armies are impressive, but their dependency on servile labor helped establish a pattern of exploitation that would only metastasize over time.

Journeying into such a storied and multifaceted past is necessarily undertaken through thoroughfares of human memory, now recorded on parchment, then orally stylized. Rather than their consideration in discrete and disaggregated form, the current study argues they are best understood when placed in mutual conversation, together with archaeological and epigraphic evidence where possible—in effect, a new archive. Such an approach best yields results when immersed in the dynamics of context, in which circumstances of production are extensively engaged. Great attention is therefore given to the personal, familial, cultural, and political dimensions of recalling the past.

What can be stated at this early juncture is that critical components of collective testimony—the written and oral documentation—were conceptually innovative and wholly unprecedented for period and place, representing either the creation or adoption of memorative technologies in response to novel developments. Oral and written tableaux center very different principals to tell stories for entirely different audiences, and for radically different purposes. Their conjunctive examination reveals a process as integral to the accounts as the characters and plots they feature. The result is a wholly new interpretation of West Africa's early and medieval history, facilitating its relocation from the periphery to the center of world history.

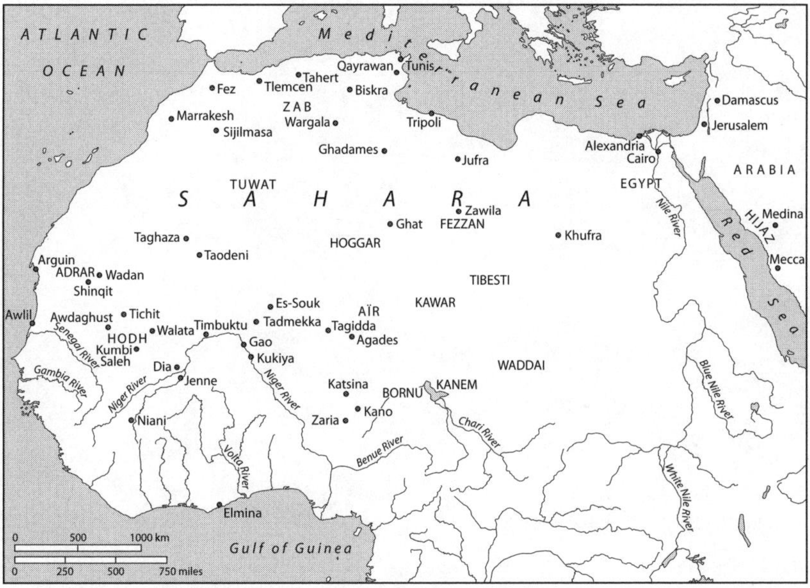

Map 1: West and North Africa, Tenth to the Sixteenth Centuries

PART I

Early Sahel and Savannah

CHAPTER ONE

The Middle Niger in Pre-Antiquity and Global Context

WORLD HISTORY PLAYS A CRITICAL ROLE within the larger discipline, providing a unitary lens, a panoptic, through which the drama that constitutes the human experience can be observed at once. The artistic achievements, the scientific breakthroughs, the political innovations, and the revelatory imagination are all on display, with an emphasis on the spectacular, the monumental. Creativity, urbanity, social and commercial intercourse, productive capacities, and the dynamics by which relations of power change or remain unaltered often form the threads by which the narrative coheres, the indices held to be common to cultures upon whom fortune smiled. By inference it follows that areas of the world consistently overlooked by scholars play no significant role in the unfolding of world history. That segments of the human family have, at no time in their existence, ever been worthy of mention, let alone included in sustained study and investigation, is a claim made indirectly, faintly whispered, with implications for the past and present.

It is therefore sobering that world history scholarship (in English) has remained fairly consistent, even formulaic, over many years. Though there is certainly organizational variation, it is often the approach to begin with ancient civilizations and to proceed in linear and diachronic fashion. Sumer, Asia Minor, and Mesopotamia are initially discussed, followed by Pharaonic Egypt. The focus then swings to the dawn of Harappan culture in the Indus valley and Vedic civilization in India in the third and second millennia BCE, after which follows a succession of Chinese dynasties from the second millennium BCE Shang all the way to the Tang of the eighth through tenth centuries CE. Graeco-Roman civilization is a staple, to which are added the rise of Islam in the seventh century CE, the Mayans of Central America from the fourth to the tenth century, and the Incas of the eleventh through the sixteenth century. The collective story then commonly features the transformation of Europe from its medieval preoccupations to a triumphalist world expansion.[1]

A developing cognate of world history is the study of empire, chiefly distinguished from the former in its preoccupation with more recent history (though with some attention to antecedent periods) that involves sweeping vistas and expansive, transregional landscapes. A "history of empire" approach can go to considerable lengths demonstrating how those under threat of subjugation resist, influence, or otherwise redirect certain consequences, and in ways that subvert if not transform the imperial project, so that imposition is an open-ended process of contestation and negotiation. As such, imperial histories are in instances quite sophisticated in their analyses, but even so, they share world history's apparent disdain for empire as envisioned and engendered by Africans themselves, as none of the texts go beyond a cursory mention of such formations as Mali or Songhay—if they are mentioned at all.[2]

What therefore unites world and imperial histories, at least for the purposes of this study, is their consistent omission, their collective silence on early and medieval Africa, of saying anything of substance about it, with the exception of Egypt, Nubia, and North Africa. West Africa is certainly left out of the narrative of early human endeavor, and only tends to be mentioned, with brevity, in conjunction with European imperialism. This sort of treatment can be observed in a leading tome of more than 550 pages, out of which the discussion of sub-Saharan Africa, in a chapter entitled "Changes in the Barbarian World, 1700–500 BC," is exemplary:

> Sub-Saharan Africa also remained apart from the rest of the world. In all probability, cultivation of edible roots and all other crops made considerable progress in West Africa, while the east coast of the continent was visited at least occasionally by seafarers from civilized ports.[3]

Later in the same volume, slightly less than four pages are devoted to a discussion of sub-Saharan Africa that includes Ghana, Mali, and the spread of Islam. The chapter is called "The Fringes of the Civilized World to 1500" and, according to the author, "rests on nothing more solid than shrewd guesswork."[4] As such, we are not at a significant remove from Hegel.[5] To be sure, world history as well as the imperial annal requires substantial preparation and endeavor, often an impressive, invaluable feat of erudition. It is therefore all the more disappointing that Africa continues to receive such short shrift.

A more promising development may be the rise of big history, resembling world history but extending it by light years, literally, connecting the immediacy of the planet's past with the universe's origins some 13.7 billion years ago. Continental shifts and drifts hundreds of millions of years old, combined with ice ages and other ecological transformations taking place 90,000 to 11,000 years ago, set the stage for the emergence of humans. In particular, big history provides a solar context for the Sahara's unfolding, central to the region's history. But once the discussion reaches Sumer, we are back to a very familiar narrative, and though Africa's consideration is at times informed by more current scholarship, the continent remains a bit player in a much larger drama, its leading roles assigned to others.[6]

Whether world or imperial or big history, none is invested in ongoing research in Africa, where developments have been considerable. Substantial archaeological work has been underway in West Africa for decades, particularly in the middle Niger valley, and should scholars of world and big histories take note, they would need to seriously revise their accounts. For it was during the period of the Shang, Chou, Shin, Han, and Tang dynasties of China, the Vedic period in India, and the Mayans in central America, that another urban-based civilization flourished in West Africa, in the Middle Niger region. From the late first millennium BCE into the beginning of the second millennium CE, a series of communities were nurtured by a floodplain that at its apex covered more than 170,000 square kilometres, comparing favorably with Mesopotamia's maximum range of cultivable land of 51,000 square kilometres, and ancient Egypt's 34,000 square kilometers. Spanning the Iron Age (from the first millennium BCE well into the first millennium CE), the region was dotted with literally hundreds of urban sites characterized by a variety of crafts and productive capacities, constituting a collective center of human organization and activity, deserving its rightful place among world civilizations customarily acclaimed. Indeed, a number of the region's six basins have yet to be adequately excavated, and even more urban settlements await discovery. Given its location, the early Middle Niger is critical to any serious investigation into the region's subsequent history—precisely the present study's major preoccupation. A consideration of what has been uncovered there is consequently both appropriate and necessary, bearing directly upon key issues reverberating well into the medieval period.[7]

To an appreciable extent, the history of civilization in the Middle Niger is a study of the multiple ways in which communities continually adjust to and engage with one of the more "variable and unpredictable" environments in the world.[8] Indeed, the story of the Middle Niger connects directly with the celestial preoccupations of big history in that much of its climatic variability is explained by slight alterations in solar radiation, produced in turn by the intricacies of the sun's cyclical patterns. The sun's behavior, in concert with shifting distributions of the earth's mass, resulted in such drastic changes that tenth millennium BCE conditions supporting teeming aquatic life together with lush flora and fauna, extending from the Middle Niger to what is now the Sahara Desert, had by 5,500 BCE undergone extensive desiccation, only to be followed by a massive dry period around 2,200 BCE, and yet another between 1,800 and 1,000 BCE. A firmament in the land had effectively taken shape, dividing Sahara and Savannah.

Though humans had entered the Middle Niger as early as 7,000 BCE, their first "serious" settlement in the region was not until 3,000 BCE.[9] Still, it was only some 2,700 years later, between 300 BCE and 300 CE, that the Middle Niger experienced a "massive influx" of human populations, corresponding to a time of dramatic decline in precipitation in West Africa as a whole, the so-called Big Dry. Rainfall patterns in the Middle Niger would stabilize from 300 CE to 700 CE, leading to an important theme that would characterize not only the narrative of the Middle Niger, but West Africa and the continent as a whole: namely, repetitive, numerically significant patterns of human migratory activity. In the case of the Middle Niger, perhaps what is most arresting is the transfer of substantial populations from the Sahara into both the southern Sahel (*sāḥil* or "shore") and the floodplain, a movement from very poor soils to those marginally less so.[10] This points to one of the signature features of the region—the perpetual transgression of differentiated landscapes by diverse communities and cultures that is only one of many reasons for conjunctively reconsidering the histories of Sahara, Savannah, and Sahel.

In response to the stresses of meteorological transformations, far beyond the capacity of anyone on earth to comprehend, populations throughout West Africa packed their belongings and sought better conditions. For the Middle Niger, the result was the gradual rise of urban culture and society, a period during which the necessary elements of urban civilization became identifiable from 800 to 400 BCE, followed by the

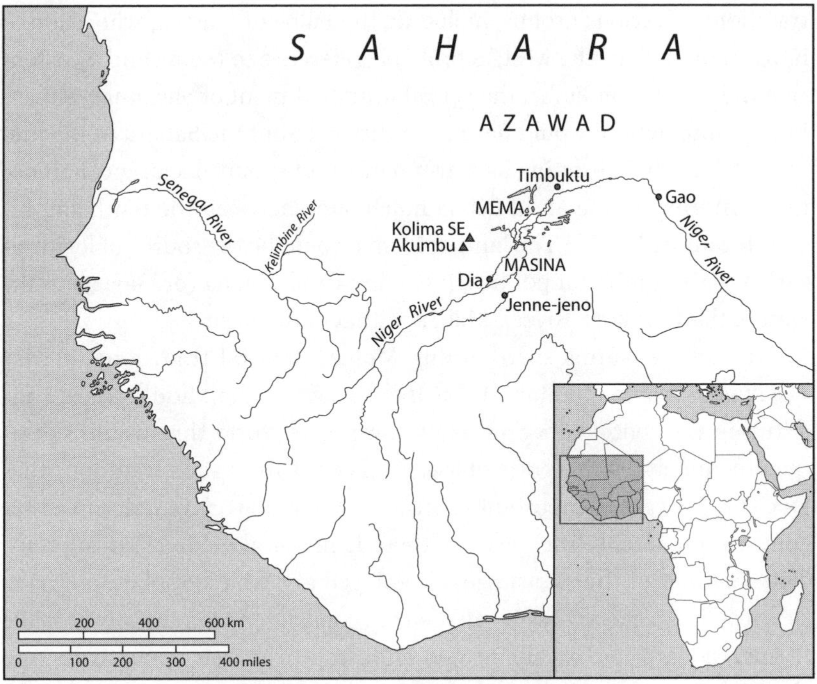

Map 2: The Middle Niger Valley in Pre-Antiquity

emergence of the first cities from 500 BCE to 400 CE. A focus of archaeological studies has been Jenne-jeno (or "original/old Jenne"), founded about 250 BCE, with some attention given to Dia/Diagha of Masina and other sites, with much work remaining to be done.[11]

Jenne-jeno and Dia/Diagha are indispensable to the history of the Middle Niger, but critical to their own development was the anterior province of Mema in the southwestern basin of the Middle Niger, where arose a "vast number and size" of urban sites (including Kolima and Akumbu) during the Iron Age, having been preceded by an "equally impressive network of clustered Late Stone Age hamlets and villages."[12] This earlier history of Mema underscores the theme of significant migratory patterns in the region, linking Savannah and Sahara in an inextricable matrix of associations and interactions, as inhabitants of the Azawad, another of the six Middle Niger basins to the north of Timbuktu, may well have traveled south to Mema with the desiccation of the basin between 4,000 and 3,200 BCE.[13] In concert, Mema's occupation began between 3,800 and 2,200 BCE, antedating the founding of Jenne-jeno by at least two thousand years. In addition to the archeological record, the vital role played by Mema in the ancient history of the region can be heard in the oral traditions of various groups, including the Fulbe of Masina, who claim to have originated in "the west," a probable reference to Mema and by extension the Sahel. The Fulbe, the veritable embodiment of Savannah-Sahara human interaction, would have been driven out of the Sahara in the first millennium BCE, existing as a group or set of groups lacking coherence until entering Mema and Masina much later, between the tenth and fifteenth centuries CE.[14] The land of Mema would be the source of legitimization for a number of polities, including Guidimakha (or Gajaga, to the west of the Karakoro River), Mali, and that of the Susu.

Not unlike claims surrounding Mema, the oral traditions of Dia/Diagha of Masina maintain it was the first city in the Middle Niger, constituting the center of a Soninke or Serrakole world that would subsequently undergo a diasporic phase.[15] It is clear from such traditions that Dia/Diagha was an important town, and although work remains to either confirm or enfeeble such claims, there is material evidence in support. The ceramics of the site suggest it enjoyed a sizable population during the early Iron Age, and when all data are considered, it is entirely possible it emerged as an urban site by 500 BCE, approximately 250 years before the founding of Jenne-jeno. Indeed, the traditions maintain that immigrants from Dia/Diagha founded Jenne-jeno, which if true may provide insight into Dia/Diagha's diminution. Situated astride a commercial axis privileging East-West exchange, Dia/Diagha may have been detrimentally impacted by the emergence of North-South trade between 850 CE and 950, prompting commercial families to relocate to Jenne-jeno.[16]

The pattern of migration from North to South, into and through Mema, is certainly supported by the flow of Saharan ceramics and semi-precious stones into the Sahel, where early urban dwellers also enjoyed the benefits of iron, produced in Jenne-jeno throughout its existence. Both *in situ* smelting (reducing the ore to a bloom) and smithing (refining the bloom and removing the slag) resulted in a product "of exceptionally high quality."[17] The two operations proceeded jointly from 250 BCE to 400 CE in Jenne-jeno, when the more polluting smelting process was relocated to surrounding sites. This was also around the time that copper made its appearance, followed by gold some four hundred years later. Rice (*Oryza glaberrina*) appears to have been the major staple, followed by sorghum and bulrush millet. These crops, together with what was gathered from undomesticated plant sources, would have been stored in pottery in Jenne-jeno, the earliest of which seems to be Saharan (and whose shards yet cover the site of Jenne-jeno as far as the eye can see). Glass beads known only to have been manufactured in Southeast Asia during the Han dynasty are proof that commerce was far from confined to the region, and that so much more awaits discovery.

Though its agricultural productivity was lacking in innovation and organization, remaining largely subsistent, Jenne-jeno nonetheless entered a more mature urban phase from 400 CE to 850, by the end of which the use of copper had developed into the manufacturing of bronze, which in turn was superseded by brass some 200 years later.[18] Copper could have been transported to Jenne-jeno from mines some 350 kilometers away, in what is now Burkina Faso, or from sources as distant as 500 kilometers in what is now Mali and Mauritania. When such importations are considered in conjunction with the presence of natron glass beads, a Roman manufacture issuing from either Egypt or (what becomes) Italy, the emerging picture is one of significant intraregional as well as trans-Saharan trading activity. Indeed, European classical sources have long suggested that commerce between the Mediterranean and the West African Sahel antedates the advent of Islam in the Maghrib, an enterprise controlled by the shadowy Garamantes, an apparent early reference to the so-called Tuareg.[19] But it was with the introduction of the camel into the Maghrib between 100 BCE and 100 CE that regularized trade between North and West Africa became viable. By 800 CE, then, Jenne-jeno had emerged as "a full and heterogeneous agglomeration of craftsmen, herders, farmers, and fisherfolk of different flavors," with a surrounding wall 2 kilometers in circumference.[20] Together with its nearby outposts, Jenne-jeno's population in 800 CE is estimated to have been from 10,000 to 26,000.

Timbuktu, that other major and far better known site of medieval West Africa, had probably assumed an urban status sometime during the first millennium CE, long before local chronicles allow, and the likelihood that it had developed trade relations with entities in the Upper Niger Delta means it was not necessarily dependent on Jenne for its foodstuffs, though such trade does not preclude the same with Jenne (or the Sahara and lands further north).[21] There will be much more to say about Timbuktu.

Constituting another of the region's six basins is the Lakes Region-Niger Bend, the northern cap of the Middle Niger floodplain, in which emerged an urban complex that would come to be associated with the town of Gao, also known by its Tamasheq (spoken language of the Kel Tamasheq, otherwise known as the Tuareg) designation as Kawkaw, along the eastern buckle of the Niger River. The archaeological record suggests the site has been occupied since the Late Stone Age, which means its settled existence antedates Jenne-jeno and Dia/Diagha by fifteen hundred years or more—more or less contemporary with early developments in

Mema, with evidence of secondary processing of copper and pottery fragments, and glass and carnelian beads between 700 and 1100 CE.[22] As the next chapter argues, Gao was critical to the formation of West African civilization and culture from earliest times, as instrumental as ancient Ghana. Indeed, Gao would maintain a more or less commanding presence in the *sāḥil* from the Late Stone Age through the seventeenth century, a remarkable longue durée rivaled only by developments bordering Lake Chad.

By 800 CE, then, there were several urban areas in the Middle Niger engaged in commerce and manufacturing and agricultural activity sufficient to support numerically significant populations. When Jenne-jeno's "satellite sites" are taken into consideration, the whole "urban cluster" increases the population to an estimated fifty thousand.[23] The Gao region was occupied as early as 2000 BCE, while cities such as Jenne-jeno and Dia/Diagha had emerged from the late first millennium BCE to the first millennium CE, by which time a number of sites near Jenne-jeno and Dia/Diagha had been abandoned, an indication of a complex early urban history about which so little is known. Urban retrenchment, however, begins to set in around 1100, lasting until about 1300. Demographic atrophy is precipitous in Jenne-jeno after 1200, and it (and its satellites) are defunct by 1400, a fate also suffered by Mema by 1300.[24]

Explanations for the demise of Jenne-jeno lay in the realm of informed speculation, beginning with the possibility of a new disease environment brought south of the Sahara through the expansion of trans-Saharan exchange or with the introduction of militaristic "Bambara" agriculturalists and/or combative Fulbe pastoralists. Its decline relative to contemporary Jenne is also matter of surmise, since it took place concomitantly with the latter's full occupation, such that it is not at all clear that Jenne-jeno's inhabitants simply resettled in Jenne, as local traditions claim. Climatic change could also have had an impact, but the rise of state formations, subject of the next chapter, cannot be removed from considerations of causation.[25] Indeed, Gao, Timbuktu, and contemporary Jenne escaped Jenne-jeno's fate, tied as they were to subsequent patterns of commerce and polity.

CHAPTER TWO

Early Gao

BY THE TIME HUMAN MEMORY in the form of written observation emerges as a principal source of information for early West Africa, transitioning from the unconscious communications of archaeological and linguistic records, Gao/Kawkaw was nearly three thousand years old. The vast majority of Arabic-language accounts mentioning West Africa between the third/ninth and eleventh/seventeenth centuries were penned far from the region, relying on the reports of merchants and travelers, or interviews with West African pilgrims to the central Islamic lands. Some accounts are pure fantasy, others a mixture of observation and mythology. Only one major source, Ibn Baṭṭūṭa, was an actual eyewitness to the events he described. The resulting picture is therefore necessarily partial and subject to ongoing emendation.

In examining the external Arabic sources for this period, the next three chapters are interwoven through sequential splicing, placing into conversation sources spatially distant yet temporally contiguous. A primary focus is Islam's emergence in the Sahel, making the point that reformist activity becomes a feature of the region as early as the fifth/eleventh century, when West Africa's "age of jihad" is usually held to begin in the twelfth/eighteenth century. Scholars have written about this earlier period, but fail to grasp its vast territorial scope as well as its interconnected nature. The fifth/eleventh-century iteration should no longer be regarded as a minor development, as its force was such that the far more illustrious Almoravid movement could have found its ideological inspiration in lands south of the Sahara.

Related to this point is the rise of new polities as well as the reinvention and reinvigoration of others, especially Ghana, the subject of chapter 3. It is commonly presented that Ghana experienced rapid decline at a point when in fact it became even more powerful than ever. The scholarship has failed to take note of the breadth of Ghana's own period of reform.

The reemergence of a more radical expression of Islam also allows for chapter 4's reassessment of domestic slavery. The evidence suggests an institution at different stages of development across the Sahel prior to the late fifth/eleventh century, and that in contrast to the Lake Chad area, Gao and Ghana were societies in which domestic slavery was initially less critical, but then began to feature with the rise of slaving activity for export purposes. This constitutes an advisory against overgeneralizing about either the antiquity or ubiquity of West African slavery.

This three-chapter sequence begins with a reconsideration of Gao's early historical significance, often relegated in the scholarship. This tendency issues from a failure to more critically assess the region's two most important thirteenth/seventeenth-century chronicles; a far more plausible rendering of Gao's importance forms when considering those chronicles in conjunction with the external sources, the archaeological record, and the epigraphic evidence. Further contesting the secondary literature is the conclusion that these very different sources are far more harmonious than has been represented. But in closely examining the sources, the very concept of *bilād as-sūdān*, or "land of the blacks" must be attenuated, as it does not conform to the demographic realities of North and West Africa.

Gao as West Africa's Starting Point

Early West African history has come to represent a sort of time before time, when Africa was powerful and free of imperial imposition. Indeed, the notion of a West African "golden age" has been critical to many antislavery, anticolonial, and antiracism campaigns, in response to a western hegemonic insistence on an Africa both backward and devoid. Within such a context, histories of early and medieval West African societies tend to emphasize the urban-based, large-scale polity, majestic in scope and lavish in lifestyle, rolling out in linear and successive fashion, beginning with Ghana, then Mali, followed by Songhay. West African history as Greek trilogy took firm hold in the historiography of the 1970s, and remains an influential template.[1]

Nothing can be more ironic, however, than the manner in which the scholarship has depicted the onset of "civilization" in the West African *sāḥil*. The chronicles of medieval West Africa, *Ta'rīkh as-sūdān* and *Ta'rīkh al-fattāsh*, have as their major focus the rise and fall of imperial Songhay, so it would have been logical as well as accurate for chroniclers to emphasize the region's deep historicity, consistent with the archaeological record.[2] And yet, though Gao's early incarnation is acknowledged, the chronicles are far more invested in connecting imperial Songhay with the earlier Mande states of Ghana and Mali. The reasons for this will be explored, but as a consequence, the orientation of the chronicles has influenced various publics that include scholars.[3]

Late fourteenth/twentieth-century scholarship concerning early West Africa therefore often begins with Ghana. This, despite the testimony of al-Ya'qūbī (d. 284/897), who in 259/872–3 wrote, "The kingdom of the Kawkaw . . . is the greatest of the realms of the Sūdān, the most important and powerful. All the kingdoms obey its king."[4] Based on his testimony, Kawkaw, Kanem, and Ghana were all important, with Kawkaw or Gao as foremost. The decision to present Ghana as the initial polity of significance, influenced by the *ta'rīkhs* (*tawārīkh*) as well as subsequent reports in Arabic, is therefore at some odds with the testimony of the period itself.

Referring to Gao as a "kingdom," al-Ya'qūbī makes clear it was centered on a town, as do contemporary al-Khuwārizmī and al-Mas'ūdī and al-Bakrī in the following two centuries. In 548/1154 al-Idrisī wrote that Gao "is large and is widely famed" with "many servants and a large retinue, captains, soldiers, excellent apparel and beautiful ornaments," with warriors who "ride horses and camels"—an allusion to the cavalry as the basis for Gao's military power.[5] While confirming domestic slavery, consistent with al-Muhallabī's observation that the king "has a palace which nobody inhabits with him or has resort to except a eunuch slave (*khādam maqtū'*)," little else is recorded that concerns slavery.[6] Gao emerges as a city-state projecting power and influence, an important model of statecraft in the early Middle Niger.[7]

Reexamination of the textual evidence therefore requires a different starting point for early West African polity, with al-Ya'qūbī's account a compelling reason to begin with Gao in the northern cap of the Middle Niger floodplain. Gao, in turn, represents a crossroads to and through which migrated whole communities across an often artificial divide between Sahara and Savannah. The Sorko were one of these communities. A portion of these "fisherfolk," along with riverine hunters known as the Gow or Gaw, moved upstream in the late first/seventh century from their base in Kukiya (near what is now Bentiya) to what would become Gao, already occupied at the time.[8] First settling in the Dendi area (a thousand kilometers to the south of Kukiya/Bentiya), the Sorko would displace the Do, the original "masters of the river," and subsequently disperse farther west and north. This first/seventh-century transition from Kukiya to Gao, possibly in response to developing trading options, may also have been due to high variability in rain patterns and seasonal flooding, causing significant sediment transfer along with sizable fish migrations.[9]

The Sorko "masters of the water" are but one strand of those who would become the Songhay/Songhoi, who would also acquire a Mande component (among others). Either complementing or in contrast to their migration are claims of origins in the "East" that, in some traditions, stretch to Yemen.[10] This is hardly uncommon in a region influenced by Islam, since similar accounts are widespread throughout the Savannah and Sahel, as will be demonstrated. While reflective of centuries-long interactions among populations inhabiting and traversing these regions, such traditions certainly seek to legitimize the authority of ruling elites by locating their origins in lands of prestige.

By the time of al-Ya'qūbī's account in 259/872–3, therefore, Gao had been invested with proto-Songhay organization and activity for some two hundred years. Kukiya remained an important base, with al-Ya'qūbī's reference to Kawkaw understood as representing the two-hundred-kilometer Gao-Kukiya nexus. Al-Ya'qūbī is hardly unique, as there are a number of external sources referencing Gao's prominence, including al-Khuwārizmī in the third/ninth century, who mentions that the "First Clime" includes

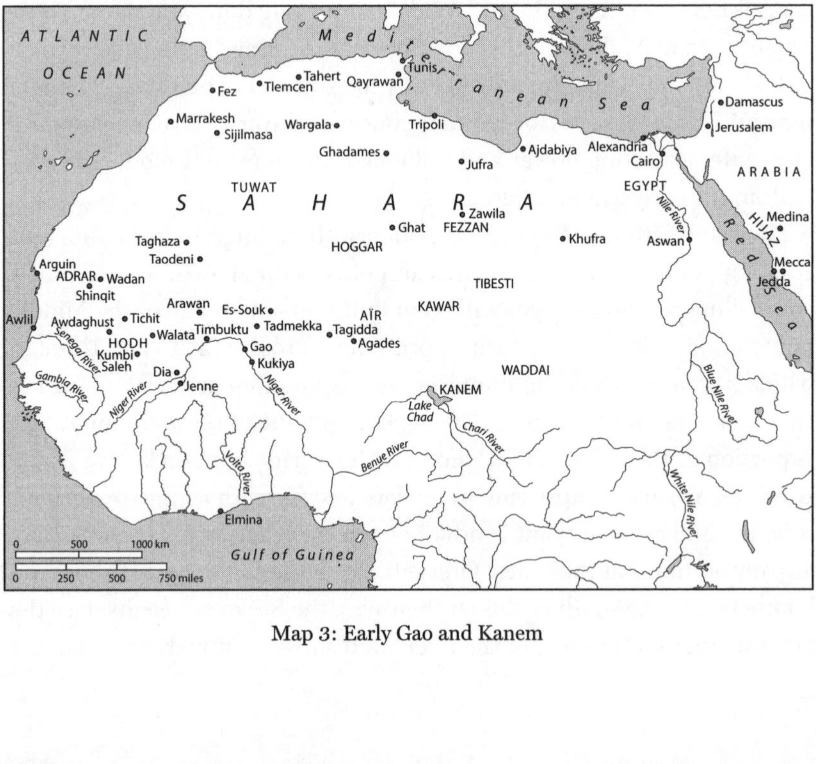

Map 3: Early Gao and Kanem

Fezzan, Sijilmasa, Ghana, "Zaghāwa," and Kawkaw.[11] Some thirty years after al-Ya'qūbī, the Iranian Ibn al-Faqīh wrote that Kawkaw was the "nation" reached in traveling from Ghana to Egypt, with al-Mas'ūdī further elaborating in the mid-fourth/tenth century.[12]

The question of what exactly transpired in Gao around the time of al-Ya'qūbī's report is the subject of considerable debate.[13] "Gao" should be understood to represent several approximate sites progressively occupied, the earliest situated on the "right" bank of the Niger River.[14] On the other side were three settlements of particular importance: Gadei, Old Gao (Gao Ancien), and Gao-Saney (Gao-Sané).[15] The archaeology suggests Old Gao was the site of the royal residence, with remains of stone structures on a significant scale dating to the fourth/tenth century.[16] Gao would become a leading entrepot between the tenth/fourth and thirteenth/ninth centuries, with networks leading to Ifriqiya, Tripoli, and Egypt, supporting al-Ya'qūbī's claims.[17]

Gao's role in connecting the western Sudan to Egypt is of considerable historicity, as Ibn Ḥawqal writes in 378/988: "Between its furthest part and the land of the Zanj are enormous deserts and sands which were crossed in olden times. The route from Egypt to Ghāna went over them."[18] This west-east axis was complemented by a south-north orientation captured in al-Zuhrī's sixth/twelfth-century description: "Caravans from the land of Egypt and from Wāraqlān reach [Gao], and a few from the Maghrib by way of Sijilmāsa."[19] Luxury imports recovered in Old Gao, including a large quantity of glazed pottery and glass in the fifth/eleventh and sixth/twelfth centuries, added to the process of social signification, casting Gao-Saney, locus of manufacturing and defense works, in the role of both servicing and protecting long-distance trade.[20] Exports apparently included ivory, as a cache of some fifty hippopotamus tusks (associated with third/ninth-century Old Gao) has been uncovered. More important than luxury items was salt, and though he stated that livestock superseded salt as a symbol and reservoir of wealth, al-Muhallabī (d. 380/990) nonetheless averred "the king's treasure-houses are spacious, his treasure consisting principally of salt."[21]

External reports undergird the archaeological findings, with al-Muhallabī describing Gao's ruler as having "a town on the Nile, on the eastern bank, which is called Sarnāh, where there are markets and trading houses (*matājir*)," and "another town to the west of the Nile where he and his men and those who have his confidence live."[22] The general sense of Gao's spatial relations are confirmed by al-Bakrī, who describes it as a "town consist[ing] of two towns . . ."[23] Settled as early as 2000 BCE, Gao had become a hub of highly significant political and commercial activity by the third/ninth century CE, and would remain so for another three-quarters of a millennium, a settlement of some 3,600 years.[24]

Islamic Conversion, Transformation, and the Reconciliation of Sources

Written sources in Arabic, in conjunction with the region's epigraphic record and oral traditions, render a composite picture of Islam's development in Gao that, with the exception of ruler-lists, is surprisingly free of contradiction. As Islam would eventually become a major organizing principle throughout the region, it is possible to plot its rise in a rather strikingly linear progression from the beginning of the fifth/eleventh to the middle of the sixth/twelfth century, when crystallizes a reformist-informed Islam either ideologically divergent or politically dissociated, or both.[25] By the latter period, Gao's royal court witnesses an expression of the faith influenced by, yet distinguished from, reform efforts characterizing a wider scope of North Africa and the western Sahel.

The analysis begins with the *ta'rīkhs'* ruler-lists and one al-Ayaman, said to be the founder of Gao's Zuwā (or Zu'a/Juwā/Jā'/Diā/Zā/Diu'a) dynasty, a "stranger from the east" who when questioned responds, "I come from Yemen," rendered simply as "he came," or *jā'*, the basis for the dynasty's name.[26] The claim is consistent with those of the Berber and Tuareg, who also maintain Yemeni origins.[27] This is arguably no idle statement, as the reference to Yemen may be a claim to Qaḥṭānī or "pure" Arab ancestry (*al-'arab al-'ārabah*), as opposed to 'Adnānī or "Arabized" Arabs (*al-'arab al-musta'ribah*), thereby favorably positioning the Zuwās relative to constituencies and potential contenders, if not a broader Muslim world.[28]

Though al-Ayaman supposedly hails from the central Islamic lands, *Ta'rīkh as-sūdān* only speculates he may have been Muslim, whereas the *Notice historique* makes no such attempt, instead identifying Kusuy/Kotso-Muslim as Gao's first Muslim ruler, fifteenth in the line of succession.[29] This is emblematic of a number of difficulties with the ruler-lists, especially their tradition of subsuming all Gao rulers into a single, Zuwā dynasty.[30] As such, the Gao ruler-lists must be treated as subsidiary to the epigraphic data and external accounts.[31]

Even so, treating the lists as subordinate should not lead to their complete dismissal, as there are critical instances in which reconciliation with both the external record and the epigraphic materials is possible.[32] To begin, al-Ya'qūbī makes no mention of Islam in Gao in the third/ninth century, and when coupled with al-Muhallabī's fourth/tenth-century depiction of Gao's ruler and his subjects as "pretenders," a picture slowly evolves of a ruler who was only nominally Muslim (or may have embraced 'Ibāḍism). This is entirely consistent with the ruler-list in *Ta'rīkh as-sūdān*, where Kusuy (or Kotso)-Muslim converts to Islam in 400/1009–10, with those preceding him having "died in ignorance, and not one of them believed in God or His Prophet, May God bless him and grant him peace."[33]

Nothing in the combined record contradicts the tradition's assertion that Kusuy/Kotso-Muslim converted at the beginning of the fifth/eleventh century, though there was an apparent lag in the response of his subjects, as al-Bakrī reports in 460/1068:

> The king [of Kawkaw] is called Qandā . . . The clothes of the people there are like those of the other Sūdān, consisting of a robe (*milḥafa*) and a garment of skins or some other material . . . They worship idols (*dakākīr*) as do the other Sūdān . . . When a king ascends the throne he is handed a signet ring, a sword, and a copy of the Koran which, as they assert, were sent to them by the Commander of the Faithful. Their king is a Muslim, for they entrust the kingship only to Muslims.[34]

Al-Bakrī's reference to clothes is no idle matter, but rather a telltale indication of contempt, as condemnatory as citing their "idol worship."[35] He does not equivocate in affirming the ruler is a Muslim but his followers are not. By casting as an "assertion" the claim that the ruler received a Qur'ān from the "Commander of the Faithful"—by whom he could only mean the ruler of the Almoravids, the fifth/eleventh century, Berber-led reform movement in al-Maghrib and al-Andalus—al-Bakrī registers his doubt. Even so, it reveals Gao saw value in such an affiliation ten years before Ghana's 469/1076 reinvention as a reform state, underscoring Gao's importance as a starting point of contextualization. This trajectory also accords with Maḥmūd Ka'ti's claim (d. 1002/1593) that Islam was later adopted by the people of Gao (not its ruler) between 471/1079 and 475/1082.[36]

Maḥmūd Ka'ti's periodization not only complements the external sources, but the area's epigraphic records as well. These materials—Arabic inscriptions on stelae and tombstones and erotic graffiti on rocks and trees in Tifinagh (the written language of Tamasheq)—represent the earliest writings of the region, with legible dates ranging from the fifth/eleventh through the ninth/fifteenth centuries.[37] Inscriptions at Gao-Saney reveal four separate series of rulers, the first two bearing the title *malik* (pl. *mulūk*), or "ruler" or "king." The tentative end date of the first series is 476/1083–4, fully congruent with Maḥmūd Ka'ti's dating of Gao's collective conversion.

Al-Zuhrī's record for this period strengthens the probability that Gao underwent significant religious transformation at this time, as he writes that in 469/1076–7 "Yaḥyā b. Abī Bakr the *amīr* of Masūfa made his appearance. [Ghana] turned Muslim in the days of Lamtūna and became good Muslims . . . [Tādimakka (*sic*) and Nslā] turned Muslim seven years after the people of Ghāna turned Muslim. There had been much warfare between them. The people of Ghāna sought the help of the Almoravids."[38] "Turning Muslim" seven years after Ghana locates the event in 476/1083–4, consistent with Maḥmūd Ka'ti and the end of the first *mulūk* series. Temporal and spatial proximities link the cultural and political shifts in Gao and Tadmekka ("the appearance of Mecca," or "verily, here, Mecca" in Tamasheq, and also known as Es-Souk/Essuk, "the market," some 390 kilometers northeast of Gao and a major entrepot for the exchange of salt and semi-precious stones), suggesting a strong connection, if not causality. "Turning Muslim" for Tadmekka most likely refers to an exchange of 'Ibāḍism for orthodoxy.[39]

The Tadmekka-Gao Connection

One facet of exchange between Tadmekka and Gao was the practice of epigraphy.[40] Commercial connections to al-Qaywaran (al-Qaywarān) and Tripoli (Ṭarābulus) suggest they were the likely source of Tadmekka's tradition, with correspondences to epigraphy's subsequent emergence in Gao-Saney. It has been argued that Tadmekka's late fifth/eleventh-century "conversion" led to expanded regional Almoravid influence that included Gao-Saney, the latter's importation of distinctively carved funerary inscriptions and marble tombstones a lynchpin, as they could have only been crafted in Almeria under Almoravid control.[41]

Though the Masūfa Ṣanhāja (one of several of Berber federations in what is now Mauritania and Morocco) may have spearheaded change in Gao, it could also have been the Soninke (northernmost Mande speakers associated with early Ghana, to be discussed shortly). Al-Bakrī noted in the fifth/eleventh century the town of Tiraqqa (whose precise location is elusive) was a market "where the people of Ghāna and Tādmakka assemble," but a century later al-Zuhrī spoke of "much warfare" between Ghana and Tadmekka, with the former seeking "the help of the Almoravids."[42] Ghana may therefore have led the campaign against Tadmekka, with the Almoravids providing assistance.[43] The notion of a new dynasty in Gao "ideologically influenced" by the Almoravids is sufficiently capacious as to include the latter scenario, though it fails to convey the arresting possibility of direct Soninke intervention.[44]

A second caveat to the hypothesis of Almoravid-influenced dynastic change and religious reform in Gao (and Ghana, discussed in the next chapter) is that the Almoravids and 'Ibāḍīs rarely employed epigraphy in their funerary customs, so that an Almoravid-inspired dynastic change may have subsequently distanced itself from that influence.[45] In this way, the correspondence of the first three rulers' names in the second *mulūk* epigraphic series to the Prophet and two of his successors does not represent initial conversion, as the Muslim pedigree among Gao rulers since Kusuy/Kotso-Muslim in 400/1009–10 is clear, but rather suggests a claim on the particular brand of Islam they were pursuing, signifying upon what preceded.[46] Rather than conversion, therefore, the second *mulūk* series reflects reform, conceivably tempered by dynastic intrigue.[47]

An Almoravid-assisted Ghanaian conflict with Tadmekka in 476/1083–4, precisely the year of the end date for the first *mulūk* series, suggests a bad ending for the latter, a possibility enhanced by al-Idrisī's 548/1154 report that the *khuṭba* (or sermon usually delivered at Friday mosque and on other special occasions) in Tadmekka-associated Tiraqqa was now delivered in the name of Ghana's ruler.[48] However, he also reports Gao's independent ruler had the *khuṭba* delivered in his name. This makes sense, as the Almoravid dynasty ended in 541/1147, though it does not preclude the second *mulūk* ruler from having become independent even before then.

Notwithstanding difficulties with ruler-lists, splicing the external, epigraphic, and local traditions together results in a rather coherent rendering of Islam's progression in Gao's royal court, some two hundred years in the making. By the end of the fifth/eleventh century, the city had converted under circumstances connected with, but not necessarily driven by, the politics of reform, issuing into a new dispensation of political (and conceivably ideological) freedom. If reform's force diminished with a new ruling family in 476/1083–4, Islam as a ruling ideology continued, linking the second *mulūk* series with a fourth, *zuwā* series by way of an intermediary third, the *malikāt,* featuring women who mostly bore the title *malika*, indicating vaunted but unspecified status.[49] The *malikāt* both spans and connects the period between the *mulūk* and the *zuwās*, so that the latter three series shared spaces of temporality, spatiality, religion, and possibly ideology.[50]

Lake Chad and the Concept of Bilād as-Sūdān

For some three hundred years, from the third/ninth through the sixth/twelfth centuries, Gao was at the center of Sahelian commerce, constituting a central node in *bilād as-sūdān*. To the east lay Lake Chad, and though spatially marginal to Gao, it is thematically central, as it not only engages with issues of slavery, but also disrupts conventional notions of the "land of the blacks."

Located on Lake Chad's northwestern edge, Kanem's meteoric rise from a territory of loosely connected nomadic groups in the fourth/tenth century to a powerful, urban-based realm in the sixth/twelfth is directly connected to slaving.[51] Slaving's importance is reflected in Ibn Sa'īd's comments during the reign of *Mai* Dunama Dubbalemi (599–639/1203–42), and concerns "Berber followers who were converted to Islam by Ibn Ḥabal the sultan of Kānim. They are his slaves. He uses them on his raids and takes advantage of their camels, which have filled these regions."[52] Ibn Sa'īd discusses the familiar notion of slavery in a most unfamiliar way, as Berbers are usually depicted as enslaving and converting "blacks." As such, he opens a very different vista onto the imprecise, fluid, and surprising configuration of *bilād as-sūdān*, revealing an evolving view of the Lake Chad quadrant, where Kanem is consistently identified with the Zaghāwa/Zaghawā (the apparent progenitors of the Kanuri).[53]

Kanem's chief trading partner to the north was the city of Zawila, in the region of the Fezzan, part of a larger 'Ibāḍī complex of cities and states that included Wargala, Djarma, Ghadames, Tahert, Wadan, and Kawar. With urban settlements founded by at least the second/eighth century, the Fezzan was the principal gateway between Lake Chad and the port cities of Ajdabiya and Tripoli.[54] Zawila was the hub of such activity, about which al-Ya'qūbī states: "They export black slaves from among the Mīriyyūn, the Zaghāwiyyūn, the Marwiyyūn and from other peoples of the Sūdān, because they live close to Zawīla, whose people capture them."[55] Al-Iṣṭakhrī, writing in the fourth/tenth century, comments that "the black slaves who are sold in the Islamic countries" come from the lands of the Sudan, and that "most of those black slaves converge on Zawīla."[56] The sixth/twelfth century *Kitāb al-Istibṣār* describes Zawila, a "great and very ancient city," as "the place of assembly for caravans and slaves are brought to it."[57]

Al-Ya'qūbī paints third/ninth-century Zawila with cosmopolitan strokes, with residents from Khurasan, Basra, Kufa, and other parts of the Muslim world. Even so, al-Bakrī considered Zawila as part of *bilād as-sūdān*, no recent, fifth/eleventh-century development, for in the *Kitāb al-ma'ārif* ("Book of Knowledge") completed in 266/879–80, the Persian Ibn Qutayba quotes Wahb b. Munabbih (d. 110/728–9 or 114/732–3) as including the Zaghāwa and the "Qazān" (Fezzan) among the descendants of Kan'ān b. Ḥām.[58] In the fourth/tenth century, al-Muhallabī maintained there were two Zawilas, one of which was "Zawīla of the Sūdān," and that the Fezzan itself was "named after Fazzān b. Ḥām b. Nūḥ, peace be upon him." Indeed, "Zawīlat al-Sūdān" was where a "majority of the people are black in colour."[59] Writing a century later, al-Bakrī corroborates:

> Zawīla is like the town of Ajdābiya . . . It is the first point of the land of the Sūdān . . . From there slaves are exported to Ifrīqiya and other neighbouring regions. They are bought for short pieces of red cloth (*thiyāb qiṣār ḥumr*).[60]

That Zawila's population "darkened" with the trans-Saharan slave trade is not at all obvious; in fact, the sources posit an ancient ancestral line of descent, as Ibn Qutayba writes: "The descendants of Kūsh and Ka'nān are the races of the Sūdān: the Nūba, the Zanj, the Qazān [Fazzān], the Zaghāwa, the Ḥabasha, the Qibṭ, and the Barbar."[61] Such consistent depiction of the Fezzan in general and Zawila in particular is at odds with the tralatitious view of what constitutes the "land of the blacks."[62]

The foregoing discussion renders untenable the concept of a *bilād as-sūdān* adhering to a divide between desert and savannah, while it reinforces an approach that places North and West Africa within a single frame of analysis. Consistent with the view that the Sahel is better understood as the northern rather than southern fringe of the Sahara, a broader canvass incorporates the desert's two "shores," with autochthonous "black" populations occupying lands below the northern *sāḥil,* alongside "non-black" communities in territories above the southern *sāḥil.*[63] With Kanem enslaving Berbers and/or converting them to Islam while projecting power and commercial control through the Fezzan, Lake Chad takes on antipodal dimensions of what obtained between Ghana and Berbers farther west, constituting an inverse reality.

The next chapter in fact turns to a Ghana resituated within a more accurate regional context relative to Gao, an operation enabled by an approach to the sources that, rather than consulting them as discrete categories, reconfigures them as a polyvocal source.

CHAPTER THREE

The Kingdoms of Ghana: Reform along the Senegal River

DEVELOPMENTS IN WHAT ARE NOW EASTERN SENEGAL, western Mali, Mauritania, and Morocco were also informed by substantial migrations and interactions between Sahelian and Saharan communities, giving rise to forms of political organization that facilitated as well as protected against commercial activity. More specifically, and in contrast to early Gao, the region would see the emergence of polities that, though vitally connected to the growing importance of Islam, were not necessarily Muslim-led. This history cannot be properly assessed without fully considering influences from the North, but the reverse is also true, and while "Maghribian" history is not the focus, it remains a tale only partially told in the absence of its considerable "sub-Saharan" elements.

The rise, fall, and rise again of Ghana is a study of why mutually beneficial commercial and political relations between Muslim and non-Muslim rulers and merchants were disrupted by the spread of reform Islam, and how the region was radically altered as a consequence. Divergent models of negotiating cultural difference lost their competition with a withering, less tolerant Islam, signaling a shift in the region's principal occupation from trafficking in gold to human beings, as well as the rise of a discourse on the relationship between phenotypic expression and "civilizational" achievement, a forerunner to concepts of "race." West Africa's renowned reform movements beginning in the twelfth/eighteenth century were therefore fully anticipated by similar ideas and developments in early Ghana and the Senegal valley.

Origins of Ghana and the Soninke

One of the earliest recorded mentions of Ghana (along with that of Gao) appears in al-Khuwārizmī's third/ninth century *Ṣurat al-arḍ* ("Picture of the Earth").[1] It next appears several decades later in al-Ya'qūbī, who, after identifying the people of Ghana as descendants of Kūsh b. Ḥām, immediately associates Ghana's ruler with gold mines, adding that "under his authority are a number of kings." Writing a century later, al-Hamdānī asserts "the richest gold mine on earth is that of Ghāna." From the onset, therefore, Ghana is identified with gold.[2]

Anthropological, linguistic, and archaeological evidence provide windows into Ghana's origins, in which ancient population movements once again feature. Dar Tichit, in what is now south central Mauritania, is a likely regional *berceau* for those who would become the Soninke—the eventual inhabitants of early Ghana.[3] Decreasing water supplies and expanding desiccation during the late Holocene period (4500 to 2000 BCE) saw northern populations move farther south, and by 1500 BCE there were a number of settlements in Dar Tichit. Between 600 and 300 BCE, the "Tichit people" were constructing small towns in defensible terrain that included Walata/Biru and Mema (or Nema), going on to establish Kumbi Saleh in the region of Wagadu (perhaps "land of the great herds" in Soninke), attracted to its network of wells and massive surrounding dunes that provided natural protection.[4] It would appear that during the first five hundred years of the current era, regional trade greatly stimulated occupational specialization, in turn contributing to Wagadu's strategic location between the Hodh in the north and Mema in the south, a crossroads for iron and copper (the latter a "durable marker of exchange networks") by the fifth century CE, with the exchange of salt for gold developing in the third/ninth century.[5]

The term Soninke (or "Soninko") as well as the Wolof name for the Soninke, "Serrakole," carry with them whispers of their origins elsewhere. The former means "inhabitant of Soni or Sana," conceivably Sanaa of Yemen (a clear stretch), whereas Serrakole may connote "clear skin," perhaps reflecting movement south from Dar Tichit and genetic exchange with the Fulbe and Berbers, themselves reflective of admixture, but also with populations moving northwest from the Niger valley.[6] The term "Soninke" is not found in the external sources, but rather the word "Farwiyyūn," while, according to al-Bakrī, "Ghāna" was the title of the ruler, subsequently adopted for the appellation for the state.[7]

That a number of these terms, including Kayamagha or Kayama'a, refer to the state of Ghana has already been demonstrated in the scholarship.[8] In parallel fashion, Mande-speaking communities renowned for their commercial networks and enterprise are called the Wangāra/Wankara in the *ta'rīkhs* and the Wangāra, Wanghāra, Wanqāra, and Banū Naghmārata in the external sources, all cognates of the Berber term for the Jula.[9]

Accounts concerning Wagadu demonstrate the independence of some origin accounts.[10] Gathered subsequently to those informing the *ta'rīkhs*, multiple versions cohere around the arrival of one Dinga from the east, progenitor of leading Soninke clans (including the Cissé or Sisse) who would rule Wagadu. That Dinga is not presented as a Muslim connotes the interstitial nature of Ghana's leadership, connecting commercially to the central Islamic lands while linking noumenally to an indigenous, authenticating cosmology. A younger son, *Magha* (or *manga*) Diabe would establish his capital at "Kumbi," haunt of the great snake Bida who provides safety, rain, and gold in exchange for an annual offering of Wagadu's most beautiful virgin. Wagadu flourishes, with the descendants of the *fado* (or governor, one for each of Wagadu's four provinces) and the *magha*—the *wago*—constituting the royal and noble clans.[11] In keeping with claims of Yemeni origins throughout the region, reflecting Islam's influence but also possibly Tichit origins, *Ta'rīkh as-sūdān* says the rulers of Ghana (Kayamagha) "were *bayḍān* ('white') in origin—though we do not know from where they were originally descended—and their vassals (*khuddām*) were Soninke (Wa'kuriyyūn)."[12]

Ghana and Awdaghust

In transitioning from origin stories to substantive history, the external record resumes centrality, focusing on Ghana's commercial relations with Sijilmasa and Awdaghust (or Tegdaoust). Awdaghust was strategically positioned to control the flow of salt from Awlil (on the Atlantic coast), while Ghana oversaw the movement of gold from deposits located in Bambuk in the southwest. Ghana and Awdaghust were therefore interdependent, separated by a journey of only ten days, with Ibn Ḥawqal reporting in the fourth/tenth century that "the king of Awdaghust maintains relations with the ruler of Ghāna," who stood "in need of the goodwill of the kings of Awdaghust because of the salt," and with whom there was "an uninterrupted trade . . . and the constant coming and going of caravans."[13]

The commercial interdependence of Awdaghust and Ghana is reflected in religion. Ibn Ḥawqal comments on al-Ya'qūbī's earlier characterization of Awdaghust's ruler as lacking religion, describing Awdaghust as resembling Mecca, suggestive when added to his observation that its salt comes "from the lands of Islam." In the fifth/eleventh century, al-Bakrī mentions a "cathedral mosque and many smaller ones, all well attended" in Awdaghust, a pattern found elsewhere in the early Sudan in which Islam gradually gathers force. However, al-Muhallabī's fourth/tenth-century claim that Awdaghust's "people are Muslims," while true of its North African merchants and even a segment of the Ṣanhāja, would not have been applicable to the town's many residents from Ghana, who were not Muslim.[14]

The residents of Awdaghust in fact boasted an assortment of origins, including "Sūdān women [who] excel at cooking delicious confections [and] pretty slave girls with white complexions, good figures, firm breasts, slim waists, fat buttocks, wide shoulders and sexual organs so narrow that one of them may be enjoyed as though she were a virgin indefinitely."[15] Here is a distillation of urban life via androgynous reverie: the culinary and sexual appetites of men, their group appellations suggesting an association with 'Ibāḍīsm, accommodated by women objectified in dichotomous racialization. Awdaghust was clearly not simply a "Ṣanhāja" town, making even more problematic and arbitrary a boundary with "the land of blacks."[16] The same can said of Sijilmasa, with residents from Basra, Kufa, and Baghdad, but also nonenslaved "blacks," its very founding in 140/757–8 attributed to 'Īsā b. Mazīd "the Black."[17] Awdaghust would play an active role in the Sahel, pillaging Awgham and killing its king in 350/961–2 with a camelry of one hundred thousand, while reportedly receiving tribute from over twenty Sudanese rulers.[18] The Almoravids would view Awdaghust as a threat the following century.

Sovereign Power in Ghana

Al-Bakrī states the "city of Ghāna" was a composite of "two towns situated on a plain." Archaeologists are divided over whether Kumbi Saleh constituted the capital in the fifth/eleventh century, with those expressing doubts growing in number.[19] Whether or not Kumbi Saleh was the "city of Ghāna" does not affect al-Bakrī's location of it "on a plain," a consideration with significance that will be demonstrated.

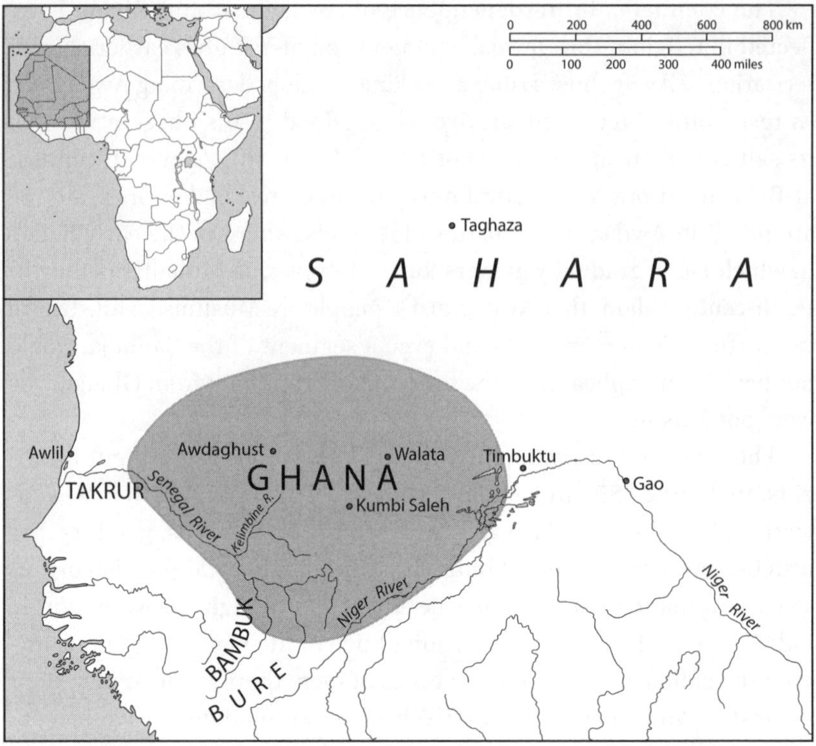

Map 4: Kingdoms of Ghana

Prior to the fifth/eleventh century, the "city of Ghāna" both reflected and facilitated a veritable power grid, within which were located four principal spheres of activity: commerce, Islam, ancestral religion, and the state. The market was by design a conjunctive space in which all four elements necessarily and frequently interacted, while the other three conformed to less-than-strict physical and cultural demarcations. The primary divide—living space—was drawn between the Muslim community and all other sectors, with the former said to constitute a separate sphere, one of the capital's "two towns" with "twelve mosques [and] salaried imams and muezzins, as well as jurists and scholars." The "king's town" was six miles away, but with "continuous habitations" between them.[20]

Al-Bakrī seems intrigued with the "king's town" and its "domed buildings and domes and thickets where the sorcerers of these people, men in charge of the religious cult, live. In them too are their idols and the tombs of their king [and] also the king's prisons. If somebody is imprisoned there no news of him is ever heard."[21] The association of ancestral religion with death—the death of former rulers, the certain death of the current ruler, the impending demise of the royal courtiers, the veneration of the dead through sacrifice, and the implied death of prisoners—is profound. This sacred grove was Ghana's existential center, intimately and inextricably connected to state authority and its power to interpret life's meaning and sanction its violation. But just as extraordinary are al-Bakrī's connections between Islam and ancestral religion, suggesting an accommodation (presumably for the sake of commerce) implicit in the mitigation of spatial distance between the two "towns" by "continuous habitations," effecting contiguity. In concert with the physical configuration were cultural approximations, as the "king's interpreters, the official in charge of his treasury and the majority of his ministers are Muslims," indicating Islam's growing influence in the royal court.[22] Through the middle of the fifth/eleventh century, therefore, Muslim scholars and jurists, non-Muslim priests and kings, the merchants, and other town dwellers all observed a certain mutual tolerance, with al-Bakrī praising one *Tunka* Basī, who "led a praiseworthy life on account of his love of justice and friendship for the Muslims."[23]

After observing that only the king "and his heir apparent (who is the son of his sister) may wear sown clothes [while all] other people wear robes of cotton, silk, or brocade, according to their means," al-Bakrī notes that the king sat in "a domed pavilion" in royal session, to his right "the sons of the [vassal] kings of his country wearing splendid garments and their hair plaited with gold." In approaching the king, the people would "fall on their knees and sprinkle dust on their heads, for this is their way of greeting him," while the Muslims "only clapped their hands."[24] Some of these protocols, especially the earthen ablution or sprinkling of dust, would extend over generations and territorial expanse to include imperial Mali and dynastic Songhay. Matrilineal succession is explained by the observation that the king "has no doubt that his successor is a son of his sister, while he is not certain that his son is in fact his own."[25] The "sons of vassal kings" also feature (a forerunner to the French "école des otages" in the thirteenth/nineteenth century), but as the fourth/tenth-century ruler of Awdaghust is also said to have received tribute from twenty kings of the Sudan, the precise nature of a kingdom's political submission is unclear.[26] Finally, as was true of Gao, adornment was a gauge of civilization as well as social differentiation.

With respect to Ghana's military, Ghana's ruler could reportedly "put 200,000 men in the field, more than 40,000 of them archers" in fighting the town of Sila (along the Senegal River). It is not clear whether this includes the one hundred thousand camelry of Awdaghust, presumably subject to Ghana's ruler by 446/1054–5 (when he was seated there), and though this may refer to a standing army, it may also reflect exigency.[27]

Al-Bakrī makes only the briefest of comments regarding taxation policies, indicating Ghana's control of access to significant gold deposits positioned it favorably in exchange for goods, especially salt, with taxation of the latter levied on both its initial importation as well as its apparent transshipment elsewhere in the Sahel and (possibly) Savannah.[28]

That the executive wielded the power of death is apparent from the description of the royal groves, to which can be added the right to dispense justice, command military ventures, and levy taxation. It would appear the ruler only heard cases concerning high officials, constituting the court of last appeal. Such authority more or less defines the fundamental prerogatives of any sovereign power, but the sources are not forthcoming as to how the apparatus was staffed and maintained, nor are offices delineated. Even so, Ghana's stature as a regional power, along with its wealth and influence, would have required an effective structural organization.[29]

Wārjābī b. Rābīs and Reform in the Sahel

It has become conventional to attribute initial Islamic reform in the Sahel to the rise of the Almoravids, though their relationship to the middle Senegal valley (or Takrur) remains opaque. There arose the (likely) Pullo leader Wārjābī b. Rābīs (d. 432/1040–1), who challenged a non-Muslim, "idol (*dakkūr*)-worshiping" population.[30] Wārjābī's activities are usually viewed as subsidiary to those of the Almoravids, but closer examination reveals the latter's close if not vital connection to the resources and politics of the Sahel, suggesting Wārjābī's endeavors may have been more generative than derivative.

Yaḥyā b. Ibrāhīm, founder of the Almoravids, hailed from the Banū Gudala division of the Ṣanhāja and lived in what is now southern Mauritania, close to the Senegal River. The community from which he sprang was closely affiliated with *bilād as-sūdān*, as was that of his mentor, ʿAbd ʿAllāh b. Yāsīn, whose own mother hailed from "Tamāmānāwt, situated on the edge of the desert which adjoins the town of Ghāna." Though Yaḥyā b. Ibrāhīm's spiritual quest took him to Mecca and then al-Qayrawan, it is worth asking whether Wārjābī helped fire the imagination of Yaḥyā b. Ibrāhīm rather than the reverse, aiding the explanation of why the Almoravids began in southern Mauritania and northern Senegal. After all, by the time Yaḥyā b. Ibrāhīm gets under way "to proclaim the Truth (*da'wat al-ḥaqq*)" in 440/1048, Wārjābī b. Rābīs had been dead for eight years, having completed his own holy war.[31] Instructively, two years following the capture of Awdaghust, the son of Wārjābī b. Rābīs, one Labbī, attempted an ill-fated rescue of 'Abd Allāh b. Yāsīn's brother Yaḥyā b. 'Umar, under siege in the Lamtuna Mountains and eventually killed by the Banū Gudala in 448/1056–7. Given Takrur's earlier example and subsequent military support for the Almoravids, it is not at all clear who preceded whom.

Takrur's rise following Wārjābī b. Rābīs was meteoric, projecting power throughout the Senegal valley by the middle of the sixth/twelfth century. Al-Idrisī writes in 548/1154 that "the Takrūrī" (Takrur's leader) possessed "slaves and soldiers, strength and firmness as well as widely-known justice. His country is safe and calm." Sila, the first town east from Awlil along the Senegal (at least in al-Idrisī's scheme), "belonged to the domains of the Takrūrī," and was "a meeting place for the Sūdān and a good market," suggesting Sila's redefinition under Takrur as a major entrepot. Barisa, the next town east of Sila, also paid "allegiance to the Takrūrī." Awlil, Sila, Barisa, and Takrur composed the land of the "Maqzāra," a term encompassing the Fulbe or Hal Pulaaren (speakers of Pulaar), Wolof, and perhaps Sereer.[32] A reasonable inference is that Takrur controlled goods and communication from Awlil to the border with Ghana, creating a uniform trading zone.[33]

Reformist activity in fifth/eleventh-century Takrur therefore precedes similar developments in Ghana, with testimony to what transpired in Ghana turning on the Almoravid defeat of Awdaghust in 446/1054–5, wresting it from Ghana's control (as it had become the residence of Ghana's ruler).[34] As al-Bakrī's account ends in 460/1068, it is al-Zuhrī who resumes the story. Concerning the "land of the Janāwa" he writes: "In former times the people of this country professed paganism (*kufr*) until the year 469/1076–7 when Yaḥyā b. Abī Bakr the *amīr* of Masūfa made his appearance. They turned Muslim in the days of Lamtūna and . . . [t]oday they are Muslims and have scholars, lawyers, and Koran readers . . ."[35] Just thirteen years after the enthroning of a new, non-Muslim king in 455/1063, therefore, something very dramatic took place in Ghana. Scholars are not agreed as to precisely what that may have been, with those insisting on a 469/1076–7 Almoravid military conquest of Ghana resisted by others citing inconsistencies in the record.[36]

Left out of the analysis is the spread of reformist Islam from Takrur to Sila, before the fall of Awdaghust, and the possibility that Ghana was already at war with Sila. It therefore cannot be discounted that either Sila or Takrur, or both, had a role to play in at least weakening Ghana prior to any possible Almoravid intervention. Whatever the verities, the end result is the same: by 469/1076–7 Ghana was a Muslim state, lauded for its adherence to Islam while engaged in slaving and militaristic promotion of its creed, garnering Almoravid support for Tadmekka's military defeat, with reverberations reaching Gao.

Whereas the external record is vague, the oral tradition employs allegory to explain the demise, or transformation, of a kingdom so powerful. When the virgin to be sacrificed to the royal snake Bida during the reign of Wagadu's seventh king is saved by a young suitor who kills Bida, the latter curses Wagadu, leading to drought and famine. Bida's severed head lands in Bure, in the land of southern Mande speakers, which becomes a new source of gold. A Soninke diaspora results from the catastrophe, and Wagadu comes to a calamitous end.[37]

Rather than Ghana's demise, the Bida allegory may be better understood as a lamentation of a late fifth/eleventh-century confrontation with a form of Islam far less tolerant than that which preceded, when Muslim merchants and learned men peacefully coexisted with a non-Muslim Ghanaian ruling elite. That ancestral religion was displaced is a primary meaning of the tale, but the fact that the Jula or Wangāra also left implies their own rejection of a rigid Islam.

Resurgent Ghana

Much of scholarly interest in early Ghana ends with the fall of the non-Muslim state, but like a phoenix it rises once more, reinvigorated, continuing well into the eighth/fourteenth century, by which time it is tributary to Mali. Neither the internal written sources, the oral traditions, nor the secondary scholarship have much to say about Ghana's reemergence as a Muslim polity, but the external record has a great deal to say. It is therefore ahistorical and misleading to only consider the early kingdom of Ghana, when the evidence is clear that there were in fact kingdoms of Ghana.

To begin, al-Idrisī's 548/1154 *Kitāb Rujār* ("Book of Roger") describes Ghana as "two towns on both banks of the river," claiming it is "the greatest of all the towns of the Sūdān."[38] This comports with archaeological finds demonstrating a long and seemingly uninterrupted trajectory associated with Kumbi Saleh, centering a beautiful mosque renovated and enlarged several times between the fourth/tenth and the eighth/fourteenth centuries, and only abandoned in the ninth/fifteenth.[39] While al-Idrisī's location of Ghana's center on a river, and not the plain initially mentioned by al-Bakrī, may echo his penchant for placing urban centers near water, it may also reflect the Muslim regime's decision to actually relocate, if not the existence of multiple capitals. But the riverine placement alludes to a much more significant development regarding a regional system of trade, as al-Idrisī asserted boats would load salt at Awlil and "then proceed up the Nīl to Silā, Takrūr, Barīsā, Ghāna and the other towns of Wanqāra and Kughā as well as to all the towns of the Sūdān"—a fascinating depiction revealing the integration of an Islamized Ghana into a regional trading system initially begun under Takrur.[40]

Ghana was a major beneficiary of the commercial network along the Senegal, with al-Idrisī claiming "all of the lands we have described are subject to the ruler of Ghāna, to whom the people pay their taxes, and he is their protector."[41] He pays particular attention to the "country of the Wanqāra" as "the country of gold," an apparent reference to Bambuk. His notion of this area as "an island" conforms well to the land between the Senegal and Faleme Rivers, referred to as *jazīrat al-tibr*, or "the island of gold," by al-Dimashqī (d. 727/1327).[42]

Consistent with the foregoing is al-Idrisī's description of an Islamized royal court whose king, "according to what is reported, belongs to the progeny of Ṣāliḥ b. 'Abd-Allāh b. al-Ḥasan b. al-Ḥasan b. 'Alī b. Abī Ṭālib. The *khuṭba* is delivered in his own name, though he pays allegiance to the Abbasid caliph."[43] The notion that the ruler was a descendant of the Quraysh and related to the Prophet is quite the departure from the prior claim of descent from Dinga. That the ruler had the *khuṭba* said in his own name reflects the Almoravid period had ended, suffering defeat in 542/1147 at the hands of the Almohads at Marrakesh. Al-Idrisī goes on to describe a palatial estate built in 510/1116–17, with "drawings and paintings, and provided with glass windows."[44] The king would appear publicly in silken clothes on "feast days," but would otherwise daily ride on horseback through the streets, and "anyone who has suffered injustice or misfortune confronts him, and stays there until the wrong is remedied."[45] In approaching the palace his commanders would have preceded him, sounding their drums, a practice that, like the earthen ablution, would survive the Ghanaian state. Though not *sharī'a*, this form of justice nonetheless gestures toward something more "Islamic," a significant evolution from judicial processes conducted in secret groves intimately associated with death.

Though Ghana had become a Muslim state by the end of the fifth/eleventh century, there were tensions with the Almohads. In a letter from

Sijilmasa's governor to "the king of the Sūdān in Ghāna" reproduced by al-Maqqarī (d. 1041/1632), the former complained of the ill treatment of his merchants, illuminating regional geopolitics in which Ghana's ruler, by having the *khuṭba* delivered in his own name while evincing nominal fealty to Baghdad, effectively rejected Almohad suzerainty.[46] Perhaps he was ill at ease with these merchants, viewing them as politically threatening, but in suggesting a "difference" in their religions, Sijilmasa's governor challenged the genuineness of Ghana's Islam (possibly a political response to Ghana's independence couched in religious discourse).

In remarkable contrast to a resurgent Ghana, Awdaghust is described in this period as a "small town in the desert, with little water [and] there is no large trade."[47] It may have never recovered from the 460/1054–5 Almoravid incursion, though commercial realignments surely played a role. Takrur and Sila's creation of a trading zone along the Senegal would have dealt a severe blow to Awdaghust as the gateway for Awlil's salt.[48] Moreover, the emergence of Walata—the Arabized form of *wala*, Manding for "shady place," also known as "Īwālātan" (its Berberized form) or Biru (its Soninke designation, "market" by implication)—to the northeast of Awdaghust would replace it as a major terminus by the beginning of the seventh/thirteenth century, signaling the dawn of new South-North commercial activity in association with stirrings in the full Savannah.[49]

Ghana's continuing development is next best illustrated by al-Sharīshī, writing from al-Andalus some fifty years after al-Idrisī and stating that "Islam has spread among its inhabitants and there are schools there. Many merchants from the Maghrib are to be found there . . . They buy there slaves for concubinage and stay with the emir, who receives them most hospitably."[50] This suggests a maturation of Islam in Ghana, with the merchant community making Ghana a permanent domicile, absent Muslim and non-Muslim demarcations.

Having reestablished a formidable regional presence since the latter quarter of the fifth/eleventh century, Ghana's power appears to have waned during the seventh/thirteenth, probably within the first third of the century, a conjecture partly driven by its relative invisibility in the sources, and by traditions concerning imperial Mali's foundation. There is a hint of regression in the sources, with ancestral religion resurgent, reinforced by the observation that, save for the Muslims, "its inhabitants go naked," with women covering their pubic areas with beads of glass or shell, or bones if poorer.[51] Such a drastic reversal in Islam's fortunes is difficult to reconcile with the preceding evidence, and may draw on assumptions in the absence of reliable information.

With al-'Umarī (d. 749/1349) there is a definitive shift in focus from Takrur and Ghana to Mali. Possibly due to Takrur's resilience from the fifth/eleventh through the seventh/thirteenth centuries, as well as its pilgrims traveling to the central Islamic lands, Mali becomes known as Takrur in Egypt and the Ḥijāz by al-'Umarī's time, although Takrur and Ghana are provinces within the Malian empire by then.[52]

Incorporated into Mali's imperial structure but honored as an ancient and storied polity, Ghana has yet to experience a definitive end by the time Ibn Khaldūn (d. 808/1406) writes his *Muqaddima*, having garnered information from one *Shaykh* 'Uthmān, "the faqīh of the people of Ghāna" who visited Cairo in 796/1394. Ibn Khaldūn presents both Ghana and Takrur as ongoing concerns, though both are subject to Mali.[53] He then says:

> Later the authority of the people of Ghāna waned and their prestige declined as that of the veiled people, their neighbours on the north next to the land of the Berbers grew . . . These extended their domination over the Sūdān, and pillaged, imposed tribute (*itāwāt*) and poll-tax (*jizya*) and converted many of them to Islam. Then the authority of the rulers of Ghāna dwindled away and they were overcome by the Sūsū, a neighbouring people of the Sūdān, who subjugated and absorbed them.[54]

Ibn Khaldūn's narrative of decline does not represent a single event, but rather collapses Ghana's initial "waning" in relation to Almoravid-related developments in the latter quarter of the fifth/eleventh century, which was then followed by a subsequent "dwindling" at the hands of the Susu in the early seventh/thirteenth century.

Ta'rīkh al-fattāsh also attempts to memorialize Ghana's final chapter, speaking of the "dying out of the rule of Kayama'a," and how "God destroyed their power, and the most vile took authority over the greatest of their people."[55] Though the text may have Ghana's ancien regime in mind, reference to the "most vile" refers to the Susu, not Muslim reformers. The *ta'rīkh* compresses centuries of Ghana's continuation under Mali, but as an eleventh/seventeenth-century document it has the advantage of describing a process that had finally run its course. Even so, the best indication of Ghana's endpoint may be the archaeological record concerning Kumbi Saleh's central mosque, abandoned at some point in the ninth/fifteenth century.

Early Ghana experienced a long existence and efflorescence, both as an independent kingdom from 300 CE to the end of the fifth/eleventh century, and as a reform Muslim state until the first third of the seventh/thirteenth, after which it lingered on in tributary form for another two hundred years. That is more than a millennium.

There was no single regime in early Ghana, but rather three (including life under Mali), and it was toward the end of its run as a non-Muslim, independent state that it became contested terrain for the claims of a militant, reformist version of Islam that spread through the whole of the Senegal valley and beyond. The twelfth/eighteenth and thirteenth/nineteenth centuries were therefore not the only age of reform in West Africa, but this initial experimentation would be assailed by many factors, including the vicissitudes of the trans-Saharan slave trade. The next chapter discusses aspects of that trade, especially its imbrications with developing notions of race and gender.

CHAPTER FOUR

Slavery and Race Imagined in *Bilād As-Sūdān*

THE FIFTH/ELEVENTH CENTURY TRANSITION to reform Islam in the western Sahel was coterminous with an intensification in slaving, generating a lively discourse regarding eligibility, within which notions of race and gender unfolded. The imbrication of slavery, race, and gender would partially inform processes by which West African elites claimed archaic origins in the central Islamic lands, creating distance from the land of their actual birth.

From the beginning, external sources associate *bilād as-sūdān* with slaving in an entirely unremarkable manner, well established by the third/ninth century given the discussion of the Fezzan.[1] Kanem would soon develop a reputation as not only a supplier of slaves, but as specializing in "black" eunuchs.[2] The area's activities must have been considerable by the eighth/fourteenth century, when Ibn Baṭṭūṭa identified Bornu as the source of "handsome slave girls (*jawarī*) and young men slaves (*fityān*)."[3] Slaving had become so profitable that Bornu's sovereign had to appeal to the Mamluks to rein in Egyptian and Syrian *jullāb* (slavers) to protect his subjects.[4]

In contrast to Kanem-Bornu, the external sources are virtually silent on Gao's participation in slaving. Though traditions maintain al-Ayaman fathered a child with an enslaved girl to begin Gao's ruling dynasty, and while Gao's sovereign had "many servants" by the sixth/twelfth century, this is not the same as procuring captives for export.[5] In discussing Gao's economy between the fourth/tenth and sixth/twelfth centuries, the sources specify livestock, rice, sugar cane, and sesame as the principal bases for Gao's wealth, while in emphasizing Gao's strategic position astride multiple axes of transregional commerce, al-Zuhrī makes no mention of slaving.[6]

It therefore cannot be assumed that all Sahelian states were similarly engaged in trafficking. Consideration of Ghana also makes this point. The earlier sources associate Ghana with gold production, and little else. Domestic slavery certainly existed in Ghana, but al-Bakrī's few references to it are in stark contrast with his delight in describing enslaved females in Awdaghust.[7] There were apparently thousands, but they were not necessarily supplied by Ghana, as Awdaghust's own king regularly raided "the land of the Sūdān."[8] It is only with al-Zuhrī's sixth/twelfth-century discussion of Ghana late in the fifth/eleventh century that its involvement in slaving becomes unequivocal, as they raided the "land of Barbara and Amīma and capture their people as they used to do when they were pagans."[9]

It is not clear who the Amīma and Barbara were (possibly "Bambara," also ambiguous), though the latter were regarded as strong, "impetuous," "brave," and skilled in war," the "most noble and aristocratic of men" to whom "the *amīr*" of Ghana was related. Said to inhabit "the middle of the desert," they may have been a branch of the Soninke. The Amīma, on the other hand, are identified as impoverished Jews who "read the Torah" and were involved in the import business.[10]

Al-Zuhrī's treatment of Ghana is confirmed by his contemporary, al-Idrisī, though the latter's emphasis shifts in saying "the people of Barīsā, Silā, and Ghāna make forays into the land of the Lamlam, and capture its inhabitants." The most distinctive quality of the "Lamlam" was their plight as prey: "Every year great numbers of them are sent to al-Maghrib al-Aqṣā. Everyone in the land of Lamlam is branded on his face with fire, which is their mark, as we have mentioned before."[11]

Ibn Sa'īd adds something both novel and suggestive in the seventh/thirteenth century, stating Ghana's ruler "often wages Holy War on the pagans; his house is well known for this."[12] For the first time, Ghana's slaving is couched within the framework of *jihād*. That Ghana had become "well known" for slaving gestures toward its waning control over the gold trade, certainly the case by the eighth/fourteenth century, when Mali eclipsed Ghana. Ibn Khaldūn's reference to the Lamlam is instructive: "The people of Ghāna and Takrūr make raids on them and capture them and sell them to the merchants, who import them beyond the Maghrib. They form the greater part of their slaves (*raqīq*)."[13] There is no mention of Ghana's gold.

The Prey of the "Lamlam"

Reference to the Lamlam brings into focus populations targeted for enslavement, with the sources employing such terms as the Mīriyyūn, the Zaghāwiyyūn, the Marwiyyūn, confined to the Lake Chad area; and the Barbara and Amīma, located within the western Sahel. In this context, the Lamlam, itself an invented term, seems to have represented a range of non-Muslim groups with whom writers were unfamiliar but who, according to al-Idrisī, specifically occupied the space to the south of Ghana (although Ibn Sa'īd's locates them principally along the Atlantic Ocean).[14]

The "Damdam" initially appear as a mere permutation, but are then distinguished in that "they eat men."[15] The fifth/eleventh-century work *Akhbār al-zamān* presents them as inhabiting a formidable realm with a "powerful" ruler, while al-Bakrī reiterates the Damdam eat "anyone who falls into their hands," qualified by the sixth/twelfth-century *Kitāb al-Istibṣār* as "any white men."[16] Al-Dimashqī divides the "heathens" into the Lamlam, "Tamīm," and Damdam, with the first two living closer to Muslims and therefore covering their "privy parts with skins," while those farther away, "namely the Damdam, eat anybody not of their own race who falls into their hands." Al-'Umarī refers to them as the "Tamtam, who eat men," with which Ibn Khaldūn does not disagree, writing that the Lamlam "are nearer to the dumb animals . . . Sometimes they eat each other and are not to be counted among human kind."[17] The Damdam were therefore differentiated by their cannibalism and powerful state, while the Lamlam were "stateless" fish-eaters. This begins a process of categorization critical to the machinery of enslavement, as it becomes increasingly important to determine who could be enslaved. Ethno-linguistic groupings in West Africa would eventually become akin to juridical categories, at least in principle if not practice.

Fantasizing West African Women

Whatever their broad distinctions, these groups were hunted and fated for export. And while men and women are mentioned, it was captive women and girls who captivated their captors. References to women are tinged with the fantastical, as in an account of Ḥabīb b. Abī 'Ubayda al-Fihrī (d. 123/741), sent by Ifrīqiya's governor to the Sus and Sudan on military expedition, who "attained success of which the like has never been seen" in his haul of gold, but whose booty included two females belonging to a "race" called *ijjān* or *tarājān*, each of whom "has but one breast."[18]

The sources reveal more about the male perspective than the "objects" of their gaze. While one-breasted women is not the stuff of most erotic dreams, it nonetheless connotes sexual exceptionality, and was but the beginning of a much more involved conversation. In the fourth/tenth century, al-Iṣṭakhrī comments that the Maghrib was the source of West African captives (*khadam*) as well as "white slaves from al-Andalus."[19] His contemporary Ibn Ḥawqal generally concurs that from the Maghrib come "very comely slave girls (*muwalladāt*) . . . and slaves (*khadam*) imported from the land of the Sūdān, and those imported from the land of the Slavs by way of al-Andalus."[20] "Black" and "white" women occupied very different servile statuses in Awdaghust, and in admiring the latter's "firm breasts" and "slim waists," al-Bakrī reveals an active imagination:

> Muḥammad b. Yūsuf says that Abū Bakr Aḥmad b. Khallūf al-Fāsī, a pious *shaykh* . . . told him: "Abū Rustam al-Nafūsī . . . informed me that he saw one of these women reclining on her side [and] her child, an infant . . . passing under her waist from side to side without her having to draw away from him at all on account of the ampleness of the lower part of her body and the gracefulness of her waist."[21]

In introducing black women as food preparers, al-Bakrī suggests they accept their plight and take pleasure in their work, whereas he associates "white" women with leisure and comfort. And though the woman in question is a mother, there is a visual fixation with and investment in her sensuality, sanctioned by no less than a *shaykh*.

Although white women may have stimulated great arousal, black women were within a similar scope of desire, as domestic service, rather than preventing sexual access, facilitated it. The allure of black women further motivated a seventh/thirteenth century-Ghana *amīr* to offer them as concubines to North African merchants as a central feature of his hospitality:

> God has endowed the slave girls there with laudable characteristics, both physical and moral, more than can be desired: their bodies are smooth, their black skins are lustrous, their eyes are beautiful, their noses well shaped, their teeth white, and their smell fragrant.[22]

On the other hand, the debilitating suffering of black women is hardly considered in the external sources. In fact, one of the most vivid recollections of the early trans-Saharan slave trade focuses on the enslaver's suffering, not that of the enslaved:

> But the *ḥaḍarī* [or urban dweller, returning north after his purchase] was exhausted with his slave women (*khadam*) and men (*raqīq*)—this woman had grown thin, this one was hungry, this one was sick, this one had run away, this one was afflicted by the guinea-worm (*al-ʿirq al-mudammir*) . . .[23]

The report only indirectly speaks of hunger, disease, melancholy, and resistance, but the allusion is a much better reflection of captive women's experiences than a voyeurism devoid of concerns with kidnapping, family dismemberment, deprivation, disease, disorientation, depression, dehumanization, humiliation, rape, gelding, and the stench of death, verities at some distance from phallocentric fantasia.

Mobilizing the Hamitic Curse

Enslaved females, like their male counterparts, were recruited from all corners of the globe into the *dār al-Islām*, with captives from Europe and Asia outnumbering sub-Saharan Africans until the twelfth/eighteenth century, while Slavs and Caucasians constituted the principal servile groups in the Ottoman empire.[24] Such miscellany underscores just how unnecessary it was for Muslims to justify slavery beyond the condition of unbelief. And yet there develops in the external sources a distinctive discourse purporting to explain the nature of somatic difference and its relationship to cultural expression, civilizational attainment, and questions of freedom and enslavement. While some views anticipate contemporary notions of racism, others, if not progressive, at least are nonjudgmental.

A panoply of considerations informs these subjectivities, including religious practice, markers of "civilization," phenotype, and slavery's expansion. The first two filters are paramount, involving the presence or absence of Islam (or another Ibrahimic religion), followed by urbanity, literacy, wealth accumulation, and clothing. Some observers were aware that West and North African societies were heterogeneous, that categories of "black" and "white" were simplistic, and were therefore more interested in other distinctions. However, the growth of the trans-Saharan slave trade homogenized and narrowed these perspectives, with those deemed "Sudan" increasingly associated with the servile estate.

The Qur'ān itself is declarative in avowing human heterogeneity as providential:

> And among His signs is the creation of the heavens and the earth, and the diversity of your languages and colors. In that surely are signs for those who know.[25]

The Grenada-born Abū Ḥāmid (d. 565/1169–70), however, preferred fables:

> In the land of the Sūdān exist people without heads . . . It is also said that in the deserts of the Maghrib there are a people of the progeny of Adam, consisting solely of women . . . These headless people have eyes in their shoulders, and mouths in their chests. They form many nations [and] reproduce and do not harm anyone, and they have no intelligence. God knows best.[26]

These stories allegorically express perspectives of autochthonous populations as female societies without and incapable of producing men—a "feminization" of the indigenous condition, an anomaly beckoning male conquest to arrest and reverse. This maps well onto their exoticization, while the acephalous condition elsewhere in the Sudan invokes an absence of government, of humanity itself, their enslavement rendering them a service. Yāqūt's seventh/twelfth century depiction of black gold producers is but a variation of Abū Ḥāmid's: "It is said that they dwell in underground hiding places and burrows, and that they are naked, like animals, covering [of the body] being unknown to them."[27]

Of course, tales of headless, single-breasted women and Amazons begin with Homer and Herodotus, refitted to North and West African contexts with Islam's spread.[28] However, a permutation apparently unrelated to Greek mythology, the so-called Hamitic curse, is circulating in the Muslim world as early as the third/ninth century, when the Persian al-Dīnawarī refers to a "nation of mankind whose eyes and mouths are on their breasts" among the Sudan, "descended from Nūḥ who incurred the wrath of God so that he changed their form," thereby linking the headless with the curse.[29] What he leaves unclear his fellow Persian and contemporary Ibn Qutayba makes plain:

> Wahb b. Munabbih said that Ḥām b. Nūḥ was a white man having a beautiful face and form. But Allāh (to Him belongs glory and power) changed his colour and the colour of his descendants because of his father's curse. Ḥām went off, followed by his children. They settled on the shore of the sea, and Allāh increased them. They are the Sūdān. Ḥām begot Kūsh b. Ḥām, Kan'ān b. Ḥām and Fūṭ b. Ḥām. Fūṭ travelled and settled in the land of Hind and Sind, and the people there are his descendants. The descendants of Kūsh and Kan'ān are the races of the Sūdān: the Nūba, the Zanj, the Qazān [or Fazzān], the Zaghāwa, the Ḥabasha, the Qibṭ and the Barbar.[30]

Here, "whiteness" is normative, an expression of divine preference and pleasure, the "change in color" a curse. A specific change of color is not specified, as it is in fact a range of colors; that people are "of color" verifies their descent from Ḥām, including Asians (Hind and Sind), Berbers (Barbars), Egyptians (Qibṭ), and all other Africans.

The author of *Akhbār al-zamān* goes further, saying "Nūḥ, peace be upon him, cursed Ḥām, praying that his face should become ugly and black, and that his descendants should become slaves to the progeny of Sām." No reason is given for Nūḥ's pronouncement, but the account goes on to say: "After Kan'ān, Ḥām begat Kūsh, who was black. Ḥām intended to kill his wife, but Sām prevented him, reminding him of their father's curse." That is, Ḥām assumed the birth of a black son was due to his wife's infidelity (requiring a black father, left unexplained), but he is reminded that it was the result of paternal and (presumably) supernatural invective. Ḥām departs and travels to the farthest west coast of Africa, followed by his sons, who stop at various stages, lose contact with each other, and develop distinct communities that include the Berbers.[31]

Yet another permutation is offered by al-Ya'qūbī: "When Nūḥ awoke from his sleep and learnt what had happened he cursed Kan'ān b. Ḥām but he did not curse Ḥām. Of his posterity are the Qibṭ, the Ḥabasha, and the Hind."[32] Whatever transpired while Nūḥ was asleep must have been fairly appalling, but in relocating the curse from Ḥām to Kan'ān (Canaan), al-Ya'qūbī says nothing about a change in color. Kan'ān is also associated with ungodly song and dance, suggesting such proclivities reside in the blood.

Al-Dimashqī adds two more variants in the eighth/fourteenth century, in the first of which Nūḥ asks God to "modify the seed" of Ḥām after the latter had sex with his wife on the ark, "so that he brought forth [the ancestor of] the Sūdān." In a second version Ḥām happens upon a sleeping Nūḥ whose private parts are exposed; his brothers Sām and Yāfath (Japheth) cover their father without looking at "his shame." Upon awakening, Nūḥ curses Ḥām.[33]

What al-Ya'qūbī assumes and al-Dimashqī revises is the Hebrew Old Testament's account of a postdiluvian, drunken Noah whose "nakedness is uncovered" by his son Ham. Awaking from his stupor and realizing "what had been done to him," Noah pronounces judgment: "Cursed be Canaan; the lowest of servants he shall be to his brothers."[34] In addition to the original offense, there are other ambiguities here, including just who was cursed—Ham or Canaan—and whether it carried divine sanction. Whatever the original intent, many interpretations settled on at least some portion of the African population, in the Muslim context a needless mechanism of justification, but just as equally an explanatory device.

In significant contrast, Ibn Khaldūn (in the *Muqaddimah*) refutes the association of blackness with the Hamitic curse:

> Genealogists who had no knowledge of the true nature of things imagined that Negroes were the children of Ham, the son of Noah, and that they were singled out to be black as the result of Noah's curse, which produced Ham's colour and the slavery God inflicted upon his descendants . . . The curse included no more than that Ham's descendants should be the slaves of his brothers' descendants.[35]

Rather than dismissing slavery as a curse upon Ḥām's descendants, Ibn Khaldūn is rejecting the notion that blackness is part of that curse, arguing instead it is atmospherically induced. In this he agrees with al-Idrisī's prior attribution of black skin and nappy hair to "the intensity of the heat and the burning sun."[36] By the same logic, Ibn Khaldūn attributes the "whiteness" of northern populations to sun deprivation.

"Blackness" and Registers of "Civilization"

Rather than viewing all "black" people as the same, the external sources differentiate according to religion, cultural affects, and physical traits. Perhaps the most enduring concept is that the closer to a center of recognized civilization, the more acceptable the black population. Thus, al-Iṣṭakhrī wrote in the fourth/tenth century:

> We have not mentioned the land of the Sūdān in the west . . . because the orderly government of kingdoms is based upon religious beliefs, good manners, law and order, and the organization of settled life directed by sound policy. These people lack all of these qualities and have no share in them. . . . Some of the Sūdān, who live nearer to these well-known kingdoms, do resort to religious beliefs and practices and law, approaching in this respect the people of these kingdoms. Such is the case with Nūba and the Ḥabasha, because they are Christians, following the religious tenets of the Rūm.[37]

Apparently ignorant of the fact that Nubia and Ethiopia antedate by millennia the rise of "civilization" in the Arabian Peninsula, al-Iṣṭakhrī assumes black civilizational distinction results from proximity to recognized models. Ibn Khaldūn would expound on this concept, viewing blackness and whiteness as polarities diverging from "the temperate regions." United in extreme circumstance, Ibn Khaldūn makes the following point:

> Their manners, therefore, are close to those of the dumb animals . . . they live in caves and in the jungle and eat herbs [and] eat each other. . . . [T]hey are not acquainted with prophethood and do not submit to any revealed law (*sharīʿa*) except for such as them as are near to regions of temperateness, which is uncommon. Such are the Ḥabasha, neighbouring the Yemen, who professed Christianity before Islam and have done so after it to this day; and the people of Mālī and Kawkaw and Takrūr, neighbouring the land of the Maghrib, who profess Islam at the present day . . . and such of the nations of the Ifranja [the Franks] and the Ṣaqābila and the Turks in the north as profess Christianity.[38]

Arguably "racist," Ibn Khaldūn's assessment is at least "balanced" in that blacks and whites are equally diminished. The analysis does not actually turn on "race," or even revealed religion, as much as it does environment, but even so, difference is embodied in divergent racial types. In discussing black stereotypical behavior, Ibn Khaldūn again locates causation in external factors:

> We have seen that Negroes are in general characterized by levity, excitability, and great emotionalism. They are found eager to dance whenever they hear a melody. They are everywhere described as stupid. . . . Now, Negroes live in the hot zone. Heat dominates their temperament and formation. . . . As a result, they are more quickly moved to joy and gladness, and they are merrier . . .[39]

While he does not reject slavery as a curse upon Ḥām's descendants, neither is Ibn Khaldūn challenging the notion that blacks are excitable and emotional, observing blacks "have little that is (essentially) human and possess attributes that are quite similar to those of dumb animals, as we have stated."[40] In tandem with his highly laudatory view of eighth/fourteenth-century Mali, however, these comments suggest he had communities well beyond recognized centers of civilization in mind.

Perhaps more surprising than the views of Ibn Khaldūn are those of the eminent eleventh/seventeenth-century scholar Aḥmad Bābā. In responding to the notion of a Hamitic curse, Aḥmad Bābā states unequivocally in *Miʿrāj al-ṣuʿūd* ("The Ladder of Ascent") that unbelief is the sole requisite condition for enslavement.[41] But in reflecting on the work of

Ibn Khaldūn and others, Aḥmad Bābā alludes to the "objectionable characteristics . . . and general lack of refinement" of blacks, and provides a rather stunning concession:

> Indeed, any unbeliever among the children of Ham or anyone else may be possessed [as a slave] if he remains in his original unbelief. There is no difference between one race (*jins*) and another. Perhaps it was that his [Noah's] curse was effective on most of them, not all of them (*la'alla du'āha 'ujību fī ghālibihim lā kulihim*).[42]

Like Ibn Khaldūn, Aḥmad Bābā does not reject the curse, but his ambivalence is all the more arresting as he was part of a West African community. His own positionality is unclear; he consistently traces his lineage to the Ṣanhāja, whereas he is often referred to as "Aḥmad Bābā al-Sūdānī," especially during and after his exile in Morocco.[43] Though possibly a phenotypic descriptor, the *nisba* "al-Sūdānī" may simply refer to his region of origin.

A Range of Opinions

Ibn Khaldūn's mention of al-Mas'ūdī, and Aḥmad Bābā's response to Ibn Khaldūn, means that from at least the fourth/tenth century the Muslim world was aware of the second-century CE Greek physician Galen's assessment of blacks, who listed ten attributes peculiar to them: "nappy hair, thin eyebrows, wide nostrils, thick lips, sharp teeth, stinking smell, an evil nature, split hands and feet (*tashqīq al-yadīn wa al-rijlīn*), long penis, and a lot of joy."[44] Al-Dimashqī reproduced this list four hundred years after al-Mas'ūdī, suggesting such views were circulating.[45] In so doing, al-Dimashqī lumps the Zanj, the Ḥabasha, the Nuba, and the "Sūdān" together, as "they are all black" due to the effects of the sun, and then goes further: "No divinely revealed laws (*nawāmīs*) have come to them nor has any prophet been sent among them, for they are incapable of unifying opposites, whereas the concept of lawfulness (*shar'iyya*) is precisely commanding and forbidding, desiring and abstaining."[46]

Mention of African sexuality connects with al-Mas'ūdī and Galen's fascination with the black male member. The sources are peppered with such comments, or insecurities, as was the case with the author of the fifth/eleventh-century work, *Akhbār al-zamān*, who wrote that one man "may marry ten women, and sleep each night with two of them."[47] Complemented by al-Bakrī's tale of a special plant, available only to Ghana's king, that greatly accentuates sexual prowess, the trope of African male hypersexuality is unmistakable, as the plant is located in *bilād as-sūdān*.[48]

Beyond the preoccupation with sex, Ṣāid b. Aḥmad Ṣāid, writing in the fifth/eleventh century, lists such groups as the Ḥabasha, Nuba, Zanj, and "Ghāna," as well as Slavs and Chinese (and others) as having no interest in science, arguing that sun and heat are also the reasons blacks living in distant lands are "utterly void of all equilibrium in judgment and certainty in evaluation. They are carried away with levity and stupidity, and ignorance dominates them."[49]

Abū Ḥāmid, on the other hand, attempts to say something affirmative, albeit qualified. Writing in the sixth/twelfth century, he says the people of Ghana "have the best way of living, are the best looking, and have the least crinkled hair." A left-handed compliment, he nonetheless applauds them for "possessing intelligence and understanding," and for making the Pilgrimage. In contrast are "the Qūqū, the Malī, the Takrūr," who are "brave people but there are no blessings in their lands . . . nor do they possess religion or intelligence."[50] As these are all Muslim societies, it would appear that blackness for Abū Ḥāmid was in instances an insurmountable condition.

Of all the external sources through the seventh/thirteenth century, al-Idrisī comes closest to offering an approbative assessment of black societies and cultures. Having mentioned the naked Lamlam, he moves to descriptions of Sila, Takrur, Ghana, and Gao, for whom he consistently employs superlatives regarding their accomplishments. He is even effusive, calling the ruler of Ghana "the most righteous of men."[51] His tone undergoes an abrupt shift, however, when he comes to the Zaghāwa, "the scabbiest of all the Sūdān," whom he then disparages: "Stealing the children of one people by another, of which we have just given an account, is a prevalent custom among the Sūdān, who see nothing wrong in it."[52] Unlike preceding commentary, al-Idrisī is less preoccupied with questions of intelligence, though he may have seen Islam as having accomplished a civilizing mission. Rather, he seems much more concerned with slaving, blaming West Africans (as opposed to external demand) for the practice.

It is therefore clear that long before the Portuguese arrived in West Africa in the ninth/fifteenth century, there was already in the Muslim world a growing association of black people with slavery, barbarity, ignorance, and licentiousness. A range of opinions existed, and as a rubric were in considerable circulation.

Bilād as-Sūdān *and the Racialization of Space*

Of course, how external views of West Africans registered is very much connected to the concept of *arḍ* or *bilād as-sūdān* itself, which not only helped shape the perception of those outside of Africa, but those inside as well. Part conjuration, part myth, part approximation of verifiable fact, it is an abstraction as significant in its implications as enduring in its ramifications, an example of the Muslim world's ability to fashion its own orientalism. The superimposition of cultural and social interpretations over an otherwise expository attempt to understand the earth's configuration, the notion of a "country or land of blacks" was a racialization of space, a fusion of verity and fantasy, with profound consequences for the African continent.

On matters approximating "race" Ibn Khaldūn would aver: "The inhabitants of the north are not called by their colour, because the people who established the conventional meanings of words were themselves white."[53] Such musings are of qualified use in the Savannah and Sahel, where significant strategies were marshaled to clarify the meaning of "whiteness" (though the more interesting challenge of defining "blackness" was far less engaged).[54] Ibn Khaldūn's position further reveals a profound nescience of the world, as ancient populations of Egyptians, Arabs, Nubians, Ethiopians, Hebrews, Berbers, and Palestinians were intimately acquainted, their referents for one another rarely betraying preoccupations with skin color.[55] In contrast, the "Ethiopian," taken from the Greek *Aethiops*, or the "Moor," from the Greek *Mavros* and the Latin *Maurus*, reflect the perceptions of Europeans. Even so, a vocabulary of physiognomic resonance/dissonance, in conjunction with cultural diversity and religion, would develop with the early expansion of Arab armies and Islam, categorizing an otherwise bewildering array of humanity.

As Islam expanded through North Africa into Iberia, Muslims slowly became aware of the enormous dimensions of Africa's upper portion, not to mention its eastern littoral.[56] The sheer size of *bilād as-sūdān*, coupled with its accessibility only through desert or ocean similarly vast, reinforced the impression of an entirely different spatial dimension. As heat was quite familiar to Arab travelers, they would have taken greater notice that everyone south of the desert was "black" (of one sort or another), as opposed to more varied expressions in Arabia, Egypt, and India. What may have been meant was *bilād as-sūdān faqaṭ*, "the land of only blacks." In any event, the effect of reifying skin color necessarily engendered new forms of consciousness.

Scholarly thinking on race in Islamic lands is largely divided into two camps, with researchers in the Indian Ocean insisting on an asymmetry that emphasizes how race and its cognates (along with "slavery," or, better, a series of inequalities and statuses of "unfreedom") are dissimilar from "western" fixations on biological or so-called scientific criteria; and those investigating societies on an arc from East Africa through Egypt into West Africa who, though also disquieted by facile adoptions of "the Atlantic model" (in stances offering an indigenous alternative), in the end propose frameworks that (unintentionally) accommodate that model remarkably well.[57]

Most such studies privilege the local context, with which this analysis agrees, but that very premise invariably leads to results that question the usefulness of the chasm between the two camps. Indeed, the Savannah and Sahel's "borderland" quality as a transitional, liminal space, within which variegated communities and cultures were in mutual exchange over millennia, facilitated the convergence of at least two conversations about race. The first, a localized, pre-Islamic notion of difference, is supported by scanty linguistic evidence whose subsequent, pejorative connotations may bear little relationship to an original signification. The Berber term for West Africans—*gnawa* or *janāwa*—at some point came to refer to "blacks," and may have been mobilized in the competition over resources with the southward movement of populations fleeing the Sahara's desiccation.[58] This suggests phenotype could have been a significant social register before Islam, but by the time the linguistics become audible in the historical record, Islam is already dominant in the region, with local meanings long infused with perspectives emanating from a much larger Muslim world and informed by scholarly disquisition.[59] This second perspective, accompanying Islam's expansion in the region, was comparative in scope, equating blackness with slavery and backwardness. Any exclusive investment in local configurations of race is therefore ahistorical, as parochial intendment in the Savannah and Sahel was clearly influenced by transregional conversations about race centuries in the making. Stories of Ḥām circulating in the region were hardly generated *in situ*.

But race making in the conjoined region also unfolded with the expansion of slaving. West African elites, like the Berbers of the region or the Safavids of Iran, would reinvent themselves through claiming descent from some progenitor in the Middle East, if not from the Prophet himself.[60] But slavery would also become a powerful ideological and economic factor, and figured in the calculus of reimagining among darker-skinned elites.[61] Race and slavery would become inextricably interwoven and mutually constitutive, notwithstanding the view that the darker and servile (or otherwise subject) strata of Berber societies were first and foremost members of those societies. Such is hardly unique to the Old World, recalling varying configurations of race in the Americas.[62]

Of course, individuals belonged to multiple groupings with respect to ethnolinguistic formation, religion, region, economic endeavor, and so on. In instances these considerations were more determinative than race, with insignia of status that could include dress, accoutrement, dietary patterns, and especially language. Various combinations of these factors reroute the process of categorizing the darker-skinned, but few of these factors negate the observation that "blackness," both within a particular social formation and between such formations, was generally a condition in need of amelioration, illustrative of analogous, if not shared values.

In a critical divergence from the Atlantic experience, race in the Muslim world was highly impacted by protocols in which children of Arab or Berber fathers followed their status (when paternity was acknowledged), as opposed to the status of the mother. This combination of patrilineality and mythology (with fictive descent claims) therefore had the potential effect of distorting if not effacing the maternal line. Here, then, is the essential problem of only recognizing a local, cultural model, as it masks a verity only recoverable through a biological forensics. In fact, fictive descent is itself mobilized through these same logics. In giving voice to the marginalized, therefore, the socio-cultural and the biological are mutually beneficial.

As such, this study understands race as referring to the culturally orchestrated, socially sanctioned disaggregation and reformulation of the human species into broad, hierarchical categories reflecting purported respective levels of capacity, propensity, and beauty, and in ways often tethered to phenotypic expression. While characteristically manipulated for advantage or to justify it, similar sentiments can be observed in African attempts to make sense of European behavior.[63] This may differ from other notions of race (with distinctions between "racism" and "racialization" of negligible significance) informed by nonsomatic, nonbiological criteria, but the models are not necessarily conflictual.[64] In traversing time and space from the specific to the global, race's precise expression has been fluid (e.g., Jews in Europe and the U.S., or the Irish in the U.S.), but the concept itself has proven rather resilient.[65]

Given the stakes of privilege and power in such societies as the Tuareg, where individuals were first Tuareg and then black, it is possible to argue that, if anything, race was more even salient. And while other darker-skinned Tuaregs were "white" by virtue of status, consideration of the actual and multifaceted nature of human descent renders a more complex picture. The same would also be true for many West African societies in which patrilineality results in significant erasure.

Evidence for the articulation of slavery, race, and gender in the early Sahel makes an argument for change over time far more compelling than assumptions regarding the antiquity and pervasiveness of slavery. Slavery's development, however, would help shape views of West African women as well as concepts of blackness. Its expansion would also stimulate debate over human difference, and in ways not terribly removed from contemporary notions of race, resting on the fulcrum of an alleged, ancient curse.

Human trafficking and intellectual exchange, in conjunction with the division of communities into civilizational registers in concert with somatic divergence, were the principal components of *bilād as-sūdān*, a construct as ideational as spatial. Slaving, together with Islam's continued rise, would constitute the double predicate upon which polity in the region would greatly expand over the next three centuries.

PART II

Imperial Mali

CHAPTER FIVE

The Meanings of Sunjata and the Dawn of Imperial Mali

TO TRANSITION FROM A DISCUSSION of the early Savannah and Sahel to the temporal threshold of that combined region's medieval history in the sixth/twelfth and seventh/thirteenth centuries is to undergo a radical shift in both the period's evidentiary base as well as its themes. With respect to the former, the interest and reliability of external Arabic documentation weakens, focused as it had been on developments within the spatial frontiers of an internal littoral. Beyond those frontiers an actual Arab or Berber presence rarely registers, such that the dawn of a different geopolitical era is at best obscure. Into the lacunae has been mobilized a genre of oral tradition, refined to an art form of exceptional quality while posing unique challenges, affording limited rather than scopic insight into a formative period of West African polity that constitutes the very core, the iconic center of subsequent lay and scholarly imagination. There emerges a new articulation in medieval West Africa—the empire—and so begins an analysis of a political formation lasting some 350 years.

Though disparate in orientation, preoccupation, and circumstances of production, written and oral sources are in other ways proximate.[1] The oral sources, through the instrumentality of the *jeli* (plural *jeliw*) or griot, are primarily concerned with the rise of imperial Mali and the life of its founder, Sunjata, the collective narrative often presented in the form of an "epic," as its various iterations contain sufficient points of correspondence and formulaic substance to more or less constitute a composite, generalized account.[2] In embracing the challenge of relating the oral corpus to other, more verifiable sources, the current approach places all into conversation, with the rise of Sunjata and Mali taking on a more complicated texture, better engaged with historicity while more dehiscent to multiple imbrications of meaning, bridging Savannah and Sahel.

As a vehicle of memorialization, oral tradition is an ingenious tool through which the severalty of "truths" and "events" is communicated. At times employing the fantastical, and often by means of the allegorical, the multiple dimensions of the human condition are re-presented in dramatic and artistic fashion, reanimating the past while resuscitating links, if not indissoluble bonds between the living with the dead, conveying purpose and identity and rank, while revealing life's mysteries and vicissitudes.

In paying serious attention to the *jeliw*, the approach here is at some variance with those for whom only verifiable fact is of interest, and for whom orality is unresponsive.[3] Though understandable, such a position can be unproductive, unnecessarily reifying dichotomies of verity and legend.[4] That *jeli* accounts are inconsistent and falter is a valid concern, but as critical is the consideration of what the griots actually convey.[5] Rather than an approach of western arrogation and assumption of vacuity, an inquiry open to cultural asymmetries is better able to navigate permutation and nuance, mitigating unnecessary tension with conventional evidentiary standards.[6]

As opposed to viewing divergent sources as hierarchical and competitive in historical claims-making, the approach here places them into dialogue, whereby the external, written record sheds light on political developments, while the oral corpus affords insights into their cultural and social dimensions—a complex of consanguinity and beliefs and retrospective that inform the historical period, resulting in a mutually disquisitional relation between the written, external record and oral, internal memory.[7]

The epic form of the Sunjata narrative is treated here as fundamentally a declaration of the integral elements of empire as understood by the Mande, featuring how it is thought to have come into being and the modalities by which it operated. As effected hundreds of years after the period in question, the corpus may serve more contemporary interests, but to the degree that earlier oral accounts were actually formed during the historical period, they represent an attempt at recording and legitimating empire.

When approached in this fashion, the oral corpus consists of three interpretive categories that are not always mutually exclusive. The first concerns historical developments corroborated by independent sources yielding high probability, examples of which include the foundational role of hunter guilds in Mande polity, Susu territorial domination followed by war, and conquest under Sunjata. Other highly probable claims not necessarily fully realized during Sunjata's lifetime include Mali's imperial organization, as evidenced in Songhay's subsequent appropriation of provinces distinctly Malian in origin.

A second interpretive category involves those developments posited by the oral corpus and unsubstantiated by sources of unrelated provenance, yet registering within a range of historical plausibility. These include dynastic rivalry and troubled familial relations, problematic aspects of Sunjata's character, and the acceleration of gender-dominated political office. Fourteenth/twentieth-century griots had little to gain by venturing so deeply into such sensitive, even embarrassing matters.

The Sunjata epic also conveys Mande values and perspectives featuring extensive, everyday interactions between the physical and noumenal, social stratification, interclan relations, gender protocols, parenting, and the etiquette of power. The traditions' didactic quality forms a matrix within which the historicity of "events" is of less significance than their instrumentality, through which mores and principles of social engagement are conveyed.[8] Achieving prescription by way of reflection, the literature (re) enacts a broad decorum of relations in recreating the social and cultural context, thus constituting a third category of analysis, an example of which is an evolving notion of caste.

In espousing a theory of empire, a process that decidedly resides within the realm of the political, the Sunjata epic delineates its constitutive elements. These crystallize with the unfolding of the epic, but their enumeration begins with the assertion of an expansive central authority that supersedes all other claims to regional sovereignty, creating in the process individuated, hierarchical relations to the center—a novel concept certainly realized by the eighth/fourteenth century.[9] A close yet fluid relationship between the state and Islam is a second component, with Islam tolerating rather than eviscerating ancestral religious practice. A third element concerns leadership qualifications trumpeting prestigious linkages to the central Islamic lands, successful navigation of trial and adversity, mastery of skills originally associated with hunters, valorous behavior in war, and manifest divine sanction. A fourth and final element reengenders the formal political sphere as an exclusively male-dominated space.

Transmission of the Traditions

Before examining how the external and oral sources relate, it would be useful to establish a sense of the latter's architecture. The narrative of Sunjata and medieval Mali's rise is one of the best known in West Africa. By its very construction as a performance, it is a balance between intellectual content and the artistic dexterity of the performer, the *jeli*. Concerns with the limitations of human memory, particularly over generations, are important, but somewhat mitigated with consideration of the epic's components. More specifically, the epic has a nucleic center composed of songs, melodies created to commemorate key or transformative events.[10] These songs, in turn, are linked through a series of narrative strategies addressing episodic moments as well as progressions in the life cycle through dialogue, speechmaking, the recounting of battles, and so on. The specifics of the "narrative links" between songs vary from version to version, but the songs themselves, the most archaic element of the epic, are more resistant to change, their metric structure requiring fidelity to a form "relatively fixed."[11]

The songs are embedded in an overall presentation often requiring musical accompaniment, and therefore classified as a specific type of performance, a *foli*.[12] Songs commemorating ancestors are *fasaw* (s. *fasa*), with the *janjon* its highest form.[13] There was necessarily drift over time in content and performance due to appropriation in various languages, changes in social and cultural insignia, fluctuating relations of audiences to the material, and innovation as well as failure in human recall. But the need to faithfully reproduce the songs remained a priority, placing constraints upon intentional emendation while reducing susceptibility to improvisation. The songs police the process, and are the anchors to which narration is moored.

Contributing to the deep historicity of at least some songs are the "first-singers," purportedly contemporaries of Sunjata, whose mention allows for a degree of corroboration. An indication of such historicity is recorded by Ibn Baṭṭūṭa during his eighth/fourteenth-century visit to Mali, when and where he paid significant attention to one "Dūghā the interpreter," who on feast days and Friday afternoons performed before dignitaries and "sang poetry in which he praises the sultan and commemorates his expeditions and exploits," followed next by the *jeliw*, who declared to *Mansā* Sulaymān (ruler at the time) that upon his royal seat (*bambī/banbī*) once sat "'such-and-such a king and of his good deeds were so-and-so . . . so you do good deeds which will be remembered after you.'"[14]

The focus of their performance is not specified, but as the subject concerned former rulers, Sunjata himself may have featured, especially as Ibn Baṭṭūṭa later actually mentions Sāriq Jāṭa, the grandfather of *Mansā* Mūsā (and likely the same person as Sunjata, or Mārī Jāṭa).[15]

Eighth/fourteenth-century recordings of Sunjata have yet to materialize, their collection dating back no earlier than the late eleventh/seventeenth century, when "crafted" under *Mansā* Saman of Kangaba.[16] Kangaba town had become a last refuge for Malian rulers reduced to the small state of Minijan, reeling from the Bambara/Bamana of Segu. Saman would initiate the tradition of reroofing the *Kama-Bolon* (*Kamabolon, Amambolon*) every seven years, a structure allegedly built by the aforementioned *Mansā* Sulaymān who, following his purported return from the Ḥijāz in 752/1352, deposited within it "holy books." The reroofing ceremony became the occasion for the gathering of representatives from the branches of the royal Keita clan, along with other Mande clans accompanied by their "traditionalists," who would listen to the Sunjata traditions as conveyed by the Jabate-Gberela griots of Keyla, five kilometers away. In fact, the traditions were in process at this time, transitioning from panegyric "metaphors and allusions" to the epic form—the *maana*—in attempting to more fully preserve the memory of Mali now under siege.[17] Language itself was impacted, as contemporary *jeliw* regard what was spoken in Sunjata's time as *kuma koro* or "ancient speech."[18]

Keyla was/is a *kumayoro* or "specialized center" from where heralds the *jeliw ngaraw* or master griots, guardians of the traditions, having inherited the responsibility from the Kuyate clan of *jeliw*.[19] The Mande were eventually joined by griots from all over the western Sudan during the reroofing of the *Kama-Bolon* for an instructional period lasting from six months to a year, explaining the epic's existence in Pulaar, Wolof, Soninke, Zarma, etc.[20] The *Kama-Bolon* reroofing was not the only occasion for reciting the Sunjata epic, but it was apparently the most critical.[21] From Kangaba, therefore, the Keyla *jeliw ngaraw* oversaw a process by which traditions were "codified" and disseminated, resulting in a measure of uniformity reinforcing the order imposed by the songs themselves. Hunter's stories (*sere*), in revealing contrast, are not subject to such controls.

The notion of the *Kama-Bolon* as a repository of books from the time of *Mansā* Sulaymān raises the question of literacy's role in the Sunjata epic, with the *jeliw ngaraw* often referring to the traditions as the Manden *Tariku*, the "book of the Manden."[22] This may relate to the claim that in Keyla resides a secret text written in *ajami* (Maninka, using Arabic script) to which no unauthorized person has access.[23] The notion of oral tradition informed by written materials is contested by scholars who maintain no such manuscripts exist, that elderly men in Keyla are "functionally illiterate," and that the *jeliw ngaraw* rely solely upon memory.[24] But as literacy has been in the western Sudan for over a thousand years, it is entirely possible eleventh/seventeenth-century griots drew upon written sources to complement what was transmitted orally. The notion of the Sunjata epic as a "literary practice" is therefore provocatively suggestive, especially in relation to Ibn Baṭṭūṭa and Ibn Khaldūn.[25]

But even if oralists knew that elements of high historical probability—the role of hunter guilds in Mande polity, Susu territorial domination and war, Sunjata's conquest, Mali's provincial composition—resided in earlier written documents, such information was neither novel nor formative, as it is too minimalist to serve as the source of such rich oral contextual information. What is more, the written accounts reveal oral performance as an ongoing process, rendering its suspension and abrupt revival three hundred years later highly unlikely.

A final consideration is the impossibility of knowing the ways in which accounts of Sunjata may have undergone alteration from the eighth/fourteenth century, to the late eleventh/seventeenth centuries, to the point at which the epic is actually recorded in the late thirteenth/nineteenth century, as they may have been influenced by local political and social spatialities. And as a function of French imperial activity, their transcription probably contributed to their further dissemination, since Kangaba's original intention could have been to limit diffusion.[26] As such, correspondences between versions uncorroborated by independent sources could reflect Kangaba-directed uniformity.

Orality and the Written Record

With an overview of orality's formation in place, its traditions can be examined alongside the written documentation. An initial inquiry demonstrates how the sources mutually reinforce the historicity of hunter guilds in Mali's formation, the rise of the Susu and war, and conquest under Sunjata. They all unfold during the "long dry" period from the sixth/twelfth to the tenth/sixteenth century, when many Mande speakers moved south and west, continuing a progression begun by the "Tichit people."[27] As such, the sources are concerned with a region in motion.

Al-Bakrī (d. 487/1094) possibly refers to the *berceau* of Mali in the fifth/eleventh century when he writes of "another great kingdom . . . the king of which has the title of Daw. The inhabitants of this region use arrows when fighting. Beyond this country lies another called Malal, the king of which is known as *al-musulmānī*."[28] He positions "Daw" (or Do) east of/along the "Nīl" (the Senegal River with its Faleme and Bafing tributaries) together with Malal, well within lands associated with ancient Mali.

According to al-Bakrī, Malal had suffered a withering drought for years, toward the end of which a guest of Malal's king, "who used to read the Koran and was acquainted with the Sunna," enjoined the ruler to convert to Islam, committing to "'pray for your deliverance from your plight. Thus he continued to press the king until the latter accepted Islam and became a sincere Muslim."[29] After the guest's partial night of intercessory prayer, rains descend. Al-Bakrī, when combined with al-Shammākhī's tenth/sixteenth century version of the same, represents a perspicacious distillation of the relationship between religion and polity at the dawn of medieval Muslim West Africa, particularly that relationship's origins in what becomes Mali.[30]

Aspects of al-Bakrī's account comport well with Mande concepts of empire as revealed in the oral corpus. The idea of leadership honed in hunter guilds is reflected in al-Bakrī's observation of inhabitants using "arrows when fighting," while his conversion tale evinces a view of political authority at its initial phase of intimacy with Islam. These are fifth/eleventh century ideas; eleventh/seventeenth century griots are not their generative source.

Though not in perfect alignment, al-Bakrī and al-Idrisī concur that a form of polity existed deep in the Savannah by the fifth/eleventh century, hardly surprising given that the middle Niger valley's urbanization antedates this moment by thousands of years. There is therefore significant irony that the land of the "Lamlam and Damdam," viewed as the heart of darkness, was in places the very essence of urban efflorescence.

Lamlam territory would have been adjacent to the heartland of the Susu, in what is now the Malian region of Koulikoro, stretching from Sikasso in the south to Mauritania in the north.[31] Associated by some scholars with the kingdom of Kaniaga, to the east of the Kelimbine River, the Susu are named in Ibn Khaldūn's eighth/fourteenth-century account as the eastern neighbors of Ghana, and as the people who defeat that kingdom.[32] The sources make clear that slaving—the targeting of the Lamlam—had become a major enterprise by the early part of the seventh-thirteenth century, as Berber imposition of tribute would have surely included slaves, with the Susu emerging as a force at that time, their own participation in slaving inferred. This is the external, written record.

As it happens, the oral corpus is in profound resonance with the external documentation on this point, presenting the emergence of medieval empire as a response to a high level of disorder, of chaos. Like some Hebraic image of an unformed cosmos just before (further) divine intervention, the articulation of empire within the western Savannah grew out of a need to counter the forces of disintegration and lawlessness, a collapse of protocol regulating relations between societies. In this way, accounts of Mali's formation read like their own creation story.

In pulling back the landscape's figurative curtains, the oral traditions reveal a scene of destruction and mayhem. Manden, or Old Mali (as "Mali" is actually a Pulaar variation), the land of Mande-speakers who called themselves Maninka (or Mandinka), is reeling from pressures brought by the Susu, a related Mande group.[33] Unidentified in the external sources, the oral accounts name the leader of the Susu: in the most popularized version, the seventh/thirteenth century opens onto the towering figure of Sumaoro or Sumanguru Kante, "king of Susu," to whom Mali had become subject.[34] Indeed, even storied Ghana, allegedly still led by the illustrious Sisse dynasty, had begun paying tribute to him. The Susu leader's reputation suffers tremendously in the traditions: he is Sumaoro the Cruel, a "plunderer," robbing "merchants of everything when he was in a bad mood." He is "an evil demon" who "forcibly abducted girls" and flogged "venerable old men." A general picture of a Savannah-Sahel under duress therefore materializes, the internal dynamics of polities and relations between them destabilized. The emergence of the Susu represents a watershed moment.[35]

The foregoing characterizations of Sumaoro are consistent with slaving activity described by Ibn Sa'īd and Ibn Khaldūn. However, it is not until the fourteenth/twentieth century that the orature specifies slaving as the catalyst for Sumaoro's organization of a Mande response.[36] When the Maninka reject his leadership, he reacts by "smashing" Manden and deporting its "inhabitants en masse as slaves."[37] The twelfth/eighteenth century example of Segu's Bambara/Bamana suggests such a response was possible, but the Jabate tradition may well reflect a western Sudan awash in domestic slavery by the thirteenth/nineteenth century, when enter the French, explaining its symmetry with developments hundreds of years earlier.[38]

If the oral and written sources concur on the role of hunter guilds and the rise of the Susu and war as instances of high probability, they are even more aligned on Sunjata as military conqueror. The oral corpus is unanimous in celebrating him as the person who defeats

Sumaoro and ends Susu rule, while mention has been made of Ibn Baṭṭūṭa's reference to Sāriq Jāṭa, most probably Sunjata.[39] The likelihood that Sunjata was the subject of performance during Ibn Baṭṭūṭa's visit is strengthened considerably by the observation that he was the center of attention just forty years later. In 796/1394, one *Shaykh* ʻUthmān, a *faqīh* (legal expert), arrived in Egypt (while making *ḥajj*) and shared information on West Africa with Ibn Khaldūn. Having established a context of regional instability through slaving and the rise of the Susu, *Shaykh* ʻUthmān said: "Later the people of Mālī outnumbered the peoples of the Sūdān [and] vanquished the Ṣūṣū. . . . Their greatest king, he who overcame the Ṣūṣū, conquered their country, and seized the power from their hands, and was named Mārī Jāṭa . . ."[40] While there may be uncertainty as to whether the Sāriq Jāṭa of Ibn Baṭṭūṭa is in fact Sunjata, there is no question that the Mārī Jāṭa of Ibn Khaldūn and Sunjata are one and the same. As *Shaykh* ʻUthmān was from Ghana, Sunjata's fame had already spread beyond Mali's core territory, a development corroborated by Ibn Khaldūn.

Mande Claim of an Early Islamic Connection

Having provided the most cursory of information regarding Mali's origins, the external accounts go largely silent, evincing little awareness of subsequent developments. It is at this juncture that the orature proceeds alone, through murky places of unsubstantiated events and exploits, but where social and cultural context become discernible. In addition to milieu, the traditions treat dynastic contention, Sunjata's bizarre behavior, a vexed if not tortured paternal relationship, and the acceleration of male-dominated political authority, all plausible matters.

The Sunjata epic is aptly called because it focuses on the purported seasons of his life. Born into a royal lineage riddled with rivalries, his exile as a young man coincides with the rising power of the Susu, who sweep through Manden and decimate the kingdom. Beseeched to return and end Sumaoro's aggression, Sunjata acquires significant assistance along the way. Sunjata defeats Sumaoro and forges a new political arrangement in the region—the empire—and is afterward occupied with expansion. Interpretive categories are embedded within a narrative arc.

Several versions of the Sunjata oral corpus discuss not only Sunjata's origins, but also those of the Maninka and other Mande speakers, conforming to a general pattern of ethnogeneic articulation found throughout West Africa.[41] In these accounts, the Keitas are said to descend from Bilāl (Bilali Bunama), elsewhere called "Sena Bilal" and obviously referring to Bilāl b. Rabāḥ (d. ca. 19/640), Companion of the Prophet and first *mu'adhdhin* (summoner to prayer) in Islam.[42] Having claimed one of the most illustrious figures in Islam, these same traditions maintain Bilāl's descendant, Mamadi Kani, becomes a "hunter king," establishing the title of *simbon* or *donso karamoko* or "master hunter," achieved through a special relationship with the *jinn* of "the forest and bush" and the special favor of *Kondolon Ni Sané*, twinned deities of the chase.[43] Mamadi Kani will rule a following of hunters, connoting the Mande idea of polity developing from hunter guilds, the *donson ton*.[44]

Examination of these traditions suggests several concerns. The Mande permutation parallels Soninke, Berber, and Tuareg notions of descent from Yemen—a transparent strategy connecting royals to a venerated Middle East—but the decision to claim Bilāl may suggest an awareness of something akin to "race" (as do the other claims, in fact), even an affirmative embrace of "blackness," which would infer a conscious decision to resituate Maninka ethnogeneity in a way that pays homage to holy lands while rejecting invidious insinuation. If true, this is a striking divergence from origin claims elsewhere in the region, consistent with the Malian oral corpus representation of black people as descendants of Ḥām sans negative connotation, with Lahilatul Kalabi considered the "first black prince to make the Pilgrimage to Mecca."

Claiming Bilāl b. Rabāḥ under any scenario asserts an ancient, powerful Muslim pedigree, for which the Maninka are revered throughout West Africa as one of the first to embrace Islam. At the same time, the elevation of Mamadi Kani as a master hunter acknowledges local connection and sensitivity. The traditions therefore present bona fides both Islamic and non-Islamic, perhaps by design, ingeniously reflecting an accommodation between Islam and anterior beliefs.

The royal lineage may begin in myth, but progresses toward verifiability with the approximation of Sunjata's birth. Of Mamadi Kani's three or four sons, it is Simbon or Bamari Tagnogokelin who becomes the great-great-grandfather of Maghan Kon Fatta or Frako Maghan Keigu, "Maghan the Handsome," or "Farako Maghan the Beautiful," Sunjata's father and member of the Keita clan.[45] Maghan Kon Fatta is himself a *simbon*, with two or three wives and six to fourteen children. He is a presence at the beginning of Sunjata's story, but he does not occupy the center.[46] Rather, the early focus concerns the experiences and roles of women, women who are not even Maninka.

Sogolon, Sunjata's Birth, and the Echo of Female Disfranchisement

Traditions concerning Sunjata's birth and early life provide insight into the possible historicity of their circumstances as well as the narrative's deep contextual setting, simultaneously occupying both the second and third categories of interpretive analysis. The relationship of women to polity is the central feature of the Sunjata saga's opening scenes, with dimensions both plausible as well as representative of social and political milieux.

To begin, there is tumult in neighboring Sangara (or Sankara), either adjacent to or conflated with the land of Do (presumably al-Idrisī's "Daw"), where a buffalo or *koba* (in some traditions, a "horse-antelope") has ravaged the land, killing farmers and terrorizing its twelve villages.[47] The buffalo is in fact Do-Kamissa, a woman who, undergoing transmogrification, has not ceased in her campaign to kill twelve people every night in each of the twelve villages. In desperation, Do's ruler Domògò Nyamògò Jata sends for hunters from surrounding lands, but they are all killed by the *koba*, with conditions continuing to deteriorate until the appearance of two young Traore brothers, "handsome and of fine carriage," Dan *Mansā* Wulani and Dan *Mansā* Wulan Tamba (the elder).[48] Having previously consulted a "sand" oracle, they then speak with an old woman in Do.[49] Their advent is a motif found elsewhere in West African folklore.[50]

Initially rude and reticent, the old woman finally reveals she is in fact the *koba*, having assumed the form "because my twelve brethren always treated me so vilely. My brethren have all the good things, villages, slaves and riches; but they gave me not one single slave to bring me water or wood for my hearth."[51] Another account equally identifies gender asymmetries as the cause of difficulties, with the sister excluded from sacrificial rites and observances of her younger brother, the ruler Domògò Nyamògò Jata, simply because she is a woman.[52] Beyond material advantage, the grievance is more concerned with political prerogative, as each brother rules over a village.[53] Sangara or Do (Daw) may therefore represent a place and time when the relationship between political power and gender, once fluid, was in the process of becoming a masculine preserve. Unacceptable to Do-Kamissa, her protest is lethal. In laying waste to the realm by way of the mystical and magical, women shift to the supernatural as a compensatory strategy.

Mande traditions in other areas where Islam becomes significant also include discussions of women who assume the *mansaya* or rulership, with accounts from the Gambia region asserting the very first *mansā* of Niumi was a woman, *Mansā* Mama Andame Jammeh, who was succeeded by another woman, *Mansā* Wame. Niumi in fact boasts twelve women who consecutively held the *mansaya*, while states all along the Gambia claim female rulers, from Baddibu to Wuli. Perhaps this was characteristic of Mande society (at least astride the Gambia) before Islam.[54]

Having wreaked havoc, Do-Kamissa tells the Traore brothers how to kill the buffalo. They do so, presenting its golden tail to Domògò Nyamògò Jata. Instead of half the kingdom (the original offer), the hunters are asked to choose one of the ruler's nine daughters (or the finest maiden of the realm, depending on the tradition). They are all brought before the hunters, save the tenth daughter, Sogolon, warned by her father to "stay where thou art," since "with thy boils and festering sores thou art too ugly."[55]

If there is unanimity within the oral corpus on any one point, it is that Sogolon Kedju—Sogolon Kèjugu, Soukoulou-Koutouma, Sukulung Konte, Sira Nyading—is "monstrously ugly."[56] One source calls her "Sogolon the Warty," with seven large, distinct bodily protuberances, having one eye higher than the other, one leg longer than the other, one arm shorter than the other, and one buttock larger than the other.[57] Another calls her "Sukuklung the Spotty," covered with pockmarks, while yet another says she has three hundred breasts and three hundred humps.[58] She is otherwise described as a hairless "hunchback," in mimicry of a buffalo.[59]

Either the sand oracle or Do-Kamissa herself instructs the Traore brothers to request Sogolon as reward, as she is Do-Kamissa's "double": "They are alike in sorcery. . . . And they are alike in power . . ."[60] The brothers comply and, after she is washed of her "fungus," they head out of town.[61] With the oldest failing to successfully bed her (her pubic hair is "like the needles of a porcupine"), they bring her to Mali's Maghan Kon Fatta the Handsome, previously alerted by a *simbon* and "seer among seers" that two hunters would arrive with an extremely unattractive woman, but that "she will be the mother of him who will make the name of Mali immortal for ever. The child will be the seventh star, the seventh conqueror of the earth. He will be more mighty than Alexander."[62]

The story of Sunjata thus begins in incongruities and contraventions. The solution to an emerging problem (Sumaoro) comes from the land of Do/Sangara, transported by the intervention of the Traore, matching the ugliest of women with the most handsome of men. But these are actually the trappings of celestial orchestration, with prophecies not simply of deliverance, but of empire on the grandest of scales, the birth of Sunjata a cosmic event. Though hardly consistent with Islam, the accounts are infused with a sense of *maktūb*—"that which is written" or destined by the will of Allāh, hearkening to a cultural matrix relating to the third category of interpretive analysis.

Accounts addressing the circumstances of Sunjata's birth also reflect multiple agendas. At the very least, they point to the role of Do/Sangara in the early formation of Manden, and stress that Keita ascension was facilitated by the Traores. The intervention of hunters points to their unique place in Mande society, as they alone possessed the supernatural power to defeat the *koba*, bringing order out of turmoil.

But the most significant observation may be the irony that Sunjata is directly linked to an embittered Do-Kamissa, her suffering displayed in Sogolon's tortured features. Not only does Do-Kamissa exact her revenge, she lives (through Sogolon) to usher into the world a person of unprecedented power and grandeur. The Do-Kamissa-cum-Sogolon Kedju saga therefore serves dual, seemingly contradictory purposes: it affirms the righteous indignation of women over the loss of political power, yet it celebrates the political sphere as the preserve of men—as Sunjata was, after all, a man. In this way, the account of Sunjata's circumstances is a mechanism of assuagement and legitimatization, a

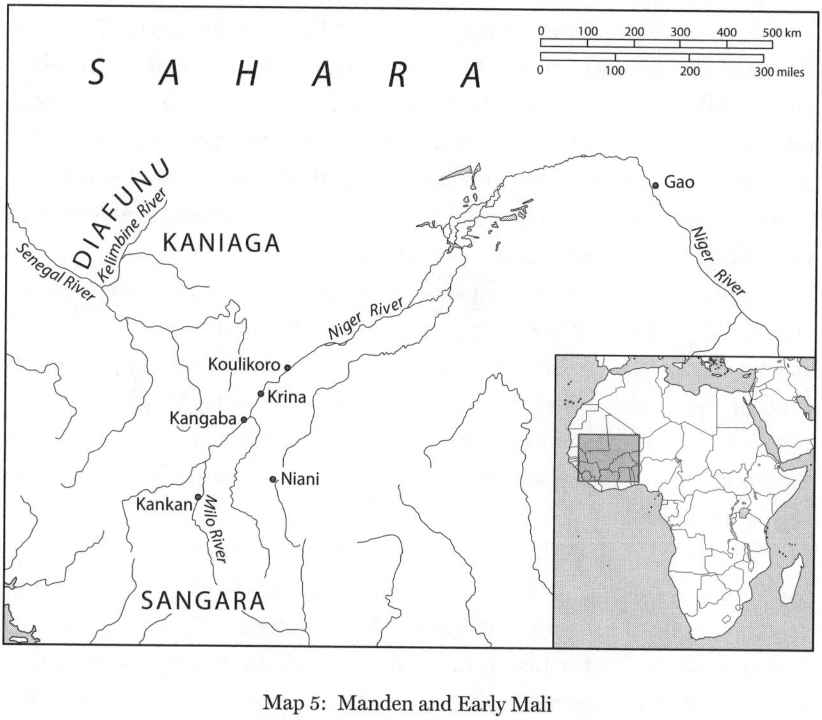

Map 5: Manden and Early Mali

double move, responding to women's resentment through their resituation as sorcerers and reification as mothers. They become alternative sites of power. The origin accounts therefore reveal a strategy of reconciliation, with Sunjata and Do-Kamissa vitally connected, sharing the same victory.

The subsequent close association between Sunjata and his mother, then between Sunjata and his sister, reflects the degree to which Sunjata is the product of women, not just in the biological sense, but also in the ideational realm, their spiritual abilities indispensable to Sunjata's survival and rise. If men are "the instruments of conquest and destruction . . . women are the *sabuw* (sources, providers) of all that these men accomplish."[63] Such information is part of a broad social and cultural setting, a third interpretive category, demonstrating Mande society's high regard for women while engendering spheres of power (political and spiritual) that plausibly reflect historical processes, thus qualifying for the second category of analysis as well.

Sunjata and the Trope of Rejection

Maghan Kon Fatta marries Sogolon and has a son by her. Throughout his adolescence, Sunjata's life is hostage to rivalries between Maghan Kon Fatta's co-wives and among his siblings.[64] The rivalries are interdependent, the former in the interests of the latter, with ever-escalating levels of vitriol. Sunjata and his mother and sister offer little resistance to various affronts and intrigues—a heavy investment in their personal character. As part of the second interpretive category, the universality of succession struggles lends credence to such rivalry (if not its particular elements), a narration from the perspective of mothers.

Sogolon's initial reception among Mali's royals is characterized by rejection, led by Maghan Kon Fatta's first wife Sassuma Berete—Sama Bérété, Siga Demba—"jealous" of her new co-wife.[65] Having "cast every kind of evil spell" to prevent the marriage, she warns Maghan, "I cannot live with her because she is too ugly . . . when you've slept with Sougoulong Kotouma, you'll need to bathe seven times before returning to my home."[66]

The initial courtship between Sogolon and Maghan Kon Fatta is nothing less than a pitched battle, with Sogolon shooting "a *subala* or sorcerer's plaiting needle" at his eye and "spraying him with scalding breast-milk to blister his skin."[67] In a herculean effort, Maghan Kon Fatta finally consummates the marriage after one week, and Sogolon immediately becomes pregnant.[68] The gestation period is unusual, signaling not only the advent of a luminary, but an exceptional bond between mother and child.[69]

Accounts diverge, not insignificantly, on the timing of Sassuma's second pregnancy. Some maintain her son Dankaran Tuman is already eight years old at the time of Sunjata's birth.[70] Others have Sogolon and Sassuma giving birth to sons on the same day, having been impregnated on the same night, recalling the Greek mythical figure Heracles, while also bringing to mind the Ya'qub-wa-al-'Īsū (Jacob-and-Esau) dynamic.[71] But it just as surely borrows from the Sāra-Ḥājar saga and (Muslim) tradition that blessing follows the one exiled.[72]

Traditions hold Sassuma returns to Bambuk and Sogolon to Do/Sangara to deliver their children, but differ as to whether Sunjata or Dankaran Tuman is born first, fueling rivalries.[73] In the case of Sunjata's birth announced first, the Ya'qub-wa-al-'Īsū signature is unmistakable, as Sunjata is described as covered with hair from head to toe, with Sassuma's mother saying of Sogolon: "The little mother has borne a 'lion thief.' Thus gave the old mother Son-Jara his name."[74]

The association of Sunjata's name with thievery indicates it has contrasting valences in the sources, suggesting an aspect of the Sunjata story with historical applicability. The most popular interpretation is that "Sunjata" conjoins "Sogolon" and "Jata" (signifying "Sogolon's lion"), adopted over time since he was originally "called Maghan after his father, and Mari Djata, a name which no Mandingo prince has ever borne."[75] Other sources emphasize "Sunjata" takes hold because, as a child, he stole so much—cattle, gold, jewelry—that he became known as "a thief like a lion," previewing subsequent imperial behavior.[76] Anger over not being recognized as the firstborn (in other accounts) explains his "hot-tempered and violent" temperament, a congenital condition so consuming he refuses to walk for years.[77]

Walking as Divine Sanction

Reference to Sunjata's refusal to walk directs attention to his abnormal childhood.[78] Many sources present this as a disability (as opposed to volition), maintaining he was either born in this condition or becomes a "cripple" later in childhood.[79] Whether congenital or subsequent, it becomes a site of miraculous transformation and verification of divine destiny.

More than one account attributes Sunjata's misfortune to Sassuma Berete, enraged over a birthing order that places her son second.[80] While this is hardly surprising, more unexpected is the assertion that Sunjata's condition is the result of his father's orders, alarmed over his son's extraordinary hunting exploits, indicating an anguished father-son relationship of possible historical verity, as it would not be a particularly popular aspect of griot performance and collective memory.[81]

Seldom speaking and taciturn, perpetually angry and braining other children, Sunjata crawls on all fours throughout his childhood.[82] A big, heavy infant who crushed midwives and then grew into a "large bull," his huge head and bulging eyes connect him to the *koba*, Do-Kamissa of Sangara. The son of Maghan Kon Fatta Sunjata, Sunjata is even more the son of Do-Kamissa's "double" Sogolon, receiving the Islamically-influenced concept of *baraka* (communicable spiritual power) from his father, while his *nyama* or life force and true Mande core emanates from his mother.[83] In some traditions Sogolon also has *dalilu*, "powers of sorcery," and it is from mothers that male heroes receive their powers.[84] As such, Sunjata becomes the vessel within which *baraka*, *nyama*, and *dalilu* are reconciled.

Sunjata's inability or refusal to walk also defines his mother, subjecting both to harsh ridicule. In one tradition he remains in the womb for seventeen years, with Sassuma Berete deriding her co-wife: "Sogolon Kèdjougou, this shit you pushed out and that you think is a baby is older than my son . . ."[85] Sogolon's ugliness is no longer mentioned with Sunjata's birth, and instead she becomes the long-suffering mother. In exasperation she laments to Sunjata: "I am so ashamed of you. . . . You can't even take yourself to the toilet, you son of misfortune!"[86] Meanwhile, Sassuma's son Danakan Tuman is by age eleven a "fine and lively boy," a hunter. Sogolon Kedju will have a daughter by Maghan, Kolokon or Sogolon Kolokon, who will also play a critical role in Sunjata's life.[87]

Sogolon Kedju's humiliation becomes the impetus for Sunjata beginning to walk, as one day she asks Sassuma for baobab leaves to prepare a meal, to which Sassuma contemptuously suggests she send Sunjata to retrieve the leaves instead. Sogolon's grief greatly impacts a seventeen-year-old Sunjata (in some accounts); enraged, he eventually enlists his father's smiths, bending and breaking one iron bar after another until one of enormous size and strength is forged, taking one year to make, and with which he finally stands.[88] "Allah Almighty, you never created a finer day," he exclaims in one version, combining Islamic influence with ancestral belief in forces associated with metallurgy. He returns not simply with a few leaves, but with the entire tree.[89]

Sunjata's newfound ability to walk signals divine designation, and he purportedly develops a youthful following that includes Fran Kamara of

Tabon and Kamanjan of Sibi, sons of rulers of their respective lands, along with "other princes whose fathers had sent them to the court of Niani."[90] Celebrating such individuals underscores the depth of their bonds as well as their subsequent preeminence in the empire's founding, while establishing Sunjata as their leader, as does the claim that he becomes a *simbon* or master hunter very early in life. But the same event reignites rivalries and stokes fears, and in an early account his father and brothers cede political power to him, in sharp contrast with most traditions characterizing Sunjata's father and brothers as so "alarmed" they seek the aid of witches and *jinn* to stop him.[91] These traditions make visible the tense nature of the *fadenya*, the set of relations between a father and offspring that includes half-brothers.[92]

A number of versions identify Sassuma Berete as the generative source behind efforts to destroy or expel Sunjata. Maghan the Handsome dies, Dankaran Tuman succeeds him, and Sassuma acts to safeguard her son's interests.[93] Few versions present Dankaran as aggressively hostile to Sunjata, but rather as someone who, while aware of the potential threat, does not wish him harm (at least initially). He therefore advises Sunjata to leave the capital, with which Sogolon Kedju concurs as Sassuma warns: "Go and seek a place to die, if not, I will chop through your necks."[94]

Exile as Empire in Embryo

The exile of Sunjata is subject to multiple interpretations, all compelling, and each making a contribution to establishing his bona fides. Though possibly whimsical, political exile has been a universal experience, a fact of political life.

Sunjata's exile in fact operates along verges of verity and fiction as it imagines the beginning of a process by which sovereign states are reconstituted as dependent provinces. One probable fiction is that all was accomplished during Sunjata's lifetime, while the veracity is that Mali was indeed an imperial formation by the late eighth/fourteenth century, made up of the very provinces identified in the tale of exile, with Ibn Khaldūn asserting Mali's "rule reached from the Ocean and Ghāna in the west to the land of Takrūr in the east."[95] What is therefore uncertain are the period and processes of such accomplishment; that is, the "myth" of Sunjata's sojourn seeks to explain a very real political transformation.

A third consideration is closely related to what precedes in that, reading the exile as substantially fabrication, its purpose is to order political relations by enshrining them in an auspicious story of origination, legitimizing claims of central authority. As such, Sunjata's banishment also serves as a primer in early Mande geography as he moves from kingdom to kingdom, establishing an arterial network through which flow alliances, hierarchies of power and privilege, and relations of subservience. In addition to serving as the memory of Manden, the traditions become a critical mechanism of Manden, the authoritative reference to which differential relations to the center adhere.

A fourth possibility is exile as a well-trod path to greatness. Examples abound in sacred writ, and in addition to Ismā'īl there is the *hijra* of the Prophet himself. More relevant to the traditionists may be the example of Yūsuf, whose brothers sell him into slavery.[96] But parallel to such examples—and probably even more compelling—is the Mande requirement that hunters enter wilderness places for considerable periods to learn their craft and survivability, and to "harness occult power."[97] Referred as the *dali-ma-sigi*, or "quest," the hunter navigates spaces in which are located reservoirs of spiritual power, constituting a "sacred geography." Though already a *simbon*, Sunjata learns much during this peripatetic phase. As such, the *dali-ma-sigi* even has implications for the *ḥajj*.

A fifth interpretation of Sunjata's exile stems from the hypothesis that the story masks the original status of the Keitas as "newcomers," who succeed in wresting authority and then enfold their imposition within an account that indigenizes their presence and authority.[98] According to one source, "Sunjata was a stranger from the north who stole the Mande heritage from the Traores and the Camaras."[99] This resonates with other aspects of the epic, including those depicting a young Sunjata as a voracious thief, providing not only another avenue of explicability, but also an additional consideration of plausible social and political circumstances within which purported events unfold.

Sassuma's threat to behead Sunjata also targets his mother Sogolon Kedju, his sister Sogolon Kolokon, and his half-brother Manden Bukari (or Manding Bori), son of Maghan Kon Fatta's third wife Namanje (of legendary beauty and daughter of the "king of the Kamaras"), a marriage strengthening the alliance between the Kamaras and the Keitas. Destined to be the right hand "of some mighty king," oralists assert Manden Bukari becomes Sunjata's best friend, and that they form a close bond with Fran Kamara of Tabon and Kamanjan (or Nan Koman Jan) of Sibi, with whom they grow up.[100] Sogolon Kedju, Manden Bukari, and an assorted host accompany Sunjata into exile.[101]

The sources diverge concerning Sunjata's itinerary upon leaving Mali, with some citing Sangara as his first port of call, while others name Mema

(Nema/Néma), yet others Tabon. One even claims he first visited Sumaoro in Susu and was well received, alluding to the conjoined nature of their respective trajectories. As most sources mention Mema as the place from which Sunjata returns to help beleaguered Mali, while Sangara, his mother's home, was much closer to Dakadiala/Dakajalan (probable village of his birth), this may have been his initial refuge (assuming there was an exile).[102] There he is protected from the murderous intentions of his brother Dankaran, who undergoes a radical attitudinal adjustment following Sunjata's departure, becoming "a man of iron."[103]

Alternatively, the most popularized version of Sunjata's sojourn begins with Jedeba, two days from Niani, and then to Tabon, "inhabited by the Kamara blacksmiths and the Djallonkés" in what is now Futa Jallon, where he is received by its ruler, Fran Kamara's father.[104] If invented, Tabon's mention grounds an important alliance in the very origins of the Malian empire. But the inclusion of Tabon is also anticipatory, as Fran Kamara informs Sunjata "'the blacksmiths and the Djallonkés are excellent warriors'," to which Sunjata vows he will make Fran Kamara "'a great general'." The brief reference underscores a larger point, that in addition to soldiering, smiths also make weapons.[105]

The popularized version is singular in claiming Sunjata next travels to Ghana, introducing the Jula while locating Sunjata in a land of renown, thus associating Sunjata with an ancient Sisse dynasty while establishing ties between the Soninke and the Maninka, reiterating Manden's claim to a venerable Muslim pedigree.[106] Though well received, Sunjata "finds no peace" and falls ill after a year, and King Sumaba Sisse sends him to his cousin Mūsā Tunkara, ruler of Mema.[107] Mema, a premier land of settlement as revealed in the archaeological record, plays a similar role as Ghana in the memory of the Mande as a source of political authority, with many accounts listing it as a critical, often final stop before the return to Mali. Mema is the place where Sunjata accepts his destiny, a consequence of Sumaoro's rise and Sogolon's death.

Sources depict Sunjata's stay in Mema as productive and mutually beneficial, as he "eclipses all the young princes" and comes to be regarded as heir to the throne (Mūsā Tunkara has no sons).[108] Further developing his skills as a hunter, within three years he is named *Kan-koro-sigui* or "viceroy," having matured into a large, "tall man with a fat neck and powerful chest. Nobody else could bend his bow. Everyone bowed before him and he was greatly loved."[109]

It is also at Mema that the full import of Sumaoro's activities hits with life-altering force.[110] The details differ, but the overall picture involves escalating conflict between Sumaoro and Dankaran Tuman, ending with Dankaran's death or flight to Guinea, where he allegedly becomes the progenitor of the Masaren of the Kisi.[111] Sumaoro also "slaughters all his brothers," enumerated as eleven in some accounts, so "tormenting" Manden that most of its brave men flee.[112] Survivors send a delegation entreating Sunjata to lead a campaign against Sumaoro.[113] They find him through his sister, who reports that Sumaoro "killed your father, [and] he killed your brother, whose head he threw down a well . . ."[114]

At this point the story enters its emotional core, as rescuing Mali turns on Sunjata's aging, ailing mother. Sunjata will not leave her, but he is torn between destiny and devotion, expressing the dilemma to his mother:

> "If I am to be king of Manding,
> Before dawn breaks tomorrow, may you be dead.
> If I am not to be king of Manding,
> May you remain ill,
> Because I will not leave you here in illness."[115]

A virtuous woman, Sogolon Kedju responds with her own prayer: "Oh God, if my son is not to be victorious in his country, then let me live! But if he is to be, on the other hand, a powerful ruler, call me to yourself."[116] Sogolon Kedju dies the next day in most accounts, making the ultimate sacrifice for him, as Do-Kamissa had done for her. Connected to Do-Kamissa through cyclical transformations, Sunjata is now free to fulfill his purpose.

Sunjata's decision to return to Mali after seven (or seventeen) years may have engendered conflict with Tunkara.[117] All turns on the burial of Sogolon Kedju, with versions more or less agreed Mūsā Tunkara requires Sunjata to pay for the burial plot, implying he is an outsider and does not really "belong" in Mema, perhaps in retaliation for his disappointing decision to leave for Mali. Sunjata complies, but the meaning of items included in the payment signals he is aggrieved and will seek retribution, deciphered by counselors who advise Mūsā Tunkara to return the payment.[118]

Mūsā Tunkara does not change his demand in other traditions, in which instance Sunjata makes an initial as well as subsequent payment for Tunkara's insolence, returning to kill him while destroying Mema.[119] Locating the issue around Sogolon's burial has the value of granting Sunjata great sympathy, if not the high moral ground, but the traditions may also reflect a level of conflict between Mali and Mema, either during Sunjata's time or thereafter. While possibly mythic, Mema's military annihilation is consistent with an archaeological record demonstrating a precipitous decline in its population around 1300 CE.

Sumaoro, Fakoli Koroma, and Legendary War

Lore enveloping Sumaoro Kante is thick with attribution. The consummate adversary, he leads a "powerful army of smiths" and reverses the relationship of Susu, "a little village of no significance" to legendary Ghana, its former "master," reducing the latter to tributary status. Susu's impenetrability is represented by a "triple curtain wall," behind which Sumaoro lives atop a seven-story tower, his "macabre chamber" filled with human heads. So mysterious a capital, it is called "Dark Forest," a stronghold of sorcery.[120]

Sumaoro is consistently (though not universally) depicted as a malevolent force, an "evil demon" unlike other men, sprouting seven or eight heads in the midst of battle while able to metamorphize into sixty-nine different bodies. He is said to have had either a *jinn* or a gorilla for a father and two mothers, going back and forth between their wombs.[121] As to his human background, he descends from the Jarisu family, smiths from the *numu* in the caste system of the Mande, having once served Ghana's rulers.[122] A hunter and great warrior, Sumaoro has encyclopedic knowledge of the supernatural.[123]

Parallels between Sunjata and Sumaoro are striking, with one version describing them as "consanguine brothers."[124] They are both exiled by half-brothers but supported by sisters, attracting large followings and achieving distinction, while in another tradition they are tied by Sumaoro's marriage to Sunjata's "nephew wife."[125] As Sunjata's antithesis, Sumaoro occupies an inverse kingdom perfectly suited to be the former's alter ego. Though the rise of the Susu is verifiable, the investment in Sumaoro as evil incarnate creates a contrast that may have little to do with an actual person.

The external sources speak of war between the Susu and the Maninka but provide nothing in the way of specifics, so that what follows is purely within the preserve of the orature. By the time Sunjata returns to Manden, Sumaoro controls both banks of the Niger River, having conquered at least half of all Mande territory and establishing his "iron rule."[126] The traditions make an immediate transition from Mema to war with Sumaoro.[127]

Assuming warfare under Dankaran Tuman, Mali could have only been a shell of its former self by the time Sunjata returns, so that he is heavily reliant, as the sources agree that most of his forces come from allies.[128] Given the heights to which Mali would rise, and the critical nature of the allies' role in that emergence, the corpus is keen to detail their involvement. The listing of allies may indeed reflect the composition of forces in a titanic struggle against Sumaoro, or they may telescope a process of much longer duration, extending well beyond Sunjata's lifetime.

With Manden Bukari at his side, Sunjata reverses the stages of his exile, picking up support as he goes along, beginning in Mema and ending in Tabon. Half of his cavalry is said to come from Mema's Mūsā Tunkara (in accounts featuring their reconciliation), the other half from Ghana. From Tabon and Fran Kamara he receives the bulk of his infantry or *sofas*, made up of smiths and "the mountain-dwelling Djallonkés," while 1,500 archers are provided by the king of the Bobo.[129] The image of Sunjata gliding from kingdom to kingdom is certainly romantic, and yet contains certain truths: that military victory was premised on manufacturing arms (thus the smiths), and that the introduction of horses into the West African Savannah revolutionized the calculus of combat.[130]

Horses were already present in Ghana, having been introduced into the Middle Niger between the first/seventh and third/tenth centuries, and were a source of "great prestige." They became much more important in the seventh/thirteenth and eighth/fourteenth centuries when deployed as cavalry, during which time large herds were actually bred in Mali. If Sunjata did not initiate what amounts to a technological innovation, he certainly benefitted from it. Indeed, one of the meanings of the term Susu is "horse" or "horseman."[131]

Sunjata's ensuing exploits include his famous generals, namely Kamanjan (Nan Koman Jan), Fran Kamara, and Tiramakan or Tiramaghan. None, however, are as intriguing as Fakoli Koroma (or Koli Mūsā Sissoko).[132] The nephew of none other than Sumaoro, he is known for his "large head and wide mouth."[133] Trained by his uncle as a skilled warrior, he grows up to serve as one of his "great commanders," if not his greatest, and learns the "secret" of Niani *Mansā* Kara Kamara, ruler of Niani and "king of iron," from the *mansā*'s wife, Niuma Demba.[134] Armed with this secret, Sumaoro overcomes Kara Kamara's fierce resistance and conquers Niani, while Niuma Demba subsequently reappears as Fakoli's wife.[135]

Niuma Demba proves exceptional, "more beautiful than all of Sumaoro's hundred wives" and "quicker at cooking." Sumaoro is equally impressed, taking Niuma Demba for his own and telling Fakoli, "You have a wife, but she is not a wife for a child." The challenge to Fakoli's "manhood" also alludes to the less than honorable way he "obtained" Niuma Demba in the first place, and Fakoli responds by swiftly joining forces with Sunjata. Laughing at Fakoli's short stature upon their initial meeting, all are soon amazed as Fakoli has to stoop to enter the enclosure, either growing until he ascends through the roof, or causing the roof to rise until it separates from the walls, revealing his own powers of sorcery.[136]

The story of Sumaoro's "theft" of "gator-mouthed" Fakoli's wife helps to explain how the latter could have turned against his surrogate father, a catastrophic defection for Sumaoro.[137] Precisely when Fakoli might have joined Sunjata is unclear (if he joined at all), but it follows several important battles between Sunjata and Sumaoro, specifically the Battle of Kankigne.[138] Fakoli goes on to an illustrious career, with Sunjata commanding: "Play the *janjon* for Fakoli."[139]

In turning to the contest with Sumaoro, Sunjata's initial step is to cross to the other side of the Niger, referring not only to transporting soldiers by way of *pirogues* or boats, but also a spiritual crossing requiring the approval of river deities.[140] The Niger's successful fording inaugurates the war, but the sources differ in describing its unfolding, with some claiming the defeat of Sumaoro after only one or two battles, while others recall a protracted struggle.[141]

It is at a point of stalemate, even despair, that sources introduce an intervention stereotypically attributed to women, but consistent with a pattern of female rescue in Sunjata's life. As was true of his mother Sogolon Kedju, his sister Sogolon Kolokon is also skilled in spiritual arts and operates independently of Sunjata, looking after his welfare.[142] To that end, she either risks or actually sacrifices her virtue, volunteering to enter Sumaoro's bedchamber to learn "the secret of his *tana*"—the object that would prove disastrous if discovered by enemies.[143] Sumaoro succumbs to the "golden pearl of the Mandé," revealing to Kolokon that his *tana* is the spur of a white rooster.[144] At its most elemental level, Kolokon's (dubious) role is key in what is otherwise an entirely masculinist enterprise, her intervention a critique of that masculinity.

Krina

With the "secret" of Sumaoro in hand, a series of clashes ensue that, given the account of war in the external sources, necessarily took place in some form. The consensus of the oral materials is that it went badly for the Susu at Kankigne, culminating in the Battle of Krina/Kirina, on the Niger, where Sumaoro is decisively defeated. Two constants thread throughout the various descriptions of these battles: animal sacrifice to the Mande deities, and Sunjata's organization of hunters into a fighting force, based upon his status as not only a *simbon*, but a *donso karamoko*, a master hunter.[145]

As far as the sources are concerned, though the Battle at Krina/Kirina involves unprecedented numbers, the real struggle is between Sunjata and Sumaoro as sorcerers, beginning either with the killing of Sumaoro's protective, twenty-seven-headed *jinn* "Susufengoto," or his monstrous, forty-four-headed snake.[146] Grazed by an arrow armed with his *tana*, Sumaoro immediately "felt his powers leave him" and flees, meeting one of two ends: either he and those with him turn into pillars of stone; or he escapes, "disappearing" into the mountains of Kulikoro, never to be heard from again.[147]

Fate of the Susu/Fissure in the Alliance

With the fall of Sumaoro, the oral sources address four further developments: the fate of the Susu, a seeming (and related) surge in slaving, the repression of revolts, and the creation of empire. With the exception of empire, none are verifiable.

Sunjata is said to utterly destroy "Soumaoro's city, Sosso, the impregnable city," massacring its inhabitants and making captives of its surviving *kèlè massa* or "war chiefs," while performing final sacrificial offerings "to fix forever the soul and the *nyama* of the dead."[148] Fakoli's loyalty is partly rewarded with "the kingdom" of Susu, while surviving Susu and their erstwhile allies are reduced to subordinate status. Responsibility becomes opportunity, as generals Fakoli, Tiramakan, and Maka Kamara ravage and reduce "the land of the Susu to slavery." The pillaging, if it occurred, has the feel of perennial enterprise, a characterization no doubt informed by subsequent thirteenth/nineteenth-century slaving in the region.[149]

The doubt is therefore substantial that Susu women and children were either domestically enslaved or rerouted through the trans-Saharan trade, or that Tiramakan and Maka Kamara dishonored Susu men by shaving their heads and converting them into *sofas* or soldiers. But as servile armies emerge in the western Sudan at some point, the traditions at least attempt to account for their origins. Whenever their precise beginnings, their rise represents an evolution, as armies (in the Mande context) initially consisted of the *donson ton* or hunter societies, perhaps later joined by farmers. As post-Sumaoro warfare seems to have increased with Mali's expansion, the inclusion of suborned soldiers could have facilitated campaigns while relieving free men, and would have been a new approach.[150]

According to the traditions, Sunjata would next face revolt, raising the question of his newcomer status. *Mansā* Kara Kamara, ruler of Niani and senior in age to Sunjata, challenges his authority: "For what reason should I accept the power of Dakadjalan? Magan Soundjata was born when I was reigning on the royal skin. Moreover, I am the first occupant of the Manden, for no one reached this land before me."[151] The situation is a bit more complex, however, as Fakoli learned the *mansā*'s "secret" from his wife, who later becomes Fakoli's wife. Suggestively, Sunjata chooses Fakoli to put down Niani's rebellion, his killing of the *mansā* characterized as an "assassination" in the sources, connoting merit in Kara Kamara's case and injustice in the way Sunjata resolves it.[152]

In putting down other revolts among the Mande, the general Tiramakan prepares to undertake his most renowned of ventures to the Jolof ruler "Surumbali," south of the middle Senegal valley, in search of horses. As Sunjata was a seventh/thirteenth century figure and the Jolof confederation began in the middle of the next, it is not clear who this ruler could have been. Even so, since the Wolof and their political formation antedate Jolof, and the area was known as a source of horses, there may well have been an attempt at procurement.[153]

Sunjata is said to have sent a delegation carrying considerable gold, but in exchange the Jolof ruler sends back leather for sandals, as "a Malinké is accustomed to going on foot, and not to mount a horse."[154] Flying into a "crazed rage" and refusing to eat for three days, Sunjata finally cedes the honor of exacting revenge to Tiramakan who, accompanied by Fakoli and Silamakan, marches to the Lower Senegal and defeats the Jolof ruler. He either beheads him and presents the grisly trophy to Sunjata, along with the "golden stool and silver lance" of the "Jolofmansa," or brings him back to Mali with seven thousand horses and seventeen thousand captives, where Sunjata himself kills him.[155]

While pursuing the Jolof campaign, Tiramakan is also said to have "ravaged" the Gambia, extending Sunjata's dominion to the middle and upper Senegal valleys, including what would become Bundu, Kingui, Karta, and Diafunu.[156] As many of these states were not in existence in the seventh/thirteenth century, the intent may have been to convey a sense of Mali's expansion by employing recognizable names. The claims also make the point that Mali is viewed as the originating source for such polities as Kabu, Niumi, Niani, Wuli, and Kantora, as well as the Gelwaar rulers of

Sin and Salum in the regions of the Sereer.[157] But this is a lot of fighting, and what Tiramakan's supposed conquests may better reflect are movements, at various times, of either Mande-speakers and/or Mande culture into the Senegal and Gambia valleys, processes that surely extended beyond the life of Sunjata.[158]

Sunjata's forces may have also been in conflict with Tuareg ("Surakas") and Arabo-Berber communities to the north. Either Fakoli or Maka Kamara is said to defeat "the Moors" en route to imposing tribute on Karta, defeating them again at Walata/Biru and pursuing them as far as Dar Tichit, with Fakoli's campaigns memorialized as "conquest."[159] This is substantial expansion if true, extending Malian interests deep into the Sahel, a development that may have taken place after Sunjata.[160]

Mande Principles and Empire

Discussion of the postwar disposition of the Susu, slaving, and repression of revolt all argue for a political center and source of directive and policy. All elements of empire may not have been in place under Sunjata, though they were in full bloom by the time of Ibn Baṭṭūṭa and Ibn Khaldūn's observations a century later.[161]

Sunjata's itinerary following Sumaoro's defeat is said to have included attacks on fabled Dia/Diagha (or Diaghan, a supposed ally of Susu), Kita (a formidable town), a brief respite in Do, and then on to either Kangaba (or, more precisely, nearby Kurukan Fugan) or Dakadiala/Dakajalan.[162] Whether at Kangaba or Dakadiala/Dakajalan, the army is divided into thirds under Fakoli Koroma, Fran Kamara, and Sunjata.[163] A tradition of interest critiques Sunjata for using "the most trivial and deceitful pretexts" to go to war, while insisting the name "Sunjata" connotes a "savage beast," a "terribly pugnacious and ferocious" creature.[164] This is consistent with the dual concept of the *n'gana* or "man of action," whose violent character contrasts with the *n'gara* or "person of words," who preserves social memory.[165]

Calling an assembly of allies to create a new political framework, the first order of business is to ensure the generals' subordination, and in response Kamanjan is said to declare: "Henceforth it is from you that I derive my kingdom for I acknowledge you my sovereign. I salute you, supreme chief, I salute you, Fama of Famas ["King of Kings"]. I salute you, Mansa!"[166] Impossible to corroborate, such a statement underscores that the process through which the Malian state evolved is a matter of speculation. Up to this point, the early Malian state could have consisted of villages grouped into *kafus* or townships, a pattern characteristic of contemporary Maninka.[167] The Keita, as possible outsiders, may have established their authority after the fifth/eleventh century, taking the title of *mansā* or "ruler."[168] In bearing the titles of *mansā* as well as *fama* of *famas* (a cognate of *farba/farma/fari*, elastic terms signifying "chief" or "governor"), Sunjata is recognized as a Mande ruler, but also as someone who transcends them, an "emperor." The transformation of the title *mansā* may therefore represent the extension of Malian power over previously independent polities, its association with Sunjata critical to its substantiation, whether achieved during his lifetime or that of *Mansā* Mūsā in the following century, by which point an imperial structure is in clear evidence.

Two major categories may have allied with Sunjata prior to the empire's founding: those within Manden itself, cohering as a loose federation of towns and villages, and sovereign Mande-speaking states territorially more distant. The sources address, perhaps entirely figuratively, how rulers invest the title of *mansā* with new meaning, as the "twelve kings of the bright savanna country . . . proclaimed Sundiata 'Mansa' in their turn. Twelve royal spears were stuck in the ground. Sundiata had become emperor."[169] Independent polities are now provinces under the suzerainty of Mali, with Ghana and Mema given elevated rank and greater autonomy, a claim of continuity between their former glory and Mali as their successor.[170] The purported ceremony may only prefigure a process that began with Sunjata.

With Mali's subsequent expansion, conquered lands may have been organized into *mamadugus* or administrative units under a lead warrior or *nwana*, and further distinguished as either "lineage territories" or "political territories," with the former presumably retaining a semblance of their existing leadership arrangements, whereas the latter were subjected to a more invasive imposition.[171] Among the latter were the Fulbe of Wassulu who, having sided with Sumaoro, were placed under a *jomba*, a royal "chief" slave.

Within the heart of Manden, exclusive of its adjoining provinces, a "Grand Council" or "General Assembly" is said to have been formed of generals and lineage heads, in addition to thirty kings or *mansās* of formerly independent Maninka.[172] Each *mansā*, based on the traditions, ruled over a collection of districts (*jamana* or *kafu*), in turn led by a senior person of royal lineage, the *jamani-tigi*.[173] Allies would have been expected to defend the interests of the center while paying tribute to it.[174]

The possibility of intensified slaving could also have contributed to empire's articulation.[175] The capture, maintenance, and transport of ever-increasing numbers would have required a broader accommodation of rising commercial activity, with domestic slavery growing in proportion, helping to explain the expansion and range of their servile functions from warring to governing, in a fashion analogous to Susu's captive smiths. The synchronous versatility of smiths and slaves in response to exigency, however, could have also led to weakened relations among communities loyal to the state, requiring leaders to adopt measures to promote social cohesion and a sense of common purpose or "unity" among disparate groups. Meeting these challenges required something more than new state structures.

Promotion of societal organization based on Mande principles could have been a mechanism through which Mali responded to these difficulties. The Sumaoro-Sunjata conflict and immediate aftermath had created bedlam, necessitating a veritable reconstruction in which societies could re-form around shared notions of order. This invites a fresh reading of widespread Mande social structures, not simply as undirected expansions of influence, but as a deliberate strategy to create a shared imperial framework and identity. The threat of instability may therefore help to explain the widespread social divisions of the Mande into the *horon* (freeborn), *nyamakala* (castes), and *jon* (slaves), perhaps initially introduced by military and commercial expansion, but then accompanied by Mande languages and culture.[176] In turn, this tripartite arrangement may be a response to the fluidity and ambiguities of the smiths and slaves, neither fully inherited nor already in place by the time of Sunjata. As so many leaders emerged from the ranks of the smiths, their subsequent segmentation may have been a means of effectively curbing their political ambitions.[177]

Smiths and Societies in Motion

Ibn Khadūn records that Mārī Jāṭa, or Sunjata, ruled for twenty-five years, and that his successor Walī performed *ḥajj* during the reign of the Mamluk ruler al-Ẓāhir Baybars (658–76/1260–77). If used to date the beginning of Sunjata's rule, the Battle of Krina/Kirina would have taken place around 630/1233, and Sunjata would have died around 656/1258.[178] He is said to have either succumbed to natural death on the banks of the Sankarani River, or to have drowned in it, and was buried in either the town of Balandugu or the forest of Nora near the same river.[179] Elaborate funeral rites are said to have delayed the burial some three months, the manner of his death uncannily similar to that of Songhay's *Sunni* ʿAlī some 250 years later.[180]

The Sunjata traditions are meant not only as rendition, but also as contemplation, valorizing developments while providing a vision for what is normative in society, culture, and politics. This prescriptive function helps explain their divergence, comprising the terrain on which subsequent contestation has been waged and retroactively applied. As such, prescriptive traditions featuring creative acts qualify for the third category of interpretation preoccupied with context, examples of which include the ancestral lines of the griots themselves, the principal maraboutic families, the relationship of the Traores to the Kamaras to the Keitas, and so on.[181]

But this prescriptive tier may also contain an unintended interlineality between certain creative acts. Although performed and recorded for didactic purposes, these acts could reveal something of actual historical import, qualifying for the second category of plausibility.

A major instance of interlineality concerns the status of smiths, through which Mande society can be observed in historical process. In presenting the Sunjata-Sumaoro conflict as an allegorical reflection of tensions between smiths and a rising mercantile community allied with warriors—and thus economic and technological transition in the seventh/thirteenth century Savannah-Sahel—scholars have already made the point that these accounts reveal something about evolving relations.[182] Generally speaking, Mali's rise was predicated on Sahelian commercial expansion deep into the Savannah, driven by slaving and the discovery of a new source of gold at Bure.[183] Further consideration of the smiths, however, leads to another hypothesis, that the era of Sunjata was one in which social relations were in negotiation. Sumaoro may have been a smith, but so was Fakoli Koroma. So was Fran Kamara, and both Fakoli and Fran Kamara become indispensable to Sunjata as generals and governors. In this way, rather than conflict between social strata, war between Sunjata and Sumaoro is more emblematic of open-ended processes. In subsequently prescribing what is normative, therefore, oralists may actually reveal social relations in formation, as historical developments.

The story of Sumaoro is particularly instructive. Emerging from a servile status and referred to as the "slave of Da" (apparently the ruler of Ghana/Wagadu), his "Kante lineage" was the "product of the servile estate in Wagadu" where, toward the end of the Sisse dynasty, privileged slaves established their own authority.[184] Sumaoro rises as a powerful, independent ruler of Susu as well as the "son of a leading blacksmith." But he is both, without obvious contradiction, mirroring the conjoined reality of Fran Kamara of Tabon.[185] Sumaoro's story therefore reflects the absence of barriers to smiths, with Mande social segmentation unfolding as a dynamic process.

The case of Fakoli Koroma provides additional insights. Scholarship maintains the "tribes of Soumaoro, especially the Kante smiths," are enslaved following Sumaoro's defeat, though sources insist the Kante smiths escape massacre.[186] When Fakoli returns from his mop-up mission in Susu, he is said to have been accompanied by a large number of smiths, as was the case when he initially defected to Sunjata.[187] Fakoli's army, composed of free smiths when he first joins Sunjata, is reinforced with servile warriors following the Battle of Krina. Though there may be confusion in the sources, Tiramakan and Maka Kamara also employ a "mixed" army. This indicates fluidity in the aftermath of Krina, with free and servile smiths serving as soldiers, under the command of other smiths, who in turn become provincial rulers and heads of state.

A common denominator in these various accounts is slavery. If, as speculated, a reimagined social order was in part fueled by an expanding slave trade, the critical questions would have included: Who could be targeted, and who is to be defended? The key criterion would have turned on Mande identity and membership in the new empire. As Mali's might grew, many would have sought its protection, for which an embrace of all things Mande, including and especially the schema of social stratification, could have been decisive. A new criterion would emerge in the coming centuries—the disposition toward Islam—with which Mande identity would become synonymous.

Sunjata and Mali's origins are at the center of an involved discussion of sources and method. This chapter reengages with materials long deemed of little historical value. But a forensics that tiers the orature into categories of high probability, plausibility, and relational context opens new vistas. Through such an approach, the decentering of women in the scholarship can be mitigated, if not reversed.

Such layering of testimony is critical to uncovering Mali's imperial transformation, and more important than whether it was completed under Sunjata is the subsequent deployment of his person and period as vehicles of authentication. Perhaps the most poignant example of this is Sunjata's exile, for which issues of historicity fade in comparison with its purpose as a charter for central and provincial power. Similarly, the conquest of the Susu, though highly probable, also establishes the basis for Mali's enduring regional claims.

The traditions also contain key insights into early Mali's relationship to Islam, evincing a careful balancing act between ancestral and Islamic principles and forces. As such, the Keitas celebrate descent from Mamadi Kani as much as from Bilāl b. Rabāḥ, and the *dali-ma-sigi* is as generative as the *ḥajj*.[188]

Islam's role at imperial Mali's beginning is therefore limited. Oral accounts of Maghan Kon Fatta praying in the mosque, or Sunjata's exchanging the garb "of a Muslim" for that of a hunter, if anything demonstrate an accommodation between Islam and ancestral religion.[189] The oral corpus is replete with sorcery and sacrifices that include those of Fakoli, leader of the *komo* society of smiths dedicated to non-Islamic practices.[190]

Even so, Islam was on the ascendance, with early Manden possibly witnessing the establishment of clerical or maraboutic communities led by the Ture, Sisse, Baghayoro, and Silla.[191] As the next chapter demonstrates, Islam would only grow stronger, ushering in an era of cosmopolitanism never before witnessed in the region.

CHAPTER SIX

Mansā Mūsā and Global Mali

AS SEEN, THE EVIDENTIARY BASE for the Savannah and Sahel, from early Ghana to the dawn of imperial Mali, shifts from external literary sources to internal, oral transcripts, the vast majority recorded since the end of the thirteenth/nineteenth century. Consistent with such unpredictability, the basis for what is known about imperial Mali from Sunjata's demise to the rise of Songhay in the ninth/fifteenth century shifts again, from the orature of Sunjata's era to (once more) external records and eyewitness accounts, this time more fully incorporating information from internally-generated written documents of the eleventh/seventeenth century.

This is the period of Mali's maturity and greatest territorial expansion, for which there are five major sources: Ibn Baṭṭūṭa, al-'Umarī, Ibn Khaldūn, 'Abd al-Raḥmān b. 'Abd Allāh b. 'Imrān al-Sa'dī (*Ta'rīkh as-sūdān*), and Maḥmūd Ka'ti and Ibn al-Mukhtār (*Ta'rīkh al-fattāsh*). The first is an eyewitness account, whereas the *ta'rīkhs* (*tawārīkh*) are internal chronicles at some three hundred years' remove from Mali's apex. This is also the moment of Mali's emergence as a transregional power, and it is through imperial Mali that West Africa literally and figuratively enters the spatial and imaginary dimensions of Europe and the central Islamic lands. Indeed, much of what is known about medieval Mali is due to a fascination emanating from far beyond its borders.

With Mali's ascent, however, the internal record falls silent, as the oralists of the region, the *jeliw*, have little to say about either medieval Mali or *Mansā* Mūsā, focused as they are on Sunjata. That the *jeliw* are mute is more than quizzical, since Mūsā is arguably Mali's most legendary figure. His absence from the orature may be explained by Islam's growing influence and preference for him, together with thorny matters of succession and legitimacy. More sobering is the realization that, absent external sources, what is known about Mali at its zenith would be very little indeed, and would give rise to significant interpretive distortion—an observation with relevance for the whole of West Africa before the ninth/fifteenth century.

Succession as a Fraught and Evolving Process

It is important to pay attention to the early succession process in Mali, as it features elements critical to the nature of polity in the region, while its lack of clarity proved to be a major cause of volatility and vulnerability for not only Mali, but Songhay as well; its conceptual framework, as well as the dynamics fueling its various resolutions, thread through the empires' respective histories in an uncannily repetitive fashion. The outcome of the process was determined by an explosive mix of variables that included questions of qualification, the splintering of royalists, the rise of non-royalist contenders, and the increasingly powerful roles of servile formations.

With respect to the specific case of early Mali, the succession following Sunjata was far from straightforward, with any understanding of it complicated by inconsistencies concerning the role of lineality in determining heirs; the effects of royal adoption; Islam's emerging profile; irreconcilable succession claims between various branches of traditionalists; and the proposed emergence of a new category of stakeholder—the *donson ton*.

The oral corpus is both internally divided as well as in conflict with Ibn Khaldūn over who actually succeeded Sunjata. They variously name as his immediate successor an eldest son; a brother; Gator-Mouthed Fakoli Koroma; or the *jomba* (royal slaves), who preside over an unstable interregnum, after which either a first cousin or a brother is enthroned.[1]

The divergence certainly owes to the challenges of oral transmission, but by way of hypothesis it also reflects the dawn of wholly new circumstances, for which prior conventions were no longer adequate. In initiating a process through which previously independent kingdoms were progressively incorporated into a novel imperial configuration, a transterritorial expansion requiring ventures into new figurative terrain, Sunjata elevated and expanded the concept of the *mansaya*. As a result, within his own lifetime he was forced to confront the *mansaya*'s changing significance, putting down challenges from rulers with greater seniority.

The hypothesis here concerns the initial stages of Mali's imperial transformation, and how succession was determined following Sunjata's demise. With the *mansaya*'s elevation, succession was no longer a local concern. The heads of thirty-three Maninka clans are presented in the oral corpus as the leadership of a broader Malian constituency, but the same corpus presents the *donson ton* or hunter societies as an independent collection of interests with its own leadership. As clan leaders were also hunters, divergence between the two groups gestures toward generational struggle, with the *donson ton* a mechanism through which younger hunters could challenge or circumvent older, established authority.[2]

Sunjata's own rise to power represents this antagonism, as he clashed with a number of senior rulers (including Mūsā Tunkara of Mema and Kara Kamara of Niani). In seeking to influence the succession, the *donson ton*, the backbone of Sunjata's support, would have followed Sunjata's personal example, setting into motion multilayered deliberations and claims-making no longer confined to customary procedure.

Further complicating matters is the question of whether the succession was exclusively matrilineal or patrilineal. Matriliny is emphasized in the external sources, with Ibn Khaldūn observing Sunjata (Mārī Jāṭa) was eventually succeeded by one Abū Bakr, "the son of his [Sunjata's] daughter. They made him king according to the custom of these non-Arabs, who bestow the kingship on the sister and the son of the sister [of a former king]."[3]

Ibn Khaldūn's report has been challenged in a secondary literature contending succession actually flowed from father to son, unless the Grand Council—presumably the thirty-three clan leaders—selected a brother, cousin, or close relative of the deceased as regent.[4] Ibn Khaldūn's own statement that two of Sunjata's sons immediately succeeded him (prior to Abū Bakr) contributes to the notion that he somehow got it wrong.

However, *Shaykh* 'Uthmān's testimony (Ibn Khaldūn's source) is not so easily dismissed, as he was well acquainted with Mande culture and history, and the Maninka would have been aware of Ghana's early succession practice as outlined by al-Bakrī, who observed that in 455/1063 *Tunka* Manīn succeeded his maternal uncle Basī, as "the kingship is inherited only by the son of the king's sister. He has no doubt that his successor is a son of his sister, while he is not convinced of the genuineness of his relationship to him."[5]

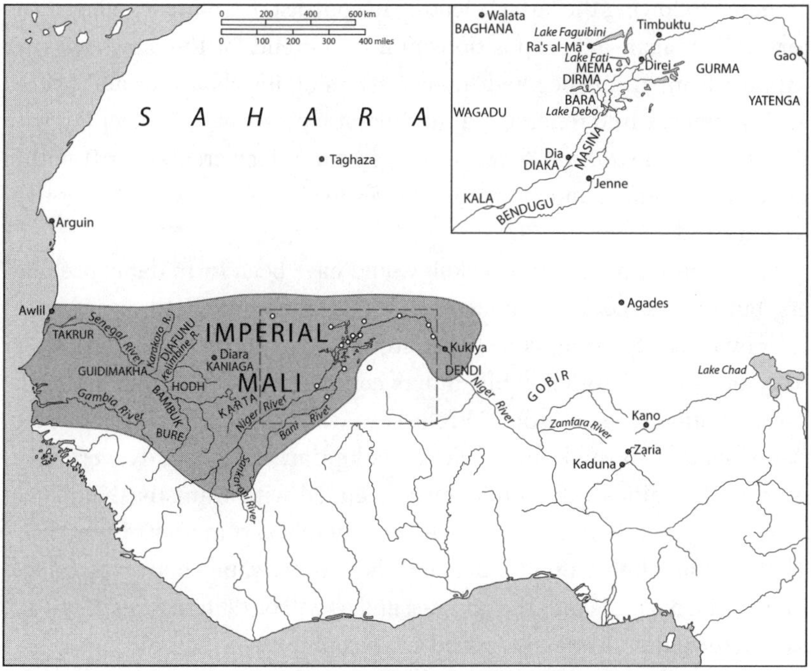

Map 6: Imperial Mali

That Ghana's succession served as the model for Mali is strengthened by Ibn Baṭṭūṭa's 753–54/1352–53 eyewitness account concerning Walata/Biru, on the fringe of Malian territorial control, deep in the Sahel, where none of its inhabitants "traces his descent through his father, but from his maternal uncle, and a man's heirs are the sons of his sister only, to the exclusion of his own sons."[6] What Ibn Baṭṭūṭa found in Walata/Biru, one hundred years after Sunjata's rise to power, suggests ongoing Soninke influence.

The proposition here is that as an emerging political force, the *donson ton* further complicated matters. This is consistent with a report that, in recognition of the *donson ton*'s supportive role, Sunjata defied the wishes of the thirty-three clan leaders to designate a successor. With no successor named for several years, the *jomba* allied with certain dignitaries to rule "without restraint," a precarious situation said to have been compounded by a Fulbe uprising at Damagan-Farani, eventually crushed by Kamanjan.[7]

This is a period characterized by some sources as a "war of succession," in which Fakoli Koroma may have also participated. Having been highly visible during Sunjata's life, he is strangely and inexplicably missing from accounts following the latter's death.[8] In contrast, Kamanjan's alleged victory at Damagan-Farani positions him to contend for the *mansaya* with support from an unspecified "many," stressing his character and overall achievement, while reflecting a meritocratic perspective in keeping with the ethos of the *donson ton*. His alleged candidacy creates a rift within the Grand Council, and Kamanjan leaves for Kong, afterward "forgotten" in Manden.[9]

To be sure, Kamanjan or Fakoli would have been formidable pretenders, but the sources actually name others as the immediate successor. At least two identify Yerelinkon (or Diourounikou or Djouroulenkoun), either Sunjata's son or brother, while others contend Sunjata had no biological sons, or only one such son—Yerelinkon, while all others were adopted: "It seems that in the imperial family, adoption and bastardy were common."[10] This jibes with traditions associated with Kangaba-Niani that assert Sunjata adopted the sons of his generals as a matter of practice.[11] That the bloodlines of pretenders may have been wholly fictive introduces substantial haziness into the process, and as will be demonstrated, opaque succession rules ultimately proved catastrophic.

Whether first or second, Yerelinkon is a likely successor as he correlates with the Ulī or Walī of Ibn Khaldūn, after which the oral traditions are less than helpful, evincing little interest or providing sketchy accounts.[12] Ibn Khaldūn, much closer to the events he describes, is more reliable, as *Shaykh* 'Uthmān (his source) was unaffiliated with any elite branch and therefore unlikely to have favored one pretender over another.

Mansā Walī or Ulī (Yerelinkon) was followed by a brother Wātī, then another brother Khalīfa, all three "sons" of Sunjata.[13] Of the three, Walī registers a presence. Indeed, Ibn Khaldūn regards Walī as one of Mali's "greatest kings," performing the Pilgrimage during the reign of the Mamluk sultan al-Ẓāhir Baybars (between 658/1260 and 676/1277). Islam had played a minor role, if any, in Sunjata's life, so the claim that his immediate successor undertook such a potentially perilous journey, owing to the distances and risks involved, is fairly dramatic. This *ḥajj*, if it took place, would have certainly shored up Yerelinkon/Walī's Islamic bona fides.

The succession from Yerelinkon/Walī through Khalīfa also affords further examination of the proposed competition between the Grand Council and the *donson ton*, since it approximates the characteristics of rival political parties. As such, the Grand Council emerges as the coterie of aristocratic privilege, imbued with a cosmopolitanism stressing transregional commerce and regional cultural plurality, while embracing

Islam as a critical corridor of connection. In contrast, the hunter guilds are more parochial in outlook, focused on domestic matters and the preservation of their core beliefs; elements of Islam could be adopted, but not to the degree of envelopment. Having fought to bring Sunjata to power, they were rewarded a seat at the table of state, where they would advocate the principle that leadership should fall to the most qualified, in the absence of which they stood no chance of assuming Sunjata's mantle.

While Yerelinkon's actual relationship to Sunjata is uncertain, he would remain Yerelinkon to the Maninka. In contrast, Ibn Khaldūn identifies him as Walī, which together with the Pilgrimage reflects a decision to Islamicize the royal persona, a strategy by which several subsequent claimants would attempt to bring order to the realm. This use of dual names is instructive, reflecting Islam's growth within a society yet wedded to its own social and cultural conventions. The pairing of Mande and Arabic names also reveals a sense of Mali as a realm of rising significance. These may be the reasons, along with stabilizing a riven Manden, why Walī came to be regarded as one of Mali's greatest kings.

Within the Mande cultural context, however, the *ḥajj* could be interpreted as a double move, a multiple and intertwining cultural signifier. In undertaking the required *dali-ma-sigi* or "quest" to enter spiritual spaces to appropriate its power, the *simbon* spent considerable time in certain natural formations and special sites—but what could be a greater source of power and blessing than the holy places of the Ḥijāz? In making *ḥajj*, therefore, Mande rulers were not only pursuing Islam, but also potentially gesturing toward indigenous, deeply embedded beliefs. Imbued with both Islamic and non-Islamic valence, the Pilgrimage is a spiritual feat like no other, representing a consummate political strategy of legitimization.[14]

While providing no information about Walī 's successor Wātī, Ibn Khaldūn describes Khalīfa as "insane," so "devoted to archery" that he "used to shoot arrows at his people and kill them so wantonly they rose against him and killed him."[15] Khalīfa (or "successor," not his actual name) could have been demented, but his penchant for "archery" may alternatively refer to an escalation of tensions between stakeholders, as archery was the preserve of the *donson ton*. If Yerelinkon/Walī constituted a victory for the Grand Council and its prioritizing bloodlines (real or imagined), Khalīfa's ascent tantalizingly suggests the pendulum swinging toward the *donson ton*. If true, the *donson ton*, having lost an initial opportunity under their champion Kamanjan, now seized upon the candidacy of Khalīfa to wrest control of the state. His assassination would signal tensions reached a point of rupture, his replacement with Abū Bakr a reclamation of the throne by royalists. But it would come at a price.

Of Metaphors and Parallels: The Curious Case of Sākūra

Ibn Khaldūn records that Abū Bakr was Sunjata's grandson through an unnamed daughter, whereas subsequent traditions assert he was Sunjata's nephew through an unnamed sister.[16] If the latter were the case, and Sogolon Kolokon the mother, her tryst with Sumaoro may have yielded more than just "insight" into his secret—quite the ironic twist. In any event, Abū Bakr's ascendance also indicates a return to genetically-related successors through uterine descent, and possible growing dissatisfaction with the practice of designating fictive scions.

Abū Bakr is a name provided Ibn Khaldūn by his Soninke informant, but in Manden he was known as Bata Manden Bori, "Bata" signifying his relationship to Sunjata through his mother. He was also known as Abubakar II, Abubakar I having been Sunjata's younger brother, Manden Bukari or Manding Bori. A subsequent shift to the exclusive use of clearly identifiable Muslim names is attributable to Islam's expanding influence and Mali's emergence as a transregional power. In turn, such a transition suggests the ultimate triumph of the royalists in their bid to control the *mansaya*.

But that triumph was not yet fully accomplished, requiring another round of developments. Neither Ibn Khaldūn nor the oral corpus provide any insight into Abū Bakr's time in office, his role in returning the throne to the matrilineal line conceivably his most significant achievement. The beneficiary of his predecessor's violent overthrow, he himself may have been the victim of a palace coup, as "their next king was one of their clients (*mawlā*) who usurped their kingship. His name was Sākūra . . ."[17] In maintaining Sākūra assassinated his predecessor, oral sources refer to him as Sekure "the usurper," a "royal slave" also known as Jonnin Sekure "the little slave." His emergence would indicate a standoff between royalists and the *donson ton*, that neither party was able to fully impose its will, with Sākūra stepping into the vacuum.[18]

While possibly a real person, parallels between his details and those of *Mansā* Mūsā are so striking as to invite an alternative analysis, one that interprets Sākūra's story as prefiguring Mūsā, incorporating aspects of the latter's reign to safely critique it from temporal distance. In discussing Sākūra and Mūsā, such a contingency must be borne in mind, offering a powerful tool of inquiry into understanding Mūsā's rise to power.

But the literal approach works just as well, as it increases the likelihood of impressive and evidently undeniable accomplishments. If Sākūra existed, he possessed extraordinary talent and leadership skills, concerning whom Ibn Khaldūn records:

> Sākūra performed the Pilgrimage during the reign of al-Malik al-Nāṣir and was killed while on the return journey at Tājūrā. During his mighty reign their dominions expanded and they overcame the neighbouring peoples. He conquered the land of Kawkaw and brought it within the rule of the people of Mālī. Their rule reached from the Ocean and Ghāna in the west to the land of Takrūr in the east . . . Al-Ḥājj Yūnus, the Takrūrī interpreter, said that the conqueror of Kawkaw was Saghmanja, one of the generals of Mansā Mūsā.[19]

Faced with obvious parallels to Mūsā, Ibn Khaldūn attempts to navigate the confusion by quoting *al-ḥājj* Yūnus on the matter of Gao's defeat, creating space between Sākūra and Mūsā, but it is not obvious that Ibn Khaldūn succeeds. To begin, relative to all predecessors mentioned by Ibn Khaldūn, Sākūra's rule is the subject of much more attention. The account alludes to matters of vast territorial expansion, heretofore unknown in the western Sudan, stretching east from Gao to the Atlantic Ocean, and north from Manden in the Savannah deep into the Sahel. However, in conferring with *al-ḥājj* Yūnus, "the interpreter for this country," Ibn Khaldūn draws attention to the parallel with Mūsā, making it an even more compelling case for its analogic value.

Ibn Khaldūn's mention of Mamluk ruler al-Malik al-Nāṣir Muḥammad b. Qalāwūn allows for dating Sākūra's alleged reign. As the former was in power in installments from 693–94/1294–95, 698–708/1299–1309, and 709–741/1309–40, and as *Mansā* Mūsā came to power in 712/1312 following two intervening rulers, Sākūra's tenure would have taken place during one of the first two installments, which would also be the approximate period of his demise, as in returning home from the Pilgrimage he is said to have died en route, possibly near Tripoli.[20] The possibility that he launched a series of military campaigns suggests he enjoyed substantial support, his Pilgrimage reflecting remarkable stability.

Although his ignoble background may have provided the motivation for seeking the legitimizing benefits of the *ḥajj*, Sākūra may have also viewed it as an opportunity to strengthen ties to the Middle East while projecting Mali's image as a growing power, such that Ibn Khaldūn repeatedly describes the realm as "mighty." It may therefore have been Sākūra who initiated Mali's rapid ascension in the Muslim world while enhancing Islam's influence at the court. If he does not prefigure *Mansā* Mūsā, he certainly anticipates him.

On Mali's Fabled Transatlantic Voyages: An Assessment

According to Ibn Khaldūn, Qū succeeds Sākūra, followed by his own son Muḥammad b. Qū, with Qū represented as either a son or grandson of Sunjata.[21] Qū is referred to as "Gao" in the oral traditions, and as an alleged son of Sunjata the thorny issue of a fictive arrangement looms here. Assuming Sākūra was actually in office and *Mansā* Mūsā succeeds in 712/1312, the time of Qū and his son Muḥammad's collective reigns would have been brief. Even so, Ibn Khaldūn's apparent lack of interest in them is curious if not stunning, given al-'Umarī's account of critical projects during their joint tenure and its relationship to *Mansā* Mūsā's meteoric rise. Qū's assumption of power would signal the end of further contestation of the succession by the *donson ton*, as the throne would be occupied by individuals related to Sunjata for many years to come. The apparent diminution in the hunters' influence was inversely proportionate to a new variable in the calculus of Malian political power and succession: the growing influence of merchants and religious elites from North Africa and the central Islamic lands.

Qū's *intronisation* was not, however, the end of intrigue. Ibn Khaldūn presents *Mansā* Mūsā as the son of Manden Bukari or Manding Bori (or Abubakar I), Sunjata's younger brother, as does the Syrian historian of the Mamluk period Ibn Kathīr (d. 774/1374), referring to him as "al-Malik al-Ashraf Mūsā b. Abī Bakr," or "the king, the sublime Mūsā, son of Abū Bakr." Ibn Kathīr's rendering is based on information garnered during Mūsā's stay in Cairo, which means Mūsā represented himself as Manden Bukari's son while there, whereas certain of the traditions state Mūsā was actually the grandson of Manden Bukari through Son Faga Laye.[22] Whether the son or grandson, power clearly shifts within the royalist camp from those claiming to be direct descendants of Sunjata to those claiming descent from Manden Bukari. This could have been one result of Sākūra's "mighty reign"—rupturing the fractious negotiation of power between hunters and royalists.

It is *Mansā* Mūsā himself who affords an important window into the aristocratic shift. While in Cairo, he was asked by the governor of Old Cairo, Abū 'l-Ḥasan 'Alī b. Amīr Ḥājib, how he came to power, and he replied as follows:

> The king who was my predecessor did not believe that it was impossible to discover the furthest limit of the Atlantic Ocean and wished

> vehemently to do so. So he equipped 300 ships filled with men and the same number equipped with gold, water, and provisions enough to last them for years. . . . They departed and a long time passed before anyone came back. Then one ship returned and we asked the captain what news they brought. He said: "Yes, O Sultan, we travelled for a long time until there appeared in the open sea [as it were] a river with a powerful current. . . . The [other] ships went on ahead but when they reached that place they did not return. . . . As for me, I went about at once and did not enter that river." But the sultan disbelieved him.
>
> Then that sultan got ready 2,000 ships, 1,000 for himself and the men whom he took with him and 1,000 for water and provisions. He left me to deputize for him and embarked on the Atlantic Ocean with his men. That was the last we saw of him and all those who were with him, and so I became king in my own right.[23]

Recorded by al-'Umarī, the account merits further consideration.[24]

To begin, Mūsā seems to intimate such a plan resided in the realm of the fantastical, that Muḥammad b. Qū (or even Qū, as will be explained) was unrealistic if not irrational, dismissing the report of the initial expedition's lone survivor. Taking a foolhardy gamble, he suffered the consequences, with Mūsā's ascension the consequence. But both the question and Mūsā's answer convey an atmosphere of crisis, of matters unfolding unexpectedly, out of anticipated sequence. That intrigue and internecine conflict informed the succession, shifting power from one royal branch to another such that Mūsā's predecessor was never heard from again, cannot be eliminated as a distinct possibility, heightened not only by preceding succession turbulence, but also by Mūsā's own undertaking of the Pilgrimage.

The mythical quality of imperial naval expeditions from Mali through the Atlantic is strengthened by the account's absence elsewhere in the sources; such a major undertaking would seemingly have registered elsewhere, leaving an indelible imprint upon the collective imagination. The failure of either Ibn Khaldūn or the oral corpus to mention it in their treatment of Qū or Muḥammad b. Qū is very odd, to say the least.

The absence of supporting evidence certainly gives pause, but on its own fails to generate skepticism sufficient to completely dismiss the possibility, as corroboration for one element of the story derives from oceanographic studies. In blaming the first voyage's failure on "a river with a powerful current," the survivor seems to refer to the

Canary Current, a year-round movement of water flowing south along the West African coast from what is now southern Morocco to Guinea; then westward in the form of the Equatorial Currents to the Gulf of Mexico, where they become the Gulf Stream; then back across the Atlantic toward Europe and North and West Africa, its southern branch developing into the Canary Current, renewing the cycle. Some one thousand kilometers in width, it would have been difficult to miss.[25] Why or how such an experience, with its basis in observable verity, would be included in a wholly fabricated story is therefore unclear. The probability that the Canary Current is referenced strongly suggests it was actually encountered.

But even if mythical, to speak of such a voyage reflects a certain aggressiveness, a kind of restlessness on the part of a growing central authority fueled by unchecked territorial expansion. A vast realm had allegedly been formed under Sākūra, reaching "from the Ocean and Ghāna in the west to the land of Takrūr in the east," and al-ʿUmarī confirms that by the time of *Mansā* Sulaymān (Mūsā's brother and successor), Mali "adjoined the Atlantic Ocean," a claim reiterated by Ibn Khaldūn, who asserts Mali extended to the domains "of Ghāna as far as the Ocean on the west."[26] It was through Malian-claimed lands, therefore, that a tremendous amount of Sahelian commercial activity was transacted. A turn to the Atlantic suggests interest in exploring additional commercial opportunities, rather than setting sail simply for the hell of it. Ships equipped with gold evince anticipation of contact and transaction.

It is not possible that coastal populations, anywhere in the world, could have failed to at least contemplate venturing into the unknown. West Africans were no different, as pilgrims, merchants, and ambassadors had long developed firsthand knowledge about North Africa and the central Islamic lands. They would also have been aware of a Mediterranean world that included southern Europe. It is hardly a stretch to imagine their interest in directly accessing those lands by water, with Ibn Saʿīd mentioning seafaring off the Saharan coast, recorded as early as the seventh/thirteenth century.[27] Al-ʿUmarī records a similar story of a maritime "commercial venture" headed for Morocco but instead redirected by the elements "into the ocean wastes to the south," making landfall and stumbling upon a coastal city "inhabited by a population of the Sūdān."[28] The foregoing are but a few examples; surely there were others.

But at least two obstacles would have faced the Malian fleet—first, a Canary Current that facilitated navigation from the north but inhibited it from the south; second, the challenges of the available technology, as West Africans possessed naval capacities ill-suited for oceanic transport, their watercraft consisting of *pirogues* or boats made of hollowed-out trees. To be sure, and according to al-Idrisī, sixth/twelfth-century Ghana as well as other polities located along the Senegal River operated watercraft from the Upper Senegal to the salt mines of Awlil off the southern Moroccan coast.[29] But observations of African naval activity near the Senegal and Gambia Rivers made by the Venetian Alvise da Cadamosto in the middle of the ninth/fifteenth century indicate ongoing limitations:

> It is asserted that when for the first time [West Africans] saw sails, that is, ships, on the sea . . . they believed that they were great sea-birds with white wings. . . . Others again said that they were phantoms that went by night, at which they were greatly terrified. . . . They have no ships: nor had they seen any from the beginning of the world until they had knowledge of the Portuguese. It is true that those who live on the banks of this river, and others along the sea coast, have canoes [called *almadie*, made from tree-trunks], the larger of which carry three or four men. In these they constantly fish, ferry across the river, or paddle from place to place.[30]

Notwithstanding Cadamosto's assumptions about the experiences of West Africans since time immemorial, the differential in technologies is on full display here, as it was along the Gambia River during the same period, when and where were sighted

> three canoes (we call them *zopoli*). . . . There were about twenty-five to thirty negroes in each; these remained for a while gazing upon a thing which neither they nor their fathers had ever seen before, that is ships and white men . . .[31]

The Gambian canoes may have been larger than those along the Senegal, but the technological divide remains evident.[32]

These challenges would be solved by combining different types of vessels, as well as tacking and the lateen sail, technology and procedures known to East Africans (and others) plying the Indian Ocean, but apparently unknown to West Africans at the time. Though Mali faced insurmountable odds in such a quest to open new vistas and circumvent overland trade routes, the elaboration of attempting it evinces a surging self-confidence. Mali was in a moment of dramatic ascent.

The Ḥajj *of* Mansā *Mūsā: Making Preparations*

Enter *Mansā* Mūsā, who would transform Mali's profile from a regional to a transregional one, completing what *mawlā* Sākūra began (assuming his historicity), with as little as three years separating their reigns. What is known about him comes mostly from external sources and the regional written texts, his virtual absence in the oral corpus a curiosity. If nothing more, it underscores the importance of the Sunjata account as a chartering mechanism, in every sense a document save the tactile.

According to Ibn Kathīr, *Mansā* Mūsā arrived in Cairo on 25 Rajab 724 (18 July 1324) en route to the Pilgrimage: "He was a handsome young man."[33] His youth is confirmed by Ibn Kathīr's contemporary Badr al-Dīn al-Halabī (d. 779/1377), who describes him as a "young man, brown-skinned, with a pleasant face and handsome appearance."[34] Now Ibn Khaldūn records that Mūsā died just after the defeat of Abū Tāshfīn, ruler of Tlemcen, by the Marinid sultan Abū 'l-Ḥasan in 737/1337, and that Mūsā's reign lasted twenty-five years, meaning he became *mansā* in or around 712/1312.[35] A "young man" in 724/1324, he would have been even younger at his ascension in 712/1312. Hazarding a guess, if thirty-five years old at the time of his Pilgrimage, Mūsā would have been twenty-three when he took the throne, obviously even younger when he was deputized (assuming the second voyage took place). That Mali would have been left in the hands of someone so young is unclear, and raises questions as to whether the shift from the house of Sunjata to that of Manden Bukari/Manding Bori was as seamless as presented.

Mūsā's youth may be indicative of developments he leaves out of his narrative. If too young, he would have required a regent, which may help explain the twelve-year gap between his taking the throne and his advent in Cairo. On the other hand, if he had not in fact been designated the heir apparent, the period may have been one of contestation. Here the characterization of Sākūra as a *mawlā* may have relevance, the discussion of his unauthorized succession or usurpation of power an instrument of critique that actually targets the circumstances of Mūsā's emergence. Ibn Khaldūn's relative silence on the reigns of Qū and Muḥammad b. Qū also invites this sort of speculation, especially when twinned with Mūsā's assertion of a spectacular attempt to cross the Atlantic. Ibn Khaldūn's reticence is in striking contrast with Mūsā's volubility, with the second voyage a site of possible intersection. Could it be that the first venture was commissioned and actually took place, whereas the second did not, but rather serves as an idiom of concealment for intrigue?

In support of an unsettled political environment is a seemingly unconnected reference in Ibn Baṭṭūṭa's *Riḥla* to the *faqīh* Mudrik b. Faqqūṣ, who told Ibn Baṭṭūṭa that a certain Ibn al-Shaykh al-Laban "made a gift to sultan Mansa Mūsā in his youth of seven mithqals. At that time Mansa Mūsā was a boy, without influence."[36] Once Mūsā became ruler, he repaid sevenfold the kindness shown him as a youth. The context of the arguably specious anecdote is a discussion of Mūsā's enviable record of bestowing more gifts upon strangers than his brother and successor Sulaymān, but it reflects not only ambiguity over who controlled the throne, but also an evolving role for foreigners in the succession. That Mūsā received such a gift while still a child and "without influence" suggests an attempt on the part of a small but growing community of expatriate merchants and religious authorities to sway the succession in a manner beneficial to their interests. The gift no doubt went to the house of Manden Bukari/Manding Bori, conceivably in anticipation that someone from that branch, possibly Mūsā, would eventually take power. But by investing in Mūsā's candidacy, expatriate support also signaled their preference, influencing a political process closely tied to cross-regional commercial relations. This suggests that Mūsā, even before coming to power, had been identified as the candidate of an internationalism closely tied to Islam.

Whether uncomplicated or achieved through vigorous disputation, Mūsā's rise to the Malian throne initiated changes that created a critical platform for Islam's emergence in West Africa. At their origin lay what is incontrovertibly one of the most important events—if not the signal event—in West African history: the *ḥajj* of *Mansā* Mūsā. As a result of this feat, *Mansā* Mūsā acquired iconic status the world over, with Mūsā, not Sunjata, dominating the visual field of imperial Mali's representation. Due to the number of people and quantity of goods involved in the journey, much of the twelve-year span between Mūsā's *intronisation* and his arrival in Cairo would have been spent in preparation.

In his *al-Bidāya wa-'l-nihāya fī 'l-ta'rīkh* ("The Beginning and End of History"), Ibn Kathīr testifies *Mansā* Mūsā was accompanied by 20,000 "Maghribīs" (presumably West Africans) and slaves upon arrival in Cairo.[37] Badr al-Dīn al-Halabī, meanwhile, states that he "appeared on horseback magnificently dressed in the midst of his soldiers," with a retinue of more than 10,000.[38] When their estimates and descriptions of Mūsā are taken together, it would appear Ibn Kathīr and Badr al-Dīn al-Halabī had access to information that al-Umarī and Ibn Baṭṭūṭa did not, as neither quantifies the *mansā*'s entourage. Neither does Ibn Khaldūn. This is somewhat surprising, since his former student al-Maqrīzī (d. 845/1442) also enumerates at least part of Mūsā's entourage: "It is said that he brought with him 14,000 slave girls for his personal service."[39]

West Africa's internal documents also score the numbers, with *Ta'rīkh al-fattāsh* stating the *mansā* embarked "with great pomp and vast wealth [borne by] a huge army" numbering 8,000 people. *Ta'rīkh as-sūdān* is far more generous, allowing Mūsā made the Pilgrimage "with great pomp and a large group, with an army of 60,000 men who walked before him as he rode. There were [also] 500 slaves, and in the hand of each was a golden staff each made from 500 mithqāls of gold." The substantial discrepancies are partially explained by what happened to Mūsā's expedition along the way: "He proceeded along the Walata route in the upper lands to the location of Tuwat, and many of his companions stayed behind there because a foot ailment, called 'Tuwat' in their language, befell them there . . ."[40] An obvious conclusion is that *Mansā* Mūsā began with many more followers than actually arrived with him in Cairo.[41]

While the numbers of the enslaved arriving in Cairo were clearly impressive, eyewitnesses were more astounded by the amount of gold they carried. *Ta'rīkh al-fattāsh* refers to the bearing of "vast wealth," while *Ta'rīkh as-sūdān* attempts a quantification, with each of 500 slaves bearing a staff of 500 *mithqāls* of gold equaling 250,000 *mithqāls* (over 900 kilograms or 2,000 pounds, nearly a ton). In like fashion, the external sources provide qualitative and quantitative estimates, with Ibn al-Dawādārī writing in the 730s/1330s that the *mansā* brought so "much gold with him" that he and "his followers bought all kinds of things from New and Old Cairo. They thought that their money was inexhaustible."[42] Approximately a hundred years later, al-Maqrīzī reiterates that Mūsā arrived in Egypt "with magnificent gifts and much gold."

Ibn Khaldūn hints at a figure, recording that the *mansā* gave the Mamluk ruler al-Nāṣir Muḥammad (708–41/1309–40) 50,000 *dīnārs* of gold (that is, 50,000 *mithqāls*, or slightly more than 180 kilograms/400 pounds), yet in another place and on the testimony of *al-ḥājj* Yūnus, estimates the Malians imported "80 loads of gold dust (*tibr*), each load weighing three *qinṭārs*"; with one *qinṭār* equaling 50.8 kilograms, 80 loads translate into 12,192 kilograms, or 26,879 pounds/13 tons of gold. Al-'Umarī, however, estimates that Mūsā "left his country with 100 loads of gold," some 15,240 kilograms or 33,600 pounds/17 tons. This is raw, unworked specie (*tibr*), and when the golden staffs of the 500 slaves are included, the total rises to just over 16,000 kilograms, or 35,600 pounds/18 tons. This is well within the conjecture that Bure produced 4 tons of gold per year and Bambuk .5 tons, or 45 tons over ten years.[43] Though only estimates, such approximations clearly convey an enormous amount of gold in transit, enough to depress its value in Cairo for some time. "They had so much gold with them that the rate of gold fell by two dirhams in each mithqal," wrote Ibn Kathīr, while al-'Umarī observed the price of gold, rarely selling for less than 25 *dirhams* prior to Mūsā's visit, never exceeded 22 *dirhams* after it.[44]

The *mansā*'s visit therefore required years to plan and prepare, and given Ibn Khaldūn's observation that within "their own country they use only slave women and men for transport but for distant journeys such as the Pilgrimage they have mounts," hundreds of camels and pack animals would have been requisitioned.[45] To gather so much gold, while procuring beasts and people and providing for their care, would have required considerable investment in time and effort.

In offering the figure of a 60,000-person entourage as far as Tuwat, *Ta'rīkh as-sūdān* indicates they constituted as many as four times the number who arrived in Egypt, but as will be seen, 15,000 is too low a figure. From all indications, the vast majority of the royal retinue was enslaved. If ten years are allowed for preparations, some 6,000 persons would have been captured per annum for this purpose, probably many more in allowing for attrition or absorption into the host society. This would necessitate expanded raiding and warfare, and what little anecdotal information is available is telling. On the basis of testimony from Old Cairo's governor Abū 'l-Ḥasan 'Alī b. Amīr Ḥājib, al-'Umarī records *Mansā* Mūsā's claim that "by his sword and his armies he had conquered 24 cities each with its surrounding district with villages and estates." Ibn Amīr Ḥājib, in turn, reveals Mali experienced interminable war with an implacable foe, who "shoot well with [bow and] arrows (*nushshāb*). Their horses are cross-bred (*kadīsh*) with slit noses."[46] This may refer to populations occupying adjoining spaces to the Maninka, even those who came to be known as the Bambara or Bamana, in accord with the servile experiences of such communities prior to their emergence as a dominant force.[47] So continuous were the slaving campaigns that al-'Umarī records: "The King of this country wages a permanently Holy War on the pagans of the Sūdān who are his neighbours."[48]

However, unlike slaving, there could be no corresponding acceleration in the accumulation of gold. Indeed, the sources are both consistent and insistent that Mali was not in control of auriferous zones, which would have been the newly developed fields of Bure, and maybe Lobi, along with existing sources at Bambuk.[49] As early as the 730s/1330s, Ibn al-Dawādārī records a conversation between *Mansā* Mūsā and the *Qāḍī* Fakhr al-Dīn, presumably in Cairo, in which the *mansā* responds to a query concerning the location of "the place where gold grows": "It is not in that part of our land which belongs to the Muslims, but in the land which belongs to the Christians [*nsārā*] of the Takrūr."[50] Fakhr al-Dīn then asks the obvious:

"Why don't you take this land by conquest?" The *mansā's* response is instructive: "If we conquer them and take it, it does not put forth anything. We have done this in many ways but seen nothing there; but when it returns to them it puts forth as usual." Mūsā's reply establishes that gold procurement was through tribute (or trade), with more coercive measures counterproductive. It is a point independently established by the *Shaykh* Abū 'Uthmān Sa'īd al-Dukkālī and subsequently recorded in al-'Umarī:

> Under the authority of the sultan of this kingdom [Mali] is the land of Mafāzat al-Tibr ["deposits of raw gold"]. They bring unworked gold (*tibr*) to him each year. They are uncouth infidels. If the sultan wished he could extend his authority over them but the kings of this kingdom have learnt by experience that as soon as one of them conquers one of the gold towns and Islam spreads and the muezzin calls to prayer there the gold there begins to decrease and then disappears, while it increases in the neighbouring heathen countries.[51]

This laissez-faire approach was not necessarily entirely lenient, however, as al-'Umarī further states the ruler of Mali "has fixed a heavy tribute on [the gold] which is brought to him every year."[52] Tribute, then, emerges as the primary mechanism by which gold flowed into Mali from the "heathen countries." As the Bure goldfields were located between the Niger and the Bakhoy (or Semefe) Rivers and to the west of Kangaba, this would have been one of the areas of "uncouth infidels."[53]

It is not clear, therefore, how Mūsā managed to increase gold production to support travel to the central Islamic lands, but one way may have involved the production and export of copper. As early as the fourth/tenth century, (the mysterious) Isḥāq b. al-Ḥusayn mentions that in the land of the Sūdān "gold dust is changed there for copper." The use of copper was widespread, as al-Bakrī reports in the following century, along with salt and cowries, reiterated in the sixth/eleventh in *Kitāb al-Istibṣār*. Al-'Umarī's eighth/fourteenth century account of Kanem mentions the use of "cowries (*wada'*), beads (*kharaz*), copper in round pieces, and coined silver as currency . . ."[54] To be sure, one source of copper was in what is now Morocco.[55] But as told to al-'Umarī by the *faqīh* al-Zawāwī, Mali controlled its own copper mine:

> Al-Zawāwī also said: "This sultan Mūsā told me that at a town called Zkry he has a copper mine from which ingots are brought to Byty [Mali's capital]. . . . 'We send it to the land of the pagan Sūdān and sell it for two-thirds of its weight in gold, so that we sell 100 mithqals of this copper for 66 2/3 mithqals of gold.'"[56]

The location of "Zkry" is illusive, but it could have been a means by which Mali stimulated gold production, facilitating Mūsā's plans for a stunning entrance into Egypt.[57]

The Ḥajj *of* Mansā *Mūsā: Motivations*

The discussion of Mūsā's preparation for the Pilgrimage does not address why he went in the first place, or why he proceeded in such an extravagant fashion. From the evidence, however, there were at least three considerations. The first concerns shoring up his claims to power, driven by the need to quell questions surrounding the succession. The second consideration was interest in expanding the spatial parameters of Mali's territorial claims to access and control a larger share of commercial markets, and in a manner that allowed Mali to maintain imperium through means other than military force. A final objective was the elevation and recognition of Mali as a transregional, if not global power, evincing a self-regard seeking to escape regional circumscription. As will be demonstrated, Mūsā would clearly achieve the first two goals, but only partially reach the third; Mali would certainly emerge as a transregional force, but witness its more global aspiration denied.

As to the initial matter, *Ta'rīkh al-fattāsh* provides a fascinating explanation:

> As for his Pilgrimage, the reason for it was told to me by the student and keeper of the traditions of the ancestors, Muḥammad Quma . . . [who] mentioned that Mali-*koi* ["king of Mali"] Kankan Mūsā is the one who accidentally killed his mother Nānā Kankan, and he was sorrowful about this and regretted it, and feared retribution for it, so he gave large amounts of wealth as alms, and resolved to fast the rest of his life. He asked some of the *'ulamā'* ["learned ones, scholars"] of his time what he should do to be forgiven for this great offense. One of them said to him, "It is my opinion that you should seek asylum with the Messenger of God, may God bless him and grant him peace . . ." That very day he resolutely made up his mind, and he began to gather wealth and provisions for the journey, calling upon his kingdom on every side in demanding supplies and assistance.[58]

The passage contains a number of suspenseful elements, beginning with the accidental killing of Mūsā's mother, "Nānā Kankan" or "Mother Kankan" (or "Grandmother Kankan"). "Kankan" is more likely "Kanku," a female Mande name, so that Kankan Mūsā would literally mean "Mūsā the son of Kanku."[59] Whether she was his mother, grandmother, or the mother of a sibling by a common father, there are weighty implications here, as matricide is a serious affair, especially the royal variety. If it occurred before or soon after Mūsā took power, the probability of intrigue is high. His attempts at appeasement (giving alms, fasting) may have entailed attempts to assuage aggrieved royal family members, with the name "Kankan Mūsā" therefore representing the strategy's failure and his unending grief and regret, the aggrieved determined to never let him forget.

The uncanny parallel between Mūsā and Sākūra is of relevance here, and returns to the question of Sākūra as factual or figurative. Though supported by the testimony of both written and oral sources, Sākūra's actual placement within the line of Malian rulers conceivably mimics the subsequent reign of Mūsā in order to register the aggrieved's protest, embedding it within the very processual fabric of memory that underscores its susceptibility to political verities as well as, or as opposed to, the more empirical variety. Such speculation is hardly at odds with the oral corpus' virtual silence on Mūsā.

In contrast to his invisibility in the oral traditions, written sources closely affiliated with Muslim interests consistently portray Mūsā as a model of piety, and are pressed to explain his inconsistencies. *Ta'rīkh al-fattāsh* introduces him as "virtuous, God-fearing, and a worshiper [of God]," and follows with examples of his virtue—building mosques, liberating slaves—before confronting the issue of matricide, thereby mitigating its egregious nature.[60] The advice to seek asylum and forgiveness in Mecca suggests an apprehension of divine punishment, but Mūsā may have been just as preoccupied with human reprisal. The *baraka* or communicable blessing of the Pilgrimage would have weakened offended factions, allying him with Muslim clerics and merchants.[61] Such a scenario of intrigue and fratricide is consistent with developments following Sākūra's curious reign, the murky tenures of Qū and Muḥammad b. Qū, and (especially) expatriate meddling in Mali's internal affairs (as indicated by the *faqīh* Mudrik b. Faqqūṣ). Mūsā's ascendance may have been entirely irregular, if not usurpacious, his hold on power dependent on the growing influence of expatriate money. From early in his tenure, Mūsā may well have been the "Muslim candidate."

Mūsā's seeking the advice of holy men to make amends is also strikingly similar to the subsequent behavior of Songhay's *Askia al-ḥājj* Muḥammad, a verifiable person (as opposed to Sākūra) who asked Timbuktu's *Qāḍī* Maḥmūd how he might avoid hellfire, having also ascended to power by irregular means.

Whether or not he killed a leading female royal, Mūsā's assumption of power signals the emergence of a new variable in the power dynamics of

Mali. The aspirations of the *donson ton* had died with Khalīfa's assassination, along with meritocracy. Royal lineage was now a prerequisite, but simply winnowing the possibilities to the consideration of bloodlines did not represent a satisfactory resolution. Islam, meanwhile, was a growing force, and those engaged in long- distance commerce would have invested in alliances that enhanced their interests. The line between support and insinuation could have been easily crossed, with Mūsā as beneficiary.

It is noteworthy that the story of Mūsā accidentally killing a maternal royal figure was never told in Cairo during his Pilgrimage, when and where so many other stories about him were generated. It would have been difficult for him to have explained it there, but its surfacing several centuries later demonstrates it was well remembered within West Africa itself.

While matricide as motivation for Mūsā's *ḥajj* is certainly plausible, as an explicatory device it falls short, when there is not only the matter of why but also how he traveled. An enormous undertaking unprecedented in scope, it was through the *ḥajj* of *Mansā* Mūsā that the central Islamic lands, cognizant of *bilād as-sūdān* (at least as a concept) for centuries, became much more aware of its wealth and potential. Europe, its ideas about Africa rather inchoate, was put on notice that a powerful and rich kingdom lay south of the Sahara. Impressing foreign powers, intertwined with the desire to be regarded as a peer, may well have been a part of Mūsā's strategy.

The failure of the eighth/fourteenth-century voyage(s) of Qū or Muḥammad b. Qū, if in fact undertaken, would have also informed the strategy, persuading Mali's leaders that oceanic endeavor was not viable, that the Sahara was the only sea by which contacts could be expanded. More specifically, strengthening commercial ties with Cairo, as opposed to North Africa, may have been part of the calculus. Even so, geopolitical considerations could have been uppermost in Mūsā's mind, with the need to position Mali within a changing Islamic landscape through an alliance with the Mamluks. Though embroidering the realm of the hypothetical, such diplomatic preoccupations merit exploration. But before doing so, the profound implications of a turn from the sea to sand require brief contextualization.

Faced with seemingly insurmountable challenges in navigating waters off the West African coast, Malians focused on the Sahara. But had they known the world was in a truly transformative period, they may have considered reinvesting in maritime endeavor, as this was precisely the moment when Asia and Europe were beginning their transoceanic voyages, ventures that would establish domination of commercial and political developments elsewhere in the world. Arabs, Indians, and East Africans had long plied the waters of the Indian Ocean, but it was Zheng He, under China's Ming dynasty in the early ninth/fifteenth century, who undertook some seven voyages, unprecedented in range, eventually reaching East Africa.[62] Meanwhile, the Portuguese and the Genoese were beginning to explore West Africa's coast, eventually culminating in the continent's circumnavigation.[63] The world, especially Africa, would never be the same.

As the examples of the Mughals and Mongols demonstrate, naval power was not a prerequisite of empire. Controlling territory the size of Africa at its apex, the Mongols' sheer numbers, light horse-archers, and double recurve composite bows, combined with such steppe tactics as the arrow storm, hit-and-run chisel attacks, and double envelopment of the enemy, led to unprecedented expansion. Mali lacked this level of military proficiency; it was not spatially positioned to benefit from the generative effects of the Silk and Spice Routes, nor did it have access to such wide-ranging expertise and productivity among subject populations. Expanding the ranks of the literate, as well as the use of literacy beyond parochial applications, may have engendered a more capable formation of individuals who, in combination with some level of recordkeeping, could have produced a more efficient, powerful state apparatus. But the minimalist impulse, combined with the rise of Atlantic markets competing with those of the Sahel and relatively sparse populations under recurrent, destabilizing threats of slaving, provided no room for such developments, either in Mali or Songhay. The former's inability to control far eastern and western provinces would encourage breakaway states and accelerate enfeeblement, whereas internal dissolution in the latter (indeed, one of those breakaway states) greatly facilitated its eventual conquest.[64] But even if these obstacles had been surmounted, it is a challenge to imagine that, given Europe's expansion over the next seven hundred years, a more robust land empire could have significantly altered eventual trajectories of subjugation and disparity.[65]

Developments beyond the region would have played an important role in shaping the timing and substance of Mūsā's Pilgrimage. North Africa was in constant political upheaval, as the Marinids, Zenata Berbers who had defeated the Almohads and taken the key cities of Fez and Marrakesh in the seventh/thirteenth century, were preoccupied with managing a complex series of relations with the Nasrid Muslim dynasty of Grenada and the Christian state of Castile, alternately allying with one against the other as circumstances dictated.[66] Though suffering a series of setbacks at the hands of Castile and the Portuguese, in 747/1347 the Marinids were able to defeat the Hafsids of Ifriqiya (in what is now Tunisia), but had ongoing difficulties with the Zayanids, also Zenata Berbers, of Tlemcen (in what is now Algeria), exchanging control of that city several times from 737/1337 to 771/1370.

In contrast, the Ayyubids, ascending to power under Ṣalāḥ al-Dīn (or Saladin) in 569/1174, had established control over Egypt and Syria in 647/1250, only to be overthrown in Egypt by the Mamluks, who went on to stem the Mongol juggernaut after the latter's capture of Baghdad in 655/1258, defeating the Mongols in 657/1260. As the only power to withstand the Mongols, the Mamluks' accomplishment was all the more impressive, with Egypt emerging as the fount of Sunni Islamic culture, establishing itself as the center of the Muslim world until their defeat at the hands of the Ottomans in 922/1517.[67] In addition to its proximity to the Ḥijāz, therefore, Egypt would have been highly attractive to Mali as a stable diplomatic as well as commercial partner, and though Mali would continue its correspondence with Maghribian states, it made sense to invest much more substantially in a polity in like ascent.

The Ḥajj *of* Mansā *Mūsā: Meeting the Mamluks*

External written sources that actually date the *ḥajj*—Ibn Kathīr, al-Maqrīzī, Ibn Ḥajar, Ibn Khaldūn, al-Dawādārī, and Badr al-Dīn al-Halabī—all agree it took place in 724/1324, with Ibn Kathīr specifying Mūsā arrived in Cairo on Wednesday, 25 Rajab/18 July.[68] *Ta'rīkh as-sūdān* routes the entourage through Walata/Biru, underscoring its rise as a major entrepot at Awdaghust's expense by the beginning of the seventh/thirteenth century.[69] The *mansā* proceeded to Tuwat, probably passing through Taghaza at Tuwat's southwest edge, a center of significant salt mining under Masūfa Berbers employing slave labor, in addition to extracting alum. Of Taghaza, Ibn Baṭṭūṭa wrote in 753/1352: "This is a village with nothing good about it. . . . Nobody lives there except the slaves of the Masūfa who dig for the salt."[70] Insalubrious habitation helps to explain why so many in the *mansā*'s entourage fell ill in Tuwat (albeit to a "foot ailment").

Ta'rīkh al-fattāsh comments that, of the various accounts of the *mansā*'s Pilgrimage in circulation, the vast majority are fabricated or significantly embellished. One such tale concerns his building a mosque in every village he passed through on a Friday, a folkloric representation of Mūsā's commitment to Islamicization. Another relates how Mūsā, with the help of his chief servant "Farba" (a title) and nine thousand slaves, recreated a body of water in the desert so that the *mansā*'s wife Inari Konte and her five hundred female servants could bathe, made possible by the *baraka* of the Prophet, a sort of pre-withdrawal of blessings that would otherwise accrue with the *ḥajj*'s subsequent completion. Understood as entirely apocryphal by *Ta'rīkh al-fattāsh*'s authors themselves, they nonetheless revel in its telling.[71] As only *Ta'rīkh al-fattāsh* discusses Mūsā's matricide, the story makes the point that Mūsā's blessings and forgiveness were predicated on the Pilgrimage.

From Tuwat, Mūsā most likely traveled to Ghat, an oasis in the Fezzan, and on to northern Sudan and southern Egypt, following the "desert route."[72] Ibn Khaldūn asserts that prior to entering Cairo, *Mansā* Mūsā "came out near the Pyramids in Egypt," while al-Maqrīzī states "Mansā Mūsā, king of Takrūr . . . stayed for three days beneath the Pyramids as an official guest."[73] While a possible romanticization, it is nonetheless the testimony of otherwise reliable sources, conveying significant symbolic import for many who study Africa and its diaspora, as ancient Egypt and medieval West Africa constitute their quintessential spatial configurations and temporal moments. That such an extraordinary convergence of space and time is only (briefly) mentioned in the external primary sources, while not at all in any indigenous account, certainly gives pause, though that same brevity might also indicate the chroniclers' underappreciation of the iconic value—an argument for its authenticity. If the *mansā* indeed passed that way, it suggests medieval Mali was well aware of Pharaonic Egypt's illustrious past, with the *mansā* purposely seeking to connect with it.

Once in Cairo, Mūsā established his residence at al-Qarāfa 'l-Kubrā with permission of the Mamluk ruler al-Malik al-Nāṣir, who reportedly also gave him a "palace" as fief, though the *mansā* would later need to sell it.[74] More specifically, and in quoting Ibn Baṭṭūṭa, *Ta'rīkh as-sūdān* states "'when the *sulṭān* Mansā Mūsā,' that is, Mali-*koi* Kankan Mūsā, made the Pilgrimage, he lodged in gardens belonging to Sirāj al-Dīn b. al-Kuwayk, one of the great Alexandrian merchants at Birkat al-Ḥabash, outside Cairo [literally "outside Miṣr"]."[75] Sirāj al-Dīn b. al-Kuwayk would feature large in the *mansā*'s adventure, while the name Birkat al-Ḥabash, located to the immediate south of the old city of al-Fusṭāṭ (Islamic Egypt's first capital, south of Cairo), can be translated as "Abyssinian Pool" or "pool of the blacks."[76] Contiguous with al-Qarāfa 'l-Kubrā, perhaps it was only coincidental that a ruler from Mali was assigned a location so named.

Just two years prior to Mūsā's arrival, Cairo witnessed a deadly outbreak of sectarian violence that destroyed nearly sixty churches and many lives.[77] As they may have been impacted by residual religious fervor, the Malians were more probably affected by the very context within which they found themselves, influencing the way they came to understand Islam. For al-Qarāfa 'l-Kubrā was in the process of becoming a vast cemetery (al-Qarāfa 'l-Kubrā means "the larger cemetery" or "Greater Qarāfa"), interspersed with gardens and abodes large and small, and with al-Qarāfa 'l-Sughrā ("the smaller cemetery") would come to comprise the City of the Dead (*madīna al-mawtā*, as it is now known). Family members of the Fatimid caliphs (296–566/909–1171) are among the buried, but more pertinently the area became a site in which the entombed were enjoined through prescribed prayer and Qur'ānic recitation (*ziyārah*).[78] Such esoterica, not unlike Shī'a notions, was similar to what would become Ṣūfī practice, which would come to undergird much of Islam's formation throughout West Africa. Living in al-Qarāfa 'l-Kubrā would have made an impression, and could have played some role in Islam's veritable transformation in West Africa.

Of course, Kankan Mūsā was passing through Cairo as head of state, and according to the governor of Old Cairo, Abū 'l-Ḥasan 'Alī b. Amīr Ḥājib, rode on horseback under very large banners or flags (*'alam*) with yellow symbols (*shi'ār*) on a red background, consistent with accounts of his traveling under standards and parasol in Mali.[79] It is not clear whether the yellow-and-red pennant displayed the colors of Mali, or was Mūsā's personal emblem; Ibn Baṭṭūṭa reports that on high holy days *Mansā* Sulaymān appeared in public behind "red banners (*'alāmāt*) of silk," but makes no mention of the yellow symbol.[80]

Mūsā may have expected such a dramatic entrance would bolster his claim as a transregional ruler if not an international one, but it did not quite work out that way. Though his status as a transregional figure would be enhanced, any ambition he harbored to be recognized as an emerging international sovereign was effectively curtailed by a series of developments, beginning with his interaction with the Mamluk leader al-Malik al-Nāṣir.

The very act of meeting with al-Nāṣir created quite the conundrum, setting the tone as well as the ceiling for expectations. By way of protocol, Mūsā as ruler of Mali should have anticipated the requirement of an audience in the Citadel soon after his arrival in Cairo, and if he did not understand this beforehand, he would have become aware of it almost immediately thereafter. Revising *Kitāb al-'ibar* until near the end of his life in 808/1406, Ibn Khaldūn simply records that after Mūsā had sent "a rich present" of fifty thousand *dīnārs* to al-Nāṣir, the Mamluk ruler "received [Mūsā] in his audience room (*majlis*), talked to him, gave him a gift (*waṣalahu*), and supplied him with provisions. He gave him horses (*khayl*) and camels (*hujun*), and sent along with him emirs to serve him until he performed his religious duty in the year [7]24/1324."[81] The picture Ibn Khaldūn presents is one of peers, more or less, co-religionists peacefully exchanging gifts and services, absent any hint of tension or deference. His student al-Maqrīzī, however, subsequently introduces an element of controversy, reporting that in going to the Citadel for his audience, Mūsā "declined to kiss the ground and was not forced to do so though he was not enabled to sit in the royal presence."[82] Ibn Kathīr records the meeting similarly: "When [Mūsā] entered the Citadel to salute the sultan he was ordered to kiss the ground, but he refused to do so. The sultan treated him with honour but he could not sit before he left the presence of the sultan."[83] In these two accounts Mūsā's reticence signals an unwillingness to acknowledge the Mamluk ruler as a superior, with al-Nāṣir saving face by requiring him to remain standing. In repeating much of this in *al-Tibr al-masbūk*, al-Maqrīzī provides a different rationale:

> The sultan al-Malik al-Nāṣir Muḥammad b. Qalāwūn sent the *mihmandār* to receive him and Mūsā rode to the Citadel.He refused to kiss the ground and said to the interpreter: "I am a man of the Malikite school and do not prostrate myself before any but God." So the sultan excused him and drew him near to him and did him honour. The sultan asked the reason for his coming and he replied: "I wish to make the Pilgrimage." So the sultan ordered the *wazīr* to equip him with everything he might need.[84]

Refusing to prostrate himself before the Mamluk ruler on the basis of adherence to the Mālikī *madhhab* or school of law (the Mamluks followed the Shāfi'ī school) was an artful dodge, but it could not mask the political implications at stake. Indeed, this becomes entirely transparent in al-'Umarī's account, in which he quotes the *mihmandār* himself, Abū 'l-Abbās Aḥmad b. al-Ḥāk:

> "When I went out to meet him . . . I tried to persuade him to go up to the Citadel to meet the sultan, but he refused persistently. . . . He had begun to use this argument but I realized that the audience was repugnant to him because he would be obliged to kiss the ground and the sultan's hand. . . .
>
> "When we came into the sultan's presence we said to him: 'Kiss the ground!' but he refused outright saying: 'How may this be?' Then an intelligent man who was with him whispered to him something we could not understand and he said: 'I make obeisance to God who created me!' then he prostrated himself and went forward to the sultan. The sultan half rose to greet him and sat him by his side. They conversed together for a long time, then sultan Mūsā went out."[85]

This is a more probable rendition of what occurred, and suggests the two leaders reached a procedural compromise. In all versions of the encounter, the two rulers get on famously, but ultimately it was Mūsā who conceded the more significant ground, whether made to stand or allowed to sit, as either scenario underscores his disadvantage: that insofar as the Mamluk ruler was concerned, the two men were not in fact peers. One source, Ibn al-Dawādārī, goes so far as to say that Mūsā, receiving a "royal robe of honour" and having been "girded with a sword by his authority," agreed to have the *khuṭba* delivered in al-Nāṣir's name, conveying an acceptance of his authority over Mali and Mūsā's deputation as his viceroy.[86] Though Ibn al-Dawādārī is singular in this regard, the whole of the evidence suggests meeting al-Nāṣir was a major disappointment for Mūsā.

Of course, Cairo was the staging area for the *ḥajj* itself. The Mamluk ruler was generous in helping the Malians prepare to travel to Mecca, no doubt in partial response to Mūsā's extravagant gifts in gold, providing the *mansā* with "camels and much equipment befitting one like him" for the next leg of the journey, "arranging for deposits of fodder to be placed along the road and order[ing] the caravan commanders to treat him with honour and respect."[87] Although al-Maqrīzī states that al-Nāṣir instructed that Mūsā be given "everything he might need," al-'Umarī actually provides details with significance.[88] The "royal robe of honour" mentioned by Ibn al-Dawādārī bore the unmistakable quality of a Mamluk aesthetic, which if cynically interpreted would identify the *mansā* as a Mamluk lieutenant, not just a person of eminence, especially with headgear insignia that could only have referred to al-Nāṣir, not Mūsā.[89]

Ibn al-Dawādārī states Mūsā arrived in Egypt in 724/1324 and stayed there an entire year before proceeding to Mecca.[90] If correct, Mūsā would have actually remained in Egypt some sixteen months before traveling to Mecca, as he needed to wait until the next Dhū 'l-Ḥijjah—the last month in the Islamic calendar and the one prescribed for the *ḥajj*.[91] Sixteen months is probably too long, especially when accompanied by so large a retinue. Ibn Khaldūn's dating of the *mansā*'s travel would appear more reliable, in asserting that Mūsā went to Mecca in 724/1324 and joined an Egyptian contingent accompanied by the chamberlain of Abū Tāshfīn, ruler of Tlemcen, whom he befriended.[92] Contrary to the testimony of Ibn al-Dawādārī, therefore, the *mansā* set off for Mecca only a few months after arriving in Cairo, an itinerary confirmed by al-Maqrīzī, who writes he entered Cairo on 26 Rajab 724/19 July 1324, and left for Mecca three months later (28 Shawwāl 724/18 October 1324).

As both al-Maqrīzī and Ibn Ḥajar describe it, although the Malians were entrusted to Sayf al-Dīn Ītmish, "commander of the caravan (*amīr al-rakb*)," they traveled "as a self-contained company in the rear of the pilgrim caravan."[93] Sayf al-Dīn Ītmish (or Ītmish al-Muḥammadī), the *maḥmil*, and the remainder of the caravan returned to Cairo on 25 Muḥarram 725/11 January 1325, the month after Dhu 'l-Hijjah.[94] Mūsā would not return with them.

Al-'Umarī questioned a guide who traveled with the *mansā* to Mecca, Muhanna b. 'Abd al-Bāqī al-'Ujrumī, who stated the Malians "maintained great pomp and dressed magnificently during the journey."[95] Mūsā traveled to Mecca as well as Medina, "accomplishing the obligations of the Pilgrimage" and "visiting [the tomb of] the Prophet [at Medina] (God's blessing and peace be upon him!)"[96] While there, Mūsā "was very openhanded toward the pilgrims and the inhabitants of the Holy Places," giving away "much wealth in alms."

Notwithstanding the benefits of the *ḥajj*, the overall experience was rather harrowing for Mūsā. Ibn Ḥajar, in mentioning the Malians spent three months in Mecca, simply says a "great number of his men died of cold."[97] Al-Maqrīzī provides only slightly more details, reducing the time spent in Mecca to "several days after the ceremonies," while stating "many of his followers and camels perished from cold so that only about a third of them arrived [in Cairo] with him."[98] It falls to Ibn Khaldūn to explain the circumstances:

> It so happened that on the way [back to Cairo] he strayed from the *maḥmil* and the caravan and was left alone with his people away from the Arabs. This route was completely unknown to them, and they could not find the way to a settlement or come to a watering place. They went toward the horizon until they came out at al-Suways (Suez). They were eating fish whenever they could find some and the bedouin (*a'rāb*) were snatching up the stragglers until they were saved.[99]

Why so many West Africans, complete strangers to the region, would somehow fail to connect with the official Egyptian caravan returning to Cairo is beyond bizarre.[100] Whatever the explanation, Mūsā would arrive in Cairo without sufficient resources to return to Mali, having lavished gold upon both Cairo and the Ḥijāz.

The Ḥajj *of* Mansā *Mūsā: Exploitation*

Back in Cairo, the Malians were once again placed under the care of the *mihmandār* Abū 'l-Abbās Aḥmad b. al-Ḥāk, who on behalf of the Mamluk ruler continued to supply the *mansā* with necessary provisions.

Additionally, and in exchange for gifts Mūsā garnered in Mecca and Medina, the Mamluk sultan sent "complete suits of honour for him and his courtiers together with other gifts," including "various kinds of Alexandrian cloth, and other precious objects."[101] The *mihmandār* himself would be richly compensated, for when he died a large amount of unworked gold worth thousands of *dīnārs* was found in his possession.[102] The Mamluk sultan's hospitality, however, was not widely emulated by the Egyptian merchant class.

When *Mansā* Mūsā first arrived in Cairo in Rajab 724/July 1324, he "and his followers bought all kinds of things. . . . They thought that their money was inexhaustible."[103] By the time they left for Mali a year later, they had to borrow the very resources they initially spent, as Ibn al-Dawādārī relates:

> Then these people became amazed at the ampleness of this country and how their money had become used up. So they became needy and resold what they had bought at half its value, and people made good profits out of them. And God knows best.[104]

Ibn al-Dawādārī collapses a process more carefully represented in other sources, but it would appear the Malians were thoroughly exploited by their Egyptian co-religionists—something remarked upon in nearly all accounts. Old Cairo's governor, Abū 'l-Ḥasan 'Alī b. Amīr Ḥājib, who had befriended *Mansā* Mūsā, told al-'Umarī the former was forced to borrow money from Egyptian merchants who made 700 *dīnārs* for every 300 they lent, "a very high rate." Though recognizing the exorbitant nature of these arrangements, Ibn Amīr Ḥājib avoids rendering judgment, perhaps owing to the fact that he himself received 500 *mithqāls* of gold as an "honorarium."[105] However, Ibn al-Dawādārī is much more critical in his assessment:

> Avaricious people lent to them in the hope of big profits on their return [that is, to Mali], but everything they borrowed fell back on the heads of the lenders and they got nothing back. Among these was our friend the *shaykh* and imam Shams al-Dīn b. Tāzmart al-Maghribī. He lent them gold of good form but none of it came back.[106]

From the *nisba*, Shams al-Dīn b. Tāzmart al-Maghribī was himself from North (or possibly West) Africa, and there are other reports stating the *mansā* indeed paid his debts upon returning to Mali, but more salient here is the merchants' unscrupulous behavior. One of the more instructive examples of Mūsā's relationship with these merchants returns to the person of Sirāj al-Dīn b. al-Kuwayk, who hosted the *mansā* at Birkat al-Ḥabash. Ibn Khaldūn records that the "Banū 'l-Kuwaykh," or his family, were among those who loaned money to Mūsā, in this case 50,000 *dīnārs*.[107] In partial repayment, Mūsā sold to Sirāj al-Dīn the "palace" given to him by the sultan al-Nāṣir, but to recover the entire amount, Sirāj al-Dīn sent agents to Mali, later followed by his son Fakhr al-Dīn Abū Ja'far. Other moneylenders did the same, and the sources disagree as to whether they were all eventually and fully compensated.[108] Whereas Ibn Khaldūn says Sirāj al-Dīn's son only collected part of the principal before Mūsā died, Ibn Baṭṭūṭa records Sirāj al-Dīn himself went to Mali, along with his son, to receive payment. Sirāj al-Dīn in fact died in Mali, but his son allayed all suspicion: "'I ate that very same food with him. If there had been poison in it would have killed us all. It is just that his time was up'."[109] As Ibn Baṭṭūṭa records seeing Sirāj al-Dīn's grave in Timbuktu, the son's account, including his insistence he was repaid (presumably in full), is reliable. Ibn Ḥajar confirms Sirāj al-Dīn died "in the land of Takrūr" in 734/1334.[110]

Merchants in fact boasted to al-'Umarī that they took advantage of the Malians across a range of transaction, "saying that one of them might buy a shirt or cloak (*thawb*) or robe (*izār*) or other garment for five dīnārs when it was not worth one. Such was their simplicity and trustfulness that it was possible to practice any deception on them."[111] Malians took for granted what many Africans would likewise assume: that foreign co-religionists, Muslim and Christian, actually practiced what they professed. They would be in for a rude awakening over the centuries, with the Malians later forming "the very poorest of opinion of the Egyptians because of the obvious falseness of everything they said to them and their outrageous behaviour in fixing the prices of the provisions and other goods which were sold to them."[112]

A related example comes from a close reading of key sources concerning one Abū 'l-'Abbās, identified as al-Dukkālī by Ibn Baṭṭūṭa and apparently the same person as the "reliable *shaykh* Sa'īd al-Dukkālī," interviewed by al-'Umarī (who also refers to him as the "truthful and trustworthy *shaykh* Abū 'Uthmān Sa'īd al-Dukkālī"). The *shaykh* claimed to have lived in Mali for thirty-five years, and was probably al-'Umarī's source regarding Mali's physical dimensions, agricultural practices, diet, and conventions and features of the royal court.[113] And yet Ibn Baṭṭūṭa paints a very different picture of the *shaykh*.[114] True enough, al-Dukkālī accompanied Mūsā back to Mali, reaching the province of "Mīma" (presumably Mema). But this is where matters get interesting, because at Mema he complained four thousand *mithqāls* given to him by the *mansā* was stolen. Embarrassed and enraged, Mūsā summoned the governor (*amīr*) of Mema, threatening him with death if he did not find the culprit. Initially failing at the task, the governor finally went to al-Dukkālī's residence (referred to as "the qadi"), where one of his female servants felt sufficiently intimidated to speak up: "'He hasn't lost anything. He has just buried them with his own hands in that place'." The governor's report of the discovery further infuriated *mansā*, and he banished al-Dukkālī "to the land of the infidels who eat mankind," where he reportedly remained four years before returning to Egypt (unharmed, as his "white" skin was unsuitable for consumption).[115] Even this "reliable and trustworthy" *qāḍī* and *shaykh* participated in the shakedown of the *mansā*.

The Malians were not entirely without blame for creating the conditions of their own exploitation. Accompanied by previously unimaginable quantities of gold, they were responsible for perpetuating myths regarding its source. To be sure, the notion of a "gold-plant" had been circulating at least since Ibn al-Faqīh's late- third/early-tenth-century report that in Ghana "gold grows in the sand as carrots do, and is plucked at sunrise."[116] Despite attempts by individuals like al-Bīrūnī (d. ca. 442/1050) to debunk such tales, the concept remained credible for centuries, with Mūsā himself encouraging it while in Cairo.[117] Having initially explained to the *faqīh* Abū 'l-Rūḥ 'Īsā al-Zawāwī that the gold came from mineral deposits, he subsequently provided a more complex explanation to the governor of Old Cairo, stating that one form of the "gold-plant" matures "in the spring and blossoms after the rains in open country (*ṣaḥrā'*) [with] leaves like the *najīl* grass and its roots are gold (*tibr*)," while the other kind can be accessed anytime near the Niger "and is dug up."[118] In part describing a factual process, Mūsā also contributed to its fabrication, reinforcing belief that West African gold was inexhaustible, thereby assuaging consciences.[119]

Having convalesced, though now burdened with luxury purchases and considerable new debt, Mūsā and his significantly reduced entourage prepared for the return trip. The Mamluk ruler once more supplied him with camels and horses, and among the purchases he retained were "several books on Malikite jurisprudence," clothing items of varying sorts, and "slave girls," a category that included both "Ethiopians" and "Turks."[120] Enslaved male Turks may have also been transported, as they were among those described by al-'Umarī as having been purchased in Egypt.[121] Al-'Umarī states Mūsā also "brought jurists of the Malikite school to his country," including the Granadian poet Abū Isḥāq Ibrāhīm al-Sāḥilī, also known as al-Ṭuwayjin.[122] In Mali he would enjoy "an esteem and consideration which his descendants have inherited after him and keep to this day."[123] Though Ibn Khaldūn says his family lived in Walata/Biru, Ibn Baṭṭūṭa records that al-Ṭuwayjin hosted Sirāj al-Dīn in Timbuktu, and was buried there (along with Sirāj al-Dīn).[124]

In addition to scholars and merchants, it is possible that Arabs from the Ḥijāz, even *sherīfian* (descendants of the Prophet) accompanied the *mansā*. *Ta'rīkh al-fattāsh* contends that while in Mecca, Mūsā had offered one thousand *mithqāls* of gold to each of four such persons to return with him to Mali, where they would serve as a blessing by their very presence.[125] Four persons said to be Quraysh (and therefore not necessarily *sherīfian*) allegedly took the offer and arrived safely with their families. The account has a ring of verity in that it questions their true background, speculating they were actually freed slaves and clients (*mawālī*) of Quraysh families. In any event, the Malian caravan returned as a mixed host that included Ethiopians, Arabs, Andalusians, and Turks.

Having suffering setbacks, the *mansā*'s Pilgrimage nonetheless achieved some of his objectives. Though recognition as a peer with the Mamluk ruler eluded him, the latter honored him as a preeminent ruler of transregional dimensions. Meanwhile, Mūsā certainly made an impression on Egypt's commercial markets that would last for centuries, by which knowledge of Mali and West Africa became widespread.

Perhaps most importantly, he now possessed the *baraka* of the *ḥajj*, political as well as spiritual currency. He would soon spend it in ways that established the template for not only Muslim polity but also Islam's practice throughout much of West Africa. Stated differently, the *ḥajj* of Kankan Mūsā was the formative period of political as well as cultural transformation in West Africa, a veritable watershed moment.

Return and Expansion: Incorporating Gao and Timbuktu

Mūsā's route in returning to West Africa is not entirely detailed, though he seems to have retraced his steps through Egypt until reaching the middle of the Sahara, where he took a decidedly different turn. This is partially based on Ibn Khaldūn's report from "our friend al-Mu'ammar Abū 'Abd Allāh b. Khadīja al-Kūmī, a descendant of al-Mu'min [the Almohad ruler]," and who was active in the Zab, what is now eastern Algeria centered on the town of Biskra (or Biskara), north of Wargala.[126] Al-Mu'ammar had been raiding the Zab when he was arrested and detained in Wargala by its ruler. Having escaped, he learned of Mūsā's Pilgrimage and waited for him at Ghadames, from where he approached the *mansā* and requested his intervention in the dispute with Wargala, a recognition of "the power of Mansā Mūsā's authority in the desert adjacent to the territory of Wārgalan."[127] This suggests the *mansā* traveled through Ghadames, a trajectory that would have previously taken him through Jufra. The sheer size of his caravan would have attracted significant attention, and al-Mu'ammar boasted he and al-Ṭuwayjin "used to keep the sultan company during his progress . . . to the exclusion of his viziers and chief men, and converse to his enjoyment. At each halt he would regale us with rare foods and confectionery."

Upon meeting up with al-Mu'ammar, the *mansā* turned south rather than continuing west toward Tuwat. The prior experience in Tuwat may have informed the detour, but given what actually followed, a clear-minded political objective was probably more determinative. He may have passed through the important entrepot of Ghat (in the Fezzan), and then either through the copper mine of Takedda or the venerable outpost of Tadmekka, after which he descended on the city-state of Gao. Such a move required prior planning, possibly even prior to the Pilgrimage. In absorbing Gao into Mali, Mūsā acted upon a range of considerations that included an anterior Malian imperial restlessness, a desire to control all commercial arteries connecting the western Savannah with the Sahel, and the perception of a certain integrity of the Niger valley and the multiple ways in which its populations were connected by way of cultural symmetries and economic relations. In seizing Gao, therefore, Mūsā realized a breathtaking political vision: the unification of the Niger, Senegal, and Gambia valleys, representing some forty to fifty million people, with the Niger valley as the realm's core.[128]

Gao's incorporation into the Malian empire recalls Ibn Khaldūn's report that it was Sākūra who in fact initially subdued it. Once again, either the character of Sākūra is meant to prefigure Mūsā, there is confusion in the sources, or Gao succumbed to Mali to Sākūra and Mūsā on separate occasions, with *Ta'rīkh as-sūdān*, as opposed to the intriguing silence of *Ta'rīkh al-fattāsh*, succinctly making the political consequences of the *mansā*'s visit to Gao clear: "Following his Pilgrimage, the Songhay people entered into his submission."[129] *Ta'rīkh al-fattāsh*'s failure to mention such a critical development suggests a divergent political orientation of its authorship, but there is no question that it took place, as Ibn Khaldūn himself confirms: "The king of Kawkaw used to be independent but the sultan of Mālī took possession of it and it became part of his kingdom."[130]

The language of *Ta'rīkh as-sūdān* suggests a peaceful submission, no doubt a practical choice with Gao facing a superior force, even though Ibn Ḥajar and al-Maqrīzī note significant diminution in those forces in returning to Cairo from Mecca. In terms of quantification, al-Mu'ammar (as recorded by Ibn Khaldūn) contends that the *mansā* departed Cairo with goods "carried by 12,000 private slave women (*waṣā'if*) wearing gowns of brocade (*dībāj*) and Yemeni silk," implying a much larger total force. Given al-Maqrīzī's estimate that the *mansā*'s entourage upon arrival in Egypt included 14,000 slave girls, al-Mu'ammar's commentary suggests they were particularly valued, as their numbers remained relatively stable.[131] If *Ta'rīkh as-sūdān*'s figure of 60,000 arriving in Cairo is combined with al-Maqrīzī's estimate of a remnant of one-third leaving Cairo for Mali, it would suggest that some 20,000 persons accompanied the *mansā* to Gao. Such notional figures support the conclusion that the size of the *mansā*'s forces may have dissuaded Gao from following a path of resistance.

It was not to military might alone that Gao acquiesced, but also to the newfound spiritual authority Mūsā wielded, and with Gao's submission the *mansā* built a mosque and prayer niche (*miḥrāb*) on the outskirts of Gao, observing Friday prayer.[132] *Ta'rīkh al-fattāsh*, distancing itself from the lore of mosques going up wherever the *mansā* might find himself on a Friday, specifies six towns in which Mūsā actually built them (omitting mention of Gao). This constituted not only a statement of religious sentiment, but also, and as importantly, a crucial means by which the *mansā* justified and maintained imperium. If there were questions about his right to reign in Manden itself, such were even more pronounced in Gao, where he was incontrovertibly a foreigner. Mūsā's pursuit of Islam was therefore as much a political mobilization as anything else. Far more than war, Islam became the quintessential implement of dominion.

From Gao, the royal caravan proceeded to Timbuktu, where *Ta'rīkh as-sūdān* says the *mansā* became the first ruler to "take possession of it," as *Ta'rīkh al-fattāsh* merely mentions he stopped there.[133] As was true of Gao, there is no hint of hostilities; indeed, Aḥmad Bābā asserts Timbuktu was sacked only three times in its history (by the Mossi, *Sunni* 'Alī, and the Moroccans).[134] There, Mūsā built Jingereber mosque, the "Great Mosque," adding to it a tower-minaret (*ṣawma'a*) while establishing a personal residence, the *ma'aduku* or "place of the ruler," most likely outside of the city, in or near Timbuktu's river port of Kabara.[135] Gao's Friday mosque and Kabara's *ma'aduku* (where Mūsā would leave a lieutenant) spatially represent an ever present but rarely intrusive political authority, near yet just beyond the center of local life, aptly illustrating a theory of empire offering economic prosperity in exchange for security and a modicum of intervention.

From the perspective of the internal written record, Timbuktu's rise progressively attracted merchants from all over the Muslim world, especially Egypt and the Maghrib, reaching a point at which they filled the city "to overflowing." Timbuktu's emergence, on the other hand, "brought about the ruin of Bīru, for its development, concerning both religion or commerce, came entirely from the west ("al-Maghrib")."[136] Though establishing control over both Walata/Biru and Timbuktu may have unwittingly hastened the former's eventual demise, it remained an important trade center at least through the period of *Mansā* Sulaymān.

The Spatial Configuration of Power

In returning to Mali around 726/1326, Kankan Mūsā established a basis for Malian dominion that could be defended ideologically as well as militarily. Doubts about the manner in which he had ascended the throne were both muted and rerouted through an imaginative oral lore. What is more, he returned not simply as the ruler of Mali, but as an international figure with greatly strengthened regional and transregional claims.

The peripheries of Malian rule would approach their limits under *Mansā* Mūsā, primarily identifiable by way of border villages and towns, with rural areas between them infrequently experiencing an imperial presence, save in times of exigency. To the northeast lay Gao, ancient and experienced in commercial and cultural exchanges with Tadmekka to its north, Kukiya to its south, and Timbuktu to its west.[137] Timbuktu's incorporation into Mali represents the addition of even more routes of concourse, largely from the upper to the western buckle of the middle Niger valley, linking old, bustling markets such as Dia/Diagha and Jenne, from which caravans connected to Walata/Biru on the southern fringe of the desert, and from where they ventured to the salt mine of Taghaza and on to Sijilmasa. Indeed, Walata/Biru, which by the beginning of the seventh/thirteenth century had emerged as Awdaghust's successor by virtue of the rise of Taghaza's salt production, marked the northern boundary of Mali's reach, and according to the oral corpus was integrated very early into Mali by Maka Kamara. Ibn Baṭṭūṭa substantiates Mali's control over the entrepot, writing that after a two-month journey from Sijilmasa he arrived in Walata/Biru, "the first district of the Sūdān and the sultan's deputy there is Farbā Ḥusayn."[138] As will be seen, the office of the *farba* or *farma* was ubiquitous, and though often rendered as "chief" or "governor," it actually describes individuals occupying an array of offices, such that Ibn Baṭṭūṭa employs *nā'ib* or "deputy," indicating its range. The *farba/farma* could have been either free or enslaved, as the latter was true of the "Farba" in the Inari Konte tale, raising questions (to be addressed) about slavery in medieval West Africa.[139]

Both internal and external written documents provide insight into Mali's eastern sphere, but they offer little in the way of its western provinces in Senegambia, tending to repeat the refrain that Mali's authority reached all the way to the Atlantic Ocean. How that was accomplished or maintained remains murky. As mentioned, both al-'Umarī and Ibn Khaldūn assert Mali's western frontier approached the Atlantic (*al-baḥr al-muḥīṭ*). Based upon the testimony of al-Dukkālī, al-'Umarī described Mali as a huge square, taking approximately four months to cross north-to-south or east-to-west, while finessing the indeterminacy of its western reach by allowing it is "not far" from the Atlantic, only to later add it "extends in longitude from Mūlī to Turā on the Ocean," with "Turā" presumably referring to Futa Toro.[140] Indeed, *Ta'rīkh as-sūdān* says Mali was a large and expansive region "in the direction of" (*ilā jiha*) the Atlantic, while *Ta'rīkh al-fattāsh* states Mali's power stretched to "Sinqilu" and "Futa," a seeming reference to the Lower and Middle Senegal.[141] *Ta'rīkh as-sūdān* also lists Sanghana among Mali's provinces, with al-Bakrī locating it adjacent to Takrur on the Lower Senegal, with "habitations [that] reach the Ocean."[142] As discussed, oral materials claiming a Malian presence in the Upper and Middle Gambia under Sunjata most likely reflect subsequent developments in evidence by the time of Portuguese and other European travelers in the ninth/fifteenth century. A reasonable conclusion, therefore, is that Mali's authority under Mūsā approximated the Atlantic and the lower Senegal valley.

According to al-'Umarī, Mali under *Mansā* Sulaymān (ruled 741–61/1341–60) was organized into fourteen provinces (*aqālīm* or *a'māl*), the first six of which were previously known to geographers, with the next seven introduced by al-'Umarī: Ghana, Zafun (or Diafunu, Zāfūn), Tirafka or Tiranka, Takrur, Sanghana, Kawkaw (or Gao), Banb'w, Zarqatabana, Damura, Dia/Diagha (or Diakha, Zāgha), Kabora (or Kābara), Bawaghuri, Bytra, and Mali itself. "The province of Mālī," he writes, "is the one where the king's capital, Byty, is located. All these provinces are subordinate to it and the same name Mālī, that of the chief province of this kingdom, is given to them collectively."[143] The geographer further noted that if the *mansā* "were to hear" that Mali was known as "Takrur" in Egypt, "he would be disdainful for Takrūr is but one of the provinces of his kingdom."[144]

In some contrast, though describing Mali as "very large," *Ta'rīkh as-sūdān* focuses primarily on political relations within the middle Niger valley, stating that Mali controlled "Songhay" (which would include Gao), Timbuktu, Dia/Diagha, Mema (to the northwest of Lake Debo), and

Baghana or Baghunu (west of Mema in what is now southeastern Mauritania), along with surrounding territories. Mema and Baghana had been closely associated with Ghana in its ascendancy, with *Ta'rīkh as-sūdān* describing Baghana as the land in which the "city" of Ghana was located and over which ruled the *tunka*, so that most if not all of these five territories are probably included in the fourteen listed in al-'Umarī.[145]

Between Mema and Baghana lay Zafun or Diafunu, mentioned by al-'Umarī, who also claims that to the north of Mali "are tribes of white Berbers under the rule of its sultan, namely: Yantaṣar, Tīn Gharās, Madūsa, and Lamtūna. They are governed by *shaykhs*, save Yantaṣar who are ruled successively by their own kings (*malik*) under the suzerainty of the ruler of Mālī."[146] Though unspecified, the areas these groups (some of whom were Ṣanhāja) inhabited would have included Mema, Baghana, and Zafun. As such, the Malian empire once again challenges conventional notions of *bilād as-sūdān* while anticipating Songhay's pluralism (though the latter would pursue policies much more concrete and extensive in integrating socially disparate elements).

In addition to these provinces, *Ta'rīkh as-sūdān* mentions that Kala, Bendugu, and Sibiridugu were under Malian control, all of which were physically proximate to Jenne, with Bendugu consisting of a string villages along the Bani River's right bank, from Jenne to just beyond (what becomes) Segu. As for Jenne itself, its status during the high period of Malian rule remains something of a mystery, best approached after further discussion of Malian administrative organization.

As both internal and external documents speak of provinces and towns as the bases for understanding Mali's physical constitution, the category of the province was not an imposition of external observers assuming or in need of a framing device to render the state more legible. On the other hand, there was recognition within Mali that vast stretches of agricultural and pastoral and waste land were one thing, and urban centers quite another, and that it was on the basis of the accumulation of the latter that a kingdom made a case for greatness. It is therefore not surprising that Mali boasted of the number of "cities" it either conquered or coerced into submission, with Mūsā claiming to have subdued twenty-four himself, "each with its surrounding district with villages and estates" per al-'Umarī.[147] Ibn Kathīr conveys this a bit differently, "that there were 24 kings under his authority, each having people and soldiers under him."[148] *Ta'rīkh al-fattāsh* is similarly invested, presenting Mali as a kingdom of urban space of some four hundred "towns" (*mudun*, also "cities"), comparing favorably with the kingdoms of the world, exceeded in beauty only by Syria.[149]

Mali therefore consisted of an ancient core made up of the heartland of old Manden in the upper Niger valley, together with territories purportedly united under Sunjata and his successors in the seventh/thirteenth century that included Ghana, Mema, Tabon, and those Mande states in close proximity to Manden. As such, the fourteen provinces listed by al-ʿUmarī are probably fairly contiguous with the original twelve territories of the "twelve kings of the bright savanna country" said to have sworn fealty to Sunjata. To this core would have been added medial provinces largely to the west, either conquered or culturally integrated, comprised of the upper through lower Senegal valley. Distinctions between the core provinces and their medial counterparts would have been both cultural and historical, with the former made up of Mande-speaking populations benefitting from a long history of interrelations, and the latter comprised of non-Mande populations (Fulbe, Wolof, for example). To the medial provinces would be added outer provinces, either under Kankan Mūsā or others in the eighth/fourteenth century, including Timbuktu, Gao, Dia/Diagha, maybe Baghana, and Walata/Biru, characterized by their more recent addition (with the exception of Walata/Biru) and by their location either in the middle Niger valley or on the fringe of the desert, with the latter further distinguished by its sheer distance from Manden's center. At indistinct points, communities from the upper to lower Gambia valleys were also incorporated.

Reconstructing Mali's imperial administrative apparatus is far from straightforward, but an overall theory of governance is discernible. To begin, whether core, medial, or outer, provinces were afforded optimal autonomy. In fact, there may have been greater intrusion into provincial affairs under Sunjata than subsequently, as the oral sources speak of the removal of disloyal or incompetent officers—perhaps indicative of a need to tightly control territories at the onset of the imperial experiment. If not directly appointed by the *mansā*, these offices would presumably have been subject to whatever internal arrangements had obtained prior to Mali's imposition, left to organize themselves as long as they remained loyal to Mali. In contrast to Mali's core, however, the principle of dual governance seems to have informed the ways in which Mali established its authority in the medial and outer provinces, allowing existing systems of self-rule to remain, but establishing parallel offices that answered only and expressly to Mali. The evidence suggests these offices were always staffed by Malians.

Aspects of Malian administration can in fact be gleaned from the discussion of imperial Songhay administration in *Ta'rīkh as-sūdān* and *Ta'rīkh al-fattāsh*, and what is instructive, even revealing, is the very terminology referring to officials. Generally speaking, officials with oversight over cities, towns, villages, and provinces are given the *koi* designation, a Songhay term conveying ownership and command, in any event reserved for the principal political official of the area in question, or in some instances the chief leader of a particular ethnic formation within an ethnically-plural municipality. Thus, under Songhay the Malian *mansā* is called the Mali-*koi*, along with the Jenne-*koi*, the Bara-*koi* (governor of Bara, north of Lake Debo), the Dirma-*koi* (governor of Dirma, south of Lake Fati between the Niger and Bara Rivers), the Timbuktu-*koi*, and so on, reflecting a Songhay cultural imprint and emergence of Songhay as an imperial lingua franca.

However, there are any number of offices within the Songhay administrative apparatus that employ such terms as *farma, farba,* and *fari* (with *faran* the Songhay derivative), as well as *mondio*, with the first three terms clearly Mande in origin, and the fourth possibly so. This strongly suggests, along with corroborating evidence, that many of these offices were inherited from Mali when Songhay rose to regional status in the ninth/fifteenth centuries, so that the Benga-*farma* and the Shā'-*farma* and the Timbuktu-*mondio* and the *Fari-mondio*, just to name a few, were already in place.[150]

It is not always possible to definitively correlate seemingly equivalent yet differently designated offices, so that while Ibn Baṭṭūṭa's "governor" of Timbuktu, *Farba* Mūsā, would appear to have been what the *ta'rīkhs* (*tawārīkh*) refer to as the Timbuktu-*koi*, alternatively he could have been the Timbuktu-*mondio*.[151] And while the responsibilities of a number of these offices are not specified, those designated in some cognate form of *farma* appear connected to the oversight of areas beyond the core areas of Mali, in which conventional rulers were allowed to continue in conjunction with the Malian agent, whereas the *mondios* were often responsible for some aspect of revenue collection (though they could also have other responsibilities). *Farmas* and *mondios* were also found working with provincial governors and their militaries to provide security for travelers, reflected in Ibn Baṭṭūṭa's observation that in traveling from Walata/Biru to Mali's capital he hired only a guide, "since there is no need to travel in company because of the security of that road."[152] While respect for the peaceful conduct of trade may have been culturally inculcated, there were also mechanisms of reinforcement, to which end such offices played a role. Another way of understanding this structure is that Mande-related offices served Songhay in an interstitial capacity, connecting to the center while linking the entire empire. That these designations continued under Songhay indicates they were not just Mande terms, but Mande concepts, having served a similar if not very same purpose under imperial Mali.

It is also conceivable that some offices appendaged with the *koi* designation actually antedate the Songhay empire, with the Mali-*koi* a prime example, and that Songhay designations in such instances merely reflect the growing importance of the language, not the creation of the post. Likewise, it is possible that certain positions in imperial Songhay evolved in some fashion from earlier iterations in Mali, for, as will be demonstrated, Songhay consciously claimed the mantle of Mali, so that a certain continuity was critical to its assertions. Songhay was therefore unquestionably indebted, so much so that Mande culture and language even informed entirely novel posts after the rise of imperial Songhay.

There are in fact a number offices associated with Songhay apparatus that qualify for a prior incarnation in imperial Mali. To begin, there was the Kala-*shā'*, the principal official of Kala, a province specifically cited as falling under Malian control upon *Mansā* Mūsā's return from the Pilgrimage. Kala was between Niger and Bani Rivers, and was the name used for the Niger south of Masina, to the west of Dia/Diagha. When first introduced, Kala is presented as a conglomeration of towns whose rulers are appendaged with *koi* (such as the Warun-*koi* and the Wanzu-*koi*), and it is only later in *Ta'rīkh as-sūdān* that the governor of the entire province, the Kala-*shā'*, is mentioned.[153] Likewise, the province to the west of the Niger River lakes, Baghana, is also mentioned in *Ta'rīkh as-sūdān* as part of imperial Mali, but it is not until information related to the beginning of the tenth/sixteenth century that the governor of the province, the Baghana-*fari*, is actually referenced.[154]

As yet another example, the post of the Benga-*farma*, governor of the area or province of Benga (which derived from *bangu*, Songhay for "lake," the lacustrine area east of Dirma and Bara, upstream from Timbuktu on the Niger River's right bank), was in existence since the time of the Sunni or Chi rulers of Songhay, who came to power late in the eighth/fourteenth century when initially subject to Mali, so it is highly probable the Baghana-*fari* had been subject as well.[155] Similarly, the post of *balma'a*, a seeming conflation of Bal-*magha* (Mande for "lord" of Bal), was a military official stationed at Timbuktu's river port of Kabara during the Malian period.[156] As late as the late tenth/sixteenth century, this person was still addressed as "Tunkara," a greeting of respect clearly related to the Soninke *tunka* for "ruler," initially reserved for the leader of ancient Ghana and, by extension, rulers of other polities including Mūsā Tunkara, ruler of Mema during the time of Sunjata.[157] Another official at Kabara was the person responsible for the port, the Kabara-*farma*, and though the sources do not discuss the origins of this office, it may also reflect the Malian era.[158] That not only Mande offices but sensibilities were transferred to imperial Songhay is confirmed by the fact that, in addition to the *balma'a*, the Kurmina-*fari* or *kanfāri*—the second most powerful position in imperial Songhay—was also honored with the greeting, "Tunkara," particularly illuminating since the office was created by the Songhay emperor *Askia al-ḥājj* Muḥammad Ture himself (ruled 898–935/1493–1529).[159]

The foregoing therefore provides a sense of Mali's organizational pattern. From the center flowed authority to the provincial levels and municipalities. The more economically profitable or strategically placed the province or town, the more important their governors and overseers, and the more important the town, the greater its profile vis-à-vis its province. Medial and outer provinces featured a system of dual authority, whereby locally determined provincial governors were paired with officials reporting directly to the Malian center, while throughout were officials primarily concerned with harvesting tax revenue.

Over such a vast territorial expanse was strategically placed a military presence that, according to *Ta'rīkh as-sūdān*, featured two paramount commanders: the *Sanqara-zūma'a* and the *Faran-sūra*, "in charge of the south" and the "north," respectively, the latter's title meaning "deputy official over the desert dwellers." As these regional commanders are not mentioned elsewhere in the sources, it is not clear whether they precede or antedate *Mansā* Mūsā. *Sūra* may refer to Suradugu or the Hodh, between Awdaghust and Walata/Biru, and though Suradugu is not mentioned as such in the aforementioned provincial lists, it is more or less contiguous with Baghana, Zafun, and Mema, with the concept of the *Faran-sūra* consistent with al-'Umarī's claim Mali ruled certain "tribes of white Berbers."[160] *Ta'rīkh as-sūdān* in fact associates the area under the *Faran-sūra*'s control with the older territory of Kaniaga (or Futa Kingui), and states that just a few years after the Moroccan defeat of Songhay in 999/1591, the *Faran-sūra* was recognized as the sultan of Diara (in what was Kaniaga).[161]

The division between the forces under the *Sanqara-zūma'a* and the *Faran-sūra* also represent differences in terrain, technology, and culture. The operations of the latter would have been informed by desert-side life and activities based on camelry and Ṣanhāja Berbers. The *Sanqara-zūma'a*, in turn, commanded forces composed of both foot soldiers and cavalry composed of Mande-speakers and other

"Savannah-dwellers," and whose Savannah terrain necessitated different tactics and technologies.

The existence of military commanders presumes persons to be commanded, and though the sources state the *Sanqara-zūma'a* and *Faran-sūra* each fielded sizable armies, what that meant quantitatively is unclear; and though it would suggest these were standing units, the degree to which "standing" requires qualification is also an open question. Al-'Umarī is almost alone in providing any insight: "The king of this country imports Arab horses and pays high prices for them. His army numbers about 100,000, of whom 10,000 are cavalry mounted on horses and the remainder infantry without horses or other mounts."[162] Since the quantity "100,000" also features in al-Maqrīzī's earlier estimate of Kanem's military, as well as in al-Bakrī's assessment of fourth/tenth-century Awdaghust, al-'Umarī may have simply borrowed a notional expression.[163] Further, the sources do not provide insight into whether waging war was the only or primary activity of those doing the fighting.[164] They do remark upon frequent campaigning, however, almost incessant under certain rulers, such that the status of those fighting could certainly approximate that of a full-time soldier. However, beginning with Sunjata and his generals, a significant portion of the Malian military was enslaved. The precise servile component cannot be determined, but the oral corpus leaves no doubt about this, while nothing in the written sources indicates the practice was at any time arrested or altered.

The *Sanqara-zūma'a* and the *Faran-sūra* clearly possessed formidable power. Under the press of imperial Songhay in the tenth/sixteenth century these regional commanders asserted their independence from a diminished Mali, but their rule became closely associated with "tyranny" and "violation," with the result that they were, according to the sources, divinely decimated.

Polity in the Medieval Savannah and Sahel

It is at this juncture, with the discussion of polity in Mali in place, that a more thoroughgoing analysis of the nature of the medieval West African state can be addressed. To be clear, as the preceding analysis indicates and the subsequent exploration of imperial Songhay will reveal, this study fully subscribes to a model of statecraft that was both hierarchical and evolving. The preceding treatment of Mali's administration is entirely consistent with such a model, as is the example of imperial Songhay, whose progression in theories of governance can be observed in the transition from the purposeful violence of *Sunni* ʿAlī, to the sophisticated pluralism of *Askia al-ḥājj* Muḥammad.

The approach adopted here is in some tension with one that categorizes states like Mali and Songhay as "composite monarchies," which feature a weak center that facilitates yet depends upon autonomous provinces, and whose authority also derives from association with cognate, mostly cultural cynosures. Secular and cultural (often religious) authority are mutually reinforcing, benefitting from "symbolic" or ritual rather (or more) than coercive power. In this way, medieval West African societies were organized by dispersed sources of authority that, when effective, worked in concert.[165]

The composite monarchy/symbolic authority conceptualization is heavily dependent on the anthropological and archaeological literature, and casts the widest of nets by which information is culled from societies throughout Africa, and from all periods, from ancient Nubia to colonial Congo. As such, this panoptic formulation envisions the whole of Africa, both spatially and temporally, as a single analytic field. Contemporary sources for medieval West Africa, while acknowledged, are rendered subsidiary to a thickly described, multidisciplinary analysis, and are discounted as revisionist in light of their political agendas.[166]

This inquiry likewise engages with the politics and circumstances of cultural production, perhaps more extensively than most. But it arrives at a different conclusion: that relations of power as described in the sources reflect actual conditions of the period, and are far too detailed and imbricated to represent the design of ideological fabrication from whole cloth. Furthermore, as has been and will be demonstrated, there are plenty of examples of coercive power in medieval West Africa, from tribute to multiple forms of taxation to military conscription, all flowing from the political center. The fact that the state would ally with either Muslim or ancestral religious officials to augment or extend its power is hardly unique to West Africa (or Africa, for that matter), but as in the case of imperial Songhay for virtually the whole of its history, the state could also be in substantial conflict with a significant component of Islam's "religious estate." And although Songhay would legitimate its rule through Islam, coercion, not symbolism, characterized many of its policies and relations.[167]

In light of the foregoing, it is more accurate to view the political center's articulation with province and periphery as a conscious decision, a philosophy of governance, as opposed to an enfeebled capacity. This was a minimalist approach that, while arguably informed by the challenges of distance and infrastructure, at least as equally (if not even more so) demonstrated a privileging of relative degrees of autonomy radiating from the center, a resolution that honored cultural sensibilities while preserving, to the extent possible, longstanding intercommunal protocols. Even so, the record registers the rise of intrusive measures across time and regimes. This is, therefore, a model of West African polity that allows for change and evolution, as opposed to temporal stasis.[168]

Aside from the scaffolding of empire—introduced for Mali and awaiting analysis for Songhay—there are just too many examples of coerced verticality to be dismissed as ideological or revisionist constructs. The sources are unambiguous that provincial governors reported to the political center, that in instances the center maintained dual administrative lines, that subject provinces were required to send their sons to live in the capital as "sons of vassals," that rulers regarded cities (especially Timbuktu and Gao) as "possessions," that taxes and tribute could be harshly imposed, that coerced labor fueled productive and extractive industries, and so on. These sorts of relations not only undergo transformation from Mali to Songhay, but the level of coercion only intensifies. Far from a presumption of conventionality, the model of an evolving, hierarchical imperial structure, relative to this place and period, emerges from careful assessment of testimony generated from both within and outside of the region.

Cohering around the Center: Of Capitals and Legendary Cities

Governors of the core, medial, and outer provinces, military commanders, and lesser officers answering to them all eventually connected to Mali's political center, the capital and main residence of the *mansā*. Al-'Umarī is the first to identify that capital as "Byty," providing the following picture:

> The city of Byty is extensive in length and breadth. Its length would be about a stage (*barīd*) and its width the same. It is not encircled by a wall and is mostly scattered. The king has several palaces enclosed by circular walls. A branch of the Nīl [the Niger] encircles the city on all four sides. In places this may be crossed by wading when the water is low but in others it may be traversed only by boat.[169]

Later in the eighth/fourteenth century, Ibn Khaldūn identifies the capital as "Bny" and—based on the testimony of Abū 'Abd Allāh Muḥammad b. Wāsūl, who lived in Gao for a period—similarly describes the capital as "'an extensive place with cultivated land fed by running water, very populous with brisk markets'," not simply the seat of government but an entrepot in its own right, a "'station for trading caravans from the Maghrib, Ifrīqiya, and Egypt'." The concept of the *barīd* is helpful in that it expands on the notion of "extensive," suggesting the dimensions of Byty/Bny covered at least seven miles.[170] Altogether, these are not the descriptions of a provincial town.

There is little doubt that Ibn Baṭṭūṭa actually traveled to West Africa, arriving in what he called "the town of Mālī" in 753/1352, but in contrast to al-ʿUmarī and Ibn Khaldūn, he says virtually nothing about it. This is curious, as he eagerly commented on Sijilmasa ("one of the finest cities"), Taghaza ("this is a village with nothing good about it"), Zaghari ("a big village"), Gao ("a great town on the Nīl, one of the finest, biggest, and most fertile cities of the Sūdān"), and other sites.[171]

Ibn Baṭṭūṭa's relative silence only contributes to the debate over the location of Mali's capital, or series of capitals, and whether Byty/Bny was legendary Niani on the Sankarani River, as maintained in the oral corpus.[172] In fact, the examination of the written sources and archaeological excavations has led to hypotheses suggesting sites other than Niani, underscoring that the Malian capital probably migrated over time, and that there were multiple capitals during any given period, with Sunjata's birth village of Dakadiala/Dakajalan a likely early political center.[173]

Much of the discussion over the Malian capital centers on Ibn Baṭṭūṭa's itinerary, which raises even more questions, especially regarding Mali's relationship with Jenne. Indeed, in all of his excursions through the Middle Niger, Ibn Baṭṭūṭa never mentions Jenne, although he refers to a number of towns far less important, including Zaghari, Karsakhu, and Quri, while he is careful to mention Timbuktu, Gao, and Takedda.[174] That he actually passed through these towns helps to explain their inclusion, but he also mentions towns he did not pass through, including Dia/Diagha (or Zāgha) and Kabora (Kābara). The failure to visit or even acknowledge Jenne is therefore mystifying.

It is tempting to venture that Ibn Baṭṭūṭa did not name the Malian capital nor acknowledge Jenne because they were one and the same, as the capital was a large and important entrepot, connoting a cosmopolitanism far beyond the provincial. Though dazzling in implication, what evidence exists is contrary and insufficient to move beyond insinuation. The first difficulty, raised by al-ʿUmarī, is that the "city of Byty is not encircled by a wall," whereas Jenne's palisades are legendary. But there is a second hurdle, potentially compelling, that suggests Ibn Baṭṭūṭa's itinerary was an intentional circumlocution around Jenne.

Jenne's relationship to Mali is one of the more fascinating features of the operation and limitations of dominion in West Africa. The evidence, when carefully sifted, reveals varying interpretations rather than straightforward divergence. *Ta'rīkh as-sūdān*, to begin, is unequivocal in its narrative:

> And in the [fullness of] their power . . . they desired that the people of Jenne enter into their submission, and they [Jenne] would not agree to this. So the people of Mali began to attack them with numerous assaults and intense, terrible battles, ninety-nine times in total, and each time the people of Jenne defeated them. And it is said [*fī al-akhbār*—"among soothsayers"?] that a hundredth [battle] between them will definitely take place at the end of the age, and that the people of Jenne will again be victorious at that time.[175]

This strongly implies that Jenne, like Gao and Timbuktu, had been offered the opportunity to peacefully submit to Mali, perhaps during Mūsā's return from the Pilgrimage. Jenne's rejection led to numerous engagements, further suggesting overall relations between Mali and Jenne were adversarial. The threat was so constant that Jenne's sultan is said to have maintained an army to its west "in the land of Sana," commanded by twelve generals responsible for protecting against Malian incursions.[176] Underscoring such pride and determination, *Ta'rīkh as-sūdān* asserts that "since its foundation, no ruler has defeated its [Jenne's] people except *Sunni* 'Alī."[177]

Ta'rīkh al-fattāsh, however, paints a very different picture:

> As for the Jenne-*koi*, he was the most insignificant of the slaves of the Mali-*koi* and the lowest of his servants; it suffices to say that he [the Jenne-*koi*] could only stand before his wife, that is, the wife of the Mali-*koi*, and it was to her that he presented the levies [*al-gharāma*] of the region of Jenne. The Mali-*koi* did not see him.[178]

Both the substance and the language employed here are in striking contrast to that of *Ta'rīkh as-sūdān*. Instead of "*sulṭān*," the Jenne-*koi* is called one of the *mansā*'s "slaves" (*'abīd*), and the least significant at that. He is not a literal slave, as the idiom is chosen to convey a humiliation deepened by the fact that he does not merit an audience with the *mansā*, but rather with the *mansā's* wife.

What goes unstated is Mali's need to put Jenne "in its place." There is an undercurrent of animosity, consistent with the claim of perennial conflict as found in *Ta'rīkh as-sūdān*. That *Ta'rīkh al-fattāsh* fails to mention the submission of either Gao or Timbuktu, while seeming to take delight in Jenne's debasement, may also signal a rivalry of sorts between Timbuktu and Jenne, at least from the perspective of the authors. In any event, it is evident that the relationship between Jenne and Mali was at least fraught. Given Jenne's central role as regional emporium, Mali would want to control it. Unlike Gao and Timbuktu, however, Jenne resisted, the supposedly large number of Malian expeditions against it the serial response. Jenne may never have been defeated militarily, but it may well have acquiesced to paying tribute, in amounts that ebbed and flowed with the level of conflict. The disdain for Jenne expressed in *Ta'rīkh al-fattāsh* was therefore an expression of frustration, as apparently Mali could never completely bring Jenne to heel.

If Mali could not impose its will directly or militarily, there remained other routes to a similar destination. Key to appreciating Jenne's dilemma is the spatial distribution of Malian governance in the vicinity.[179] To the immediate west and south of Jenne were the provinces of Kala, Bendugu, and Sibiridugu, with part of Kala comprising the land between Niger and Bani Rivers. Each of the three provinces featured twelve "*sulṭāns*" or rulers over components of each province, with one of the Kala sultans, the Kokiri-*koi*, positioned on the western border of the important village of Dia/Diagha (Zāgha), and over whom governed the Kala-*shā'*, in charge of the entire province. Sibiridugu was farther south, between the Niger and the Bani, whereas Bendugu consisted of villages beginning at Jenne's southern border, and extending along the bank of the Bani. When the fact that Mali also controlled Baghana—to the west of the Niger Inland Delta, the floodplain from the lacustrine to the riverine area as far south as Jenne—is taken into consideration, it means Mali controlled river routes from the Upper Niger to the border of Jenne, as well as the overland route on the western edge of the Niger all the way to Timbuktu. That is, Jenne was caught in a veritable vise, with Mali controlling strategic positions along thoroughfares to its north and south. That control may have fluctuated, but a significant amount of Jenne's commerce flowed through territories claimed by Mali. If Jenne was required to pay tribute, at least on occasion, its relationship to Mali may be more aptly described as coerced, as opposed to the utter domination presented in *Ta'rīkh al-fattāsh*.

This helps explain Ibn Baṭṭūṭa's overland return route from the Malian capital to Timbuktu, at which point he took a boat to Gao. In moving by camel to Timbuktu, he traveled along corridors controlled by Mali, bypassing Jenne. It was a time of high tension, and as a guest of Mali, the traveler may not have been welcomed in Jenne.

Ibn Baṭṭūṭa's Account of the Royal Court

Ibn Baṭṭūṭa's discussion of the Malian capital and omission of Jenne are therefore very useful. Though he exoticizes, he also goes beyond the exercise of rendering intelligible the arcane. For accompanying his depiction of the pomp and circumstance of the royal court, and undergirding his account of the pageantry and performance of power and privilege, are descriptions of the mechanisms of power that resonate with corroborating materials. Not unlike the power grid of Ghana's capital in its former glory, spatial configurations attendant to the staging of the magisterial reveal relations of rank and position consistent with Malian governance as outlined up to this point.

Ibn Baṭṭūṭa describes two principal arenas, apparently fairly close together, as the conjunctive locus of state power in the Malian capital: the *qubba* and the *mashwar*.[180] In the *qubba* or domed pavilion sat the *mansā* "for most of the time," indicating his formal office. "When he is sitting," conducting matters of state, the town would come alive, mobilized around the protocol and substance of power. The commencement of a royal session was signaled by flying a "patterned Egyptian kerchief" attached to a "silken cord" from a pavilion window, signaling drummers and trumpeters to alert everyone else. An armed guard of approximately "300 slaves"—archers and those with "short lances and shields"—formed ranks on either side of the gate, the lancers standing and the bowmen sitting, the latter honor possibly indicative of continued reverence for the hunter and Sunjata as his idealization. Two horses, saddled and bridled, were present along with two rams, warding away the evil eye.

The *qubba* may or may not have also served as the ruler's residence. Ibn Khaldūn records that upon returning from the Pilgrimage, *Mansā* Mūsā commissioned the Granadian poet al-Ṭuwayjin to construct a house "with plaster on account of its unfamiliarity in their land," and al-Ṭuwayjin did so, possessing "a good knowledge of handicrafts and lavished all his skill" in making "something novel for him by erecting a square building with a dome."[181] Plastered over and covered with "colored patterns so that it turned out to be the most elegant of buildings," the edifice caused "great astonishment" in Mali. In potentially describing the same structure, Ibn Baṭṭūṭa was not as impressed.

Once the *mansā* was actually seated in the *qubba*, three slaves would locate an important deputy (or *farba*, Qanjā Mūsā at this time), together with the *farāriyya* or "emirs," the *khaṭīb* (the Friday mosque speaker or preacher), and the *fuqahā'* (singular *faqīh*, experts in legal matters). They would all sit before the *mashwar* or meeting place of the Grand Council, partitioned from an otherwise open area and at a short walking distance from the *qubba*. Each of the *farāriyya* remained on horseback with a quiver "between his shoulders" and a retinue in front "with lances and bows, drums and trumpets." At the gate of the *mashwar* stood "Dūghā the interpreter," the *jeli*, enturbaned and resplendid in silk, gold and silver lances in either hand, a golden-sheathed sword about his waist.

Ibn Baṭṭūṭa's observations suggest that whenever the *mansā* was in executive session in the *qubba*, the rest of the court sat aside the *mashwar* in case there was need to consult them. In such instances, the *mansā* would leave the *qubba* and walk "with great deliberation," led by singers with "gold and silver stringed instruments" and followed by the royal guard of three hundred. Once inside the *mashwar* the *mansā* would sit on the *banbī* (or *bembe*, a raised platform upholstered with silk, with cushions on top and over which was a parasol of silk)—a smaller version of the *qubba* with a golden bird atop "the size of a falcon"—with drums and trumpets sounding, prompting the three slaves to usher inside the *farba* and *farāriyya* while leaving the others in the tree-shaded street.

Al-'Umarī's description of the Malian royal is contemporary with that of Ibn Baṭṭūṭa and specifically concerns the *mashwar*. Both an executioner and a "poet" were central to the proceedings, the latter an intermediary between the ruler and the ruled and apparently a reference to Dūghā. Behind the *mansā* stood thirty slaves, and in referring to them al-'Umarī uses the term *mamlūk* (as opposed to *'abīd*), probably because they were "Turks and others who are bought for him in Egypt," perhaps the same ones who accompanied *Mansā* Mūsā.

If read absent context or attribution, it would be difficult to determine whether the foregoing pertains to eighth/fourteenth-century Mali or fifth/eleventh-century Ghana, given correspondences that include the enturbaned ruler, the domed pavilion, the human cordon with golden swords and shields, the heralding drums.[182] Even more striking is the earthen ablution. Appearing in early Ghana, it had become an even more critical component of acquiescence by the time of imperial Mali (together with crawling on all fours after prescribed movement of the right hand).[183] Al-'Umarī writes of emirs and others who entered the royal session:

> When he reaches [the opposite end of the room from the *mansā*] the slaves of the recipient of the favour [to approach the throne] or some of his friends take some of the ashes . . . and scatter it over the head of the favoured one, who then returns groveling until he arrives before the king. Then he makes the drumming gesture as before and rises.[184]

Such submission by high officials, otherwise allowed to remain on their steeds, was particularly imperative.

Ibn Baṭṭūṭa witnessed a similar production, writing that at the ruler's summons the invited "takes off his clothes and puts on ragged clothes . . . and advances with submissiveness and humility." The supplicant, striking the ground "with his two elbows," then stands "like one performing *rak'a*" (bowing, which together with *sujūd* or prostration form the basic physical movement in Muslim prayer). Upon invitation, the supplicant removes his clothes and sprinkles "dust on his head and back, like one washing himself with water. I used to marvel how their eyes did not become blinded." The earthen ablution's centrality is underscored by Ibn Baṭṭūṭa's comment that *Mansā* Sulaymān's ambassador to the Marinid ruler actually brought with him a "basket of earth and sprinkled dust on himself whenever our Lord [the Marinid ruler] spoke kindly to him . . ."[185] No wonder *Mansā* Mūsā dreaded an audience with Cairo's Mamluk ruler, possibly fearing he would have been expected to perform the same.

Royal sessions were also occasions for the *mansā* to serve in a juridical capacity, with al-'Umarī noting that he heard "complaints and appeals against administrative oppression (*maẓālim*)," delivering "judgment on them himself." His purview therefore seems to have been restricted to the conduct of state officials, leaving other matters to a growing coterie of *qāḍīs*, *faqīhs*, and other such officials.[186] Ibn Baṭṭūṭa attests, however, that there were times when state and mosque worked together, as in an instance in which the *mansā*'s ruling also involved the *qāḍī*. The case concerned the *mushrif* or "overseer" of Walata/Biru, responsible for helping to regulate its market.[187] Also known as *manshājū* (Mande for "the emperor's servant or slave"—*mansā jon*), he was accused by a scholar of taking "'from me something worth 600 mithqals and wishes to give me for it 100 mithqals only,'" at which point the *mushrif* was tried before the *qāḍī*. When the claims of the scholar were upheld, the *mansā* removed the *mushrif* from office.

The case of the *mushrif* also partially illuminates the circumstances of Ibn Baṭṭūṭa's shadowy *farāriyya* or "emirs," seemingly the same as the "emirs" of al-'Umarī seated near the *mansā*, presumably the *farmas* and *kois* of a far-flung imperial apparatus.[188] But the *mushrif* had to be summoned to the capital to answer charges of misconduct—he was not already there. That is, those in charge of towns and cities and provinces were at their posts, often at some remove from the capital. So then, who were these *farāriyya* who appear to have been a constant presence in the capital?

The possible answers to this query are speculative. First, what Ibn Baṭṭūṭa and al-'Umarī report may concern special occasions, when officials throughout the realm were required to appear at the capital. Ibn Baṭṭūṭa was in Mali from Jumādā 'l-Awlā 753/July 1352 to Muḥarram 754/February 1353, encompassing the Muslim high festivals of *'Īd al-Fiṭr*, ending the Ramaḍān fast (celebrated in 753/1352 on 1 Shawwāl 753/9 November); and *'Īd al-Aḍḥā*, the "Feast of the Sacrifice" honoring Ibrāhīm's willingness to sacrifice Ismā'īl while also marking the end of the *ḥajj* (celebrated in 753/1353 on 10 Dhū 'l-Ḥijja/17 January). It would make sense that officials would gather at the capital on such occasions, further signaling Islam's increasing insinuation into the meaning of Malian dominion.

On the other hand, an ongoing, uninterrupted presence of *farāriyya* in the capital, augmented by the occasional visitation of officials stationed elsewhere, would suggest identifying the former as "emirs" may not be entirely accurate. Instead, the category may have consisted of lineage heads and councillors, the legacy of the Grand Council originally formed under Sunjata, and junior leaders from around the empire, selected to live in the capital for protracted periods. Insight into their circumstances is provided by *Ta'rīkh as-sūdān*'s account of the progenitors of the Sunni or Chī dynasty of Songhay, 'Alī Kulun and his brother Silman Nāri. Upon reaching "the age of service," they were placed in the care of the Malian ruler (as Gao was subject to Mali), since "it was customary for the sons of rulers who were subordinate to [the *mansās*]. This custom is in force among all the *sulṭāns* of the *Sūdān* down to the present time"[189] The practice of subject rulers sending their sons to the capital echoes ancient Ghana and the "sons of vassal kings" at its royal court; in Mali they would have been among the *farāriyya*.[190]

In addition to the *farāriyya*, the Malian court also featured scribes who composed correspondence intended for recipients in North Africa and Egypt. As one example, both al-'Umarī and al-Qalqashandī refer to a letter from Kankan Mūsā to the Mamluk ruler of Cairo, "written in the Maghribī style" and following "its own rules of composition although observing the demands of propriety."[191] While not reproduced, al-ʿUmarī says its content consisted of "greetings and a recommendation for the bearer," and a gift of five thousand *mithqāls* of gold.

Literacy was not used, however, to record the *mansā*'s domestic policies, nor judicial decisions, nor commercial transactions, for according to al-ʿUmarī, "as a rule nothing is written down." Rather, the *mansā*'s "commands are given verbally," though "he has judges, scribes, and government offices (*dīwān*)."[192] The early tenth/sixteenth-century traveler Valentim Fernandes would make a similar observation regarding the Jula, stating they viewed written records as antithetical to principles of trustworthiness.[193] As such, though Mali could produce many written transcripts, convention dictated oral media and memorization. The alternate use of oral and written technologies for different purposes has origins in early Ghana, its continuation in medieval Mali facilitating their connection.

But this also means that so much is unrecoverable about medieval Mali, that had it not been for travelers and internal written sources recorded much later, a transregional power of enormous expanse and duration, perhaps West Africa's greatest, would have remained in historical obscurity, an irony as troubling as it is inescapable.

The aftermath of Sunjata's reign saw a succession struggle pitting the principle of privilege (led by royalists) versus the proponents of meritocracy (championed by the *donson ton*). A remarkable period of stability and expansion ensued under the legendary *Mansā* Mūsā, resulting in a West Africa at its pinnacle. Mali was a realm of cities, through which flowed rivers of commerce, connecting to Mediterranean and Red Sea worlds in an unprecedented continuity of cosmopolitanism. While tales of transoceanic misadventure are shrouded in uncertainty, a Pilgrimage just as spectacular, whose likes had never been seen, introduced to the world the aspirations of a realm in rapid ascent. This dramatic unfolding of West African possibility rested on the empire's unification of the region's three major river systems—the Niger, Senegal, and Gambia—heretofore unrivaled in scope, further facilitating integration into a trans-Saharan trading network of untold value.

Mūsā would embrace Islam emphatically, breaking with predecessors by building mosques in key cities, laying the foundation for Mali's reputation as a Muslim land. Islam would soon become a principal cultural signifier, articulating a realm of growing ethnic diversity while compensating for an imperial presence guided by a minimalist theory of governance.

For all of Mūsā's accomplishments, he would never fully escape rumors of matricide and intrigue, with Sākūra a possible vehicle of remonstration. But in paying close attention to what the sources say, it is as critical to note what they do not say, which leads to the stunning realization that the very zenith of the Malian moment is essentially disregarded in the oral traditions. Even so, in their silence the traditions reflect brilliance, reinforcing the foundational role of the Sunjata epic.

CHAPTER SEVEN

Intrigue, Islam, and Ibn Baṭṭūṭa

DEVELOPMENTS THROUGH THE NINTH/FIFTEENTH CENTURY constitute a period of Malian retrenchment, reflected in a loss of interest in the external Arabic sources. At the same time, this is precisely the dawn of European activity along the West African coast, from where observations open a (distant) window onto the West African interior. Consistent with their purpose, seafaring accounts are preoccupied with entrepots and trade organization, with Jenne, Timbuktu, and the Jula networks as their focus, and in privileging cities add to the impression of a diminished Malian state. Ominously, the early European presence is also a harbinger of the region's future, with human trafficking beginning to flow to the Mauritanian coast.

It is through the writings of Ibn Baṭṭūṭa, who in visiting the realm records Qāsā's remarkable bid for power, that a glimpse into Mali's debilitation is afforded, recalling a pre-imperial time when women were full participants in the political realm. The famous traveler could not have fully appreciated the significance of what he witnessed.

Though waning as a regional power, Mali was highly successful in achieving a paradigm in which Islam and polity worked in close cooperation. This intimate association of culture and statecraft would completely transform the politics of the region for centuries to come. Critical to this new model of West African statecraft were efforts to reimagine and situate the region within the larger Muslim context.

Mali and the Marinids

Both Ibn Ḥajar and Ibn Khaldūn record that *Mansā* Mūsā reigned for twenty-five years (711–37/1312–37), the latter stating he was succeeded in death by a son *Mansā* Maghā (or Maghan).[1] Ibn Khaldūn notes Maghā means "Muḥammad," so this could be the same son al-ʿUmarī mentions Mūsā leaving in charge of Mali upon departing for the Pilgrimage.[2] As Mūsā is described as a young man at that time, Maghan must have also been young at his succession, possibly requiring a regent. This same Maghā is referred to in the oral traditions as Maghan Soma Buréma Kéin, or "Maghan the Sorcerer, Ibrāhīm the Handsome," with implications for Islam and religion in the realm.[3] He would die soon after taking office, his own son far too young to succeed, so that the crown fell to Mūsā's brother Sulaymān, who would die in office twenty-four years later.[4]

Sulaymān's image suffers from an unfavorable comparison with Mūsā, with travelers drawn to Mali because of Mūsā becoming the sources for his immediate successors, especially Sulaymān. Efforts to place Sulaymān and Mūsā on a similar footing include traditions of the former returning from the Pilgrimage in 753/1352 and depositing "holy books" in the *Kama-Bolon*.[5] These efforts are unsuccessful, however, as Sulaymān's *hajj* is unsupported in the written documents; Ibn Baṭṭūṭa was in Mali during Sulaymān's reign but makes no mention of any such journey, which suggests that the "books" probably refer to the Mālikī texts Mūsā brought back from Cairo.[6] Even so, Sulaymān's tenure was not without significance, witnessing momentous—if not extraordinary—developments in foreign diplomacy, as well as internal intrigue.

Egypt's instability after Mamluk ruler al-Malik al-Nāṣir Muḥammad b. Qalāwūn's death in 741/1341, followed by the arrival there of the Black Death toward the decade's end, may have informed *Mansā* Sulaymān's shift in focus from Egypt to the Maghrib, where he concentrated on relations with the Marinids.[7] These Zenata *Imazighen* (Berbers, s. *Amazigh*) began challenging the Almohads as early as 539/1145, taking control of Fez in 641/1244 and Marrakesh in 667/1269. Their control of the Maghrib would fluctuate until the dynasty's demise in 869/1465, though they were a formidable power under Abū ʾl-Ḥasan (731–51/1331–51), whose reign overlapped with those of Mūsā, Maghā, and Sulaymān. The Marinid ruler may have had a personal interest in Mali, his dark complexion attributed to his "Sūdān" mother.[8]

Marinid ascendance was accentuated by Abū ʿl-Ḥasan "the Black's" dramatic defeat of Abū Tāshfīn, ruler of Tlemcen, in 737/1337, and *Mansā*

Mūsā responded by sending a delegation to Fez.[9] The *mansā*'s spectacular feat in Egypt and Abū 'l-Ḥasan's Tlemcen victory resulted in mutual recognition, initiating a long-term relationship. When first discussing this development, Ibn Khaldūn speaks of "diplomatic relations and exchanges of gifts," and that "high-ranking statesmen of the two kingdoms were exchanged as ambassadors," a reciprocation between peers.

But in subsequently returning to Malian-Marinid relations, Ibn Khaldūn states Abū 'l-Ḥasan received the Malian delegation "with honour" and, known for his "ostentatious ways," sent back "the rarest and most magnificent objects of Maghribī manufacture," along with a freed eunuch named 'Anbar. Mūsā was dead by this time, at which point Ibn Khaldūn characterizes Malian-Marinid relations very differently, mentioning the Marinid delegation

> returned to the one [Abū 'l-Ḥasan] who had sent them accompanied by a deputation of Mālī grandees who lauded his authority, acknowledged his rights, and conveyed to him that with which their master had charged them, namely [the expression of] humble submission and readiness to pay the sultan his due and act in accordance with his wishes. Their mission being carried out, the sultan had achieved his aim of vaunting himself over other kings and exacting their submission to his authority and so he fulfilled God's due of thanks for His favour.[10]

This was not the first time a foreign power claimed Mali's fealty, as Ibn al-Dawādārī stated *Mansā* Mūsā agreed to have the *khuṭba* performed in the name of Mamluk ruler al-Nāṣir.[11]

There are several possible explanations for Ibn Khaldūn's restatement. The first is that such representations reflect a Marinid-Mamluk rivalry, while a second either misrepresents or misunderstands Mali's disposition, entirely compatible with the first. Regarding the second explanation, cultural differences could have led to interpretations of political symbolism and ritual at variance, as when *Mansā* Sulaymān's ambassador to Abū 'l-Ḥasan performed the earthen ablution, conceivably miscoded as Mali's ritual submission rather than perfunctory Mande protocol.[12] Yet another possibility is that Mali calculatingly entered into such agreements for the purpose of enhancing the domestic, Malian perception of its authority through associating with such foreign powers. This last possibility, however, is mitigated by evidence that Malian rulers did not actually regard themselves as subject, as Ibn Baṭṭūṭa observed Mali's queen and king were mentioned "from the pulpit," a reference to the *khuṭba* that signified Mali accepted neither Marinid nor Mamluk suzerainty.[13] If fealty was feigned in North Africa while rejected in West Africa, Sulaymān may have seen little downside in maintaining dual, spatially distinct political claims.

Two months following Ibn Baṭṭūṭa's arrival in Mali's capital in 732/1352, *Mansā* Sulaymān "gave a memorial feast for our Lord Abū 'l-Ḥasan," who had died the year before.[14] Political and religious luminaries were invited to the gathering, where the Qur'ān was recited and prayers offered for both Abū 'l-Ḥasan and Sulaymān. While certainly a service to honor the deceased Marinid ruler, it may have been also something more obligatory. The *khuṭba* was said in Sulaymān's name following Abū 'l-Ḥasan's death, but this does not address how it was previously delivered. Had Mali in fact entered into a subordinate position vis-à-vis the Marinids, at least in North Africa, it would have reflected a decision made by Sulaymān, not Mūsā.

Sulaymān had earlier sent a delegation to Abū 'l-Ḥasan in 749/1348–9 in celebration of the latter's recent military victory in Ifrīqiya. Sulaymān then reportedly busied himself "collecting wonderful and strange objects of his country," but only managed to send them north in 760/1358–9, seven years after Abū 'l-Ḥasan's demise.[15] If this was meant to be understood as tribute in North Africa, but not in Mali, it may have contributed to a subsequent context of contested claims between Morocco and Songhay.

Ibn Baṭṭūṭa, Sulaymān, and Qāsā's Gambit

Ibn Baṭṭūṭa arrived in Mali as a Marinid emissary with the highest self-regard, anticipating a certain level of accommodation and assuming he would be the recipient of Malian largesse. He experienced just the opposite. His assessment of Sulaymān as a "miserly king from whom no great donation is to be expected" was conditioned by the vast sums of wealth Mūsā had previously lavished upon favored foreigners. He was sorely disappointed by what he himself received, and following a two-month convalescence from sickness, registered his displeasure after attending a gathering that included the *mansā*:

> Ibn al-Faqīh . . . came in to me saying: "Come! The cloth (*qumāsh*) and gift of the sultan have come for you!" I got up, thinking that it would be robes of honour and money, but behold! It was three loaves of bread and a piece of beef fried in *ghartī* and a gourd containing yoghourt. When I saw it, I laughed . . .[16]

Ibn Baṭṭūṭa would complain to various officials for the next two months, and was finally granted an audience with Sulaymān, to whom he put the matter through Dūghā "the interpreter": "I have journeyed to the countries of the world and met their kings," stated Ibn Baṭṭūṭa, and given the lack of a suitable reception gift, "What shall I say of you in the presence of other sultans?" "I have not seen you nor known about you," the *mansā* replied, subsequently giving the world traveler over 33 *mithqāls* of gold, followed by another 100 *mithqāls* upon his departure—a paltry sum in comparison with the 4,000 *mithqāls* al-Dukkālī allegedly received from Mūsā, or the multiple hundreds of *mithqāls* he distributed in Cairo.

The relatively small gifts afforded Ibn Baṭṭūṭa, combined with the *mansā*'s seeming dismissal of his importance, may have been intended as a message to Abū 'Inān, the recently-installed Marinid sultan, that whatever had obtained between Sulaymān and his father, the *mansā* was now pursuing a different policy. The performance of the *khuṭba* in his own name rather than Abū 'Inān's would support this view.

Ibn Baṭṭūṭa was convinced, however, that Sulaymān's lack of attention was due to the latter's character flaws, as even "the Sūdān disliked Mansā Sulaymān on account of his avarice."[17] The tendentious nature of Ibn Baṭṭūṭa's claim is clear when considering his overall assessment of Mali, though he reports two episodes that strengthen his assertion of Sulaymān's unpopularity. The first concerns the report of a *faqīh* who, returning from "a distant country," informed the *mansā* that locusts had descended in Mali, with one of the locusts verbalizing: "God sends us to the country in which there is oppression in order to spoil its crops." The "oppression" may refer to inordinate taxation and relate to Sulaymān's "avarice," hinting at dissatisfaction, at least in the peripheral provinces. Addressing the *farāriyya*, the *mansā* declared his innocence.[18]

A second episode concerns the conspiracy of Qāsā, Sulaymān's chief wife and first cousin (daughter of a maternal uncle).[19] The *mansā* became displeased and imprisoned her in the house of one of the *farāriyya*, replacing her with the nonroyal Banjū. In the ceremony to recognize her elevation, Sulaymān's paternal female first cousins placed dust or ashes on their forearms but not their heads, performing the full earthen ablution only after Qāsā was released from confinement, signaling their rejection of Banjū as chief wife. When Banjū complained, the cousins did penitence by appearing naked before the *mansā* for seven days, having initially sought asylum in the mosque.

Though freed, Qāsā was not restored as chief wife, and she responded by undertaking the decidedly political performance of riding daily with enslaved men and women in tow, dust on their heads, after which she would stand veiled at the gates of the *mashwar* or council place. As this became a much-discussed scandal, one of her "slave girls" was summoned before the *mansā* and the Grand Council, where she confessed she had served as Qāsā's envoy to the *mansā*'s paternal first cousin Jāṭil, who had taken refuge from the *mansā* for some offense. Qāsā allegedly encouraged Jāṭil to "depose the sultan from his kingship, saying 'I and all the army are at your service'." Upon hearing this, the *farāriyya* exclaimed Qāsā had committed "a great crime and for it she deserves to be killed!" Qāsā would seek sanctuary with the *khaṭīb*, and nothing more is recorded of the affair.[20]

Such an open display of intrigue is remarkable, involving both branches of the Keita family. As a paternal first cousin, Jāṭil may have been a direct descendant of Sunjata (as opposed to Sulaymān and Mūsā, from the line of Sunjata's brother Manden Bukari/Manding Bori), and the brother of the paternal first cousins who could not abide Banjū's selection. In any event, they were closely related, their public humiliation of Banjū perhaps more a protest of Jāṭil's exile than Qāsā's demotion. Jāṭil may have been on the run because he was a strong pretender, with Qāsā's overture an effort to exploit a rivalry. Her standing at the gates of the *mashwar* suggests at least some among the *farāriyya* sided with her, and though her pledge to deliver the entire military may have been hyperbole, it reveals she understood the elements of a successful revolt. This has all the marks of a serious push for power, and could explain her imprisonment at its beginning, the specifics of which Ibn Baṭṭūṭa was only vaguely aware. As the daughter of a maternal uncle, presumably the brother of Mūsā's mother Kankan, Qāsā's demotion and imprisonment may have also reopened wounds.

Insecurities resulting from burdensome exactions and palace intrigue may explain al-'Umarī's otherwise curious comments concerning Sulaymān's policies: "Among their chiefs are some whose wealth derived from the king reaches 50,000 mithqāls of gold every year, besides which he keeps them in horses and clothes. His whole ambition is to give them fine clothes and to make his towns into cities."[21] As it was usually the provincial and urban governors who financially supported the political center, it is also true that most were not gold- and copper-producing provinces. Al-'Umarī's statement implies an expectation of the distribution of such wealth to the governors of mineral-deficient provinces, with more than a hint of anxiety, reflecting a need to ensure loyalty in uncertain times.

Ibn Khaldūn's assertion that Sulaymān ruled for twenty-four years following Maghā's four-year term cannot be accurate, as Mūsā died around 737/1337 and Sulaymān around 761/1360. For the arithmetic to work, Maghā's rule would have been much briefer, possibly four months rather than four years.[22]

Succeeding Sulaymān

Ibn Khaldūn observes "dissension broke out" following Sulaymān's death, in accord with the oral corpus' claim of intense postmortem competition.[23] Tantalizingly, Ibn Khaldūn lists one Qāsā as Sulaymān's son and successor, and though this could have been the son of the former chief wife, alternatively it could have been Qāsā herself, depicted as a man in keeping with convention. Ibn Baṭṭūṭa had mentioned the queen's name was included in the *khuṭba*, suggesting she once wielded real power, strengthening this possibility. Qāsā may have also served as regent. Any of these scenarios is consistent with Ibn Khaldūn's characterization of the period, as Qāsā would rule only nine months.[24]

Qāsā b. Sulaymān was succeeded by Mārī Jāṭā b. *Mansā* Maghā, in power from approximately 761/1360 to 775/1373–4.[25] This could have been the aforementioned Jāṭil, Sulaymān's first cousin, whose return may have been facilitated by Qāsā. Referring to him as Konkodugu Kamissa, the oral traditions maintain he suffered a rivalry with Sulaymān's son Kamba.[26] Scholarship has noted that, beginning with Mārī Jāṭā b. *Mansā* Maghā, Ibn Khaldūn's ruler list bears an uncanny resemblance to his cyclical theory of empire formation and dissolution, raising questions about its reliability.[27]

Mārī Jāṭā is said to have been "a most wicked ruler" who "ruined their empire, squandered their treasure, and all but abolished the edifice of their rule."[28] Whatever the assessment's accuracy, he managed to attend relations with the Marinids, evidenced by gifts that included a giraffe.[29] Mārī Jāṭā died of "sleeping sickness," and if this were trypanosomiasis (which can induce death within six months of its onset), he would have been incapacitated toward the end of his life.

Mārī Jāṭā was succeeded by his son Mūsā (d.789/1387), otherwise known as Fadima Mūsā, who "adopted a way of justice . . . and quite abandoned the way of his father."[30] But this Mūsā could not reverse Mali's downward spiral, and at some point his authority was usurped by his *wazīr*, yet another Mārī Jāṭā. This second Mārī Jāṭā is said to have placed Mali on a war footing to subdue "the eastern provinces," suggesting the emergence of a resistance encouraged by Mali's weakening, with Gao conceivably at its epicenter. Mūsā's death also ended his *wazīr*'s power, with his brother *Mansā* Maghā taking power. Referring to him as Kita Tenin Maghan, the oral traditions maintain that, rather than being assassinated a year later (per Ibn Khaldūn), he was forced to flee to the Upper Niger, where he established the Hamana branch of the Keita clan.[31] Yet another *wazīr*, one Sandakī, assumed power, but was quickly killed. Ibn Khaldūn then records the arrival of one Maḥmūd "from the lands of the pagans," said to be related to Qū, the aforementioned son or grandson of Sunjata. He adopted the name of Maghā once in power in 792/1390, at which point Ibn Khaldūn's account ends.[32]

Though Ibn Khaldūn attributes Mali's faltering to Mārī Jāṭā b. *Mansā* Maghā, it seems to have actually begun with the end of Sulaymān's reign, if not with Qāsā's revolt. Mali's center would shift to the Upper Niger with the establishment of the Hamana and Dioma branches of the Keita by the beginning of the ninth/fifteenth century, and while Mali would continue into the eleventh/seventeenth, Songhay would establish mastery in the Middle Niger. It is probable that, coupled with the challenges of succession, Mali's expansion had simply surpassed its ability to govern such a vast domain. In reporting the subversive activities of Qāsā, Ibn Baṭṭūṭa was an unwitting eyewitness to Mali's unraveling.[33]

At Mali's Verges: The Genoese and Portuguese

Much of what is known about Mali in the ninth/fifteenth century comes from sources at a considerable territorial remove. Although geographers apparently lost interest in West Africa, and the oral corpus is thin, internal written records continue to mention Mali, suggestive of its displacement yet ongoing aspirations. An important source on Mali for this period, however, is a new genre—European seafarers. Informed by their observations, scholars have sketched Senegambia's broad contours, arguing the waning of Malian influence following *Mansā* Sulaymān encouraged the formation of the Jolof confederation under Njajane Njaye, consisting of Walo, Cayor or Kajor, and Baol. Though it lost influence along the Senegal, Mali would retain a presence along the Gambia.[34]

An early account comes from the Genoese traveler Antonio Malfante, who in 850/1447 traveled overland to Tuwat. In discussing the Tuareg (whom he calls "the Philistines"), Malfante names polities "in the land of the Blacks" bordering the "states which are under their [Tuareg] rule," and lists Takedda ("Thegida"), perhaps Tadmekka ("Checoli"), Gao-Kukiya

("Chuciam"), Timbuktu ("Thambet"), and Jenne ("Geni"). He also mentions Mali ("Meli"), "said to have nine towns."[35] Mali was therefore understood as a collection of urban centers, its waning force suggested by the featured order.

Meanwhile, the Portuguese, largely under the direction of the Infante Dom Henrique (Henry the Navigator, d. 865/1460), were making contact along the West African littoral, with Gomes Eannes de Zurara producing a narrative of slave raiding along the Mauritanian coast in the 840s-850s/1440s. João Fernandes, while a captive of the "Azanegues" (speakers of *Znāga*, ancestors of the area's Berbers or Imazighen, singular Amazigh), learned that "in the land of the Negroes there is another kingdom called Melli, but this is not certain; for they bring the Negroes from that kingdom, and sell them like the others, whereas 'tis manifest that if they were Moors they would not sell them so."[36] Malfante and Fernandes create a composite picture in which Mali is heavily involved in slaving, though now trading in the west as well as the north.

Fernandes's capture helped the Portuguese realize that raiding had its limits, as coastal populations adjusted to better defend themselves. The establishment of trade relations therefore became a point of emphasis, aligning with Dom Henrique's original motivation, as he was inspired by reports of abundant "Arab gold" in Timbuktu.[37] To that end, the Venetian Alvise da Cadamosto (Alvide da Ca' da Mosto) would play a critical role in gathering intelligence for the Portuguese, boarding caravels bound for West Africa in 859/1455 and 860/1456 and providing more information on Mali.

Cadamosto identified several nodes of commercial activity connecting the Savannah with the Sahel. Six days inland from Arguin was the market of Wadan ("Hoden"), "where the caravans arrive from Tanbutu [Timbuktu]," and from where "brass and silver from Barbary" are sent back to Timbuktu, along with horses: "These Arabs also have many Berber horses, which they trade, and take to the Land of the Blacks, exchanging them with the rulers for slaves. Ten or fifteen slaves are given for one of these horses, according to their quality."[38] There was also Taghaza, where "a very great quantity of rock-salt is mined. Every year large caravans of camels . . . carry it to Tanbutu; thence they go to Melli, the empire of the Blacks . . ."[39] Horses and salt were Timbuktu's major imports, consistently distinguished from Mali by European travelers, with Cadamosto's estimating distances between Taghaza and Timbuktu (forty days on horseback) and Timbuktu and Mali (thirty days). These reports portray the "Emperor of Melli" as "so great a lord," indicating it remained a regional power whose reach extended along the Gambia, where titles such as the "Farosangoli," the "Batimaussa," and the "Gunimenssa," incorporating the Mande terms *Faran* and *mansā*, were encountered.[40] Though the relationship to Mali's center is not clarified, these designations imply something more than Mande cultural influence, as the Farosangoli was "subject to the Emperor of Melli, the great Emperor of the Blacks . . ."[41] In contrast to the Gambia, there is no mention of a Malian presence along the Senegal.[42]

The observations of Diogo Gomes comport well with those of Cadamosto. Arriving on the Gambia in 860/1456, he met "Frangazick," grandson of the aforementioned Farosangoli, the "great power of the blacks." Venturing farther inland to Cantor/Kantora on the Gambia's southern bank, the visitor learned about Timbuktu and "Kukia," perhaps Gao-Kukiya, and of war between "Sambagenii" and "Samanogu," a possible reference to the leader of Jenne and Sulaymān Dāma, a predecessor of *Sunni* ʿAlī in Gao-Kukiya, with Samanogu emerging victorious.[43] This would seem to concern imperial Songhay in early formation; Diego Gomes is told that the "king Bormelli," or *Buur* or ruler of Mali, controlled the "land of the gold," and that "all the land of the blacks on the right bank of the river [Gambia] were under his dominion . . . and that he lived in the city of Kukia." Here, then, is a conflation of Mali and Gao by those in the Gambia, not yet fully aware of their growing divergence.[44]

Diego Gomes had ventured to Cantor aboard one caravel, while two others moored elsewhere along the Gambia. One encountered the "Batimansa" or *mansā* of Bati, close to the Gambia's southern aperture, while the other came into contact with the "Ulimansa." In expelling a Muslim "cleric" bested by Diego Gomes in a religious debate, the Batimansa displayed the limitations of Malian influence so far west.[45]

Two major accounts of West African voyages were compiled between 910/1505 and 913/1508 by the Portuguese Duarte Pacheco Pereira and the Moravian Valentim Fernandes.[46] Though Fernandes uses the term "Mali," Pacheco Pereira does not, suggesting the waning of Mali's influence over the Gambia. The latter speaks of "the great kingdom of Mandingua," identified as Cayor ("Encalhor"), intriguing since Cayor/Kajor was ruled by Wolof sovereigns, indicating either misinformation or Mande cultural encroachment.[47] More curious is his failure to mention Mali even when discussing the interior, though he references Timbuktu, Jenne, and Bitu/Bughu.[48]

In contrast, Valentim Fernandes records that salt taken from Walata/Biru to Timbuktu was then shipped by boat to the walled city of Jenne "in the kingdom of Mali."[49] As there is no other evidence that Jenne formed part of Mali at this time, Fernandes speaks of general rather than specific truths, and in discussing Jenne he associates its prosperity with the Jula (whom he calls "Ungaros" or Wangāra):

> The merchants belong to a particular race called *Ungaros*. . . . When the *Ungaros* arrive in Jenne, each merchant has with him 100 or 200 black slaves or more, to carry the salt on their heads from Jenne to the gold mines, and to return from there with gold. . . . The merchants who conduct the trade with the gold mines are very wealthy. . . . They trust each other, without receipts, without written records, without witnesses. They extend credit. . . . because the *Ungaros* only come to Jenne once a year.[50]

There is much to absorb here: impressive wealth, trade monopolies and their cyclical seasonality, massive use of slaves in commerce, and human memory as the ledger of business. In learning about West African trade, Timbuktu, Jenne, and the Jula occupy the center of the European imagination, at Mali's expense.

European travel reports refer to Mali well into the tenth/sixteenth century, by which time political developments challenging its dominant position are unmistakable. The very advent of the European presence along the West African coast is itself generative. But Mali's immediate challenge lay deep in the interior, stimulated by a centuries-old orientation toward the sea of sand.

Clerical Towns and the Project of Indigenization

As the foregoing indicates, Islam and slavery were two aspects of an expansive medieval Mali, and though both were present before Sunjata, qualitative evidence strongly suggests they grew as closely linked phenomena. Indirect testimony to Islam's gathering strength is the sources' virtual silence regarding Mande non-Islamic religions, with much of what is known about them deriving from later travel literature and ethnographic studies. When the external Arabic sources therefore present Mali as a Muslim realm, they are referring to conditions in urban areas and the royal court, where it was decidedly in the interests of government and expatriates to be considered part of the Muslim world. But the reality of religious practice was much more complicated.

Consequently, it is hardly surprising that Islam's development in Mali is best legible as a component of its political narrative. That Islam emerges as a powerful, state-sanctioned force is discernible in imperial signage, constituting the site of its most compelling claim. Indeed, in making the

Pilgrimage, *Mansā* Walī (Yerelinkon) distinguishes himself from his father Sunjata, nominally Muslim at most, marking the debut of the religion as a significant influence in the affairs of state. The very use of his double moniker—*Mansā* Walī and Yerelinkon—reveals a developing sense of connection to a larger world, with rulers soon shifting to Muslim designations as their sole, or at least most recognizable names.

Mansā Mūsā's Pilgrimage was itself undertaken on the advice of unspecified *'ulamā'*, possibly non-West African elites. Their influence was only enhanced with Mūsā's return, accompanied by Granadian poet al-Ṭuwayjin, Arabs from the Ḥijāz, and unspecified experts in *fiqh*. The expatriate community was still a considerable presence during Ibn Baṭṭūṭa's visit; he lodged with them in the "white" quarter, there meeting a relative of Muḥammad b. al-Faqīh al-Gazūlī, a *faqīh*, as well as 'Alī al-Zūdī al-Marrākushī, a "scholar."[51] As earlier evidence and the example of Gao's *qāḍī* Abū 'Abd Allāh Muḥammad (from Sijilmasa) illustrates, expatriates were in fair number, occupying offices associated with Islam. Those in the Malian capital developed ties to the state.[52]

Without question, the *ḥajj* of *Mansā* Mūsā represents a pinnacle of achievement, both for Mali and the whole of West Africa. He would return deeply affected, his association with the construction of many mosques emblematic of his connection to Islam's subsequent expansion. It is also possible that the experience of living in Birkat al-Ḥabash, placing the Malians in direct contact with the venerational culture of al-Qarāfa 'l-Kubrā, conditioned the West African perspective toward subsequent esoteric practice within the sacred space of the *zāwiya*.[53]

While in Cairo, Mūsā openly declared that he was "of the Malikite school," underscoring an attempt to maintain political distance if not independence from the Shāfi'ī-affiliated Mamluks, while acknowledging Malikism's prior ascendance in West Africa. It was precisely this difference in *madhhabs* (*madhāhib*) that allowed Mūsā to inaugurate a process by which he could contribute to Islam's institutionalization while simultaneously strengthening Mali's claims to sovereignty, accomplishing both through a project of indigenization.

When Ibn Baṭṭūṭa visited the Malian capital, he met a number of expatriate religious leaders, but he also met 'Abd al-Raḥmān, a *qāḍī* of Mali and "one of the Sūdān, a respectable pilgrim of noble virtues."[54] Rare praise for Ibn Baṭṭūṭa, but 'Abd al-Raḥmān reflected Mūsā's decision to adjust the profile of religious elites in Mali. Mūsā's experience in Egypt, where he had been pressured to swear allegiance to the Mamluk ruler, was an opportunity to reconsider his dependence on foreign expertise. They may have been instrumental in his ascent, remaining critical in diplomatic and commercial relations, which suggests a need to at least balance their influence. Political considerations were therefore as much a consideration in the formation of West African Muslim elites as the religious imperative itself.

According to *Ta'rīkh as-sūdān*, the jurist Kātib Mūsā was the last of the "Sudanese" *imāms* of Timbuktu's Jingereber mosque, holding the post for forty years through both Malian and Tuareg rule. Blessed with exceptional health, Kātib Mūsā never missed a day nor delegated his authority, and, like *Mansā* Sulaymān, sat on a dais to adjudicate cases beneath a large tree in Susu Debe Square.[55] He was "one of the *'ulamā'* of the Sūdān who traveled to Fez to study knowledge (*'ilm*) during Malian rule (literally, "during the reign of the people of Mali") and by order of the just *sulṭān al-ḥājj* Mūsā." Sending black students to Fez was both the beginning and focus of *Mansā* Mūsā's indigenization program, and the aforementioned Malian *qāḍī* who met with Ibn Baṭṭūṭa may have been one of the program's beneficiaries, as there is every evidence the *mansā*'s initiative was wildly successful. Such can be gleaned from 'Abd al-Raḥmān al-Tamīmī, relocating to Timbuktu at a time when the city was "completely overtaken with Sūdānese *fuqahā'* (jurists)." Impressed with the city's level of scholarship and realizing the "Sudanese" scholars surpassed him in the [knowledge of] *fiqh*," he himself traveled to Fez to study.[56]

Of particular relevance to *Mansā* Mūsā's new policy was the *qāḍī* of Timbuktu, the *shaykh* and *faqīh* and holy "friend of God" (*walī*) Abū 'Abd Allāh *Modibo* Muḥammad al-Kāborī, who settled in Timbuktu in the mid-ninth/fifteenth century.[57] The contemporary of a number of scholars central to the discussion of Songhay, *Modibo* Muḥammad al-Kāborī is said to have achieved the highest levels of knowledge (*'ilm*) and righteousness, and was so elevated that at one point he guaranteed Paradise to those giving alms of one thousand *mithqāls* of gold to assist the poor (only to be admonished to "not obligate Us again" in a dream). He served as the teacher of such luminaries as 'Umar b. Muḥammad Aqīt and the illustrious *Shaykh* Sīdī Yaḥyā al-Tādalisī. Such was his spiritual standing that a scholar "of far-reaching influence" from Marrakesh died from leprosy after criticizing *Modibo* Muḥammad al-Kāborī, having made a play on his name in calling him "al-Kāfirī" or "heathen."

As his name suggests, *Modibo* Muḥammad came from the town of Kabora (or Kābara, not to be confused with Kabara, the port village of Timbuktu), located in Masina upstream from Dia/Diagha. Both Kabora and Dia/Diagha were Malian provinces, as Ibn Baṭṭūṭa confirms "Kābara and Zāgha have two sultans who owe obedience to the king of Mālī."[58] Though students assigned to Fez may have come from various Malian provinces, the *mansā* seems to have targeted Kabora for his indigenization project. *Ta'rīkh as-sūdān* states that during *Modibo* Muḥammad's time, the Sudanese students filling Timbuktu were "people of the west who were diligent in knowledge [*'ilm*] and righteousness, so much so that it is said that, interred with him in his mausoleum (*rawḍa*) are thirty people of Kābara, all of whom were righteous scholars." The "people of the west" appears to refer to Kabora.[59]

It is not clear how the traditional maraboutic families—the Ture, Sisse, Baghayoro, Silla, and Berte, with claims to an Islamic pedigree antedating *Mansā* Mūsā—may have fit into his program, but relations between the Berte and the Keita, for example, were particularly strong. Originating in Mali's core area, well to the south of Kabora, these families may have also been among the recruited.[60]

Though the sources are clear that physically proximate Dia/Diagha and Kabora (Kābara) were under Malian control, their respective relationships to the *mansā*'s undertaking could not have been more divergent. In contrast to Kabora, there is no mention of individuals hailing from Dia/Diagha. This is peculiar, as Ibn Baṭṭūṭa reports "the people of Zāgha are old in Islam," suggesting they either refused to participate in the *mansā*'s initiative, or were excluded from it.[61]

A possible explanation may be found in the reputation and oral narratives of the town's clerical communities, to which the Jula or Maraka are also connected, centering on Dia/Diagha and *al-ḥājj* Salīm Suwāre, a possible seventh/thirteenth-century figure, though certainly alive by the ninth/fifteenth.[62] *Al-ḥājj* Salīm Suwāre was the founder of the Jakhanke, a Mande clerisy, and the traditions strongly intimate that both commercial and religious estates grew out of Dia/Diagha's unique circumstances. In states led by Muslim elites, the clerisies were viewed as scholars, whereas in polities ruled by non-Muslims and dominated by indigenous cultural values, they were regarded as religious specialists, if not subsumed as caste groups. Independent sources have little to say about them.

The Jakhanke of Dia/Diagha under *al-ḥājj* Salīm Suwāre eschewed ties to political elites, viewing them as spiritually compromising. If founded in the seventh/thirteenth-century, they may have resisted the *mansā*'s recruitment efforts. The establishment of the Jakhanke in the ninth/fifteenth century, in turn, may itself have been in response to the *mansā*'s initiative. In either scenario, opposition to ties with the state may explain the absence of these scholars.

Muslim practice in Dia/Diagha was a conscious choice, as the village was not far from "Zāgahrī" of the Wangāra ("Wanjarāta"), where also lived "Kharijites of the Ibāḍī sect called Saghanaghū."[63] As Saghanaghu became a common Jula clan name, this may reflect an early schism among the

Jula. There were therefore three different religious traditions in towns fairly proximate—'Ibāḍism in Zagahri, apolitical Suwarianism in Dia/Diagha, and Fez-trained, state-aligned scholarship in Kabora. Islam in Mali was becoming diverse rather than uniform very early on.

Ta'rīkh al-fattāsh provides an important window into Dia/Diagha's relations with Mali, adding critical depth:

> Diaba was the city of jurists (*fuqahā'*), located in the middle of the land of Mālī. The *sulṭān* of Mālī does not enter it, and no one exercised judicial authority in it except the *qāḍī*. Those who entered it were safe from the injustice of the *sulṭān* and his tyranny, and [even if] someone killed the son of the *sulṭān*, the *sulṭān* could not ask for his blood. It is called the city of God.[64]

Save in a context in which Dia/Diagha recognizes the political claims of Mali, this depiction makes no sense.

In pursuing his strategy, *Mansā* Mūsā demonstrated an awareness of the limits of military power, and that he needed an alliance with state-sponsored religious authorities that would liberate him from reliance on expatriates. His decision to educate "Sudanese" scholars in Fez was therefore ambidextrous in promoting both Islam and the polity, creating an interlacing not easily unraveled. In the same way, commissioning the construction of Jingereber mosque in Timbuktu certainly elevated the profile of Islam, but the very fact that it was built at the command of the *mansā* enhanced his own political authority as well.[65] *Mansā* Mūsā's investment in Timbuktu helps to explain its continuing economic prosperity and the relocation of Sudanese *'ulamā'* there.

Mūsā's pro-Islamic policies may have suffered a setback under his successor, "Maghan the Sorcerer," but Sulaymān would then rule for twenty-four years, giving the new Muslim elites additional time to regain momentum. Evidence for their resurgence includes Sulaymān's court fully observing the Muslim high festivals of *'Īd al-Fiṭr* and *'Īd al-Aḍḥā* , along with Ibn Baṭṭūṭa's visit with *Farba* Sulaymān, who was literate and had in his possession a copy of Ibn al-Jawzī's *Kitāb al-mudhish*.[66] Ibn Baṭṭūṭa also generalizes, stating the "Sūdān" are "assiduous" in prayer, and that Friday mosque was fully attended, with individuals sending their prayer mats through servants to secure spaces ahead of time. Children were severely disciplined until they succeeded in memorizing the Qur'ān: "I went into the house of the qadi on the day of the festival and his children were fettered so I said to him: 'Aren't you going to let them go?' He replied: 'I shan't do so until they've got the Koran by heart'!"[67]

Empire's Underbelly: Mobilization of the Enslaved

As demonstrated in the 1375 Catalan Atlas attributed to Cresques Abraham of Majorca, *Mansā* Mūsā's Pilgrimage created an indelible impression of Mali as the quintessential land of gold, and reports generated out of Cairo were dominated by its discussion.[68] Observed but obscured in the process was the otherwise equally impressive display of slaves bearing the gold (and other goods), providing security, and attending to the whims of notables. Mali as a critical source of servile labor is overshadowed in the immediacy of the eighth/fourteenth century by its mineral resources, so much so that the extensive nature of slavery in Mali is not readily grasped. But from every indication, slavery was entrenched and ubiquitous, hidden in plain sight.

Though Mūsā intended to mesmerize with minerals, there can be no doubt he also meant to openly flaunt his many servants. The enslaved beneath *Mansā* Mūsā were the collective insignia of royal status, an over-the-top performance of vast, unbridgeable social difference and unchecked monarchical privilege. They were the mascots of Malian power.

While estimates of the enslaved accompanying the *mansā* vary, all agree there were thousands upon thousands, with several reports particularly taken with the high number of females, perhaps as many as fourteen thousand. Given their vulnerability to sexual exploitation, they may have been viewed by Egyptians as a veritable harem in motion, a misogynistic moveable feast, the largest ever witnessed. The potential for such an interpretation is implicit in an exchange between Old Cairo's governor Abū 'l-Ḥasan 'Alī b. Amīr Ḥājib and the *mansā* himself:

> And it is the custom of his people that if one of them should have reared a beautiful daughter he offers her to the king as a concubine (*ama mawṭū'a*) and he possesses her without a marriage ceremony as slaves are possessed. . . . I said to him that this was not permissible for a Muslim, whether in law (*shar'*) or reason (*'aql*), and he said: "Not even for kings?" And I replied: "No! Not even for kings! Ask the scholars!" He said: "By God, I did not know that. I hereby leave it and abandon it utterly!"[69]

As the females described by Ibn Amīr Ḥājib were freeborn and presumably Muslim, their enslavement would have been illegal. But no such restrictions applied to the vast numbers of enslaved females in the royal caravan. A commentary on an imperfect and uneven Islamicization process in Mali, the anecdote also resonates with an uninhibited appropriation and objectification of women long in formation. Mūsā's acceptance of Ibn Amīr Ḥājib's rebuke did not alter his fundamental view of such women one iota, and in returning to Mali he secured a number of "slave girls" that included Ethiopians and Turks. Such foreign women, though rare, were not the exclusive property of the king, however, as *Farba* Sulaymān had in his employ "an Arab girl from Damascus."[70]

Enslaved women and girls were valued in Mali precisely because of their dual subjectivity to domesticity and sexual exploitation, but there is little mention of Malians selling slaves during Mūsā's *ḥajj*, especially the females, even when struck by economic hardship. This is rather surprising, considering that they were presumably uneducated and therefore not as prized as those described by Ibn Baṭṭūṭa, who in visiting Takedda found "its people are comfortable and well off and proud of the number of male and female slaves which they have. The people of Mālī and Īwālātan also are like this. They sell educated slave girls but rarely, and at a high price."[71] He then tells of two instances in which he bought "an educated slave girl" in Takedda, and in both cases the owners subsequently sought to abrogate the sale, one of whom "almost went mad and died from grief. But I let him off afterwards."

Notwithstanding Mūsā's apparent decision not to sell slaves, or many slaves, in Egypt, there remained substantial demand for West African females, and Ibn Baṭṭūṭa reports that upon returning from Takedda to Morocco in 754/1353, he joined a large convoy in which were transported some six hundred captive females (*khādim*). Ibn Baṭṭūṭa himself traveled with a young enslaved boy who had been given to him as a gift, and to whom he became attached.[72]

With respect to domestic slavery, women regularly appear in accounts of Mali, as they were indispensable to the lives of elites. As an example, "Dūghā the interpreter" performed before *Mansā* Sulaymān with his four wives and a hundred of his enslaved women (*jawārī*), all wearing "fine clothes" and head-dresses with "bands of gold and silver adorned with gold and silver balls."[73] This contrasts with circumstances in which women appeared before powerful men without any clothing, about which Ibn Baṭṭūṭa appears to complain:

> One of their disapproved acts is that their female servants and slave girls (*al-khadam wa-'l-jawārī*) and little girls appear before men naked, with their privy parts uncovered. . . . Another is that their women go into the sultan's presence naked and uncovered, and that his daughters go naked. On the night of 25 Ramaḍān I saw about 200 slave girls bringing out food from his palace naked, having with them two of his daughters with rounded breasts having no covering upon them.[74]

There is a quality of voyeurism here, although female nudity was not only emblematic of servitude, but also a gendered act of political submission if not humiliation, as Sulaymān's female cousins' punishment for supporting the deposed Qāsā was to appear before the *mansā* naked.[75]

By virtue of intimacies with slaveholders, enslaved women were often either entrusted with secrets or positioned to learn them, and their testimony could be critical to rendering justice and resolving intrigue. So it was that al-Dukkālī was proven a liar by a female servant who demonstrated ultimate loyalty to the ruler.[76] In the case of Qāsā, however, her female servant was "bound and shackled" and forced to divulge Qāsā's plot. Qāsā's rebellion was in fact heavily dependent on women, with royals having protested her removal while Qāsā rode "every day with her slave girls and men (*jawārīhā wa-ʿabīduhā*)."

If women and girls were used principally as domestics and concubines, men and boys appear primarily as soldiers and attendants, though women were also attendants, especially bearers, and when journeying a slaveholder was "followed by his male and female slaves (*ʿabīduh wa-jawārīh*) carrying his furnishings and the vessels from which he eats and drinks made of gourds."[77] As for soldiers, Ibn Baṭṭūṭa reports the *mansā* was always accompanied by 300 armed slaves, while al-ʿUmarī distinguishes between these 300 and the thirty *mamlūks* or "Turks and others" brought from Egypt.[78] These would have comprised a palace guard, while each of the *farāriyya* also had a (presumably servile) armed guard "with lances and bows, drums and trumpets." In addition to these, al-ʿUmarī writes of a standing army of 100,000 distributed throughout the realm, at least a portion of which was on display during Mūsā's Pilgrimage, as *Ta'rīkh as-sūdān* specifies Mūsā was accompanied by "an army of 60,000 men."[79] A possibly inflated figure, many would have been enslaved.

The enslaved served in other capacities, working in the salt mines of Taghaza and, as Ibn Baṭṭūṭa records, both enslaved men and women (*al-ʿabīd wa-'l-khadam*) performed the arduous work of mining copper at Takedda (and maybe "Zkry").[80] Their participation in agriculture, however, is less clear, as it was often the domain of free persons, if not the defining element of their status. With that said, al-ʿUmarī states the *mansā* gave fiefs (*iqṭā'ā*) and benefits (*in'āmāt*) to his *amīrs* and soldiers, so that slaves, who by the thousands prepared and served food to nobility and royalty, may have played a major role in its cultivation, even on such latifundia.[81]

Imperial Mali's fiefs may bear some relationship to the twenty-four tribes allegedly inherited from Malian emperors by Songhay's rulers, discussed in the forged manuscript C of *Ta'rīkh al-fattāsh*. The text says these tribes became "vassals" to Mali, but the relationship of Mali's rulers to these groups is an open question, given manuscript C's disqualifying nature.[82] Even so, its resonance with al-'Umarī is striking.

Yet another task assigned to the enslaved, male and female, was transporting commodities. As previously cited, Ibn Khaldūn mentions the Malians "use only slave women and men for transport but for distant journeys such as the Pilgrimage they have mounts," a convention confirmed by Valentim Fernandes, who wrote that "each [Jula] merchant has with him 100 or 200 black slaves or more, to carry the salt on their heads from Jenne to the gold mines, and to return from there with gold."[83] Human lorries are often overlooked in the scholarship, but this was a critical form of exploitation, as they headloaded goods both within and between Sahel, Savannah, and forested areas to the south. Based on Fernandes, 100 traders would have required 10,000 workers to perform this task annually, and this is the lower end of the estimates, and only for Jenne.

Finally, slaves in imperial Mali were also state functionaries, though they become much more prevalent in imperial Songhay. The fable of Inari Konte and the recreation of the Niger in the desert features "Farba," a royal slave in charge of others, but whose title is also used for free officials, suggesting it bears no relationship to a person's status as free or enslaved. And there was also the case of the *mushrif* or "overseer" of Walata/Biru, a state official also called the *manshājū* or "emperor's slave."[84]

This mostly qualitative evidence indicates slavery was rapidly evolving in the region, and while a more thorough analysis awaits the recovery of greater detail with the emergence of imperial Songhay, what can be stated here is that these differentiated servile deployments—from domestics to soldiers, and from office holders to their exploitation in mining and possibly agriculture—represent, in the aggregate, something distinct from earlier epochs in Ghana and Gao. There is a noticeable increase in their numbers as well as the variety of their occupations under Mali, further suggesting such expansion was part and parcel of the imperial project in West Africa, and predicated on such myriad mobilization. As a principal adhesive, the enslaved would have served as the collective living tissue more firmly connecting Mande *kafus* with non-Mande towns and rural areas.

Mali and Mombasa: Comparative Commentary

Mansā Mūsā's Pilgrimage may have required others to reconsider condescending opinions about West Africa, as by all accounts he succeeded in presenting Mali as a Muslim polity in control of inexhaustible resources. As West Africa had long been associated with gold and slaves, what was new in the equation was Islam's prominence, and from an external perspective, Mali's rise meant that parts of West Africa had undergone a transformation. In this way, Islam functioned as an instantiation of *la mission civilisatrice*, antedating its Christian European iteration by a thousand years.

A perspective that lauds the effect of Islam while deploring antecedent cultural and social expression is on full display in the evaluative commentary of Ibn Baṭṭūṭa. Upon entering Walata/Biru, he misunderstands the role of the intermediary in West African political protocol, interpreting an exchange between Walata/Biru's *farba* and its merchant as "ill manners and contempt for white men." Ibn Baṭṭūṭa's discussion of West Africa constantly draws distinctions between "black" and "white," so that phenotype clearly has significance for him. After fifty days in Walata/Biru, he headed for the Malian capital, making a beeline for the "white" quarter, having previously written to its "white community." Upon receiving a disappointing reception gift, Ibn Baṭṭūṭa laughed in derision, "and was long astonished at their feeble intellect and their respect for mean things."[85]

Ibn Baṭṭūṭa's remarks are at odds with those recorded during an earlier visit to the East Africa littoral (729–31/1329–31), when and where he characterized Mombasa's inhabitants as "people of [Islamic] faith, virtue, and piety." While describing most of Kilwa's residents as "Zanj and deeply black in color" (*al-zunūj al-mustaḥkamū al-sawād*), and remarking on the resemblance of their facial scarification with that of the "Līmī of Janāda" (*sharaṭāt fī wujūhihim kamā fī wujūh al-līmīin min al-janāda*), he distinguishes the Muslim Zanj from the neighboring, "unbelieving" Zanj (*kuffār al-zunūj*), as the former are "people of *jihād* because they are in a single land adjoining that of the unbelieving Zanj." He goes on to describe Kilwa as "the loveliest of cities with the most skillfully constructed dwellings (*'imāra*)," all made of wood, and under a *sulṭān* admired for his generosity and adherence to Islam. Known for their "[observant] faith and piety" (*al-gālib 'alīhim al-dīn wa al-ṣalāḥ*), Kilwa's Muslims, like those of Mombasa, adhered to the Shāfi'ī school.[86] There is no hint of "racism" or bias here, only respect, if not admiration.

Twenty years later, a very differently disposed Ibn Baṭṭūṭa arrived in Mali, his new attitude potentially explained by an acquired sense of privilege, but also informed by Mali's reputation as a wealthy kingdom. His reference to the "feeble intellect" of blacks, however, links with racialized stereotypes and fantasies previously discussed, and suggests Ibn Baṭṭūṭa may have been aware of that literature. The signal trope of such sentiment is cannibalism. In mentioning the infamous al-Dukkālī, Ibn Baṭṭūṭa states his punishment for lying was banishment "to the land of the infidels who eat mankind." Ibn Baṭṭūṭa commits to the theme and immediately follows with a similar account concerning emissaries from gold-producing lands. Part of their reception gift from the *mansā* was a young girl, who they "slaughtered . . . and ate her and smeared their faces and hands with her blood and came in gratitude to the sultan." Ibn Baṭṭūṭa adds "they say that the tastiest part of women's flesh is the palms and the breast," the ultimate in sexualized phantasmagoria, but key to Ibn Baṭṭūṭa's perspective is the comment that such was "their custom whenever they come in deputation" to the *mansā*. There is a hint of condemnation here, that the *mansā* is complicit in the anthropophagy of others by way of vicarious and serial participation, an early articulation of the savage heart beneath civilized skin.[87]

Notwithstanding Ibn Baṭṭūṭa's own participation in mythologizing the African, when confronted with other evidence he was capable of reevaluation. Thus, Ibn Baṭṭūṭa describes the *Qāḍī* ʿAbd al-Raḥmān as a "respectable pilgrim of noble virtues," and Dūghā the griot as "one of the respected and important Sūdān."[88] It helped that he received a bovine from both, but Ibn Baṭṭūṭa acknowledges the serious pursuit of Islam in general, as well as registers his objections to certain practices, and given his overall caustic attitude, his commendations are high praise indeed.

And then there is his encounter with *Farba* Sulaymān, "well known for his courage and strength. . . . I did not see among the Sūdān anybody taller or more heavily built than he." Awed by his imposing physical stature as well as his array of weapons ("shields, bows, and lances"), Ibn Baṭṭūṭa was even more impressed with his facility in Arabic and possession of Ibn al-Jawzī's work. "I did not see among the Sūdān anyone more generous or worthy than he," concluded Ibn Baṭṭūṭa. "The lad whom he gave to me has remained in my possession until now," suggesting his retention was a way of remembering the *farba*. Ibn Baṭṭūṭa may therefore have left Mali with a more "complicated" view of "blacks" than he registered upon his arrival.

The foregoing is the record of a post-*Mansā* Mūsā Mali in initial decline. Suffering from invidious comparison with his brother, Sulaymān's reign is yet remarkable in including an episode featuring a demoted wife, Qāsā, challenging for the leadership of his vast empire. It is also with Sulaymān that the pivot to North Africa begins. However, relations between the regions are less than transparent, an opacity reflecting ambiguity that would lead to misunderstanding and, eventually, open conflict.

Though there would be a waning, in its heyday imperial Mali achieved unprecedented success, displaying genius in bringing together powerful political and cultural currents in a mutually complementary fashion. Politically, the state built upon local and regional forms of governance, folding them into a more capacious and broader configuration of hierarchical power. The formula of integrating the local into the regional, in turn, provided a grid across which political authority was extended over a territorial expanse never before witnessed in West Africa, uniting the Niger and the Senegal and Gambia under a single centralized power. The achievement of such vast dominion resulted in control over multiple trade routes, entrepots, and mining centers, and an accumulation of wealth possibly unrivaled anywhere in the world for much of human history. The kingdom's political and economic pillars were in turn strengthened by a cultural approach that embraced Islam's universality while eschewing its forceful imposition. This approach enshrined mutual respect between practitioners of Islam and ancestral religions, while laying the foundation for an efflorescence of urban Islamic culture and learning in the decades and centuries to follow. A diverse Islam, Mande political and cultural innovation, and Jula commercial indispensability connected the far-flung reaches of a realm that would assume iconic proportions, West Africa's greatest.

PART III

Imperial Songhay

CHAPTER EIGHT

Sunni 'Alī and the Reinvention of Songhay

THE MID-NINTH/FIFTEENTH CENTURY arrival of the Portuguese along the West African coast was not the principal reason for a reorientation of power in the region, as that process had actually begun at least fifty years prior. In the aftermath of *Mansā* Sulaymān's reign, Mali faltered due to succession disputes, in tandem with a central administrative apparatus challenged by a sprawling territorial expanse. Growing Malian weakness encouraged the rise of alternative political formations, and though Mali would continue well into the eleventh/seventeenth century, it would do so in diminished form, losing control over vital spaces of commercial and cultural exchange in both the Senegal and Niger valleys. The Middle Niger is the focus of what follows, where dawned a polity that, though tethered to the Malian antecedent in important ways, nonetheless forged a model of state power never before witnessed there. The onset of Songhay was in fact a reemergence, in that it recentered the ancient town of Gao, capital of the novel experiment. Inheriting the mantle of Mali, Songhay would undertake important innovations in meeting the demands of international commerce, ethnic diversity, and Islam's expansion.

By way of serial effort, experimentation, and even regime change, Songhay boldly attempted the realization of a pluralist society fully reflective of its multiple constituencies—an approach premised on a new theory of governance in which spheres of influence were distributed to shareholders as self-organized groupings or communities, a policy made evident and articulated through practice and convention. Spheres with the highest levels of influence were those of the mosque and the state, intersecting with each other as well as with other spaces largely defined by ethnic and occupational interests. Informed by both local practice and international engagement, Songhay would eventually achieve a remarkable social compact by which new levels of mutual respect and tolerance were reached, and through which Songhay came to be characterized. In this way, it distinguished itself from its Malian predecessor, for—although inclusive of non-Mande elements—the Malian empire was first and foremost a Mande operation, in which the Mande sought to control all levers of political, social, and cultural power, something even *Mansā* Mūsā sought to consolidate through his indigenization program. In contrast, Songhay would evolve differently, becoming a much more ethnically heterogeneous society in which allegiance to the state transcended loyalties to clan and culture, with its leadership becoming much more diverse.

Circumstances of Production: The Songhay Chronicles as a Political Archive

But the turn away from Mali to imperial Songhay involves, once again, the engagement with a different source base, though consulted in previous chapters. The externally-written Arabic sources, in conjunction with the archaeological and linguistic data upon which knowledge of the early Sahel and imperial Mali heavily depends, is of tertiary importance for imperial Songhay, as little of it pertains to the ninth/fifteenth and tenth/sixteenth centuries. Likewise, internal oral materials of the kind devoted to Sunjata are of far less significance or centrality. In their place are materials written in Arabic during the period of imperial Songhay and after its fall in 999/1591. As such, these records represent an entirely new development in West Africa, as the first written documentation intentionally created to record its history. Eyewitness accounts of foreigners, combined with records from Morocco, help to round out the picture, with ethnographic research gathered since the thirteenth/nineteenth century extrapolated (at considerable risk) for social and cultural explication. As a result, imperial Songhay's history very much rests on a penned indigeneity.

Until this reconstitution of Songhay, so much of what is known about West Africa is based on external sources and foreign traveler reports, while oral traditions tend to be highly stylized and parochial in temporal scope and concern, preoccupied with origins and foundational relationships.[1] The latter is also true of imperial Songhay, for which the oral record provides an alternative, often countervailing perspective, more impressionistic than declarative.[2]

To be sure, oral traditions are included in the written histories of the tenth/sixteenth and eleventh/seventeenth centuries, but their appropriation represents a dramatic shift in West African processes of memorialization. Why the approach to recalling the past changed with imperial Songhay is far from obvious, as writing had been utilized in the region for centuries, in both Arabic and Tifinagh (the written language of Tamasheq, beginning no later than the fifth century CE), so it is not a matter of new technology.[3] The primary sources for the period remain ʿAbd al-Raḥmān b. ʿAbd Allāh b. ʿImrān al-Saʿdī's *Taʾrīkh as-sūdān*, and *Taʾrīkh al-fattāsh*, begun by the *qāḍī* (judge) and *faqīh* (jurist) Maḥmūd Kaʿti b. *al-ḥājj* al-Mutawakkil Kaʿti al-Kurminī al-Waʿkurī (otherwise known as Maḥmūd Kaʿti b. *al-ḥājj* al-Mutawakkil ʿalā ʿllāh) and completed by his grandson Ibn al-Mukhtār.[4] There is also an anonymous, untitled work written between 1067/1657 and 1079/1669 and published as a second appendix to the French translation of *Taʾrīkh al-fattāsh* called *Notice historique*. These are supplemented by the extraordinary scholarship of Aḥmad Bābā, in particular his *Miʿrāj al-ṣuʿūd* ("The Ladder of Ascent") and *Kifāyat al-muḥtāj li-maʿrifat man laysa fī ʾl-dībāj*, an abridgement of his *Nayl al-ibtihāj bi-taṭrīz al-dībāj* (found on the margins of Ibn Farhūn's *al-Dībāj al-mudhahhab fī aʿyān ʿulamāʾ al-madhhab*), together with the writings of Muḥammad ibn ʿAbd al-Karīm al-Maghīlī, the recordings of Leo Africanus (or al-Ḥasan b. Muḥammad al-Wazzān al-Zayyātī), and Moroccan correspondence that mostly pertains to the post-999/1591 period. Foregrounding the backgrounds and interests of the principal works' authors greatly facilitates the analysis, while providing insight into the innovation of an internal, written record.[5]

Taʾrīkh as-sūdān *and the Arma*

To begin, the author of *Taʾrīkh as-sūdān*, al-Saʿdī, was born in 1002/1594 and died at some point after 1065/1655–56, the last date mentioned in the *Taʾrīkh*. This means he was born after Morocco's defeat of Songhay and spent his entire life under the occupation and authority of the "Arma," officials and soldiers who, after conducting the military operation, settled in Songhay, marrying local women and raising families over the course of the eleventh/seventeenth century, so adjusting they eventually functioned independently of Morocco. Al-Saʿdī was in fact part of the Arma regime, initially serving as *imām* of the Sankore mosque in Jenne in 1036/1626–27, then as a bureaucrat in Jenne and Masina, and finally as chief secretary for the Arma in Timbuktu by 1056/1646, all of which suggests a certain loyalty.

As the second half of *Ta'rīkh as-sūdān* concerns the Arma occupation, with which al-Sa'dī was directly familiar, he was necessarily dependent on other sources as well as eyewitnesses for what preceded—"reliable persons" whom he infrequently but anonymously acknowledges. Of the *Ta'rīkh*'s first half, approximately fifty percent is political history, beginning with the twelfth chapter and the reign of *Sunni* 'Alī. Prior to this chapter, al-Sa'dī's tome is a curious mix of folktales, accounts of prior empires, urban history, and a panegyric to important scholars and saints. The *Ta'rīkh* begins with ancient Gao during the time of the Zuwās/Juwās/Jā's, followed by a brief account of the Sunni dynasty (linking the two), after which is an account of *Mansā* Mūsā and Mali's rise, underscoring the former's elevated status. Several chapters concern the histories of Jenne and Timbuktu under Malian and Songhay hegemony, with one exclusively dedicated to Jenne's religious elite. Al-Sa'dī then pivots, ruminating on the origins of the Tuareg, after which are three important chapters on the scholars and saints of Timbuktu, along with a separate chapter on the imams of Jingereber and Sankore mosques in Timbuktu. Al-Sa'dī acknowledges that the celebration of Timbuktu's *'ulamā'* (Chapter Ten) is derived from the *Kifāyat al-muḥtāj li-ma'rifat man laysa fī 'l-dībāj* of the luminary Aḥmad Bābā, a work more simply referred to as *al-Dhayl*.[6]

In his introduction, al-Sa'dī offers an explanation as to why he wrote *Ta'rīkh as-sūdān*, through which he provides a picture of what appears to have been a diminution in the role of the griot, as well as corruption in the latter's professionalism. He says that "our forefathers used mainly to divert one another in their assemblies by talking of the Companions and the pious folk—may God be pleased with them, and have mercy on them"—clearly a reference to the Companions of the Prophet and their accounts through standard written texts. Al-Sa'dī then becomes much more local in his meaning, stating that the forefathers would then "speak of the chiefs and kings of their lands, their lives and deaths, their conduct, their heroic exploits, and other historical information and tales relating to them." This is much more within the wheelhouse of the griot, though not necessarily confined to their expertise. Al-Sa'dī then makes a startling claim: "Then that generation passed away. . . . In the following generation, there was none who had any interest in that, nor was there anyone who followed the path of their deceased ancestors, nor anyone greatly concerned about respect for elders." Circumstances of modalities by which the past was recalled had become so dire that "the only folk remaining" with the requisite skills "were those whose motivations were base, and who concerned themselves with hatred, jealousy, back-biting, tittle-tattle, scandal-mongering, and concocting lies about people. God preserve us from such things, for they lead to evil consequences." In response to such misinformation, al-Sa'dī took the responsibility upon himself:

> Now when I saw that branch of learning [recounting the past] fading away and disappearing, and its coinage being debased. . . . I sought the help of God—Sublime is He—in recording the stories and historical traditions that have been handed down about the kings of the *sūdān*—the people of Songhay (*ahl Sughay*)—their conduct, and their military exploits, recounting the foundation of Timbuktu, the kings who ruled it, and some of the scholars and pious folk who settled there, and so forth, down to the end of the Aḥmadī, Hāshimī, 'Abbāsī dynasty, [that of] the *sulṭān* of the Red City, Marrakesh.[7]

There are several issues here difficult to disentangle. As previously discussed, oral historians were especially critical to elite narratives. Al-Sa'dī's comments seem to relate to griots, at least in part, their "passing away" possibly connected to the demise of the Askia dynasty. This would make sense, as there was no longer a royal formation to which griots were attached, and though a remnant of the Askia dynasty would remain in the Dendi region to the south of Gao, al-Sa'dī would not have been in contact with them. But even if he consulted griots, al-Sa'dī clearly was not proceeding as one, as he *writes* his history, in a fashion very different from stylized conventions. So it is very curious when he says he is responding to the "fading away" of a "branch of learning," which might be alternatively translated as the "disappearance of this knowledge and its study," for within the western Sudan no such branch had been established. Rather than reviving a regional tradition of writing history, therefore, Maḥmūd Ka'ti and al-Sa'dī were *inventing* it, and in that order, pioneering a new technology of memory stimulated by an engagement with scholarship from across the Muslim world. Rather than extending the griot tradition, they were in effect breaking from it.

Although the reasons al-Sa'dī gives for writing *Ta'rīkh as-sūdān* are seemingly innocuous, he was in fact also pursuing a political project: the legitimization of Arma rule. To begin, he asserts that the first rulers "of Songhay" were the Zuwās/Juwās/Jā's, and having presented the early Zuwās/Juwās/Jā's as originating in Yemen (or *al-yaman* as simply "the east"), he makes the connection to the subsequent Sunni dynasty by claiming that the first Sunni ruler, 'Alī Kulun, was the son of one *Zuwā/Juwā/*

Jā' Yāsiboy.[8] He then brings the account back to the first *zuwā/juwā/jā'*, al-Ayaman, to suggest that in killing the demonic creature, al-Ayaman was Muslim. The issue here is not whether al-Ayaman was indeed Muslim, or if he or any of these connections are valid or historical, but that al-Sa'dī makes them.

Having proffered the argument that both Songhay dynasties trace their heritage to Yemen, al-Sa'dī then does the same for the Arma, claiming the Ṣanhāja (with whom al-Sa'dī equates the Masūfa) originated in Himyar, Yemen, and that upon the conversion of one of their rulers to Islam, those who followed his example were driven out, leading them to slowly drift westward until they reached al-Maghrib, where they intermingled with the "Berbers," adopting their language and intermarrying.[9] This is the same alleged origin of the Sankore scholars, who comprise the core and focus of al-Sa'dī's chapters concerning Timbuktu. The Arma, therefore, as extensions of the Sa'dians with alleged origins also in the Arabian Peninsula, inherit the mantle of the Zuwās/Juwās/Jā' and Sunni dynasties.

Instructively, al-Sa'dī does not dwell on *Askia al-ḥājj* Muḥammad's Mande background. Indeed, the inappropriate and corrupt behavior of his successors explains their defeat by the Moroccans, such that in the Arma there is a restoration of divine order that connects with an initial political and spiritual authority hailing from Arabia. Al-Sa'dī's perspective is decidedly informed by the theme of Sankore exceptionalism, as he emphasizes the people of Mali were *sūdān*, whereas the progenitors of ancient Ghana were *bayḍān*, as were the Ṣanhāja, who "are of the religion of Islam and follow the Sunna and wage jihād against the blacks (*as-sūdān*)."[10] *Ta'rīkh al-fattāsh* is less preoccupied with such matters, simply stating that, notwithstanding speculation concerning the origins of Kayamagha's (Ghana's) progenitors, it is clear they did not originate "from among the blacks."[11] Though such depictions in both *ta'rīkhs* (*tawārīkh*) may relate much more to cultural than phenotypical differences, the latter is inescapably inferred, especially when considering Ibn Baṭṭūṭa or Ibn Khaldūn, who use these terms to convey not only cultural but also "racial" or ethnic divergence. The *ta'rīkhs* were written in dialogue with such writers.[12]

If legitimization of the Arma was part of al-Sa'dī's agenda, a close second objective would have been to remind the Arma that, as their power was dependent on their treatment of the scholarly community, the latter's abuse would result in the regime's providential demise. As such, *Ta'rīkh as-sūdān* is both an appeal and a caution, no doubt crafted in view of the Moroccan *Pasha* Maḥmūd b. Zarqūn's 1002/1593 crackdown on the descendants of *Qāḍī* Maḥmūd b. 'Umar and the Aqīt family, a powerful Sankore formation in Timbuktu. The Aqīts and their associates had been suspected of fomenting unrest in Timbuktu two years earlier, so that a number of them were arrested, with some facing immediate execution while others were later exiled to Marrakesh (from 1002/1594 to 1004/1596), among them the illustrious Aḥmad Bābā (who would not return to Timbuktu until 1016/1608).[13] The personal fate of *Pasha* Maḥmūd b. Zarqūn was therefore all but assured, as he was subsequently decapitated by "infidels." His fate paralleled that of *Sunni* 'Ali, who in 873/1469 began a serial persecution of the same family that also led to death and exile. Instructively, both *Pasha* Maḥmūd b. Zarqūn and *Sunni* 'Ali suspected the Aqīts of an alliance with hostile Tuareg forces, and *Sunni* 'Ali's pogrom would feature waves of harassment over many years. Like *Pasha* Maḥmūd b. Zarqūn, his life would end abruptly.[14] Born two months after the scholars' exile from Timbuktu, al-Sa'dī alludes to the fate of any state abusing the *'ulamā'* in describing Mali's enfeeblement, relating that an army of "human-like children" appeared and disappeared in the span of an hour "by the power of the Mighty and Powerful One," decimating the Malians as punishment for its rulers' "tyranny and high-handedness."[15] His concern with scholars explains the structure of *Ta'rīkh as-sūdān*, as it dwells on this community before undertaking Songhay's political history, with Aḥmad Bābā's *Nayl al-ibtihāj*, completed in 1004/1596 while in exile in Marrakesh, taking center stage. Such an organizing principle also helps explain al-Sa'dī's experimentation with historical writing itself, as there was a need to appropriate a more capacious apparatus by which to defend the *'ulamā'*.

Ta'rīkh al-fattāsh *and the Askias*

If *Ta'rīkh as-sūdān* sought to indigenize yet proscribe the power of the Arma, the objectives of *Ta'rīkh al-fattāsh* were very different. Maḥmūd Ka'ti, who died in 1002/1593, was the originating author of a project subsequently revised and embellished by his daughter's son, Ibn al-Mukhtār, to whom the volume is often credited and who wrote of developments as late as 1065/1655–56, with three of his maternal uncles, a cousin, and his own father making minor contributions.[16] Having therefore died the year before al-Sa'dī was even born, Maḥmūd Ka'ti's personal experience with occupation was brief, so that the two men were writing out of radically different contexts. To political and generational divergence must be added the observation that, although both chronicles were completed around the same time in the second half of the eleventh/seventeenth century, it is very possible—if not probable—that an earlier version of *Ta'rīkh al-fattāsh* was known to al-Sa'dī, in which case *Ta'rīkh as-sūdān* serves as a response, if not a corrective. Al-Sa'dī was certainly aware of Maḥmūd Ka'ti, mentioning him twice and referring to him as the "erudite scholar and jurist."[17]

Maḥmūd Ka'ti's family enjoyed an intimate association with Tendirma, to the southwest of Timbuktu along the Niger, where both he and his son Ismā'īl served as the town's *qāḍī*.[18] Tendirma was a critical site of power under *Askia al-ḥājj* Muḥammad in the early tenth/sixteenth century, so that the Ka'ti family's subsequent prominence in Timbuktu is partially explained by the Tendirma connection, a religious as well as political linkage suggestive of *Ta'rīkh al-fattāsh*'s central purpose—the legitimization of the Askia dynasty.[19] Such an objective is buttressed by the organization of the text itself, which begins with a discussion of a divine orchestration of political succession and regimes, followed by disquisitions on the anterior polities of Mali, Kaniaga, and Kayamagha or Ghana.[20] In moving past *Sunni* 'Alī's controversial reign over Songhay, *Ta'rīkh al-fattāsh* launches into a straightforward political history of the Askias through the period of the Moroccan conquest and initial occupation. Religious and scholarly figures certainly appear, but the focus is squarely on the policies, triumphs, and failures of the state.

As such, *Ta'rīkh al-fattāsh* differs in emphasis and substance from *Ta'rīkh as-sūdān*, and like the oral corpus concerning Sunjata, seems to have been initiated to both legitimate and shore up *Askia al-ḥājj* Muḥammad's claims to an authority to which neither he nor the ensuing Askia dynasty were legally entitled, as they were neither royals nor were they even ethnically Songhay. Maḥmūd Ka'ti and Ibn al-Mukhtār skillfully accomplish this objective by connecting *Askia al-ḥājj* Muḥammad to imperial Mali, divinely favored as a consequence of the Pilgrimage of *Mansā* Mūsā, and about which the authors go into detail; next, to Kaniaga, a kingdom from which subsequently issued the city of Diara, governed by the Soninke clan of the Diawara; and then to Kayamagha or Ghana, the ancient kingdom of the Wangāra, a Soninke-related formation. Following rumination on the exploits of *Sunni* 'Alī, which does little to explore his ethnic background or claims to power (itself an instructive maneuver), the authors pivot and return to the Mande imperative, linking *Askia* Muḥammad's father to the Soninke Silla clan (said in this instance to derive from Futa Toro). The authors present *Askia* Muḥammad as "prince of the believers and *sulṭān* of the Muslims" by means of veritable hagiography, trumpeting his spiritual virtues as a rightly guided ruler who makes his own Pilgrimage, thereby addressing discomfort over his spiritual fitness to rule, as he was not Songhay's rightful heir. The authors attempt to resolve the controversy by placing *Askia al-ḥājj* Muḥammad within a distinguished Mande ruling lineage tracing to ancient Ghana itself.

Although not without controversy, Maḥmūd Ka'ti's own pedigree may itself constitute an additional window into the design of *Ta'rīkh al-fattāsh*, for as the name "al-Sa'dī" gestures toward Arabia, so "Ka'ti" equally directs attention to a different set of lineage claims. On the one hand, Ka'ti, the vowelization of which is only proximate in the Arabic, could be rendered Kante or Konte, and therefore Soninke.[21] If so, and as opposed to al-Sa'dī, Maḥmūd Ka'ti and his grandson adopt a legitimization strategy that doubles down on a regional authenticity heavily invested in the widely-recognized success of the Mande, a tactic that, beyond the question of accuracy, may have been dictated by the need to govern local constituencies at Gao. On the other hand, relatively recent research argues that Maḥmūd Ka'ti's father (or possibly grandfather) al-Mutawakkil was himself the son of a Spaniard, 'Alī Ziyād al-Qūtī (as the nisba "al-Qūtī" means "Gothic"), and documents associated with him connect him to Toledo, from where he is alleged to have emigrated to West Africa by way of Tuwat.[22]

Even if Ka'ti is a corruption of al-Qūtī, more than linguistic adjustments might have been in operation, as there is also the suggestion that 'Alī Ziyād al-Qūtī was a Muslim convert of Jewish ancestry. This would have been a matter of considerable discomfort, especially in light of the vitriolic role and politics of Muḥammad ibn 'Abd al-Karīm al-Maghīlī (d. 908 or 909/1503 or 1504) in West Africa.[23] The decision to choose Soninke over Jewish affiliation would therefore have been logical as well as consistent with the maternal line, insinuating the political position of the Ka'ti family within the power structure of the Mande-related Askia dynasty. And yet, the possibility of a Ka'ti Jewish connection is sustained well into the thirteenth/nineteenth century, with the claim that the founding of Tendirma, the Ka'ti family redoubt, involved seven Jewish princes with large retinues and considerable resources.[24]

In further assessing the purpose of *Ta'rīkh al-fattāsh*, questions concerning the circumstances of its production and distribution are paramount, but the determination that one of its manuscripts is actually a thirteenth/nineteenth-century forgery, apparently written by one *Alfa* Nūḥ b. al-Ṭāhir b. Mūsā al-Fulānī, does little to diminish the argument for the text's principal objective, and in fact strengthens it.[25] The infamous manuscript C, a copy of a manuscript first obtained by the French administrator Brévié in 1912, contains materials that include a prophecy featuring *Shehu* Amadu Lobbo (d. 1260/1845), ruler of Masina from its capital of Hamdullahi, as the last of the twelve caliphs foreseen by Prophet Muḥammad. It would appear that a widespread operation was undertaken to weave the prophecy (and other information) into as many copies of *Ta'rīkh al-fattāsh* as possible, while destroying others not so emended. Such tampering requires careful use of *Ta'rīkh al-fattāsh*, but its very targeting for manipulation suggests it was understood throughout Muslim West Africa as a vehicle of legitimization—that *Shehu* Amadu Lobbo's self-promotion involved exploiting the very means by which *Askia al-ḥājj* Muḥammad's own legitimacy had been certified. Nearly half of the volume is compromised, demonstrating its purchase.

A final consideration in assessing *Ta'rīkh al-fattāsh*'s purpose concerns the period in which Maḥmūd Ka'ti actually lived, and as opposed to the date of his death (1002/1593), the date of his birth is neither without controversy nor significance. Manuscript C records a statement long attributed to Maḥmūd Ka'ti, that he began writing *Ta'rīkh al-fattāsh* in 925/1519, which if true is itself a critical indication of its agenda.[26] That he could have begun the work in 925/1519 may have been occasioned by the death of Muḥammad's brother, the *Kanfāri* 'Umar, that same year, a huge blow to the aging *askia*, further debilitating his grip on power.[27] As Muḥammad was a usurper, this would have been the generative moment to mount a vigorous defense against all detractors and pretenders, in particular the rightful heirs to the throne. Scholars, however, have serious reservations that Maḥmūd Ka'ti could have begun writing *Ta'rīkh al-fattāsh* at that time, qualms which under careful scrutiny largely rest on the improbable estimate that he was born in 872/1468, which if true means he died at the age of 125. The 872/1468 date issues from a claim, made only in manuscript C, that he was twenty-five years old in 898/1493. This date was accepted by the orientalist community for many decades, defending it by imaginatively translating a passage of *Ta'rīkh al-fattāsh*'s manuscript A concerning Maḥmūd Ka'ti and certain other *'ulamā'* as having been "born during the lifetime" of *Askia* Muḥammad, though "during the reign" of the *askia* is a more logical rendering of "*fī ayyām*" (literally, "in the days of"). Consistent with the former translation and manuscript C's problematic nature (as well as other considerations), the argument is made that Maḥmūd Ka'ti could not have begun *Ta'rīkh al-fattāsh* in 925/1519, and that he was actually much more closely affiliated with *Askia* Dāwūd.[28]

Reexamining the evidence suggests, however, that two separate matters have been conflated, and that there is no compelling reason to conclude that an unacceptable birth date of 872/1468 rules out Maḥmūd Ka'ti having begun *Ta'rīkh al-fattāsh* in 925/1519. Consistent with the logical rendering of *fī ayyām*, Maḥmūd Ka'ti could have born much later, even around 898/1493, which would have made him twenty-six years old when he began the project, the same age as the eminent scholar Aḥmad b. Muḥammad b. Sa'īd when he began teaching in 960/1553. He then would have died near the age of one hundred, not so far-fetched since his colleague, (Abū Ḥafṣ) 'Umar b. Maḥmūd b. 'Umar b. Muḥammad Aqīt, also died at an unspecified but advanced age, and was as senior as Maḥmūd Ka'ti when they both attended the sessions of the much younger Aḥmad b. Muḥammad b. Sa'īd.[29] Furthermore, there is no relationship whatsoever between the ambitions of *Shehu* Amadu Lobbo and 925/1519 as *Ta'rīkh al-fattāsh*'s beginning, and therefore no reason for the *Shehu* to have concocted that date. Treading warily, this suggests that, although a forgery, manuscript C yet retains elements which, while not found in the more reliable manuscripts, may yet be of value for the tenth/sixteenth century. In any event, the claim that Maḥmūd Ka'ti began writing in 925/1519, some ten years before the end of *Askia al-ḥājj* Muḥammad's tenure, is both reasonable and consistent with *Ta'rīkh al-fattāsh*'s overall arc.

The Rise of the Sunnis

Analysis of the divergent agendas of *Ta'rīkh as-sūdān* and *Ta'rīkh al-fattāsh* is critical to the discussion of Songhay, whose origins are linked to ancient Ghana but whose imperial history begins with Mali's weakening in the last quarter of the eighth/fourteenth century. The full spectrum of the response to Mali's decline includes transformations in the lower and middle Senegal valleys, where the Jolof confederation arose under Njajane Njaye, tying together the Wolof states of Walo, Baol, and Cayor.[30] Mali's western reach was now confined to parts of the Gambia.

Mali's retreat from the middle Niger valley was even more pronounced, as it had major investments there. Careful analysis of accounts for the eighth/fourteenth and ninth/fifteenth centuries provides insight into the period as well as subsequent developments, including *Askia al-ḥājj* Muḥammad's reign. To begin, traditions recorded in the *ta'rīkhs* suggest Gao-Kukiya's transition from the Zuwā/Juwā/Jā' dynasty to Malian authority was much more gradual than precipitous. Indeed, the accounts could only mean that the Zuwā/Juwā/Jā' dynasty, rather than being dismantled under the Malians, was subsumed under an imperial apparatus in which it played an instrumental role in Mali's ability to govern the city. That the Zuwās//Juwās/Jā's would be allowed to continue in power aligns with the absence of a confrontation with *Mansā* Mūsā upon returning from the Pilgrimage, with Mali adopting its own version of indirect rule.

Consideration of the Zuwās/Juwās/Jā's relationship to both Mali and the succeeding Sunni or Chī dynasty affords further insight into how the divergent *Ta'rīkh* agendas shape their respective narratives. *Ta'rīkh as-sūdān*, for example, is much more insistent on underscoring tensions between an insurgent Gao-Kukiya and an oppressive Mali, though an examination of the last six Zuwā/Juwā/Jā' rulers mentioned in the *Ta'rīkh*—Bīr Falaku, Yāsiboi, Dūru, Zunku Bāru, Bisi Bāru, Badāas—as well as their possible relationship to the figure of 'Alī Kulun strongly suggests the Zuwās/Juwās/Jā's continued under Malian domination.[31] Although Kusuy/Kotso Muslim is considered the first *zuwā/juwā/jā'* to convert, few of his successors are known by Muslim names, raising questions about Islam's rigor in the royal court. In fact, only Bīr Falaku is affirmed by the scribe's proclamation, "May God Most High be merciful upon him." Bīr Falaku's relationship to his successor, Yāsiboi, is unspecified, but Yāsiboi becomes the father of brothers 'Alī Kulun and Silman Nāri. 'Alī Kulun is said to have led an independence movement after escaping obligatory service in Mali, and is lauded in *Ta'rīkh as-sūdān* as "the one who cut the yoke of dominion on the necks of the people of Songhay from the people of Mali, and God Most High aided him in this."[32] Yet the same text lists four more Zuwās/Juwās/Jā's who succeed Yāsiboi, perhaps viceroys in Gao-Kukiya while Yāsiboi's two sons served in Mali.

Ta'rīkh as-sūdān identifies 'Alī Kulun as the founder of a new dynasty, though an obvious resonance with Sunjata-Dankaran Tuman in the circumstances of his birth, combined with the similarity of their names to subsequent *Sunni* rulers Sulaymān Dāma and 'Alī Ber, have led some to dismiss the entire 'Alī Kulun-Silman Nāri tradition.[33] Though conceivably rhetorical, it should be remembered that name repetition is common in Mali and Songhay ruler-lists, and that, unlike the Sunjata-Dankaran Tuman account, rivalry does not develop between 'Alī Kulun and Silman Nāri. Rather, the brothers fight against Mali side-by-side, with 'Alī Kulun emerging as the leader, succeeded by Silman Nāri without trace of intrigue. Aspects of the 'Alī Kulun-Silman Nāri story are therefore open to challenge, but someone, at some point, founded an independent Sunni/Chī dynasty. *Ta'rīkh as-sūdān* makes a case for 'Alī Kulun.

In contrast to *Taʾrīkh as-sūdān*, the Maḥmūd Kaʿti-associated *Notice historique* states that ʿAlī Kulun was actually born in Mali and raised in the service of the *mansā*, suggesting a natural intimacy rather than conscription.[34] To be sure, the "notoriously brave, highly energetic and extremely valiant" ʿAlī Kulun eventually elects to leave Mali, but as opposed to al-Saʿdī's account, the decision is not explicitly characterized as a move to "liberate" Songhay from "the yoke" of Mali. Rather, the text simply says ʿAlī Kulun "abandoned" Mali's ruler for reasons "too many to enumerate." Though it says little else about him, *Notice historique* frames the relationship between Mali and Songhay as cooperative and cordial, making the subtle point that legitimacy and imperium were transferred from the former to the latter, rather than wrested.

In departing from Mali, Songhay independence may not have been ʿAlī Kulun's initial objective. Such a conclusion is certainly embedded in *Notice historique*, but it can also be found in *Taʾrīkh as-sūdān*, where, while presenting the goal of Songhay independence as a given, there is a focus on ʿAlī Kulun's preparations.[35] These measures involved identifying and hiding resources for an eventual secession attempt, but unfold within a context of his "seeking fortune" on journeys successively venturing farther away from the Malian capital. Beyond insinuating a relationship with the Jula and larger Mande world, such activity metaphorically represents Mali's gradual loss of control over the eastern Niger buckle. And if the Zuwās/Juwās/Jā's continued to rule Gao-Kukiya in Mali's name, as the ruler-lists imply, ʿAlī Kulun's may have originally been more interested in contesting the right to rule Gao-Kukiya while remaining under Malian suzerainty. Whatever his early goals, Gao would experience increasing autonomy, with the sources commemorating ʿAlī Kulun as the progenitor of a new Sunni/Chī dynasty.

It has been argued that the Zuwā/Juwā/Jāʾ dynasty in Gao-Kukiya extended through the seventh/thirteenth century, ending in either 678/1280 or 698/1299.[36] This neatly wraps up the dynasty and period, but these proposed dates are inconsistent with the implications of the *taʾrīkhs*.

Taʾrīkh as-sūdān states that *Mansā* Mūsā established Malian control over Gao upon his return from the Pilgrimage (in 726/1326). When conjoined with the tradition of ʿAlī Kulun delivering Songhay from the yoke of the Malian ruler, the logical deduction is that ʿAlī Kulun appeared at some point after *Mansā* Mūsā, presumably following the end of his reign in 737/1337. This is also consistent with the epigraphic evidence.

However, *Notice historique* actually places *Mansā* Mūsā's reign after ʿAlī Kulun, locating his Pilgrimage during the reign of *Sunni* Mākara

Komsū, fourth in the order of succession from 'Alī Kulun.[37] If true, this would mean either Songhay was never actually liberated from Mali (consistent with *Notice historique*'s general presentation), or that, when combined with the perspective of *Ta'rīkh as-sūdān*, 'Alī Kulun's liberation of Songhay was short-lived, followed by a resubjugation under *Mansā* Mūsā. The second option redirects attention to Sākūra as the one who (at least initially) captured Gao, though the significance of 'Alī Kulun's "liberation" dissipates if it only lasted a decade or two.

Given the inconsistent and conflicting accounts, although Gao-Kukiya had become subordinate to Mali by the first third of the eighth/fourteenth century, its transition to independence before the ninth/fifteenth century is not at all certain. And if, as these same accounts intimate, the Zuwās/Juwās/Jā's were the rulers of Gao under Mali, Sunni/Chī origins may well originate in this former dynasty.[38]

This lack of clarity over when Songhay achieved independence also yields related yet distinct hypotheses as to how dynastic change in Gao-Kukiya might have eventually disrupted relations with imperial Mali. The first interprets 'Alī Kulun as representing evolutionary rather than precipitous change, through which a newly formed Sunni/Chī dynasty incrementally realizes increasing autonomy, culminating in an unqualified independence under *Sunni* Sulaymān (Sulīman) Dāma in the ninth/fifteenth century. Such a gradual process is consistent with the observation that Timbuktu remained a Malian possession until the Maghsharan Tuareg takeover in 837/1433–34.[39]

A second hypothesis differentiates between Gao and Kuikya, and allows for the possibility that Sākūra initially conquered Gao (presumably by 708/1309), which was subsequently liberated by 'Alī Kulun. Under this scenario, *Mansā* Mūsā could have indeed retaken Gao, but without necessarily capturing Kukiya (some two hundred kilometers to the south). This possibility restores a bit of luster to the latter's independence narrative, for which there is support in *Ta'rīkh al-fattāsh*. The chronicle notes that the Sunnis/Chīs lived in Kukiya, not Gao, until the time of *Sunni* 'Alī, who was the first to build a royal residence in Gao (as well as in Kabara and Wara, though maintaining the one in Kukiya).[40]

The question of Mali's political relationship to Gao-Kukiya is important in understanding the nature and context of Songhay's emergence in the ninth/fifteenth century. But if the chronicles differ in depicting Gao-Kukiya's interactions with Mali, they more or less agree that prior to Songhay expansion under the Sunnis, Gao's territorial control did not extend beyond the Gao-Kukiya corridor.[41]

The Image of Sunni *'Alī*

The coming of *Sunni* 'Alī was an event of vast proportions and profound implications, occupying a status proximate to that of Sunjata himself. In parallel fashion, *Sunni* 'Alī was largely responsible for exponentially increasing the territorial reach of Songhay; in a real sense the empire begins with him. And like Sunjata, he is intimately associated with war, emerging as an indefatigable warrior, the consummate general of his time, veritably transforming both physical and human landscapes through incessant campaigning. But unlike Sunjata, he is also recognized for establishing political control over leading commercial entrepots, in particular Timbuktu and Jenne, and doing so in a manner strikingly different from the efforts of *Mansā* Mūsā. And unlike Sunjata or Mūsā, he acquired quite the reputation, notorious as well as controversial, for his treatment of Muslim elites. *Sunni* 'Alī's imperial policies and their relation to religious communities would long animate the decision-making process in imperial Songhay.

Degenerate, accursed, despotic, godless, profligate, arrogant, cold-hearted, the Shedder of Blood, the Great Tyrant, the Notorious Evil-doer, the Killer of So Many People that only God Most High Knows the Count.[42] Such are the characterizations of *Sunni* 'Alī in the chronicles, initially suggesting a uniform assessment of his reign and its meaning.[43] However, more careful consideration of what the *ta'rīkhs* actually say, or more precisely, their strikingly different foci following such general pronouncements, once again points to their divergent agendas. While *Ta'rīkh as-sūdān* is preoccupied with condemning *Sunni* 'Alī, *Ta'rīkh al-fattāsh*'s denunciation, though forceful, is more obligatory, as it seeks a different outcome. That is, *Ta'rīkh al-fattāsh* is concerned with something other than censure, and adopts the language of condemnation as a necessary means of disarming resistance to its larger project. As such, it is a more nuanced approach than that of *Ta'rīkh as-sūdān*, whose harsh criticism of *Sunni* 'Alī's person and policies are, in turn, absolutely critical to its own objectives.

The account of *Sunni* 'Alī's reign in *Ta'rīkh al-fattāsh* is heavily skewed toward summaries of military itineraries, conquests, and territorial expansion, subjects that either receive short shrift or are contextualized differently in *Ta'rīkh as-sūdān*. To be sure, *Ta'rīkh al-fattāsh* criticizes *Sunni* 'Alī's war conduct, specifically his cruelty, and subjects his general character to a generous sprinkling of opprobrium, but what emerges most saliently is the recognition, if not celebration, of an imperialism that equates with greatness and glory. For in the final analysis, *Sunni* 'Alī was also 'Alī Ber, 'Alī "the Great," with *Ta'rīkh al-fattāsh* as principal witness.

The trope of conquest actually begins with *Sunni* 'Alī's predecessors, for which there are two independent traditions. The first concerns one Mādao (alternatively, Māda'o, Muḥammad Dao, Muḥammad Dā'o, Muḥammad Dā'u), the father of *Sunni* 'Alī.[44] According to *Ta'rīkh al-fattāsh's* manuscript C, Mādao was responsible for the defeat of the Malian emperor, after which he took possession of the controversial twenty-four tribes.[45] The dubious placement of *Shehu* Amadu Lobbo's thirteenth/nineteenth-century claim to these groups within a transfer of authority between Mali and Songhay some five hundred years prior, however, does not eviscerate the notion that the imperial impulse began with Mādao.

A second tradition of Songhay imperialism is associated with Sulaymān (Sulīman) Dāma, otherwise known as "Dāndi," credited with an assault on the "irresistible" power of Mema. *Ta'rīkh al-fattāsh* states Mema province had broken away from Mali, further indication of Mali's weakening condition. *Sunni* Sulaymān Dāma sacked the land of Mema, "annihilating them and destroying their power."[46]

Timbuktu's Sack/Jenne's Surrender

Sunni 'Alī succeeded Sulaymān Dāma in 869/1464, and would rule until 897–98/1492, between twenty-seven and twenty-eight years.[47] As previously established, he is identified as the son of Mādao.[48] Both *Ta'rīkh al-fattāsh* and *Notice historique* list four rulers between Mādao and 'Alī, whereas *Ta'rīkh as-sūdān* lists seven. The relationship between Sulaymān Dāma and 'Alī is unspecified, though there is evidence of conflict. Indeed, the *Replies* of al-Maghīlī state that with his father's death, 'Alī "sought power" and "rose up against Songhay," fighting them "until he overcame them and gained dominion over them, as his father and other *sulṭāns* of Songhay had done before him."[49] Precisely who he fought against is unclear—a royal faction, a segment of the population, a region; all are possibilities—but the succession process was far from smooth. His father's death apparently sparked a struggle, as 'Alī was not next in line. The absence of clear succession rules, together with conventions encouraging competition, were aspects of governance that passed from the Keitas of Mali to the Sunnis of Songhay, and would directly contribute to the ruin of the subsequent Askia dynasty and Songhay itself.

Ta'rīkh al-fattāsh purports to present 'Alī's campaigns, thirty-four expeditions over a span of twenty-eight years, in diachronic fashion, whereas *Ta'rīkh as-sūdān* mentions about one-third that number, some eleven expeditions.[50] 'Alī's warring takes on a different valence in *Ta'rīkh as-sūdān*, as it is experienced through the prism of the scholarly community's suffering, denying 'Alī's glory while excoriating him. In some contrast, the scholars' plight is but part of the imperial trajectory in *Ta'rīkh al-fattāsh*, the antagonistic nature of these relations captured in the pithy remark that "this profligate (*fājir*) campaigned incessantly."[51]

Placing the *ta'rīkhs* into conversation reveals the *sunni* was concerned with expansion and key cities as well as perennial adversaries. Regarding the former, the primary targets were Timbuktu and Jenne, with 'Alī's activities in areas relatively proximate, undertaken to secure his hold on these cities. But his itineraries also reveal a strategy that sought mastery over the entire middle Niger valley, from Jenne to Kukiya. There were major threats to that mastery, including the Kel Tamasheq to the north of Timbuktu in the Azawad region, referred to in the sources as the Maghsharan Tuareg, and the Mossi to the south of the Niger buckle, mostly located at Yatenga. As such, and in striking dissimilitude from the international profile of *Mansā* Mūsā, *Sunni* 'Alī's policies were entirely regional in scope; with the exception of Walata/Biru, he evinced little interest beyond the immediate orbit of the Middle Niger.

Consultation with *Ta'rīkh as-sūdān* suggests *Ta'rīkh al-fattāsh* is not reliable in its temporal progressions, with some events haphazardly sequenced. As an example, *Ta'rīkh al-fattāsh* states that the *sunni*'s campaigns began with an advance on Direi, along the Niger between Tendirma and Timbuktu, but upon hearing of the Mossi's assault on Walata/Biru, 'Alī changed plans and met the Mossi in battle at Kubi (or Kobé), to the south of Lake Debo. After many years of subsequent campaigns, the chronicle recounts that the *sunni*, learning the Mossi were headed for Walata/Biru, traveled to Sama (between Segu and San) and seized the family and possessions of the Mossi ruler, after which he headed for Direi, only to confront the Mossi at Kubi. Such apparent repetition represents a seam (of which there are other examples), a less than careful revision of an earlier version. The current study proposes 888/1483 as the date for 'Alī's encounter with the Mossi, which in turn could not have been the start of his campaigning, as he had taken control of Timbuktu as early as 873/1469.[52]

Pairing the chronicles clarifies that *Sunni* 'Alī's first order of business, certainly the target of his first major military campaign, was Timbuktu. The evidence depicts a leader less motivated (at least initially) by glory than effrontery. While *Ta'rīkh as-sūdān* supplies details, *Ta'rīkh al-fattāsh* has more to say about subsequent events in Timbuktu, mentioning the year of conquest (873/1469) very late in the chain of 'Alī's military feats, in reverse order of their occurrence.[53]

Ta'rīkh as-sūdān's account of 'Alī's sack of Timbuktu begins with statements attributed to the Timbuktu-*koi Shaykh* Muḥammad Naḍḍa and his son and successor, 'Umar.[54] The former had sent salutations to 'Alī upon the latter's taking power, asking him to not "forsake his pact with him" as he considered himself part of 'Alī's family.[55] Implicit in the entreaty is a willingness to render tribute. Upon his father's demise, however, 'Umar wrote to convey "just the opposite," to 'Alī, boasting his father "left for the other world with only two linen cloths [a reference to his burial shroud], but that he ['Umar] had abundant power, and whoever opposed him would see this power." 'Alī would remark, "What a difference in understanding between this young man and his father!"[56]

Timbuktu had experienced the waning of Malian authority, inviting the establishment of the Maghsharan Tuareg (*tawāriq maghsharan*) over the city in 837/1433–34.[57] Akil, "*sulṭān* of the Tuareg," controlled Timbuktu through Muḥammad Naḍḍa. Signaling *Ta'rīkh as-sūdān*'s didactic purpose in warning the Arma, al-Sa'dī records that following Muḥammad Naḍḍa's death, the Tuareg committed "many gross injustices and great tyranny," as they "forcefully removed people from their homes while violating their women."[58] Muḥammad Naḍḍa had been a righteous man by way of association with *Sīdī* Yaḥyā al-Tadallisī, the "perfected pole" (*quṭb al-kāmil*), for whom he built a mosque (the Mosque of *Sīdī* Yaḥyā), and shortly after whom he died (and next to whom he would be buried). Their collective demise allowed the forces of darkness to take hold of the city.[59]

Divine retribution would be precipitated through Akil's decision to deny the Timbuktu-*koi* his customary right to a third of all taxation, instead apportioning it to others who may have been castes.[60] Infuriated, Muḥammad Naḍḍa's successor 'Umar sent word to 'Alī that he would assist him in conquering the city, after which *Sunni* 'Alī's cavalry soon appeared near the city on the Niger's right bank. The sack of Timbuktu was underway.

'Umar's actions suggest 'Alī had designs on Timbuktu, but that he was uncertain he could defeat the Tuareg, until he received 'Umar's invitation. The latter would in fact flee the city, perhaps fearing retribution for his earlier message of defiance. What happened next in Timbuktu is the source of considerable consternation, best left to examination upon the completion of 'Alī's martial itinerary.

Jenne appears to have been the *sunni*'s next port of call and second campaign, though unlike the assault on Timbuktu, the chronicles do not provide a definitive date for the Jenne campaign. Even so, the evidence suggests it ensued immediately after Timbuktu had been secured, as *Ta'rīkh as-sūdān* states the *sunni* continued "killing and humiliating" members of Timbuktu's scholarly community until the year 875/1470–71, when a segment of this community took flight to Walata/Biru.[61] When combined with *Ta'rīkh al-fattāsh*'s testimony that 'Alī, while laying siege to Jenne, sent a threatening message to Timbuktu upon learning scholarly groups had fled, the siege may have begun that same year.[62] The reason for attacking Jenne would have been compelling: complete control over the major entrepots of the western Niger buckle, establishing mastery over the entire arc from the Inland Delta to Gao.

The chronicles differ in their accounts of Jenne, beginning with the duration of the siege. Emphasizing that, with the exception of 'Alī, no ruler had ever sacked the city, *Ta'rīkh as-sūdān*'s versions may be influenced by the mystical import of numbers. Establishing that Jenne was territorially connected to 7,077 villages, all in close proximity, al-Sa'dī initially reports the siege lasted seven years, seven months, and seven days, only to later include a story that the siege took four years, representing the first four caliphs of the early Muslim state—Abū Bakr, 'Umar, 'Uthmān, and 'Alī—who served as the city's sentinels at its four corners until abandoning their posts due to an injustice (possibly a poor man's wife abducted by an army official). In contrast, *Ta'rīkh al-fattāsh* maintains the siege lasted six months, a reasonable amount of time.[63]

Jenne's location near the Bani River, together with the latter's perennial flooding, feature prominently in the sources, but in contrasting ways. In *Ta'rīkh as-sūdān*, the flooding protects the city, as the *sunni* would daily assault the city until the waters rise, forcing him to retreat to Nibkat Sunni ("the *sunni*'s hillock"). This is said to have gone on for seven years, until famine hit the city. The *sunni* was on the verge of returning to Gao when a Jenne senior military official secretly sent word of the city's plight. The sultan who capitulated was only a lad, his father having died during the siege, prompting 'Alī to remark, "Have we been fighting a boy all this time?" Sharing the same rug, 'Alī asked for permission to marry his mother, giving him as a gift the horse that carried her into 'Alī's camp.[64]

Ta'rīkh as-sūdān's account of the siege conveys the city's formidability, with 'Alī's success lessened by the claim of treason. Its version also underscores a different relationship with Jenne than Timbuktu, as Jenne became ʿAlī's ally, albeit subordinate, the bond sealed through marriage, a significant departure from his reputation of forcibly taking any woman he found desirable. Gao's ties to Jenne became enshrined in the protocol of meeting, with successive city sultans sharing the same rug with Songhay rulers.

Taʾrīkh al-fattāsh's version of the siege of Jenne is rather different.[65] In this account, the river's flooding actually makes the city vulnerable, as a military official called the *kuran* attacks the *sunni* at night in a place called Shitai (Shītai). By daybreak the *sunni* had "annihilated" the *kuran*'s forces, as he would those of the *tunkoi* and the *surya*ʿ, also military commanders. A confident Jenne-*koi* or sultan of Jenne, having blissfully slept through the night, went out to meet the *sunni* on the proverbial next day, with an army so large as to be uncountable. Daily pitched battles ensued for the next six months, but with the Bani's flooding and four hundred "pirogues" (or vessels, *sufun*), ʿAlī allowed neither ingress nor egress until the city surrendered. Initially seeking accommodation in the royal residence, the *sunni* was driven out by "snakes" and "scorpions," evocative of resident evil (and in concert with *Taʾrīkh as-sūdān*'s citing a wife's abduction as the cause of Jenne's fall). ʿAlī would settle in a house south of the royal residence and east of Jenne's Great Mosque, which became the residence of *Askia al-ḥajj* Muḥammad when visiting.[66]

Western and Northern Campaigns

Following the successful siege of Jenne, the *sunni* would launch a series of expeditions bordering the town, beginning with forays into "Bambara country" and ending in the village of Tamsaʾa, near Bandiagara's sandstone escarpment.[67]

While likely an attempt to create a *cordon sanitaire* around Jenne, these offensives also have the feel of slaving, as the next target of operations, the "*bayḍān*," led him to Daʿ, between Bandiagara and Douentza, where he killed *Modibo* Wāra, apparently an important leader. He then returned to Gao following engagements in Sura Bantanba, a general area north of Timbuktu that includes the Azawad and the Hodh (in southeastern Mauritania).[68]

Taʾrīkh al-fattāsh employs Ramaḍān as a dating device, identifying successive locations where he would celebrate the end of the fast.[69] If he left Jenne circa 878/1473–74, he would have returned to Gao in 881/1477, well within a frame that finds him fighting the Mossi in 888/1483. From the seizure of Timbuktu in 873/1469 until his return to Gao in 881/1477, the *sunni* was at perpetual war.

The campaign against the *bayḍān*, often translated as "white" in referring to Arabs and Tuareg, in this instance alludes to the Hal Pulaaren or Fulbe.[70] Key to 'Alī's targeting this community was an extreme hatred, which *Ta'rīkh al-fattāsh* emphasizes without benefit of explanation:

> There were no enemies more loathsome to him than a Peul (*fulan*), and he only wanted to kill any of the Fulbe (*al-fulāniīn*) that he saw, whether he was learned or a fool, man or woman. He did not give any learned Peul either wages (*sarf*) or justice. He decimated the tribe of the Sangara, allowing only a tiny fraction to survive, such that they could all fit under the shade of a single tree.[71]

'Alī would send another expedition against the Fulbe in the town of Numa, ordering his Dendi-*fari* Afumba to "kill them."[72] The *sunni* was not alone in his hatred of the Fulbe, as Muḥammad Aqīt, progenitor of the illustrious Aqīt family of Timbuktu and grandfather of Timbuktu *Qāḍī* Maḥmūd, is said to have left his home of Masina for Walata/Biru out of deep disdain for the Fulbe, fearing his progeny would intermarry with them.[73] The irony is that al-Sa'dī himself was of Fulbe descent, as the *imām* of Timbuktu's Jingereber mosque, 'Abd Allāh al-Balbālī, had married 'Ā'isha al-Fulāniya, from whom issued one Nāna Bēr Tūre, al-Sa'dī's paternal great-grandmother. 'Ā'isha al-Fulāniya had been taken captive in one of 'Alī's raids against the Fulbe of Sunfuntir (or Sonfontera, in Masina, relatively close to Numa), and she was part of the "many" women sent to Timbuktu's elites as "gifts." Rather than treat her as a concubine, 'Abd Allāh al-Balbālī married her. Perhaps 'Alī's command to "kill" the Fulbe applied only to males.[74]

Returning to Gao upon completing his western tour, *Sunni* 'Alī began planning a second, largely northern campaign, initially targeting the Azawad. He could not have spent much time convalescing, for *Ta'rīkh as-sūdān* locates him in Kabara (Timbuktu's port) in 882/1477, presumably on his way to the Azawad. He had placed part of his army under *Askia* Baghna for an assault on Tusku (or Tusuku, presumably near Timbuktu). But as *Askia* Baghna would remain on the battlefield, the *sunni* went to Tusku himself in 884/1479. As neither chronicle discusses the outcome, the fighting may have been indeterminate, and the *sunni* next proceeded to Na'siri "in the land of the Mossi," where he celebrated the end of Ramaḍān.[75]

The Mossi and the Southern Strategy

Ending his second, northern tour, the *sunni* replenished his forces in Lulu, in Borgu province just south of Dendi, where he raised and placed a large army under the Dendi-*fari* Afumba. Several other high officials were involved, including the *Fārin* 'Uthmān, the Tondi-*farma* Muḥammad (who would become *Askia* Muḥammad), his brother the Kutalu-*farma* 'Umar Kumjāgu (who would become the *kanfāri* under *Askia* Muḥammad), and the *Hi-koi* Bukar. Dendi region was a major source of support for Gao-Kukiya, and when the Moroccans invaded in 999/1591, Dendi would remain defiant, ungovernable, a place of refuge for the surviving Askias. 'Alī's turn to Dendi also suggests Songhay benefitted from a possible movement of militarized Sorko into the area at that time.[76] Adjacent to Kebbi, these Sorko may have included Hausa elements. The genius of *Sunnis* Sulaymān and 'Alī may have been their ability to harness that surge.

'Alī commissioned this large force either in Kankoi or against the *kankoi* (the passage is obscure), close to Hausaland, lending some credence to *Ta'rīkh as-sūdān*'s contention that he conquered Kebbi ("the land of Kanta," an apparent reference to Kebbi since *kanta* was the title of its rulers in the ninth/fifteenth and tenth/sixteenth centuries).[77] He was unsuccessful, however, in neighboring Borgu (on the west side of the Niger, with Kebbi on the east).

With the Dendi-*fari* leading the fight against Kebbi and Borgu, the *sunni* turned his sights on the Mossi as part of this third, southern strategy.[78] From Dendi he set out for Yatenga, purportedly destroying a royal Mossi residence while mercilessly killing its residents. He then marched on Muli and put its residents to flight, returning to Dendi to raise and place yet another army under the *Hi-koi* Ya'ti, who then attacked the *Tenka-Ya'ma'*, apparently a high official of Yatenga.[79]

The Mossi remained *Sunni* 'Alī's focus, as the Mossi-*koi* Komdāo (or Nasséré I or Nāssadoba) of Yatenga had assaulted on Sama, between Segu (to the southwest) and San (to the northeast) in 882/1477.[80] This was the beginning of Komdāo's own campaign, who in the summer of 885/1480 sacked Walata/Biru, taking spoils and demanding the daughter of the virtuous scholar *Sayyid* Anda-Naḍḍa 'Umar b. Alī b. Abī Bakr. She would remain in this coerced, unlawful marriage until *Askia al-ḥajj* Muḥammad rescued and married her years later.

Closely monitoring the Mossi campaign against Walata/Biru, *Sunni* 'Alī attacked their camp at Sama and seized persons and property left behind three years earlier. Returning to Sama from Walata/Biru, the Mossi-*koi* set out to retrieve his "family" and goods, sometime after 885/1480.[81]

Although *Ta'rīkh al-fattāsh* states 'Alī departed for the confrontation with the Mossi from Direi, *Ta'rīkh as-sūdān*'s alternatively places him in Jinjo (a town just north of Lake Debo), absorbed in an engineering effort to hollow out a canal to connect the lake at Ra's al-Mā', on the western edge of Lake Faguibine, with Walata/Biru, some four hundred kilometers (approximately 250 miles) away.[82] This was an extraordinary undertaking, possibly out of recognition of Tuareg mastery over the territory between Timbuktu and Walata/Biru.[83] It was not the only such feat attempted under imperial Songhay, as Timbuktu's port at Kabara was also widened. 'Alī's motives in pursuing the canal are not evident, though *Ta'rīkh as-sūdān* claims it was to facilitate pursuit of scholars fleeing Timbuktu. Commenting that the Mossi-*koi*'s advance forced 'Alī to abandon the project, al-Sa'dī opines, "Thus, God Most High saved the people of Bīru from his wickedness."

For six years, from 882/1477 to 888/1483, 'Alī made no attempt to prevent the Mossi's western march nor their assault on Walata/Biru, but rather took strategic advantage, both at Na'siri and Sama. It was probably his calculation that any conflict between the Mossi and Walata/Biru could only strengthen his own position, so it was only after the Mossi-*koi* directed his attention toward the *sunni* that the latter responded frontally. They finally met at the town of Kubi, south of Lake Debo in 888/1483.[84] Both chronicles state the Mossi-*koi* was put to flight, the *sunni* pursuing him all the way to Mossi territory.[85]

This was an important victory in that it eliminated the Mossi as a serious threat to Songhay suzerainty for many decades. 'Alī would then "conquer the mountains," a reference to either Bandiagara to the south, or to Azawad in the north. His last operation was against Gurma, usually a reference to land within the Niger buckle (the right side of the river) between Gao and Timbuktu, but in this instance, perhaps the area between Timbuktu and the lakes west of it.[86] Whatever Gurma's precise location in this instance, the operation demonstrates a preoccupation with threats near Timbuktu and Jenne. By the end of his reign, 'Alī had solidified his control over these towns while shoring up claims to Jinjo. Smaller but regular skirmishes against Yatenga and in Bandiagara to the south, and in the Azawad to Timbuktu's north, served to maintain control of Gurma and Hombori (farther south of the Niger buckle, east of Bandiagara).

This discussion of an imperial shift in the region requires analysis of the sources, as they transition from the combination of external and internal written documentation for Mali, to a nearly complete reliance on the latter concerning Songhay. Examination of the principal *ta'rīkhs* (*tawārīkh*) reveals the divergent agendas of the respective authors, with *Ta'rīkhs as-sūdān* attempting to indigenize while cautioning a Moroccan-based occupation, while *Ta'rīkh al-fattāsh* began as an initiative to justify the Askias usurpation of power. Both represent a novel element in the region—historical writing. Through it, the various campaigns of *Sunni* 'Alī, a veritable force of nature, reveal a determination to protect the Timbuktu-Jenne corridor, a major focus for the succeeding Askia dynasty as well. What is more, the chronicles demonstrate how Timbuktu and Jenne differ in their relationship to centralized power, with Timbuktu's relations registering as far more turbulent. This tension will develop into a major focus for the *ta'rīkhs*.

CHAPTER NINE

The *Sunni* and the Scholars: A Tale of Revenge

THE MOSSI ASSAULT ON WALATA/BIRU IN 885/1480 sought to take advantage of a major disruption in power relations in the Middle Niger, highlighting antagonisms between Timbuktu's scholarly community and *Sunni* ʿAlī. The chroniclers characterize the tensions with sweeping generalizations, but the *sunni*'s relationship with the scholars was in fact more complicated than straightforward, with some in persecuted families willing to broker an accommodation with the ruler. In the end, however, the *sunni* seriously miscalculated in alienating such a powerful coalition of the learned and the moneyed.

What follows is an examination of how *Sunni* ʿAlī sought to balance his fear of opposition in Timbuktu with his need for alliances by which he could rule the city. He would embark upon a strategy of attacking one community of scholars associated with his political nemesis, while embracing an alternative group of more neutral elites. Those he favored would remember him in a fairly favorable light, while those antagonized with death and exile would recall the *sunni* as evil incarnate. The latter would not simply revile; they would organize an insurgency.

Other important aspects of early imperial Songhay are visible during *Sunni* ʿAlī's tenure. These include the origins and interconnections of Timbuktu's powerful Muḥammad Aqīt and Anda ag-Muḥammad families; the emergence of the oft-overlooked Mori Koyra, a scholarly community with a major role in the unfolding of Songhay history; and the ways in which servile formations impacted Songhay policy and military operations.

A Foundation of Hostility

Before *Sunni* 'Alī ever stepped foot in Timbuktu in 873/1469, a number of scholars had already fled. Learning of the *sunni*'s approach, the Tuareg leader Akil is said to have assembled a thousand camels to transport Timbuktu's scholars to Walata/Biru, as "their fate was of upmost importance to him."[1] This was a curious decision; since the *sunni*'s principal military challenge would have been Akil, why take the scholars? A plausible explanation is that they were politically aligned with Akil, and therefore anticipated mistreatment by the *sunni*, Akil's efforts to protect them suggesting their sentiments were well known.

But there seems to have been something else at work here, a consideration having to do with the scholarly community's perception of 'Alī. Al-Sa'dī writes that the *sunni* "hated" them for their "elitism," with the wellspring of such a visceral response 'Alī's sense of rejection by the scholars, that there was something disqualifying about him.[2] This was undoubtedly informed by the *sunni*'s practice of Islam, and the judgment that he was either not a Muslim, or a very poor one. Scholarly condescension may help explain the intensity of 'Alī's reaction to the *'ulamā'*, and that their condemnation of the *sunni* was not wholly based on their persecution.

Ta'rīkh as-sūdān specifies Akil placed the "*fuqahā* (jurists) of Sankore" on those thousand camels, a reference to Sankore quarter and mosque. One of their leading members, the jurist 'Umar b. Muḥammad Aqīt, was fleeing to Walata/Biru with his three sons 'Abd Allāh, Aḥmad, and Maḥmūd, the youngest at five years of age. Maḥmūd could not ride a camel, and so was carried on the shoulders of a family slave, Jiddu/Hiddu Makkankī. In addition to the Aqīts was the prominent Anda ag-Muḥammad family, featuring al-Mukhtār al-Naḥwī ("the Grammarian"), also the maternal uncle of 'Abd Allāh, Aḥmad, and Maḥmūd—an example of interfamilial alliances. Al-Sa'dī discusses the practical challenges to organizing the exodus, including the *'ulamā'* trembling before dromedaries, as they had no riding experience, having lived largely indoors, their privilege sheltering them. The flight from Timbuktu would occasion their rethinking, and upon their eventual return they would free their children from such "confinement," allowing them to play outside and experience such things.

Some, however, remained in Timbuktu, where many would suffer at least five distinct waves of persecution, a serial pogrom. The chronicles are agreed that 'Alī "killed and humiliated" them, alleging they were friends of the Tuareg. Al-Sa'dī offers the example of Sita bt. Anda ag-Muḥammad the Elder, the sister of al-Mukhtār al-Naḥwī and, more importantly, the mother of Maḥmūd b. 'Umar b. Muḥammad Aqīt. She was imprisoned, while her jurist brothers Maḥmūd and Aḥmad were put to death. The chronicle does not explain why they were left behind.

As he was just getting started, 'Alī would visit "insult after insult and humiliation after humiliation" upon the Sankore *(ithāya' ba'da ithāya' wa ihāna ba'da ihāna)*. From Kabara, 'Alī launched a second wave, demanding thirty virgin daughters of the Sankore be brought to him on foot to become his concubines, a decidedly offensive and illegal move. Having lived in *purdah* (actually *al-khudūr*, sections of the abode reserved for women, as *purdah* is a Persian term) and therefore accustomed to neither strange men nor outside conditions, they began the forced trek to Kabara (6.4 kilometers or five miles from Timbuktu), collapsing from exhaustion and fear. 'Alī would put them to death, the site of their execution known as *Finā' qadar al-abkār*, "the door of destiny of the virgins."[3]

The persecution's third phase began at some point in 875/1470–71, when remaining Sankore also fled to Walata/Biru. The *sunni* sent the Timbuktu-*koi* al-Mukhtār b. Muḥammad Naḍḍa (having replaced his brother 'Umar) to pursue them, and al-Mukhtār overtook them at Ta'jiti, where the "flower of the scholars" died in battle. 'Alī then targeted the descendants of *al-Qāḍī* al-Ḥājj living in Alfa Gungu or "Scholar's Island," a fourth wave of repression, so "affronting and humiliating them" that some fled, this time to Tagidda with Tuareg assistance.[4] Al-Ḥājj and his brother *Sayyid al-faqīh* Ibrāhīm, originally from Walata/Biru, eventually resettled in Bangu (either Benga east of Bara, or Mussabangu, east of Kabara). Al-Ḥājj served as the *qāḍī* of Timbuktu "during the last days of Malian rule," and was so virtuous he was considered a *badal*.[5]

For those remaining in Alfa Gungu, they were either killed or imprisoned, both men and women. Their leader, the *faqīh* (jurist) Ibrāhīm b. Abī Bakr b. *al-Qāḍī* al-Ḥājj, was made to stand in the sun all day, to "humiliate and torture" him. In the midst of the ordeal he is said to have received a vision in which his father beat *Sunni* 'Alī with a stick, saying, "'May God scatter your children as you have scattered mine'." Thirty of "their finest" then fled to Shibi village (possibly near

Direi), where they napped under a tree while fasting. Upon waking one reported a dream in which

> they were all "breaking the fast that night in Paradise (*al-janna*)." Scarcely had he finished speaking when the messengers of the wicked tyrant rode upon them and killed them all. May God Most High spare us [from such things] and have mercy on them and be pleased with them all.[6]

A fifth wave of repression would take place relatively late in the *sunni*'s tenure.

Sunni *'Alī and the Scholars: Attempts to Differentiate*

Given the experience of the Sankore, the *ta'rīkhs'* decidedly unfavorable characterization of *Sunni* 'Alī is understandable. But by the testimony of the very same *ta'rīkhs*, the representation of *Sunni* 'Alī as one-dimensional is contestably unfair. *Ta'rīkh as-sūdān* in particular allows for a more complex and layered personality, thereby enhancing its credibility (though also raising questions and inconsistencies). Taken together, the sources form a composite picture of a man clearly driven and deeply flawed, who, in resorting to extraordinary violence, displayed both a theory of governance as well as deep-seated insecurities.

Ta'rīkh as-sūdān records that with the scholars' departure from Timbuktu, 'Alī appointed as *qāḍī* Ḥabīb, the grandson of 'Abd al-Raḥmān al-Tamīmī (who had relocated from the Middle East when Timbuktu was "completely overtaken with Sūdānese *fuqahā'* [jurists]," probably in the ninth/fifteenth century). Ḥabīb was closely associated with Sudanese scholars, and his appointment indicates the *sunni*'s decision to fill the vacancy with someone independent of the Sankore, especially the Aqīts. The appointment in turn fostered a close friendship with al-Ma'mūn, Ḥabīb's first cousin. The *sunni* referred to al-Ma'mūn as "my father," and when many denounced 'Alī after his demise, al-Ma'mūn refused to join the chorus, vowing, "'I will not speak ill of *Sunni* 'Alī, since he treated me well and did not do evil unto me, as he did other people.'" Al-Ma'mūn's stature was such that his neither "praising nor condemning" 'Alī was respected by none other than the *faqīh* Abū 'l-Barakāt ("father of blessings") Maḥmūd b. 'Umar b. Muḥammad Aqīt, who at age five had been spirited out of harm's way.[7]

The regard, even admiration, of Maḥmūd for al-Ma'mūn's impartiality is situated in a rather bizarre set of circumstances requiring reconsideration of *Sunni* 'Alī's character, while calling into question a rather uncomplicated picture of Sankore suffering. For in 885/1480, Maḥmūd actually returned from Walata/Biru to Timbuktu.[8] He must have been around sixteen years old, and the context suggests he left Walata/Biru just as the Mossi began laying siege to the town. Presumably there were other options, but not only did he return to Timbuktu; he also began to study with the *Qāḍī* Ḥabīb, the *sunni*'s handpicked appointee, who became Maḥmūd's *shaykh*. Given this development, and that Ḥabīb and al-Ma'mūn were closely related, Maḥmūd's acceptance of the latter's impartiality is less surprising. What remains a puzzle, however, is the nature of Maḥmūd's relationship with 'Alī.

Maḥmūd lived in Timbuktu for some thirteen years before 'Alī's death, with the latter very aware of it, given his relationship with al-Ma'mūn. Maḥmūd's father 'Umar b. Muḥammad Aqīt remained in Walata/Biru until he died, while his brother 'Abd Allāh would reside in Tazakht until his death, refusing to accept Maḥmūd's invitation to join him in Timbuktu, as he did not want to live in the same location as 'Alī's children.[9] His uncle al-Mukhtār al-Naḥwī, however, also returned to Timbuktu with Maḥmūd (Maḥmūd's brother Aḥmad would reenter the city at a later point), and the fact that al-Sa'dī's ancestor 'Abd Allāh al-Balbālī married 'Ā'isha al-Fulāniya as a "gift" from 'Alī means he must have also returned to Timbuktu around this time (if he ever left). Their collective decision to return (or remain) therefore uncovers a breach within the Aqīt and Anda ag-Muḥammad families. Maḥmūd and his uncle may have returned to learn what became of Sita, Maḥmūd's mother and al-Mukhtār al-Naḥwī's sister. Though her ultimate fate is unknown, the fact that her son and brother lived peacefully in Timbuktu until late in *Sunni* 'Alī's reign suggests an accommodation was reached, that the *sunni* was not so irrevocably disposed against the Sankore.

Appointing Ḥabīb as *qāḍī* of Timbuktu, embracing al-Ma'mūn as a father figure, and allowing members of the Aqīt and Anda ag-Muḥammad families to return required al-Sa'dī to provide some balance in his assessment, grudgingly offering that "in spite of all the evil he perpetrated against the scholars, *Sunni* 'Alī recognized their worth (*yuqirru bifaḍlihum*), saying that 'if it were not for the scholars life would not be agreeable or pleasant,' and he treated others better and respected them."[10] This passage takes on a very different valence if a key phrase, *yuqirru bifaḍlihum*, is understood as "in spite of all the evil he perpetrated against the scholars, *Sunni* 'Alī decided to treat them with kindness," capturing a change in the *sunni*'s approach to the scholarly community over time. This would have gone beyond mere personal sentiment, involving policy adjustments.

The *sunni* realized he needed some portion of the *'ulamā'* to successfully govern the city, given their status, visibility, and Timbuktu's potential as an important site of learning, probably informing the rapprochement with Maḥmūd b. ʿUmar and al-Mukhtār al-Naḥwī. The objective of restoring at least functional if not amicable relations with the *ʿulamāʾ* was no doubt also the rationale behind ʿAlī supplying them with captive Fulbe women from Sunfuntir—no small operation as *Taʾrīkh as-sūdān* states "he sent many" such women.[11] Given the *sunni*'s hatred of the Fulbe, combined with the possibility that he was also aware of Muḥammad Aqīt's similar disdain, such "gifts" may have been a gesture of contempt, a huge jest. Even so, it yet demonstrates a calculation to gain the allegiance of a group devastated by earlier persecution, if at little cost to the *sunni*.

Notwithstanding efforts to woo remaining luminaries, the evidence suggests resistance to the *sunni* was forming, and that of lethal variety. In an anecdotal frame of mind, al-Saʿdī reports on a curious but telling encounter concerning two mothers affected by ʿAlī's alleged mood swings. Kasay (or Kāsay), the mother of the future *Askia al-ḥājj* Muḥammad, would frequent the home of Nānā Tinti, daughter of Abū Bakr b. *al-Qāḍī* al-Ḥājj, whose family had been targeted in Alfa Gungu. Nānā Tinti was the sister of the *faqīh* (jurist) Ibrāhīm b. Abī Bakr b. *al-Qāḍī* al-Ḥājj (who was made to stand in the sun all day), and apparently she had also relocated to Timbuktu by the time of Kasay's visits. Kasay requested prayer for her son, from time to time beleaguered by the *sunni* under circumstances to be examined. Her solicitations are evidence of belief in the efficacy of Nānā Tinti's prayers as a descendant of the *badal* al-Ḥājj. The phrasing in *Taʾrīkh as-sūdān* is instructive: Kasay would visit Nānā Tinti "and ask her to pray that God Most High would cause him [Muḥammad] to triumph over *Sunni* ʿAlī. 'If God accepts this prayer', [Kasay] said, '[Muḥammad] will make your children and relatives rejoice, God willing'. And this promise was fulfilled with his [*Askia* Muḥammad's] reign."[12]

This is not the only time al-Saʿdī indicates such entreaty was instrumental in *Sunni* ʿAlī's demise. Having related Ibrāhīm's vision, in which he saw his father Abū Bakr b. *al-Qāḍī* al-Ḥājj thrashing the ruler, al-Saʿdī also reports that in 892/1486–87, some six years before ʿAlī's death, the *sunni*'s name was invoked in the presence of the *faqīh* ʿAbd al-Jabbār at Mount Arafat (east of Mecca), petitioning God to punish the *sunni*.[13] The implication is significant, as the invocation may have taken place on the ninth day of Dhū ʿl-Ḥijjah (the month of *ḥajj*), when Muslims gather for the afternoon at Mount Arafat, in this way making the *sunni* a matter of concern for the entire Muslim world. *Taʾrīkh al-fattāsh* echoes this theme, recording that the father of a maiden raped by the *sunni* remonstrated, only to be threatened with death by fire. Weeping and raising his hands to the sky, the father faced Mecca and implored God's aid.[14] His petitions were joined by those of *Mōri* al-Ṣādiq and *Mōri* Jayba, members of the Mori Koyra (or Mōri-Koïra) community, whose complaints led to their arrest and exile on a deserted, unidentified island. They prayed one after the other:

> Oh God, protect us from this man, and destroy him before he is able
> to [even] stand up from where he sits.
> And may he not die in Islam, but in unbelief!

The imprecations and their timing will be consulted in unveiling circumstances toward the end of the *sunni*'s reign, but according to *Ta'rīkh al-fattāsh*, the day of these petitions is the very day 'Alī died.

In attributing regime change as divine response to human intercession, the chroniclers were dancing around a highly delicate issue. The context of faith is to be taken seriously, but the anecdote concerning Kasay and Nānā Tinti goes beyond prayer and piety, and more than implies intrigue and conspiracy between powerful families colluding in "prayer." And in fact, though there is something in the interaction between Kasay and Nānā Tinti that transcends a strictly Muslim belief in the power of prayer—a hint of a heightened spirituality often associated with women (and mothers in particular)—it does not exclude them from having actually participated in, or even headed a plot against, the *sunni*, not unlike Qāsā in eighth/fourteenth-century Mali.

The Savaging of Sunni *'Alī's Character*

While acknowledging the Sankore scholars' alliance with Tuareg overlords as an issue for *Sunni* 'Alī, the documentation goes to extraordinary lengths to attack his own religious standing, a two-pronged strategy that involved ridicule while intimately linking him to non-Islamic practices, ultimately making the case that he was not a Muslim. Such efforts are not dissociated from intrigue, helping to explain as well as justify 'Alī's fate. Thus, al-Sa'dī records:

> Among the characteristics of this nefarious tyrant was to make a mockery of his religion. He would leave the five daily acts of worship until the night, or until the following morning. Then, from a sitting position he would incline himself repeatedly [ignoring the prescribed motions of *rak'a* and *sujūd*], mentioning the names of the acts of worship. After saying a single salutation [*as-salāmu 'alaykum*] he would then say, "You know one another best, so share [my salutation] among you."[15]

In a similar fashion, *Ta'rīkh al-fattāsh* states that the *sunni*'s actions were so evil and unacceptable that

> some of the *shaykhs* (*shuyūkh*) of his time, from the people of Mori Koyra, were asked if he were a Muslim or an unbeliever (*kāfir*), as his deeds were the deeds of unbelief, yet he utters the double *shahāda* ["There is no god but God, and Muḥammad is the messenger of God"]. And those who were powerful in knowledge considered his deeds to be godless.[16]

The "people of Mori Koyra" (Mōri Kuyra), who take center stage later in the study, were a scholarly and saintly community, their pronouncements carrying weight. So did those of al-Maghīlī, who in his *Replies* to the queries of *Askia al-ḥājj* Muḥammad repeats several of the chronicles' accusations. In the *Replies*, 'Alī is accused of having made "a lip profession of the two *shahādas* and other similar words of the Muslims without knowing their significance." In giving an example of 'Alī's alleged ignorance in the form of an inversion, the complaint borders on the ludicrous: "Sometimes he heard the name of the Prophet (may God bless him and grant him peace) and would say: 'Glory to Him', or he would hear the name of God and say, 'May God bless him and grant him peace'." In yet another correspondence between the *Replies* and *Ta'rīkh as-sūdān*, the former renders a rather bracing characterization of the *sunni*'s practice of Islam, intertwining themes of ignorance and arrogance:

> As for him, he memorized neither the *Fātiḥa* nor any other verses, nor did he pray any prescribed prayer at its appropriate time, nor did he perform bowing and prostration during his prayer. He would simply leave the five prayers until the end of the night or until the following day in the forenoon. Then he would sit in the *tashahhud* posture and make gestures indicative of the *sujūd* from his sitting position, though he was in good health and strong, and not suffering from any physical disability. During his prayer he recited nothing [of the Qur'ān]—he merely mentioned the name of the prayer. . . . Thus during the bowing of the *Maghrib* prayer and during the prostration he would say "*al-Maghrib, al-Maghrib*" and at the *'Ishā'* prayer "*al-'Ishā', al-'Ishā'*," and similarly during the other prayers.[17]

To be ignorant of the *Fātiḥa*, the opening *sūra* of the Qur'ān, is fairly egregious, while refusing to pray in the prescribed manner when healthy completely unacceptable. If true, and based upon this alone, the *sunni*'s Islam would have been suspect, and it may have been because of such deficiencies that the *sunni* was never seen in a congregational or ordinary mosque, "on a Friday or any other day."

There are also ambiguities concerning ʿAlī's behavior during Ramaḍān. *Ta'rīkh al-fattāsh* employs successive Ramaḍāns to follow his military campaigns, often saying he was "overtaken" (*ṭuli'u*, from *ṭala'a*) in a given locale when Ramaḍān began and there would observe *ʿĪd al-Fiṭr*, but that does not mean he observed the fast itself, even though al-Maghīlī's *Replies* states he fasted Ramaḍān, "making abundant alms of slaughtered beasts." It is a challenge to imagine he actually observed a month of fasting every year—a fairly serious commitment, given his lax adherence in other areas. The *Replies* in fact state that of the thousands in the *sunni*'s entourage, none prayed a "single prescribed prayer nor fasted a day of Ramaḍān for fear that he would punish them for that. None of them, free nor slave, prayed or fasted unless in secret, for fear of him." This begs the question as to why they would fear someone who was himself observing.

The sources agree that ʿAlī took any woman he wanted, married or not, free or enslaved, and "put her in his house and in his bed. . . . He would keep her and her mother at the same time," though it should be remembered that *Mansā* Mūsā, prior to his enlightenment in Egypt, was similarly unencumbered. Potentially as heinous was his treatment of scholars and others in the community, which according to the *Replies* included castration.[18]

The case against *Sunni* ʿAlī turned not only on his dubious practice of Islam, but also on his alleged polytheism. One indictment concerns official protocol, that the *sunni* was regularly regaled with the honorific title of *dāli* or the "Most High," reserved for God alone, and that his servants were called *dūlinta*, or "servant of the Master," also a transgression of holy terrain. *Qāḍī* ʿAbū al-Abbās Sīdī discouraged Muslims from so addressing the *sunni* and his servants.[19]

While the *ta'rīkhs* insinuate, the *Replies* are much more direct, featuring an examination of the culture of *Sunni* ʿAlī's mother. In contrast to the mother of *Askia al-ḥājj* Muḥammad, who sought saintly intervention, ʿAlī's mother is said to have come from "Fār," potentially Fari village in Dendi, a land consisting of

> an unbelieving people who worship idols among trees and stones; they make sacrifices to them and pray to them for their needs. If good befalls them they claim that it is those idols who gave it to them.These idols have custodians who serve them and act as intermediaries between the people and them. Among these people are diviners and sorcerers who likewise serve them.[20]

Because ʿAlī grew up in his mother's culture and among maternal uncles, he allegedly became "imbued with their idolatrous nature and practices."

Once in power, he continued to worship and offer sacrifices to these deities, consulting diviners and sorcerers "in all or most of his affairs," a phrase suggesting they were part of his administration.

Al-Maghīlī's discussion is not limited to *Sunni* 'Alī. In his third question, *Askia* Muḥammad observed that in freeing those enslaved under the *sunni* who claimed to be Muslims, he inquired about their cultural backgrounds. Their answers referred to beliefs not unlike those attributed to 'Alī's maternal family:

> But in spite of [professing *shahāda*] they believe that there are beings who benefit them and those who harm them other than God, Mighty and Exalted is He. They have idols and they say: "The fox said so and so, and thus it will be," and "If [it said] something else, then it will be that." They venerate certain trees and make sacrifices to them. They have their shrines and they do not appoint a ruler or decide a matter great or small unless ordered by the priests [*sadana*] of their shrines concerning it.[21]

Reference to the fox resonates with Dogon beliefs to the south of Songhay, rendering them unbelievers in al-Maghīlī's judgment, eligible for reenslavement or slaughter.[22] But their particular circumstances raise questions about Islam's practice throughout Songhay, beyond urban centers, for which answers are not obvious. The extent to which rural populations were impacted by Islam is far from clear, and even when discussing towns the sources whisper of variant approaches, an example of which concerns the mid-ninth/fifteenth-century figure Fūdiye *al-faqīh* Muḥammad Sānū al-Wangarī of Jenne, whose house was previously a worship center dedicated to a local deity. Though no longer devoted to such use, why was it allowed to remain so long?[23] Al-Wangarī's experience may have relevance for *Sunni* 'Alī's inability to reside in the royal compound due to snakes, creatures often associated with ancestral practice.[24]

Gao itself is a question mark. Islam had been a presence there for hundreds of years prior to *Sunni* 'Alī, but it is seldom identified as a center of learning and rarely associated with leading scholars (with Ṣāliḥ Diawara a notable exception). Given 'Alī's dubious embrace of the religion, there were surely others like him in Gao. The capital's ambiguous position would become a factor in the politics of *Askia al-ḥājj* Muḥammad.

As the *Replies* nor the *ta'rīkhs* provide much information on non-Islamic practices, extrapolation from the anthropological literature is not without peril.[25] Religions in Africa, as elsewhere, have been neither stagnant nor impervious to external influence, demonstrating resilience as well as adaptation. It is therefore difficult to know with any precision what non-Muslim Songhay believed during the period of *Sunni* ʿAlī, or how those beliefs might have been incorporated into the Islam practiced in the area.

Even so, the outlines of ninth/fifteenth-century Songhay religion become less faint when tracked with categories described in the *Replies*. In particular, the allegation that the *sunni*'s maternal family worshiped, consulted, and sacrificed to deities among natural formations, and that these deities were attended by specialists in conjunction with diviners and "sorcerers," is amply supported in the anthropological testimony as well as oral tradition.[26] The latter posits worship of the *tōru*, deities led by "Dandu Urfāma," who had many offspring, while the former evinces Islamic influence as it enumerates various categories of worship or veneration, including the worship of Allāh, Iblīs (Satan), the *zin*, ancestors, angels, and the *holey*. The first of the four features Islam itself, while the second is a society about which little is known, but whose very name suggests an import from Islamic teachings. The cult of the *zin* venerates spirits of the original masters of lands and water, and as a cognate of *jinn* (the Muslim category for the disembodied made of fire), may have recontextualized preexisting beliefs within an Islamic framework.

As for the cult of the ancestors, it is closely associated with the *zin*, as these are the initial, human "arrivants" in given locales, revered as especially powerful, and for whom ancestral shrines were erected.[27] The veneration of "angels" may or may not represent Islamic influence, though *malaika* ("angel") refers to beings who surveil the earth while residing in the seventh heaven.

The *holey* cult refers to the "true" overseers of the earth and water and lowest sky, central to which are possession and dance, as it is the *holey* who enter the human soul. As the "most important and most widespread cult," it features in observances of the preceding categories, and is not unlike the practice of *bori* found throughout North Africa, Egypt, and parts of the central Islamic lands. Like *bori*, women are the principal conduits through whom the *holey* manifest.[28] As a widely spread yet highly gendered set of practices, it may help to explain Sufism's appeal as a sphere within which men participate in the experiential.[29]

Consideration of all the evidence concerning *Sunni* ʿAlī's spiritual practice weighs most heavily in favor of a political leader who first and foremost understood Islam's importance in facilitating his authority. Public affirmation, even observance of Islam, would have been of critical significance in the western half of the realm. Given his conflict with a significant proportion of Timbuktu's *'ulamā'*, the *sunni* needed to demonstrate that his policies were politically driven, rather than evidence of conflict with Islam. This he attempted to do, though ultimately without success.

At the same time, 'Alī was clearly not Islam's model practitioner. Detractors may have overstated their case, but that he may have been an adherent of non-Islamic Songhay religion, or sought to pursue it along with Islam, or favored the former while exploiting the latter, are all possibilities. In attempting to stake out a midway between Muslim and non-Muslim polarities, he exposed his vulnerability.

The Timūr Lang of West Africa

The contretemps between *Sunni* 'Alī and segments of the scholarly community also turns on the former's use of violence; 'Alī's reputation for cruelty and carnage was so great as to reach ears far removed from the middle Niger valley. The Egyptian luminary al-Suyūṭī (d. 911/1505), who met *Askia al-ḥājj* Muḥammad as well as other dignitaries from Songhay and other parts of West Africa (and was therefore hardly impartial), would list 'Alī's reign as one of the three great catastrophes of the ninth/fifteenth century, characterizing him as "a sort of Timūr Lang who destroyed worshipers of God and cities," while his student al-'Alqamī, in a commentary on al-Suyūṭī's *al-Jāmi' as-saghīr* ("The Smaller Compendium"), echoed having heard that "there appeared in al-Takrūr a man called Sunni 'Alī who destroyed both lands and people."[30] It was not simply that he was always at war, but rather the way he went about it, hurling infants into mortars and ordering their mothers to pulverize them with pestles, then feed them to horses; burning people alive; committing myriad mutilations, including severing noses and hands; authorizing castrations; and splitting open the wombs of pregnant women to remove the fetuses, a practice associated with ancient Ghana's moral degradation and portent of their doom. Together with the rapine of women, it is obvious that 'Alī sought to shock, and he more than succeeded, so much so that both al-Sa'dī and al-Suyūṭī assign him the epithet of *khārijī*, "the Kharijite." There is debate over what this meant, from the *sunni* adhering to Kharijism owing to the earlier presence of 'Ibāḍism, to the view that he was a *khārijī* in the strictest sense of making himself "a lord, or chief, and goes forth, and becomes elevated." Though called *dāli*, a reasonable conclusion is that he was branded a Kharijite for his heterodoxy (possibly at the expense of Khariji elements in the region).[31]

In discussing *Sunni* 'Alī's use of force, the sources depict him as mercurial, becoming enraged and ordering an execution, only to later change his mind. Maybe he suffered from a personality disorder, though this should not obfuscate his deployment of violence as a deliberate strategy. In assuming power through violence, he lacked *Mansā* Mūsā's Islamic bona fides to command fealty. In striking contrast to Mūsā, 'Alī did not enjoy the respect of Timbuktu's elites. This does not excuse his sadism, but rather repositions the optic from his perspective.

Sunni *'Alī's Curious Death: The Makings of a Conspiracy*

In 890/1485, Aḥmad b. 'Umar b. Muḥammad Aqīt, brother of jurist Maḥmūd who had returned to Timbuktu five years earlier, made the Pilgrimage.[32] He came back from *ḥajj* "during the time of troubles (*fitna*) launched by the *khārijī Sunni* 'Alī," apparently in the year 893/1487–8, when "the people of Timbuktu went to Hawkī," where they remained until 'Alī's demise five years later. *Ta'rīkh as-sūdān* states that 'Alī was in Tusku (probably near Timbuktu) at that time, but an account in *Ta'rīkh al-fattāsh* refers to an episode that occurred while he was allegedly laying siege to Jenne. Other than placing the *sunni* in Jenne, the account's details conform well to this 893/1487–8 Hawki displacement.

According to the report, having received word that the "people of Timbuktu" were fleeing the city—some heading for Walata/Biru and others for Fututi and Tichit—the *sunni* sent word to Timbuktu that all who remained loyal to him should leave the city for "Hawkiyi," on the other side of the Niger, and that any who remained would be killed. Upon hearing the public crier's noon decree, all fled in such panic that many carried neither food nor blankets, leaving behind horses and unlocked homes. By nightfall, the city was deserted save for the sick and the blind. The terror of 'Alī had returned, a fifth wave of repression against the scholarly community.[33]

There may be a relationship between this 893/1487–88 purge and the *ḥajj* of *al-ḥājj* Aḥmad b. 'Umar. In 891/1486, the year following the latter's departure for Mecca, the Timbuktu-*koi* al-Mukhtār b. Muḥammad Naḍḍa, who had replaced his brother 'Umar and hunted down fugitive scholars fleeing Timbuktu, was arrested and imprisoned by the *sunni*. The sources do not provide the reason, but Aḥmad b. 'Umar's Pilgrimage is a consideration. Aḥmad may have passed through the Timbuktu area en route without the Timbuktu-*koi* reporting his movements to 'Alī. Given the early conflict between the *sunni* and the Aqīt family, combined with the troubled history of the Timbuktu-*koi*'s own family with the *sunni*, failure to inform ʿAlī may not have been viewed as an oversight.

ʿAlī could have been concerned that the return of Muḥammad Aqīt's eldest son, preceded by that of his brother Maḥmūd and uncle al-Mukhtār al-Naḥwī, signaled an attempt to reestablish their influence, and even that of the Tuareg, an interpretation strengthened by the assertion that Muḥammad Aqīt himself once entertained designs on the city (to be examined). If he was a threat before making *ḥajj*, Aḥmad was even more so upon his return, graced with *baraka* of the *ḥājj* as well as the prestige of having met such Egyptian notables as Jalāl al-Dīn ʿAbd al-Raḥmān b. Abī Bakr al-Suyūṭī (d. 911/1505) and grammarian Khālid b. ʿAbd Allāh b. Abī Bakr al-Azharī (d. 905/1499). Such would be Aḥmad b. ʿUmar's renown that he would become a celebrated teacher, circulating as far as Kano while amassing some seven hundred volumes in his personal library. If his return in fact alarmed the *sunni*, the latter's response would anticipate that of the Moroccan *Pasha* Maḥmūd b. Zarqūn one hundred years later, who also suspected the Aqīts of fomenting unrest in close association with the Tuareg. The imprisonment of the Timbuktu-*koi*, whether or not connected to Aḥmad, nonetheless coincided with the beginning of a purge that would (again) target the Aqīts. Those departing for Hawki would include Aḥmad b. ʿUmar and his brother Maḥmūd, the latter's accord with the *sunni* apparently undone.

Five years following this fifth purge, *Sunni* ʿAlī was dead. The sources do not address what transpired between Gao, Timbuktu, and Hawki in those years, but circumstantial evidence indicates a high level of tension between an elite, targeted scholarly community and Songhay's head of state. Matters were at an impasse, and though a coup d'état cannot be unequivocally demonstrated, the necessary elements were coming together. If encouraged by the scholars, military capability would be required.

Enter Muḥammad Ture. As ʿAlī's Tondi-*farma*, or "Governor of the Rock" (or "Mountains"), he was probably responsible for the security of the western Gurma region, the southern hemisphere of the empire from Bandiagara escarpment to Hombori, with the Mossi a particular concern.[34] He was therefore strategically positioned, and unless the post of Tunki-*farma* (mentioned subsequently in *Taʾrīkh as-sūdān*) is a corruption of Tondi-*farma*, the latter's lone mention in the *taʾrīkhs* suggests it came into existence with *Sunni* ʿAlī, with Muḥammad Ture its sole occupant.

As Tondi-*farma*, Muḥammad Ture was in the upper chain of command, and along with his brother ʿUmar the Kutalu-*farma* accompanied

'Alī on at least two of his campaigns, suggesting a high level of trust between all three men.[35] Yet the fact that Kasay sought the protection of the Aqīts for her sons reveals significant tension. Kasay worried about the *sunni*'s penchant for ordering executions without cause, "even if they were the most dear to him." As *Ta'rīkh as-sūdān* states:

> This happened in the case of his official, *Askia* Muḥammad more than once, as *Sunni* 'Alī condemned him to death or imprisonment because of [the former's] stout heart and great courage, placed in his nature and disposition by God, and at times [the *sunni*] would rescind his order. . . . As for the *Askia*'s brother 'Umar Kumadiagha, since he strictly obeyed [the *sunni*], as he was wise and prudent, the tyrant never did him any harm.[36]

The Tondi-*farma*'s defiance presumably concerned differences over military strategy; he may have openly opposed the *sunni*'s policy of terror. Beyond mood swings, therefore, the *sunni* felt insecure around Muḥammad Ture, who must have exhibited special qualities to have been appointed Tondi-*farma* in the first place. Indispensable as well as threatening, he mirrored the Sulaymān-Dāwūd relationship in the Hebrew Old Testament.

If *Ta'rīkh al-fattāsh* and *Notice historique* merely mention *Sunni* 'Alī's death in 898/1492, *Ta'rīkh as-sūdān* provides brief commentary and tantalizing circumstance, observing that the *sunni* died upon returning from campaigning in Gurma, where he had fought against the Zughrānī.[37] The victim of sudden flooding near Kuna village, al-Sa'dī asserts the *sunni* "was destroyed through the power of the Mighty and Powerful One."[38] If true, this natural occurrence would constitute a supernatural response to the many aforementioned prayers inveighed against the *sunni*. If the Gurma cited in this anecdote refers to the area between the lacustrine region and Timbuktu, the sudden burst may have indeed been a flash flood. But if it was the Gurma farther southeast and under the jurisdiction of the Tondi-*farma* Muḥammad, the implications are explosive. Indeed, the oral traditions are emphatic in accusing the Tondi-*farma* of assassinating *Sunni* 'Alī, while Kasay's promise that in return for Nānā Tinti's intercessory prayers her son Muḥammad Ture would "make you rejoice in your children and relatives" assumes a tangible quality, as the al-Ḥājj and Aqīt families were the major beneficiaries of Muḥammad Ture's emergence. "When *Askia* Muḥammad acceded to power," *Ta'rīkh as-sūdān* remarks, "he kept this promise."[39] This comes well nigh to acknowledging a prior conspiracy.

A Military Blend of Free and Servile

In discussing *Sunni* ʿAlī, the sources pay scant attention to how he constructed his empire, with most references contained in *Taʾrīkh al-fattāsh*. For example, in a rare instance of specifying a secular post, *Taʾrīkh as-sūdān* mentions the *sunni* had a scrivener or scribe (*kātib*) named Ibrāhīm al-Khiḍr from Fez; the *sunni* may have appointed him because he lived in the vicinity of Jingereber mosque and not Sankore.[40] It is likely, however, that most of the offices mentioned after his reign (under the Askias) were also in existence during it. For example, the previously explained office of *mondio* would have extended from Mali to the Askia dynasty through the Sunnis, as would have been true of the Jenne-*koi* and Timbuktu-*koi*. Other offices designated by the appendage *koi* or *farma* (and its cognates) would have been responsible for cities, towns, villages, and provinces, consistent with the Malian model and quite apparent under the Askias.[41]

In mentioning the offices of the *Farans* Afumba, Abū Bakr, and ʿUthmān, along with the *Kanfāri* or Kurmina-*fari* ʿUmar and the *Askia* Muḥammad, the sources underscore their importance.[42] All of them are initially connected with campaigns, suggesting their primary responsibility was of a military nature. The *Faran* Afumba would later be identified as the Dendi-*fari*, and given his prominence in battle, he may have been second only to the *sunni* in actual power, as he was given command of armies on at least two occasions, on one of which he was assisted by the *hi-koi* (apparently a purely military post at Gao, overseeing the *sunni*'s river fleet). Only he could freely speak his mind in the ruler's presence, a privilege under the Askias that presumably began with or before ʿAlī. The Dendi-*fari* may have been rivaled if not outranked, however, by the Dirma-*koi*, governor of Dirma (south of Lake Fati between the Niger and Bara Rivers), who alone could enter the royal palace still mounted on his steed, or build a two-story residence, honors that before ʿAlī were enjoyed by the *sunni* alone.[43]

In introducing the "Askia" Baghna, *Taʾrīkh al-fattāsh* points out that the title did not originate with *Askia* Muḥammad.[44] Indeed, the epigraphic evidence reveals its use in Gao as early as 631/1234.[45] But *Askia* Baghna is not to be confused with the Baghana/Bāghana-*fari*, governor of the province to the west of the lacustrine region. Though said to be a part of imperial Mali, the Baghana-*fari* is not actually mentioned until the beginning of the tenth/sixteenth century.[46] As for other offices, the Benga-*farma*, governor of Benga (the lacustrine area east of Dirma and Bara) was apparently already in existence by the time of the Sunnis, while the *balma'a*, a military official stationed at Kabara as early as the Malian period, was evidently restored after the Maghsharan Tuareg interregnum, perhaps by *Sunni* 'Alī.[47]

According to al-Sa'dī, indiscriminate conscription was the main apparatus by which the *sunni* raised armies: "regarding the military [*Askia* Muḥammad] made a distinction between civilians and soldiers, as opposed to the situation in the days of the Khārijīte [*Sunni* 'Alī], when everyone had been a soldier."[48] The *sunni* drew heavily from his base of support in the Dendi area, from where he raised at least two "large" armies, the vehicles through which the *sunni* pursued his special brand of terror.[49]

The frontal assault or siege of urban strongholds required supply lines and mobility, and necessitated a cavalry. As the Malian army was cavalry-based, the same was true of imperial Songhay, certainly by the time of 'Alī. Control of the Middle Niger, from Jenne to Gao-Kukiya, was highly dependent on the use of horses and camels, and in addition to the Dirma-*koi*, *Ta'rīkh al-fattāsh* places 'Alī at the head of his cavalry (literally, "on his horse") in pursuit of his various campaigns.[50] Given that a number of his campaigns targeted Azawad, he would have also needed experienced and amenable Tuareg and camels.

While the cavalry and infantry would have included free persons, consideration of shifting social circumstances during *Sunni* 'Alī's reign suggests servile formations were also part of the Songhay military, consistent with their use in imperial Mali. 'Alī entered into unequal relationships with a variety of groups, resulting in widespread subjugation. Many, even most, of the conquered may not correspond to the twenty-four servile groups of *Ta'rīkh al-fattāsh*'s problematic manuscript C, but for those engaged in riverine activity the collective evidence suggests a surprising convergence.

According to this thirteenth/nineteenth-century document, there were several communities whose activities bore some relationship to the military, even if they themselves did not serve as soldiers.[51] It claims that both the "Arbi" from whom young men marched before and after the ruler en route to battle, and the "Jindikita" (or "grass cutters'), responsible for feeding the Malian royal horses, continued in the service of the Sunnis and Askias. It also claims that other groups (the "Jam Tene," the "Jam Wali," the Sorobana," and the "Samashaku") were blacksmiths who supplied the Songhay dynasties (but not the Malians) with lances and arrows.[52]

It is hardly remarkable that communities would provide such services, whether the actual groups specified or others. In fact, the Arbi are actually mentioned in manuscript A, and therefore not a thirteenth/nineteenth-century concoction.[53] More pertinent at this juncture, however, is manuscript C's claims about another group, the so-called Zanjī (pl. Zanājiyya), aspects of which are consistent with what is actually known about the period in question. The "Zanjī" were supposedly owned by the Malian *mansā*, and described in the document as a series of fishing communities located along the Niger River from Kanta in the east to Sibiridugu in the west—that is, from one end of ʿAlī's Songhay to the other. They were required to provide fish and potentially other river creatures for Malian and Songhay rulers, but they were also said to provide another critical service: they built watercraft. One passage reads, "And each time he [the ruler?] came to them in need of boats, he would take from them a boat and crew [*mallāḥīn*, "sailors"]."[54]

Manuscript C's use of the term "Zanjī" is probably of thirteenth/nineteenth-century derivation, since it is often associated with populations from the interior of East Africa's coast, but, more importantly, its use suggests these fishing communities were viewed as autochthonous to the rivers, as the term denotes early if not original inhabitants. The word does not appear in *Ta'rīkh as-sūdān* (nor does the discussion of the twenty-four tribes), but more critical than what these people are called is the service they performed, and in this instance there can be no doubt the word refers to the Sorko and Somono, the fisherfolk.[55] The Sorko are in fact named in *Ta'rīkh al-fattāsh*'s manuscript A, and as they may have built the watercraft that gave the *sunni* an advantage over Jenne, they may have also figured into his vision of a canal connecting Ra's al-Mā' to Walata/Biru.[56] As the *sunni* needed the Sorko to construct watercraft and to watch over successful navigation, they were necessarily incorporated into the naval effort.

These strands come together at the moment when the *sunni* travels to Lulu, south of Dendi, to raise an army. The precise phrase in *Ta'rīkh al-fattāsh* states he "traveled to the river at Lulu," placing the army under the command of the Dendi-*fari* in the presence of the *hi-koi*, the official in charge of the *sunni*'s river fleet.[57] As the term *hi* means "canoe," the Sorko under the *hi-koi* are deeply insinuated in the mobilization.

Amadu Lobbo's dubious claim to the twenty-four tribes is not the issue here. Rather, it is recognition that for ʿAlī to succeed, he needed smiths, fishers, boat-builders, etc. The precise nature of these relations is unclear, but by all accounts, *Sunni* ʿAlī was a violent force of nature, readily resorting to coercion when deemed necessary.[58]

The Fulbe and Slavery under 'Alī

The question of servile military formations obviously connects to the issue of slavery in Songhay, a full theorization of which awaits an evidentiary base only provided during the reign of *Askia* Dāwūd (chapter 13). The institution emerges at this junction, however, in such sources as *Askia* Muḥammad's correspondence, which makes clear the institution was robust under 'Alī, who had "amassed wealth and slaves [*khuddām*] from diverse sources."[59] The "amassing" was apparently no exaggeration, as the *askia* referred to "thousands of men and women" in the royal entourage, either accompanying 'Alī or living on royal grounds. These would have included free persons, but given what follows, the enslaved would have been well represented.[60]

Specific references to slavery during the period of *Sunni* 'Alī are actually rare, and when mentioned are presented as normative. 'Alī was in perpetual campaign mode, and though death and destruction are usually provided as the end results, many captives were taken. In charging *Sunni* 'Alī with seizing free Muslims and dispersing them as gifts, *Ta'rīkh al-fattāsh* seems to refer to the Fulani women, though *Askia* Muḥammad alleges 'Alī "seized property, took captive free women (*ṣabā man al-ḥarīm*) and sold free men (*bā'a man al-iḥrār*) to an extent that cannot be measured."[61] Even so, the *askia*'s complaint may largely pertain to the Fulbe, as they are the only group actually singled out for captivity, and the only captive group whose relocation to Gao is chronicled.[62] The origins of the Kurtey, descendants of Fulbe mixed with Sorko in the Tillabery archipelago and along the banks of the Niger (between what is now Niamey and Say), could trace to this period.[63]

In sum, the sources treat slavery in Songhay under *Sunni* 'Alī as unremarkable. When slaves are specifically mentioned, it is in the capacity of concubines and menials. The latter's widespread exploitation can safely be assumed, as they no doubt were among *Sunni* 'Alī's reportedly large retinue, and are incidentally mentioned in hagiographies, including that of *Sīdī* Yaḥyā al-Tādalisī, whose "slave girls" (*juwārī*, probably *ḥuwārī*) tried to prepare fresh fish for him one day, cooking from morning to nightfall, only to later learn the *Sīdī*'s foot had accidently brushed against the fish, rendering the fish impervious to fire.[64]

The importation of such groups as the Fulbe into Songhay territory, where they would inhabit various statuses, as well as the integration of the Sorko into Songhay's military, convey broader implications, including certain transformations within Songhay society. While these began with

Sunni ʿAlī, they reached a more definitive stage under the Askias, when a more thoroughgoing analysis of slavery can be provided.

Excavating the Mori Koyra

In discussing the *Sunni* dynasty and its turbulent relations with Timbuktu scholars, the secondary literature neglects other developments in Islam that were quite significant. As mentioned, *Mansā* Mūsā's indigenization project promoted the formation of an Islamically-educated West African elite who could reinforce the Keita dynasty and redirect religious power and influence from expatriate authorities. There is every indication that Mūsā's effort was a resounding success, though it would eventually be decoupled from its political agenda as regional power shifted to Gao under *Sunni* ʿAlī some 127 years later. West African scholars and saints from the southern Sahel would continue to emerge, but now complemented by those from the Sahelian north.

One of the communities from the southern Sahel figuring prominently in Songhay under the Sunnis, potentially constituting a remarkable link to the pioneering efforts of *Mansā* Mūsā, was that of the Mori Koyra (or Mōri Koïra), a Songhay-Mande conjunction meaning "village of the saints."[65] As demonstrated in chapter 11, though introduced in the sources as a single town, the broader evidence invites an understanding of the Mori Koyra as a community of learned individuals from multiple Inland Delta locales. *Ta'rīkh al-fattāsh* makes a qualified assertion regarding their origins, stating that the Sunnis, the Askias, and the people of Mori Koyra were all descendent from "Yara," from where also migrated Wangāra and Wa'akore families, thus identifying the Mori Koyra as a Mande people.[66] In making the association between the Sunnis, the Askias, the Mori Koyra, and the Wangāra (or Jula), *Ta'rīkh al-fattāsh* shrewdly insinuates a connection between the glories of early Ghana and subsequent Songhay, consistent with its overall agenda.

Mōri Hawgāru is said to have been Mori Koyra's progenitor, notwithstanding more ancestral ties to Kaniaga. While not mentioned in *Ta'rīkh as-sūdān*, *Mōri* Hawgāru makes a number of appearances in *Ta'rīkh al-fattāsh* as a *faqīh*, and as the great-grandfather of *Mōri* al-Ṣādiq, who along with *Mōri* Jayba inveighed against *Sunni* ʿAlī and were rescued from exile by ʿAlī's own forces the day after his death.[67] This would suggest *Mōri* Hawgāru was active in the late eighth/fourteenth and/or early ninth/fifteenth-centuries.[68] Revered as a saint, *Mōri* Hawgāru's tomb in legendary Yara was once a site of intercessory prayer.[69]

The Mori Koyra will again feature, but their connection with *Mōri* Hawgāru and Kabora (Kābara), focus of *Mansā* Mūsā's project, could have been in the person of *Mōri* Magha (Maghan) Kankoi.[70] Described as a *faqīh*, a scholar (*ʿālim*), and a saint, he is said to have come from the village of Tayu.[71] *Mōri* Magha Kankoi would study in Kabora, and if he had no direct connection to the Mori Koyra, the fact that he studied in Kabora means the village remained an active site of Islamic formation well into the middle of the ninth/fifteenth century, when *Mōri* Magha Kankoi arrived in Jenne. He would emerge as an important figure in the reign of *Askia* Mūsā (935–37/1529–31), his imprecations against the *askia* understood as a major reason for the latter's abbreviated tenure and violent end. By extension, the subsequent mistreatment of the Mori Koyra community was believed to be a leading reason for the fall of Songhay itself.[72] The Mori Koyra community therefore emerges as a source of potent spiritual power. More than one hundred years after *Mansā* Mūsā's death, his investment continued paying dividends.

And it was to Jenne, not Timbuktu that *Mōri* Magha Kankoi relocated. There he developed a sizable following and was in perpetual teaching mode, holding classes in the congregational mosque from the middle of the night until the morning prayer, from the morning prayer until noon, and again after the midday prayer to the mid-afternoon prayer. He developed a reputation not only for erudition and piety, but for strict discipline, so much so that in overhearing someone next to him pray, "Oh God, *Mōri* Magha Kankoi has made matters difficult for us in this land; take him away from us," he immediately left Jenne and settled in Jinjo (on Lake Debo's northern edge), after spending an unspecified period in Kona (Kūnā), suggesting he interpreted the lament as widely shared within Jenne.[73] The *mōri* relocated to Jinjo during the reign of *Sunni* ʿAlī, and as was true of *Mōri* Hawgāru, his tomb became a site of veneration.

A contemporary of *Mōri* Magha Kankoi also associated with Jenne was Fūdiye *al-faqīh* Muḥammad Sānū al-Wangarī, a jurist, scholar, and saint, whose *nisba* relates his Mande, perhaps Jula/Maraka origins. Settling in Tura village, apparently near Jenne, he regularly attended Friday mosque in the latter until "one of the *sulṭān*'s chief officers (*kubarā' sulṭān*)" dreamed he was Jenne's protector.[74] This suggests al-Wangarī was frequenting Jenne just before *Sunni* ʿAlī captured it, as the text's language implies an immediacy between the revelation and the sultan's destruction and rebuilding of a structure previously dedicated to a local deity as the saint's residence. Though accepting the new abode, al-Wangarī steadfastly refused to visit Jenne's sultan until an apparently innocent man on the verge of execution pleaded for his intervention. The sultan granted clemency on condition the saint share a meal with him, but the holy man's hand swelled upon touching the ruler's food. Others would emulate this early, apolitical posture.

Al-Wangarī's life spanned the period before *Sunni* 'Alī's takeover of Jenne to that of *Askia al-ḥājj* Muḥammad, who appointed him *qāḍī* of Jenne after the *askia*'s return from the Pilgrimage and upon the recommendation of Maḥmūd b. 'Umar b. Muḥammad Aqīt, who in visiting Jenne was most impressed with him. His elevation to *qāḍī* initiated a new era in Islam in Jenne, as the position apparently did not previously exist there. Al-Wangarī is said to have been the first to adjudicate according to *sharī'a*, and that prior to his appointment, the "blacks" (*as-sūdān*) had their legal disputes settled by a *khaṭīb* (the Friday mosque speaker or preacher), while the "whites" (*al-bayḍān*) went to *qāḍīs*. As was true of *Mōri* Hawgāru and *Mōri* Magha Kankoi, al-Wangarī's burial site in the congregational mosque's courtyard became a site of veneration and source of *baraka*.[75]

Southern Sahelian scholars were not only in Jenne, but in Timbuktu as well. The ninth/fifteenth century *Sīdī* 'Abd al-Raḥmān al-Tamīmī studied in Fez in emulation of the numerous "Sūdānese *fuqahā'* [jurists]" in Timbuktu, and one of his exemplars was the jurist Kātib Mūsā, last of the "Sudanese" *imāms* of the Great Mosque of Timbuktu, whose service of forty years saw the transition from Malian to Tuareg rule.[76] Kātib Mūsā had been one those who studied in Fez "by order of the just *sulṭān al-ḥājj* Mūsā," and he was succeeded as *imām* by 'Abdallāh al-Balbālī, the al-Sa'dī ancestor who married 'Ā'isha al-Fulāniya, and for whom the *sunni* had great respect.[77]

Yet another "Sudanese" luminary who would have left an indelible impression upon al-Tamīmī was the *qāḍī* of Timbuktu, the *shaykh* and *faqīh* and holy "friend of God" (*walī*) Abū 'Abd Allāh *Modibo* Muḥammad al-Kāborī, who arrived in Timbuktu in the middle of the ninth/fifteenth century. Examples of his elevated piety include walking on water, and it was asserted he had reached the ultimate registers of knowledge.[78] *Modibo* Muḥammad al-Kāborī was a crucial link between scholars under Malian rule and their subsequent transformation under imperial Songhay, as he led a community at a time when Timbuktu was replete with "Sūdānese students, people of the west"—most likely a reference to Masina, the location of Kabora (Kābara), consistent with *Modibo* Muḥammad's *nisba*. The *qāḍī* was therefore the embodiment and living expression of a policy initiated a hundred years earlier that focused on Kabora, and as a teacher of progenitors from whom subsequent leaders would emerge, he was both foundation and bridge for all that would transpire in Songhay's ensuing history.[79]

Modibo Muḥammad al-Kāborī would have been a successor (though perhaps not directly) of *al-Qāḍī* al-Ḥājj as *qāḍī* of Timbuktu.[80] If *Modibo* Muḥammad al-Kāborī never actually met al-Ḥājj, he certainly knew the founders of other leading clerical families in Timbuktu. For example, he taught *Sīdī* Yaḥyā al-Tādalisī as well as ʻUmar b. Muḥammad Aqīt—he was their *shaykh*.[81] He was also the contemporary of *Sīdī* ʻAbd al-Raḥmān al-Tamīmī and Abū ʻAbd Allāh Anda ag-Muḥammad the Elder. All of these associations are significant, because the next generation of religious leaders in Timbuktu in large measure descended from these men. Al-Tamīmī was the grandfather of *Qāḍī* Ḥabīb, a future luminary, whereas Abū ʻAbd Allāh Anda ag-Muḥammad the Elder and ʻUmar b. Muḥammad Aqīt were the grandfather and father, respectively, of Maḥmūd b. Umar b. Muḥammad Aqīt, the city's future *qāḍī*. They were all closely connected via familial, marital, and spiritual ties, enjoying mutual bonds of admiration, with *Sīdī* Yaḥyā al-Tādalisī admonishing his students to follow al-Tamīmī's example of studying in Fez.

Muḥammad Aqīt and Commerce in Timbutku

As was true of *Modibo* Muḥammad al-Kāborī, *Sīdī* Yaḥyā al-Tādalisī arrived in Timbuktu during the reign of the Tuareg and died in 866/1461–62.[82] He therefore may have witnessed the coming of Muḥammad Aqīt, ʻUmar's father, who settled his family in Timbuktu during the time of the Tuareg ruler Akil. Muḥammad Aqīt's individual story is suggestive, to say the least. According to al-Sa'dī (and based on Aḥmad Bābā), he was living in Masina when, motivated by his "hatred of the Fulani living nearby," he left for Walata/Biru, suggesting an interest in trade.[83] There are no details of what else may have transpired either in Masina or Walata/Biru to affect Muḥammad Aqīt, but al-Sa'dī's observation that Timbuktu's commercial rise "brought about the ruin of Bīru" more than hints at Muḥammad Aqīt's commercial motivation in relocating to Timbuktu.[84]

It is the account of what happens on the way to Timbuktu that holds fascination. Halting midway between Timbuktu and Ra's al-Mā', Muḥammad Aqīt needed the intervention of the grandfather of Masire Anda ʻUmar (a future prominent jurist) to gain entrance into the city. Akil had initially responded to the grandfather's pleas by emerging from a tent to display a shield shattered by spear and sword: "'Look at what Muḥammad Aqīt has done to me: How can one settle a quarrel in his land with an enemy who has done such a thing'?" The grandfather explained Muḥammad Aqīt had changed, and had "'become tranquil and has dependents, and only wants a quiet life'." Akil would yield to further entreaty.

This exchange reveals Muḥammad Aqīt was no stranger to Akil, that they had previously met in a circumstance of conflict, if not combat. Though the confrontation could have been over anything, the Tuareg sultan clearly saw Muḥammad Aqīt as a threat, which also suggests that, since he was acquainted with weapons, Muḥammad Aqīt had not been unaccompanied. This time, only family and (surely) servants were with him.

This early incident casts a very different light on the Aqīts. Muḥammad Aqīt was no scholar; Aḥmad Bābā, a descendant of Muḥammad Aqīt, states that it was Abū 'Abd Allāh Anda ag-Muḥammad the Elder, another of his ancestors, who was the first in his lineage to pursue erudition.[85] If his confrontation with Akil was a contest over the control of Timbuktu, the subsequent history of the Aqīts takes on a more intriguing quality, as their phenomenal clerical rise could have realized a similar objective. The period of Tuareg domination was therefore formative, with the al-Ḥājj, Aqīt, and Anda ag-Muḥammad families forging alliances through marriage and religious endeavor, providing the basis for a new source of power. This would have been more than apparent to *Sunni* 'Alī.

Abū 'Abd Allāh Anda ag-Muḥammad the Elder served as Timbuktu's *qāḍī* under the Tuareg, which means he enjoyed their confidence.[86] It would appear his entire family followed suit, with impressive results. Presumably listed in order of preeminence are two sons—al-Mukhtār al-Naḥwī ("the Grammarian") and 'Abd al-Raḥmān—and two grandsons, *al-faqīh* Abū 'l-'Abbas Aḥmad Buryu ("the Handsome") b. Aḥmad, and Abū 'Abd Allāh Anda ag-Muḥammad b. al-Mukhtār al-Naḥwī. Al-Sa'dī states that in spite of his physical attractiveness, Abū 'l-'Abbas Aḥmad Buryu "sought little of this world while humbling himself before God Most High," becoming a highly-regarded teacher, whereas Abū 'Abd Allāh Anda ag-Muḥammad would become *imām* of Sankore mosque. A great-grandson, al-Mukhtār b. Muḥammad b. al-Mukhtār al-Naḥwī, is also listed as both a jurist and eulogist of the Prophet. These accomplishments would of course take place during the Askia dynasty, but are mentioned here to underscore the preeminence and longevity of the Anda ag-Muḥammad lineage. There are many more.[87]

Anda ag-Muḥammad the Elder's son al-Mukhtār al-Naḥwī is described as not only a grammarian but also "a scholar in all branches of learning," the same al-Mukhtār who returned to Timbuktu with his nephew Maḥmūd b. 'Umar during *Sunni* 'Alī's reign. Though he traveled with Maḥmūd, he and Anda ag-Muḥammad the Elder provided instruction to Maḥmūd's brother Aḥmad, who later made *ḥajj*.[88] As mentioned, al-Mukhtār al-Naḥwī's brothers Aḥmad and Maḥmūd were put to death by the *sunni*. In addition to being the father of Abū 'l-'Abbas Aḥmad Buryu, Aḥmad was the grandfather of Abū Muḥammad 'Abd Allāh, said to have been an unassuming "*muftī*, grammarian, and lexicologist, renowned in his day for his knowledge of the Qur'ān."[89] As for his brother Maḥmūd, he was the grandfather of Abū 'l-'Abbas Aḥmad b. Anda ag-Muḥammad, also learned in "a variety of knowledge" that included grammar and poetry.

Al-Sa'dī observes that the sons of 'Umar b. Muḥammad Aqīt—'Abd Allāh, Aḥmad, and Maḥmūd—were the (maternal) grandsons (*asbāṭ*) of Anda ag-Muḥammad. Sita is mentioned as the mother of Maḥmūd alone, which suggests there was at least one other, unnamed sister involved in this process. These sisters, daughters of Anda ag-Muḥammad, would marry 'Umar b. Muḥammad Aqīt, and Aḥmad Bābā states 'Umar was a "learned and righteous jurist," having studied under *Modibo* Muḥammad al-Kaborī.[90]

There is some evidence for the scholar-entrepreneur during this period, and surprisingly it comes from the illustrious and divine *quṭb* ("pole"), *Shaykh Sīdī* Yaḥyā al-Tādalisī, concerning whom Abū Zayd 'Abd al-Raḥmān b. *al-Qāḍī* (of Timbuktu) Maḥmūd b. 'Umar declared it incumbent upon believers to visit his tomb every day to benefit from his *baraka*. Since the beginning of his career, al-Tādalisī had seen the Prophet every night in a dream, but toward the end of his life the visits began to taper off to once a week, then once a month, then once a year. Asked the reason he surmised, "I believe it simply has to do with my preoccupation with business," but he continued in it because he "did not want to be dependent on people."[91] Al-Tādalisī's participation in both scholarship and commerce was hardly unusual, and was bracketed by the same practice on the part of Khārijī and 'Ibāḍī communities in Awdaghust and Sijilmasa in the fourth/tenth century; by expatriates to sixth/twelfth century Ghana, about whom al-Sharīshī wrote, "Islam has spread among its inhabitants and there are schools there [with] many merchants from the Maghrib"; and by the Kunta *shaykhs* north of Timbuktu, as well as other merchant-scholar families who continued to dominate commerce in those same regions well into the thirteenth/nineteenth century.[92] Rather than establish a precedent, al-Tādalisī followed a trajectory that may explain Muḥammad Aqīt's move to Timbuktu.

Inspired by Mali's assimilation of multiple urban centers, *Sunni* 'Alī ventured far beyond the traditional parameters of Gao-Kukiya, wresting control over the entire middle Niger valley through military conquest. Practicing a ruthlessness possibly unparalleled in the region, his relentless campaigning resulted in a surge of captives as well as a more effective integration of servile communities into his war machine. He would remain in power some twenty-eight years, testifying to his abilities of intimidation.

While impressive, *Sunni* 'Alī's accomplishments relative to those of *Mansā* Mūsā qualify him as a regionalist. He neither made nor attempted to make the Pilgrimage, and if he maintained diplomatic relations with powers in either the Maghrib or Egypt, the records are silent. For all of his territorial expansion, it came at a time when European maritime ventures would ultimately place West Africa in a decidedly disadvantaged position. By 875/1471, just a few years after *Sunni* 'Alī came to power, the Portuguese had reached São Tomé and Principe and Elmina; by 886/1482, with 'Alī preoccupied with the Mossi, the Portuguese were exploring the Congo River.

But it was neither the threat of regional foes nor a gradually gathering storm along the West African littoral that led to *Sunni* 'Alī's undoing. Rather, it was the transition of spiritually-premised power from established locals to the more recently indigenized. There were at least two simultaneous processes, moving in opposite trajectories, unfolding in the urban west of imperial Songhay from the period of the Maghsharan Tuareg through the end of *Sunni* 'Alī's reign: the maturation of the "Sudanese" scholarly ranks as initiated by *Mansā* Mūsā, most impressively represented by the Mori Koyra, and the rise of a new cynosure of spiritual and political power, specifically in Timbuktu and located within the intertwined families of Masūfa and Ṣanhāja immigrants, who would come to call Timbuktu home. The former would facilitate the latter, and by various means the *sunni* sought to debilitate their power, but his embrace of violence had its limits. A remnant would remain, and would identify a champion to take up their cause. Given 'Alī's fate, the irony (from the *sunni's* perspective) is that he was not ruthless enough.

CHAPTER TEN

Renaissance: The Age of *Askia Al-Ḥājj* Muḥammad

THE ASKIA DYNASTY represents the return of a cosmopolitanism absent from the region since *Mansā* Mūsā. Like the Malian achievement more than one hundred years earlier, Songhay's internationalism would emphasize cities, nurtured and sustained by ongoing transregional commerce, combined with social experimentation and the privileging of Islamic cultural practices. While this sense of heightened West African urbanity is certainly a function of the sources' focus, it yet qualifies as distinctive for place and period.

The concept of "renaissance" under Muḥammad Ture is appropriate not only for the manner in which urbanity was emphasized and supported by state policies, but also by reconnections with polities and luminaries in the central Islamic lands. As will be seen, the restoration of ties regaled as indispensable insignia under *Mansā* Mūsā once again become emblematic of the state under Muḥammad Ture, and as such constitutes a dramatic rejection of *Sunni* 'Alī's policies. Indeed, it is striking that in a reign spanning some thirty years, virtually nothing is recorded of foreign diplomacy under *Sunni* 'Alī, his activities vaguely and briefly mentioned by chroniclers in Egypt. In contrast, *Askia* Muḥammad inaugurates a new era of diplomacy, reinvigorating relations with the centers of the Muslim world.

Askia Muḥammad's investment in cultivating foreign relations was to some extent a consequence of resettling leading clerical families in Timbuktu previously targeted by *Sunni* 'Alī. But connections with notables in Egypt and the Arabian Peninsula were also critical to the *askia*'s claim to power, as his ascendance constituted its usurpation. Association with clerical communities in Timbuktu and Jenne was insufficient to assuage concerns in Gao, the ancient political capital of Songhay, as well as in the Dendi region, its traditional source of support. *Askia* Muḥammad therefore borrowed a page from *Mansā* Mūsā's book, and though his own Pilgrimage is a far cry from the *mansā*'s at levels of opulence and spectacle, he succeeded in mimicking its essentials.

Askia Muḥammad would reign some thirty-six years, from 898/1493 to 935/1529, longer than Sunjata (twenty-six years), *Mansā* Mūsā (twenty-five years), or *Sunni* 'Alī (twenty-seven to twenty-eight years). Originally affixed to clerical and commercial interests, the *askia*'s arrogation of power would encourage a review of those relations, leading to a series of challenges to Timbuktu and Jenne's self-promotion as bastions of autonomy and self-regulation. The *askia's* policies are therefore not unlike those of *Mansā* Mūsā, who paired internationalism with indigenization. These challenges would endure throughout Songhay's existence, and require rethinking Timbuktu exceptionality.

Notwithstanding difficulties, Songhay's cosmopolitanism reached a height of sophistication never before witnessed in the region. More specifically, it is with Songhay that a variety of ethnicities—Songhay, Hal Pulaaren, Mande-speakers, Kel Tamasheq, etc.—undergo a process through which their allegiance to the state begins to supersede group loyalties, resulting in the formation of a new political identity. As opposed to the Soninke of Ghana—or Mande-centered Mali, whose peripheral inclusion of others, such as the Wolof and Fulbe along the Senegal, and the Songhay in the eastern Niger buckle, did not affect its political core—Songhay represents a novel political project that reified the state while seeking the full incorporation of its constitutive parts. As an experiment in pluralism it was unprecedented.

Like *Mansā* Mūsā, *Askia* Muḥammad would embark upon a campaign of significant territorial expansion, extending well into the northern Sahel, while evincing substantial interest in the Hausa city-states to the east. With the Niger buckle having been secured under *Sunni* 'Alī, the *askia* pursued a northward projection to realize a greater share of trans-Saharan commerce. At its height, the realm would cover more than 1.4 million square kilometers (500,000 square miles), its principal urban centers of Gao, Timbuktu, and Jenne potentially boasting populations of 100,000, 80,000, and 40,000, respectively.[1] Notwithstanding his accomplishments, Songhay would be slowly circumscribed by breathtaking transformations on a global scale, so that a different outcome in struggles with the Hausa would not have significantly altered the region's future trajectories.

Revolt of the Tondi-farma

Following the mysterious death of *Sunni* 'Alī's on 15 Muḥarram 898/6 November 1492, his son Abū Bakr Dā'u, also known as Bāru (an apparent contraction of Bakr Dā'u) was declared *sunni.*[2] *Ta'rīkh al-fattāsh* provides 2 Rabī II 898/20 January 1493 as the date of his taking power, consistent with the notion that it was swift and relatively unencumbered, as one month later he was under heavy assault by the pretender Muḥammad Ture, 'Alī's Tondi-*farma*. 'Alī's sons would replace his entrails with honey to combat putrification.

According to *Ta'rīkh as-sūdān*, 'Alī's army struck camp at Ba'aniyya following his demise, whereas *Ta'rīkh al-fattāsh* states it was the army that declared Bāru the next *sunni*. That both *ta'rīkhs* (*tawārīkh*) mention the army underscores it had assumed a critical role in determining the succession.[3] But the army may have been divided at this juncture, for in less than one month the Tondi-*farma* attacked *Sunni* Bāru with lethal force. While *Ta'rīkh al-fattāsh* does not address his reasons, al-Sa'dī says that upon learning of 'Alī's death, the Tondi-*farma* "kept to himself [his desire to] to succeed, attending to his ambition in many details, and when he had finished bringing together the various strands of his scheme," he took action.[4] One "detail" very likely consisted of collusion with exiled clerical families, a negotiation that could have started before Bāru was named the next *sunni*.

The Tondi-*farma*'s offensive against *Sunni* Bāru saw two major battles, the first at Danagha on 14 Jumādā 'l-Awlā 898/8 February 1493, resulting in the latter's defeat and retreat to Anku'u near Gao; and then on the 14 or 24 of Jumādā 'l-Thāniya 898/2 or 12 of April 1493, which according to both *ta'rīkhs* was epic in scope. Al-Sa'dī says "the combat was intense, the bloodletting so great (*ḥarb shadīd wa qitāl 'athīm*), and the fighting so horrific that [the two armies] were on the verge of annihilating each other." *Ta'rīkh al-fattāsh* provides a very similar description: "The combat was intense, the bloodletting so great (*ḥarb shadīd wa qitāl 'athīm*) that everyone believed ruin had befallen them."[5] One of the authors (most likely al-Sa'dī) had clearly read the other.[6]

The indeterminate struggle ends with "God granting victory" to "the most felicitous and well-guided" Muḥammad Ture, and *Sunni* Bāru fleeing to either Ayan/Ayar (plausibly Air) or the more likely destination of Dia/Diagha, where he remained in exile. Songhay traditions also present the encounter as a victory for Islam, in which *Sunni* Bāru refuses to turn away from ancestral religion, igniting Muḥammad Ture's response.[7] Dendi-*fari*

Afumba remained loyal to Bāru, and was probably the force behind the army declaring him *sunni*. However, his fate following Bāru's defeat is unclear, as *Ta'rīkh al-fattāsh*, after lauding his courage, goes on to say he flung himself into the Niger and drowned. *Notice historique*, identifying him (apparently mistakenly) as the Bara-*koi*, provides a different account, stating he was able to harass Muḥammad Ture's troops with exacting nocturnal raids until his capture and execution.[8] Whatever his precise end, his opposition to Muḥammad Ture signaled a serious problem, as Afumba was governor of Dendi. Muḥammad Ture would have to go to great lengths to overcome the misgivings of the region, but such weakness at the historical core of Songhay power would contribute to difficulties, including Songhay's defeat at the hands of Morocco one hundred years later.

The war against *Sunni* Bāru reveals some of the "details" and "various strands" of Muḥammad Ture's probable conspiracy, with *Ta'rīkh al-fattāsh* stating that at the decisive second battle, and in contrast to Afumba's support of *Sunni* Bāru, "the *Askia* Muḥammad had with him the Bara-*koi* *Mansā* Kūra, but not one of the other rulers of Takrūr or Songhay was with him; no one else responded to his call other than [*Mansā* Kūra]."[9] Bara province was north of Lake Debo, and its governor's support suggests Muḥammad Ture had cultivated a relationship with him as Tondi-*farma*. But the passage also unveils that the Tondi-*farma* had failed in soliciting additional support for his cause.

Ta'rīkh al-fattāsh's discredited manuscript C provides an account of the encounter between the Tondi-*farma* and *Sunni* Bāru that, at least in part, is consistent with its more reliable manuscripts while offering potentially very useful information. It states that the *sunni* had over ten "ministers" (*wuzarā'*) with him, and that in contrast to the Bara-*koi*, all remained loyal to the *sunni*, including the Taratan-*koi*, the Dirma-*koi*, the Bani-*koi*, the Kara/Kala-*koi*, and the Jenne-*koi*. The location of Taratan is unclear, though likely in the vicinity of Dirma (to the north of Bara along the Niger), Bani (between the Bani and Niger Rivers to the south of Jenne), and Kala (along the Niger from Sansanding in the south to Dia/Diagha). These provinces (including Bara) were contiguous, extending from (what is now) Sansanding to just south of Timbuktu, so that Bara was alone in its support of the Tondi-*farma*. Indeed, this portion of manuscript C is entirely plausible and could represent an inherited tradition as opposed to one wholly fabricated in the thirteenth/nineteenth century. In describing the Bara-*koi* as an old man with ten children it may reflect an unintended moment of candor in the conflict's collective account, suggesting he was either liberated in his thinking or not thinking very clearly.[10]

Five years following the fifth pogrom against Timbuktu *'ulamā'*, 'Alī was dead and Bāru defeated. Muḥammad Ture had successfully seized power, establishing the Askia dynasty, with the likelihood that intrigue connects all of these events quite high. Consideration of the brevity of time between *Sunni* 'Alī's death (15 Muḥarram 898/6 November 1492), *Sunni* Bāru's succession (2 Rabī II 898/20 January 1493), and the commencement of hostilities with the Tondi-*farma* (14 Jumādā 'l-Awlā 898/18 February 1493)—some three months—only heightens suspicion. But the revelation that the Tondi-*farma* canvassed widely in the effort to overthrow *Sunni* Bāru, given the distances involved, the time it would take to travel those distances, and that potential allies would need time to weigh their options strongly intimates the two months between *Sunni* Bāru's succession and the outbreak of hostilities were insufficient to accomplish it all.[11] Rather, the short, three-month span between *Sunni* 'Alī's demise and *Askia* Muḥammad's ascension suggests plans were in the works prior to 'Alī's death, with the Tondi-*farma* nursing his ambitions and "keeping to himself [his desire to] succeed" long before 15 Muḥarram 898/6 November 1492.

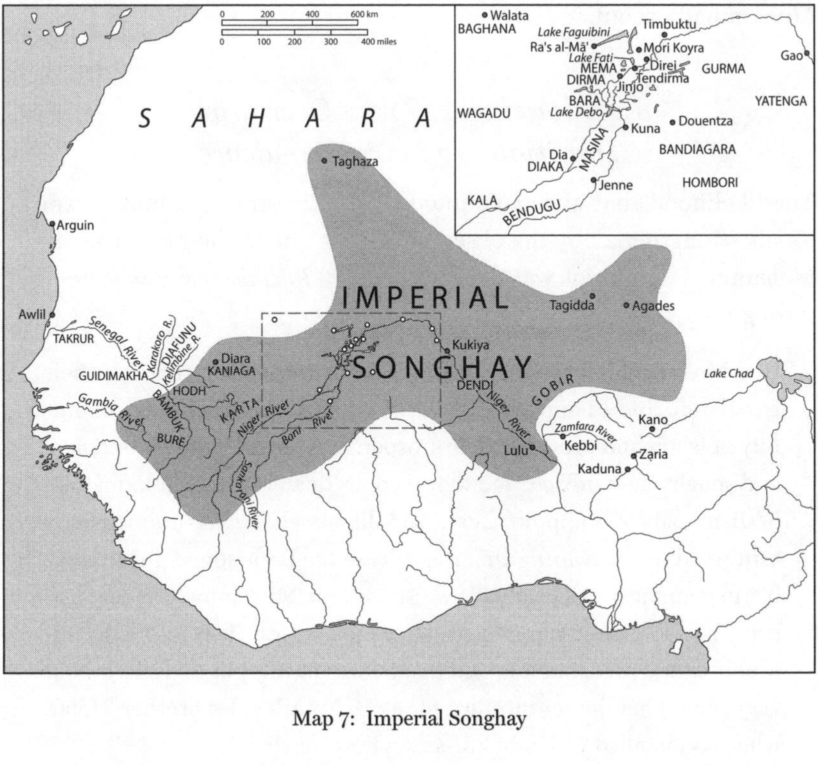

Map 7: Imperial Songhay

It is instructive that both *Sunni* 'Alī and Dendi-*fari* Afumba (at least in one account) died through the agency of a river—the former an "act of God," the latter of his own volition. These drownings may euphemistically represent assassination, but given the characterization of *Sunni* 'Alī as a godless and tyrannical butcher, it is not obvious why the sources would not be forthright. However, the fact that the Tondi-*farma* did not enjoy the support of the vast majority of Songhay's governors and generals indicates that, whether resulting from intimidation or the distribution of spoils, or a combination thereof, the Sunni dynasty commanded loyalty. Openly celebrating the Tondi-*farma*'s role in 'Alī's assassination would have been unacceptable, not only to high officials but to constituencies in Gao and its base in Dendi, and as Afumba was the Dendi-*fari*, the circumstances of his demise may also reflect an attempt to avoid antagonism. As such, Muḥammad Ture's overthrow of Bāru would have been less unsavory than the assassination of his father, who despite his faults was a living legend. The emphasis on Bāru's defeat therefore redirects attention from 'Alī's ignominious fate, while drawing attention to Muḥammad Ture's military prowess. The transition was nonetheless messy, and would continue as a problem well into *Askia* Muḥammad's reign.

Legitimizing a Violent Overthrow: Traditions and Correspondence

The likelihood that exiled Timbuktu *'ulamā'* were principal conspirators is strengthened by the observation that one of the first tasks *Askia* Muḥammad undertook was their restoration. *Ta'rīkh as-sūdān* states that through the *askia*

> God Most High relieved the Muslims of their grief, and removed their tribulation and calamity. (The *askia*) strove to establish the community of Islam and promote their prosperity. He befriended the scholars and sought their advice, and they were intimately involved in matters of dismissals and appointments and dismissals. . . . He immediately sent word to the *Khaṭīb* 'Umar to release the imprisoned al-Mukhtār b. Muḥammad-n-Allāh (that is, al-Mukhtār b. Muḥammad Naḍḍa) and bring him so that he could be reinstated in his post. He was told that al-Mukhtār had died, but it is said that he was hastily put to death at that very time. Then he sent to Biru for al-Mukhtār's elder brother 'Umar, who was installed as Timbuktu-*koi* in his place.[12]

This remarkable passage establishes three independent yet closely related decisions: the return of the beleaguered clerical community to positions of privilege, consultations over the articulation of a new administrative regime, and the decision to reinstate in municipal authority a family with whom the clerics were familiar. Al-Mukhtār b. Muḥammad Naḍḍa is the same person imprisoned by *Sunni* 'Alī in 891/1486, the year following Aḥmad b. 'Umar's *ḥajj* and approximately two years before the fifth purge of Timbuktu. His elder brother 'Umar was the same 'Umar who had fled from *Sunni* 'Alī upon the latter's approach to Timbuktu in 873/1469. The clerical community therefore sought to restore all that had obtained prior to the *sunni*, and *Askia* Muḥammad was eager to accommodate. However, the relationship with Timbuktu would grow complicated.

With the recovery of Timbuktu underway, the *askia* quickly turned to securing the western interlacustrine region. This was a critical matter since, with the exception of the Bara-*koi*, all of its governors had given their allegiance to *Sunni* Bāru. Jenne, previously in support of *Sunni* Bāru, had already submitted to the *askia* upon his ascension, but the region as a whole needed to be secured.[13] Therefore, in 899/1494—his second year in power—Muḥammad sent his brother 'Umar to defeat Dia/Diagha (strengthening the probability that *Sunni* Bāru had taken refuge there). 'Umar's victory at Dia/Diagha was of such magnitude that he would become as 'Umar Kumadiagha, "'Umar, the conqueror of Diagha [Diakha]."[14]

But 'Umar was not sent into the western region simply to deliver a surgical strike, but rather to reconfigure the region's governance. This led to the most important political innovation in imperial Songhay's history: the creation of the office of *kanfāri* (or Kan-*fari* or Kurmina-*fari*), first occupied by 'Umar and located in Tendirma, within Dirma province. The *kanfāri* differed from the Dirma-*koi* in that the latter was a provincial governor, while the former was responsible for the whole of the empire's western half.

Ta'rīkh as-sūdān does not provide any context for the office's creation and evolution, simply introducing 'Umar as the Kurmina-*fari* in mentioning the defeat of Dia/Diagha. Ironically, it is (again) manuscript C of *Ta'rīkh al-fattāsh* that contains such context, and when divested of references to subaltern communities, is again consistent with other testimony. In this instance, it asserts that in 900/1494–95 (a year later than recorded in *Ta'rīkh as-sūdān*) the *askia* created the office of the *kanfāri* and placed in it his brother 'Umar, who two years later built the village of Tendirma to serve as the western regional capital. 'Umar identified Tendirma as the site after a long search throughout the lacustrine area, with the text claiming it was once a Jewish settlement that, by the time of ʿUmar's arrival, had become the home of a single Sorko named "Tendi."[15] Whatever the verities, Tendirma became an indispensable administrative center of stabilization as well as expansion.

The return of the *ʿulamā'* to Timbuktu and establishment of the *kanfāri* at Tendirma were critical steps reinforcing the new regime, but the very fact that it was new, that it represented rupture, meant that as a usurper *Askia* Muḥammad faced significant opposition in various sectors. In addition to his failure to win support from Songhay governors and military leaders in his campaign against Bāru, there was also resistance among surviving Sunni royals. The latter is evident in the response of *Sunni* ʿAlī's daughters (and therefore Bāru's sisters) to learning of Muḥammad Ture's claim to the throne after defeating *Sunni* Bāru, declaiming: "'Askīyā'," which *Ta'rīkh as-sūdān* translates to mean, "It is not his" (*lā yakūna ʿiyāhu*). Apparently amused, Muḥammad is said to have responded by embracing the designation.[16] As discussed, however, the adoption of the title confirms its evolution from at least 631/1234.[17]

At the same time, oral sources generated in the eastern Niger buckle reveal a different, though not necessarily incongruent understanding of circumstances at the beginning of the Askia dynasty.[18] More specifically, there are symmetries between the Sunni-Askia conflict and stories of Mamar (or Māmar), son of the *sunni* character's sister (*tūba* or *weyma-ije/ize*, "sister's child"). A point of convergence between the oral account and *Ta'rīkh as-sūdān* is the former's identifying Kasay as the sister of the *sunni* figure and mother of the child, the name of *Askia* Muḥammad's mother in the latter. According to the former, diviners warn the *sunni* that his sister's son would become his rival and replace him, to which the *sunni* responds by killing all sons of his sisters save Mamar, who survives by being switched with the son of a slave woman and raised as a slave, a *baniya*. Mamar's abilities eventually betray his true identity, and after escaping the *sunni*'s murderous attempts, he returns and indeed kills the *sunni*, assuming power.[19]

The beginning of the account features a curious inversion in that Mamar, the son of a *jinn* who lives beneath a river where he rules a town, receives from him the weapons he would use to kill the *sunni*, depicted as an observing Muslim. Though the *jinn* inhabit an unseen world in the Muslim perspective, the association with water clearly connects to a non-Islamic regard for riverine spirits, and implies it was this spiritual force that overcame the *sunni*—a stark reversal of the conventional relationship between *Sunni* ʿAlī and *Askia* Muḥammad. It could be surmised that as a rendition intended for only certain Songhay publics, the *jinn*-centric version sought to resolve tensions over *Sunni* ʿAlī's death by portraying Muḥammad Ture as the elect of the unseen world. Further, as Mamar's immediate motivation for assassinating the *sunni* was to avenge a mother who had endured the serial loss of infants, the story links to ʿAlī's reputation as quintessentially violent, providing justification for regicide. *Askia* Muḥammad's image as a serious Muslim and reformer is quickly reestablished in the account, but as a matter of how he governs, not of how he reaches that point.

The Mamar story maps onto a parallel Tuareg account in which one Adelāsegh is the son of the ruler Aligurran's sister (or al-Igurran, Arigullan, Aniguran), who is likewise warned that a sister's son would contest the throne, causing Aligurran to eliminate all such nephews save Adelāsegh, who like Mamar survives via exchange for an enslaved woman's child, growing up as a slave or *asku* (or *askiw*, Tamasheq for "young male slave"). In uncovering his true identity (through recognizing his intelligence), and in realizing he was a threat to his own son, Aligurran forces Adelāsegh into exile. But Adelāsegh (also) returns to kill and replace Aligurran.

These obviously analogous tales are not unlike those of Sunjata, and even more reminiscent of Mūsā in sacred scripture. As such, their purpose—the legitimization of a new dynasty—is also clear, rendering usurpation less egregious when undertaken by someone who is in truth a royal, not a slave. This explains the production and dissemination of such narratives in the eastern buckle, where *Askia* Muḥammad likely had difficulties with elites related to or allied with the Sunnis. Scholarly speculation that Songhay possession dances arose in the aftermath of the Sunnis' overthrow suggests elite discontent was shared with other Songhay sectors, with spirit possession a form of cultural resistance and political protest.

As to the placement of Mamar and Adelāsegh in servitude, it is an artifice, accentuating the point that, in emerging from servility, these individuals fulfilled destiny. That Mamar lived as an *asku*, and that *asku* and *askia* may be related etymologically, may well indicate the latter term's servile associations. However, given the seventh/thirteenth-century appearance of *askia* on an area tombstone, such origins, assuming a correlation with *asku*, were already temporally distant by the time of *Askia* Muḥammad.

If Songhay and Tuareg oral traditions were created in the immediate aftermath of Bāru's defeat and Muḥammad's rise, it would mean they are older than the *ta'rīkhs*, that chroniclers may have been aware of their circulation and content. As discussed, al-Sa'dī refers to the diffusion of oral accounts that "spoke of the chiefs and kings of their lands, their lives and deaths, their conduct, their heroic exploits, and other historical information and tales relating to them." This would certainly have been inclusive of, but not limited to, the professional activities of the griot, or *jèsérè* (pl. *geseru*). The Songhay term *jèsérè* derives from the Mande *jeli*, and when combined with the observation that Soninke is the conventional language of oral tradition among the Songhay people, makes a persuasive case that this form of recalling the past represents either a Mande cultural importation or imposition, in the latter instance possibly displacing an indigenous Songhay griot formation (at least at the level of royalty). As such, this heightens the possibility that the Mamar story was generated with the *askia*'s blessing.[20] In stating that the generation providing this information "passed away," with no succeeding generation "who had any interest in that, nor was there anyone who followed the path of their deceased ancestors," al-Sa'dī seemingly alludes to griots, among others, whose alleged demise (before a subsequent reemergence) could have been a result of the Askias' defeat at the end of the tenth/sixteenth century.[21]

In incorporating oral accounts, *tawārīkh* authors were highly selective, appropriating the name Kasay as that of *Askia* Muḥammad's mother and casting dynastic change as violent, while dismissing other aspects, a process al-Sa'dī may have had in mind when referring to "those whose motivations were base, and who concerned themselves with hatred, jealousy, back-biting, tittle-tattle, scandal-mongering, and concocting lies about people."[22] Such a display of critical facility is present in the *ta'rīkhs'* rejection of the oral traditions' resituating Muḥammad Ture within the royal family, and through minimalist reconstruction they locate those origins elsewhere. In so doing, the chronicles embrace an organizing principle at variance with the specifics of the oral accounts, but not necessarily with their objective.

Though both oral and written accounts are invested in legitimating the Askia dynasty, and as such reconciling a society torn by civil strife, they operate according to very different criteria. While the oral sources pursue a strategy of royal lineality, *Ta'rīkh al-fattāsh* attempts a correlation of dynastic continuity protracted over many years and regional in scope. In referring to the *askia* as Muḥammad b. Abū Bakr al-Tūrudī, the chronicle provides a *nisba* potentially referring to Futa Toro (in the middle Senegal valley), but subsequently comments on a more distant derivation that connects *Askia* Muḥammad to ancient Ghana through Kaniaga (at one point governed by the Soninke Diawara clan). In a final clarification, the

Ta'rīkh claims Muḥammad's father Abū Bakar is from the Silla (a Soninke clan), and originally from Toro, while his mother Kasay is the daughter of the Kura-*koi* Bukar, a descendant of one Jābir b. 'Abd Allāh, allegedly from the Anṣār.[23]

Al-Sa'dī adds a bit of variance in discussing the *askia*'s father, though essentially agreeing with *Ta'rīkh al-fattāsh* by introducing the *askia* as "Muḥammad b. Abī Bakr al-Tūrī, or al-Sillankī, as some say," later stating his father was also called "Bāru," with opinion was divided over whether he was "Tūranke or Silankī," referring to the Ture and Silla clans.[24] As opposed to water *jinn*, therefore, *Askia* Muḥammad's paternity was Soninke, and as such he was heir to a heralded Mande world.

The challenges *Askia* Muḥammad faced upon initially seizing power are also reflected in an encounter with the Timbuktu *Qāḍī* Maḥmūd b. 'Umar. Though appearing early in *Ta'rīkh al-fattāsh*'s account of *Askia* Muḥammad's reign, it necessarily took place years after his assuming power in 898/1493, as Maḥmūd b. 'Umar did not become *qāḍī* until 904/1498–99, the year of his predecessor Ḥabīb's death. This particular encounter is tantalizingly presented in true-to-form minimalist fashion, yet filled with innuendo, providing substantial insight into relations between Gao and Timbuktu. A portion of the dialogue is highly relevant for present purposes, its context a confrontation over the limits of imperial power in Timbuktu. At a critical juncture, the *qāḍī* reprimands the *askia*:

> "Have you forgotten, or are you pretending to have forgotten the day when you came to find me in my house and, grasping my feet and clothes said to me: 'I place myself under your inviolable sacred protection (*ḥurma*) and safekeeping, that you might intervene between me and hell. Please help me and take my hand lest I fall into damnation. I place myself under your charge.'"[25]

While the urgency of the *askia*'s concern is apparent, its content is not. Even so, the violent and troubling circumstances of the *askia*'s ascendance, involving the killing of either *Sunni* 'Alī, his son *Sunni* Abū Bakr Dā'u (Bāru), or both, could have been the issue. Given Muḥammad Ture's lack of support, more blood may have flowed in the removal of provincial governors, not only a matter of eliminating legitimate Songhay leaders, but leaders who were also Muslims. This may explain *Ta'rīkh al-fattāsh*'s manuscript C's characterization of Muḥammad Ture's offensive against *Sunni* Abū Bakr Dā'u as a legally prescribed *jihād*, complete with three prior missions—progressively led by the *sherīfian* Muḥammad Tule, the trusted counselor and *alfa* (or *alf'a*, *alfā*, "learned one") Ṣāliḥ Diawara, and finally Maḥmūd Ka'ti himself—to entreat the *sunni* to convert to Islam. Abū Bakr Dā'u's rejection of each delegation was increasingly vociferous, instructing Ṣāliḥ Diawara to go back and tell Muḥammad Ture to prepare for battle, as the *sunni* "does not accept his invitation [to convert], nor will I ever accept it." Depicting Abū Bakr Dā'u as an unrepentant *kāfir* is certainly one way to navigate the treacherous shallows of arrogation.[26]

Muḥammad Ture's correspondence with al-Maghīlī also addresses the circumstances of his rise to power. It is not clear when al-Maghīlī visited Gao, but it was after 898/1493 and even as late as 907/1502, by which time *Askia* Muḥammad had returned from the Pilgrimage. If the latter, his *Replies* would indicate an extended, ongoing challenge to the *askia*'s authority, and, to a degree, that al-Maghīlī's prominence and erudition were enlisted to help quell the controversy. The scholar refers to the matter repeatedly, and after finding that "the case of *Sunni* 'Alī is a mark of unbelief without doubt," goes on to argue that "*Sunni* 'Alī carried his own burden on his neck (*hamala himlahu 'alā 'unuqihi*) and acquired what he acquired while carrying it until his appointed time (life) ended (*'anqada*, or 'was destroyed'). That burden was then cast down before you (*bainakum*), and you were the one who took it up." This would have been sufficient to resolve the debate, but al-Maghīlī takes pains to make his position wholly transparent:

> *Sunni* 'Alī and all his officials and followers and helpers are no doubt among the most evil tyrants and miscreants . . . so that the *jihād* of the *Amīr Askia* against them and his seizing of power from their hands is among the most worthy and important of *jihāds*.[27]

The resonance between *Ta'rīkh al-fattāsh*'s manuscript C and al-Maghīlī's characterization of the coup as a *jihād* is striking, a sanctioning that could not be more declarative.

Becoming Askia al-Ḥajj *Muḥammad*

It is therefore within such controversy and facing possible threats to his reign that *Askia* Muḥammad, having reestablished the *'ulamā'* at Timbuktu and his brother 'Umar as *kanfāri* at Tendirma, prepared for the Pilgrimage. No other reason was necessary beyond fulfilling the obligation, but a political calculus was also in operation. The circumstances of Muḥammad's emergence are uncannily similar to *Mansā* Mūsā's (accidental) killing of his mother (or grandmother) Nānā Kankan.[28]

The *askia*'s objectives in making *ḥajj* were not confined, however, to issues of legitimization or personal guilt. As will be demonstrated, he also had in mind a new theory of governance, a strategy for ruling Songhay that would be effectively inaugurated and sanctioned by the *ḥajj*. Such a theory involved reimagining Songhay as a multi-ethnic political and social space, whose very identity would be known not only by its adherence to Islam, but by its heterogeneous and cosmopolitan character. This was a novel approach to statecraft in West Africa, developing neither accidentally nor haphazardly, but rather with all intentionality.

With related motivations, then, *Askia* Muḥammad made his preparations. Before departing Gao, he summoned *Kanfāri* 'Umar, who was "left behind to look after [the *askia*'s] kingdom with complete authority."[29] In contrast to *Ta'rīkh as-sūdān*, *Ta'rīkh al-fattāsh* takes more interest in this arrangement, stating the *askia* "deputized him and appointed him [to govern] in his place (*anābahu wa istakhalafahu*)."[30] This required the *kanfāri* to leave Tendirma before completing its fortification (as 'Umar had only arrived in 899/1494), a task then entrusted to *Bar-koi* Bukar "the Zughrānī" (Zoghrānī or Joghoranī) and his brother Armayizzi, sons of the Dendi-*fari*, while actual governance of the western region was given to *Balma'a* Muḥammad Kiray and Benga-*farma* 'Alī Kindānkangai.[31] The relationship between the *askia* and the *balma'a* is more than intriguing; as the son of *Sunni* 'Alī's sister, his loyalty to the *askia* must have been unassailable (perhaps he was disaffected by his uncle's heinous policies).[32] In any event, the move reveals the risk involved in the *askia*'s Pilgrimage: Tendirma and control of the empire's western hemisphere were critical, but the stakes at Gao were so high the *askia* could only rely upon 'Umar. At the same time, the relocation of the Dendi-*fari*'s sons was a stroke of political genius, removing a potential source of instability far from their base of support in the east.

With reliable lieutenants and a balanced political apparatus in place, *Askia* Muḥammad selected 1,000 infantry and 500 cavalry (or camelry), while transporting some 300,000 *mithqāls* of gold (*dhahab*, about one ton), taken from funds *Sunni* 'Alī had entrusted to the *Khaṭīb* 'Umar (presumably the same *Khaṭīb* 'Umar commanded to release al-Mukhtār b. Muḥammad Naḍḍa from prison). This was apparently one of the *sunni*'s personal stashes, as opposed to the royal treasury, which "was already gone" without a trace.[33] The large retinue and considerable gold prompt comparisons with *Mansā* Mūsā some 170 years before, which no doubt *Askia* Muḥammad invited. As Mūsā's Pilgrimage was legendary, what better way to vault the complexities of usurpation than retrace his steps, addressing both guilt as well as effectively transferring the spiritual authority for temporal power from belief in non-Islamic, noumenal powers to the *baraka* (communicable spiritual power) of Islam alone?[34]

In accepting the *askia*'s invitation, however, comparisons with the Pilgrimage of *Mansā* Mūsā yield mixed results. The figure of a 1,500-armed escort is far less than the estimates provided for the *mansā*, one-tenth of the average given for those who survived the journey to Cairo, and only 2.5 percent of the 60,000 *Ta'rīkh as-sūdān* estimates to have embarked from Mali. The actual figures may have been closer since the Malian estimates include the enslaved, whereas the sources are silent on slave participation in the *askia*'s venture (though they presumably played some role).

It is with the relative amounts of gold that *Ta'rīkh as-sūdān* seeks to draw a favorable contrast, stating that of the *askia*'s 300,000 *mithqāls*, he dispensed 200,000 in charitable giving, whereas *Mansā* Mūsā gave away only 27,000 *mithqāls*. Though the total amount of gold transported by the *mansā* (some 18 tons) vastly outweighed that of *Askia* Muḥammad, the point concerning charitable giving may have validity, as providing the Mamluk ruler 50,000 *dīnārs* of gold—one example of the *mansā*'s beneficence—does not occupy the same category of giving.

Al-Sa'dī's argument that *Askia* Muḥammad's Pilgrimage should be afforded similar status is therefore not without merit, and in qualitative terms compelling. Just as *Mansā* Mūsā's return from the Pilgrimage stimulated Islam's indigenization in Mali and the Savannah, *Askia* Muḥammad's *ḥajj* was the beginning of far-reaching developments in West African polity, initializing an era of Islamic reform not only in Songhay, but in Hausaland as well. As a consequence, Songhay would come to be regarded as a "Muslim state," with Islamic law influencing not only the ruler's personal conduct, but also his administrative policies.

In undertaking the Pilgrimage to explore a different way of governing, the *askia* departed from *Sunni* 'Ali's strategy of intimidation and fear. Both *ta'rīkhs* provide insight into this theory by discussing just who accompanied the *askia* to Mecca. According to manuscripts A and B of *Ta'rīkh al-fattāsh*, the Bara-*koi Mansā* Kūra and one Yāyi Katu Wakāri ("the Wangārī") were fellow travelers, along with four "leaders of the whites" (*aqyāl kuray*), eight officials (*aṣḥāb*), and seven jurists (*faqīh*) "from his land."[35] Concerning these jurists, *Ta'rīkh as-sūdān* mentions only *Mōri* Ṣāliḥ Diawara, a Soninke from Tendirma, but this is significant in that it alludes to that city's growing concentration of political, military, and spiritual authority, helping to counterbalance the weight and prestige of the *'ulamā'* in Timbuktu.[36]

Ta'rīkh al-fattāsh's manuscript C also lists jurists while supplying other details, placing the *aqyāl kuray* (without enumeration) among the eight *aṣḥāb*, with the other four in this category consisting of the *askia*'s son Mūsā (presented as "*Askia* Mūsā," in anticipation of his subsequent rule); Yāyi Katu Wakāri; the Bara-*koi Mansā* Kūra; and the famous ʿAlī Fulan (perhaps ʿAlī the Fulānī), also mentioned in *Ta'rīkh as-sūdān* as a fellow pilgrim and as the *huku-kuri-koi* or "master of the palace interior" (akin to a *wazīr*), who served under Muḥammad for virtually the whole of his reign.[37]

The remaining five jurists mentioned in manuscript C are *Mōri* Muḥammad Hawgāru, *Mōri* Muḥammad of Tinenka, Gao Zakaria (with "Zakaria" possibly referring to a section of Gao), the *Qāḍī* Maḥmūd Niandobogho, and *Alfa* Muḥammad Tule. Their participation would appear apocryphal, but precisely who accompanied *Askia* Muḥammad to Mecca is less important than the communities they represented.[38] The *askia* was well aware of these implications, with his choice of companions as political as it was spiritual.

Al-Sa'dī thus observes the *askia* was escorted by "a group of leaders from every community (*qabīla*)."[39] That is, while lacking the specificity of *Ta'rīkh al-fattāsh*'s manuscripts, *Ta'rīkh as-sūdān* emphasizes that multiple constituencies were represented, referring to "others" after mentioning *Mōri* Ṣāliḥ Diawara, Muḥammad's son Mūsā, and ʿAlī Fulan. Indeed, al-Sa'dī's refusal to name individuals only reinforces the point that through their participation the *askia* symbolically included their communities in a seminal act of reenvisioning the Songhay state. Thus, the ethnic Songhay, various Mande speakers, and the Fulbe were represented, as were the *kuray* or "whites," a possible reference to the Ṣanhāja and Masūfa, the Kel Tamasheq, Arabs, and immigrants from elsewhere in the Muslim world. This is all the more arresting as these were the very groups antagonized by *Sunni* ʿAlī, who despised and enslaved the Fulbe, was in a constant state of belligerency against the Kel Tamasheq, and targeted families in Timbuktu as well as oppressed the scholarly community of the Mori Koyra. Indeed, it was likely under *Askia* Muḥammad that the Mori Koyra experienced heightened influence, prompting interest in an antecedent history that included *Mōris* al-Ṣādiq and Jayba's opposition to *Sunni* ʿAlī.

The *askia*'s politics of inclusion was therefore more than a shrewd maneuver to address his seizing power, as it evinces a concept of how to move forward in governing effectively. By involving representatives of these groups in the launch of a new Songhay, the *askia* laid the groundwork for variegated populations to begin seeing themselves as integral to the state, recreating the kingdom as a cosmopolitan space accommodating assorted ethnic and regional interests.

The *askia*'s journey to the central Islamic lands, having begun in the second month of the Islamic lunar calendar (Ṣafar) in 902/1496, reached Cairo within ten months, traveling on to Mecca in *Dhū 'l-Ḥijja*, the month of the Pilgrimage and the last month of the year.[40] As was true of *Mansā* Mūsā, *Ta'rīkh al-fattāsh* tells of miraculous developments along the way. All are recorded in manuscript C, including a conversation between *Mōri* Ṣāliḥ Diawara, *Alfa* Muḥammad Tule, and *jinn* led by one Shamharūsh who, after speaking with them (and actually shaking their hands), repeats the prophecy of a twelfth caliph to come, a reference to *Shehu* Amadu Lobbo. An account in *Ta'rīkh as-sūdān* also elevates the stature of *Mōri* Ṣāliḥ Diawara, who, near death from heat and thirst between Mecca and Cairo, intercedes for a royal caravan, and is answered by so much rain that a stream forms, allowing pilgrims and animals to drink and bathe. Refusing to call upon the *ḥurma* of the Prophet for deliverance (as it is too exalted for such a purpose), *Mōri* Ṣāliḥ Diawara instead invoked the Almighty in his own humility.[41]

Though the site of the miraculous may have been the central Islamic lands, the real context and audience was the West African Sahel. As mentioned, before their apparent conversion to Islam in the eighth/eleventh century, the Soninke believed the great snake Bida provided rain as a divine prerogative. Al-Bakrī's account of the ruler's conversion operates within this framework in highlighting famine and drought, with the intervention of a Muslim holy man ending the crisis. *Mōri* Ṣāliḥ Diawara's intercession proceeds similarly, the rain once more confirming divine approbation of the *mōri* as well as *Askia* Muḥammad's rejection of *Sunni* 'Alī's heterodoxy.

Askia Muḥammad would have passed through Cairo en route to and from the Ḥijāz, but in contrast to *Mansā* Mūsā, it was his visits to Mecca and Medina that garner most attention. In both places he made charitable contributions totaling some 100,000 *mithqāls*, while in Medina he spent another 100,000 *mithqāls* on the purchase of "gardens" he converted into an "endowment for the people of Takrūr," and yet another 100,000 *mithqāls* on items for himself. He may have elected to invest in Medina (and even Mecca, where *Ta'rīkh al-fattāsh* claims he built a house) to distinguish himself from Kanem's *Mai* Dunama Dubbalemi (ruled 599–639/1203–42), who had purchased properties in Cairo to support West African pilgrims. It was in Medina, at the tomb of the Prophet, that *Mōri* Ṣāliḥ Diawara prayed for *Kanfāri* 'Umar, left behind in Gao, and though *Ta'rīkh as-sūdān* records he did so because of 'Umar's great affection and support, the anecdote equally makes the point that the *kanfāri*'s success in holding together the realm was, like the rain, dependent on the *mōri*'s intercession.

While the *askia* chose Medina to make Songhay's presence felt in the Muslim heartland, it was in Mecca and Cairo that he connected with key figures, receiving important political and religious support. Among the "many scholars and holy men" and "illustrious *'ulamā'* and the pious and venerated" he met in Cairo was al-Suyūṭī (d. 911/1505), who had also met with Aḥmad b. 'Umar twelve years earlier. *Ta'rīkh al-fattāsh* even claims the *askia* made the acquaintance of al-Maghīlī in Cairo.[42] And in one of these two cities, or perhaps both, he was anointed *khalīfa* (in this context "vice-regent") over Songhay. *Ta'rīkh al-fattāsh* records he was made such by the "*sharīf* of Mecca," who placed a blue turban on his head and named him "*imām*," while *Ta'rīkh as-sūdān* says it was the "Abbasid *sharīf*," who enturbaned him a "true *khalīfa* in Islam," suggesting it was the Abbasid caliph of Cairo who appointed the *askia* as his deputy for the "land of Songhay."[43]

Whatever this may have meant in Cairo or Mecca, how it was represented in Gao is another matter. In emphasizing the *sherīfian* dimension's fused political-spiritual cachet, the chronicles effectively diminish the importance of any particular political connection. This makes sense, as the Mamluks, in power at the time of the *askia*'s visit, would be defeated by the Ottomans in 923/1517. Muḥammad would therefore reinterpret his initial investiture toward the end of his life, calling himself the representative of "the great Ottoman *sulṭān*."[44] The central Islamic lands as a source of legitimization were therefore clearly understood in Songhay, beyond which it operated independently, the Ottoman presence there nonexistent.

Askia al-ḥājj Muḥammad's return to in Gao in *Dhū 'l-Ḥijja* 903/July-August 1498, some two years after his departure from Gao, was nothing short of triumphant.[45] He had met with renowned spiritual leaders, and had been appointed *khalīfa*. But he was also the recipient of unusual divine blessings. Embellishing this point, *Ta'rīkh al-fattāsh* gives an account in which the *askia* meets a person alleging to possess strands of the Prophet's hair, soaking it in water and selling the water for consumption or ablutions. When shown the hair, the *askia* seizes a strand and swallows it.[46]

The *ḥajj* did not completely debilitate disaffection for the *askia*, but it proved a powerful weapon against opposition while providing the basis for a spectacular expansion of personal and imperial authority. *Askia al-ḥājj* Muḥammad's activities in Medina would be considered the generative source of military victories deemed miraculous, as well as decisions judged extraordinarily wise. He had undertaken a remarkable transformation of not only the basis for temporal power, but the very nature of the Songhay state.

The Mossi, Mali, and Agades

Having adopted the *din-tūr* or "burning brand" as the insignia of the new dynasty, *Askia* Muḥammad immediately set about redefining Songhay, undertaking two projects that would launch the empire into an orbit consistent with that of a Muslim polity, thereby establishing its trajectory for the remainder of the *Askia* dynasty.[47] One such order of business, if not the very first, was to reconstitute relations with the critically important entrepot of Timbuktu. The *askia* laid the foundation for this by appointing Maḥmūd b. ʿUmar b. Muḥammad Aqīt as the city's *qāḍī* in 904/1498–99, just months after his return from the *ḥajj*. It may have been entirely coincidental that it was the year of the death of his predecessor Ḥabīb (appointed by *Sunni* ʿAlī), though human intervention cannot be ruled out.[48] Indeed, there are compelling reasons, already explored, to interpret the appointment as the culmination of a quid pro quo extending back to *Sunni* ʿAlī's opposition. But as will be seen, there is considerable nuance in both the circumstances of the appointment and the dynamics of the relationship between Timbuktu and Gao under the Askias.

The other endeavor pursued by the *askia* that same year was a military campaign against the ruler of the Mossi kingdom of Yatenga.[49] The decision to go to war underscores the realm's ongoing vulnerability to incursions from south of the Niger buckle, partially animating the campaigns of *Sunni* ʿAlī, but the way the *askia* went about it signaled a very different approach. Counseled by *Mōri* Ṣāliḥ Diawara to transform the campaign into a legally prescribed *jihād*, the *askia* sent the *mōri* to Yatenga to enjoin its ruler to convert to Islam. After consulting their ancestors, the Mossi rejected the invitation, after which the *askia* launched his campaign. Killing the Mossi and decimating their lands, he also took captive children who "became blessed of God," a stunning euphemism for their enslavement and forced conversion. It was also during this campaign that the *askia* rescued and later married the daughter of Anda-n-Allāh ʿAlī b. Abī Bakr of Walata/Biru, who in 885/1480 had been given in marriage to the Mossi ruler.[50]

Al-Saʿdī maintains this was the only *jihād* undertaken by *Askia al-ḥājj* Muḥammad, framing it as a seminal act, a struggle between Islam and heathenism, good and evil. He claims that *Mōri* Ṣāliḥ Diawara actually visited a Mossi sacred place (*bayt ṣanam*, "idol house"), where he observed a consultative process during which the apparition of an old man warned them to reject the summons and fight Songhay until one or the other was destroyed. The old man, adjured by the *mōri*, identified himself as "Iblīs" (Satan), who leads the Mossi "'astray so that they may die in unbelief'." The anecdote is less fascinating as a site of verifiability than a window into a (Muslim) Songhay world in which such forces were very real. In fact, *Askia* Muḥammad would later fell a tree, at whose base was a Mossi "idol," by simply pronouncing the *shahāda*—a measure of how seriously ancestral religion was taken, as well as the *askia*'s own *baraka*.

He would remain on a war footing for the next three years, traveling to Tendirma in 905/1499–1500 to combat and arrest the Baghana-*fari* (who apparently resided there, though he governed territory to the west of the Inland Delta), while executing Dimba Dumbi al-Fulānī, presumably a leader in Masina. In 907/1501–2, after being turned back at the town of Dialan (or Diala) by *Qāma* Fatī Qallī (or *Kama* Fati Kalli), a governor loyal to Mali, *Kanfāri* 'Umar sent for reinforcements from the *askia*, who arrived in person to defeat Fatī Qallī, razing a royal Malian residence at Tinfarin (near Dialan).[51]

This western activity represents growing preoccupation with developments in the Sahel that would culminate in a major war in the upper Senegal valley, reflecting Songhay's dramatic expansion. Baghana's prior association with Mali indicates the arrest of the Baghana-*fari* and the fight against Dialan-Tinfarin were related, evidence of Mali's attempt to defend its interests in the Sahel. Tinfarin's strategic significance was underscored by the *askia*'s tarrying after the battle to rebuild the town, "laying a foundation different from its first foundation" in an effort to transform it into a Songhay possession. Slaves were taken, including Marīam Dābo, a Soninke woman ("Wānkarīa"), who would become the mother of Ismā'īl, son of the *askia* and future ruler.

In the middle of mobilizations in the west, the *askia* also attacked Agades in the northern region of Air in 907/1501–2, some 750 miles (860 kilometers) from Gao, sending into flight its ruler Tilẓa Tanat, or Muḥammad b. 'Abd al-Raḥmān, while incorporating from Air the *kakaki*, large trumpets used by the cavalry. As the major commercial thoroughfare through which flowed goods from Egypt and the Maghrib in exchange for the gold of the Akan fields circulating through Hausaland, its seizure would have been a threat to the Hausa city-states. As such, the move demonstrates the *askia*'s designs on Hausaland itself, revealing a substantial imperial imagination that stretched from the Upper Senegal to Lake Chad.

These campaigns would imply concerns over the *askia*'s seizure of power had greatly subsided. But in fact, circumstances surrounding his very next expedition (after a three-year lull) reveal that tensions continued to simmer. In 911/1505–6, the *askia* campaigned against Borgu (or Baribu, as the majority in Borgu were called). Located to the west of the Niger River and across from Kebbi, Borgu was key to commerce moving between the Nupe and Yoruba to the south and Hausaland to the northeast, connecting with Agades. But Borgu had also been a site of extensive recruitment under *Sunni* ʿAlī at Lulu, so its targeting implies relations with Gao had undergone alteration since the *askia*'s ascent. In any event, he needed to bring it under control.

And the way he went about it is a study in perspicacity. Central to his plans were the *Juwā-ber-banda*, or "the descendants of the great Juwā," elites associated with *Sunni* ʿAlī and decidedly not on the best of terms with the Askias. This is borne out in an exchange between Muḥammad and his brother ʿUmar, who after witnessing so many *Zuwā Ber-banda* perish at Borgu, turned to the *askia* weeping: "You have annihilated Songhay." The *askia* would reply:

> "Actually I have given life to Songhay. These people whom you see will [not] make life pleasant for us in Songhay as long as they are with us. But we cannot do such a deed with our own hands, and it is for this purpose that I brought them to this place so that they might annihilate each other, and we would be free of them, since I know they fight to the death and never flee." And he [ʿUmar] left his brother without grief or regret.[52]

This riveting exchange exposes a strategy that pitted a fifth column—Songhay elite who did not follow *Sunni* Bāru into exile but remained disaffected from the *askia*—against external opposition in an area where the Sunnis had previously enjoyed tremendous support. It was daring, even brilliant, but also a high-risk gamble that nearly ended the new dynasty before it could really begin. This is suggested in *Taʾrīkh as-sūdān*, where the high casualty rate among the *Zuwā Ber-banda* features, but the actual outcome of the battle does not. And though *Taʾrīkh al-fattāsh* asserts the *askia* routed Borgu, the account reflects just how close death came. Indeed, in this rendition Borgu initially puts the army of the *askia* to flight, isolating and surrounding him and his brother ʿUmar with one hundred of their children. Dismounting from his steed, the *askia* prays toward Mecca for deliverance, and recalls the day he swallowed the Prophet's strand of hair. Remounting, he turns and defeats the enemy without suffering a loss, a miracle indicative of his own *baraka*. Given these accounts, it is not at all clear which side "won" the battle, if it was conclusive at all.[53]

Whether victorious or barely escaping, the *askia* left with captives, most notably Zāra Kabirun-*koi*, who would become his concubine and mother of the future *Askia* Mūsā. She had previously been the Kabirun-*koi*'s concubine, by whom she also bore a son (who would also become a ruler). Zāra Kabirun-*koi* was apparently highly desirable, for after being taken by the *askia* she was later captured in battle by the Busu-*koi*, by whom she would again give birth to a future ruler in Busa (a Borgu town west of the River, between Kebbi and Oyo Ile).[54]

The Borgu campaign was forerunner to forays in the east, attesting to the *askia*'s aspirations to expand into Hausaland itself.[55] Taking eight years to recover from what may have been a debacle at Borgu, Muḥammad returned to the area in 919/1513–14, this time with sights trained on Hausaland proper, striking at Katsina deep inside the heartland. According to *Ta'rīkh as-sūdān*, the *askia* renewed his attack on Katsina the following year, and again at the end of 921/1516, while in 922/1516–17 he fought against al-'Adāla, the sultan of Agades. Although the campaigns against Katsina are contested in the scholarship, they are consistent with efforts to control the region's commerce, with Songhay but one of several contenders. The *askia* would renew his campaign against Hausaland in 923/1517–18, this time targeting the more proximate Kebbi (*kanta* in the Arabic), but "without any success."[56]

Confronting Tengela

In the eight-year interim between his assault on Borgu in 911/1505–6 and his 919/1513–14 attack on Katsina, the *askia* would renew his interest in the west, with far-reaching and long-lasting consequences for the whole of West Africa. Having previously moved against the forces of the Baghana-*fari* and Mali at Dialan-Tinfarin, around 913/1507–8 he attacked Kilanbut/Kilanbuti/Kalanbut, a Malian province as far west as the upper Senegal and Faleme valleys, returning there in 915/1509–10. Two years later he (again) confronted the Baghana-*fari*/*faran*, one Ma' Qutu Kayta (or Magha Kutu Keita), against whom he sent *Huku-kuri-koi* 'Alī Fulan along with Muḥammad Kiray, the *balma'a* (military commander of Timbuktu's port of Kabara). And as late as 924/1518–19, the *askia* sent the *kanfāri* against *Qāma* Qatiya, whose title also suggests a

Malian connection.[57] The cumulative evidence therefore indicates control of Baghana was being fiercely contested between an emerging Songhay and a struggling yet defiant Mali, with Mali as the *askia*'s primary preoccupation in the west. Even so, there was another concern whose resolution was as consequential, if not more so.

The retreat of Malian power created a vacuum between Baghana and the upper Senegal and Faleme valleys, particularly in the lands of Karta to the south and adjacent Kaniaga to the north, far from Songhay's center in the eastern Niger buckle. Following the *huku-kuri-koi* and *balma'a*'s offensive against the Baghana-*fāri* in 917/1511–12, the very next year saw the *askia*'s forces move even farther west to Kaniaga, where they confronted the "accursed false prophet" (*al-mutanabbī*) "Tayanda" or "Tanyeda," better known as Tengela/Tenguela. This individual led a considerable following from Futa Jallon to the town of Diara (in Kaniaga, also referred to as Futa Kingui, suggesting a demographic shift from Soninke to Fulbe), where he perished, but from where his community continued their circumlocutions, eventually settling in the middle Senegal valley. There his son Koli Tengela would establish the Denyanke dynasty over Futa Toro. The rise of the Denyankes would lead to a series of developments, with Futa Toto emerging in the late eleventh/seventeenth century as a key locus of tension emanating (in part) from the expansion of transatlantic and trans-Saharan slaving, targeting Muslim and non-Muslim populations alike.[58]

Efforts in the middle Senegal valley to protect Muslims from the tentacles of the slave trades can be traced to Nāṣir al-Dīn (d. 1084–85/1674), who led a clerical community against the Arab-descended, warrior-minded Ḥassān, who, with Moroccan forces, formed "Ormankobe" slaving incursions into Senegambia from the late eleventh/seventeenth through the twelfth/eighteenth centuries.[59] Basing his opposition in the prohibition against enslaving fellow Muslims, Nāṣir al-Dīn would begin his effort south of the Middle Senegal, where it was known as the *tubenan* (from the Arabic *tawba*, "repentance" or "return"). The cause quickly extended north of the Middle Senegal, where it was called the *shurbubba*. Nāṣir al-Dīn's efforts are connected to the twelfth/eighteenth-century theocracies of Bundu, Futa Jallon and Futa Toro, from which would emerge reformers and movements across the expanse of the West African Sahel, including those led by *al-ḥājj* ʿUmar and Usuman dan Fodio in the thirteenth/nineteenth century. As such, the activities and movement of Tengela and Koli Tengela were highly generative, for had they settled in Kaniaga/Futa Kingui instead of Futa Toro, they may not have been as affected by slaving, with much of the region's subsequent history possibly evolving very differently.[60]

The reason for the Tengelan community's detour from Kaniaga to the Middle Senegal was the encounter with *Askia al-ḥājj* Muḥammad at Diara. As both al-Sa'dī and al-Suyūṭī refer to *Sunni* 'Alī as a *khārijī*, the former's use of *al-mutanabbī* or "accursed false prophet" in characterizing Tengela has a similar sense. *Ta'rīkh al-fattāsh* adopts comparable language in calling him "a deceiver (*kadhdhāb*) who claimed (*idda'ā*) prophethood and the status of a messenger (*nubūwa wa risāla*), God's curse be upon him."[61] It therefore cannot be ruled out that Tengela was an "innovator" of a religious approach at variance with Sunni Islam (perhaps Kharijism, once again). Use of the ascriptions "prophet" and "messenger" was highly inflammatory, as Muḥammad is the seal of the prophets, in this context burnishing *Askia al-ḥājj* Muḥammad's credentials as a Muslim reformer. Tengela's defeat at the hands of Songhay is treated in the *ta'rīkhs* as necessary and providential, forcing his son Koli Tengela to leave Kaniaga. The precise Denyanke succession thereafter is less important than orthodoxy's eventual victory, made possible by Tengela's defeat but realized under *Satigi* (or Sila-*tigi*/Sira-*tigi*) Galajo b. Koli Tengela b. Tengela (circa 970–86/1563–79), Tengela's grandson.[62]

But even if he were a religious leader, Tengela's struggle with Songhay was probably not over religion. Other than leveling the false prophet allegation, al-Sa'dī does not actually provide a reason, whereas *Ta'rīkh al-fattāsh* gives two different explanations, an indication that its compilers, at a temporal distance, were themselves attempting to unravel what might have happened. According to one account, a Zughrānī who traveled annually to trade in "Futa" (probably Futa Kingui or Kaniaga) was seized and violently stripped of his merchandise by Tengela. Escaping death, the Zughrānī fled to Tendirma and informed *Kanfāri* 'Umar he had been contemptuously slandered by Tengela. Incensed, the *kanfāri* marched on Tengela.[63]

The other story is that Tengela migrated to Kaniaga/Futa Kingui and began conducting himself as its ruler, clashing with the Kaniaga-*faran* at Diara. Tengela's military superiority "in horses and men" led to the Kaniaga-*faran* requesting help from the *kanfāri*.

If the Kaniaga-*faran* indeed requested Songhay's assistance, it would have reflected the dissipation of Malian influence in the area, whose interests were represented by the *Faran-sūra*, the "deputy official over the desert dwellers," possibly Suradugu or the Hodh. Precisely where the *Faran-sūra* resided is not specified, but just a few years after the Moroccan defeat of

Songhay in 999/1591, the *Faran-sūra* is referred to as "the sultan of Diara," conceivably the office of the Kaniaga-*faran*. This suggests the *kanfāri*'s assault on Tengela was the cause of Mali losing all claim to Kaniaga.

The two accounts converge in maintaining Tengela originated from outside of Kaniaga, and that commerce was at the heart of the dispute. Encouraged by Mali's Sahelian twilight, Tengela pursued his own brand of expansionism. Both versions also agree Songhay fought against Tengela, though al-Sa'dī makes no specific mention of *Kanfāri* 'Umar, but simply says "the *askia* campaigned against the accursed false prophet and killed him in Diara." In contrast, *Ta'rīkh al-fattāsh* states the *kanfāri* marched on Tengela with neither the approval nor prior knowledge of the *askia*.

The Songhay army under the *kanfāri* was large and "well versed in the art of war," but the trek of more than two months across "vast and desolate desert" to confront Tengela's forces, already superior in number and "strength," was so exacting that only divine intervention saved the *kanfāri*. Hauling enormous booty, 'Umar returned to Tendirma, where he is said to have buried Tengela's head.[64]

Vying with Hausaland

The analysis of *Askia al-ḥājj* Muḥammad's various military campaigns is critical to understanding Songhay's territorial dimensions during his tenure, as well as how his administrative structure may be distinguished from that of the Sunnis. As for Songhay's parameters, *Ta'rīkh as-sūdān* makes the breathtaking assertion that the *askia* ruled over all lands from Kebbi (on the western edge of Hausaland) in the east to the Atlantic Ocean in the west, and from the Taghaza salt mines in the north to Bendugu (the territory from Jenne to Segu along the right bank of the Bani River) in the south, "conquering all of them with the sword."[65] However, these dimensions are not entirely supported by the evidence, especially the western frontier.

That Bendugu constituted Songhay's southern frontier would seem a fair representation, as the *jihād* against the Mossi of Yatenga apparently crippled the latter, effectively eliminating them as a factor for the remainder of the *askia*'s reign (as opposed to that of *Sunni* 'Alī, for whom they remained a constant adversary), while the assertion that Taghaza constituted the northern imperial edge is supported by the demand from Moroccan ruler *Mawlay* Aḥmad al-A'raj (ruled 930–52/1524–45, and 954–56/1547–49) that *Askia* Isḥāq Bēr relinquish it. Taghaza may have fallen to Songhay under *Askia al-ḥājj* Muḥammad, though the absence of its mention is quizzical.[66]

As for the east and northeast perimeter, the final battle against Agades took place in 922/1516–17, from which booty was amassed, suggesting a successful campaign. Agades's tributary status to Songhay therefore began with its initial defeat in 906/1500–1, and was reinforced in 921/1516, and again the following year.[67]

If Agades and Air were subject to Songhay, the same was far from the case for Kebbi and Katsina of Hausaland. After surviving the Borgu disaster, *Askia al-ḥājj* Muḥammad attacked Katsina eight years later, and again set his sights on Kebbi four years thereafter. The battle against Kebbi was unsuccessful, probably also true of Katsina, as the sources do not discuss the outcome. It is possible that other parts of Hausaland were subject to Songhay, as the aforementioned assault against Agades in 922/1516–17 involved the *Kanta* Kuta, ruler of Leka (near what is now Maleh, north of Gande), who led a rebellion against Songhay over the tardy distribution of spoils, "casting off his allegiance to the *amīr Askia al-ḥājj* Muḥammad, [a condition that continued] to the demise of the state of the people of Songhay. The *kanta* 'stood' on his own." Given its location, it makes sense that Leka was part of Songhay until Kuta's revolt, and nearby settlements may have also been under Songhay's limited and episodic control.[68]

Running counter to the testimony of the *ta'rīkhs* is the account of Leo Africanus (al-Ḥasan b. Muḥammad al-Wazzān al-Zayyātī), who maintained he passed through Hausaland and Bornu in the early tenth/sixteenth century (challenged in the scholarship).[69] Africanus, who likely garnered information from others while visiting Gao or Agades, states the *askia* defeated Gobir, executing the ruler while reassigning his castrated grandsons to the royal palace at Gao; and that he also defeated Kano, Katsina, Zamfara, and Zaria (Zegzeg), "seizing their kingdoms" and imposing an annual tribute of one-third on Kano's revenue, making its ruler's daughter his wife. Such success surely would have registered in the *ta'rīkhs*, or even the *Kano Chronicle*, so that Africanus may have been given inaccurate information that confused Songhay with Kebbi, which had experienced successful expansion into other parts of Hausaland.[70] What the oral tradition does support, however, is that the *askia* took the wife of Gobir's ruler (not the daughter of Kano's), but this may well confuse Gobir with Borgu.

The Air and Hausaland campaigns targeted Muslim rulers, and were therefore very different from the expedition against the Mossi. How the *askia* justified attacking Muslim-governed territories is unclear, but the correspondence with al-Maghīlī provides clues. His fourth question is particularly illuminating:

> If there is a land in which there are Muslims and their *sulṭān* is tyrannical or their chief seizes their wealth in an unjust and hostile way, does it fall to me to drive away the oppressor from them, even if this leads to his being killed, or does it not?

The complete question is more complicated, but essentially reveals an interest in identifying circumstances under which the *askia* might legally intervene in Muslim-governed territories. Al-Maghīlī carefully words his response, warning the *askia* to "beware lest you change one reprehensible state of affairs for another like it or worse." With that said, he then provides cover:

> A [third category is] land having an *amīr* from among those chiefs whom you described as levying unlawful taxes (*maks*) and being oppressive and depraved and lacking in virtue. If you are able to end his oppression of the Muslims without injury to them so that you can install among them a just *amīr*, then do that, even if this leads to killing, and the killing of many of the oppressors and their helpers and the killing of many of your helpers, because whoever is killed from among them is the worst of those who fall in battle (*qatīl*), but whoever is killed from among your people is the best of martyrs (*shahīd*).[71]

Reference to *maks* is ironic, as it would be an issue for the *askias* themselves, but the Air and Hausaland campaigns indicate Muḥammad may have found justification in al-Maghīlī's *Replies*.

With Taghaza and Bendugu as the imperial boundaries to the north and south, and with Songhay's eastern reaches established along a line from Air to Dendi, rimming Hausaland, it remains to establish Songhay's western frontier. Al-Sa'dī's claim that Songhay authority reached the Atlantic appears more aspirational than factual, as there is no mention of any campaign beyond the Upper Faleme (if any went that far), with the Tengela operation a single episode after which Songhay's military returned to Tendirma. That Diara's ruler may have requested Songhay's assistance in the struggle with Tengela implies Diara (and by extension the province of Kaniaga/Futa Kingui) was then reduced to tributary status within Songhay. But Kaniaga is a long way from the Atlantic.

At the same time, the sources mention the *askia* fighting the Baghana-*fari* and Mali as early as 905/1499–1500 and as late as 917/1511–12, and these struggles, together with events in Diara, represent Songhay's successful encroachment upon the embattled Mande state. Baghana's strategic location south of Walata/Biru explains its importance, and as the Baghana-*fari* is henceforth unambiguously included in *Ta'rīkh as-sūdān* as part of imperial Songhay, the 917/1511–12 encounter under *Askia al-ḥājj* Muḥammad may have been the moment when Songhay largely ended its struggle with Mali over Baghana (though there would be subsequent flare-ups).[72] Baghana was thereafter a medial Songhay province, distinguished from Kaniaga/Futa Kingui's tributary status. Events in both Baghana and Kaniaga demonstrate that Songhay did not only benefit from an enfeebled Mali, but contributed directly to the reduction of its Sahelian footprint.

Though not extending to the "sea of salt" (the Atlantic), imperial Songhay was nonetheless enormous in size. Its core consisted of territory originally conquered by *Sunni* 'Alī—the Niger buckle from Dendi in the east to Jenne in the west, with Timbuktu to the Bandiagara escarpment to the south—while its outer territories included Air, Taghaza, and Kaniaga/Futa Kingui, distinguished from the former in that its governors were chosen by the *askia* and regularly called upon to participate in military campaigns, as they were also expected to provide an annual tribute, as will be examined.

The Imperial Architecture under Askia al-ḥājj *Muḥammad*

Rather than disrupt, it would appear the Askia dynasty sought to improve on imperial structures inherited from the Sunnis, whose approach in turn had been similar to that of imperial Mali. One such improvement involved reimagining the realm as a conventional Islamic polity, rather than a peripheral Islamic land, signaled by al-Sa'dī's designation of *Askia al-ḥājj* Muḥammad as *khalīfa* ("successor") and *amīr al-mu'minīn* ("Commander of the Faithful"). Depending upon the Sunni or Shi'a perspective, either 'Umar or 'Alī was the first *amīr al-mu'minīn*, a title then adopted by the Umayyads and Abbasids to represent their authority over a theoretically unitary Muslim world. In deference to the Abbasids, the Almoravid rulers would call themselves *amīr al-muslimīn*, but with the 923/1517 removal of the Abbasid caliph from Cairo to Constantinople, the Sa'dians reappropriated *amīr al-mu'minīn*.[73]

As both *ta'rīkhs* refer to *Askia* Muḥammad as *amīr al-mu'minīn*, the adoption of the title may have been a response to the Sa'dians, an imperial claim of both independent as well as competing status. Songhay rulers would maintain the claim, as in a colophon dated 995/1587 (concerning a copy of Ibn Abī Zayd's *Risāla*) in which *Askia* Muḥammad Bāni (ruled

995/1586 to 996/1588) is called *amīr al-mu'minīn*, as is *Askia* Dāwūd (his father) and *Askia* Muḥammad (his grandfather).[74] In any event, the chronicles alternately refer to Muḥammad as *amīr al-mu'minīn* and *askia*, and like the meaning of the Malian *mansā* in coming to signify "emperor" or *fama* of *famas*, the title *askia* also underwent transition from more modest associations, commensurate with Muḥammad's success.

Under *Askia al-ḥājj* Muḥammad, Songhay's administrative scaffolding cohered around a double nucleus, with the capital at Gao and a second, very powerful site of political authority at Tendirma. While the sources do not clearly delineate the *askia*'s inner circle of royal counselors and officials at Gao, their existence and roles can be inferred from a sprinkling of evidence throughout the texts, and from which it seems the circle was dominated by the *huku-kuri-koi* 'Alī Fulan. This is underscored by not only his accompanying the *askia* on *ḥajj*, but also by his role in a military capacity when, together with the *Balma'a* Muḥammad Kiray, he fought against the Baghana-*fari* in 917/1511–12. It is also probable that 'Alī Fulan was a eunuch, as there is mention of a subsequent *huku-kuri-koi* leading a cavalry of eunuchs toward the end of the Askia dynasty, and as *huku-kuri-koi* is essentially the same construction as *hu-kokorey-koi*, "head of the palace eunuchs."[75] Such an influential position may have its origins in a similar arrangement in late fourth/tenth century Gao, for which al-Muhallabī reports its ruler "has a palace which nobody inhabits with him or has resort to except a eunuch slave (*khādam maqtū'*)."[76]

Uncertainty over 'Alī Fulan's personal circumstances is introduced, however, by al-Sa'dī's subsequent reference to one Bukar 'Alī Dūdu b. 'Alī Fulan, otherwise identified as Bukar Shīlī-ije ("son of Shīlī," his mother) in a series of references that, if not handled carefully, introduces significant confusion. Bukar 'Alī Dūdu or Bukar Shīlī-ije is not be confused with 'Alī Dādu, who served as *hi-koi* under two different Askias (Mūsā and Dāwūd). The name Bukar 'Alī Dūdu b. 'Alī Fulan appears only once in the sources—probably an error, since al-Sa'dī immediately identifies Bukar Shīlī-ije as the son of 'Alū Zalīl, the son of *Kanfāri* 'Umar.[77] Given 'Alū Zalīl's clear paternity, 'Alī Fulan was not the father, with developments under *Askia* Dāwūd rendering the following sequence of events: *Hi-koi* 'Alī Dādu was killed in battle in 961/1553–54, and was replaced as *hi-koi* by Bukar Shīlī-ije, who in being named Dendi-*fari* in 970/1563 is called "*Hi-koi* Bukar 'Alī Dūdu." Hence Bukar 'Alī Dūdu and Bukar Shīlī-ije are one and the same.[78]

The case of 'Alī Fulan, therefore, actually strengthens the likelihood that the position of *huku-kuri-koi* was reserved for a eunuch, consistent with the *askia*'s interest and investment in women (to be examined).[79] 'Alī

Fulan's influence in the royal court steadily increased as the *askia* aged, leading the *askia*'s son Mūsā to resent a relationship so close the *hukukuri-koi* effectively controlled the state. Mūsā would complain "the *amīr* did nothing except what 'Alī Fulan told him to do."[80]

If 'Alī Fulan was the *askia*'s principal counselor at Gao, *Kanfāri* 'Umar was his right hand at Tendirma, reflecting a harmonious partnership in evidence since the days of *Sunni* 'Alī. In contrast to his outspoken brother, 'Umar was far more circumspect, but his guarded behavior concealed a fierce loyalty to Muḥammad, and once situated in Tendirma, the *kanfāri* proved a consistently reliable and indispensable lieutenant, a leading member of the inner royal circle, albeit from a distance.

Other persons in that circle can be identified in the list of those who made *ḥajj* with the *askia*, the purpose of which was to establish a cartography of power for subsequent relations of authority. Prominently situated within the list is the Bara-*koi Mansā* Kūra, who alone supported the revolt against *Sunni* Bāru. Such was the *askia*'s regard for him that only the Bara-*koi* had the right, or, even more correctly, the responsibility to veto a poor decision made by the *askia*, whether the latter "liked it or not."[81] Already advanced in age early in the *askia*'s reign, Bara-*koi Mansā* Kūra may have died soon after the Pilgrimage, when he disappears from the record.

While the *ta'rīkhs* do not precisely agree on who made the Pilgrimage, and with *Ta'rīkh al-fattāsh*'s manuscript C presenting special challenges, someone who appears in all lists is Muḥammad's son Mūsā, the son of Zāra Kabirun-*koi* of Borgu.[82] The oral traditions associate her with Gobir, and unless they are asserting that is her origin, Gobir's position so deep within Hausaland's interior raises doubts the *askia* found her there. A thornier issue is al-Sa'dī's claim that she only becomes the *askia*'s concubine with the 911/1505–6 campaign, some eight years after his return from Mecca. As the chronicles insist Mūsā was Zāra Kabirun-*koi*'s son, a possible reconciliation is that he was retroactively included in the *askia*'s *ḥajj* to explain his subsequent rise to power, or to facilitate it.[83] In any event, as her son matured, Mūsā Zāra Kabirun-*koi*'s stature and influence grew as well. Regarded as the *askia*'s firstborn son, he became the *fari-mondio*, overseeing revenue collection throughout the empire, a platform from which several would succeed to the *askiyate* (*al-taskiya* or *al-askuwīya* in the Arabic).[84]

The examples of *Kanfāri* 'Umar and *Fari-mondio* Mūsā illustrate that the *askia*'s family served in critical roles. Yaḥyā, at times presented as the brother of Muḥammad and 'Umar, would become *kanfāri* with the latter's death, the post thereafter remaining, with few exceptions, the exclusive preserve of the progeny of Muḥammad and 'Umar, beginning with 'Umar's sons Muḥammad Bonkana Kirya and (conceivably) 'Uthmān Tinfarin, followed by *Askia* Muḥammad's sons 'Alī Kusira, Dāwūd, and Ya'qūb. In addition to the post of *kanfāri*, several of the *askia*'s sons, including Balla, Sulaymān Kangāga, 'Alī Yandi (or Bindi-Kanyiya or Gandānkiyya), and Ḥabīb Allāh (or Muḥammad) served as Benga-*farma*. Those occupying the position of *balma'a* included his sons Muḥammad Dundumiya and Khālid. Posts of lesser yet significance were also entrusted to the *askia*'s scions, including that of Hari-*farma* ("chief of water," to which 'Abd Allāh was assigned); the Wanay-*farma* ("chief of property," an obscure post held by Mūsā Yunbul); the Kuray-*farma* (given to *Mori* Mūsā, with responsibilities concerning the Tuareg and Arab-Berbers); the *bābali-farma* (perhaps "minister of agriculture" and held by one Fāma); and the Kalisi-*farma* (given to Sulaymān Kundi Kurya and apparently related to gold, the Mande meaning of "kālisi"). His sons not only held these posts, but also took turns succeeding him as *askia*.[85]

After the *huku-kuri-koi*, *Ta'rīkh as-sūdān* conveys the strong sense that the *kanfāri*, *balma'a*, and Benga-*farma* were the most important offices, as those in them are listed together with future rulers.[86] This is significant, as all three were concerned with the empire's western half: the Benga-*farma* governed Benga, the lacustrine area east of Dirma and Bara; the *balma'a* was the military leader at Timbuktu's port of Kabara; and the *kanfāri* supervised the entire western sphere from Tendirma. The concentration of western high officials with military capacity merits greater scrutiny, especially in relation to Timbuktu and Jenne. But there were other critical posts, including the Dendi-*fari*, already distinguished by Afumba under *Sunnis* 'Alī and Bāru. A source of trouble for the new *askia*, by 922/1516 the post had recovered some of its luster, as it was the Dendi-*fari* who opposed *Kanta* Kuta of Leka's request for the spoils from Agades.[87] But the post may have never been fully restored, as this Dendi-*fari* is unnamed, while none of the *askia*'s sons or nephews were ever appointed to it. Even so, the Dendi-*fari* remained the only official who could candidly address the *askia*, a privilege that, together with that of the Bara-*koi*, had the very practical purpose of checking executive excess.

In addition to provincial governors and transregional posts, there was government at the town and village levels, the most salient of which were the municipalities of Timbuktu and Jenne. Because of their unique circumstances, their governance cannot be properly understood without fully taking into account corresponding religious authority, a subsequent focus. What can be noted here, however, is that the stature of an official at any tier did not derive solely from the relative importance of his or her function, but also from circumstances of instantiation. Just as the Bara-*koi*'s enduring relationship to the *askiyate* stemmed from his having aided the Tondi-*farma*, so too the tradition of the *askia* sitting with the Jenne-*koi* (afforded no other official) issued from *Sunni* ʿAlī's exceptional treatment of Jenne's young ruler. Rather than disrupting such arrangements, the *askia* dynasty continued to honor them.[88]

In visiting the western Sahel between 911/1506 and 915/1510 (and even a few years later), Leo Africanus describes Gao as a "very large town" and "very civilized compared to Timbuktu," whose "houses are in general very ugly," but with "a few of very fine appearance where the king and his court live."[89] The royal compound was in fact a complex, with a public and private gate, between which was a large walled courtyard. On either side of the courtyard were loggias for royal audiences, and presumably behind the private gate were the royal chambers. A "special palace" separately housed "a huge number of wives, concubines, slaves, and eunuchs assigned to watch over these women." The *askia* was surrounded by "numerous functionaries," including "secretaries, counselors, captains, and stewards."

While providing a sense of the general layout of the royal compound, Africanus apparently did not actually witness any audiences there, as opposed to Timbuktu, where he depicts a "royal court . . . very well organized and magnificent."[90] This is no doubt a reference to the *ma'aduku* (*mādugu, ma'a dugu, ma'a dugu, ma'aduku*), the "place of the ruler" probably built in or near Kabara, Timbuktu's river port, by *Mansā* Mūsā. Africanus further comments that when the *askia* travels "from one town to another with his courtiers, he rides a camel, and the horses are led by grooms."

Timbuktu was the site of a reenactment probably more than one thousand years old, as Leo Africanus recounts:

> When anyone wants to address the king, he kneels before him, takes a handful of dust and sprinkles it over his head and shoulders. This is how they show respect, but it is demanded of those who have never addressed the king before, or ambassadors.

The earthen ablution therefore persisted into imperial Songhay. As a staple of politesse and protocol and performance of submission and loyalty, it had no rival. In ancient Ghana, Muslim dignitaries were not required to submit to the rite, but neither *Mansā* Mūsā's Islamicization project nor the full embrace of Islam under *Askia al-ḥājj* Muḥammad could eradicate it. In commenting on the relative entitlements, *Ta'rīkh al-fattāsh* notes that exceptions or modifications were important indicators, such that the Jenne-*koi* could substitute ground meal (*daqīq al-ṭaʿām*), while the *kanfāri* could wear headgear during the sprinkling.[91]

The various privileges of high officials were for public consumption during official audiences. Other examples include the right to speak candidly, the right to remain seated on steeds, and the right to announce their presence through drums. The few enjoying this distinction were drumlords (*arbāb al-ṭabl*), their drums sounding until they reached a threshold, beyond which only the *askia*'s drums could be sounded.[92] Though a performance of submission, such drumming clearly bordered on the subversive, and in fact would be employed to signal as much later in Muḥammad's reign.

If the pattern under *Askia* Dāwūd had been established earlier under *Askia al-ḥājj* Muḥammad, then royal audiences were typically held on Friday, presumably after Friday prayer, as well as on holidays.[93] The *askia* only rose to his feet for scholars and those just returning from the Pilgrimage, while no one could even whisper his name save the *jèséré-dunka* or *gissiri-dunka*, head of the griots. Any communication between the *askia* and supplicants, or even high officials, was transmitted through the "*askia*'s mouth," the *wanadu*. Finally, the only people who could sit on the royal dais were *sherīfians*, who together with the *ʿulamāʾ* and a category known as the *san* were also afforded the honor of dining with him.[94] Precisely who the *san* may have been is a matter of conjecture.[95] In Songhay the term means "ruler, lord, chief," and once the Moroccan occupation begins, the *san* are identified in *Taʾrīkh al-fattāsh* as "the most sublime of the servants of God" in "generosity, maintenance of virtues, and discretion, paying no attention to meaningless issues while remaining in their homes, assisting the Muslims and aiding those in need, something innate and natural for them."[96] In fondly remembering Songhay in its heyday, the writer may refer to the scholars of Sankore mosque, a speculation supported by the incorporation of the honorific title into the name of a descendant of Anda ag-Muḥammad, one Muḥammad San b. *al-faqīh* al-Mukhtār.[97]

A major challenge with the term *san*, however, is that it rarely appears, and though it may have been reserved for leading religious families, the reference to dining with the *askia* "even if they were very young" also resonates with the well-entrenched custom of subject rulers sending their children to reside in the imperial capital. Leo Africanus seems to refer to this custom in stating Jenne's ruler was taken to Gao where he remained until death, though this may actually refer to the ruler's son, as the bond formed with Jenne under *Sunni* ʿAlī was honored by the Askias.[98] The concept can also be found in his discussion of Gobir's ruler and his castrated grandsons (though it is unlikely that the *askia* ever defeated Gobir). Called the *farāriyya* by Ibn Baṭṭūṭa, these "sons of vassal kings" represent a tradition that, together with the earthen ablution, traversed considerable distance and time, from ancient Ghana through imperial Mali into tenth/sixteenth century Songhay.

The Songhay Military

Leo Africanus also states that, while traveling from town to town, the *askia*'s entourage could quickly change to a war footing.[99] This is consistent with evidence that both provincial as well as "national" or central forces directly under the *askia* could be mobilized for a given expedition, and that one of the primary responsibilities for at least some governors was to provide for the security of their provinces as well as for Songhay's overall defense. In listing the various governors who remained loyal to *Sunni* Bāru against Tondi-*farma* Muḥammad Ture—the Dirma-*koi*, the Taratan-*koi*, the Bani-*koi*, the Kara-*koi*, the Jenne-*koi*, and others—*Ta'rīkh al-fattāsh* states each commanded a numerous army.[100] As none of these governors is mentioned as a military leader under the *askia*, he may have reduced their military capacity—perhaps refocusing their armies under the command of the *kanfāri* at Tendirma. Hence, it is no surprise that it was the *kanfāri* who in 907/1501–2 fought against *Qāma* Fatī Qallī at Dialan/Diala, and again in 924/1518–19 against *Qāma* Qatiya. And according to *Ta'rīkh al-fattāsh*, it was the *kanfāri* who alone defeated Tengela in 918/1512–13.

In coming to the aid of his brother 'Umar against Fatī Qallī, and in sending 'Alī Fulan to fight alongside the *balma'a* against the Baghana-*fāri*, the *askia* provides examples of instances when provincial and central forces were conjoined, indicating a "national" force existed, presumably at Gao. As military commander at Kabara, the *balma'a* (like the *kanfāri*) would have had a standing force, but the *askia* had forces at Gao as well. The Gao contingent can be approximated by combining reports, including the number of soldiers accompanying the *askia* to Mecca—some 500 cavalry and 1,000 infantry—with Leo Africanus' estimate of the *askia*'s cavalry at 3,000, along with a "huge number of infantry armed with bows made of wild fennel [who] fire poison arrows."[101] Assuming a similar cavalry-to-infantry ratio as obtained for the Pilgrimage, such a military force may have consisted of 9,000 soldiers, and since the context suggests the *askia* was actually in Timbuktu at the time of

Africanus's visit, it could be assumed these troops followed him back to Gao, where Africanus says the ruler maintained "a sizeable guard of horsemen and foot soldiers with bows." If forces permanently garrisoned at Kabara, Gao, Tendirma, and the Dendi region (under the Dendi-*fari*) were each only half that of the 9,000 estimated to have passed through Timbuktu during Africanus's visit, the combined estimate would be some 27,000 troops, not taking into consideration forces commanded by the provincial governors.

Askia Muḥammad "made a distinction between civilians and soldiers, as opposed to the situation in the days of the Khārijīte [*Sunni* 'Alī], when everyone had been a soldier."[102] This suggests a more deliberate process in determining military eligibility, and when taken together with the observation that "the people of Songhay were well versed in the art of war and the science of combat, extremely brave and daring, and most expert in the ruses of war," it implies a degree of professionalization.[103] In maintaining a trained standing army, it is possible some form of conscription of the peasantry existed.

The circumstances of the Sorko under the *hi-koi*, commander of the royal river fleet, would have continued under the *askias*, so that a percentage of the army would have been enslaved or otherwise servile.[104] The same may have been true for the cavalry during the reign of *Askia* Muḥammad Bāni, as *Ta'rīkh as-sūdān* mentions a "eunuch cavalry" (*fārisān min khaṣī*) numbering some 4,000 during the final days of Songhay's independence.[105] This could also, however, represent a development over the course of a century.

Taxation in Songhay

Like any empire, Songhay required resources. If the administrative features of imperial Songhay are nowhere clearly articulated, its methods of taxation and revenue procurement are even more elusive, as formal or official tax records were apparently not maintained. Even so, there is sufficient evidence that the empire raised revenue from at least six major sources: possessions confiscated from the Sunni dynasty; inheritance duties; assessments on agricultural production within the empire; tribute assessed from outlying, subject provinces; the spoils of war; and customs paid on goods passing through such entrepots as Timbuktu, Jenne, and Gao, as well as the Taghaza salt mines.

The very first category—the properties and claims of *Sunni* 'Alī—was a preoccupation of some complexity placed before al-Maghīlī. Its consideration lays bare the *askia*'s interest in not only justifying his seizure of power, but of appropriating the *sunni's* wealth. The *Replies* make clear that something was at stake, and that as a Muslim reformer, the *askia* could not simply seize properties without legal foundation.

Having repeatedly asserted *Sunni* 'Alī had all the characteristics of an infidel, with which al-Maghīlī agreed, the *askia* made his case for the confiscation of his possessions by outlining the circumstances as he saw them: 'Alī and his supporters had enslaved and killed self-proclaimed Muslims, illegally appropriating their property. Some had since displayed idolatrous behavior, raising serious doubts as to whether they were ever Muslim, but others were certainly so. The *askia*'s queries (found in his second and third questions) therefore followed: As the *sunni* and his accomplices were not Muslims, can property they took from Muslims now be reappropriated, and by whom? Can the *sunni*'s heirs be enslaved or put to death, and what is to be done with their concubines and offspring? Who bears the burden of proof in the case of those claiming to have been enslaved as Muslims, and, finally, what is to be done with professing Muslims who refuse to abandon idolatry?[106]

Al-Maghīlī's answers to these queries were highly contingent and not entirely responsive; informed by scholarly consensus, they could not have been everything the *askia* wanted to hear. Establishing the concept of a public treasury (*bayt al-māl*), and the criteria by which unbelief can be identified as well as its categories, it was al-Maghīlī's view that in the case of "born unbelievers" (as opposed to apostates), offspring and wives could be enslaved and property seized. Property taken from Muslims could be claimed by the aggrieved, but those refusing to repent of their unbelief should be killed, their concubines subject to sale, their children forced into Islam and not enslaved. The assertions of those claiming to have been free Muslims before their enslavement must be honored. As al-Maghīlī may have arrived in Gao after the *askia*'s Pilgrimage, for which he paid with funds recovered from *Sunni* 'Alī's *Khaṭīb* 'Umar, these questions evince an abiding interest in the considerable wealth the *sunni* had accumulated but had yet to be recovered. Of course, the *askia* occupied a powerful position from which to interpret individual circumstances.

A second category from which the state derived revenue was inheritance, and the sixth question put to al-Maghīlī demonstrates the ways Islam could be highly beneficial to the *askia*. At issue was matriliny and the widespread custom of inheriting through the female line, such that nephews inherited from their maternal uncles, a practice dating back to ancient Ghana. Here the scholar's response was far more straightforward: if, after being given an opportunity to change their ways, such persons continued to reject the patriliny of Islam, they were to be considered infidels, with the *askia* free to confiscate everything they own. But even if they repent and accept Islamic law, they could only retain what was inherited according to those laws, while the *askia* could take half of what remained.[107] This could have been a significant source of state income, as the *askia* contended he had "found large amounts of [such] wealth."

With respect to the third classification of agricultural produce, livestock, and fishing, several sources indicate this was an important revenue stream. In his fifth query, the *askia* asserts that in taking control of Songhay he now led people with "many fields under cultivation (*mazāri' kathīra*) and a wide river teeming with life," and asks: "Is it for me to impose taxation (*kharāj*) on their land or not, for *Sunni* 'Alī had greatly oppressed them in matters of taxation (*kharāj*) and other things?"[108] Al-Maghīlī responds that a just ruler has an obligation to appoint agents to collect *zakāt* (obligatory alms) on the productivity of the land and herds, and in levying *kharāj* he is to distribute the proceeds to the eight Qur'ānic categories of persons (*aṣnāf*) eligible to receive them.[109] So the issue was benefitting from the land, and here the *askia* was on firm legal ground. Agents appointed for such taxation may have included the *fari-mondio* (literally "chief of fields"), the Wanay-*farma*, and the *bābali-farma*.

The *askia*'s reference to the Niger re-centers the plight of the Sorko. Together with the shallow-fishers of the Sorogo or Bozo, and the deep-channel activities of the Somono, these fisher communities would have been expected to provide a portion of their catch for the benefit of the state, in addition to their naval responsibilities. While references to these and the "twenty-four tribes" are largely confined to manuscript C, all versions of *Ta'rīkh al-fattāsh* contain a soliloquy attributed to *Askia al-ḥājj* Muḥammad in which he refers to the Sorko and the "Arbī" as "our slaves" (*mamlūkān linā*).[110] This necessarily had a productive component, and since the Sorko were fisherfolk, manuscript C's claim that the "Zanjī" were required to provide quantities of dried fish each year is consistent with the overall evidence.

The observations of Leo Africanus are instructive here, as he mentions agricultural produce accounting for a considerable proportion of Songhay's market activity. Concerning Gao he records "bread and meat are abundant," while "melons, cucumbers, and excellent squash are plentiful, and there are enormous quantities of rice," with many "sweet water wells," though wine and fruits were difficult to locate (as should be expected with the former). In Jenne and Timbuktu he similarly found "a great abundance of barley, rice, livestock, fish and cotton," with a "great abundance of cereals and livestock" in the latter, "hence the consumption of milk and butter is considerable." However, he directly contradicts the *askia*'s assertions regarding *Sunni* ʿAlī, alleging it was actually the *askia* who "taxes them so heavily that he barely leaves them enough to subsist on."[111] It would therefore appear that the *kharāj* on agriculture and livestock was a substantial source of state income.[112]

There is no indication in the sources as to how *kharāj* was determined, but it may have been an annual levy paid in kind. The fourth category of revenue—tribute assessed on subject provinces not fully integrated into Songhay proper—is universally characteristic of empire, and would have been similar to *kharāj* if also collected yearly, the detritus of negotiation between unequals. Subject provinces would have included Air and Kaniaga/Futa Kingui, where the governor, though initially toppled by Songhay in the case of the former, was thereafter selected by a mechanism internal to the province (while subject to Gao's approval).

As an example of how tribute from subject provinces worked, and with respect to Air and its town of Agades, Africanus reported that its ruler "earns a large revenue from the dues which the foreign merchants pay, and from the products of the country, but he emits a tribute of some 150,000 ducats (i.e., *mithqāls*) to the king of Timbuktu" (that is, *Askia al-ḥājj* Muḥammad), paid in gold.[113] To put this in some perspective, this amounts to one-half of what the *askia* reportedly transported during *ḥājj*; Air's annual tribute to Gao was therefore considerable, if not staggering.

This fourth category of state revenue partially coincides with the fifth, the spoils of war or *fay'* in Islamic law, as the latter covers not only the initial spoils but also subsequent tribute from territories militarily defeated.[114] Regarding the former, Songhay amassed booty in every successful campaign, with the *askia*'s expeditions against the Mossi, the Malians at Tinfarin, and the *kanfāri*'s foray against Tengela resulting in enormous hauls. Conflicts with Borgu and Hausaland also provided Songhay with significant spoils, with all of the campaigns acquiring captives, a circumstance in which women feature.

By every indication, therefore, Songhay achieved extraordinary levels of prosperity under *Askia al-ḥājj* Muḥammad. Food was plentiful, with Jenne making "considerable profit from the trade in cotton cloth which they carry on with the Barbary merchants," its residents "very well dressed, [wearing] a large swathe of cotton, black or blue, with which they cover even the head," while the inhabitants of Timbuktu were "very rich, especially the resident strangers," serviced by "numerous artisans' workshops, merchants, and in particular, weavers of cotton" imported from Europe.

Africanus describes Gao as "very civilized compared to Timbuktu," also made up of "rich merchants," but of the peasantry he simply says

> the remainder of the kingdom is made up of towns and villages, where cultivators and herdsmen live. In winter they dress in sheepskins. In summer they go naked and barefoot. . . . These are men of total ignorance.[115]

Though such comments suggest bias, differences in materiality between city and countryside were probably substantial. The metrics by which "civilizations" are assessed are often principally informed by the urban setting, and by such measures imperial Songhay fares well. Al-Sa'dī may have summed it up best when asserting that with the success of the *askia*'s Pilgrimage, Islamic reforms, and military conquests also came "expansive prosperity and widespread blessings."[116]

References to cotton and commerce concern the final category of revenue—customs paid on goods passing through Timbuktu, Jenne, and Gao, as well as profits from the Taghaza salt mines—and this category could have been the most consequential, as it has been speculated that income from the trans-Saharan trade, which would have flowed through Agades and Walata/Biru (to a lesser extent), was far greater than revenue raised from the peasantry (*kharāj*).[117] The importance of such revenue is also made clear from the number of officials responsible for gathering it, who were strategically placed throughout the wide expanse of Songhay's domains, which included the Timbuktu-*mondio* and Jenne-*mondio*, but also the Tasara/Tusur-*mondio* and the Masina-*mondio*, all concerned with tax collection in their towns or provinces.[118] *Mondios* were likewise assigned to tax other sources, and officials such as the Barbūshi-*mondio* and the Taghaza-*mondi*o were responsible for trans-Saharan caravans passing through other, lesser entrepots as well as the Taghaza salt mines.[119] The array of such officials means that Gao was fairly focused on the economy, as every sector of society contributed to the imperial coffers, be it agrarian, fishing, urban, commercial, or industrial. There is more to investigate regarding taxation in Timbuktu and Jenne, but as will become clear, it is not easily disentangled from religion, internal mechanisms of municipal self-governance, or the nature of relations between political and cultural-economic hubs.

In sum, a likely conspiracy between powerful Timbuktu interests and Tondi-*farma* Muḥammad led to the overthrow of a Sunni dynasty with roots deep in the ancient pedigree of the Zuwās/Juwās/Jā's. The resulting resistance was deep and widespread, generating efforts to legitimate the new Askia regime that would include not only the Pilgrimage, but the diffusion of new traditions in an extensive propaganda campaign.

Askia al-ḥājj Muḥammad was not simply interested in power, however, but in the reinvention of Songhay as a Muslim state, advancing beyond and transitioning from the perception of Mali as a Muslim land. Such a transformation would not only involve the implementation of Islamic law—at least in the major urban areas—but also the creation of a Songhay imperial identity, to which multiple communities and regions could owe their ultimate allegiance. This was a very different vision for Songhay, a political project never before seen in the region, facilitating its reintegration into the international context.

It is with the Askia dynasty that features of government come into sharper relief, and though the analysis is hampered (again) by an absence of notarial documentation, the evidence is sufficient to discern the broad contours of Songhay administration. Divided into eastern and western spheres and led by an inner circle in which the *kanfāri* and *huku-kuri-koi* loom large, Songhay's territorial claims extended far and wide. Provincial status, methods and principles of taxation, and the apparatus through which all was articulated take on definitive form. No facet of imperial formation, however, holds greater fascination than Gao's relations with Timbuktu, subject of the next chapter.

CHAPTER ELEVEN

Of Clerics and Concubines

AS IT CONCERNS IMPERIAL SONGHAY, fewer themes have received greater attention than the relations between Gao and Timbuktu. An edifice of Timbuktu exceptionalism is the result, but closer examination of the testimony challenges the consensus. Framed by regional offices and protocols, a startlingly different composite picture forms, with a much-neglected Inland Delta assuming major proportions. As such, the inquiry attenuates the idea of Timbuktu as a political locus, while accentuating its position as a spiritual and cultural center. The reorientation proves entirely revelatory, with women emerging as spiritual and political power brokers. In fact, it is the concubine who features as the conduit of new political experimentation in West Africa, a pursuit of pluralism, reflecting ethnicity's evolving relevance.

The Inland Delta and the Mori Koyra

It is useful to recall that the *ta'rīkhs* (*tawārīkh*) trace the lineage of *Askia al-ḥājj* Muḥammad's father to the Mande-speaking, ancient Ghana-associated Wangāra, with a more specific membership in either the Silla or Ture clan of the Soninke. His mother was from Kara or Kura, daughter of the Kara/Kura-*koi* Bukar.[1] Kara (or Kala) was a province east of Jenne, whereas Kura seems to be the name of a lake south of Timbuktu. Whatever the correct rendering, Kasay was from the Inland Delta, with maternal bonds one reason for the *askia's* strong ties to the region. Indeed, the connection to the Inland Delta may explain why *Ta'rīkh al-fattāsh*, in making the point that the Bara-*koi* was alone in supporting Muḥammad Ture, only mentions rulers of provinces in or connected to the Delta; this was Muḥammad Ture's regional home, beyond which he could not have expected assistance.

The possibility that Muḥammad and his brothers ʿUmar and Yaḥyā hailed from the Inland Delta also helps to explain the choice of Tendirma as the site of the western capital. Strategically located to the north of Lake Debo, near the Niger, to both regulate and protect Timbuktu's commerce, Tendirma was also a place where Soninke culture had a presence, as both the *kanfāri* and the *balmaʿa* of Kabara, Timbuktu's river port, were greeted with the title of "Tunkara" ("Your Excellency"), tracing back to the early Soninke state of Ghana.[2] As the office of *kanfāri* was created by *Askia al-ḥājj* Muḥammad and (with that of the *balmaʿa*) was associated with Soninke culture, it is even possible that Soninke was the *askia*'s native tongue.

Given the *askia*'s roots and heritage in the Inland Delta, it is hardly surprising that the Soninke *jèséré* or *gesere*, entrusted with maintaining and reproducing the past (particularly of nobles and royals), are said to have followed the *askia* from the Delta to Gao, where they were the generative source of royal traditions.[3] But they were not the only ones to have made that west-to-east trek.

The prior introduction of the Mori Koyra (or Mōri-Koïra), the "village of saints" and scholars, posits that the Mande term *mōri* (like *karamoko*) was apparently used to distinguish Mande holymen from those of other ethnic and cultural backgrounds.[4] It is presented in the sources as a specific place, as in the case of Ḥaddu b. Yūsuf, a Moroccan occupational official who around 1013/1604 fled from Tendirma to Mori Koyra in fear for his life, or when *Sunni* ʿAlī is alleged to have given a leading female captive as a gift to "the village of Mori Koyra."[5] Though such spatiality is reflected in the contemporary village of Morikoira's identification with this clerisy, the community's location in the sources can be ambiguous. Even so, the sources consistently associate the people of Mori Koyra with the Inland Delta.[6]

Emerging from the associations of the late eighth/fourteenth and/or early ninth/fifteenth-century *faqīh Mōri* Hawgāru—celebrated as Mori Koyra's founder, along with such luminaries as *Modibo* Muḥammad al-Kāborī and *Mōri* Magha Kankoi—is the observation that both Kabora and Jinjo were important centers for the Mori Koyra.[7] Serving as the centerpiece of *Mansā* Mūsā indigenization strategy, Kabora's connection with Jinjo is of significant historicity, a fusion wonderfully demonstrated in the person of the *faqīh* Ṣiddīq b. Muḥammad Tagalī, *imām* of Jingereber mosque in Timbuktu, who is described as "a Kābarī by origin, born in Jinjo."[8]

Mori Koyra-affiliated scholars could therefore be found in settlements that included not only Kabora and Jinjo but Tendirma as well, and this conjoined relationship, in addition to its strategic location and site of Soninke settlement, helped to inform the choice of Tendirma as the seat of the *kanfāri*'s authority. The Inland Delta was thus a vital source of support for the *askia*, with the Mori Koyra as a principal component, having backed the Tondi-*farma* in the high stakes gamble against *Sunni* ʿAlī. With the Tondi-*farma*'s victory, the Mori Koyra were handsomely rewarded, most apparent in the example of the most powerful cleric to journey with the *jèséré* from the Inland Delta to Gao—the aforementioned *Mōri* (*Alfā*) Ṣāliḥ Diawara, a Soninke (*wankorī*), from the village of Tawta Allāh "in the land of Tendirma."[9]

While the *taʾrīkhs* differ on precisely who accompanied the *askia* on the Pilgrimage, they agree that Ṣāliḥ Diawara and ʿAlī Fulan were among them; together with the *Kanfāri* ʿUmar, they were probably the three most influential individuals in the kingdom other than the *askia* himself. It was the intervention of Ṣāliḥ Diawara that saved the royal caravan from sure death in traveling between Mecca and Cairo; it was Ṣāliḥ Diawara who in Medina prayed for *Kanfāri* ʿUmar left behind in Gao. And it was Ṣāliḥ Diawara, not the clerics in Timbuktu or Jenne, who not only instructed the *askia* in pursuing a legally-prescribed *jihād*, but who led that effort in serving as an emissary to the ruler of Yatenga. In playing such a prominent role in the early part of the *askia*'s reign, he is to be credited with a movement from diffidence to alacrity in the royal court's embrace of Islam, as he provided much of the knowledge base upon which a new, Islamically-oriented Songhay was constructed. It is difficult to identify anyone in Gao approximating his stature or influence following his death, which is simply recorded as having occurred during the *askia*'s reign.[10]

Ṣāliḥ Diawara was not the only *mōri*/*alfa* to have achieved notoriety. Though apocryphal, the very fact that *Mōri* Muḥammad Hawgāru, *Mōri* Muḥammad of Tinenka, and *Alfa* Muḥammad Tule are placed with the *askia* during his Pilgrimage underscores the prestige that only their presence could afford. In fact, it is *Mōri* Hawgāru's descendant *Mōri* al-Ṣādiq, who with brother *Mōri* Jayba railed against *Sunni* ʿAlī, who is claimed as the source in manuscript C for a version of Tendirma's past that includes seven princes descended from Jews, each with 12,000 cavalry and infantry without number; profoundly deep wells sustaining incredible agricultural yields; 100 masons who build the new capital in less than one year (in 902/1496–97); and the controversial "Zanjī" and Sorko. That is, the story seeks credibility by linking with the venerable community of the Mori Koyra.[11]

Apocrypha and verity come together in unique state privileges bestowed upon the Mori Koyra.[12] Though there are discrepancies among the manuscripts of *Ta'rīkh al-fattāsh*, all agree the community enjoyed preferential treatment. As the story goes, in the course of 913/1507–08 the *Mōri* brothers al-Ṣādiq and Jayba, along with a third brother Muḥammad, appealed to the *askia* in Kabara, complaining of their exile and egregious suffering under *Sunni* ʿAlī. The *askia* responds by giving each of them ten slaves (*ʿabīd*) and one hundred head of cattle as compensation. The brothers then encounter five more brothers who, upon learning of their good fortune, demand that all be equally divided. An angry dispute results in their return to the *askia*, who indicates that all along he had assumed there were other descendants of *Mōri* Hawgāru to whom he could be generous, and promptly gives to each of the five additional *mōris* ten slaves and one hundred head of cattle, adding that he would pay them the same compensation (*gharāma*) every year for as long as he lived.

It gets even better for the Mori Koyra. Guaranteed an annual allotment of slaves and livestock, they are also provided a letter of safe conduct throughout the realm, protecting against soldiers' arbitrary seizure of their property. Ibn al-Mukhtār, Maḥmūd Ka'ti's maternal grandson and the one who completes *Ta'rīkh al-fattāsh*, claims to have read this letter himself, describing its frayed condition. It stipulates that the Mori Koyra are to be exempt from all royal levies and fines (*waẓā'if sulṭana wa gharāmatahu*) in perpetuity, and that they may take wives from any community in the empire save the Sorko and the Arbi, who are the "property" (*mamlūkān*) of the *askia*.[13] These privileges were to be honored by all subsequent Songhay rulers.

This remarkable correspondence, allegedly written by ʿAlī b. ʿAbd ʿAllāh b. ʿAbd al-Jabbār al-Yemenī and witnessed by the *faqīh* Abū Bakr b. *Alfa* ʿAlī Kāra b. *al-Khaṭīb* ʿUmar, *Alfaka* (presumably similar to *Alfa*) ʿAbd ʿAllāh b. Muḥammad al-Aghlālī, and al-ʿĀqib b. Muḥammad al-Sharīf, is then proclaimed before an assembly of dignitaries: the Kalisi-*farma* Sulaymān Kindankaria (or Kundi-Koray), the Wanay-*farma* Mūsā Yunbul (or Yanbalu), the Shā'-*farma* ʿAlū, the Hari-*farma* ʿAbd ʿAllāh, and the *Kanfāri* ʿAlī Kusili (or Kusira), who swear to honor it.[14] The challenges in this account begin with the alleged letter writer and a witness, the one supposedly from Yemen and the other a *sherīfian*. While possible, high regard for both statuses is a caution, further strengthened by considering those to whom the decree was supposedly read. These officials actually served, but precisely when they served is another matter. Though 'Alū seems to have been in office by the end of *Askia al-ḥājj* Muḥammad's reign, it cannot be verified that Sulaymān Kindankaria, Mūsā Yunbul, or 'Abd 'Allāh were also in office at that time, while 'Alī Kusili does not become *kanfāri* until *Askia* Ismā'īl.[15] Perhaps their offices are mentioned to represent what they would become, as opposed to what they actually were in 913/1507–08. Potentially more critical, however, is that they were all sons of *Askia al-ḥājj* Muḥammad, reinforcing that his pledge was to be maintained by his progeny. Key to understanding the exceptionalization of the Mori Koyra community is that the *askia* was repaying them for their active opposition to the *sunni* and, by implication, their support of the Tondi-*farma* in his time of need.

The relationship between the royal family and the Mori Koyra was therefore close, if not intimate, and as the sources give the title *mōri* to two of the *askia*'s sons, 'Uthmān Sayyid and Muḥammad Kunbu, they may have pursued scholarship in association with the clerisy.[16] Maḥmūd Ka'ti himself studied under the *mōris*, stating he learned an aspect of *Mansā* Mūsā's Pilgrimage from "our *shaykh Mōri* Bukar b. Ṣāliḥ the Soninke (*wangarbe*)."[17] Ka'ti's reference ties together the Mori Koyra, their Soninke background, and their influence in the royal sphere. As *Ta'rīkh al-fattāsh* asserts kinship ties between the Sunnis, the Askias, and the Mori Koyra as descendants of the Wangāra (or Jula), the verifiability of such claims is less important than their acceptance as verity, a basis for very real political alliances.

In fact, the family of Maḥmūd Ka'ti was a major conduit for interactions between the *askia*, the *kanfāri*, and the Mori Koyra. Though manuscript C's inclusion of Maḥmūd Ka'ti in the *askia*'s Pilgrimage of 902/1496 is highly unlikely (as he would have been an infant if born as early as 898/1493), he is listed, as are the additional *mōris*, to both exploit and enhance the status of the Ka'ti family in Songhay. The Ka'tis were not only tied to the Askias through arguable myth, but also through very tangible linkages of power, and in ways that once again connect with the Mori Koyra. Thus, both Maḥmūd Ka'ti and his son Ismā'īl served as Tendirma's *qāḍī*. The purported Jewish origins of Tendirma, as contained in *Ta'rīkh al-fattāsh*, become all the more intriguing given speculation that the Ka'ti family shared those same origins. But in identifying its initiating author as Maḥmūd Ka'ti b. *al-ḥājj* al-Mutawakkil Ka'ti al-Kurminī al-Wa'kurī (*wangarī*), *Ta'rīkh al-fattāsh* itself serves as a mechanism of connectivity, employing the idiom of family in the service of privilege.[18]

The prestige enjoyed by the Mori Koyra in Gao may in fact explain the initial, rather odd question (purportedly) from *Askia* Muḥammad to al-Maghīlī in the *Replies*:

> Concerning the first [matter] you raised: Since God blessed us with Islam, a disaster has overtaken us in this land, explaining our lack of confidence in those in our land in whom is attributed learning [based on the Qur'ān]. One of their characteristics is that they are non-Arabs, who understand nothing of the Arabic language save a few words spoken by Arabs in their midst, [resulting in] tremendously distorted and corrupted and un-Arabic [meanings], to the degree that they do not know the arguments of scholars, where distortion and corruption have no place. Even so, they have books and stories and information that they teach, and among them are judges and exegetes who talk about the religion of God, claiming they are among the scholars who are heirs of the prophets, and that we must emulate them. . . . Is it permissible for me to do as they say regarding God's religion . . . ?[19]

The group under assault is unidentified, but presumably it would not have been the learned clerics of Timbuktu and Jenne, some of whom claimed Arab ancestry, and among the most prominent of whom had tremendous facility in the Arabic language. This leaves open the possibility, purely conjectural, that al-Maghīlī targets the Mori Koyra, or some other group, to enhance his own cachet. If viewed as an impediment, Mori Koyra influence could have been mitigated by way of placing the query in the mouth of the *askia*.

Whoever may have been the object of al-Maghīlī's critique, the Mori Koyra were clearly prominent under *Askia* Muḥammad, with one source synopsizing their role: "We are the marabouts of the Songhay. They consult with us concerning everything they do."[20] Marginalized in *Ta'rīkh as-sūdān* and virtually dismissed in the scholarship, they are overshadowed by the stature of Timbuktu.

Timbuktu, Jenne, and the Imperial Center

The close connection between Gao, Tendirma, and the Inland Delta, greatly facilitated through intimacy with the Mori Koyra, provides the most appropriate context for understanding the relationship between Gao and its two most important commercial and cultural centers—Timbuktu and Jenne. It is fair to say the collective scholarly perspective is uniform, that there is consensus. Summarily, the view is that Timbuktu in particular, and Jenne by extension functioned as autonomous political spaces, in which the authority of the *qāḍī* and other prominent religious figures and scholars was paramount and unencumbered by interference from Gao, such that "Timbuktu was part of the Songhai empire, but was not strictly ruled or dominated by the Songhai."[21] According to this view, the imperial administration in Timbuktu was nominal: "Under the Askiya Muḥammad and his successors the *qāḍīs* held real authority in Timbuktu and seem to have been more influential than the governor of Timbuktu (*Timbuktu-koi*). The *qāḍī* acted independently, and even prevented messengers of the *askiya* from carrying out their duties in the city."[22] Though appointed by the *askia*, "in reality the essence of power was in the hand of the qāḍī named by the Askia and was independent of the Timbuktu-koi."[23] This notion is best summarized as follows:

> It was, perhaps, during the sixteenth century that Timbuktu enjoyed its greatest degree of independence, and also of security. Though an integral part of the Songhay empire, with a governor (the Timbuktu-*koi*) appointed by the Askia as well as other officials of secondary importance . . . the city, through the enormous prestige of its *qāḍī* and the veneration in which its scholars and holy men were held, managed to be virtually self-governing and to be sheltered from arbitrary exactions by either Songhay officials or the desert-dwellers.[24]

Indeed, so great was the weight of Timbuktu's religious establishment that not only is it argued it was virtually independent of Gao's authority, but that its reach extended to Gao, where it was highly influential in shaping state policy. In adopting such a position, scholars have essentially embraced the written sources' characterization of these relationships, as *Ta'rīkh al-fattāsh* asserts: "And indeed, at that time Timbuktu had no authority except for the authority of divine law, and there was no ruler in it; the *qāḍī* was the ruler, and in his hand alone was the power to loose and to bind."[25] But in accepting this representation, scholars have not fully considered all of the evidence the *ta'rīkhs themselves* provide. What follows, therefore, is an interrogation of the Gao-Timbuktu-Jenne nexus that diverges from both the consensus as well as the propaganda of the *ta'rīkhs*, arguing that just the opposite was true: that Gao so drained the resources and revenue of Timbuktu and Jenne that the latter had great difficulty fending off excessive and frequent demands, leaving little doubt Gao enjoyed firm control over the entrepots, and that, in turn, Gao was virtually free of influence stemming from Timbuktu or Jenne (as opposed to the Mori Koyra).[26] It is within this context that Islam's expansion within the empire can be properly understood, as they were mutually constitutive.

A reconsideration of the political apparatus in Timbuktu reveals the now familiar dual administrative approach: an imperial arrangement with clear lines of authority leading directly to the *askia* in Gao, and a municipal government under the authority of the *qāḍī*. Concerning imperial authority, the Timbuktu-*koi* headed the delegation, and as discussed, the office was formally integrated into Songhay under *Sunni* 'Alī and remained so under *Askia* Muḥammad.[27] Following the Timbuktu-*koi* was the Timbuktu-*mondio*, who could have been responsible for collecting city revenues, beyond whom were four additional offices: the Tasara/Tusur-*mondio*, who apparently worked closely with the Timbuktu-*mondio*; the Yubo-*koi* or "commissioner of the market"; the Koyra-*banda-mondio*, who had a supervisory capacity over areas outside of the city's perimeter; and the Ashar-*mondio*, either an assistant to the *qāḍī* or the chief of police, and, if the latter, possibly part of the *askia*'s coterie. Altogether, these posts constituted Timbuktu's imperial administration. In addition, the heterogeneity of the city was managed by officials responsible for its various quarters and ethnic groups, including the Barbūshi-*mondio*, who liaised with Arabo-Berbers within the city, and the Maghsharan-*koi*, head of the Kel Tamasheq living north of the city.

In conjunction with offices inside Timbuktu were those associated with its port town of Kabara (five miles to the south): the powerful position of the *balma'a*, the town's military leader and commander of its garrison; and the Kabara-*farma*, who oversaw the town's quotidian affairs that probably included customs collection.[28]

As for Jenne and the Jenne-*koi* as its traditional head, the dual administrative scheme can be observed in the office of the Jenne-*mondio*, who as its "governor" answered directly to the *askia*, an arrangement made visible late in the history of imperial Songhay, when the Moroccan invasion and the death of the Jenne-*koi* Waybu'alī shifted attention to its Jenne-*mondio* Bukarna. That the chief imperial officer of the town was called the "Jenne-*mondio*" equally underscores his principal responsibility—overseeing revenue collection. Jenne also had an Ashar-*mondio*, with more details about the town's administration lacking.[29]

Given their high commercial and cultural profile, Timbuktu and Jenne formed a corridor with its own military capabilities, which was then folded into a regional system of security under the authority of the *kanfāri* of (relatively) nearby Tendirma, so vital that it could only be entrusted to Muḥammad's brother and closest confidant, 'Umar. It is beyond credulity that the *askias* would maintain such an impressive array of officials and military potential did they not intend to fully control the corridor.

It could be asserted that these arrangements were in place not solely as security measures, but also out of recognition that Timbuktu's *qāḍī* indeed exercised unique and appreciable power. To be sure, he was responsible for adjudicating cases on the basis of *sharīʿa*; however, as his influence was not limited to juridical matters but extended into multiple arenas, it has been argued he was the virtual leader of the city, in conjunction with others of the scholarly community.[30] The *jamāʿa* or association of the learned enjoyed incomparable prestige among the city's inhabitants by virtue of their scholarship, piety, and wealth, the last further evidence of their *baraka*.[31] These factors would suggest the *qāḍī* wielded a form of politico-administrative authority that transcended the limits of posts under his direct control (such as the *imāms* of some, but not all of the mosques).

Bolstering this contention is the observation that a prospective Timbuktu *qāḍī* had to meet qualifications that placed him in the most rarified of atmospheres. In addition to a high level of erudition, he required an intimate knowledge of the city as well as an independent and sufficient means of income, mitigating susceptibility to bribery while ensuring implementation of his *fatwās* (legal decisions). But most importantly, he needed the approbation of the *ʿulamā'*. As has been and will be further discussed, the office was restricted to members of the Aqīt family after the demise of *Sunni* ʿAlī.[32]

Given both the *qāḍī*'s prominence and the existence of an imperial staff in and around Timbuktu, the lines of authority are not always readily apparent, leading some to maintain that imperial officials actually answered to the *qāḍī*.[33] However, there are two separate passages in *Ta'rīkh al-fattāsh* revealing that, among other things, the imperial administration was indeed under the *askia*'s direct control. The first involves a conversation between *Qāḍī* Maḥmūd and *Askia* Muḥammad, a portion of which was examined in relation to the latter's probable participation in *Sunni* ʿAlī's assassination. The entire incident reveals the *qāḍī*'s vehement refusal to comply with an imperial directive, followed by the beating and expelling of imperial representatives from the city. Rather than the *qāḍī*'s actions, more instructive here is the *askia*'s attempt to realize material benefits that the *qāḍī* found objectionable, thus exposing the dual administration of (and fissures within) the city.[34]

The second bit of evidence emanates from the reign of *Askia* Dāwūd (956–90/1, 1549–82/83), who apparently visited Timbuktu on a regular basis and followed a prescribed itinerary.[35] According to *Ta'rīkh al-fattāsh*, it was his custom first to visit the Yubo-*koi*, the Timbuktu-*koi*, the Barbūshi-*mondio*, and the Koyra-*banda-mondio* in Balma-Dyinde, the northern quarter of the city, and it was only after conferring with the imperial staff that he would seek an audience with the *qāḍī*.[36] He would then greet the *'ulamā'* at Jingereber mosque and return to Balma-Dyinde, where he held audiences with the merchants and other notables. The pattern of royal visits clearly adheres to an administrative dichotomy, just as the fact that Dāwūd frequented the city manifests, in conjunction with a considerable imperial staff and military presence, keen interest in the city's affairs. The existence of imperial officials residing in Timbuktu further militates against the concept of the city's independence, with imperial fiscal policy rendering the idea even more implausible.

A proper evaluation of such evidence returns to a discussion of Songhay taxation, specifically pertaining to the sixth and final category or revenue—customs paid on commercial goods passing through the major entrepots—and necessarily approached through Islamic legal prescription. In fact, questions over the legality of certain taxes provide the means to assess claims of Timbuktu and Jenne autonomy. Though often indirect and imprecise, references to taxation suggest Islamic law provided its approximate parameters, and that the overwhelming proportion of revenues from Timbuktu derived from the trans-Saharan trade. Such a twofold thesis is based on the reputation of the city as a paradigm of Islamic culture, as well as its preeminent position vis-à-vis other commercial centers.

The Muslims of Timbuktu and Jenne paid *zakāt* (obligatory alms) to the legal treasury at Gao. As the tax applied to urban dwellers, this should have meant they paid *zakāt* upon their personal property, gold, and commercial goods to the value of one-tenth of the whole. Therefore, it is likely that merchants paid at least a tenth of the value of trade commodities imported into Timbuktu. This revenue would have been collected within Timbuktu itself rather than Kabara, as the Kabara-*farma* did not collect *zakāt*, but *gharāma*, a kind of extralegal levy in accordance with the general practice of Islamic rulers. At Timbuktu, the collection of the legal tax may have been the responsibility of the Tasara/Tusur-*mondio*, who with the Timbuktu-*mondio* appears in *Ta'rīkh al-fattāsh*. Such double taxation, Islamic and non-Islamic, would not have been unusual, and although a portion of the taxes collected by the Tasara/Tusur-*mondio* may have been surrendered to the *qāḍī*, the size of the trans-Saharan trade and the general prosperity of the city guaranteed that Gao's share would be substantial.[37]

The most salient point to emerge from this discussion is the probability of two different sets of taxes: those prescribed by Islamic law, and those imposed by the imperial regime. Based upon this arrangement, it is possible to take the question of a self-governing Timbuktu and Jenne still further. Specifically, the data where available suggest that not only did Gao benefit enormously from taxing Timbuktu-Jenne commerce—in itself sufficient evidence Gao realized its economic objectives—but also that it did so through imposing illegal as well as legal taxes. The problem of non-*sharīʿa* taxation is a recurrent theme in the history of the *dār al-Islām*, and falls under the rubric of *maks* (pl. *mukūs*)—a toll, a customs duty, or a form of market dues. Under the Fatimids and Mamluks, a variety of items were taxed in this way, with rulers demonstrating their piety by repealing *mukūs*, only to reimpose them.[38]

The *gharāma* collected in Kabara by the Kabara-*farma* is one example of dual taxation, but the real question concerns taxation in Timbuktu itself. There it would appear the basic tax was the legal *zakāt*, whose payment to Gao implies a degree of control over the former by the latter, but also supports the image of Timbuktu as a center of piety, since from that perspective it was less a matter of Gao imposing its will than Timbuktu complying with divine law. However, if it can be demonstrated that Gao also sought to extract *maks* from Timbuktu, its image as an imperial force aggressively exploiting its main commercial market would be burnished.

Maks *and the* Qāḍīs

A guiding hypothesis for the establishment of the Askia dynasty is a probable conspiracy involving the Tondi-*farma* and the Timbuktu *'ulamā'* who suffered murder, exile, and humiliation under *Sunni* ʿAlī, and that an early agenda item for the new *askia* was the restoration of these clerical families. It is not clear precisely when that community, and particularly the Aqīt family, returned from exile to Timbuktu, but at least some were already back by the death of the *Qāḍī* Ḥabīb in 904/1498–99, at which point Maḥmūd b. ʿUmar was appointed by *Askia* Muḥammad as Ḥabīb's successor.

Notwithstanding the need to repay the Aqīts for their support, there is no reason to doubt the *askia*'s sincerity in reinventing the new regime as an Islamic one. But the *askia* surely nursed a strong interest in restoring the town's commercial health, which had suffered under the mercurial *Sunni* ʿAlī, resulting in the flight of commerce east to Hausaland.[39] The Sankore connection with northern Arabo-Berber merchants was therefore indispensable, with any disturbance to it proving highly disruptive. No scholar argues for an autonomous Timbuktu under ʿAlī's thirty-year reign, but as will be demonstrated, the new regime's commercial interest was qualitatively no different than that of its predecessor.

The post-904/1498–99 encounter between *Askia* Muḥammad and the *Qāḍī* Maḥmūd, in which the former expressed angst, if not guilt over the deposition of *Sunni* ʿAlī, offers a clear indication of that interest, its details recorded for posterity:

> Then he [the *askia*] said to him [Maḥmūd] after the completion of the greetings and salutations, "I sent to you my envoys bearing my concerns—did you carry out my order in Timbuktu? No! Rather, you sent back my messengers and forbid them from making my concerns evident. Did not the Mali-*koi* rule Timbuktu?" The *shaykh* [Maḥmūd] replied, "Without question, he ruled it." He [the *askia*] continued, "In those days, was there not a *qāḍī* in Timbuktu?" He [Maḥmūd] said, "There certainly was." He [the *askia*] said, "Are you greater than that *qāḍī*, or is he greater than you?" He answered, "No doubt, he is greater than me, and more illustrious." Then the *askia* said, "Did his [the Mali-*koi*'s] *qāḍī* prevent him from acting freely in Timbuktu?" He [Maḥmūd] replied, "No, he did not prevent him." Then the *askia* said, "Were not the Tuareg the rulers (*sulṭāns*) of Timbuktu?" And he replied, "They certainly were." He [the *askia*] continued, "Was there not a *qāḍī* in it in those days?" He answered, "Certainly it was so." The *askia* said, "Are you greater than that *qāḍī*, or is he greater than you?" The *shaykh* replied, "Surely he is greater than me and more illustrious." Then he [the *askia*] said to him, "Did not *Chi* [*Sunni* ʿAlī] rule Timbuktu?" The *shaykh* said, "He surely did." He [the *askia*] continued, "In those days, was there not a *qāḍī* in it?" He replied, "There was." Then he [the *askia*] said, "He feared God more than you, or do you fear [God] more than he, and are you more illustrious?" He replied, "Without question, he was more God-fearing than I, and more illustrious." Then he [the *askia*] said, "Did these *qāḍīs* prevent these rulers from acting freely in Timbuktu, or were they able to do in the city whatever they wanted regarding matters of government and taxation?" Then he [Maḥmūd] answered, "They did not place an obstacle between them and their desires." Then he [the *askia*] said, "Then why do *you* [emphasis added] prohibit me [from doing the same], and restrain my hand and reject my messengers whom I sent to carry out my wishes; and [why did you] beat them and order their expulsion from the land [the city]? What's wrong with you? What's going on here? How do you explain this?!"[40]

The confrontation between these two powerful figures is jaw-dropping, with the key to the *askia*'s consternation the phrase "matters of government and taxation" (*min amr wa nahy wa akhdh wa ʿatā*ʾ, literally, "commanding and forbidding, and taking and giving"): the two areas in which imperial authority over Timbuktu, from the Malians and Tuareg through *Sunni* ʿAlī and the Askias, took on concrete form. Whatever the full range of *Askia* Muḥammad's concerns, taxes and his right to levy them were at their core. For his part, Maḥmūd's intrepid response indicates the *qāḍī* was himself upset; it is highly unlikely he would have taken such bold action had he not felt justified by the law. It therefore makes sense that the bone of contention between the two men was the problem of *maks*, non-*sharīʿa* taxation, which the *askia*, in accordance with traditional practice, was trying to impose. In response, the *qāḍī* felt compelled to resist such attempts in the effort to observe *sharīʿa*, as well as protect the scholarly and commercial community of the city he represented, and would have given a stern warning to the *askia*'s envoys sent to investigate his lack of cooperation. Relations between Gao and Timbuktu would have become strained over their public flogging, leading the *askia* to make personal inquiry into the *qāḍī's* insolence. In defense of his actions, Maḥmūd made the deft maneuver of referencing the *askia*'s prior request of assistance in avoiding hellfire. In recalling the earlier consultation, Maḥmūd implied his response to the *askia's* messengers was part of that assistance. Invoking holy law, the *qāḍī* stood his ground; the *askia*, his legitimacy premised entirely on his embrace of Islam, could in this instance only yield.

In describing the *qāḍīs* at Timbuktu, the sources portray them as defiant toward the rulers at Gao, in keeping with the normative conduct of holy men. A future *qāḍī* of Timbuktu, al-ʿĀqib, who took office in 973/1565, is said to have reached such heights that all were in "great awe of him," even rulers for whom he "cared nothing, and with whom he clashed," who would "yield to him and were in awe of him, obeying him in whatever he wanted." If he observed behavior he "abhorred" (highly suggestive of *maks*), he withdrew and "shut his door," and would have to be entreated to return to his post, a cycle repeated several times.[41] In a similar fashion, his nephew (and Aḥmad Bābā's father) Aḥmad b. *al-ḥājj* Aḥmad is described as greatly revered by "rulers and ruled," who treated rulers and their agents "harshly," such that they would "submit themselves to him with the greatest of submission" while visiting him in his home. The precise form of this "submission" is unclear, but given that Aḥmad b. *al-ḥājj* Aḥmad held no office, it most likely involved spiritual rather than political matters.[42]

Some three centuries later, Muḥammad Bello reiterated the principle: "Now the pious learned man is the one who does not envy what money you possess and treats you as you deserve in his preaching and his talk."[43] The behavior of *Qāḍī* Maḥmūd was therefore prescribed, but his success in this instance is also explained by his unique leverage owing to the circumstances of the *askia*'s seizure of power, and by the *askia*'s reluctance to offend the city's *'ulamā'* and return to an era of antagonism.

The preceding quarrel, however, also demonstrates that in pressing his authority, the *askia*'s view of the Aqīts had evolved. Though allied with the clerics, the *askia* was obviously feeling more secure in his position, more assertive some ten years after taking power. Though not at the same spiritual level as the Timbuktu *'ulamā'*, he himself had made *ḥajj*, had met renowned scholars, and was in possession of his own *baraka*. The effort to impose *maks* was therefore a statement of growing confidence, an indication he was becoming less dependent on the Aqīts and Anda ag-Muḥammads. In his response, *Qāḍī* Maḥmūd perspicaciously reminded the *askia* of all that was at stake.

Maḥmūd may have paid a price for his daring. In 915/1509–10, he made his own *ḥajj*, receiving the *askia*'s approval to appoint his maternal uncle al-Mukhtār al-Naḥwī as interim (literally, "deputy") *imām* of Sankore mosque, and 'Abd al-Raḥmān b. Abī Bakr as "deputy" *qāḍī*.[44] On the very day of his return the following year, Maḥmūd reclaimed the *imām* post from his uncle (surprising many who thought he would allow his uncle to remain in the position), but he did not seek the return of the *qāḍī* post from 'Abd al-Raḥmān, who continued in it another two years. Maḥmūd's immediate recovery of the *imām* position, but not that of the *qāḍī*, suggests humility was not a primary factor, evidenced when Maḥmūd later disagreed with a ruling (*fatwā*) of 'Abd al-Raḥmān, saying it contradicted the Qur'ān, the *sunna* (teachings and personal example traditions of the Prophet), and *ijmā'* (scholarly consensus). When 'Abd al-Raḥmān refused to alter his ruling, Maḥmūd made no further objection, but when informed of the dispute the *askia* sent messengers to Timbuktu, who convened the *'ulamā'* at Sīdī Yaḥyā mosque. 'Abd al-Raḥmān was reprimanded for not immediately relinquishing the post upon Maḥmūd's return, and ordered to vacate the post. It would take a second delegation of notables from Gao, however, to persuade Maḥmūd to resume his term as *qāḍī*. The notion of a substantially autonomous Timbuktu does not square with *Qāḍī* Maḥmūd's need for the *askia's* approval to name interim officials (the very arena in which one would expect such autonomy), while the implication of the entire affair is that the *askia* was quite content to be rid of the combative Maḥmūd as *qāḍī*, a sentiment apparently fully appreciated by Maḥmūd. With 'Abd al-Raḥmān's position becoming untenable, the *askia* had no choice except to seek Maḥmūd's reinstatement, though the fact that he was forced to intervene makes the point that the appointment of the *qāḍī*, as well as other, lesser religious offices, was ultimately the prerogative of the ruler.

There was gravity to an appointment as *qāḍī*. Although Aḥmad Bābā writes of the "honor" of being a *qāḍī*, it was also controversial, especially in Timbuktu, where the post was the interface between local and imperial forces.[45] The fuss surrounding Maḥmūd's original appointment at the death of Ḥabīb illustrates this very well. Maḥmūd had been nominated to the *askia* by Abū Bakr b. al- Ḥājj, to the outrage of al-Mukhtār al-Naḥwī: "Why did you suggest my nephew? Do you not have a son capable of performing the duties of a *qāḍī*; why was *he* [emphasis added] not suggested?"[46] Al-Mukhtār al-Naḥwī's agitation can be explained, in part, by his firsthand knowledge of the challenges of dealing with rulers, going back to *Sunni* ʿAlī, but also by a reticence, customary throughout the Muslim world, to accept a position, however prestigious, which carried with it the risk of mortal sin. The sin in question stemmed from the very nature of a position that pronounced the judgments of God, but also from the possibility that the *qāḍī* might receive some benefit from the illicit revenues of the state. At Timbuktu in 904/1498–99, such considerations would have been compounded by its inescapable politics. The deceased *Qāḍī* Ḥabīb had been *Sunni* ʿAlī's choice, the latter an unmitigated scoundrel in the eyes of the Timbuktu *ʿulamāʾ*. Reservations concerning Ḥabīb could register in the fact that, though revered, relatively little is written about him.[47] *Sunni* ʿAlī's association with Ḥabīb and his office may have therefore tainted both, with the surviving scholarly community reluctant to again affiliate with either the ruler or the post, even during the early years of *Askia* Muḥammad.

Instances of refusing to occupy posts could be rather entertaining, including one concerning Sankore mosque.[48] Nearing death (which would arrive in 991/1583), *Qāḍī* al-ʿĀqib wanted his nephew Muḥammad al-Amīn b. *Qāḍī* Muḥammad to become Sankore mosque's *imām*, as al-ʿĀqib had also occupied this office, but his nephew's mother Nānā Ḥafṣa bt. *al-ḥājj* Aḥmad b. ʿUmar objected. The *qāḍī* then turned to the *faqīh* Muḥammad Baghayughu, who also declined, citing his responsibilities to a different mosque. Another nephew of *Qāḍī* al-ʿĀqib was then chosen, the *faqīh* Abū Bakr b. Aḥmad Bēr, who against his will led the prayers until the end of the very day of his installation, after which he bolted for another town. Finally, the *qāḍī*'s brother, the *faqīh* ʿAbd al-Raḥmān accepted the responsibility, though ill and perhaps not in a position to decline, serving until the Moroccan invasion several years later. While the reasons for these serial rejections are not provided, the ruler's required approval may have been an issue.

If there is uncertainty whether *maks* was a serious problem at the beginning of Maḥmūd's career as *qāḍī*, there is no question that such was the case toward its end. The evidence comes from the reign of *Askia* Isḥāq Bēr ("Isḥāq the Great," 946–956/1539–49) who, though depicted as virtuous and honorable, is also accused of illegally taking goods worth seventy thousand *mithqāls* in gold from Timbuktu's merchants through his servant (*khadīm*) Maḥmūd Yāza, "who moved back and forth between Gao and Timbuktu, extorting from every merchant according to his means."[49] Maḥmūd's authority was waning at the time; having assumed office at the age of thirty-five, he was at least seventy-seven at the beginning of Isḥāq Bēr's tenure. In contrast to his encounter with *Askia* Muḥammad, the *qāḍī* may have been too enfeebled to resist *Askia* Isḥāq Bēr's exactions, and "no one mentioned this [the exactions] during the *askia's* lifetime for fear of reprisal (*saṭwatihi*, literally "his ability to attack")."

Indirect evidence of *maks* also comes from the reign of *Askia* Isḥāq Bēr's successor Dāwūd (956–90 or 91/1549–82 or 83). With a reputation second only to *Askia al-ḥājj* Muḥammad in piety, and otherwise enthusiastically supported by the *'ulamā'*, Dāwūd nonetheless had conflicts with Timbuktu's *qāḍīs*, who, following the death of Maḥmūd (955/1548), were his sons Muḥammad (d. 973/1565) and al-'Āqib (d. 991/1583).[50] One misunderstanding had to do with the struggle over preeminence in the construction of Jingereber mosque.[51] But Aḥmad Bābā also writes of frequent, unspecified disagreements, and according to him, Dāwūd was repeatedly in violation of *sharī'a*.[52] Once again, the problem with *maks* may lie at the core of difficulties, indicating the *askia* was unwilling to relinquish the extralegal profits enjoyed by his predecessors, particularly in the case of Isḥāq Bēr.

Scenes from Jenne

This entire argument, from the economic motives of the rulers of Songhay to the conflict with the *qāḍīs*, may be corroborated with the experience of Jenne, Timbuktu's mirror (if slightly lesser) image at the Inland Delta's southern end, under the *Askias* Isḥāq Bēr and Dāwūd. Most illustrative of circumstances in Jenne is *Ta'rīkh al-fattāsh*'s rich and fascinating anecdote, dripping with irony, of an encounter between *Askia* Isḥāq Bēr and Maḥmūd Baghayughu, one of Jenne and Songhay's leading scholars, with whom the *askia* had managed to develop an adversarial relationship almost as soon as the latter took office.[53] Convening the whole of Jenne, both "commoners and the elite," before the grand mosque of Jenne, the *askia* pledged to resolve the city's festering discontent by punishing those guilty of harming the Muslim community and "oppressing" the people. The crowd remained silent for some time, until Maḥmūd Baghayughu, seated near the *askia*, spoke up:

> "Are you sincere in what you're saying, oh Isḥāq?" "By God, I am in earnest," the *askia* responded. "If we make known this tyrant to you, what will you do to him?" [The *askia* replied to the *faqīh*], "I will give him what he deserves, whether it is death, or a beating, or imprisonment, or exile, or restoring whatever property he destroyed, making him pay a fine." The *faqīh* Maḥmūd Baghayughu, may God be pleased with him, replied, "We know of no one here more tyrannical than *you* [emphasis added], as you are the father of and reason for all that is unjust, for no one here illegally seizes [wealth] by force except you, by your authority and on your orders. If you want to kill the tyrant, begin with yourself, and be quick about it! This wealth that you have taken from here to enrich yourself, is it [really] yours? Do you have slaves here who cultivate the soil for you, or assets that generate wealth for you?"

Such chippiness was not totally unprecedented, as can be observed in an earlier exchange between *Askia al-ḥājj* Muḥammad and the *Qāḍī* 'Umar of Yindubughu village, very close to Timbuktu.[54] The latter had been appointed by the *askia*, but *Qāḍī* Maḥmūd began to complain that 'Umar's nephew was in the habit of frequenting Timbuktu, only to return to "sow discord" with the inhabitants of Yindubughu, suggesting he took exception to Maḥmūd's rulings. Upon meeting the young man, the *askia* said: "So, you are the one sowing discord between the jurist Maḥmūd and your maternal uncle [*Qāḍī* 'Umar]," to which a greatly annoyed 'Umar interjected: "You are the sower of discord, who appointed a *qāḍī* in Timbuktu and another in Yindubughu," indicating the town and village were too close to warrant separate judges. The *askia* made no reply.

The encounter in Jenne between *Askia* Isḥāq Bēr and Maḥmūd Baghayughu, however, had far greater invective and proved far more consequential. In response to what can only be described as a stunning rebuke, a dazed, deeply sighing *askia* is said to have burst into tears, making such a visible display that the crowd began to pity him, his entourage staring menacingly at Maḥmūd Baghayughu. The "despicable and ignorant and lowly" then challenged the *faqīh*: "Is this the way you speak to the *sulṭān*?" On the verge of attacking him, they were prevented by the *askia*, who in humility turned to the *faqīh* and said, "By God, you have spoken the truth. I repent before God, and I ask your forgiveness." He continued shedding large tears upon returning to his camp from the mosque.

What happened next, however, was a masterstroke of political genius. Learning of the death of the *Khaṭīb* Aḥmad Turfu (or Aḥmad Sunkumū) in Jenne, the *askia* decided to name Maḥmūd Baghayughu as the *qāḍī* of Jenne, sending military officers to install him. Arriving in Jenne and gathering the people (including the "*sulṭān* of Jenne," apparently the Jenne-*koi*), the officers invested the *faqīh* with robes and a turban. It was now Maḥmūd Baghayughu's turn to cry, returning home to an incredulous wife.

> "Why did you consent to become *qāḍī*," she asked. "I did not consent to this," the *faqīh* replied, "They forced me and commissioned me." "It would have been better [the wife continued] if you had chosen death, and if you had said, 'Kill me, but I will not accept.'"

Now the wife began weeping, inconsolably, for days. The *faqīh* became so distraught he took ill, and died within weeks.

Isḥāq Bēr had extorted large sums of money from Timbuktu, and based upon his public confession in Jenne, he treated that town no differently. Rather than rewarding Maḥmūd Baghayughu, the *askia*, known as a "shrewd" man, was chastising him for his insolence, the decision to enturban him the most ironic of punitive measures.

Such a display of bitterness and reticence at assuming Jenne's most prestigious office suggests something was terribly amiss, that the office of *qāḍī* had become severely compromised as one of corruption and collaboration with imperial agents. Implicit in *Askia* Isḥāq Bēr's appointment of Maḥmūd is a cruel jest, repaying the cleric's insults by making him a part of the evil he decried. Whatever Isḥāq Bēr's intent, it is clear that *maks* had driven Jenne to despair.

Disdain for the *qāḍī* post at Jenne continued into the reign of *Askia* Dāwūd. In 973/1566 he sought to name Muḥammad, one of Maḥmūd Baghayughu's two sons (Aḥmad was the other), to the position. In light of their parents' experience, they refused and together took refuge in the mosque for several months. The crisis was only resolved when the brothers agreed to visit Dāwūd in Gao, but it underscores the problems with the office, along with the investiture of a town's *qāḍī* as ultimately a royal prerogative, not wholly internal to the locale.[55]

Reading Against the Grain of Timbuktu Political Influence

The evidence against Timbuktu's autonomy is therefore mutually reinforcing in at least two ways. First, imperial officials in Timbuktu were not subject to the *qāḍī* but to the *askia*. Second, Gao was highly successful in exploiting the commercial benefits of the entrepot, given the evidence concerning *Askias* Isḥāq and Dāwūd. Timbuktu would resist, now successfully in the encounter between *Qāḍī* Maḥmūd and *Askia* Muḥammad, later unsuccessfully under Isḥāq Bēr and Dāwūd. Brief and often indirect glimpses into the relationship between Gao and Timbuktu consistently reveal unrelenting pressure on the latter to contribute to the royal coffers, even and especially by illegal means. Evidence for Jenne confirms Gao's overall exploitative bent toward the Timbuktu-Jenne corridor.

As for the consensus that Timbuktu wielded significant influence over Gao and imperial policy, the observations of Felix Dubois, writing toward the end of the thirteenth/nineteenth century, have been influential:

> The marabouts regained their lost ground, however, under the Askias. The founder of the dynasty, whether from conviction or expediency, showed himself their ardent and untiring friend, and we have seen them lending devoted support to the usurper in return, and legitimizing with sacred texts his assumption of the throne. They were kept constantly about his person, and he consulted them in everything, even asking their advice in matters of war. He appealed to them in all legal affairs, and treated them, in short, as his ministers.[56]

Similarly, it has been asserted that "the cadi or judge of Timbuctoo became the Supreme Justice for the entire Songhoi Empire"; that *'ulamā'* in Timbuktu fully expected to regularly voice their opinions on political as well as judicial matters, with the Askias invariably responding by "promoting the *'ulamā'*'s interests"; that "throughout the sixteenth century the authority of the *qāḍī* in Timbuktu was uncontested and the *askiyas* rarely intervened in the internal affairs of the city," while "the Muslim scholars of Timbuktu exerted influence over the imperial policy of the *askiyas*"; and that Timbuktu was deeply involved in Gao's civil strife just prior to 999/1591.[57]

To the contrary, with the exception of the years 995–99/1586–91, the sources uniformly reveal that Timbuktu exerted little appreciable influence over the decision-making process at Gao. First, as has been established, the scholars of Mori Koyra occupied the highest rung of clerical authority in Gao. Second, the evidence does not support the characterization of Timbuktu *'ulamā'* "surrounding" the Askias, or that they even frequented

Gao. *Askia* Muḥammad received Maḥmūd at Gao on the occasion of the cleric's return from the Pilgrimage (having departed in 915/1509–10), but such does not represent a regular pattern.[58] On the possibility that the Askias customarily visited Timbuktu for advice, Aḥmad Bābā mentions *Askia al-ḥājj* Muḥammad's visit to Maḥmūd to obtain a blessing, but this hardly constitutes a political consultation.[59] *Askia* Dāwūd indeed took an active interest in Timbuktu, but there is no basis for the contention that his primary (or even secondary) reason for visiting the city was to solicit political counsel. In frequenting Timbuktu as a matter of policy, he was not seeking advice as to what that policy should be.

Al-Maghīlī certainly stressed the need to be well advised, and *Ta'rīkh al-fattāsh* asserts the *askia* was obedient to this admonition. However, the advisors he sought were not the scholars of Timbuktu.[60] Rather, there was al-Maghīlī himself, along with al-Suyūṭī, with whom the *askia* consulted while in Cairo. On a regular basis, his key advisors were in Gao and included 'Alī Fulan and *Mōri* Ṣāliḥ Diawara, who enjoyed the highest profile from among the Mori Koyra. These individuals were far more critical to policy formulation at Gao than scholars in Timbuktu.

The reasons for this state of affairs are unclear, but it must be kept in mind that Gao was itself an ancient town, in existence some eight hundred years before imperial Songhay's dawn. A major entrepot, Gao enjoyed significant commercial activity throughout the tenth/sixteenth century, with connections to Walata/Biru, Air, and Ghadames, and by extension Egypt and al-Maghrib. Islam had made its presence felt very early, with local traditions developing independently of those in either Jenne or Timbuktu. Individuals had long pursued the Islamic sciences, though with few exceptions is there evidence of marked erudition in Gao. Notwithstanding their perceived mediocrity, they served the Askias, with others of the Mori Koyra, to the virtual exclusion of more learned colleagues at Timbuktu.

The rare exception to the foregoing, and the only mention of political advice emanating from Timbuktu that was actually followed, concerns *Qāḍī* Maḥmūd's counsel to *Askia* Muḥammad regarding imprisoned Tuwatī merchants at Gao.[61] Beyond this, there is no evidence of Muḥammad deferring to Timbuktu on matters of imperial policy. To the contrary, he maintained distance from Timbuktu in decision-making.

Though the sources fail to treat successive reigns evenly after *Askia* Muḥammad, it would appear relations took a turn for the worse under his successor Mūsā. In a series of developments that included eliminating competitors for the throne, Mūsā would march on the *kanfāri* and the Benga-*farma* Balla. *Qāḍī* Maḥmūd would give refuge to the Benga-*farma*, but Mūsā refused to recognize the *qāḍī's* house as inviolate, seizing and later executing the Benga-*farma*.[62] So much for Maḥmūd's influence with *Askia* Mūsā.

Muḥammad Bonkana Kirya (937–43/1531–37) would succeed Mūsā. Following a military defeat, he expressed concern over "what the people of Timbuktu will say when the news reaches them, and the gossipers will wag their tongues when they gather behind Sankore mosque."[63] This episode has been offered as an example of Timbuktu's involvement in imperial politics, but unlike other Askias, Muḥammad Bonkana Kirya's father, the *Kanfāri* ʿUmar, had sent him to study in Timbuktu as a lad, explaining his familiarity with its gossip, as opposed to fretting over its political ramifications.[64] When overthrown by the Dendi-*fari* and replaced by Ismāʿīl in 943/1537, Muḥammad Bonkana Kirya would indeed flee to Timbuktu for asylum, underscoring his personal relations with the town. He would have to flee again to Tendirma's *kanfāri*, as Timbuktu's *qāḍī* could not protect him.

It is with Muḥammad Bāni's reign (beginning in 995/1586) that Timbuktu becomes appreciably involved in imperial politics. The city's merchants and part of the scholarly community favored Muḥammad's brother, the *Balma'a* Ṣādiq, to become the new *askia*. Ṣādiq would march on Gao, only to be defeated by Isḥāq b. *Askia* Dāwūd (or Isḥāq II), who had replaced Muḥammad Bāni with the latter's sudden death. With the Moroccan invasion underway, Isḥāq b. *Askia* Dāwūd convened his cabinet to discuss the challenge. A Timbuktu *ʿālim* was present, but his advice was rejected.

The commercial benefits of controlling the Timbuktu-Jenne corridor were of the highest priority for Songhay rulers, from *Sunni* ʿAlī to *Askia* Muḥammad Gao, who deployed an array of officials to ensure security and fiscal oversight. The Askias so pressed their advantage that Timbuktu, far from enjoying autonomy, was firmly under Gao's authority.

Timbuktu's Spiritual Gravity

In adhering too closely to the chronicles' characterizations of relations between Gao, Timbuktu, and Jenne, scholars have exaggerated the centers' autonomy while granting them a measure of political clout they did not actually wield. But this is not to say religious elites did not exercise extraordinary influence. They certainly did. Righteous rulers like *Askia al-ḥājj* Muḥammad were acknowledged for their pursuit of Islam, and respected as sovereigns favored by God, but they were not necessarily holy men or scholars. On the other hand, the saints and scholars of Timbuktu,

Jenne, Dia/Diagha, Mori Koyra, and other centers acquired substantial authority from two primary sources: erudition and piety. The two were intimately related, as the former was often a factor in achieving the latter, involving an interaction between teacher and pupil that led to the persistent, everyday application of what was learned. Erudition, however, could also be the result of such factors as family connections and wealth, potential determinants in the quality as well as the degree of knowledge. But in sum, spiritual authority derived from a command and performance of knowledge.

Related to and complementing spiritual authority was a second dynamic, a power or force emanating from the spiritual plane and bestowed by the Almighty—*baraka*—which could be transmitted from person to person. Those possessing both spiritual authority and *baraka* commanded enormous respect. What therefore follows is informed by and pivots from the preceding discussion of political dimensions of Timbuktu and Jenne, first examining the nature of spiritual authority derivative of scholarship, then pursing a consideration of spiritual power, of *baraka*, and how concentrations of such authority and power formed a critical foundation for the ways in which Islam would unfold in West Africa.

Reminiscing about Timbuktu's former glory, *Ta'rīkh al-fattāsh* paints the following idyllic portrait:

> Before the arrival of the Moroccan ordeal (*fitna*), and prior to the exile of the children, grandchildren, and relatives of *Qāḍī* Maḥmūd b. ʿUmar, Timbuktu had reached the height of loveliness, beauty, and elevation in religion and the *sunna* [teachings and personal example of the Prophet], lacking nothing in religion or material goods. . . . At that time Timbuktu had no equal throughout the territories of the lands of the blacks, from the land of Mali to the farthest limits of the land of the West, with respect to virtue (*murūʾa*), freedom (*ḥurrīya*), purity, security and protection throughout the land, mercy and compassion for the poor and strangers, and friendliness and assistance to the students of knowledge.[65]

Though nostalgic, there is a substantive core to the *Ta'rīkh*'s recollection that finds an echo in Leo Africanus's description of Timbuktu, in which were

> numerous judges, scholars and priests, all well paid by the king. Many manuscript books coming from Barbary are sold. Such sales are more profitable than any other goods.[66]

Africanus's focus on scholars and books is in fact the substance of *Ta'rīkh al-fattāsh*'s lament of a former Timbuktu in its heyday, a prime reason for the captivation with Timbuktu and Jenne throughout the centuries. *Ta'rīkh al-fattāsh* makes this very clear, transitioning from the general to the particular in estimating between 150 and 180 Qur'ānic schools (*maktabān*) in the city, with one instructor (*mu'allim*) receiving 1725 cowries in payment every Wednesday, his students paying between five and ten cowries each, averaging just under 250 pupils in that one school.[67] By extension, this suggests a city with a sizable student population, entirely consistent with Africanus's general impression. Attempts at quantification are simply that, but a range of 7,500 to 9,000 students in such schools does not seem an unreasonable estimate.[68] By these and other indices, Timbuktu and Jenne emerge as vibrant centers of culture and commerce.

A rich and engaging literature has developed within recent years that in multiple ways connects with Timbuktu and Jenne's early scholarly tradition. In trading on the cities' prominence and profile to emphasize a much broader regional erudition, studies have made critical interventions in addressing the relative lack of attention to West African Islamic scholarship in the western academy, while pointing out how West African thinkers directly contributed to the Islamic sciences.[69] These approaches are not simply invested in relocating West Africa from an intellectual periphery, but in challenging prevailing notions regarding the nature of "West African Islam" through an emphasis on not only the relational dimensions of "embodied" knowledge formation, but an incisive analysis of how this process—an important counterweight to colonial imposition—has been caricatured by the latter.[70]

Such scholarship significantly expands a preceding literature that, like Africanus, invests substantially in the intellectual activity of Timbuktu and Jenne.[71] Four themes are particularly salient in this literature: curricula through which erudition commended itself to a broader Muslim world of letters; levels of scholarship; the relationship between teacher and pupil and ensuing chains of transmission over generations; and the financial support of scholars. Following a discussion of these four areas, the focus will shift to a fifth that has received less attention—the metaphysical dimension of the scholarly community, as it provided a basis for the growth and expansion of esoteric practice, including Ṣūfīsm, throughout West Africa in subsequent generations.

Centers of Erudition: Jingereber, Sīdī Yaḥyā, and Sankore

To characterize the pursuit of the Islamic sciences as "curricular" is to adopt an idiom often associated with a university or circumstance of advanced study, and, indeed, learning in Timbuktu has been characterized as something similar, with the "University of Sankore" at its core.[72] While somewhat problematic in its conjuring of western institutions (with which circumstances in Timbuktu are then compared), advanced study existed in many parts of the world, including (or especially) the *dār al-Islām*, and the latter is the better frame of reference for understanding Timbuktu and Jenne as cultural centers.[73] The notion of a "University of Sankore," however, is not inconsistent with spheres of influence and prestige within Timbuktu, as much of its cultural activity revolved around the mosques of Jingereber, Sīdī Yaḥyā, and Sankore. To be sure, there were other city mosques, including that of the main market (*sūq*), the ʿAlī b. Yūsuf mosque, and the mosque of the Tuwātīs, but the first three were the major ones.[74] Jingereber, Songhay for the "Great Mosque," was otherwise known as the congregational mosque (*masjid al-jāmiʿ*), first constructed by *Mansā* Mūsā upon returning from the Pilgrimage.[75] Mūsā would add a tower-minaret (*ṣawmaʿa*) to Jingereber, and its long association with imperial authority may explain why *Askia* Dāwūd convened the *ʿulamāʾ* there when visiting the city. Located in the southwestern quarter of town, Jingereber saw luminaries, including the *Qāḍī* Maḥmūd, gather in their finest apparel every week to observe Friday prayer (*ṣalāt al-jumuʿa*), the main worship service that began after noon.[76] Prayer would follow the *khuṭba* (a sermon usually delivered at Friday mosque), often acknowledging the political authority in place.

Jingereber was also distinguished in the selection of its *imāms*, who tended to come from either outside of Songhay or from groups not associated with the Aqīt and Anda ag-Muḥammad families. Their review is most revealing. As mentioned, the jurist Kātib Mūsā was the last of its "Sudanese" or "black" *imāms*, who saw the transition from Malian to Tuareg rule during his forty-year term.[77] Kātib Mūsā had been one of those sent by *Mansā* Mūsā to study in Fez, and upon returning to Timbuktu was accompanied by ʿAbd Allāh al-Balbālī, al-Saʿdī's ancestor through the Fulani woman.[78] Al-Balbālī succeeded Kātib Mūsā as *imām*, and is considered the first *bayḍān* or "white" *imām* of Jingereber, and was in turn followed by *Sīdī* Abū ʾl-Qāsim al-Tuwātī (d. 935/1528–39), then by his student *Sayyid* Manṣūr al-Fazzānī, and then the *Sayyid al-faqīh* Ibrāhīm al-Zalafī (who taught al-Saʿdī's father). The next *imām* was Aḥmad the father of Nānā Bēr, the consensus candidate of the "people of the Great Mosque" (apparently notables associated with Jingereber) and approved by *Qāḍī* Maḥmūd.

When the son of *Sīdī* Abū 'l-Qāsim al-Tuwātī arrived from Tuwat two months later, some mosque leaders sought to have him replace *Imām* Aḥmad, but *Qāḍī* Maḥmūd refused, threatening them with prison. The son returned to Tuwat, but when Aḥmad died seven months thereafter, a "newcomer," one *Sayyid* 'Alī al-Jazūlī, was appointed by *Qāḍī* Maḥmūd.[79] Al-Jazūlī's deputy was the *faqīh* 'Uthmān b. al-Ḥasan b. *al-ḥājj* al-Tishītī, and he resisted *Qāḍī* Maḥmūd's efforts to name him *imām* at al-Jazūlī's death eighteen years later. Instead, 'Uthmān successfully nominated the learned *faqīh* Ṣiddīq b. Muḥammad Tagalī, the "Kābarī by origin, born in Jinjo." 'Uthmān served as deputy *imām*, becoming close friends with *al-faqīh* Ṣiddīq, and when the latter died after twenty-four years as *imām*, 'Uthmān became *imām* upon threat of prison by *Qāḍī* Maḥmūd. 'Uthmān would die in 977/1569–70, and was succeeded by *al-faqīh* Gidado al-Fulānī (d. 989/1581), and then *Imām* Ṣiddīq's son Aḥmad (d. 1005/1597), the latter two appointed by *Qāḍī* al-'Āqib.[80]

As their *nisbas* indicate, many of these individuals either arrived from elsewhere, or were descendants of foreigners (to Timbuktu): Tuwat, the Fezzan, Morocco, Tishit, Jinjo, etc.[81] Like al-Balbālī, many or most were characterized as *bayḍān* or "white." None of the *imāms* during the period of imperial Songhay were Aqīts or Anda ag-Muḥammads, so that Jingereber mosque as a site of the imperial presence was accentuated by an *imām* post apparently reserved for (non-Aqīt) immigrants and their descendants. It is unclear if advanced scholarship was pursued there, as only children are mentioned studying in its environs during the period of *Sīdī* Abū 'l-Qāsim al-Tuwātī.[82] But though Jingereber mosque was distinguished as an international space, the city's official interface with the world, there seems to have been a quid pro quo with Gao by which Timbuktu's *qāḍī* could name Jingereber's *imām* on his own authority.

In contrast to Jingereber and Sankore mosques, relatively little is recorded about the *masjid* at Sīdī Yaḥyā, also known as the mosque of Muḥammad-n-Allāh. Located near the town's center, it was built by the Timbuktu-*koi* Muḥammad-n-Allāh (or Muḥammad Naḍḍa) in honor of *Sīdī* Yaḥyā al-Tādalisī. The Timbuktu-*koi* had appointed his cherished friend *Shaykh* al-Tādalisī, the "perfected pole," as *imām*, and al-Tādalisī apparently convened classes at Sīdī Yaḥyā mosque, since scholars (or "students," *ṭalaba*) from Sankore would study with him there.[83] It may have been viewed as a "neutral" site between Jingereber as an international space, and the Aqīt and Anda ag-Muḥammad-associated Sankore mosque, since it was at Sīdī Yaḥyā that *Askia* Muḥammad gathered the *'ulamā'* to reinstate Maḥmūd as Timbuktu's *qāḍī*. Its unaffiliated quality is also suggested by the fact that during an interregnum under *Askia* Al-Ḥājj, when the city was without an official *qāḍī*, the *faqīh* and *imām* Muḥammad Baghayughu carried out those responsibilities at the door of Sīdī Yaḥyā mosque following morning prayer. As he was accompanied by his students, learning necessarily took place, though this may have been an exceptional rather than normal arrangement.[84] Because of the sources' focus on Sankore, it is unclear if many pursued erudition at Sīdī Yaḥyā mosque, but such pursuits may pale when compared with the mosque's more profound reputation as a site of supernatural activity.

Relative to Sīdī Yaḥyā and Jingereber, Sankore mosque clearly emerges in the writings of al-Sa'dī and Aḥmad Bābā as the very heart of the pursuit of Islamic sciences. Translated to possibly mean "white nobility" in a fashion similar to the Arabic *bayḍān*, and therefore as complicated as the Ṣanhāja community was multi-phenotypical, Sankore quarter was located in the northeast of Timbuktu, where its mosque was built (at an unknown date) by a single, very wealthy woman "of the Aghlāl" (perhaps from the western Sahara) as an act of piety.[85] Sankore became an enclave for Ṣanhāja immigrants from Walata/Biru in the early ninth/fifteenth century, including the *badal* al-Ḥājj, Timbuktu's *qāḍī* toward the end of Malian control.[86] Other immigrants were Muḥammad Aqīt, *Sīdī* 'Abd al-Raḥmān al-Tamīmī, *Modibo* Muḥammad al-Kāborī, and possibly Abū 'Abd Allāh Anda ag-Muḥammad the Elder, and while al-Tādalisī also immigrated around this time, he settled elsewhere, perhaps because he was from North Africa as opposed to Walata/Biru.[87] These men built upon a foundation laid by Fez-trained scholars during the Malian period, becoming the progenitors of successive generations of highly educated religious elites. The atmosphere created by these first- and second-generation immigrants was so exceptional that *Modibo* Muḥammad al-Kāborī would make the boldest of comparisons: "I was the contemporary of the righteous people of Sankore, who were equaled in their righteousness only by the Companions of the Messenger of God—may God bless him and grant him peace, and may He be pleased with them all."[88]

It is therefore with activity in Sankore quarter that the contours of high erudition take form, and as the secondary literature has well established, the basis of the Islamic sciences was the Qur'ān and its exegesis, or *tafsīr*, followed in importance by the study of *ḥadīth*, or traditions of the Prophet via the *Ṣaḥīḥ* of Muslim (d. 261/874–75) and *Ṣaḥīḥ* of al-Bukhārī

(d. 256/870), along with such interpretative works as *Kitāb al-shifā* (*al-shifā bi-ta'rīf ḥuqūq al-muṣṭafā*) of *Qāḍī* 'Iyāḍ.[89] Following *ḥadīth* was the study of jurisprudence or *fiqh*, and given that Songhay and most of West and North Africa adhered to the Mālikī *madhab*, it was informed by the *Muwaṭṭa'* of Mālik b. Anas (d. 179/795); the *Mudawwana* of Saḥnūn (that is, 'Abd al-Salām b. Ḥabīb al-Tanūkhī al-Qayrawānī, d. 240/854–55) and its abridgement, the *Tahdhīb* of al-Barādhi'ī (that is, Khalaf b. Abī 'l-Qāsam al-Azdī al-Qayrawānī, d. ca. 430/1039); the *Risāla* of Ibn Abī Zayd (Abū Muḥammad 'Abd Allāh b. Abī Zayd 'Abd al-Raḥmān al-Qayrawānī, d. 386/996); and the *Mukhtaṣar* of the Egyptian Khalīl b. Isḥāq al-Jundī (d. 776/1374, the latter requiring a commentary to make sense of it). In addition to these disciplines, Arabic grammar (*naḥwa*) and syntax and rhetoric and logic were also studied, as was astronomy, critical for lunar-based cultures engaged in extensive cross-regional travel.[90] History was not formally studied, viewed from the Islamic perspective as "worldly" if it did not pertain to the early Muslim *ummah*, or as the preserve of the griots in the indigenous context. Ṣūfīsm as an intellectual field is poorly represented; there is the book the *Ḥikam* of Ibn 'Aṭā' Allāh al-Iskandarī, d. 709/1309, and the treatises of Abū Bakr b. *al-ḥājj* Aḥmad (b. 932/1525–26)—remarkable since it was becoming an important if not critical aspect of Muslim life in Sankore.

Studying the various branches of Islam began with Qur'ānic school, or *maktab*, where students learned Arabic grammar and Qur'ānic recitation. The sources from the period do not specify, but if similar to later Qur'ānic schools in West Africa, boys and girls would learn in separate spaces, with boys of sufficient means continuing their education beyond a certain level. In later centuries, the term *madrasa* would become more commonly used for the same school and early process, but for the period in question *madrasa* seems to have been reserved for schools led by individuals with the capacity for more advanced study, and was used interchangeably with the term *majlis*, in this context "teaching circle." The latter is also employed for the study of specific books or in conjunction with prominent teachers, suggesting very focused, intense learning on the part of well-educated individuals. This latter point underscores that the sources are preoccupied with elites; non-elites, with limited finances, may not have attended the same classes or been exposed to the same teachers as those for whom erudition was a constitutive part of an elevated status.

The physical setting of the *maktab*, *madrasa*, or *majlis* was in or near a mosque or home of the instructor, and examples of the pedagogic process include those of Abū 'l-Abbās Aḥmad b. *al-faqīh* Muḥammad (or Aḥmad) al-Sa'īd, whose *majlis* was attended by the likes of *Qāḍī* Maḥmūd and the *faqīh* brothers Muḥammad and Aḥmad b. Maḥmūd Baghayughu; and by Aḥmad Bābā, who provides limited vistas into the relationship between teacher and pupil in speaking of studying with two other students under 'Uryān al-Ra's ("the Bald-Headed," otherwise known as Abū 'Abd Allāh Muḥammad b. Muḥammad b. 'Alī b. Mūsā, d. 1027/1618).[91] In another anecdote he recounts not being allowed to participate in the reading and analysis of *Kitāb al-Shifā* in *madrasa* (attended by his father Aḥmad b. *al-ḥājj* Aḥmad and the *faqīh* 'Umar b. Muḥammad b. 'Umar), until, one day, only he correctly answered a question (concerning transitive or intransitive verb tense), at which point the instructor "lifted his gaze to me and smiled."[92] These circles of advanced study could be intimate, even though the teacher and subject were popular; *Modibo* Muḥammad al-Kāborī had so many students that a month did not end without his completing the *Tahdhīb* of al-Barādhi'ī with at least one of them.[93]

With the successful completion of a book, the instructor would provide the student with an *ijāza* (pl. *ijāzāt*) or license qualifying the person to teach the same; Aḥmad Bābā records he received licenses from his father to teach all the books for which he had been licensed, in addition to licenses he gave on his own.[94] He also records that when traveling to the central Islamic lands Songhay scholars obtained *ijāzāt* there, as was true of Muḥammad b. Aḥmad b. Abī Muḥammad al-Tāzakhtī and Timbuktu *Qāḍī* al-'Āqib.[95] With that said, the study of these books could take years, requiring multiple readings, and it is not clear if an *ijāza* was issued with the initial completion of a book, or every time it was finished; Aḥmad Bābā states that with his principal *shaykh* Muḥammad Baghayughu he read the *Mukhtaṣar* of Khalīl eight times and the *Uṣūl* (or *Jam' al-jawāmi'*) of al-Subkī (Tāj al-Dīn 'Abd al-Wahhāb b. 'Alī al-Subkī) three times, spending three years studying the *Tas'hīl al-fatwā'id wa takmīl al-maqāṣid* of Ibn Mālik.[96]

The foregoing underscores that knowledge was a process of transmission, involving not simply intellectual endeavor but also observation and adoption of habits and lifestyle, underscoring the critical nature of the teacher-student relationship. These were bonds, with the transfer of knowledge over generations forming *isnāds* (*asānīd*) or *silsilas* (*salāsil*)—chains of transmission. These *isnāds* could span centuries, and the more illustrious the teachers in the chain, the more prestigious the *isnād*.[97] The close connection to and adoption of the master teacher's lifestyle in subsequent Ṣūfī orders throughout West

Africa were conceivably informed, to some degree, by these anterior teacher-student relations.[98]

Those providing instruction and attaining appreciable levels of education were acknowledged and honored with various titles, though it is not obvious that the titles always corresponded to different levels of erudition. Some seem to have been used interchangeably, representing both degrees of academic attainment as well as cultural divergence. This is further complicated by the fact that *Ta'rīkh as-sūdān*, *Ta'rīkh al-fattāsh*, and Aḥmad Bābā do not necessarily employ the same nomenclature. The generalizations that follow, therefore, are not always consistent, but are nonetheless instructive. For example, it would appear that although Aḥmad Bābā uses the title *sīdī* for such prominent contemporaries as 'Uryān al-Ra's, *al-Qāḍī* Aḥmad, and his uncle 'Abd Allāh b. 'Umar b. Muḥammad Aqīt, he usually reserved the title for very prominent scholar-saints of a preceding era, especially in the ninth/fifteenth century, when founders of the scholarly tradition at Timbuktu were just arriving. These scholar-saints tended to come from North Africa and Egypt, and include *Sīdī* Yaḥyā al-Tadallisī, *Sīdī* 'Abd Allāh al-Balbālī, and *Sīdī* Abū 'l-Qāsim al-Tuwātī, and while *Ta'rīkh al-fattāsh* also makes reference to *Sīdī* Yaḥyā al-Tadallisī, it expands the pool of luminaries to *Sīdī* al-Suyūṭī, *Sīdī* Maḥmūd b. 'Umar, and *Sīdī* Aḥmad Bābā himself.[99] So while there is flexibility, the use of *sīdī* seems to have been restricted to very exclusive company.

In discussing Timbuktu's *imāms*, al-Sa'dī sometimes uses *sayyid* ("lord" or "master"), as in *Sayyid* Manṣūr al-Fazzānī, and also refers to *Mōri* Ṣāliḥ Diawara as *sayyid*, while calling Abū 'l-Qāsim al-Tuwātī *sayyid* as well as *sīdī*, along with his student Manṣūr.[100] As other Timbuktu *imāms* were not so addressed, there apparently was no fast rule, and though *sayyid* does not seem to fully approach the loftiness of *sīdī*, it is reasonable to conclude only exceptional individuals were honored in this way.

Relationships between the terms *faqīh*, *mōri*, and *alfa* (or *alf'a*, *alfā*) are more fluid. The first refers to a jurist, with many if not most of the scholar-saints called "jurists." What qualified a person as a *faqīh* is not made explicit, but one would assume a threshold was met concerning such canonical works as the *Muwaṭṭa'* of Mālik b. Anas, the *Mudawwana* of Saḥnūn, the *Tahdhīb* of al-Barādhi'ī, the *Risāla* of Ibn Abī Zayd, and the *Mukhtaṣar* of Khalīl. Even so, there were jurists, and there were jurists of very high caliber, with *al-faqīh Modibo* Muḥammad al-Kāborī occupying a unique orbit.[101] In some contrast, Ṣāliḥ Diawara is only called a *faqīh* in problematic manuscript C, though *Ta'rīkh as-sūdān*, addressing him as *Mōri* Ṣāliḥ Diawara, also confers upon him the title *sayyid*.[102]

As observed, the term *mōri* is closely connected with Mande religious specialists, many associated with the Mori Koyra community. *Ta'rīkh al-fattāsh* refers to *Mōri* Hawgāru as "the ancestor of the people of Mori Koyra and its *faqīhs* (*fuqahā'*)," creating an equivalence between title and religious community, a perspective reinforced by *Askia* Muḥammad's letter of protection in which the Mori Koyra are called the "sons of *al-faqīh Mōri* Ma'ma' b. *Mōri* Ma'mak b. *al-faqīh Mōri* Hawgāru."[103] This equivalence is also found in al-Sa'dī, who calls *Mōri* Magha Kankoi a *faqīh* and a scholar.[104]

In addition to *mōri*, *Ta'rīkh al-fattāsh* also uses the term *alfa*, and Maḥmūd Ka'ti is called *Alfa* Maḥmūd Ka'ti as well as *al-faqīh*.[105] An aide to *Askia* Dāwūd is referred to as *Askia-alfa*, and Ṣāliḥ Diawara is presented as an *alfa*. When treating the subject of Maḥmūd's return to Timbuktu from Walata/Biru in 885/1480, *Ta'rīkh as-sūdān* refers to Timbuktu's future *qāḍī* as *Alfa* Maḥmūd.[106]

The mention of *alfas* returns to the 150 and 180 Qur'ānic schools in Timbuktu, each headed by an instructor (*mu'allim*).[107] Immediately preceding that discussion is reference to some 126 tailoring shops called *tindes*, each headed by a master teacher also called a *mu'allim*, each with 50 to 100 apprentices. Scholars have noted the mention of tailoring shops and the discussion of Qur'ānic schools in the very next breath, surmising a strong association between them, the former helping to finance the latter and resulting in "tailor-alfas." The period of the Askias in Songhay may have been their beginning, but as the status of an *Alfa* Maḥmūd Ka'ti or an *Alfa* Maḥmūd b. 'Umar b. Muḥammad Aqīt could not have been the same as a tailoring apprentice, the term *alfa* may have become more widely used subsequently.[108]

These *mu'allims*, *kātibs*, *alfas*, *mōris*, *khaṭībs*, *sayyids*, *faqīhs*, *shaykhs*, *imāms*, and *qāḍīs*, comprising Songhay's "religious estate," were supported through student tuition, book copying, family commercial activities, and alms from the faithful. As an example, Jingereber's *imām* received 500 *mithqāls* in alms from the congregation every Ramaḍān, and when only 200 *mithqāls* were collected one year, *Qāḍī* Maḥmūd insisted the people make up the difference.[109] With respect to the largesse of the state, its level of support for the *'ulamā'* must have been considerable, taking many forms that often directly targeted individuals, especially Timbuktu's *qāḍīs*. It was said, for example, that *Qāḍī* Maḥmūd, a man of "irreproachable character," would ignore the solicitations of sultans who persisted in sending him many "gifts and presents."[110] In such passages resides a certain tension between claims of religious figures resisting imperial pressures, and the fact that imperial gifts, often involving slaves, were many times accepted. This is yet another lens through which to view relations between Gao and Timbuktu and Jenne, where many of the religious elites were wealthy. It was therefore critical for the *qāḍī* to formally reject all forms of corruption and extralegal exaction, alleviating any suspicions that he himself was a beneficiary.

Timbuktu as the Locus of Spiritual Power

With scholarship and learning providing context, the complement of spiritual authority—spiritual power—can be explored, beginning again with the Mori Koyra. Their mention brings to the fore a divergence between *Ta'rīkh al-fattāsh*, *Ta'rīkh as-sūdān*, and the writings of Aḥmad Bābā. Nearly all of what is known about the Mori Koyra comes from *Ta'rīkh al-fattāsh*, for which themes of spiritual authority and registers of knowledge are less important than the spiritual power capable of intervening into and affecting material circumstances. While highly laudatory of luminaries in Timbuktu and Jenne, *Ta'rīkh al-fattāsh* does not discuss in any appreciable detail their intellectual achievements, nor does it attend to the specifics of their erudition. Al-Sa'dī and Aḥmad Bābā, on the other hand, are heavily invested in demonstrating just how prolific and accomplished were the scholars of Timbuktu, and while they do not neglect manifestations of *baraka*, they are preoccupied with favorably comparing the city's scholarship with that of other centers in al-Maghrib and the central Islamic lands. As a consequence, sites of learning such as Dia/Diagha, Jenne, and possibly Gao, suffer.

While virtually nothing is said of the *faqīh Mōri* Hawgāru's scholarship, his burial site is duly noted, as it was a location at which his *baraka* could be accessed by the faithful.[111] Likewise, *Askia al-ḥājj* Muḥammad's counselor Ṣāliḥ Diawara, rather than presented as a scholar, is a veritable saint, whose activities and interventions have already been delineated.[112] In both *ta'rīkhs* he is called a "friend of God" (*walī*), reflecting an unusual intimacy with the Almighty, as was true of *Modibo* Muḥammad al-Kāborī.[113]

Luminaries affiliated with the Mori Koyra, but who settled in either Jenne or Timbuktu, receive more attention, as their contributions to the intellectual profiles of these centers were important. The ninth-tenth/

fifteenth-sixteenth century *Mōri* Magha Kankoi, for example, was a noted juriconsult and scholar in Jenne, with whom many of "the learned" studied. But like *Mōri* Hawgāru, his tomb was also a shrine, his *baraka* so powerful his curses ended the reign of *Askia* Mūsā.[114] Magha Kankoi's contemporary Fūdiye *al-faqīh* Muḥammad Sānū al-Wangarī was so holy his hand swelled from merely touching a ruler's food, and like *Mōris* Hawgāru and Magha Kankoi, Fūdiye *al-faqīh* Muḥammad Sānū's interment in the courtyard of Jingereber became site of veneration.[115] Such practices may be linked to *Mansā* Mūsā's experience in Cairo at al-Qarāfa 'l-Kubrā, but in any event, accessing the spiritual power of the entombed, a major Ṣūfī practice in West Africa, was well under way by the ninth/fifteenth century in Songhay.[116]

In contrast to the Mori Koyra, a number of Timbuktu *'ulamā'* (and, to a lesser extent, Jenne) are featured in the works of al-Sa'dī and Aḥmad Bābā as exemplars of both erudition and piety. The focus of these authors is again Sankore mosque, where *Qāḍī* Maḥmūd was a towering figure. Repeatedly referring to him as *Shaykh al-Islām*, al-Sa'dī leaves the full elegiac statement to Aḥmad Bābā, whom he quotes:

> Maḥmūd b. 'Umar b. Muḥammad Aqīt b. 'Umar b. 'Alī b. Yaḥyā al-Ṣanhājī al-Tinbuktī and its *qāḍī*, Abū 'l-Thanā' ("father of [to whom is due] praise"), Abū 'l-Maḥāsin ("father of good qualities"), the saint, teacher (*mudarris*), jurist, imām and scholar of Takrūr who had no equal. He was one of the best of God's righteous servants who was intimate (*al-'ārifīn*) with Him, who possessed great circumspection in matters and was perfectly guided. He was calm and dignified, even majestic. He became famous throughout the land for his knowledge and righteousness, his fame spreading to all regions—east, west, south and north—as his *baraka* became manifest in his practice of religion, righteousness, asceticism, and blamelessness, and regarding matters of God he did not fear any censure of man. Everyone, from the *sulṭān* to those below him, fell under his command, visiting his house to receive *baraka* from him, and he would pay them no attention though they continually sent him gifts and presents.[117]

Here Aḥmad Bābā introduces *Qāḍī* Maḥmūd to the world as the leading spiritual authority for the whole of the western Sudan ("Takrur"). It is instructive that in making this claim, Aḥmad Bābā emphasizes his personal traits, continually mentioning his *baraka* while asserting he enjoyed an experiential intimacy with the Almighty. It is only after laying such a foundation that Aḥmad Bābā provides any details into his scholarship.

Aḥmad Bābā also says *Qāḍī* Maḥmūd "revived scholarship in his land" through his devotion to teaching (for which he was gifted), resulting in a large increase in the number of students studying Islamic jurisprudence.[118] His standing was no doubt elevated by his Pilgrimage in 915/1509–10, when he met the Shāfiʿī scholars Ibrāhīm al-Maqdisī (d. 923/1517) and Zakariyyā al-Anṣārī (d. 926/1520); and the Mālikī jurists Shams al-Dīn Muḥammad b. Ḥasan al-Laqānī (d. 935/1528) and Nāṣir al-Dīn Muḥammad b. Ḥasan al-Laqānī (d. 958/1551), his younger brother.

In using the *kunya* (honorific title) "Abū 'l-Barakāt," or "father of divine blessings," al-Saʿdī identifies Maḥmūd as a conduit of that power. While the pursuit of scholarship can be one fount of *baraka*, the way it is pursued is critical, since it involves conforming to life practices as well as being embedded in a community through which *baraka* flows. Maḥmūd therefore acquired such power through adherence to the *sunna* (which includes prescribed and supererogatory prayer and reading the Qur'ān), performing *ḥajj*, and from his place within the *silsila* or *isnad* of *baraka*-possessing shaykhs. So positioned, Maḥmūd was blessed with *mukāshafa* or "clairvoyance," which refers to the lifting of a veil that prevents sight into other, unseen worlds. Thus, after the burial of his brother *al-ḥājj* Aḥmad, Maḥmūd sighed and declared, "Now my brother Aḥmad has parted company with the angels," by which it is believed he actually witnessed the angels Munkar and Nakīr remove Aḥmad from the grave, a "great example of miracles (*karāmāt*) and clairvoyance (*mukāshafa*)." Indeed, al-Saʿdī asserts Maḥmūd was "the locus of many manifestations of miracles (*karāmāt*) and *baraka*."[119]

Reference to *al-ḥājj* Aḥmad underscores that all three of ʿUmar b. Muḥammad Aqīt's sons were held in great esteem, as testified the gnostic and *quṭb* ("pole") *Sīdī* Muḥammad al-Bakrī: "Aḥmad is a friend of God (*walī*), Maḥmūd is a friend of God, and ʿAbd Allāh is a friend of God, though he lives in a village [Tazakht]" where he remained until he died."[120] But *Qāḍī* Maḥmūd occupied a truly exceptional status, and was not only the "father of divine blessings" in a spiritual sense, but also in a very literal sense, fathering children who would become distinguished scholars and saints in their own right. Indeed, Masire Anda ag-Muḥammad (whose *kunya* means the "blessing of Islam") and the "righteous *shaykh*" Masire Bēr maintained Maḥmūd "did not excel us except in fathering righteous sons."[121] Maḥmūd in fact fathered five sons and a number of daughters, among whom *Qāḍī* Muḥammad, mentioned first, was regarded as "a revered scholar, sagacious and clever. During his lifetime he had no equal in understanding, astuteness, intellect, or his worldly wealth."[122] An "illustrious jurist" described as "nimble-minded" and "an intellectual genius," at the age of forty-five he would become *qāḍī* with the death of his father in 955/1548, and would remain in office until his death in 973/1565, at the age sixty-three.[123] Another son, al-ʿĀqib, born in 913/1507–8, became *qāḍī* with Muḥammad's death in 973/1565, "filling the land with justice" for the next eighteen years, never in error, "as if he could see the future," with "penetrating insight into matters."[124] Blessed with wealth and "fortunate in his affairs," he studied with both his father and uncle, and in making *ḥajj* met with leading scholars that included al-Nāṣir al-Laqānī, who certified him to teach a number of books. Al-ʿĀqib in turn became one of Aḥmad Bābā's instructors, granting him an *ijāza*, and at his passing in 991/1583 was succeeded as *qāḍī* by his brother Abū Ḥafṣ ʿUmar (in 993/1585).[125]

Abū Ḥafṣ ʿUmar executed the office for nine years, an expert on the life of the Prophet and *ḥadīth.* He "excelled in the histories and times of the people" (*bara'a fī . . . tawārīkh wa ayyām al-nās*), excelling even more in the study of *fiqh.*[126] Unlike Abū Ḥafṣ ʿUmar and the other two brothers, ʿAbd Allāh held no office, but he was a scholar, jurist and teacher. Though he scorned "worldly wealth," he managed to accumulate quite a bit of it. Matters of *baraka* and divine manifestations therefore re-center with Maḥmūd's son Abū Zayd ʿAbd al-Raḥmān, as he was a "friend of God" (*al-walī bi-Allāh*), a recluse (*al-nāsik*), an ascetic (*al-zāhid*), and a gnostic (*al-ʿārif*), "rejecting the world in its entirety." He was also clairvoyant (*thā mukāshafāt*), alerting Timbuktu on the very day the Moroccan army set out from Marrakesh to conquer Songhay.[127]

Relative to *Qāḍī* Maḥmūd, his older brother *al-ḥājj* Aḥmad (d. 943/1536) emerges as the second most prominent of ʿUmar b. Muḥammad Aqīt's three sons, as Aḥmad Bābā, his grandson, took greater interest in him. Described as "one of the righteous servants of God and a practicing scholar," he was instructed by both Anda ag-Muḥammad the Elder and al-Mukhtār al-Naḥwī, and taught his brother Maḥmūd the *Mudawwana.*[128] His possible role in unsettling the delicate situation in Timbuktu under *Sunni* ʿAlī has been discussed, but beyond the Pilgrimage, he is also noted for divine manifestations (*karāmāt*), with one of the most "celebrated" the unassisted, supernatural opening of the door to the Prophet's tomb in Medina after a guard's refusal to do so. He would reject an invitation to serve as *imām* of an unspecified mosque.

Not unlike Maḥmūd, *al-ḥājj* Aḥmad's greater legacy may have been a significant number of sons and grandsons who would distinguish themselves in the Islamic sciences and in manifestations of *baraka.* His son

Abū Ḥafṣ 'Umar was a grammarian who eulogized the Prophet day and night, and was a lynchpin in connecting the Aqīt network, "maintaining the ties of kinship and fulfilling his obligations to his relatives, calling on them in sickness and in health." He was arrested by the Moroccans in 1002/1593 and exiled to Marrakesh, where he "died a martyr."[129]

Another son of *al-ḥājj* Aḥmad, Abū Bakr or Abbeker Bēr (b. 932/1525–26), was an ascetic and scholar known for almsgiving (despite his limited personal means), performing the Pilgrimage twice, the second time returning with his family to live in Medina, departing the world in 991/1583. He was known to have often experienced "exalted [spiritual] states" (*aḥwāl jalīla*) and teleportation, as related by his brother Aḥmad b. *al-ḥājj* Aḥmad, who claimed (on the testimony of *Sīdī* Muḥammad al-Bakrī himself) that Abū Bakr traveled every day from Timbuktu to Cairo to perform the second evening worship (*ṣalāt al-'ishā'*)—a stunning demonstration of his status as a "friend of God."[130] As mentioned, Abū Bakr b. *al-ḥājj* Aḥmad b. 'Umar b. Muḥammad Aqīt also wrote treatises ("small books") on Ṣūfism (*al-taṣawwuf*).

Aḥmad Bābā's own father, the aforementioned Aḥmad b. *al-ḥājj* Aḥmad (b. 929/1522), was a versatile scholar, "upon whom God perfected beauty in all of its forms—physical appearance, complexion, speech, handwriting, and eloquence."[131] Described as a "sensitive" man (literally, "a slave to a big heart" *raqīq al-qalb 'athīm*), he was beloved and respected by all men, reciting the *Ṣaḥīḥs* of Muslim and al-Bukhārī in Sankore mosque during the months of Rajab, Sha'bān, and Ramaḍān. He wrote commentaries on Ibn Mahīb's presentation of al-Fāzāzī's (d. 627/1230) elegiac *'Ishrīniyyāt*, Khalīl's *Mukhtaṣar*, al-Sanūsī al-Tilimsānī's (d. 892/1486) popular text *Ṣughrā*, al-Maghīlī's poem on logic, and so on. Making the Pilgrimage in 956/1549–50, he also met with al-Nāṣir al-Laqānī, and became close to *Sīdī* Muḥammad al-Bakrī, from whom he received *baraka*. He would receive the same from his uncle *Qāḍī* Maḥmūd, the "blessing of the age," with whom he studied. Amassing a large library of his own, Aḥmad b. *al-ḥājj* Aḥmad was held in the highest esteem by temporal rulers. He would die one month after his brother Abū Bakr in Sha'bān 991/August of 1583.

As for 'Abd Allāh, the brother of Maḥmūd and Aḥmad and 'Umar b. Muḥammad Aqīt's third son, he was a *faqīh* with tremendous powers of recall and an especially effective Qur'ān memorizer, a God-fearing ascetic and righteous "friend of God." He had refused to return to Timbuktu with Maḥmūd and al-Mukhtār al-Naḥwī, electing instead to remain in Tazakht, near Walata/Biru, where he died in 929/1522–23.[132] It was there he taught his star pupil Makhlūf b. 'Alī b. Ṣāliḥ al-Balbālī (d. 940/1533–34), who would also go on to become a leading *faqīh* and memorizer of the Qur'ān himself.[133] Makhlūf al-Balbālī read the *Risāla* with 'Abd Allāh, evincing such potential that 'Abd Allāh encouraged him to travel to North Africa, where Makhlūf al-Balbālī studied with the most learned Ibn Gāzī of Fez, after which he taught in Kano, Katsina, Timbuktu, and Marrakesh. Miracles (*karāmāt*) were displayed through 'Abd Allāh, even after death, as when his student extinguished a lamp and washed his corpse by the light of the *faqīh*'s prayer beads.

Manifestations of divine grace were not limited to the Aqīt and Anda ag-Muḥammad families. Al-Ḥājj, the *qāḍī* of Timbuktu toward the end of Malian rule and considered a *badal*, pronounced a blessing, over a meal of millet, that preserved the lives of all who fought the Mossi.[134] His descendant 'Umar, *qāḍī* of Yindubu'u (near Timbuktu), could walk on water; and as further demonstration of al-Ḥājj's *baraka* and its communicable quality, it was the efficacious prayers of his granddaughter Nānā Tinti that led to the downfall of *Sunni* 'Alī. As for *Modibo* Muḥammad al-Kāborī, he also walked on the waters of a river during *'Īd al-Aḍḥā*, responding incredulously to a pupil who sank while trying to emulate him: "How can you compare your foot to one that has never walked in disobedience [to God]?" Likewise, *Sīdī* Abū 'l-Qāsim al-Tuwātī, *walī* and *imām* of Jingereber mosque, was said to have been the "locus of miracles (*karāmāt*) and divine power (*barakāt*)," including trapping and (later) forgiving a date-stealing thief, who became lodged in his tree one night; head loading wood that cured the disease of all who used it for fuel; and rescuing a man from drowning in Lake Debo 125 miles away, only to be back in minutes (if not seconds) to lead the early morning prayers.[135] Finally, *Sīdī* 'Uryān al-Ra's, one of Aḥmad Bābā's illustrious *shaykhs*, is said to not only have received a visitation from *Sīdī* Muḥammad al-Bakrī (who lived in Cairo but was yet able to daily visit Timbuktu), but to have even seen the Almighty, adversely affecting his mental state.[136]

A Foundation for Sufism's Regional Ascendancy

As veneration of the tombs of the saints had become a critical practice among the Muslims of imperial Songhay, an account relating to *Sīdī* Abū 'l-Qāsim al-Tuwātī, buried in a new cemetery adjoining Jingereber mosque at his passing in 935/1528–39, underscores the view of the dead as very much alive. As the story goes, one night during Ramaḍān a *sherīfian* exited the rear door of Jingereber mosque to relieve himself. In so doing he walked through the cemetery, and upon his return he "became aware" of a seated group of white-robed, enturbaned men through whom he attempted to pass, who exclaimed: "Give praise to God! How can you tread upon us with your sandals on?" The *sherīfian* removed his footwear.[137]

Sīdī Yaḥyā mosque was also sacred in that it contained *Sīdī* Yaḥyā's tomb. *Ta'rīkh al-fattāsh* emphasizes that large numbers visited his tomb, all testifying to its efficacy. Aḥmad Bābā and the sons of Aḥmad Baghayughu—Ibrāhīm and Muḥammad—also frequented the tomb, "without ceasing." And as Abū Zayd 'Abd al-Raḥmān b. *al-Qāḍī* Maḥmūd b. 'Umar b. Muḥammad Aqīt declared it incumbent upon believers to visit the tomb every day to benefit from his *baraka*, no less than four leaders of the Moroccan occupation—*Qa'ids* Bū Ikhtiyār, Manṣūr, Muṣṭafā al-Turkī, and al-Ḥasan b. Zubayr—were buried there "under the protection of Sīdī Yaḥyā."[138]

Sankore mosque was no less sacred a place, where a number of renowned scholar-saints were interred, including *Modibo* Muḥammad al-Kāborī and thirty others from Kabora. A "locus of miracles (*karāmāt*) and wonders (*'ajā'ib*)" while alive, this friend of God's mausoleum was strategically located between that of another *walī*, *al-ḥājj* Aḥmad b. 'Umar b. Muḥammad Aqīt (died either 942/1535 or 943/1537), and the site where petitioners prayed for rain (*ṣalāt al-istiqṣā'*).[139] *Ta'rīkh al-fattāsh* lists a number of tombs in the western reaches of the empire known for their efficacy.[140]

The twelfth/eighteenth and thirteenth/nineteenth centuries would see the establishment of Ṣūfīsm in West Africa in the form of such *ṭarīqas* (*ṭuruq*) as the Qadiriyya and Tijaniyya, and later the Muridiyya and others. Not everywhere embraced in the Muslim world, the Ṣūfīsm of these *tarīqas* would emphasize an experiential dimension of Islam very much premised on the discipline and *baraka* of a teacher or *shaykh*, a process involving not only (or in some instances not even) book learning, but the emulation of the example and lifestyle of the *shaykh*, in which the tombs of scholar-saints are important locations. The scholar-saints from the days of imperial Songhay laid a foundation for these formal networks. After all, individuals like 'Uthmān b. Fūdī (Usuman dan Fodio) and his son Muḥammad Bello—Qadiriyya adherents and founders of the Sokoto Caliphate—viewed aspects of the reign of *Askia al-ḥājj* Muḥammad as a model for Muslim polity, and held the scholarship of Aḥmad Bābā in esteem (though there were quibbles), while the Kunta *shaykhs*, leaders of the Qadiriyya *ṭarīqa* in West Africa, would be headquartered proximate to Timbuktu.[141]

Women and the Circuitry of Spiritual Power

A cursory review of the documentation for imperial Songhay seems to offer little insight into the ways in which women contributed to scholarship and esoteric practice in the region. Upon closer examination, however, one of the striking features of the dense node of Sankore saints and scholars are "unofficial," back-channel *silsilas*, or lines of transmission, often composed of women, usually unnamed, through whom individuals were vitally connected. If only descent through the paternal line is considered, recognition of ancestors responsible for the rise of many of Timbuktu's elites would be impossible, their heritage eviscerated. This is particularly true of the Aqīts. *Qāḍī* Maḥmūd's father 'Umar b. Muḥammad Aqīt was apparently not very accomplished, though Aḥmad Bābā says he was a "learned and righteous jurist" who studied under the eminent *Modibo* Muḥammad al-Kaborī.[142] 'Umar's father Muḥammad Aqīt, in turn, was wholly unrefined, unrelated to scholarship. Such combined lackluster no doubt contributes to the chroniclers' emphasis on the Anda ag-Muḥammad ancestry of the subsequent Aqīts—that is, their maternal line.

Aḥmad Bābā, a descendant of Muḥammad Aqīt, states that it was Abū 'Abd Allāh Anda ag-Muḥammad the Elder who was the first in his lineage to pursue erudition.[143] But it is through the female line that Aḥmad Bābā is related to the Anda ag-Muḥammads. As previously mentioned, a number of Anda ag-Muḥammad family members became impressive scholars, including two sons: al-Mukhtār al-Naḥwī ("the Grammarian") and 'Abd al-Raḥmān.[144] Al-Mukhtār al-Naḥwī was *Qāḍī* Maḥmūd's uncle and the brother of Sita bt. Anda ag-Muḥammad the Elder, Maḥmūd's mother. His two (older) brothers, 'Abd Allāh and Aḥmad, are with Maḥmūd referred to as the (maternal) grandsons (*asbāṭ*) of Anda ag-Muḥammad. As Sita is identified as the mother of only Maḥmūd, she and possibly another sister would marry 'Umar, the son of Muḥammad Aqīt, and it is with 'Umar b. Muḥammad Aqīt that the tradition of erudition begins within the Aqīt family.[145]

The importance of the maternal line continues through *Qāḍī* Maḥmūd, as his *baraka* flowed not only through sons, but through daughters as well, so that Abū 'l-Abbās Aḥmad b. *al-faqīh* Muḥammad al-Sa'īd, otherwise known as Aḥmad b. Muḥammad b. Sa'īd and Maḥmūd's grandson "through a daughter," was considered a "righteous friend of God" as well as a divine. He had a direct relationship with his grandfather Maḥmūd, studying with him the *Risāla* (presumably of Ibn Abī Zayd) and *Mukhtaṣar* of Khalīl, and would later teach the *Mukhtaṣar*, along with the *Mudawwana* (of Saḥnūn) and *Muwaṭṭa'* (of Mālik b. Anas) to the *faqīhs* Muḥammad and Aḥmad Baghayughu (sons of the illustrious Maḥmūd Baghayughu). Maḥmūd Ka'ti and Aḥmad Bābā would also join his teaching circle (*majlis*), as would his own uncle, *Qāḍī* 'Umar b. *al-faqīh* Maḥmūd. Yet another of *Qāḍī* Maḥmūd's grandsons through a daughter, Abū Bakr b. Aḥmad Bēr, was so righteous that his paternal uncles agreed he should lead the worship when *Qāḍī* al-'Āqib fell ill.[146]

A wonderful illustration of how the *baraka* of Anda ag-Muḥammad the Elder continued to extend to descendants through their mothers is the case of *al-faqīh* and *Imām* Abū 'Abd Allāh Anda ag-Muḥammad, or simply *Imām* Anda ag-Muḥammad, who became *imām* of Sankore mosque when an aging *Qāḍī* Maḥmūd finally relinquished the post.[147] Best known as a eulogist (*mādiḥ*) of the Prophet, the "divinely favored" (*mubārak*) *Imām* Anda ag-Muḥammad had five "divinely favored" (*mubārakāt*) daughters, who in turn gave birth to "divinely favored" (*mubārakīn*) sons: one was the mother of Muḥammad San; another the mother of two brothers, *Qāḍī* Muḥammad Qaryanki and *Qāḍī Sīdī* (possibly *Sayyid*) Aḥmad; a third daughter the mother of *Imām* (of Sankore mosque) Muḥammad b. Muḥammad Koray; a fourth the mother of "the Bearer of the Book of God Most High" (*ḥāmil Kitāb Allāh Ta'ālā*, or memorizer of the Qur'ān) Muḥammad b. Yumthughurbīr; and a fifth the mother of Aḥmad Mātinī b. Asikala. Al-Sa'dī makes absolutely clear that though known as the sons of this or that man, they inherited their *baraka* through their mothers.

Other than serving as vessels through whom illustrious sons were born, mothers were also important to their formation as scholars and saints. Al-Sa'dī may evince the greater sensitivity to and awareness of the role of women in this capacity, as he is careful to acknowledge his descent from 'Abd Allāh al-Balbālī through his Fulani wife.[148] And it is al-Sa'dī who reports on the compact between Kasay and Nānā Tinti.[149] Though the *baraka* that made her prayer against *Sunni* 'Alī efficacious may be attributed to her father, it was nonetheless channeled through Nānā Tinti, and as such is an example of how the sources implicitly embed the spiritual qualities of women.

Beyond the foregoing, it is a challenge to locate references to women as spiritual agents and actors. There is the aforementioned 973/1565 episode in which Nānā Ḥafṣa bt. *al-ḥājj* Aḥmad b. 'Umar successfully objects to *Qāḍī* al-'Āqib naming her son Muḥammad al-Amīn as *imām* of Sankore mosque, indicating her own, independent influence.[150] In yet another example, al-Sa'dī mentions the death of both the *sharīfa* Nānā Bēr and her daughter the *sharīfa* Nānā 'Ā'isha (seven days later) in

1019/1611, suggesting they enjoyed a level of prestige.[151] Though scarce, such evidence, when combined with consideration of mothers as sources of *baraka*, suggests there were more Songhay women who were spiritual leaders in their own right.

Gendered Notions of Political Power in Songhay

In addition to achieving levels of recognition and prominence as unofficial bearers of spiritual power, royal women in Songhay were also recognized, though it is not clear if their circumstances translated into formal positions of political authority. At the very least a designation of respect, the title *waiza* precedes the names of several daughters of *Askia al-ḥājj* Muḥammad—*Waiza* Bāni, *Waiza* 'Ā'isha Kara, *Waiza* Ḥafṣa, and *Waiza* Umm Hāni. Following these four women are others to whom the title of *waiza* is not attached, yet they were important individuals: 'Ā'isha Bonkana, the mother of the *Balma'a* Muḥammad Kurbu (or Kūba); 'Ā'isha Kara, the mother of *Balma'a* Muḥammad Wa'aw; Hāwa Da-*koi*, the mother of the Hombori-*koi* Mansa or Munsu; Farāsa, the mother of the Dirma-*koi* Mānankā; and Aryu the mother of the *Kanfāri* Hammād (and wife of the *Balma'a* Muḥammad Kiray). Like women associated with religious elites in Timbuktu, they derived status as the daughters of the *askia*, or as mothers of leading officials. *Waiza* Umm Hāni is similarly identified as a mother (of Hāni), but otherwise the first three women bearing the title *waiza* are not associated with children, signifying the title may have been an office rather than a status.[152]

This title reappears for two daughters of *Askia* Dāwūd, again without relation to marriage or motherhood: *Waiza* Ḥafṣa and *Waiza* Akībunu/Kaybunu. That it carried some political connotation is further suggested by al-Sa'dī's mention of *Waiza* Ḥafṣa's death in 967/1560, stating that in the following year "*Waiza* Kaybunu assumed office," only to pass away in 972/1565. These are the only two women mentioned in conjunction with an "office" for the whole of imperial Songhay in this text, but the office was probably significant, as their deaths are mentioned in conjunction with such prominent figures as the Shā'-*farma* Muḥammad Konāte (d. 967/1559–60), the *faqīh* al-Mukhtār b. 'Umar (d. 968/1560), and *Qāḍī* Maḥmūd himself (d. 973/1565).[153]

Otherwise, several of Dāwūd's daughters are noted for their position as wives: Kāssa (or Kāsā) the wife of the Jenne-*koi* Manaba'la (or Wainba'alī); Binta (or Bita), the wife of the Maghsharan-*koi* Maḥmūd Bēr *al-ḥājj* b. Muḥammad al-Līm; Ṣafiyya ("the pure"), wife of *Sīdī* Sālim al-ʿAṣnūnī; Umatullāh, spouse of the *Khaṭīb* Darāmi; and ʿĀʾisha Kimari (or Ḥafṣa Kīmari), wife of Maḥmūd Kaʿti (who sent her to Timbuktu without having relations with her). The examples of Umatullāh, Ṣafiyya, and ʿĀʾisha Kimari suggest a development under Dāwūd whereby royal daughters began marrying religious figures. Speaking specifically of Dāwūd's daughters, al-Saʿdī indeed writes: "Many of them were married to scholars, jurists, merchants, and army commanders."[154]

The apparent rerouting of female power in West Africa from the political to the noumenal was initially examined regarding Do-Kamissa and Sunjata in chapter 5, and what little evidence exists of Songhay female office holders is not inconsistent. However, on Songhay's southeastern border were women serving not only as officials, but as sovereigns, with Hausa women rulers long attracting attention, especially the tenth/sixteenth figure Āmina or Aminatu of Zaria.[155] She can be located within a broader territorial spectrum of women rulers, from the very famous (e.g., Nzinga of Angola) to those with less legible power. The literature tends to emphasize women controlling certain spheres of endeavor, exercising power by virtue of their position relative to the male ruler (such as queen mothers), influencing such processes as succession, or becoming prominent within periods of liminality, such as regency.[156]

Women also wielded power originating in spaces that were not formally political, subsequently undergoing translation, by which it became decidedly political, a critical example of which is Dona Beatriz Kimpa Vita of Kongo.[157] Examples of political authority with either formal or unorthodox beginnings resonate with developments along Songhay's western frontier, where the sources provide two examples of female rulers during the time of *Sunni* ʿAlī. The first is said to have conquered the land of the Ṣanhāja Nono, a group living in Masina, under the leadership of one Queen (*Malika*) Bīkun Kābi.[158] The other example is a fascinating account of resilience as well as resurgence in the struggle against *Sunni* ʿAlī, centering on one Yānū of Anganda village (presumably east of Lake Debo), who established a community in the mountainous Hajar between Hombori and Danaka. The origins of her authority are unspecified, but it was manifestly political by the time *Sunni* ʿAlī assaulted the area in 997/1588, putting Yānū to flight while capturing her niece Jata. He would give Jata to the people of Mori Koyra as a "gift," and she would marry the (unnamed) brother of *Mōri* Hawgāru and have a child, Munsu ʿAlū Maidaʾa. At *Sunni* ʿAlī's demise, Yānū traveled to Budara (perhaps east of Bara province), where she reemerges as a "great ruler," evidently possessed of considerable leadership skills.

Yānū's political and military prowess were on full display when the Bara-*koi Mansā* Mūsā asked for her help in putting down a revolt led by one "Mindi Jam," an iron-worker (*ḥaddād*). At the head of some fifty cavalry, Yānū led the charge, defeating and killing Mindi Jam, after which she established the town of Buyo on choice land in Bara province, the condition for her assistance. Yānū died with no heir save nephew Munsu 'Alū Maida'a, so the people of Buyo went to Jata and returned with Munsu 'Alū Maida'a to Buyo, where he became Bana-*koi*, the first to bear that title. He and *Kanfāri* 'Umar developed a close friendship, celebrating "*'Īd*" (presumably *'Īd al-Fiṭr* at Ramaḍān's end) in Tendirma every year. Though male leaders round out the story, Yānū's leadership and bravery in these circumstances constitute its compelling core.[159]

Consistent with what little is known about the *waizas* under *Askias al-ḥājj* Muḥammad and Dāwūd, Yānū is not explicitly associated with marriage, and the text specifically states she left no heirs, seeming to signal a belief that marriage and maternity were seen as antithetical to political power, that women could only hold office, or at least this type of office, outside of such disqualifying statuses. That female political authorities are rarely mentioned in the chronicles further points to a prevailing phallocentric notion of authority connected with war and plunder, best epitomized by *Sunni* 'Alī, who, in his defeat of Yānū, reinforced the paradigm. That she reemerges as a political leader, steed-mounted and handling a sword as skillfully as any man, does not disrupt so much as strengthen the view that Yānū was becoming an exception to what were otherwise masculine performances.

Concubinage and the Fashioning of an Ethnic and Cultural Mosaic

While female political leaders seem to have been rare in Songhay, giving birth to children within elite formations was a far more predictable route to recognition, prestige, and even power. The mothers of sons who rose to prominence as scholar-saints or as political figures have been discussed, but there is another category of mothers whose rise to notoriety is altogether counterintuitive, yet critical to understanding the experiences of women and concepts of gender, as well as theories of governance and slavery in imperial Songhay. This is the category of the concubine, by definition an enslaved female, which *Askia* Muḥammad reconfigured into one of the most influential positions in the realm.

Confirming the potential influence of those living within the *askia's* circle of intimacy, al-Sa'dī names the mothers of the successors to *Askia al-ḥājj* Muḥammad as well as some of his other sons, beginning with *Askia* Mūsā's mother Zāra Kabirun-*koi* (or Kurbu), originally a slave girl (*jāriya*) to the Kabirun-*koi* ("Zāra" may be a local generic for "female slave" and not a personal name); followed by Marīam Dābo, a "Wangāra" or Soninke woman, who became the mother of *Askia* Ismā'īl; then Kulthūm Barda of Daram/Dirma, possibly Tuareg and the mother of *Askia* Isḥāq Bēr; then Sāna bt. Fāri-*koi* or Sāna Fāriu, *Askia* Dāwūd's mother (also called Bunkānū Fāriyu in *Ta'rīkh al-fattāsh*); and so on, listing eleven women altogether.[160] Other than Zāra Kabirun-*koi*, the statuses of these women are not provided, but they were in fact all concubines, as *Ta'rīkh al-fattāsh* maintains that save for *Askia al-ḥājj* Muḥammad himself, all of the Askias were the sons of concubines (*sarārīy*).[161]

The implications for concubinage's high profile in the royal court are no less than stunning. To begin, a valid assumption is that *Askia al-ḥājj* Muḥammad was married, presumably to no more than four wives at a time (the limit in Islam). The *askia*, or any free slaveholder, could marry a concubine upon first manumitting her, but the fact that none of his wives are named, nor their children explicitly identified, is astounding. Second, Muḥammad must have been around fifty-two years old when he became *askia* in 898/1493, as he was ninety-seven when he died in 944/1538.[162] He had therefore probably fathered children before wresting power, and would end up with "many" children, apparently in the hundreds. Though there was a succession order loosely based on age and lineal proximity, it is not consistently in evidence, a degree of flexibility and absence of precision inherited from the Malian model. Under normal circumstances, this allowed for the succession's contestation without necessarily endangering the realm, but in times of crisis—as the Moroccan invasion constituted like no other—it contributed to the forces of destabilization. Dāwūd would follow his father's example in producing numerous progeny.[163] It is not possible that, given so many potential pretenders for the throne as well as other plum assignments, the mothers of these children did not play a vital role in promoting the interest of their children against those of others. Rivalries were therefore probably intense, the royal court heavy with intrigue. No outcome was guaranteed, opening the door to such machinations that the sons of the *askias'* wives lost out every time.

Rivalry between children of free and enslaved women within complex, large harems was hardly unique to Songhay.[164] The anthropological record for the Songhay-Zarma suggests enmity between the sons of concubines and wives had become an anticipated social feature, informed by a dichotomous framing within which children of the same mother (the *nya-ize*) experienced affectionate bonds, in contrast to sons of the same father (the *baab-ize*) who viewed each other adversarially. The children of concubines (the *wahay-ize*) would come to suffer stigmatization—though they could aspire to high office—but this is nowhere in evidence during the tenth/sixteenth century.[165]

Referred to in the Qur'ān as "that which your right hands possess" (*mā malakat aymānukum*), a concubine's status changed to that of an *umm walad*, or "mother of a child," once she bore a child for a free man (and paternity was acknowledged), after which she could not be sold for as long as that man lived, and was freed upon his death. Her children, however, were born free, inheriting the status and identity of their father. This was apparently the case for hundreds of children and their mothers under the Askias. That all of *Askia al-ḥājj* Muḥammad's successors were the sons of concubines is no greater testimony of adherence to these principles.

Though status and inheritance flowed through the paternal line, it is fascinating that the identities of these enslaved mothers were not erased, but in fact preserved, as opposed to the names of royal wives. Though matriliny may have been "unofficially and discreetly" recognized among the Songhay, royal concubines of the imperial era were more than acknowledged—they were celebrated, in part a reflection of their giving birth to rulers.[166] Thus, Zāra Kabirun-*koi* is conspicuous in her mention, sought out by several rulers and having children by at least three of them. Her son Mūsā is in fact regarded as *Askia al-ḥājj* Muḥammad's first son, instructive given the high probability that Muḥammad already had adult children before he even became *askia*. Like Zāra Kabirun-*koi*, Fāṭima Buṣ Zughrānī, the mother of *Askia* Isḥāq, left such an imprint that her son was known as *Askia* Isḥāq Zughrānī, or "*Askia* Isḥāq the Zughrānī"—probably a curious if not conflictual experience for him, as the Zughrānī (or Joghoranī) were the Diawambe clients of the Middle Niger Fulbe, and the name therefore a reminder of a servile heritage. These examples demonstrate that women subjugated in this way could nonetheless reinvent themselves and influence the direction of the empire itself.

In addition to the mothers of future rulers were other royal concubines, such as Tāti Za'ankoi (or "the Za'ankī," perhaps Jakhanke and the mother of Benga-*farma* 'Alī Bindi-Kanyiya); the "Ajur woman of mixed ancestry from the people of Kīsu," Āmina Kiraw (of Kiraw); Āmina Wāy Bardā (of Bardā); Amisi Kāra (of Kāra); and Kamsa Mīman-*koi* (related to the ruler of Mīman, possibly Mema).[167] Their variegated appellations, beyond simply indicating a diversity targeted by the Songhay military, allude to something more profound in *Askia al-ḥājj* Muḥammad's theory of governance.

Such relative and qualified privilege, however, was little compensation for the experience of the many more women and girls uprooted from their homes and families to be objectified, assaulted, and violated. No matter its size, the royal harem could not account for the untold numbers trafficked into this condition and unable to significantly alter their trajectories. There were concubines and there were concubines, with those bearing sons for rulers, clerics, and merchants occupying a very different space, figuratively and literally.

Further underscoring the rule was the exceptional female captive who underwent a rather dramatic transformation in her circumstance, as in the case of al-Sa'dī's ancestor *Imām* 'Abd Allāh al-Balbālī, who married the Fulani captive 'Ā'isha.[168] In like spirit, 'Uryān al-Ra's (d. 1027/1618) would "purchase many slaves (*al-mamālīk*) and manumit them for the sake of God Most High and the Hereafter," exhibiting the principle that manumission, though not obligatory, was a laudable act before God.[169] But al-Balbālī and 'Uryān al-Ra's were probably exceptional, for as *Ta'rīkh as-sūdān* asserts, *Sunni* 'Alī sent many captive Fulbe "as gifts to the eminent men of Timbuktu, and to some of the scholars and holymen, ordering them to take them as concubines," consistent with "gifting" a leading female captive to "the village of Mori Koyra" and giving Jata, the niece of Yānū, to *Mōri* Hawgāru's brother (who married her).[170] *Askia* Muḥammad likewise awarded the *Mōri* brothers al-Ṣādiq and Jayba and other siblings ten slaves (*'abīd*) each, and some may have become concubines. The latter were certainly among the "gifts" rulers regularly sent to the *'ulamā'* of Timbuktu, including *Qāḍī* Maḥmūd.[171] In support of its acclamatory introduction of *Askia* Muḥammad as the "*sulṭān* of the Muslims," *Ta'rīkh al-fattāsh* is explicit on this point, stating the *askia*

> demonstrated his love for the scholars and saints and students with many alms and deeds both prescribed and superogatory, as he was a person most discerning and shrewd, showing humility toward the scholars, showering (*bathala*) them with slaves (*nufūs*, literally "people") and wealth to promote the interests of the Muslims and to aid them in their obedience and service to God.[172]

Seizing women and girls from communities throughout the western Sahel and Savannah was certainly a function of imposition, but their subsequent treatment by the *askia* was no unintended consequence. Rather, the elevation of royal concubines reveals itself as a well-considered policy of the state, the reasons for which are several and compelling. First, although *Sunni* 'Alī and *Askia al-ḥājj* Muḥammad were similar in capturing and enslaving females, the latter's subsequent policy of inclusion was altogether distinguishing. Second, the reification of concubines who bore children for the *askia* had the effect of encouraging their communities of origin to identify with Songhay and the new regime, as they were now represented at the highest levels of society and government. Third, by acknowledging the children of women from such disparate backgrounds, the *askia* pursued a policy of political unification through the recognition of ethnic and regional diversity, in this way becoming the father, literally and symbolically, of the Songhay empire.[173] And fourth, as a Muslim ruler embracing such miscellany, he encouraged submission to Islam throughout the realm. As such, the *askia* encouraged all who participated in the cultural and political life of Songhay to think of themselves as members of the state, especially in Timbuktu and Jenne. From every indication, notwithstanding the clerical rhetoric of resistance, they fully embraced that membership and were loyal to it, an orientation that became more than apparent with the dawn of the Moroccan occupation.

Askia al-ḥājj Muḥammad was therefore far wiser than his predecessor in understanding the political potential of concubinage, but even though he chose an approach more in keeping with legal prescription than *Sunni* 'Alī', at the end of the day he also succeeded in acquiring so many that a "special palace" was established to house "a huge number of wives, concubines, slaves, and eunuchs assigned to watch over these women."[174] This was a harem in the classically stereotypic, orientalist imagination, with gelded males and plenty of intrigue, entirely analogous to the Ottoman counterpart.[175]

Slavery and the Calculus of Ethnicity

Askia al-ḥājj Muḥammad's policies toward concubinage also point to the maturation of a process by which the enslavement eligibility of whole communities was determined, with far-reaching implications for West Africa itself. Its foundation is certainly suggested in the correspondence between *Askia* Muḥammad and al-Maghīlī, with the former referring to those claiming to be Muslims yet retaining "idols"—a seeming description of the Dogon. Naming the backgrounds of royal concubines further suggests an unfolding of this identification process, a necessary development in distinguishing between Muslims and non-Muslims subject to enslavement.

This is a far cry from an earlier period, when such ambiguous categories as the Lamlam and Damdam were invoked. The previously mentioned Makhlūf b. ʿAlī b. Ṣāliḥ al-Balbālī (d. 940/1533–34), the *askia*'s contemporary and ʿAbd Allāh b. ʿUmar b. Muḥammad Aqīt's star pupil, confirms that a system of differentiation based on community or land of origin was indeed well under way, stating in a *fatwā* that the "people of Kano, some of Zakzak [Zaria], the people of Katsina, the people of Gobir, and all of the Songhay . . . are all Muslims and it is not lawful to possess them. Likewise all the Fulani."[176] Makhlūf al-Balbālī goes on to articulate the concept that serves as the bedrock for determining slavery eligibility. Having listed the ineligible groups, he declares:

> Anyone who is known to be from those lands, which are known to be [lands of] Islam . . . and who mentions that he is from those lands, should be let go, and should be adjudged free. This was the ruling of the jurists of Andalusia . . . [and] a similar ruling was given by the people [*ahl*, presumably judges] of Fez, and likewise by *Sīdī* Maḥmūd, *qāḍī* of Timbuktu. He would accept their claim [of freedom], though he would charge them with establishing that they were from [one of] those lands. Whoever seeks salvation for himself should only buy of such persons those who name their land [of origin], and after an investigation as to whether he is from that land or not, meaning whether he is from a land of Islam or a land of unbelief. By means of this great calamity [enslaving free Muslims] tribulation has spread widely throughout the lands in this age. And God knows best.[177]

Makhlūf al-Balbālī's anxiety does not concern slaving itself, but rather its victimization of Muslims. More critical is his declaration that it is the status of the land—Muslim or non-Muslim—that dictates whether someone from that land can be enslaved. By means of this concept, he provides a list of polities as well as communities (including the Fulbe and the Songhay, the latter conceivably representing both the state and the ethnolinguistic group) who were not to be subjugated in this way.

The following century saw both the confirmation and further elaboration of this principle. Aḥmad Bābā composed his *Miʿrāj al-ṣuʿūd* or "The Ladder of Ascent" in 1024/1615 in response to queries from one al-Jirārī, who apparently lived in Tuwat.[178] Writing the *Miʿrāj* after his exile in Morocco (between 1002/1593 and 1016/1608), Aḥmad Bābā affirms that unbelief is the sole basis for enslavement, whatever a person's "race" or ethnolinguistic community, but that in cases of contested individual status, the condition of unbelief is a function of the status of the land of origin, with the clear inference that recognition of a land as Muslim was predicated upon whether its inhabitants had originally embraced Islam willingly, or by coercion:[179]

> You [al-Jirārī] asked: "Were these aforementioned lands belonging to the Muslims of the Sūdān conquered and their people enslaved in a state of unbelief, while their conversion to Islam occurred subsequently, so there is no harm [in owning them], or not?" The Reply is that they converted to Islam without anyone conquering them, like the people of Kano, Katsina, Bornu, and Songhay. We never heard that anyone conquered them before their conversion to Islam. Among them are those who have been Muslims since long ago, like the people of Bornu and Songhay.[180]

This question of the mechanism by which a land or community became Muslim is also implicit is al-Jirārī additional queries: "Reveal to us the true state of affairs of these lands. . . . Was their land taken by force, or peacefully, or what? And at what time did Islam reach them? Was it during the period of the Companions or later?"[181] Citing Ibn Khaldūn and the examples of Kanem-Bornu, Gao and Mali, Aḥmad Bābā answers that "it is clear from Ibn Khaldūn and others that they became Muslims of their own volition."[182]

Having clarified that unbelief is the basis for enslavement, and that a land whose inhabitants voluntarily embraced Islam qualifies as Muslim and is therefore exempt from slavery, Aḥmad Bābā gets to the practical application, as revealed in *Mi'rāj al-ṣu'ūd*'s alternative title: *al-Kashf wa'l-bayān li-aṣnāf majlūb as-sūdān*, "The Disclosure and Enumeration of the Categories of Transported Black Slaves." Conflating polity and ethnolinguistic community while repeating Makhlūf al-Balbālī's ruling that the people of Bornu, Kano, Songhay, Katsina, Gobir, Mali, "most" of the Fulbe, and some of the inhabitants of Zaria ("Zakzak") are Muslim, Aḥmad Bābā goes further, listing those lands and groups eligible for enslavement: the *ṣanf* or "category" of the Mossi, followed by the Dagomba (a branch of the Mossi), the Gurma (or Gurmanche, east of the Mossi), Borgu (land of the Bariba), Busa (a Borgu town west of the River Niger, between Kebbi and Oyo Ile), the Kotokoli (in what is now northern Togo), the "Yoruba" (*yurba*), the Tombo (the Dogon of the Bandiagara escarpment) and Kumbe (the Dogon of the plains), the Bobo (south of Jenne), and the unidentified "Krmu."[183]

The Moroccan Yūsuf b. Ibrāhīm b. 'Umar al-Īsī had in fact posed similar questions to Aḥmad Bābā before he wrote *Mi'rāj al-ṣu'ūd*, apparently during the latter's exile in Morocco. Indeed, it is al-Īsī who specifies that the Gurma, Borgu, "Irbā" (which could refer to the Yoruba), Dagomba, Mossi, Kotoloki, "Tondinke" (cliff dwellers from Hombori to Bandiagara), and the unidentified Kurwā are unbelievers (according to what he had heard), while he raises questions about the ambiguous status of the "Sīwī Arabs" (apparently the Shewa Arabs near Lake Chad), along with "Jolof and Jenne."[184] In responding, Aḥmad Bābā clarifies that the "Jolof" or Wolof are Muslims as far as he could determine, as are the people of Jenne, and that the Tondike are subdivided into different groups, some Muslim and some not, while jurists are divided over the Sīwī Arabs. But Aḥmad Bābā confirms the others as enslavable, adding to them the Arbinda and Armina, as well as the "Bambara" and Bobo south of Jenne. In a postscript to his second reply to al-Īsī, he names no less than 107 Muslim "tribes" (*qabā'il*, though the list is actually a mix of ethnicity and clan names, such as "Kabā" and "Sillā," together with "the tribes of the Fulanī"), followed by a collection of thirty-one groups and place names characterized by unbelief. Members from these groups had entered Morocco as slaves, and it was important to resolve the legality of their circumstance.

The delineation of groups subject to enslavement represents a significant development in West African slavery. That both the *Mi'rāj al-ṣu'ūd* and Aḥmad Bābā's replies to al-Īsī were written between two to twenty-five years after the fall of Songhay suggests the question of eligibility had been in formation at least since the reign of *Askia* Muḥammad, especially as Makhlūf al-Balbālī was the *askia*'s contemporary, while the groups subject to enslavement are consistent with the derivations of some of his concubines, such as Zāra Kabirun-*koi* of Borgu, as well as with areas Songhay regularly targeted for raids. Given the expansion of both Islam and trafficking in the western Sudan, notions of origins and group affiliation had become critical to differentiating between exempt and subject populations, with ethnicity in West Africa emerging as a juridical category in tandem with other cultural and social insignia, long before the arrival of European colonialism.[185]

The Eunuchs of Songhay

Another genus of slaves was that of the eunuch. There is little to gain in comparing his plight to that of the concubine, though it can be remarked that with the latter there was some possibility of mitigation through childbirth, even of freedom, with the owner's death. Not so for the eunuch, whose condition was permanent and immutable. Both forms of enslavement involved violation of an egregious nature, and it was precisely the alteration of their sexuality that facilitated their access into the intimacies of elite circles. For the concubine, such admission potentially carried future reward, however dubious. For the eunuch, certain possibilities were forever foreclosed.

As observed, al-Muhallabī mentions the presence of eunuchs in the royal court at Gao in the fourth/tenth century.[186] By the time of *Askia al-ḥājj* Muḥammad, it would be reasonable to assume eunuchs were recruited from the same populations as concubines, so that eunuchs and concubines from the same communities could have built on existing cultural affinities. Given their placement and close association with females in the royal harem, it is also appropriate to speculate they were involved in strategies supporting the interests of children they favored. The *askia*, busy with empire, religion, and impregnating women, would have had little time to attend to actually raising so many children, and would have depended on eunuchs, thus deepening their influence. The likelihood that *Huku-kuri-koi* ʿAlī Fulan, the *askia's* chief of staff, was a eunuch only strengthens the notion that their influence could be considerable.

But eunuchs were hardly confined to the care of royal concubines. Some seven hundred, each outfitted in silken attire, stood behind the *Askia* Dāwūd during royal audiences.[187] In fact, the use if not dependence on eunuchs may have grown over time, as some four thousand comprised a "eunuch cavalry" (*fārisān min khaṣī*) led by the *huku-kuri-koi* during the final days of Songhay's independence.[188] Whether eunuchs were used in such a capacity as early as *Askia al-ḥājj* Muḥammad is unclear, though the "expedition of the four thousand" seems to echo ʿAlī Fulan's foray (along with Muḥammad Kiray) against the Baghana-*fari*/*faran* in 917/1511–12.[189] The inclusion of eunuchs in what was a professional standing army underscores its servile component.[190] By the reign of *Askia* Muḥammad Bāni (995–96//1586–88), the position of Kabara-*farma* was also held by a eunuch.[191]

Of course, the enslaved included more than concubines, eunuchs, and soldiers, serving in capacities related to production, among whom the Sorko fisherfolk feature. The Sorko and the Arbi are the only two groups to escape the confines of *Taʾrīkh al-fattāsh*'s manuscript C, and are specifically mentioned in the letter written by *Askia al-ḥājj* Muḥammad's scribes to protect the interests of the Mori Koyra. Considered the exclusive "property" (*mamlūkān*) of the *askia*, little is known about the Arbi (as opposed to the Sorko) save that the apparent meaning of their name suggests they were indigenous to the land, maybe as cultivators. What little insight is given into their circumstances is from manuscript

C, where they are identified as the special servants of the *askia*, their daughters as ladies-in-waiting for the royal wives, others as domestics. Messengers and escorts for the military, they also cultivated and prepared food for the royal family.[192] To the extent this information is of some use, it suggests a level of agricultural productivity primarily for royals. That level will greatly expand under *Askia* Dāwūd, but beyond the Arbi, agriculture based on servile labor is not directly addressed during the reign of *Askia* Muḥammad, suggesting a reliance on heavily taxed peasant communities.

It is under *Askia al-ḥājj* Muḥammad, therefore, that royal slaves, especially concubines and eunuchs, begin to assume power and influence, both formally and informally, emerging as veritable elites. Though they could be rivals, they could come together to promote their own interests, as well as those of favored mothers and sons. A collective consciousness and solidarity was forming that in time would express itself as an organized, if loyal constituency.

The Waning of the Age

On 3 Rabī' al-Awwal 926/22 February 1520, *Askia al-ḥājj* Muḥammad's brother and trusted confidant *Kanfāri* 'Umar died, sending *Mōri* Ṣāliḥ Diawara, with whom 'Umar was very close, into seclusion for three days. He was replaced as *kanfāri* by their brother Yaḥyā, but it was the beginning of the end for the *askia*, as 'Umar's death left an enormous vacuum in the structure of power and consultation. According to *Ta'rīkh al-fattāsh*, the *askia* arrived in Tendirma the same night 'Umar passed away, and was so distraught he spent ten days away from Gao in mourning. Clearing his head while following the meandering path of a Niger tributary, he lamented the loss of so valuable a counselor: "How beautiful and excellent is this land, but its leaders can never agree on a single thing!" When asked his meaning, he explained: "[Just as] this river's course is contorted, so are those who drink from it; their advice is unreliable, and the leaders do not agree with each other."[193]

In attempting to help fill the void, or perhaps taking advantage of it, 'Alī Fulan may have offered the *askia* poor advice, revealing 'Alī Fulan's sensitivity to, if not actual participation in, an atmosphere of intense rivalry between the *askia*'s many scions. This is supported by *Ta'rīkh as-sūdān*, where the *huku-kuri-koi* urges the *askia* to replace the deceased Benga-*farma* 'Alī Yamra/Yamara with Balla, one of the *askia*'s younger sons, setting into motion a series of visceral reactions from the older siblings. Balla had occupied the undefined post of Adiki-*farma*, while the office of Benga-*farma* was one of the three most important in the realm, and came with an estate (*tarika*). Though respected by his brothers for his courage and bravery, Balla's nomination so angered the older ones they vowed to "split open his drum" when he came to Gao, a reference to the Benga-*farma* as one of the drum lords.[194]

Balla indeed proved fearless, and upon learning of these threats responded that "for anyone who wanted to split open his drum, he would split open their mother's ass," a crude but insightful reflection on maternal involvement in jockeying for power. On approaching Gao, the newly appointed Benga-*farma* had his drum sounded all the way to the palace gate, an affirmation that not only did he intend to remain Benga-*farma*, but viewed himself as the heir apparent. His brothers, grumbling "in envy" before his arrival, joined the military commanders in welcoming him at the palace gate, dismounting from their horses in acknowledgement of his rank, suggesting the military commanders, following the *huku-kuri-koi*'s lead, were in full support. The brothers deemed it prudent to momentarily fall in line.

All save *Fari-mondio* Mūsā, regarded as the *askia*'s oldest son. Refusing to alight, he spoke to Balla with a slight nod of his head: "I have nothing to say about this matter, though you know that if I speak, I keep my word." None of the military commanders "dared oppose this offense" (of not dismounting), and in so characterizing Mūsā's actions, al-Sa'dī lays the groundwork for a critical assessment of Mūsā's role in overthrowing his father, further stating that it was because of his "arrogance" (*al-ṭulū'*), as well as the fact that he was a man of great valor, "surpassing [his brothers] in courage in many exploits and battles," that "animosity thickened" between not only Mūsā and Balla, but also between Mūsā and other siblings. Allegiances between the brothers were strategic rather than permanent, and by delving into motivations, al-Sa'dī depicts an atmosphere rife with jealousy and insecurity.

The breaking point was reached in 934/1527–28, when Mūsā "swerved from the ways of his father" and threatened to kill 'Alī Fulan, accusing him of exercising undue influence over the *askia*, who by then was not only old but blind, a condition 'Alī Fulan "kept hidden," which can only mean he controlled access to the *askia* and was therefore in command for all practical purposes. Exposed, the *huku-kuri-koi* fled to *Kanfāri* Yaḥyā at Tendirma, and the next year Mūsā fully "broke with his father," relocating to Kukiya with some of his brothers, a move approximating rebellion. Attempting to calm the situation, the *askia* asked *Kanfāri* Yaḥyā to go to Kukiya and "straighten out these children" with restraint and diplomacy. But upon his arrival there, he was confronted and overpowered by his nephews. Knocked to the ground, he would remain lying face down, exposed and injured. Several standing over him would eventually succeed to the *askiyate* (*al-taskiya* or *al-askuwīya* in the Arabic), a portent of trouble to come as well as commentary on their character.[195] Dāwūd kept silent while Ismā'īl covered his uncle's nakedness with a garment: "I knew you would be the only one to do that, Ismā'īl, as you honor kinship," the *kanfāri* replied. In contrast, Muḥammad Bonkana Kirya, son of the deceased *Kanfāri* 'Umar, began accusing Yaḥyā of lies and deceit, to which the latter replied: "You are the one known for deceit. You will never hear such a thing [from me], you who sever kinship ties!" Yaḥyā expired while lying there, and upon hearing the news, the *askia* named his son 'Uthmān Yawbābo as the next *kanfāri*.

Ta'rīkh al-fattāsh's version of the story bypasses the intrigue, simply saying *Kanfāri* Yaḥyā became aware of Mūsā's plan to seize power from his aging father and traveled to Gao to stop it. After warning Mūsā to turn from the path of sedition, the *kanfāri* carelessly rode his horse to the outskirts of town, where he was caught off guard and killed by Mūsā and his "corrupt and depraved and rebellious brothers."[196] In either scenario, Mūsā emerges as the transgressor.

Following the more detailed narrative of al-Sa'dī, the selection of 'Uthmān Yawbābo as *kanfāri* was the last straw, and that same year (935/1529) Mūsā came out in open revolt. Choosing *'Īd al-Aḍḥā* (on 10 Dhū 'l-Ḥijja/15 August) as the occasion, Mūsā traveled to the capital with his brothers. As the *askia* was about to participate in the worship service, Mūsā interrupted, vowing they would not continue unless he was named the new *askia*. With his brothers 'Umar and Yaḥyā dead, and 'Alī Fulan in full flight, the eighty-eight-year-old *Askia* Muḥammad acquiesced, having been in office for thirty-seven years and six months.[197] Mūsā led the worship service and the people followed, signifying their acceptance of the transition. For al-Sa'dī, however, this seizure of power was an unforgivable offense, even though Mūsā allowed his father to continue living in the palace.[198]

Al-Sa'dī's perspective is certainly justifiable, as the Age of *Askia al-ḥājj* Muḥammad had been extraordinary. Under his leadership the empire had expanded significantly, reaching north to Taghaza and Agades, south to the border with Mali along the River Bani, east to the frontier with Hausaland, and west to Diara in Kaniaga/Futa Kingui. From every indication, commerce was robust, especially in Timbuktu, where the *askia* had successfully restored the Sankore *'ulamā'* after a period of intense persecution under *Sunni* 'Alī. Their return sparked a veritable cultural renaissance in which scholars and saints enjoyed security and freedom, pursuing erudition at levels commensurate with leading centers elsewhere in the Muslim world. The pursuit of religion in Timbuktu and Jenne was matched by the *askia's* own embrace of reform, beginning with his Pilgrimage and followed by his efforts at expanding *sharī'a* with the appointment of *qāḍīs* in key urban areas and their environs. These efforts were connected to a renewed interest in internationalism and in refreshing ties with the central Islamic lands, raising Songhay's profile to attract such luminaries as al-Maghīlī.

Reconsideration of the sources, however, does not sustain the view that Timbuktu and Jenne were exempt from Gao's political control, nor that they exerted political influence on the capital. Rather, the Askias were highly successful in serially exacting wealth from the entrepots. Even so, under the Askias Timbuktu and Jenne became major cultural centers, as well as founts of spiritual power and practices.

While the religious leaders of Timbuktu and Jenne enjoyed unrivaled prestige, there were other actors who, though receiving scant attention in the secondary materials, were nonetheless significant figures. Specifically, holy men associated with the Mori Koyra community played influential roles, as did royal women, including, and especially, the royal concubines. Indeed, women were a critical component of the *askia*'s strategy in realizing an ethnic pluralism that would transform relations between the clan and the state, such that loyalties to the former could be accommodated within the latter. Buoyed by a resurgent economy, stellar scholarship, and the reconfiguration of political fealty, Songhay experienced a new age of cosmopolitanism.

With so many accomplishments, it is little wonder *Askia al-ḥājj* Muḥammad is revered as one of the most important leaders in West African history, his policies a template for Muslim reformers for centuries to come. Though advanced in years and impaired by the time of his removal from power, he remained in al-Sa'dī's eyes "Commander of the Faithful."[199]

PART IV

Le Dernier de l'Empire

CHAPTER TWELVE

Of *Fitnas* and Fratricide: The Nadir of Imperial Songhay

THE ENSUING TWENTY YEARS following the toppling of *Askia al-ḥājj* Muḥammad were filled with intrigue and bloodletting and death, as aspirants to the *askiyate* contended full tilt. The general protocols of succession, acknowledging seniority and proximity, were vulnerable to and often challenged by the ability of pretenders to influence circumstances and marshal support. The next four Askias—Mūsā, Muḥammad Bonkana, Ismā'īl, and Isḥāq Bēr—would come to power via such means, exposing a fraught process riven by unabated rivalry and disaffection. Scores of royals would be killed or exiled, and the absence of clear-cut succession rules, combined with an inability or disinterest in achieving a more reliable mechanism, would eventually prove lethal for both individuals and the empire itself.

The imperial nadir does not unveil itself so much as its silhouette becomes discernible. That is, the instability of succession creates space in which new stakeholders form and increasingly assert their influence. Referred to as the "people of Songhay," their precise composition is a matter of speculation approximated through a triangulation that eliminates certain possibilities while rendering others plausible.

Slaving's seeming increase during the nadir is related to market forces, with an eye toward exportation as well as internal consumption. A presumption is that captives were principally sent into the Sahara in exchange for horses, but as this is precisely the time when European demand was beginning to register along the West African littoral, it is possible some were diverted there, resulting in compensatory measures to meet northern demands.

Askia *Mūsā and Civil War*

"Then *Askia* Mūsā initiated the process of killing his brothers (*dakhala . . . fī qatl*)."[1] Thus begins al-Sa'dī's assessment of the nadir. Mūsā's time in office was transitory, only two years (935–37/1529–31), the destruction he visited on family members so swift and intense he either planned it immediately upon taking office, or as early as his confrontation with Benga-*farma* Balla, after which Mūsā broke ranks with his father. Al-Sa'dī consistently blames Mūsā for beginning what he calls a *fitna*, a time of trouble and instability in Songhay.[2]

Facing death at the hands of his nephews, the *Kanfāri* Yaḥyā would reiterate that they were guilty of "rupturing the ties of kinship" in refusing to honor conventions by which elders were respected and fraternal affinities affirmed. In pleading for his life, he becomes the vessel of an analysis of a root cause of Songhay's downfall, epitomized by the shockingly violent and brutal nature of *Askia* Mūsā's tenure. Indeed, the fractured fraternal bonds could not have been in greater contrast to the intimate ties enjoyed by *Askia al-ḥājj* Muḥammad and his brothers 'Umar and Yaḥyā.[3]

Mūsā's behavior was so alienating that al-Sa'dī could not bring himself to repeat *Ta'rīkh al-fattāsh*'s charge that Mūsā, like some imitation of Absalom's "going in" to his father King David's concubines, not only put his father out of the royal palace, but kept his wives and concubines for himself.[4] In response, the deposed Muḥammad allegedly prayed, "Oh God, uncover his [Mūsā's] genitals and shame him," answered the next day when Mūsā fell from his horse, his private parts exposed before his entire army. *Ta'rīkh al-fattāsh* pulls no punches, saying that of all who would claim the *askiyate*, no one was more despicable or insignificant (*akhaff*) than Mūsā, and that the office of *askia* was far too lofty for someone of his "impudence" (or "stupidity," *safāha*).

Al-Sa'dī had observed that during *Kanfāri* Yaḥyā's visit to Kukiya "animosity thickened" between the brothers, most apparent once Mūsā became *askia*. Seeing a different side of Mūsā, Ismā'īl fled to Tendirma and, with his brothers 'Uthmān Sīdī and Bukar Kirin-kirin, sought refuge with the *Kanfāri* 'Uthmān Yawbābo, *Askia al-ḥājj* Muḥammad's son and replacement for the slain Yaḥyā.[5] Benga-*farma* Balla would join them, constituting a Tendirma rebellion-in-formation against Gao.

The role of mothers in navigating relations between half-brothers is on full display here. Resolving to end the stalemate with the western capital, *Askia* Mūsā initially opted for diplomacy, sending an envoy with two letters—one for the *kanfāri*, and another for the *kanfāri*'s mother—with instructions that if *Kanfāri* 'Uthmān Yawbābo refused to read the letter, the messenger was to convey the second to Kamsa Mīman-*koi*.[6] As the *kanfāri* did not even acknowledge the royal envoy, the second letter was brought to Kamsa, in which the *askia* requested her intervention to avoid bloodshed, placing himself under her *ḥurma* ("protection"), along with that of his father. Kamsa "read the letter and understood its contents," which suggests she was literate though a concubine, and persuaded her son to reconsider a confrontation with Mūsā. In response, the *kanfāri* prepared to visit the *askia* in peace, loading his boats with provisions and setting off with his army.

A funny thing happened on the way to Gao. The *kanfāri*'s griot (*mughanī*) began singing, so incensing the *kanfāri* that he halted the journey, vowing "this head of mine will never again have dirt on it for anyone." Perhaps the griot reminded 'Uthmān Yawbābo that he had been named *kanfāri* by his now deposed father, or was subtly ridiculed for following his mother's advice.[7] In returning to Tendirma, he "left no doubt" of his sedition.

Seeing matters unfold, *Qāḍī* Maḥmūd sought to intervene, intercepting *Askia* Mūsā's army en route to Tendirma and meeting him in Tiryi village. The *qāḍī* kept his back turned the entire time, refusing to look at the one who had overthrown *amīr al-mu'minīn*. In defending his actions, Mūsā complained his father only did the bidding of 'Alī Fulan, whom he feared would one day turn father against son ("one day order evil against me"), a concern heightened by younger Balla's appointment as Benga-*farma*. There is a certain paranoia in this reasoning, resonating with his assessment of *Kanfāri* 'Uthmān Yawbābo: "I know my brother 'Uthmān. He has no mind of his own, but rather does what he is told by his courtiers, who are only rascals and fools."

The *qāḍī* pleaded with Mūsā to forgive the *kanfāri* and avoid *fitna*, as it would violate "the ties of kinship"—the essence of al-Sa'dī's critique of *Askia al-ḥājj* Muḥammad's sons. Mūsā's cynical response was laced with sarcasm: "Be calm and patient until they burn in the sun, then they will scurry for shade." Pointing to a bag of large poisoned lances, the *askia* explained, "These are the sun, and you are the shade. When they suffer pain they will rush to you, and then I'll forgive them." The *qāḍī* could only conclude Mūsā was bent on violence, and returned to Timbuktu.

Mūsā's stop near Timbuktu also helped him gauge the support of the *Balma'a* Muḥammad Kiray, stationed at Kabara. Having helped govern the realm's western sphere during *Askia al-ḥājj* Muḥammad's Pilgrimage, he later accompanied 'Alī Fulan against the Bāghana-*fari*, so he was very experienced. They met at Toya village (southwest of Kabara), and Muḥammad Kiray shared his concern that the skills of 'Uthmān Sīdī and Bukar Kirin-kirin, 'Uthmān Yawbābo's brothers, were so formidable that either could emerge victorious, whether they fought for or against the *askia*.[8]

The Toya meeting resulted in a shift in alliances, as both 'Uthmān Sīdī and Bukar Kirin-kirin switched from the *kanfāri* to the *askia*, not wanting to be counted among "the losers."[9] But there is also the riddle of *Balma'a* Muḥammad Kiray himself. The context could support he was siding with *Askia* Mūsā, though this is never made clear. But as Mūsā later kills him in Mansur (or Mansura, a village just outside of Gao), the *askia* may have never trusted him.[10]

The first full-scale battle between the sons of *Askia al-ḥājj* Muḥammad, with *Askia* Mūsā on one side and *Kanfāri* 'Uthmān Yawbābo on the other, was finally joined in 936/1529–30 at Akagan/Akenken, east of Timbuktu, just months after Mūsā seized power. Heavy losses on both sides included the deaths of the intrepid 'Uthmān Sīdī, but the *askia* prevailed. 'Uthmān Yawbābo fled to Tumni, where he would remain until his death in 964/1556–57, while former *Huku-kuri-koi* 'Alī Fulan relocated to Kano, where he would die, his plans to live out his days in Medina unfulfilled. Mūsā would name Muḥammad Bonkana Kirya, son of *Askia al-ḥājj* Muḥammad's brother 'Umar, as the new *kanfāri*.[11]

Ismā'īl also managed to escape, but to Walata/Biru, along with his brother-in-law Akbaran Kasu, the Maghsharan-*koi* and leader of the Tuareg north of Timbuktu. Akbaran Kasu was the grandson of Akil, who governed Timbuktu before *Sunni* 'Alī as the "*sulṭān* of the Tuareg." The shift to "Maghsharan-*koi*" indicates the transformation of a formerly independent office into one now subject to Gao, a transition supported by Akbaran Kasu's marriage to Ismā'īl's sister Kibiru, and further substantiated by the marriage of the future *Askia* Dāwūd's daughter Binta to an unnamed Maghsharan-*koi*.[12] That Akbaran Kasu and Ismā'īl fled together indicates ongoing ties, and given their historical connection, suggests Timbuktu may have supported *Kanfāri* 'Uthmān Yawbābo over *Askia* Mūsā. Mūsā may have understood this, explaining his dismissal of *Qāḍī* Maḥmūd's mediation.[13]

Benga-*farma* Balla, whose promotion precipitated all of these events, likewise fled the battle, but to *Qāḍī* Maḥmūd in Timbuktu.[14] "Anyone who enters [the *qāḍī*'s] house is safe, with the lone exception of Balla," was *Askia* Mūsā's response to Maḥmūd's request for clemency, to which the Benga-*farma* then raised a set of books over his head: "[In that case], I have entered under the protection (*ḥurma*) of these books." The *askia* rejected this attempt as well, and Balla resolved to surrender at Tila, the royal walled encampment at the Timbuktu port of Kabara. As Balla entered Tila, Mūsā's son exclaimed, "O father, do not kill my father the Benga-*farma*," but Balla consoled him: "My son, for me there is no escape from death, since there are three things I will never do: I will not address him as *askia*, I will not pour dirt on my head for him, and I will not ride behind him."

Al-Sa'dī portrays *Askia* Mūsā as impervious to reason or mercy, but Mūsā would have remembered Balla's threat to crack his mother's anus. The *askia* therefore had him arrested and taken to Alfa Gungu ("Scholar's Island"). There, together with his cousin Alfaqi (or al-Faqqi) Dunku, a son of *Kanfāri* 'Umar, Balla was buried alive in a deep pit.[15]

So there would be no doubt *Askia* Mūsā's reprehensible behavior was deserving of the whirlwind he would reap, al-Sa'dī records the intervention of the *walī* and *shaykh Mōri* Magha Kankoi, who along with followers from Jinjo met the *askia* on his return to Gao from fighting the *kanfāri*.[16] After offering the customary prayer, the *walī* implored the *askia* to spare the lives of the Dirma-*koi* and Bara-*koi*, "as they did not join the revolt willfully, but did so out of fear for their lives, being forced and coerced and unable to abandon [*Kanfāri*] 'Uthmān." But either the deed had already been done or the order given, as the *askia* replied, "They are beyond my control and out of my hands." It made strategic sense for the *askia* to move against the two governors to solidify his control of the western empire, but in putting both to death he was now awash in the blood of royals and nobles. "Do not do that—do not dismiss my intercession!" pled the *shaykh*, recounting that in praying for the longevity and success of *Askia al-ḥājj* Muḥammad, the *'ulamā'* had inquired as to whether there was a divinely favored son "in whom the Muslims might place their hope." "Mūsā" was the name the Commander of the Faithful uttered in response, so the saints

> "prayed for you to succeed him, and God heard our prayers. But if you cause our efforts to fail and refuse our protection, then the palm of the hand that remains raised to God Most High in prayer for you will be raised to Him against you."

The *Bana-farma* Isḥāq, another of *Askia al-ḥājj* Muḥammad's sons, later swore that as *askia* he would have killed the *walī* for his insolence, even if it meant eternal damnation, and accused Mūsā of being afraid to act.

Mūsā would respond that during the entire conversation the *shaykh* was holding back two lions with upraised palms (another dimension of the "the palm of the hand that remains raised"). "If [*Bana-farma* Isḥāq] had seen what I saw," Mūsā reflects, "he would have died on the spot from fear and alarm." Far from idle threats, *Mōri* Magha Kankoi's words were understood to issue from a spiritual authority that placed the *askia*'s fate in his hands. But none of these interventions—by mothers, *qāḍīs*, *shaykhs*, *mōris*, or *walīs*—could deter the *askia*.

Upon returning to Gao, paranoia and gamesmanship alloyed in lethal form. After killing as many as thirty-five cousins—sons of the defunct *Kanfāri* 'Umar—Mūsā turned to his own brothers, arresting the *Faran* 'Abd Allāh, the full brother of *Bana-farma* Isḥāq.[17] He then displayed 'Abd Allāh's clothes to Isḥāq: "Your brother 'Abd Allāh is a coward. We shut him up in a room and he died from fright"—a riposte to Isḥāq's earlier ridicule of Mūsā fearing *Mōri* Magha Kankoi. Reduced to tears, Isḥāq consulted the Shā'-*farma* 'Alū Wāy, another of *Askia* Muḥammad's sons.[18] "Shut up! Are you a woman? This is the last of us he will kill." Undertaking a two-day revolt with brothers who apparently included Muḥammad Bonkana Kirya, the Shā'-*farma* injured and finally killed a valiant *Askia* Mūsā on 24 Sha'bān 937/12 April 1531 in the village of Mansur.[19] There was deep irony as well as poetic justice for al-Sa'dī, who recalls that Mūsā "had killed *Balma'a* Muḥammad Kiray" in Mansur.

Having deposed his father, Mūsā inhabited a fratricidal space from which he could not escape, in which he "not once ever rested."[20] He was "always depressed and preoccupied with thoughts about [his hostile relatives] and anxious, forever on guard while taking precautions until he died (*maḍā li-sabīlihi*)." Though brief, his tenure was remarkably sanguinary.

Askia *Muḥammad Bonkana Kirya, the Enslaved, and Gao's Shifting Dynamics*

After killing Mūsā, the Shā'-*farma* 'Alī Wāy returned to Gao only to find *Kanfāri* Muḥammad Bonkana Kirya enthroned "between the stakes" (*al-a'wād*): "Who is that sitting between the stakes? I don't smash a tree with my head so that someone else can eat its fruit." But before he could reach Muḥammad Bonkana Kirya, 'Alī Wāy was overpowered and forced to flee by a younger brother, 'Uthmān Tinfarin, disqualifying him from the *askiyate*. With Muḥammad Bonkana Kirya now installed and the "people swearing fealty to him," 'Alī Wāy sought refuge with Gao's "harbor people."

Their leader, the Kūma-*koi*, promptly beheaded him, sending the grisly trophy to Muḥammad Bonkana Kirya. The new *askia* would thank the Kūma-*koi*, then later kill him.[21]

There is tension in the sources over *Askia* Muḥammad Bonkana Kirya (or Mār-Bonkan). On the one hand, the *ta'rīkhs* agree he expelled an aging *Askia al-ḥājj* Muḥammad from Gao to the island of Kangaga, where he was imprisoned.[22] He would languish there, and later complain to his son Ismā'īl: "Praise God that your arm is [as strong] as this, yet you abandon me to mosquitoes that bite and frogs that leap all over me!"[23] Lore held Muḥammad had been warned by none other than *Sunni* 'Alī who, upon hearing an ominous wail from a difficult birth (one meaning of Mār-Bonkan is "cut from the womb"), ordered the infant's death, to which Muḥammad and 'Umar pleaded for the child's life, as he was 'Umar's son (through a concubine). Learning the infant was born with a mouth full of teeth (a sign of greedy ambition), the *sunni* turned to Muḥammad: "This child will be wretched and debauched, but I will let him live. But you are the one, Ma'a Kīnā [addressing Muḥammad with a term of affection], who alone will suffer, and you and your children will see what emanates from him against you."[24] The story's apocryphal quality makes the point that Muḥammad Bonkana Kirya's birth was of such portent that even *Sunni* 'Alī was alarmed.

And yet, the chronicles cast Muḥammad Bonkana Kirya in a light very different from *Askia* Mūsā. Acknowledging the injustice of *Askia al-ḥājj* Muḥammad's exile, the sources are quite reluctant to actually condemn him for it. *Ta'rīkh al-fattāsh* is even laudatory, calling him a "brave and heroic" leader, who would alight from his horse and fight on foot. What is more, this same source credits him with elevating the stature of the *askiyate*, introducing elements of pomp and circumstance that include adornment and jewelry for his eunuchs (*khadam*), along with musical instruments such as the *futurifu* (a horn from Air), and the *gabtanda* (a distinctly-sounding drum), while playing tambourines when traveling by boat.[25] *Ta'rīkh as-sūdān* concurs, saying he enlarged and enhanced the court's dimensions while providing "sumptuous garments, different types of musical instruments, and male and female singers."[26] In contrasting *Askia* Muḥammad Bonkana Kirya's enlivened court with his predecessors', al-Sa'dī explains Mūsā was consumed with internal challenges, while *Askia al-ḥājj* Muḥammad "had not longed for the things of this world (*dunyā*) out of fear of the [evil] eye, and frequently forbade his brother *Faran* [*Kanfāri*] 'Umar from it [pursuing materialism]."

This curious treatment of Muḥammad Bonkana Kirya may be explained by al-Sa'dī's identifying him as the source of "many gifts and benefactions," and that "during his reign divine favors (*barakāt*) descended while doors of blessings were opened." This no doubt refers to the *askia*'s relationship with the *'ulamā'*, especially in Timbuktu, the most likely recipient of his philanthropy. This is even more probable as Muḥammad Bonkana Kirya spent his youth studying near Sankore mosque, and would seek asylum with *Qāḍī* Maḥmūd following his ouster.[27] Sankore may have even supported his taking power in the first place, given its antipathy toward *Askia* Mūsā.[28]

Muḥammad Bonkana Kirya's emergence represents an important shift in the dynamics of power at Gao, mirroring and encouraging changes in the makeup of an elite that would survive his reign. To begin, he was the first and only person to assume the *askiyate* who, though the son of a concubine, was not the son of *Askia* Muḥammad, but rather *Kanfāri* 'Umar.[29] Muḥammad Bonkana Kirya's mother was Āmina Kiraw, while Tāti Za'ankoi (or "the Za'ankī," possibly Jakhanke) was the mother of his younger brother 'Uthmān Tinfarin, appointed as the new *kanfāri*. Having wrested the succession from *Askia* Muḥammad's descendants, Muḥammad Bonkana Kirya exiled *Askia* Muḥammad from Gao while recalling Ismā'īl from Walata/Biru. Though they had been close since childhood, he nonetheless made Ismā'īl take an oath on the Qur'ān, after which he married him to his daughter Fati. The coup de grace, however, was requiring *Askia* Muḥammad's daughters to listen with heads uncovered to a (presumed) griotte Yāna Māra continuously declaim, "A single ostrich chick is better than a hundred hen chicks," favorably comparing Muḥammad Bonkana Kirya to the many sons of *Askia al-ḥājj* Muḥammad.[30]

The expulsion of *Askia al-ḥājj* Muḥammad, combined with his daughters' humiliation and Ismā'īl's neutralization, was a serial political performance designed to persuade certain constituencies while reassuring others. Through such a demonstration, Muḥammad Bonkana Kirya both recognized and further stimulated the rise of differentiated sectors of influence, and it is with his empowerment that faint outlines of reconfiguration become discernible, a rearticulation that becomes increasingly more critical with the unfolding of time.

Suggestions of such a new formation begin with the affirmation of Muḥammad Bonkana Kirya as *askia* by "the people" (*al-nās*). This could not be a reference to ordinary persons, but rather constituencies whose support had become crucial. Adopting a forensics of triangulation directs attention to the three royal branches of Songhay, beginning with the scions of *Askia al-ḥājj* Muḥammad, known as the *Mamar hamey*. They would continue constituting some part of the new dynamic under *Askia* Muḥammad Bonkana Kirya, but with diminished influence. A second branch, less prominent, would have been the surviving family of *Sunni* ʿAlī. Together with the descendants of the Zuwā/Juwā/Jāʾ dynasty, they were known as the *Si hamey* (or *Sohantye* or *Sohance*), and are said to have maintained various village strongholds following ʿAlī's overthrow, developing a reputation as "grand masters of sorcery." If the example of *Balmaʿa* Muḥammad Kiray, the son of ʿAlī's sister, is any indication, they exerted influence and occupied key positions.[31] Muḥammad Kiray was appointed by *Askia al-ḥājj* Muḥammad himself, marrying the *askia*'s daughter Aryu (or Aryaw) and having a son with her, Ḥammād. *Sunni* ʿAlī's legacy would continue, as Ḥammād became *kanfāri* under *Askia* Ismāʿīl.[32]

With Muḥammad Bonkana Kirya's investiture as *askia*, the family of *Kanfāri* ʿUmar would have become the third royal branch. The office of *kanfāri* had essentially been their preserve until then, but according to *Taʾrīkh al-fattāsh*, though they were numerous and courageous "people of war," most of ʿUmar's sons did not amount to much (*lam yaṣib ismān wa lā mawḍiʿān yashtahiru bihi*; literally, "did not leave a name or [achieve] a rank worthy of celebration").[33]

The *fitna* started by *Askia* Mūsā continued, at least initially, under *Askia* Muḥammad Bonkana Kirya, reducing the power (and numbers) of the first two branches through war, exile, and assassination. And while *Taʾrīkh as-sūdān* suggests this phase of the internecine struggle was less bloody than that of Mūsā, *Taʾrīkh al-fattāsh* asserts Muḥammad Bonkana Kirya killed some fifteen sons of *Askia al-ḥājj* Muḥammad in one battle.[34] Given such attrition, who else might have constituted "the people" (*al-nās*), Gao's stakeholders?

There are two primary candidates for this evolving elite formation. The first would have been the leaders of the royal eunuchs, and the second the leading royal concubines, wives, daughters, and sisters. As to the former, al-Saʿdī offers clues that they became more visible under Muḥammad Bonkana Kirya as a function of their growing influence. The first clue concerns the new *askia* lavishing the court with "more courtiers than ever before," but who were these courtiers, and did their increased numbers also represent augmented clout?[35] The answers are arguably found in the relationship between Muḥammad Bonkana Kirya and the royal eunuchs, as indicated by his decision to fashion new clothing and jewelry for them. Rather than simply trumpet the *askia*'s authority, the new wardrobe may have signaled an increase in their own power. Their visibility and sumptuary embellishment only grew over time, and by *Askia* Dāwūd's tenure, some seven hundred eunuchs were outfitted in special, exquisite silken attire, prominently on display. Their elevation was not simply for visual consumption, however, as toward the end of the Askia dynasty there were some four thousand of them, comprising a special "eunuch cavalry" under the *huku-kuri-koi*.[36]

The rise in the profile of royal eunuchs indicates they came to function as a virtual bureaucracy at Gao. As the royals battled and eliminated one another, there was an ongoing need to keep the ship of state afloat. Eunuchs, with their intimate knowledge of the court and affairs of state, would have been uniquely qualified to fill the void, for which they were rewarded sumptuarily. Their rise is not unlike that of the Janissaries and Mamluks, servile officers more than capable of exploiting access, and in ways resulting in the dramatic augmentation of their power.

Directly related to a rise in the influence of royal eunuchs was a corresponding increase in the influence of royal women, especially concubines and wives, but also daughters and sisters. This is even more speculative, but it stands to reason that such women, given their proximity to royal males and privileged eunuchs, would have identified various informal channels to effect outcomes, particularly those involving rivalries. One has to consider, for example, how the former *Huku-kuri-koi* ʿAlī Fulan ever came to recommend the promotion of Balla to the post of Benga-*farma* in the first place—surely not with the counsel or support of *Askia* Muḥammad's other, more senior sons. And as soon as Balla learned of opposition to his appointment, he threatened harm to mothers, not his brothers, suggesting the former were active in promoting the interests of their sons. Such advocacy, in turn, would have been communicated through eunuchs, as well as through direct contact with fathers. ʿAlī Fulan, as a probable eunuch, headed an extensive informal network of information and gossip controlled by concubines and wives. This may help explain how he became aware of Balla's potential, informing his recommendation to the *askia*.

The influence and power of royal concubines also helps to explain *Askia* Mūsā's request to Kamsa Mīman-*koi*, *Kanfāri* ʿUthmān Yawbābo's mother, to intercede on his behalf. He placed himself under her *ḥurma* or "protection" in recognition of her influence and strategic position; indeed, she may have been the only person in the realm capable of averting war, and was nearly successful. In a maneuver acknowledging such potential, the daily humiliation of the daughters of *Askia al-ḥājj* Muḥammad in Muḥammad Bonkana Kirya's court was designed to disable an otherwise potent mechanism of insurgency.

In addition to the *Mamar hamey*, the *Si hamey*, *Kanfāri* ʻUmar's descendants, and the leaders of the eunuchs and royal women, "the people" would have also included the heads of leading families and clans, and given Gao's deep historicity, they would have enjoyed considerable prestige. Eunuchs and other male slaves were important ligatures between these different groups, their liminality facilitating their access as they moved from sector to sector. Having previously referred to Songhay's inhabitants as the "Songhay people," al-Saʻdī becomes more parochial in his meaning during the nadir. Initially employing *al-nās*, he then adopts *ahl Sughay*, or "people of Songhay," a stylistic change possibly reflecting the stakeholders' changing profile.[37]

There is also an inference that slaving increased during Muḥammad Bonkana Kirya's approximately six-year reign, as the lavishing of "gifts and benefactions" surely involved captive humans, adding to the presence of royal servants, including eunuchs. If estimates for the gelding process elsewhere hold true for imperial Songhay, through which only ten percent survived, then by the time of *Askia* Dāwūd's rule some 7,000 male captives would have been required to produce 700 eunuchs, a figure that increases exponentially by the end of Songhay independence, when approximately 40,000 males would have been needed to create a eunuch cavalry of 4,000.[38]

Consistent with intensified raiding, the "most felicitous *sulṭān*" was said to have been "hell-bent (*mūlaʻ*) on campaigning and *jihād*, pursuing them so frequently that the [people] of Songhay grew tired of him, loathing him."[39] To achieve his objectives, he added another 1,700 men to the standing army under his direct control, and if these were free men, conscription may have been involved, helping to explain the response of the Songhay elite.[40] It is not clear if the territory covered in his raids was extensive, or if he confined himself to the two areas actually mentioned by al-Saʻdī: Gurma and "Kanta." In this instance, the former appears to apply to the broad area south of the Niger buckle, its inhabitants referred to as "the Gurma" and infidels, thus the characterization of his slaving as *jihād*. The campaign flirted with failure once the "infidels" resisted the *askia*'s forces, and was saved only by Dankulku, a military leader ("Lord of the Route," *rabb al-ṭarīq*) reluctant to interrupt his game of "Sudanic chess" (*al-shiṭranj al-sūdānī*). "Slaughtering [the 'infidels'] until the following morning," Dankulku reprimanded the panicked *askia*: "You are nothing but a coward. You do not deserve to be an *amīr*." The *askia* appoint Dankulku as Kala-*shā* or governor of Kala (east of Jenne), thus getting him out of Gao. But Muḥammad Bonkana Kirya's support was now beginning to crumble.[41]

The other campaign was against "Kanta"—Kebbi in prior instances, though in this case it was probably the *kanta* or ruler of Leka, who had led a rebellion against *Askia al-ḥājj* Muḥammad, reemerging as a force under *Askia* Dāwūd.[42] Muḥammad Bonkana Kirya suffered a "terrible" defeat at his hands at Wantaramasa, and had to be carried by the *Hi-koi* Bukar 'Alī Dūdu through swamp to escape (al-Sa'dī later refers to him as Bukar Shīlī-ije, the son of 'Alū Zalīl b. *Kanfāri* 'Umar). The swamp in fact saved the *askia*'s life, and in projecting how the defeat would be discussed near Sankore he imagined it would be said: "The one who revolted against *Askia* Muḥammad is the one against whom he campaigned"—a likely reference to *Kanta* Kuta.[43]

Fatigued from war and the Wantaramasa debacle, the Songhay stakeholders began to "talk about Muḥammad Bonkana among themselves due to their weariness of him."[44] Apprised, the *askia* queried his inner circle (*khawāṣṣ*), who demanded to know who had provided such information, "sowing discord between us." His hand forced, the *askia* gave up confidant Yāri Sunku Dibī, who was then painted red, black, and white, and paraded around town on a donkey.

What transpired next points to the fractured and incohesive nature of Songhay's stakeholders, for while part of the inner circle may have been loyal, others were not (as Yāri Sunku Dibī dutifully reported). Pitching camp at Mansur on yet another campaign, Muḥammad Bonkana Kirya sent Dendi-*fari* Mār Tumzu on a separate mission, only to be followed by select members of his inner circle (*khawāṣṣ*) to spy out his activities. Mār Tumzu not only placed the *askia*'s inner circle in chains, but returned to Mansur to depose the *askia* himself (Mār Tumzu means "deposed"). The date was 2 Dhū 'l-Qa'da 943/12 April 1537, the "month of rest" in Songhay. At the start of his mission, the Dendi-*fari* had said God would cause all to turn out well, and that "we shall all rest, God Most High willing."[45] The *askia* would appreciate his real meaning only after Mansur, now a veritable site of destiny, where Muḥammad Bonkana Kirya had deposed Mūsā, who before had there slain the venerable *Balma'a* Muḥammad Kiray.

Ismā'īl's Betrayal

Having removed Muḥammad Bonkana Kirya, al-Sa'dī records Dendi-*fari* Mār Tumzu named Ismā'īl as *askia* in Tara village, returning power to the scions of *Askia al-ḥājj* Muḥammad. However, the circumstances of Ismā'īl's rise to power are far from straightforward, with *Ta'rīkh al-fattāsh* presenting it as a putsch by Ismā'īl, who proclaimed himself ruler while still outside the walls of Gao.[46] That Ismāʿīl and not Mār Tumzu initiated the revolt sheds light on an otherwise murky *Taʾrīkh as-sūdān* account in which Ismāʿīl visits his father at Kangaga Island. Muḥammad, after admonishing his son for allowing him to suffer in fetid conditions, instructs him to go to a certain eunuch (*wāhid min khadiānihi*) and request gold he had been safekeeping "to buy men secretly."[47] He then tells Ismāʿīl to seek the guarantee of "safe conduct" from the *Fari-mondio* Sūma Kutubāki, Muḥammad Bonkana Kirya's close friend. Once "you obtain what you desire, then kill me immediately. You must, you must," was Sūma Kutubāki's reply, expressing inner conflict between repaying *Askia al-ḥājj* Muḥammad for previous assistance, and his current loyalty to Muḥammad Bonkana Kirya. Ismāʿīl's moves have all the earmarks of a conspiracy, with Dendi-*fari* Mār Tumzu possibly one of those paid (from the gold stash) to fight for him. Muḥammad Bonkana Kirya's earlier efforts to secure Ismāʿīl's loyalty demonstrate he understood Ismāʿīl could become an adversary.

Ismāʿīl was twenty-seven years old when he became *askia*, his time in office (943–946/1537–1539) only slightly longer than that of *Askia* Mūsā.[48] His reign saw a marked increase in the power and visibility of the stakeholders, along with a series of natural challenges that included drought and famine. In fact, it inauspiciously began with the onset of *kafi*, a plague akin to yellow fever that probably claimed the life of the *faqīh al-ḥājj* Aḥmad b. ʿUmar b. Muḥammad Aqīt.[49]

In full flight, the deposed Muḥammad Bonkana Kirya first sought refuge with *Qāḍī* Maḥmūd in Timbuktu. Upon realizing the *qāḍī* could not protect him, he joined his brother *Kanfāri* ʿUthmān Tinfarin in Tendirma, where they successfully defended against a reconnaissance cavalry team from Gao. ʿUthmān Tinfarin encouraged Muḥammad Bonkana Kirya to return to Gao, but he refused: "We cannot do that, as the number of men in the Songhay army was expanded during my reign, so that your entire army would be no match for them." Even more insightful was his next observation: "Besides, when the people of Songhay (*ahl Sughay*) hate you there is no cure." Songhay's stakeholders had taken control of events.[50]

When a second reconnaissance team reached Tendirma, Muḥammad Bonkana Kirya and ʿUthmān Tinfarin escaped for the "land of the *Sanqara-zūmaʿa*" in Mali.[51] Muḥammad Bonkana Kirya's son Bukar would marry there, indicating initial Malian approval, yet time reveals they were never really accepted by the Malians, who began humiliating them, so angering ʿUthmān Tinfarin that, according to al-Saʿdī, he left for Walata/Biru. In contrast, *Taʾrīkh al-fattāsh* speaks of a rancorous split between

Muḥammad Bonkana Kirya and 'Uthmān Tinfarin, resulting in the latter's death along with fifteen of his "brothers."[52] The sources are agreed, however, that Muḥammad Bonkana Kirya resettled in Sama (or Taba), "at the farthest reaches of the land of the *sulṭāns* of Kala," where he and his family would remain a source of anxiety for subsequent Askias.[53]

The Death of Amīr al-mu'minīn

At some point after Ismā'īl's "selection" as *askia*, there was an official enthroning ceremony, but al-Sa'dī records that with the declamation of the griot (*al-mughanī*), the new *askia* suffered a heart attack.[54] With blood flowing from his rectum, Ismā'īl concluded he was being punished for betraying Muḥammad Bonkana Kirya: "That is what got ahold of me and pierced me. I shall not remain in the sultanate long." Defending his actions, Ismā'īl pointed to the rescue of his father from exile, as well as his sisters from ignominy (going without the *ḥijāb*), but al-Sa'dī didactically underscores that disloyalty has consequences, adding that not long thereafter *Fari-mondio* Sūma Kutubāki, Muḥammad Bonkana Kirya's close friend, came to the *askia* demanding to be executed for having assisted his insurgency. Ismā'īl imprisoned him instead, replacing him as *fari-mondio* with the future *Askia* Dāwūd, whose habit of mounting Ismā'īl's horse every time the latter alighted revealed his own ambition.

If he accomplished nothing else, Ismā'īl indeed rescued his father from Kangaga in Dhū 'l-Ḥijjah 944/June 1537, returning him to the palace. The failing *askia* then performed a royal investiture of his own, dressing Ismā'īl with the robe, white cap, and green turban from Mecca, placing a sword nicknamed *angurji* (Songhay for "battle worthy," also a gift from Mecca) on his son's neck, declaring that while the "godless" Mūsā had usurped the throne only to be deposed by Muḥammad Bonkana Kirya, both were outside the succession (*khārijāni*). Ismā'īl was the true successor, the legitimate *khalīfa*. As *Askia al-ḥājj* Muḥammad had been made the *khalīfa* of the Abbasid *sharīf*, now Ismā'īl was the *khalīfa* of the *khalīfa* of the *sharīf*, who in turn was "the *khalīfa* of the great Ottoman *sulṭān*."[55] *Askia al-ḥājj* Muḥammad would leave the world on the eve of *'Īd al-Fiṭr* (ending Ramaḍān) 1 Shawwāl 944/3 March 1538.[56]

Beyond the restoration and death of his father, effectively bookending his short tenure, there are two other noteworthy matters relating to Ismā'īl. His appointment of Ḥammād as the new *kanfāri* was as much the result of his female forbears as his male progenitors (if not more), as he was the son of *Askia al-ḥājj* Muḥammad's daughter Aryu/Aryaw and the celebrated *Balma'a* Muḥammad Kiray, the son of 'Alī's sister.[57] The second development is that through *Kanfāri* Ḥammād, slaving reached a point of saturation. This can be seen in his pursuit of the ruler Bakabūl in the "land of Gurma," presumably the same Gurma targeted by Muḥammad Bonkana Kirya. The ensuing battle was a gruesome, nearly Pyrrhic encounter in which some nine hundred Songhay cavalry lost their lives, but Bakabūl's losses were even greater. Ḥammād took "so much booty that one slave (*'abd*) sold for three hundred cowries in the market of Gao." Based on Leo Africanus, three hundred cowries would have represented one-sixtieth the normal price, but the larger point is that the operation flooded the Gao market with slaves.[58]

Isḥāq Bēr and Conflicting Testimony

Ismā'īl died in 946/1539, in the midst of a campaign accompanied by unidentified stakeholders (suggesting royal slaves).[59] The latter raced back to Gao before the *balma'a* could get there (suggesting his interest in the *askiyate* were known), who at this point may have been 'Alī Kusira, another son of *Askia al-ḥājj* Muḥammad.[60] The stakeholders instead chose his brother Isḥāq Bēr, who with Hari-*farma* 'Abd Allāh were sons of the concubine Kulthūm Barda of Dirma (or Daram and possibly Tuareg). Isḥāq Bēr, also known as Isḥāq Kadibini (Isḥāq "the Black Stone" in Soninke), would rule for nine years and six to nine months, from 946/1539 to 956/1549.[61]

The disparity between the *ta'rīkhs* (*tawārīkh*) in assessing the character of Isḥāq Bēr's tenure could not be more striking. As far as *Ta'rīkh al-fattāsh* is concerned, *Askia* Isḥāq Bēr was "a virtuous man with whom God was pleased and blessed for giving many alms and assiduously observing collective prayer. He was highly intelligent as well as shrewd."[62] An anecdote demonstrating his piety follows, in which Isḥāq Bēr reaches the mosque on a rain-soaked night for the final prayer, ahead of the *imām* and the *mu'adhdhin*. The two officers arrive and, believing they are alone, decide to proceed, concluding no one would venture out in the rain and mud, least of all the *askia* who, they mused, lay in a silk-covered bed. The *askia* startles them from the shadows, announcing his presence. It is Isḥāq Bēr who named Maḥmūd Baghayughu as *qāḍī* of Jenne, setting off waves of consternation.

This is in stark contrast to *Ta'rīkh as-sūdān*, whose treatment of Isḥāq Bēr brings the Songhay nadir to a dramatic end. If *Askia* Mūsā's fratricidal tendencies were fed by insecurities not entirely of his own making, *Askia*

Isḥāq Bēr was a clear-thinking, bloodcurdling, stone cold killer, representing a return to Mūsā's murderous ways, only more methodically. Al-Sa'dī writes:

> As for Isḥāq, he was the most regal of those who entered the sultanate, and the one who inspired the most fear and dread. He executed many men of the army. It was said of him that if he imagined anyone making the least move against the throne, he would have him killed or banished without fail. This was his habitual practice.[63]

Such practice began immediately, with the new *askia* sending an assassin, a "lone Zughrānī man," to Walata/Biru to kill former *Kanfāri* 'Uthmān Tinfarin. Carrying out the mission, the Zughrānī was awarded thirty cows, only to be executed by the *askia* on his way home. He then killed *Kanfāri* Ḥammād w. Aryu, replacing him with 'Alī Kusira, after which he put to death Sūma Kutubāki, to whom he had offered the office of *fari-mondio* for assisting Ismā'īl, but who insultingly responded: "The blessed and rightly-guided *sulṭān* [Ismā'īl] asked this of me to no avail, and frankly [in contrast] you are worthless." This was followed by Isḥāq Bēr ordering the Hombori-*koi* to arrest the *Hi-koi* Bukar 'Alī Dūdu, of whom the *askia* had become apprehensive, but who escaped death by resigning first.[64]

Sūma Kutubāki's harsh characterization may have been based on the *askia*'s homicidal tendencies as well as policies of extralegal expropriation, as he was accused of confiscating thousands of *mithqāls* in gold from the merchants of Timbuktu.[65] According to al-Sa'dī, the issue was intimidation; not only did few challenge the *askia*—with the notable exception of Jenne's Maḥmūd Baghayughu—but they were too afraid to even mention such deeds until he was dead, as the *askia* had created an atmosphere of "fear and dread."

In either 946/1539–40 or 949/1542–43, Isḥāq Bēr led an expedition to Taba in the "farthest reaches of the *sulṭān* of Bendugu," no doubt in search of the deposed *Askia* Muḥammad Bonkana Kirya. *Ta'rīkh as-sūdān* states the latter had found asylum in Sama, but it is with Isḥāq Bēr's excursion to Taba, where *Ta'rīkh al-fattāsh* claims Muḥammad Bonkana Kirya fled, that the sources begin to converge. According to *Ta'rīkh al-fattāsh*, Muḥammad Bonkana Kirya suddenly died upon Isḥāq Bēr's arrival, leaving the *askia* to preside over his funeral (*ṣallā 'alīhi*, "he prayed for him"). *Ta'rīkh as-sūdān* maintains it was actually during a visit to Sama by *Askia* Dāwūd, sometime after 966/1558–59, that Muḥammad Bonkana Kirya unexpectedly expired. The accounts, though varying, both make the point that the deposed *askia* was a threat, and though neither ruler is said to have actually executed Muḥammad Bonkana Kirya, his death is connected with their efforts to reach him.[66]

It was from Taba that *Askia* Isḥāq Bēr went to Jenne for his memorable encounter with Maḥmūd Baghayughu, but upon returning to Gao, *Kanfāri* 'Alī Kusira made several attempts to kill him, coming very close. Once in Gao, Isḥāq Bēr ordered the "people of Tendirma" (presumably officials loyal to him) to expel the *kanfāri*, and 'Alī Kusira fled to the Ūdāya, a branch of the Banū Ḥassān Arabs living between Wadan and Walata/Biru. Taken captive and placed in chains, he watered gardens as a slave, until one day he was recognized by an Arab who sold him horses in "the days of his arrogance and tyranny" ("Say! Aren't you *Faran* 'Alī Kusira?"). So he committed suicide by leaping down a well, an act viewed as divine retribution since in exchange for horses he "egregiously violated [the rights of] the free born, selling them [as slaves]."[67] *Qāḍī* Maḥmūd is said to have warned him: "Do not sell free men, as you should fear that [one day] they will sell you."[68]

'Alī Kusira was replaced as *kanfāri* by Dāwūd, who in 952/1544–45 led an expedition into Mali, from which the Malians fled.[69] Entering Mali's "capital," Dāwūd enacted the ultimate display of contempt, ordering his men to defecate in the royal palace for seven days, after which they returned to Songhay. The people of Mali were horrified, but Dāwūd was staking an unmistakable claim: Songhay, not Mali, was now the premier western Sahelian power.

It was during *Askia* Isḥāq Bēr's reign that a portent of the future arrived. The Wattasid Moroccan Sultan *Mawlāy/Mawlāya/Mawlā* Abū 'l-Abbas Aḥmad "the Great," or Aḥmad al-A'raj (ruled 930–52/1524–45, and again 954–56/1547–49), wrote a letter to the *askia* demanding the Taghaza salt mine—an indication of its value as well as its location deep in the Sahara, nearly midway between Marrakesh and Gao. Isḥāq Bēr responded that the Aḥmad who would receive such a concession was not the one who had sent the emissary, for the Isḥāq who would make such a concession had yet to be born. Demonstrating Songhay's resolve, Isḥāq Bēr sent a force of two thousand Tuareg camelry to raid the Dar'a valley near Marrakesh, with instructions to avoid killing anyone. Carrying out the *askia*'s orders, the Tuareg pillaged the market of Banī Asbah, Dar'a's leading entrepot.[70] Morocco would not forget.

Askia Isḥāq Bēr fell ill in Kukiya toward the beginning of 956/1549, succumbing just months later in Ṣafar 956/March 1549. He was preceded in death in Ramaḍān 955/October 1548 at the age of eighty-eight by the

Shaykh al-Islām, *Qāḍī* Maḥmūd b. ʿUmar b. Muḥammad Aqīt, who was succeeded as *qāḍī* by his forty-five-year old son Muḥammad in Shawwāl of 955/November of 1548. Like his older brother Aḥmad b. ʿUmar, *Qāḍī* Maḥmūd had been a victim of the *kafi* plague, though advanced age surely played a role.[71]

Songhay's twenty-year nadir was first and foremost a time of myopia relative to the expansive, internationalist age of *Askia al-ḥājj* Muḥammad that preceded it, its parochialism a function of an unprecedented rivalrous spirit invested in sanguinary practice distinctive in both elevation and scope, reaching the most privileged while encompassing a broad expanse of social formations. A collective royal neurosis of the most toxic variety enveloped Songhay's elite, as a result of which many sons, and even daughters, of *amīr al-mu'minīn* were cut down by blood relatives, and precisely for that reason.

Because intimacies necessarily attended these intrafamilial conflicts, the level of intrigue must have been extraordinary, aided by privileged slaves who stepped into breaches left by the serial elimination of their masters, advantaged by administrative experience combined with their nonthreatening, liminal status. This was not a novel development, as Sumaoro may have had servile origins, while the *jomba* were said to have assumed power in the wake of Sunjata's demise. In Songhay, the process was led by eunuchs, who leveraged their skills in both their own interests as well as those of their patrons, becoming indispensable. As a result, royal slaves and the royal women they served became a powerful component of the "people of Songhay."

The growth of the servile estate, in turn, was enabled by an apparent surge in slaving, swelling not only the ranks of the dispossessed but constituting the principal "commodity" for which mounts could be imported into the empire, stimulating further slaving.

The intensification in slaving came at a critical time in West and West Central African history, unfolding in parallel with the gradual establishment of European coastal trading posts. By the mid-tenth/sixteenth century, the Portuguese and others were successfully pursuing trade relations at São Tomé, Elmina, and São Salvador, by which time some 250,000 Africans had been exported from the continent via the Atlantic. Europe was occupied with improving seafaring techniques, expanding participation in international commerce, and negotiating across cultural chasms, steadily adding to their knowledge base. Songhay royals, at the head of the most powerful empire in West Africa at the time, were, by contrast, immersed in wholesale mutual recrimination and destruction. Europe was not without its own rivalries, but the broad comparisons suggest trajectories that could not have been any more divergent.

As it turns out, Songhay was spared incursions from forces capable of exposing a vulnerable and at times inchoate central command. The Mossi were quiet, while Songhay's periodic forays into Mali kept the latter on the defensive. Only Morocco, quite possibly aware of Songhay's bloodletting, probed the integrity of Songhay's outer provinces at Taghaza. They received a stinging rebuke, but would probe again.

CHAPTER THIRTEEN

Surfeit and Stability: The Era of *Askia* Dāwūd

THE THIRTY-FOUR-YEAR REIGN of *Askia* Dāwūd (from 956–90/1549–82) punctuates the bloodletting of the nadir, with Dāwūd turning from his remaining brothers to his own children to fill key positions of authority.[1] This essentially meant the descendants of *Askia al-ḥājj* Muḥammad, the *Mamar hamey*, were now favored over the scions of *Kanfāri* ʿUmar, the third royal branch. In the process, Dāwūd reclaimed some of the power previously ceded to Songhay's stakeholders (*ahl Sughay*).

Askia Dāwūd's reign saw the dramatic expansion of domestic slavery. Though significant throughout the dynasties of the Sunnis and the Askias, the numbers under Dāwūd become so pronounced, their exploitation so extensive, that the period constitutes a stage of evolutionary development. Slavery as *qualified reciprocity* is the mechanism by which its relationship to servitude and caste will be explored, as well as its intimate connection to spirituality.

The reign is bracketed by epidemics and ends with a preview of Songhay's fate: in 957–58/1550–51, a pestilence called *kurzu* killed "many people" in the region of Tendirma, while in 990/1582–83 a deadly infectious disease (*waba' ʿaẓīm*) spread through Timbuktu. Venereal disease is even mentioned, as Dāwūd's son Muḥammad Bonkana suffered from "syphilitic ulcers" (*qarḥ*, but presumably *qurūḥ masar* is meant).[2] More menacing than plague and contagion, however, was Morocco's increasingly intrusive behavior—a harbinger of things to come.

Suspension of Tumult

Nearing his life's end ("despairing of life"), *Askia* Isḥāq Bēr selected forty of his bravest cavalry to escort ʿAbd al-Malik to the home of Gao's *khaṭīb*, to be placed under the latter's protection (*ḥurma*). The *askia* had designated his son as his successor, but the stakeholders were opposed due to his "haughtiness and tyranny," and were declarative in their preference for Dāwūd, and would "not accept anyone except" him.[3] Dāwūd was the son of Sāna bt. Fāri-*koi* or Sāna Fāriu.[4] *Ta'rīkh as-sūdān* makes no effort to characterize his reign, whereas *Ta'rīkh al-fattāsh* is effervescent, reflecting his close bond with Maḥmūd Ka'ti:

> [Dāwūd] had worldly fortune, with as much power and authority as he desired, acquiring immense worldly possessions. His father *Askia* Muḥammad and his brothers had all toiled in sowing for him, and when he arrived he reaped; they prepared the soil, so that when he came he rested (*nāma*, literally "he slept").[5]

The beneficiary of his father's prophesy that he would eclipse all other descendants, effacing their memory while reducing some to subservience (*taba'ān*), he is described as eloquent and magnanimous, a noble and distinguished leader who, though "dreaded," could also be a practical joker. The first *askia* to establish "treasury depositories" (*khazā'in al-māl*) and "book repositories" (*khazā'in al-kutub*, essentially libraries), he had copies of books made and gave them to scholars. He also memorized the Qur'ān, while completing the *Risāla* of Ibn Abī Zayd with a *shaykh* in midday lessons.[6]

Receiving the investiture in Kukiya and traveling the short distance to Gao, *Askia* Dāwūd immediately made his son Muḥammad Bonkana the new *Fari-mondio*—an office Dāwūd had occupied under Ismā'īl—and named his son al-Ḥājj as the Korey-*farma*, who may have been charged with the affairs of "whites" or Arabo-Berbers in Songhay. An important military post, it liaised with the Maghsharan Tuareg to the north of Timbuktu, possibly connecting expatriate networks that included Gao.[7]

Naming al-Ḥājj as Korey-*farma* represents a development, as the office had been a lesser-known post, mentioned only once before in *Ta'rīkh al-fattāsh*.[8] To the extent it regulated the affairs of "whites" in Gao, it reflects the growing influence of expatriate merchants, active in Gao for hundreds of years, but further enriched by slaving's dramatic increase. Leo Africanus also commented on these "rich merchants who continually roam around the region," with profits that translated into political capital.[9]

Unlike *Mansā* Mūsā, *Askia* Dāwūd responded by formally incorporating their influence into the structure of governance. Timbuktu had a parallel office in the Barbūshi-*mondio*, responsible for the affairs of the Barābīsh Arabs (also only mentioned in conjunction with Dāwūd).[10] Al-Ḥājj would use the opportunity as a stepping-stone to the post of *fari-mondio* (986–91/1579–83) and then to the *askiyate* itself (991–95/1583–86).[11]

Placing his sons in key positions, Dāwūd ended an era of turmoil. His naming Kashiya b. 'Uthmān Tinfarin, of Zughrānī origin maternally, to the post of *kanfāri* was consistent with this strategy. In stressing Kashiya's maternal heritage, al-Sa'dī alludes to the irony of the "lone Zughrānī man" who assassinated *Kanfāri* 'Uthmān Tinfarin, Kashiya's own father and son of *Kanfāri* 'Umar. Kashiya's appointment may therefore have been an attempt to recapture the dynamic between *Askia* Muḥammad and *Kanfāri* 'Umar.[12]

With these appointments accomplished, Dāwūd turned to the *Hi-koi* Mūsā, who had sternly rebuked Dāwūd when he arrived in Kukiya just before *Askia* Isḥāq Bēr's death (and in anticipation of it): "Who ordered you to [to come here under these circumstances], and with whom did you seek counsel? Go back immediately!"[13] Dāwūd complied and did not return to Kukiya until *Hi-koi* Mūsā summoned him following the *askia*'s death (soon thereafter). Dāwūd did not forget the *hi-koi*'s intervention, for which Dendi-*fari* Muḥammad Bonkana Sinbilu counseled he should not be punished. But Dāwūd was threatened by the *hi-koi*, "intimately acquainted with boldness, bravery, and strength," and instructed his nephew Muḥammad to kill him at an opportune time.[14] Once carried out, *Askia* Dāwūd named 'Alī Dādu as the new *hi-koi*.[15]

The Campaigns of Askia *Dāwūd*

Songhay under *Askia* Dāwūd experienced accelerated material accumulation, accomplished through at least twenty military operations. All were not successful, but the overall result was enormous booty, especially in captives.

The *ta'rīkhs* diverge dramatically regarding these campaigns, with *Ta'rīkh al-fattāsh* evincing virtually no interest. In contrast, *Ta'rīkh as-sūdān*'s discussion of Dāwūd is largely structured around this theme. Though not a preoccupation, *Askia* Dāwūd would attack the familiar Mossi upon taking office in 956/1549 and again in 969/1561–62, the latter resulting in significant loss of life for Songhay.[16]

The *askia* also probed the perimeter defenses of the Hausa. A "quarrel" (*khuṣūma*) broke out with the now-independent *kanta* of Leka in

959/1551–52, perhaps related to the subsequent expedition of twenty-four Songhay cavalry to Katsina in 961/1553–54. Their small numbers could only mean it was a reconnaissance mission, but when discovered they were soundly defeated by four hundred Katsina cavalry in quilted armor, following the "fiercest and most protracted of battles."[17] Fifteen of the Songhay lost their lives, including the *Hi-koi* 'Alī Dādu. The remaining nine were treated for their wounds and returned to Songhay in recognition of their fighting spirit. Among them was 'Alū/'Alā Zalīl, another son of *Kanfāri* 'Umar, along with Bukar 'Alī Dūdu/Bukar Shīlī-ije. 'Alī Dūdu/Bukar Shīlī-ije would replace 'Alī Dādu as *hi-koi*, and then replace Muḥammad Bonkana Sinbilu as the Dendi-*fari* with his death in 970/1563.[18]

Some may have seen the Katsina mission as Dāwūd's attempt to eliminate the Umarian branch altogether, as at least three of those killed or injured were sons of *Kanfāri* 'Umar. When Dāwūd initially selected Kamkuli as the new Dendi-*fari*, Bukar 'Alī Dūdu interpreted it as prefiguring his own imminent elimination, and appealed to *Fari-mondio* Muḥammad Bonkana. Apprised, Dāwūd announced the next day that "God has shown me that no one except *Hi-koi* Bukar 'Alī Dūdu" should be the next Dendi-*fari*. Performing the earthen ablution, *Huku-kuri-koi* Kamkuli reacted viscerally: "Is not the *amīr* lying? I swear by God, it was not God who showed you this; you picked him yourself." Though stinging, his rebuke was within the context of submission, demonstrating the qualities of a Dendi-*fari* in speaking candidly. Kamkuli would be named the new Dendi-*fari* in 973/1565–66 at Bukar 'Alī Dūdu's death.[19]

In 966/1558–59, the *askia* attacked the town of Busa in Borgu province, south of Dendi; its capture would mean effective control over much of the trade between Hausaland and the Nupe in the north, and the Yoruba to the south. The attack left devastation in its wake, and five years later (971/1563–64) the *askia* again attacked "the land of Barka," confronting one Bani in a "mountain," a foe "most wily, dashing (*ghandūr*), smart, and cautious."[20] Led by Dendi-*fari* Bukar 'Alī Dūdu, with *Fari-mondio* Muḥammad Bonkana second in command, the Songhay killed Bani and all of his followers.

The *askia* also targeted the northern sphere of Mali's faltering empire, and in 957/1550, five years after literally laying waste to the Malian capital, he raided Toya (or Tu'u) in Baghana, fighting the Fulani under *Fondoko* Jājī Tumāne.[21] Less than ten years later, in 966/1558–59, the *askia* was again in Mali, first Suma, then Dibikarala, where he defeated the Malian war general Magha or Ma' Kanti Faran.[22]

Finally, in 978/1570, *Askia* Dāwūd ventured into "Sūra Bantanbā in the land of Mali," his last campaign in "Ataram." As "sūra" in this instance refers to Berbers in southern Mauritania, this was a raid on lands to the west of Baghana. The *askia* sent Korey-*farma* al-Ḥājj in his role as military leader of the "whites," with forces of some twenty-four thousand camelry divided into two divisions, each under a "*sulṭān*." One of them, the Maghsharan-*koi al-ḥājj* Maḥmūd Bēr and leader of the Tuareg north of Timbuktu, was married to *Askia* Dāwūd's daughter Binta/Bita.[23] The other, the Indāsan-*koi*, presumably led another group elsewhere in the region.[24] The Songhay "wandered about (*'āra*) [attacking] the Arabs in these outlying areas and returned" from this last Malian venture.

The resolution of the first expedition against Mali is much clearer, as Dāwūd returned to Gao with "many artisans male and female (*al-qainīn wa al-qaināt*) called *mābī*, creating a special quarter for them as *Askia al-ḥājj* Muḥammad had done for the Mossi."[25] The term *mābī* (Pulaar, *maabo*; Songhay, *maabe*) refers to ironworkers, weavers, and griots, indicating *Askia* Dāwūd sought to benefit from caste expertise. The results of the second campaign were also evident, and included Nāra, daughter of the Malian sultan, apparently given in marriage to *Askia* Dāwūd as part of ending the conflict. Dāwūd sent her back to Gao along with "a great deal of jewelry, male and female slaves (*'abīd wa imā'*), furnishings, and household items and utensils, all covered in gold leaf, in addition to water vessels, mortar and pestle, and other goods."[26] The enslaved had presumably already been made so by the Malians themselves (as Malians were Muslims and legally ineligible).

In addition to *Askia* Dāwūd's better known campaigns, he also fought marauders in relatively lawless places, focusing on al-Hajar (*al-Ḥajar*, "the Stone") in the Bandiagara escarpment and sending both *Huku-kuri-koi* Kamkuli and the Soninke ("Wangarī") Shā'-*farma* Muḥammad Konāte in 962/1554–55 into the "mountains" (*al-jibāl*).[27] The results were uncertain—unsurprising, as the challenges of highland fighting were noted by the Jenne-*mondio* al-Amīn, who, upbraided by the *askia* ("We made you governor (*ḥākim*) over the land, but you are not taking care of it, so much so that the infidel Bambara (*banbara*) have multiplied and settled in it, and you're not doing anything about it"), quoted *Askia al-ḥājj* Muḥammad in defending his reticence: "'The *sulṭān* who is not wary of campaigning in al-Ḥajar and in the forest of Kubu seeks only ruin and destruction for his army.'"[28] Dāwūd apparently took heed, as it was only after 986/1578, twenty-four years following the expedition of *Huku-kuri-koi* Kamkuli and Shā'-*farma* Muḥammad Konāte, that he again ventured into the mountains to attack its "Dum" inhabitants (recalling the "Damdam" of early chroniclers while resonating with Dāwūd's "infidel Bambara"). As the

Dum had successfully resisted *Sunni* 'Alī and *Askia al-ḥājj* Muḥammad (*mā nālān minhum nailān*, "[the *sunni* and *askia*] made no headway against them"), Dāwūd ordered *Huku-kuri-koi* Yāsī to attack, yet avoid placing soldiers "in danger and peril." Assessing a charge up the mountain as too risky, Yāsī refused Dāwūd's son *Kanfāri* Muḥammad Bonkana's advice to do so. Rather, one Muḥammad w. Mawri stealthily ascended on horseback and killed the "dashing (*ghandūr*) and widely-renowned" Ma'a, leader of the Dum. The Dum did not completely surrender, but they grew "fearful of the Songhay cavalry," and became a lesser threat.[29]

The difficulties in Bandiagara suggest its populations were emboldened by the previous infighting among Songhay royals, with Gao needing to restore its authority. These include post-978/1570 raids on the town of Zubanku in Gurma, followed by forays into the contiguous provinces of Kala and Bendugu, on opposite sides of the Bani River near Jenne.[30]

Royal Women

In addition to aforementioned *Waiza* Ḥafṣa and *Waiza* Akībunu (or Kaybunu) and their unspecified office, *Askia* Dāwūd had many other daughters, using them to effect political alliances and gain currency among powerful constituencies.[31] Thus al-Sa'dī writes: "Many of [his daughters] were married to scholars, jurists, merchants, and army commanders."[32] Marriages to eminent religious figures suggest growing ties between the political and religious estates, especially at Gao and Tendirma, as Timbuktu's Aqīt and Anda ag-Muḥammad families seem uninvolved. These arrangements reflect a view of the royals as serious, observing Muslims, concomitant with an emerging profile of nonroyal clerics and merchants.

The concubines and wives of *Askia* Dāwūd are far less conspicuous than those of his father *Askia* Muḥammad, their relative omission the consequence of an abbreviated dynastic succession following Dāwūd. Even so, several are mentioned as mothers to his sons, including Muḥammad Sorko-ije ("Muḥammad, son of a Sorko woman") and Hārūn Fāta Ṭuru/Fati Tura-ije ("Hārūn, son of Fāta Ṭuru or Fati Tura"). Dāwūd's sister Dalla may have been favored, as Dāwūd gave her son Muḥammad the assignment of killing *Hi-koi* Mūsā, and then named him to replace *Balma'a* Khālid b. *Askia al-ḥājj* Muḥammad at his death in 986/1578.

On occasion, Dāwūd undertook military expeditions accompanied by royal women, including the 978/1570 assault on Sura Bantanba, when his son Hārūn was conceived, and later in the march on Dendi, where his own mother Sāna bt. Fāri-*koi* or Sāna Fāriu died. Inari Konte had accompanied *Mansā*

Mūsā on *ḥajj*, so there was precedent, though in contexts outside of Mali and Songhay this was hardly a royal prerogative, as even enslaved soldiers on long campaigns brought their wives to carry supplies, cook, and care for the camp. In the case of royals, however, security concerns may have also informed the decision to bring wives, and would have required making choices—Dāwūd had at least sixty-one concubines, along with 333 children.[33]

Servility and Slavery: The Tale of Misakul Allāh

Institutions of servility and "unfreedom," ranging from occupational castes to "serfdom" to those approximating chattel slavery, come into full view with *Askia* Dāwūd, providing a remarkable opportunity to revisit relations of inequality, exploitation, and subjugation. If royal women are given attention and nonroyal females essentially ignored in *Ta'rīkh as-sūdān*, the opposite is true in *Ta'rīkh al-fattāsh*, informing much of the following discussion. At the same time, *Ta'rīkh as-sūdān*'s focus on Dāwūd's many campaigns explains slavery and servility's greater visibility, the chronicles' combined evidence both quantitative and qualitative.

Ta'rīkh al-fattāsh's discussion of slavery and servility under *Askia* Dāwūd begins with seemingly disjointed tales that, upon review, are very much interlaced. Though the first story is attributed to an anonymous source (of "great confidence") and a purported eyewitness (Bukar b. ʿAlī Dantūru), the accounts share an allegorical quality. That aspects are spun more out of imagination than observation need not be of inordinate concern, as they are anchored in realities of the day and, more importantly, neither occlude nor diminish the stories' didactic purposes, revealing much about "unfreedom" in imperial Songhay.

The serial saga begins with Misakul Allāh, from the land of "Barma" (perhaps Baguirmi, southeast of Lake Chad), whose name could mean "force of nature." He is head manager of a royal rice "plantation" (*ḥarth* is used interchangeably with *majra'a*) called "Abdā," in Dendi province.[34] It is large, taking Misakul Allāh three days to canvass, and on which two hundred "slaves" (*ʿabīd*) work under four sub-managers or drivers called *fanāfī* (singular, *fanfa*). The plantation is expected to produce one thousand *ṣunūn* (singular *ṣunnīa*) or animal-hide sacks of rice annually—a quota that never changes, critical to the account.[35]

Askia Dāwūd supplies seed and animal skins for the *ṣunūn*, reflecting his ownership of a harvest levied upstream by ten boats to Gao, which upon receipt the *askia* sends Misakul Allāh one thousand *gūro* or kola nut, a large bar of salt, a black kaftan, and a large measure of black cloth for his wife.[36] These are gifts rather than payments, tokens of the *askia*'s satisfaction with the head manager's productivity. But the gifts distinguish Misakul Allāh and raise questions about his status.

The arrangement works well until, one year, Misakul Allāh goes to the nearby village of "Denkidumdi" and convenes the *imām*, students, indigent, and widows—that is, the needy—telling them the plantation is his that year, and that he is giving them its harvest as alms "to get closer to God," in preparation for the Hereafter. He gives each of the four *fanāfī* a bit of land on which they might subsist, but nothing is directly said about the workers.

The news reaches *Askia* Dāwūd and his council is scandalized, concluding Misakul Allāh is either *jinn*-possessed or gone mad, with some calling for his death. The *askia*'s response is to proceed with sending the boats and *ṣunūn* to Abda to collect his customary quota, and that the head manager is not to be arrested unless he is unable to meet expectations. Learning of his dilemma, Misakul Allāh hurries to Gao and pleads his case, disavowing his actions were in any way rebellious (*mā dakhaltu lahu fī al-fitna*, "I did not enter into sedition against him"). He reaches an agreement with the *askia*: if he fills the 1,000 *ṣunūn* with rice stored in his home in Gao (where he also has a large habitation and another wife), he can avoid arrest. The *askia* charges a eunuch (*'abd al-khaṣī*, "castrated slave") and 50 other slaves (*'abdān*) with making sure the quota is filled, and Misakul Allāh assigns his own head slave and doorkeeper (*'abd al-kabīr*) with overseeing the task. Misakul Allāh not only fills the 1,000 *ṣunūn* from two different storage facilities; he fills 230 more.

The story provides a number of insights into Songhay slavery and servitude, beginning with the plantations themselves. In establishing the context, *Ta'rīkh al-fattāsh* states *Askia* Dāwūd in fact had a number of such plantations, and though they are first mentioned in connection with Dāwūd, they represent expansion on an exponential scale, rather than innovation.[37] Just how many plantations may have existed is unclear; outside of the Abda farm, only one other plantation name ("Jangaja") is provided in the chronicle.[38] However, *Ta'rīkh al-fattāsh* cites at least twelve areas in which plantations were located, essentially along the Niger River, beginning south of the eastern buckle with Irya (downstream from Dendi), then Dendi, Kulani (in the Niamey-Say area), Karai Hauṣa and Karai Gurma (left and right banks of the Niger), then lands around Gao and Kukiya. The text moves next to the western side of the Niger buckle, featuring Kiyusu (between Timbuktu and Gundam), "the isles of Bamba and Benga" or the lacustrine area itself, Ataram (to the west of Baghana), Futa Kingui/Kaniaga, Buyu or Bunyu (to the north of Lake Debo), to the end of Lake Debo. In providing these locations, *Ta'rīkh al-fattāsh* traces Songhay's vast territorial claims, intimating the scope of such agricultural servitude was novel for medieval West Africa.[39]

The establishment of royal plantations throughout the realm may have been a response to drought and famine under *Askia* Ismā'īl (943–46/1537–39). If so, the experiment in food security wildly exceeded all expectations, as the "harvest could neither be counted or estimated." *Ta'rīkh al-fattāsh*, however, attempts to do just that, estimating the *askia* received over four thousand *ṣunūn* in a peak year, a surfeit of alimentation. The number four thousand is notional, as it is the same figure used for Dāwūd's annual donations to Timbuktu's poor. Even so, it establishes a correlation between the plantations and the *askia*'s almsgiving.

Dendi province, supposed location of Abda farm, is where the factual meets the allegorical. Whether the story actually happened is far less consequential than the assumptive nodal verities built into it, as the account's efficacy is premised on actual circumstances of unfree labor. In fact, the story was of such importance that it occupies the center of *Ta'rīkh al-fattāsh*'s discussion of *Askia* Dāwūd.

In describing the plantation chain of command, the chronicle organizes slaves (*'abīd*) into units of twenty to sixty, each under a *fanfa*, the "chief of slaves" (*ra'īs al-'abīd*).[40] The status of the *fanfa* is not evident, though Misakul Allāh as head manager is called *ra'īs al-fanāfī*, and since Misakul Allāh is later identified as a "slave," the *fanāfī* probably were as well. Misakul Allāh only features as a slave, however, in royal discourse, when his actions become the subject of debate and consternation, and the term *'abd* is repeatedly used. Misakul Allāh, lamenting the distrust generated by his actions, observes: "There is no trust between a slave (*'abd*) and his master (*sayyid*)."[41]

If a slave, Misakul Allāh is among the most privileged, with one wife at Abda and at least one other (in a large residence) at Gao. Though Dāwūd early refers to Misakul Allāh's "abasement and poverty and wretchedness," the story unfolds to reveal he is actually wealthy, with at least one slave of his own and significant accumulations of rice at Gao, as he only had to meet the annual quota, with any surplus his to keep. That he is expected to provide the *askia* with one thousand *ṣunūn* of rice per annum, when four thousand *ṣunūn* represent a peak year, is probably a seam in the *Ta'rīkh*, but the larger point is that such an individual could be very successful, leading *Askia* Dāwūd to exclaim to his courtiers: "Did I not tell you that this slave had become so sated [with wealth] that he had no equal except for us and our children?"[42] The question therefore becomes: In what sense is Misakul Allāh a slave?

The chronicle anticipates this very question, and in response his courtiers declare: "Since all slaves (*'abīd*) are the same, not one of them can become great unless it is based on the greatness of his master (*sayyid*), for he [the slave] and his property (*rijq*) are the property of his master." This succinct statement encapsulates three seemingly incongruent principles that in practice work quite well together, outlining the fundamental contours of Songhay slavery. The first, that a slave could achieve tremendous importance, is very much in dialogue with the second, that a slave's profile was in relation to that of the master, which therefore does not contradict the third, that the enslaved was the property of the master.

Placing the three concepts into conversation with how the enslaved actually lived reveals that, in relation to each other, principles are active or latent depending upon the context. Misakul Allāh's story suggests that the third, proprietary principle was far more latent than active as a social dynamic—that a slave could acquire a status (albeit qualified) informing and complicating the slaveholder's claims. Such attenuated servility is borne out in the *askia*'s response to Misakul Allāh's activities, as he does not confiscate any of the latter's resources, but proceeds as if those resources indeed belong to Misakul Allāh.

Askia Dāwūd's refusal to seize Misakul Allāh's property, or otherwise mistreat him, conforms to his portrayal as wise, pious, and secure. But the respect afforded Misakul Allāh is hardly confined to an imagined encounter, and can be observed in instances in which enslaved authority was very much respected. A striking example concerns the *askia*'s campaign against the Dum mountain people. Dāwūd's son *Kanfāri* Muḥammad Bonkana lobbied for the campaign, and having formerly served as the *fari-mondio*, he had been named *kanfāri* around 986/1578, as "[Dāwūd] entrusted Kurmina-*fari* Muḥammad Bonkana with all the affairs of the western region."[43] And yet, Dāwūd placed the Dum campaign under the *Huku-kuri-koi* Yāsī. Muḥammad Bonkana may not have enjoyed his father's full confidence, or, as he now controlled western Songhay, the *askia* had second thoughts about expanding his portfolio. In any event, the *Huku-kuri-koi* Yāsī twice rejected the *kanfāri's* insistence that they ascend the mountain, leading an exasperated *kanfāri* to call him an "emasculated slave." Yāsī responded: "You go too far in saying that. Rather, refer to me as 'you unfortunate slave,' as is indeed the case."[44] The bottom line is that *Kanfāri* Muḥammad Bonkana followed the eunuch's orders, rather than the opposite.

The cases of Misakul Allāh and Yāsī concern royal slaves, not those enslaved to clerics and merchants and other nonroyals, who presumably did not wield similar authority, nor were afforded the same respect, but this very observation reinforces the principle that a slave's achievements were very much dependent on the master's status, the former in effect an extension of the latter.

Servility and Slavery: The Tale of Mūsā Sagansāru

The tale of Misakul Allāh provides insight into Songhay slavery and servitude, but that is not its purpose. Rather, its objective comes to light by way of an ensuing account concerning a second farm, also placed in Dendi, and the death of the *Jango* Mūsā Sagansāru several months earlier.[45] The office of *jango* is not defined, but Mūsā Sagansāru is called a *khadīm* and seems to be a royal slave.[46] Interestingly, the "property" in question, including the slaves, is considered the property of the *jango*, and with his death its disposition falls to the *askia*. This differs from Misakul Allāh, who manages an Abda plantation that clearly belongs to the *askia*, but as the two stories run consecutively, the discrepancy is hardly attributable to emendation.

Askia Dāwūd's handling of the deceased's affairs reveals the ambiguous yet discernible nature of the latent-versus-active principle of appropriation in an owner's claims over a slave's possessions. Theoretically, the property is the *askia*'s all along (the reason it is brought to his attention), but its resolution indicates *de jure* versus *de facto* conventions; even how the *askia* learned of the property is suggestive. Still debating the challenge posed by Misakul Allāh, another servant (*rajul min khadam*) enters with news of the *jango*'s property. Preoccupied, Dāwūd has to be reminded the *jango* had died, and that he had previously sent the servant with instructions to return with what remained of the *jango*'s estate (*mīrāth*). The servant approaches the *askia* to inform him privately, but the *askia* demands that he speak openly: "Why not declare [the value of the estate] publicly before the people? Did we steal it? Either declare it in the hearing of the people or get out!"[47]

As was true of Misakul Allāh, *Askia* Dāwūd is not prepared for the news; the royal servant was overwhelmed by what he found and unable to transport five hundred slaves (*'abīd* male and female), fifteen hundred *ṣunūn* of grain, seven cows, thirty goats, fifteen horses (seven of which are purebred), saddles, clothes, weapons and shields, and utensils.[48] What Mūsā Sagansāru had amassed far exceeds anything the *askia* had anticipated, and together with Misakul Allāh, is a portrait of material overflow. Though entitled, the *askia*'s response makes clear he views confiscating the *jango*'s possessions as theft, consistent with his view of property in Misakul Allāh's care.

Aspects of the tales of Misakul Allāh and Mūsā Sagansāru accord remarkably well with colonial testimony in what would become western

Niger/eastern Mali, strengthening their probable reflection of actual practice. Commenting that villages wholly inhabited by domestic slaves (*captifs de case*) were in instances located next to those of free persons, it was observed that the former paid their owner a yearly levy (*impôt*) of twenty bags of grain, and that while such slaves could "acquire" goods and livestock, it was understood "the master could take everything they possess as his right." Farther east (in what would become northern Nigeria and Niger), the Sokoto Caliphate as well as Damagaran also featured plantations, with most slaves in the latter settled in villages or on "special farms and gardens dispersed throughout the kingdom."[49]

The two chronicle accounts merge at this juncture, with the *askia* addressing the central conundrum. The real issue is not the potential loss of production, but that Misakul Allāh has in effect set a new standard of piety in donating Abda's harvest to religious leaders and the indigent, challenging that of the *askia*: "Misakul Allāh wanted nothing more than to elevate his name above ours, as [it has not been our custom] to give 1,000 *ṣunūn* at a time; so how is it that one of our slaves surpasses us in generosity and liberality?" His courtiers' reply anticipates what would follow: "God forbid such a thing, as he himself does not equal a drop in the ocean of your generosity and liberality, and if you choose you would prove yourself more generous than he with all of his material wealth."[50]

Jango Mūsā's estate gives the *askia* an opportunity to resolve the dilemma, beginning with an elderly matriarch who pleads to keep her children, grandchildren, and great-grandchildren together, as she breastfed the *jango* and her mother the *jango*'s father, a relationship of servility spanning generations. The *askia* manumits her entire family, some twenty-eight persons, "the most attractive and most beautiful in appearance and stature," emphasizing financial loss. "Go with your family," Dāwūd declares, "I have freed them and released them, manumitting them for [the love of] God, Who gave me 500 slaves at one time. I did not have to trade or travel or war against anyone to obtain them."[51]

The *askia* is far from finished. Offered five thousand *mithqāls* in gold for the five hundred slaves by expatriate merchant 'Abd al-Wāsi'a al-Masrātī, the *askia* "articulates" the accounts: "By God, I will only sell them to the Almighty Creator (*lā abiya'uhum illā lilkhālifi ta'ālā*) and not to the created, and by them [that is, in so doing] purchase (*ishtarā*) Paradise (*al-janna*) from God. One of my slaves . . . named Misakul Allāh purchased his share of Paradise for 1,000 *ṣunūn*, so how can I [do any different] given my many sins?"[52] "Selling them to God" meant giving them away as gifts, with the *askia* making donations in allotments of twenty-seven to various parties, beginning with the *Askia-alfa* Bukar al-Anbārī (or Bukar Lanbār, Abū Bakr Lanbāru). This is the office's first mention, perhaps formalizing Mori Koyra influence in Gao; Bukar al-Anbārī would remain a royal scribe and advisor to Dāwūd's successors.[53]

Following the *askia-alfa*, Dāwūd gives allotments of twenty-seven slaves to Gao's grand mosque and then its *imām*, repeating the pattern with the *khaṭīb* and *qāḍī* of Gao, Muḥammad Diakite, who is to divide them among those with a right to these "alms"; then with Muḥammad Diakite himself; then the *sherīfian* 'Alī b. Aḥmad; and with others unnamed. To Timbuktu *Qāḍī* al-'Āqib the *askia* sends one hundred slaves, and when he finishes handing out people, he distributes animals and cereals from the *jango*'s farm to orphans and widows and *mu'adhdhins* of Gao's mosques, purportedly giving *Qāḍī* "Hind" Alfa's sister one thousand head of cattle, keeping only the horses for the cavalry. Motivated "for [the love of] God Most High," "for the Hereafter," "to purchase Paradise from God," and "for forgiveness and pardon," Dāwūd's desire to best Misakul Allāh is made clear by the *wanadu* (the royal spokesman): "As the sun appeared and ascended and blotted out the light of the stars, so has your generosity and magnanimity blotted out that of Misakul Allāh. . . . What a difference between the elephant and the mouse!"[54]

News of the *jango*'s property, on the heels of Misakul Allāh's challenge, was certainly opportune. The name 'Abd al-Wāsi'a al-Masrātī is suspect, as is Hind ("Hindī"?) Alfa. But there are verities within these accounts, including reference to slaves sold to the *sherīfian* 'Alī b. Aḥmad and later manumitted, who falsely present themselves as *sherīfian*.[55] There is also the matter of *Askia* Dāwūd's wrestling with guilt and enlisting religious leaders to intercede, consistent with other evidence. And then there are allotments to actual individuals and destinations.

The *askia*'s adjudication of the *jango*'s estate, however, is at odds with conventions made visible in the colonial period, by which both royal and nonroyal slaves were progressively integrated into Songhay-Zarma families over generations, becoming *horson*—a category of domestic slaves viewed as human (as opposed to *cire banniya* or beasts, the characterization of the newly-acquired), so integrated into the master's family that their sale or manumission was unimaginable, as their condition was regarded as permanent and unmodifiable.[56] If an enslaved wet nurse suckled her own son as well as the son of her master, bonds between the *frères du lait* were nearly as strong as those between blood brothers. Feared as the locus of supernatural powers potentially malevolent, while specializing in practices that included amulet making, circumcision rites, spirit possession, and divination, the *horson* were not to be mistreated.

As the accounts reveal, however, *Askia* Dāwūd does not follow these protocols, freeing the elderly matriarch and multiple generations of her family while giving away many others as gifts. Thirteenth/nineteenth century conventions may therefore represent a permutation, or alternatively, indicate royal behavior was less subject to scripting.

Notwithstanding such external evidence, other aspects of the Misakul Allāh and Mūsā Sagansāru accounts are supported by additional details in *Ta'rīkh al-fattāsh* itself. For example, Ibn al-Mukhtār cites an account from his maternal uncle, the son of Maḥmūd Ka'ti, in which the latter arrives in Gao and is warmly received by *Askia* Dāwūd.[57] Maḥmūd Ka'ti then enlists *Askia-alfa* Bukar al-Anbārī to present certain requests to Dāwūd, to which the *askia-alfa* assents, as he was "without question [Maḥmūd Ka'ti's] messenger," an allusion to their membership in the Mori Koyra community. Among his requests (all in writing) are eighty *mithqāls* of gold to purchase al-Fayrūzābādī's (d. 817/1414–15) lexicon *al-Qāmūs al-muḥīṭ*, and clothes to replace those worn out by his four accompanying students.[58] He also asks for four slave girls (*imā'*), four carpets, and four coverings or veils for the trousseaux of his four daughters (of marriageable age). But it is his request for his five sons that is most revealing, for in addition to turbans, vestment, cattle, and horses, he also requests cultivable land, seed, and slaves to work that land.

In fulfilling these requests, the *Ta'rīkh* specifies the *askia* gives Maḥmūd Ka'ti a plantation (*ḥarth*) called "Jangaja" in Yuna (near Lake Koratu, in what is now the Mopti region), with thirteen enslaved workers, their *fanfa*, and seed.[59] This plantation was apparently already in operation and may have been the property of the eunuch and Kabara-*farma* 'Alū, leading to a dispute between him and Maḥmūd Ka'ti. Maḥmūd Ka'ti's behest supports the factual nature of these plantations.[60]

Rethinking Slavery

Carefully considered, the stories yield critical insights, and though not necessarily entirely "factual," need not masquerade as such. Their most striking aspect is the perception of the relationship between spirituality and slavery. They are closely, intimately associated, such that the enslaved serve as spiritual currency.[61] When Dāwūd stated he would purchase his share of Paradise, he understood slaves as the tender. And though manumission is encouraged in Islam, giving slaves to religious elites and mosques was manumission's equivalent. Indeed, while the pleas of the elderly matron were heeded, nearly ninety-five percent of the *jango*'s slaves remained just that, their use as gifts every bit as efficacious as manumission. In fact, in all probability elites would view their ongoing subjugation to be in their interests, not unlike the Mossi children who, in being taken captive by *Askia al-ḥājj* Muḥammad, became "blessed of God."

The foregoing is consistent with another, possibly factual account of a Hausa slave who returns to Gao from the Pilgrimage with others. The account operates at the interstices of royal benevolence and the status-altering potential of Islamic conversion. At his customary reception, the *askia* grasps and kisses their hands one by one, and is about to do the same with the Hausa man when interrupted by the *wanadu* who, in leveling all manner of imprecation, recommends amputation. An uncertain *askia* turns to Maḥmūd Ka'ti for advice: "Just cut off his hand," he responds, "as it is the appropriate thing to do." "But I implore you in God's name," the *askia* demands, "is it permitted (*yajūzu*) to amputate his hand for this offense?" The *alfa* would provide the most shrewd and sagacious of counsel:

> How is it not lawful to cut off the hand of someone who stood at Arafat, who circumambulated the Ka'ba, who placed that hand on the Black Stone, and then touched the Yemeni Corner (*rukn al-yamānī*), and with that hand participated in the two stonings [at Mina], then visited the Messenger of God [in Medina] (may God bless him and grant him peace) and placed this hand on the chair (*maq'ad*) of the Messenger of God's noble pulpit (may God bless him and grant him peace), and then entered the garden (*al-rawḍa al-sharīfa*) [in the Prophet's mosque, between the pulpit and the room where he is buried], and placed this hand on the grate that surrounds [the Prophet's tomb], and then placed it on the tombs of Abū Bakr and 'Umar (may God be pleased with them). But not satisfied with all these privileges and advantages and commendable acts, [he] came to you to place this hand in yours, by so doing he might achieve the most modest and fleeting of earthly goals . . .

Given the exceptionality of the Hausa's experience, the *askia* can only acknowledge the effective transformation of his status, striking and imprisoning the *wanadu* instead. He not only pardons but also manumits the slave, along with one hundred members of his family, releasing them from ever having to pay taxes.[62] In an act showing the fluidity and equivalency of piety, manumission, and slavery, having just manumitted the Hausa family, he then rewards Maḥmūd Ka'ti with five others, remarking, "Without the *'ulamā'*, I would be lost."

From every indication, Songhay under *Askia* Dāwūd was awash in slaves. They were everywhere, performing services both menial and significant, fighting as soldiers, collecting taxes, providing counsel as advisors, occupying political office, serving in greatly expanded plantation agriculture, and featuring as intimates of the royals. These experiences were hardly unique to Songhay, and could be observed elsewhere in Muslim Africa (and beyond).[63] In Songhay, however, the servile were emerging as a crucial segment of the Gao-based stakeholders, the "people of Songhay."

But it is also the case that slavery under *Askia* Dāwūd was variegated and incongruous, raising fundamental questions as to its nature and meaning. Apparently, thousands of slaves directly owned by the *askia* labored on large-scale farms under enslaved managers, while some royal slaves were not simply managers, but were themselves owners of large farms with hundreds of enslaved workers in tow. At the same time, the "enslaved" could be intergenerationally tied to the land in a manner reminiscent of serfdom, a circumstance found elsewhere in West Africa, as was slavery and serfdom's simultaneity.[64]

Nonagricultural operations were also entrusted to persons of servile status, as the head official of the Taghaza salt mines, the Taghaza-*mondio* Muḥammad Ikumā, is referred to as the *khadīm* of *Askia* Dāwūd.[65] Such arrangements were by no means confined to productive endeavors, however, as the servile also occupied high political and military positions, as was true of the *Huku-kuri-koi* Yāsī. Indeed, as will be seen, the Kabara-*farma* 'Alū 's position was so sensitive that his assassination by the *balma'a* would unleash the mother of all Songhay civil wars.[66]

Slavery and servitude's crescendo under *Askia* Dāwūd also included the military. Before him, the *askia* "inherited" (*waratha*) only the weapons and horses of deceased soldiers. Under Dāwūd, however, something called "military inheritance" was instituted, by which he could lay claim to everything a soldier owned, with the soldiers themselves now referred to as "his slaves" (*'abīduhu*). This brief mention might indicate yet another important military development, though referring to the entire army as slaves may simply have been a figure of speech adopted to facilitate royal expropriation.[67]

Though extensive, slavery and serfdom did not represent everyone in servitude, with the previously mentioned endogamous castes brought to Gao by Dāwūd as examples that expand the register of forced labor, requiring a more capacious, flexible categorization.[68] The very consideration of a servile "range" invites a reconsideration of Songhay slavery, as slaves could own other slaves, inherit other forms of property through spouses and children over successive generations, and could wield considerable political and military power. What, then, was the practical meaning of "slavery" in medieval Songhay?

To be sure, much has been written on slavery in Africa.[69] As the range of experience is considerable, so are scholarly efforts to define slavery in a fashion that makes sense in most, if not all, cultural contexts and historical periods, reflecting the position that a common idiom is requisite in rendering meaning. The present study is less sanguine about this approach, though acknowledging great merit in monophysite framings that either rearticulate proprietary principles, or understand slavery as a progressive amelioration of "acquired outsider" status relative to kinship, or that posit some iteration of social death. Heeding sage advice, the approach here is to understand slavery in its local and temporal context.[70]

As such, slavery in medieval Songhay can be understood as a socially sanctioned, highly exclusive relationship of subjugation between parties in one-to-one correspondences, constraining the dominated party to fully submit or yield to the will of the dominant for as long as the relationship is sanctioned.[71] Consistent with governance in the region and period, the actual experience of subjugation, though potentially all-encompassing in scope, tended to be relatively proscribed, characterized instead by a flexibility or autonomy serving the interests of the dominant as well as the dominated. With exploitation and power as the objectives of the dominant, the dominated were the vehicle through which those objectives were often realized. Labor was central to production, as agency was critical to governance, with the former taking place on farms and battlefields, in mines and households, and the latter in positions of responsibility, if not privilege. In enough instances, individuals performed on both sides of a dichotomy: eunuchs were both soldiers and officials, concubines both sexually exploited and mothers (even royals), with female domestics one act removed from either of the latter categories.

As the extension of the master's power and authority, the enslaved was simultaneously vessel and receptacle, a subject often in command of others, whether free, royal, or otherwise. The enslaved were the insignia of the slaveholder's rank, with the potential of operating at a similar level of influence. Rather than a contradiction, there was alignment between a slave's status as personal property and his or her elevation as agent.[72] In this way, human bondage was a model for religion itself, reflecting submission as the means to extraordinary achievement.

As such, a *qualified reciprocity* model of slavery remedies an asymmetric emphasis on the acquisition of slaves to boost the status and/or lineage of slaveholders, or a focus on "natal alienation and general dishonoring," as the latter reifies slaveholder motivations without necessarily addressing the range of the enslaved's potential (albeit ultimately constrained) to reinvent (or resurrect) themselves.[73] Reciprocity also helps to explain why servile transfiguration tended to reinforce rather than threaten power disequilibria.

Qualified reciprocity is therefore akin to marginality amelioration in its approach, but better accounts for the experiences of royal slaves, especially eunuchs. For though the eunuch could become very intimate with the royal family, he could never fully become part of it, nor without offspring was there any capacity for amelioration over successive generations. Though bonds of affection certainly developed, the possible quid pro quo for him was not familial integration, but influence and power.

As such, the concubine and eunuch would have the greatest potential to wield authority in Songhay society. Having suffered and survived so much loss, they had the potential to emerge as socially transformed, the violation of their person the very mechanism by which they were now entrusted with position and responsibility.[74] They could have paid no greater price.

Askia *Dāwūd and* Qāḍī *al-ʿĀqib of Timbuktu*

Relations between Gao, Timbuktu, and Jenne continued to be complicated under Dāwūd. *Ta'rīkh al-fattāsh* follows the plight of Muḥammad and Aḥmad, *al-faqīh* Maḥmūd Baghayughu's sons in Jenne, where Muḥammad refused Dāwūd's pressure to become its *qāḍī*, leading to both brothers taking refuge in the mosque for months. They were assisted by Aḥmad b. Muḥammad b. Sa'īd, grandson (*sibṭ*) of *Qāḍī* Maḥmūd, who taught the Baghayughu brothers as well as Maḥmūd Ka'ti.[75] Aḥmad b. Muḥammad b. Sa'īd would return to Timbuktu (apparently accompanied by the Baghayughu brothers), where he soon died in 976/1568.

Relations between Dāwūd and *Qāḍī* al-ʿĀqib were tense as well as competitive. Becoming Timbuktu's *qāḍī* following his brother Muḥammad's death in 973/1565, al-ʿĀqib remained in the post until his own demise in 991/1583 at the age of seventy-eight.[76] He and Dāwūd were therefore elderly men when their terms began running concurrently. Al-ʿĀqib is described as Timbuktu's greatest *qāḍī* in impartiality (*ʿadl*) and juristic reasoning (*ijtiḥād*), so "unflinching in judgments that were firmly anchored in truth" that he sentenced Jingereber's *mu'adhdhin* to death for mispronouncing a word in a poetry reading and refusing correction.[77] He is closely associated with mosque renovation, the specific site of his rivalry with *Askia* Dāwūd. In 976/1569 he began rebuilding Sīdī Yaḥyā mosque, completing "beautiful alterations" the following year, and in 977/1570 began Jingereber's renovations, followed by the *sūq* mosque in 985/1577–78. Sankore mosque was rebuilt the following year, for which he is said to have precisely adopted the Ka'ba's measurements.[78]

The *askia* took great interest in the Jingereber project, symbol of the city's cosmopolitanism, and trouble between the two men may have represented a struggle over its association with secular power.[79] Strongly worded correspondence originating with unnamed "calumniators" sowing "discord" (*wa qad sa'ā bainamā wushāh*) led to a direct exchange between the two, with the *askia* making "unhelpful remarks" (*al-aqāwīl lā yanbigā*) and the *qāḍī* responding in a manner that "only someone of the stature of Dāwūd could weather."[80]

In returning to Timbuktu from Sura Bantanba in 978/1570, the *askia* displayed "excellent comportment" (*wa unẓur ḥusn mulāṭafatihi*) toward the *qāḍī*, visiting the city at a time when "the rebuilding of [Jingereber mosque] had not yet been completed."[81] The *askia*, however, was made to stand "for a long time" outside the *qāḍī*'s locked gate, and only after a leading *'ulamā'* interceded was the *askia* allowed to enter.[82]

Dāwūd continued abasing himself, and when the *qāḍī*'s anger subsided the two men entered an agreement that probably concerned Jingereber.[83] *Ta'rīkh al-fattāsh* would indicate this, referencing "the year when [the *askia*] quarreled with the *qāḍī* over the building of this mosque." With the work nearing completion, the *askia* complained: "You haven't left anything for me to do!" The *qāḍī* suggested the ruler build a structure connecting the tomb of *Sīdī* Abū 'l-Qāsim al-Tuwātī (d. 935/1528–39) with those of "his companions," a compromise the *askia* happily accepted. Though *Ta'rīkh as-sūdān* asserts he completed what remained of Jingereber's restoration, both sources suggest al-'Āqib succeeded in minimizing Dāwūd's role.[84]

Sa'dian Specter

While *Askia* Dāwūd was busy campaigning against Borgu in 966/1558–59, an ill wind was gathering at Taghaza, where in 964/1556–57 al-Filālī al-Zubāyrī, ostensibly angry over the *askia* appointing a nephew to lead the mining operation, killed the Taghaza-*mondio* Muḥammad Ikumā, the *khadīm* (slave) of *Askia* Dāwūd.[85] However, Morocco's *Mawlāy*

Muḥammad *al-Shaykh al-Kabīr al-Sharīf* al-Drawī al-Tagmadert, founder of the Sa'dian dynasty (ruled 951–64/1544–57), had authorized (*bi-ithn mawlāya*) the attack, taking advantage of al-Filālī's resentment. Songhay had last been tested under *Askia* Isḥāq Bēr, when the Wattasid Moroccan Sultan *Mawlāy* Abū 'l-Abbas Aḥmad "the Great" demanded the mine. The rise of the Sa'dians saw Muḥammad *al-Shaykh* defeat the Portuguese at Agadir in 948/1541, the Wattasids and Zayanids at Fez and Tlemcen in 956/1549, and successfully defend Fez five years later.[86] Taghaza must therefore be understood within a broader context that includes Europe, the Ottomans, and Morocco.

Morocco's interest in Taghaza only intensified with the coming to power of *Mawlāy* Aḥmad or al-Manṣūr (986–1012/1578–1603), who demanded a year of taxes (*kharāj*) from Taghaza.[87] Unlike Isḥāq Bēr, Dāwūd conceded, sending him ten thousand *mithqāls* of gold as a "goodwill gift." Al-Manṣūr is said to have "marveled" at the *askia*'s generosity, establishing a "close friendship" with him, and would grieve at Dāwūd's death. Even so, Dāwūd's gesture was likely interpreted as weakness, only whetting al-Manṣūr's appetite. He would become known as Aḥmad al-Dhahabī ("Aḥmad the Golden") with Songhay's subsequent conquest.

The end of *Askia* Dāwūd's life saw signs and wonders auguring ill. In 990/1582–83 a "great plague" killed many in Timbuktu, and was followed by an ill-advised foray into Masina in retaliation for rogue Fulbe brigandry. *Kanfāri* Muḥammad Bonkana, failing to consult with the *askia*, laid waste to Masina, killing "many of its virtuous scholars and holymen . . . from whom emanated many manifestations of divine grace after their death." Dāwūd would bitterly disapprove of his son's action, as it was a "bad omen" for Songhay and the *askia*. Al-Sa'adī implies a correlation between the slaughter of clerical innocents and the *askia*'s own death that same year (or the next) at his Tondibi estate. His body was prepared and transported south to Gao for burial.[88]

The reign of *Askia* Dāwūd compares favorably with others, second only to that of *Askia al-ḥājj* Muḥammad in significance. He ended interminable infighting among royals, established the equivalent of public libraries, and created a more systematic state treasury. If he achieved no further territorial expansion, he successfully projected power throughout the region, with the dramatic rise in servile plantation agriculture a result. Indeed, Dāwūd's reign allows for a sustained discussion of slavery and servitude in Songhay, as he accelerated a practice whereby slaves became spiritual currency, the living tender through which religious elites were honored and Paradise approximated. As such, Songhay under Dāwūd was a slave society in every sense of the concept.

The empire remained connected to the world principally via an immense expanse of sand. Transformative changes were taking place in that world, with al-Maghrib's participation becoming ever more robust. Their capacities strained, Moroccan regimes needed additional resources.

CHAPTER FOURTEEN

The Rending Asunder: Dominion's End

BETWEEN *ASKIA* DĀWŪD'S DEATH IN 990–91/1582–83 and the Battle of Tondibi in 999/1591 that marked the beginning of Morocco's occupation, the empire endured the tumultuous reigns of four *askias*, the depravations of famine, and a civil war so destructive that Timbuktu's religious elites felt compelled to intervene. It is no small irony that an enslaved official was at the epicenter of exigency, nor that slaves were strategically positioned to influence events, nor that those events prominently featured enslaved soldiers. Elites, whether political actors or *shaykhs*, were therefore as dependent on as they were dominant over slaves. The Moroccan invasion would arrive at a most unpropitious time.

Return to Instability

As probably Dāwūd's oldest son, Muḥammad Bonkana had a most curious career.[1] Named *fari-mondio* in 956/1549, he became *kanfāri* in 986/1578, by which time he had helped lead three major military campaigns. But he was entrusted with commanding none of them, suggesting he did not enjoy his father's full confidence.

Dāwūd's appointment of Muḥammad Bonkana as *kanfāri* toward the end of his reign, however, suggests his son's longue durée of seasoning was ending, and that the *askia* was maneuvering to ensure his succession.[2] Al-Sa'dī says that all of Dāwūd's elder sons were present at his passing, but Muḥammad Bonkana was apparently the exception, as it was only upon hearing of his father's faltering that he departed Tendirma for Gao.[3] Upon reaching Timbuktu, he learned his father had already expired, and that his brother al-Ḥājj was now *askia*. The *kanfāri* hurried to Tendirma to assemble his army "to go to Gao to fight," but in passing (back) through Timbuktu his army revolted and fled to Gao, having heard rumors the *kanfāri* had in the interim requested *Qāḍī* al-ʿĀqib's protection (*ḥurma*), and that he had written to *Askia* al-Ḥājj swearing allegiance, asking permission to remain in Timbuktu to study.

Initially acceding to the *qāḍī*'s intercession, *Askia* al-Ḥājj would later send Amar b. *Askia* Isḥāq Bēr to arrest and imprison Muḥammad Bonkana in Kanatu.[4] Al-Hādī b. Dāwūd became *kanfāri* as reward for his allegiance to al-Ḥājj, but as he would later lead a failed revolt, he would be imprisoned with Muḥammad Bonkana in Kanatu (effectively replacing Kangaga Island as the site of imprisoned or banished royals).

Al-Ḥājj was actually named *al-ḥājj* Muḥammad for his grandfather *Askia al-ḥājj* Muḥammad, but the honorific title became his personal name (with no indication he ever made the Pilgrimage).[5] The son of Āmina/Mina Gāy Bardā, he was presumably Dāwūd's second eldest son and the oldest present at his passing, having previously been named Korey-*farma*. His investiture included a public demonstration of fealty by enslaved elites, indicating their prominence.[6]

Both *ta'rīkhs* (*tawārīkh*) treat al-Ḥājj favorably, with *Ta'rīkh al-fattāsh* claiming he "spoke the language of soothsaying and had knowledge of that which was concealed, with most of what he said concurring with what God had decreed." This allegedly included the sobering prediction that the next person to appear before him would be the *askia* to witness Songhay's end, at which point Muḥammad Gao, the last of imperial Songhay's Askias, entered the palace.[7] Al-Ḥājj began suffering from "ulcers in his lower bowels" (*bi'illa al-qurūḥ fī asfalihi*) rendering him incontinent ("prevented him from being master of himself"), a "chronic illness" disabling him from ever campaigning.[8]

There were four major developments during al-Ḥājj's tenure: the submission of Masina's sultan *Funduku* Būbu Maryam, *Qāḍī* al-ʿĀqib's death, *Kanfāri* al-Hādī's revolt, and a decided shift in Moroccan policy from diplomacy and threats to actual military intervention. As to the first, relations between Songhay and its tributary Masina had been troubled following *Kanfāri* Muḥammad Bonkana's murderous assault in 990/1582–83. The *askia* instructed Bukar b. *Askia* Muḥammad Bonkana Kirya to take *Funduku* Būbu Maryam into custody and bring him to Gao, where he remained for so long it was assumed he had died.[9] Satisfied he was no longer a threat, al-Ḥājj offered to restore him in Masina, but the *funduku* allegedly preferred to continue in service to the *askia* in Gao. Al-Ḥājj responded by giving him a residence, horses, and servants, appointing Ḥammad Āmina as sultan of Masina in his stead.

The second development was the death of *Qāḍī* al-ʿĀqib on 21 Rajab 991/10 August 1583 at age seventy-eight, either thirteen months or four days after *Askia* Dāwūd's own demise.[10] A year and a half would pass before the office was filled by Abū Ḥafṣ ʿUmar b. Maḥmūd in 993/1585, *qāḍī* until 1002/1593 and his arrest and exile to Marrakesh, where he "died a martyr."[11] The *ta'rīkhs* differ over why the post remained unoccupied for two years.[12]

In the interim, *Muftī* Aḥmad Mu'yā (or Mughyā), of the *san* or *'ulamā'* of Sankore (among nine slain by the Moroccans in 1002/1593), heard cases involving the Sankore, while Muḥammad Baghayughu b. Maḥmūd adjudicated cases for those of "mixed ancestry" (*al-muwalladūn*, with unclear meaning in this instance), as well as those from elsewhere in the Muslim world (*al-musāfirūn*), in front of Sīdī Yaḥyā mosque.[13] Muḥammad Baghayughu's justice included jailings and beatings, engendering opposition from "agitators and depraved persons and fools" who railed: "Observe this man, who claims to not love the things of this world and that he is an ascetic (*zāhid*), but who in fact loves power, having made himself *qāḍī* without anyone appointing him to [the office]." Letters sent to his home challenged him: "Oh Muḥammad Baghayughu, who made you *qāḍī*?" Muḥammad Baghayughu's response was gentle yet spirited:

> "We have been appointed to this [responsibility], as God demands from us an account of all that goes unattended during this period. As far as we know, not one complaint has been raised about our rulings [literally, "that which we have been appointed to do"], and we fear the full wrath of God if we neglect His charge."

A third event, the revolt of *Kanfāri* al-Hādī in Ṣafar 992/ February 1584, is as intriguing as it is revealing.[14] Al-Sa'dī reports he had been encouraged to overthrow al-Ḥājj by their brothers in Gao, but that those same brothers then betrayed him. Wearing a coat of mail (*dir' min ḥadīd*) underneath his clothing, the *kanfāri* approached Gao with horns and drum, only to be challenged by Ṣāliḥ, Muḥammad Gao, Nūḥ, and other siblings. If once complicit, their questions suggest they were either excellent prevaricators or not the brothers conspiratorially involved:

> "What have you brought here [referring to the horns and drum]? What do you seek? With whom have you consulted, and from whom have you received support? You must think we are all women here! Wait right here, and you'll see what we carry [whether a penis or a vagina]!"

Al-Sa'dī later identifies a maternal uncle, the brother of Āmina Gāy Bardā (al-Ḥājj's mother), as the force behind the intrigue, implicating Āmina Gāy Bardā as well.

With whatever support al-Hādī may have had in Gao now dissipated, *Hi-koi* Bukar Shīlī-ije agreed to arrest him in exchange for becoming Dendi-*fari*. A deeply disappointed *askia* addressed the outlaw: "You are nothing but an ungrateful wretch, al-Hādī!" Turning to the *kanfārī*'s exceptional horse, al-Ḥājj concluded: "Only this horse could have caused my brother al-Hādī to pursue *fitna*!" He then imprisoned al-Hādī in Kanatu, where he joined Muḥammad Bonkana b. *Askia* Dāwūd.

A fourth development portended Songhay's destiny. *Mawlāy* al-Manṣūr (ruled 986–1012/1578–1603) had embarked upon a series of expensive building projects best exemplified by the extravagant Marrakesh palace of *al-Badī'*, commissioned upon his arrival in power, that would take another twenty-five years to complete. Ransom paid by the Portuguese following their defeat at the 986/1578 Battle of the Three Kings (at Wadi al-Makhazin, near *al-Qaṣr al-Kabīr* or Alcazar) was a source of funding, but al-Manṣūr's projects, expanded military, and lavish lifestyle required additional revenue.[15]

Al-Sa'dī records *Mawlāy* al-Manṣūr sent remarkable gifts to *Askia* al-Ḥājj as a pretext for "spying out the land of Takrūr," with al-Ḥājj sending back presents double in value.[16] Soon came word that a Moroccan expeditionary force of twenty thousand soldiers had been sent to Wadan, but "God dispersed that army through hunger and thirst, scattering them in all directions." Undeterred, al-Manṣūr sent a much smaller force of two hundred musketeers (*rumā'*, from singular *rāmī*, literally "shooter" of matchlocks) to a largely deserted Taghaza, its inhabitants previously alerted. With the musketeers returning to Marrakesh, some salt traders went to Taoudeni, south of Taghaza, where they renewed their activities.[17]

In Dhū 'l-Ḥijja 994/November-December 1586, unnamed siblings deposed al-Ḥājj and named Muḥammad Bāni as *askia* in Muḥarram 995/December 1586.

Already in very poor health, al-Ḥājj was exiled to Tondibi and soon died, having ruled for four years and five months.[18]

The Enslaved at the Epicenter of Conflict

Muḥammad Bāni's reign of one year and four months (until Jumāda al-Awwal 996/April 1588) was one of drought-inflicted "misery," resulting in famine and inflation.[19] It marked the beginning of yet another prolonged fratricidal war, "the reason for the ruin of Songhay, as it opened the door to domestic calamity, corrupting its rulers while severing their ties (*qaṭa'a silk niẓām*) just when an expedition from Marrakesh arrived, and so on."[20] The irony is that this final *fitna* erupted over the high profile of slaves, demonstrating their influence as well as the extent to which the lines between enslaved and free, including royals, had become blurred.

Learning of Muḥammad Bāni's ascension, the imprisoned al-Hādī exclaimed, "God's curse upon hasty decisions! The most idiotic of all to come from our father's loins has become *sulṭān*." He proved prescient, as *Askia* Muḥammad Bāni would execute both al-Hādī and Muḥammad Bonkana, burying them side-by-side.[21] All three were sons of *Askia* Dāwūd, and as neither his surviving brothers "nor anyone else" approved, his siblings began plotting against him.

With such intrigue as context, conflict between *Balma'a* Muḥammad al-Ṣādiq b. Dāwūd and Kabara-*farma* 'Alū provides the specific moment of disintegration. Here *Ta'rīkh al-fattāsh* acknowledges dependence on the yet-to-be-recovered work *Durar al-ḥisān fī akhbār mulūk al-sūdān* ("Exquisite Pearls in the Annals of the Rulers of the Sudan"), describing Kabara-*farma* 'Alū as "a tyrannical, unjust, debauched, deceitful, domineering, ignorant, arrogant and pigheaded eunuch."[22] By custom, the Kabara-*farma* was a slave (*gulām*) of the *askia*, and 'Alū fit the bill.[23] His eventual death at the hands of the *balma'a*, Kabara's military commander, was considered providential by al-Sa'dī, an example of God "delivering the Muslims from his wickedness." Charges of tyranny and debauchery probably relate to extralegal taxation, as the Kabara-*farma* levied duties on goods entering and exiting Kabara.

The incident precipitating the clash between Muḥammad al-Ṣādiq b. Dāwūd and 'Alū centered on slaves, with the former's male slave (initially *khadīm*, later *gulām*) accused of stealing cloth from the latter's female slave (*jāriya*, pl. *jawārīn*). The Kabara-*farma* demanded the cloth or the thief, but the *balma'a* believed the male slave's denial. "Ugly" words ensued, with the Kabara-*farma* seizing, flogging, and imprisoning the accused. In response, the *balma'a* walked to the Kabara-*farma*'s house, confronted him, and knocked him to the ground. He then drove a large lance through his heart, throwing his body out of the house and confiscating his wealth. *Ta'rīkh al-fattāsh* concurs with al-Sa'dī in asserting 'Alū suffered what he deserved, but for his mistreatment of Maḥmūd Ka'ti. 'Alū had not only taken his rice field, a gift from the *askia*, but he seized and threw the *shaykh* to the ground in the process.[24]

The chronicles diverge as to whether the *balma'a* attacked the Kabara-*farma* as part of a predetermined plot to challenge for the *askiyate*.[25] In either case, the episode reflects just how extensive and defining intimacies between royals and their slaves could be: 'Alū was a slave, lower in many respects than the most humble peasant, yet superior in authority to the vast majority of Timbuktu elites.

Realizing, at the very least, that his actions were an affront to *Askia* Muḥammad Bāni, the *balma'a* asked *Kanfāri* Ṣāliḥ to join him from Tendirma and together march against Gao, where they would establish Ṣāliḥ as the next *askia*. The *kanfāri* accepted and the two men met at Toya.[26] Al-Sa'dī writes, however, that "perceptive" individuals counseled the *kanfāri* to demand from the *balma'a* all he had seized from the Kabara-*farma*, as he had a greater right to it, and as a test of the *balma'a*'s sincerity.[27] They would turn on each other with the *balma'a*'s refusal, but unlike *Ta'rīkh as-sūdān*'s questioning of the *balma'a*'s motives, *Ta'rīkh al-fattāsh* faults the *kanfāri*, a "stupid man" (*rajulān khurqān*) who confronted the *balma'a* with forty of his bravest soldiers. Initially fleeing, the *balma'a* eventually killed the *kanfāri*; upon learning of learning of Ṣāliḥ's death, his army pledged loyalty to the *balma'a*.[28]

Askia Muḥammad Bāni therefore prepared to confront a revolt of essentially the entire western sphere, as *Balma'a* Muḥammad al-Ṣādiq b. Dāwūd was joined by Baghana-*fari* Bukar, Hombori-*koi* Mansa, Bara-*koi* Amar, and Kala-*shā'* Bukar, "among others." This was a "large army" of some six thousand soldiers, according to *Ta'rīkh al-fattāsh*, which asserts the whole of Ataram followed the *balma'a*.[29]

Muḥammad Bāni waited for the *balma'a* to approach Gao, having assembled thirty thousand soldiers. The moment of truth arrived on 12 Jumādā 'l-Awlā /9 April 1558, but before the two forces could meet the *askia* died mid-siesta from either a "fit of rage" or the combination of heat, his coat of mail, and extreme corpulence.[30] His young eunuchs (*gilmānuhu al-khiṣyān*), responsible for his massage, bathing, and teeth cleaning, discovered the body, and what happens next unveils much about the ever-evolving role of the enslaved.

The eunuchs informed other courtiers of their discovery, presumably also slaves, who then told the *huku-kuru-koi* and the *bārai-koi* ("master of horses"); as the *huku-kuru-koi* was a eunuch, the *bārai-koi* may also have been a slave.[31] Together with military commanders that included the *hi-koi*, these stakeholders decided to conceal the *askia*'s death from Dāwūd's sons, and instead sent for the Benga-*farma* Maḥmūd b. *Askia* Ismā'īl. "Oh Maḥmūd," they began, "we fear this day is the last of the days of the state (*daula*) of the Songhay people, the day of their perishing (*yaum fanā'ihim*)." In view of the Benga-*farma*'s superior organizational skills, these elite slaves determined that he should become *askia* immediately, before Dāwūd's sons learned of Muḥammad Bāni's death. They further vowed:

> "Everyone who you order us to arrest and imprison [we will do so], and those who deserve death we will execute upon your order. Then we will beat the royal drum for you and swear fealty to you, and you will be *askia* without anyone being able to contest it. Then we will march to battle against *Balma'a* Ṣādiq and kill him. This is our counsel, and it is sound, and by it our lives will be secure. As for the sons of *Askia* Dāwūd and their descendants, we will never consent to any of them assuming power over us due to their evil and tyranny, given how they sever ties of kinship."

Maḥmūd b. *Askia* Ismā'īl accepted the slaves' offer.[32]

The problem with their plan, however, was that the loyalty of other slaves lay elsewhere. The eunuch Tabakali was to invite Isḥāq b. Dāwūd (Isḥāq "the Zughrānī" or Isḥāq II) to meet with Muḥammad Bāni (without revealing he had died), but instead he told Isḥāq b. Dāwūd of the plot. The oldest of more than seventy sons and grandsons present that day, Isḥāq b. Dāwūd gathered his brothers and allies (about one hundred altogether) and rode to Muḥammad Bāni's tent, demanding Maḥmūd and the scheme's leaders either surrender or die. Begging for their lives, these same slaves then named Isḥāq b. Dāwūd as *askia* on 13 Jumādā 'l-Awlā 996/10 April 1588, pledging fealty on the Qur'ān and performing the earthen ablution, a decision ratified by the army to the sound of the royal drum.[33] Muḥammad Bāni had been *askia* for one year, four months, and eight days. His body was washed and buried in Gao, behind the tomb of *Askia al-ḥājj* Muḥammad.

The Empire Unravels

The battle between the *balma'a* and the *kanfāri* exposed *Askia* Muḥammad Bāni's vulnerabilities as well as the fraught succession process. With so much at stake, many in Timbuktu felt compelled to choose sides and swore allegiance to *Balma'a* Muḥammad al-Ṣādiq, including "common people," merchants, imperial officials, and some of the *'ulamā'*. Even the tailors participated by outfitting the *balma'a*'s army.[34]

Led by Timbuktu-*koi* Abakar, Maghsharan-*koi* Tibirt ag-Sīd, and one al-Kayd b. Hamza al-Sanāwī, Timbuktu doubled down on its choice with the 19 Jumādā 'l-Awlā 996/16 April 1588 arrival of the news that Isḥāq b. Dāwūd was now *askia*, seizing and imprisoning the royal messenger. Widespread "merriment" followed, with drums "erupting" from rooftops. The *balma'a* was "greatly loved" in Timbuktu, a city in open revolt.

The *askia*'s impending battle with the *balma'a* was announced with *Askia* Isḥāq b. Dāwūd recruiting his two nephews, 'Umar Katu b. Muḥammad Bonkana and Muḥammad b. *Askia* al-Ḥājj ("full of *baraka*" and fighting prowess), the day before.[35] The battle itself would involve sizable forces that included Tuareg cavalry allied with the *askia*, descending upon the *balma'a* "like locusts." Muḥammad al-Ṣādiq was routed by day's end, with the *askia* sending *Ḥaṣal-farma* 'Alū w. Sabīl and (yet another) eunuch Atakurma Diakaté to pursue him at the head of fifty cavalry. In full flight, the *balma'a* reached Timbuktu days later on 28 Jumādā 'l-Awlā 996/25 April 1588.[36]

Though the chronicles qualify Timbuktu's support of the *balma'a*, the city's embrace of his cause is difficult to mask. Instructively, the *balma'a* went first to the house of Muḥammad Baghayughu, huddling with supporters and spending the night, after which he left for Tendirma. Arriving in Timbuktu soon thereafter, *Ḥaṣal-farma* 'Alū w. Sabīl jailed the Timbuktu-*mondio*. Timbuktu had backed the wrong horse.[37]

As to the fate of *Balma'a* Muḥammad, the sources diverge. *Ta'rīkh al-fattāsh* says he initially vanished in Hajar, later meeting his demise in a surprise raid by the "mountain people."[38] Al-Sa'dī, however, maintains he was eventually captured, imprisoned, and executed in Kanatu, where he was buried next to Muḥammad Bonkana, al-Hādī, and *Bana-farma* Daku: "The four graves are well known."[39]

The *balma'a*'s *fitna* affected the whole of the empire, resulting in the most dire of consequences. *Askia* Isḥāq b. Dāwūd punished the *balma'a*'s allies—governors and military leaders of the western hemisphere, especially officers in and near Timbuktu. *Hombori-koi* Mansa was buried alive in a palm frond sack. Timbuktu-*koi* Abakar and Maghsharan-*koi* Tibirt ag-Sīd were likewise killed, while Bara-*koi* Amar and Kala-*shā'* Bukar were imprisoned (though released under the Moroccans). The *askia* would later execute his brother Yāsī Buru-Bēr b. Dāwūd, accused (falsely, according to al-Sa'dī) of plotting insurrection. Baghana-*fari* Bukar initially took refuge under the *ḥurma* of Maḥmūd Ka'ti in Tendirma before escaping to Kala, but "many" in provinces allied with the *balma'a* were imprisoned or killed. "Yet others were lashed with a heavy twined belt; Muḥammad Koi-je, son of the former [*Kanfāri*] Ya'qūb [b. *Askia al-ḥajj* Muḥammad] died from such a beating."[40]

Al-Sa'dī criticizes Isḥāq b. Dāwūd's execution of the Timbuktu-*koi* and Maghsharan-*koi*, but *Ta'rīkh al-fattāsh* is wholly laudatory, describing *Askia* Isḥāq b. Dāwūd as "noble and generous and openhanded, as well as handsome." The "Anonymous Spaniard," in Marrakesh in 999–1000/1591, related a similar profile:

> It is said that Isḥāq of Gao is a man of 45 years. Although black, he is truthful and faithful to his word, and has a very gentle nature, and many good qualities; he is well loved by his subjects. He is not depraved as are the Moors of Marrakesh and Fez, and has no other vices than those permitted by his religion.[41]

Such was his beneficence that *Ta'rīkh al-fattāsh* asserts not one person in Gao could deny having personally benefitted, quite a claim given the capital consisted of 7,626 houses, not including "dwellings built with straw" (*gairu buyūt mabniyāt bi-l-ḥashīsh*), qualifying it as a contender for the foremost town in the western Sudan.[42]

With the end of reprisals, Isḥāq b. Dāwūd began replenishing his administration, naming his first cousin Maḥmūd b. *Askia* Ismā'īl as *balma'a* and Muḥammad Hayku b. *Faran* 'Abd Allāh b. *Askia al-ḥājj* Muḥammad as Benga-*farma*.[43] He also undertook two campaigns against the "infidels" of Gurma, and was preparing to march on Kala in 999/1590–91 when the Moroccan incursion required that he abandon his plans. He would be deposed by his brother *Balma'a* Muḥammad Gao in 1000/1591–92, having spent three years and seven months in office.[44]

A Calamitous End to Calamity: The Moroccans Invade

The 999/1591 Moroccan invasion of Songhay consisted of a combined cavalry and infantry of 3,000 to 4,000 soldiers or "musketeers" (or *rumā'*, from the singular *rāmī*), and another 6,000 auxiliaries that included medical and other skilled staff. It was actually led by a Spaniard, a "short, blue-eyed eunuch" (*fatā qaṣīr azraq*) named Jawdar (or Jawdār or Jūdār). As the principal *qā'id* or general, *Pasha* Jawdar commanded ten lesser *qā'ids* (*quwwād*, but *qiyād* in al-Sa'dī) and two *kāhiyas* (*kawāhin*) or lieutenants, including *Qā'ids* 'Ammār the Eunuch (*al-fatā*) "the Former Infidel" (*al-'iljī*), 'Alī b. al-Muṣṭafā "the Former Infidel," as well as *Kāhiya* Bā-Ḥasan Firīr (that is, Ferrer) "the Former Infidel." As the term *al-ʿiljī* was applied to Muslim converts, at least four of the military leaders were Europeans.[45] Furthermore, according to the Anonymous Spaniard, although 1,500 lancers were "from among the local people," half of the 2,000 infantry were "renegade musketeers," while the other half were émigrés from Granada (presumably Arabo-Berbers). Most of the 500 mounted soldiers (*spahis*) were also "renegades."[46] The Spaniard's mention of auxiliaries lists 600 sappers and 1,000 camel-drivers (leading 8,000 camels and 1,000 pack-horses). Therefore, a substantial proportion of the invading army was not "Moroccan" at all, but rather European, principally Spaniards.

With Timbuktu under a thick cloud of suspicion, Tendirma a shell of its former self, the empire's western half reeling from retribution, and numerous royals and leaders either dead or imprisoned, the empire's cohesion was effectively undone. One Wuld Kirinfil, a royal slave imprisoned at Taghaza, escaped to Marrakesh, where he wrote to *Mawlāy* al-Manṣūr in Fez, "informing him of the weakness of Songhay's leadership (*ahl Sughay*) and providing intelligence about them concerning their desperate circumstances, their depraved natures, and their enfeebled power, urging him to take the land from their hands."[47] Al-Manṣūr included the letter in a missive to the *askia*, again demanding taxation (*kharāj*) from Taghaza, arguing he had a right to it and would use the money to finance "the armies of God" against the infidel (Christian Europe), whose "flowing torrents would inundate you, its pouring rain would flood your land. [These armies of God] have reined in unbelief, so that you have slept securely under their surety, and in equanimity and peace of mind under their protection."[48]

Perhaps precisely because Songhay was so wounded, *Askia* Isḥāq b. Dāwūd roared back with a "strongly worded" (*qabīḥ*) letter, conveying insult and threatening war, accompanied by a lance and two iron shoes.[49] But al-Manṣūr, armed with new intelligence and acutely aware of Songhay's vulnerability, decided to once again attempt a full-scale invasion.

The expedition under *Pasha* Jawdar left Morocco in Muḥarram 999/November 1590, and on 4 Jumādā ʿl-Awlā 999/28 February 1591 reached the Niger River, where Jawdar held a feast to celebrate their safe arrival.[50] On 17 Jumādā ʿl-Awlā /13 March they engaged the Songhay army at the Battle of Tondibi (more accurately at Tankondibogho, near Tondibi). Estimates of the Songhay force fluctuate wildly, from 18,000 cavalry and 9,700 foot soldiers (*Taʾrīkh al-fattāsh*), to 12,500 cavalry and 30,000 infantry (al-Saʿdī), to 80,000 soldiers in total (the Anonymous

Spaniard). Many Songhay warriors died that day, their lines broken "in the twinkling of an eye," overcome by the superior firepower as well as the introduction of battle tactics unknown to the Songhay.[51] The Anonymous Spaniard maintains Songhay archers valiantly "bent the leg and fastened it below the knee," rendering them immobile. Other Songhay soldiers, "seeing them remain firm, [would] fight with greater courage and not run away," but "the [Moroccan] musketry did great damage among them." Al-Sa'dī similarly records Songhay soldiers sat on their shields rather than retreat, and were killed "in cold blood," the invaders stripping their wrists of gold bracelets.

With *Askia* Isḥāq b. Dāwūd ordering Gao's evacuation, Jawdar entered a largely deserted capital. The *askia* sued for peace, offering 100,000 *mithqāls* of gold and 1,000 slaves in exchange for the Moroccans' return to Marrakesh. Jawdar relayed the offer to al-Manṣūr, along with his view that the head donkey-driver's house in Marrakesh was better than the royal palace in Gao, implying the expedition was not worth the effort.

While awaiting al-Manṣūr's reply, Jawdar headed to Timbuktu, having spent seventeen days in Gao. They remained just south of Timbuktu for thirty-five days, finally entering on 6 Sha'bān/30 May, and found it much more to their liking. Al-Manṣūr's angry response to Isḥāq b. Dāwūd's peace offer arrived with *Pasha* Maḥmūd b. Zarqūn and eighty musketeers on 26 Shawwāl/17 August, deposing Jawdar and recommitting the expedition to the occupation. *Pasha* Maḥmūd would fight the *askia*'s army a second time on 25 Dhū 'l-Ḥijja/14 October, at the Battle of Zanzan, routing the Songhay and forcing the *askia* to flee to Dendi. Songhay's military leaders soon declared Muḥammad Gao the new *askia*, stripping Isḥāq b. Dāwūd of all insignia and escorting him to Songhay's borders. He headed to Tinfini in Gurma, where he was killed in Jumādā 'l-Thāniya 1000/March-April 1592. Only forty days later, *Askia* Muḥammad Gao would be arrested and executed by *Pasha* Maḥmūd. The *askiyate*, such as it was, passed to his brother Nūḥ.

Imperial Songhay was no more. The Moroccan occupation would eventually become independent of the Moroccan sultan and increasingly indigenized through intermarriage, establishing a series of puppet Askias through which the *pashas* attempted to govern, confining the rump, "legitimate" Askias to the Dendi region. However, the story of the Moroccan occupation and its aftermath are for another day.[52]

Interpreting the Fall

Ta'rīkh al-fattāsh's assessment of 999/1591, in appropriating the lens of religion, reveals an acute awareness of certain social transformations:

> Why was the power of Songhay ruined and their unity shattered by God, so that they were overtaken by that which they derided [as not possible]? It was because of their neglecting the laws of God, the wickedness of slaves, and the haughtiness and arrogance of pride. During the days of [*Askia*] Isḥāq, Gao had reached the limits of moral depravity and the display of atrocious and reprehensible sins, spreading such filth until adulterers practiced openly, having created a [unique] drum by which they would call (*yutaḥākimūna*) to one another. And there were other such acts too disgraceful to mention by a virtuous narrator. We belong to God, and to Him we must return.[53]

Only eight years following the death of *Askia* Dāwūd, Songhay was finished—an unfathomable development on the order of the cataclysmic. Beyond moral turpitude, the analysis makes two critical points. The first concerns the consequences of the pursuit of self-interest. The civil war led

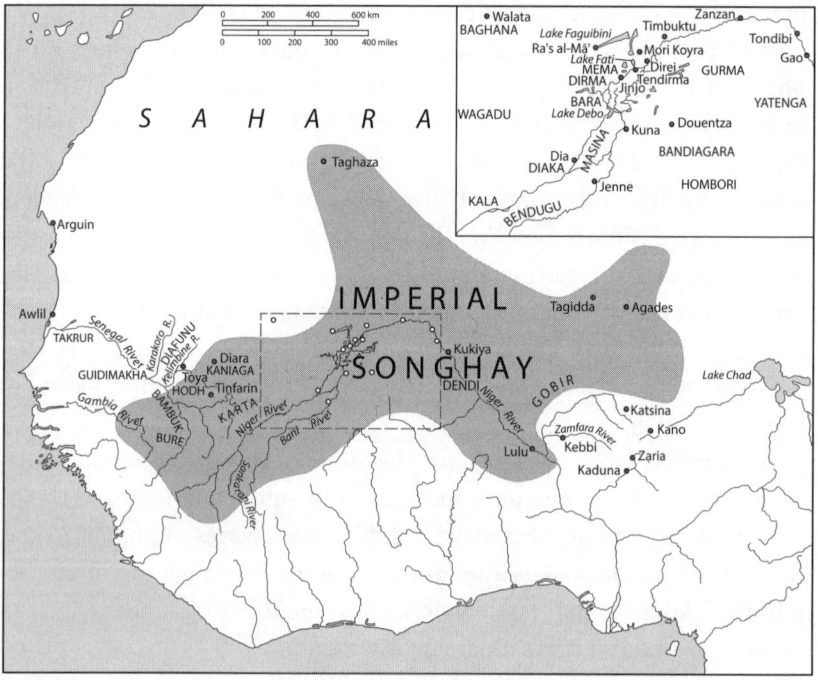

Map 8: Imperial Songhay at the Fall

by *Balma'a* Muḥammad had been encouraged by the ineffective tenures of *Askias* al-Ḥājj and Muḥammad Bāni, in turn emanating from sibling rivalries that had reached new lows. Even without a Moroccan invasion, the empire may have been irreparably crippled.[54]

The second point concerns "the wickedness of slaves," whose high profile is on full display with Kabara-*farma* 'Alū, and again following the death of *Askia* Muḥammad Bāni. They arguably came to constitute the most important of stakeholders, benefitting from while contributing to the dysfunction of the Askias.

Al-Sa'dī's critique also makes the point that the technical reasons for Songhay's crushing defeat are less important than factors underlying its weakened condition. The intensification of plantation slavery under Dāwūd, a possible response to famine, would have also been highly disruptive of the social fabric, as increasing numbers were recruited to labor on these farms. As such, social insecurity and political instability would have been mutually reinforcing.[55]

Less than ten years following the death of *Askia* Dāwūd, second only to *Askia al-ḥājj* Muḥammad in accomplishment and renown, imperial Songhay lay in utter ruin, never more to rise. The carnage that followed Dāwūd's reign, largely a consequence of a challenged succession process, simply could not be managed by an empowered servile elite. This time, transregional developments would intervene at a moment of high vulnerability. This time, there would be no recovery.

EPILOGUE

A Thousand Years

SOME FOUR HUNDRED YEARS AFTER ITS FALL, the world was reminded of imperial Songhay's former glory when, in early January of 2012, the National Movement for the Liberation of Azawād, or the MNLA (*Mouvement national de Liberation de l'Azawad*), attacked the towns of Menaka and Aguelhok, leading to the collapse of the national army in northern Mali. A 22 March military coup in Bamako would accelerate developments, with insurrectionary forces establishing control over Kidal, Gao, and Timbuktu by 1 April.

Though uprisings in northern Mali were nothing new, developments in 2012 were precipitated by Libya's experience of the "Arab Spring," where unrest in February of 2011 led to western military intervention. With Muammar al-Qadhafi's death that October, at least two thousand heavily armed loyalists crossed the border into Mali, among other places, emboldening elements already in opposition to the government.

With the fall of Gao and Timbuktu, the fraught and contingent nature of rebel alliances came into relief. Overwhelmingly Tuareg and secular, the MNLA had been joined by al-Qaeda in Islamic North Africa (or AQMI, *al-Qaïda au Maghreb islamique*) under the command of the Algerian national Abdelhamid Abu Zayd. Ansar Din ("Defenders of the Faith"), under the leadership of Iyad ag Ghali and composed of Tuareg, Arabs, and other ethnicities, constituted a third group seeking to establish *sharīʿa* in northern Mali, while the Movement for Unity and Jihad in West Africa, or Mujao (*Mouvement pour l'unicité et le jihad en Afrique de l'Ouest*), drew its membership from across the expanse of West Africa. Having splintered from AQMI in October of 2011, Mujao allied with Ansar Din and was subsequently joined in Gao by Mokhtar Belmokhtar, another Algerian.

Differences between the groups were exposed on 27 June 2012, with Mujao driving the MNLA out of Gao. Its citizens had come to see the MNLA as oppressive and racist, their anger further fueled by reports of rapine and violent seizures of property. Ansar Din and Mujao enjoyed some success in recruiting the local population, but the introduction of *sharīʿa* was brutal, with amputations, public floggings, and stonings, while in Timbuktu shrines were destroyed. At least four hundred thousand citizens would flee northern Mali.

The January 2013, French-led intervention of *Operation Serval* would return a modicum of stability in the north under a reconstituted Malian central authority. But the conflagration of the preceding twelve months had halted, at least temporarily, the important work of preserving Timbuktu's intellectual treasures, with their basis in the period under study here.

The twenty-first century was not the first instance in which the modern world reflected on West African anterior history, though prior occasions were largely artistic in nature. Yambo Ouologuem's 1968 novel, *Le Devoir de Violence* ("Bound to Violence"), is a critical assessment of West African sovereignty (and complicity) in self-destructive processes, including slaving, that begin with fictional Nakem, an empire representing medieval Mali. Winner of the Prix Renaudot, the controversy engendered by *Le Devoir de Violence* was more than matched by the exuberance of *The Lion King*, the proverbial flipside of Ouologuem's written coinage. Appearing in 1994 as a musical film and later as a theatrical adaptation, its similarities with oral traditions have sparked debate over its relationship to the Sunjata epic. In any case, through both real-world events and artistic creativity, enactments of West Africa's medieval past have filtered into contemporary consciousness.

Even so, in turning from the popular to the academic, histories purporting to convey a sense of global development since antiquity continue to ignore Africa's contributions, not merely as the presumed site of human origins, but as a full participant in its cultural, technological, and political innovations.

The full trajectory of West African history begins with early polities along the Niger and Senegal Rivers, where human trafficking was overshadowed by the trade in gold. This pattern would change toward the end of the fifth/eleventh century, with militant states beginning to invest heavily in slaving.

The notion of *bilād as-sūdān* appears to take much of its practical implication from this expansion in trafficking, inviting invidious comparisons with other parts of the world. However, the spatial imagination of a "land of the blacks" involves an imprecise and problematic concept that vacillates and equivocates with respect to areas in the Sahara and North Africa.

In the full Savannah, fabled Manden would emerge as victor in a monumental struggle, establishing the foundations of West Africa's most illustrious empire, its founder's accomplishments so far-reaching as to be immortalized. Sunjata's story is performed in the key of subtextual concern for women's diminished political capacity, his success attributed to their intervention.

Mali would undergo dramatic transformation with the Pilgrimage of *Mansā* Mūsā, arresting the world's attention while enshrining its iconic dimension in written reportage. Mūsā's case for Mali as a transregional power lays the groundwork for Islam's ascent, and while he may not have fully succeeded, Mali's image as a land of unbelievable wealth was burnished. By means of his Islamic bona fides, Mūsā expanded Mali's spatial dimensions from the eastern Niger buckle to the Atlantic Ocean, uniting the Niger, Senegal, and Gambia valleys in unparalleled fashion.

Encumbered by a flawed succession process, Mali may have also fallen victim to its own success, exceeding its capacity to effectively govern lands so vast. A weakened eastern presence encouraged Songhay secession and the emergence of *Sunni* 'Alī, who would wrest the Middle Niger from Mali and the Tuareg, leaving the region reeling from elevated levels of pillage and rapine. With Timbuktu elite families as his most significant challenge, 'Alī's demise would come at the hands of his own lieutenant, in likely alliance with those elites.

Like *Mansā* Mūsā, *Askia al-ḥājj* Muḥammad Ture used the Pilgrimage to legitimize his rule, while embracing an internationalism that privileged relations with the broader Muslim world. In expanding Songhay suzerainty, Muḥammad would again borrow from the Malian paradigm. But unlike the *mansā*, the *askia* embraced a novel approach, pursuing pluralist policies that encouraged the reimagination of Songhay as a multiethnic state. Concubinage proved to be a critical vehicle, with successive Askias the very embodiment of political innovation.

The restoration of Timbuktu's leading families facilitated a culture of erudition never before witnessed in the region, with the secondary literature exaggerating the scholar's political influence, to the neglect of the experiential dimension.

In control of major trade routes and markets, Songhay was also involved in slaving. With Islam's increasing integration, issues of eligibility had a generative effect, their resolution requiring a more precise determination of the disposition of lands and inhabitants at the moment of Islam's introduction. With imperial Songhay, demographic differentiation was also mobilized for juridical purposes, constituting a watershed moment of ethnogenesis.

Songhay's commercial success attracted expatriates, who with servile elites would join the exclusive "people of Songhay." Royal slaves in particular succeeded in exerting an increasingly intrusive as well as determinative level of influence, more than matched in sheer numbers by counterparts moored to latifundia, their use as currency no less important.

As royals engaged in ever-quickening mutual slaughter, the enslaved played an expanding role in state affairs. The unraveling could not have come at a more inconvenient time, with Morocco in need of assets. Songhay's death knell would reverberate for centuries.

West Africa now entered a period of direct contact with Europe. *Mansā* Mūsā could not have foreseen the cataclysm.

NOTES

Chapter 1: The Middle Niger in Pre-Antiquity and Global Context

1. World history texts include William H. McNeil, *A World History* (New York: Oxford U. Press, 1999); Chris Harman, *A People's History of the World* (New York: Verso, 2008); Richard Bulliet, Pamela Crossley, Daniel Headrick, and Steven Hirsch, *The Earth and Its Peoples: A Global History*, 4th ed (Boston: Houghton Mifflin, 2008); Kenneth Pomerantz, *The Great Divergence: Europe, China, and the Making of the Modern World Economy* (Princeton: Princeton U. Press, 2000); Peter Liddel and Andrew Fear, eds., *Historiae Mundi: Studies in Universal History* (London: Duckworth, 2010); B.V. Rao, *World History: From Early Times to AD 2000*, 3rd ed. (Elgin, IL: New Dawn Press, 2006); J.M. Roberts, *The New Penguin History of the World*, 5th ed. (London: Penguin, 2007); ___, *A Short History of the World* (New York: Oxford U. Press, 1993); ___, *The New History of the World* (New York: Oxford U. Press, 2003); Peter Stearns, *Globalization in World History* (London and New York: Routledge, 2010); Robert L. Tignor, Jeremy Adelman, Stephen Aron, and Stephen Kotkin, *Worlds Together, Worlds Apart: A History of the World from the Beginnings of Humankind to the Present*, 2nd ed (New York: W.W. Norton, 2008); Ranajit Guha, *History at the Limit of World-History* (New York: Columbia U. Press, 2002); Pamela Kyle Crossley, *What is Global History?* (Cambridge: Polity Press, 2008); Jared Diamond, *Guns, Germs, and Steel: The Fates of Human Societies* (New York: W.W. Norton, 1997).

2. See Jane Burbank and Frederick Cooper, *Empires in World History: Power and the Politics of Difference* (Princeton: Princeton U. Press, 2010); John Darwin, *After Tamerlane: The Global History of Empire since 1945* (London: Bloomsbury, 2008); David Abernathy, *The Dynamics of Global Dominance: European Overseas Empires, 1415–1980* (New Haven: Yale U. Press, 2000); Ronald Findlay and Kevin H. O'Rourke, *Power and Plenty: Trade, Power, and the World Economy in the Second Millennium* (Princeton: Princeton U. Press, 2007).

3. McNeil, *A World History*, 113. The author cites three sources, all published in the 1950s.

4. Ibid, 275–78.

5. "At this point we leave Africa, not to mention it again. For it is no historical part of the World; it has no movement or development to exhibit." G.W.F. Hegel, *The Philosophy of History*, trans. J. Sibree (New York: Dover Publications, 1956), 99.

6. Examples of big history include Cynthia Stokes Brown, *Big History: From the Big Bang to the Present* (New York: New Press, 2007); Fred Spier, *The Structure of Big History* (Amsterdam, Amsterdam U. Press, 1996); ___, *Big History and the Future of Humanity* (West Sussex, UK: Wiley-Blackwell, 2010); Donald R. Kelley, "The Rise of Prehistory," *Journal of World History* 14:1 (March 2003): 17–36; David Christian, *Maps of Time: An Introduction to Big History* (Berkeley: U. of California Press,

2004); Tom Gehrels, *Survival through Evolution: From Multiverse to Modern Society* (Charleston, S.C.: BookSurge, 2007).

7. The groundbreaking publications of the McIntoshes include Roderick J. McIntosh, *Ancient Middle Niger: Urbanism and the Self-Organizing Landscape* (Cambridge: Cambridge U. Press, 2005); ___, *The Peoples of the Middle Niger: The Island of Gold* (Oxford: Blackwell Publishers, Inc., 1988, 1998); ___, "Clustered Cities of the Middle Niger: Alternative Routes to Authority in Prehistory," in David M. Anderson and Richard Rathbone, eds., *Africa's Urban Past* (Oxford: James Currey and Portsmouth, N.H.: Heinemann, 2000); ___, "Africa's Storied Past. Once a 'People Without History,' Africans Explore a Vibrant Precolonial Landscape," *Archaeology* 52 (4): 54–60, 83; Susan Keech McIntosh, ed., *Excavations at Jenne-jeno, Hambarketolo, and Kaniana (Inland Niger Delta, Mali): The 1981 Season* (Berkeley: U. of California Press, 1995); ___, "A Reconsideration of Wangāra/Palolus, Island of Gold," *Journal of African History* 22 (1981): 145–58; ___, "Changing Perspectives of West Africa's Past: Archaeological Research since 1988," *Journal of Archaeological Research* 2:2 (1994): 165–98; Roderick J. McIntosh and Susan McIntosh, "The Inland Niger Delta before the Empire of Mali: Evidence from Jenne-jeno," *Journal of African History* 22 (1981): 1–22; ___, "Recent Archaeological Research and Dates from West Africa," *Journal of African History* 27 (1986): 413–42; ___, "Cities without Citadels: Understanding Urban Origins along the Middle Niger," in T. Shaw, P. Sinclair, B. Andah, and A. Okpoko, eds., *The Archaeology of Africa: Foods, Metals, and Towns* (London: Routledge, 1993).

8. McIntosh, *Ancient Middle Niger*, 73.

9. Ibid, 81–89.

10. Ibid, 89–90, 174–91. Lydon writes that the "western African" perspective locates the *sāḥil* on the Sahara's northern fringe (subsequently misunderstood and redirected to the south by the French), while from the Algerian vantage point the *sāḥil* constitutes the southern fringe. As the Sahara is analogous to a body of water, and most such bodies have more than one shore, there is no inherent contradiction here. See Ghislaine Lydon, *On Trans-Saharan Trails: Islamic Law, Trade Networks, and Cross-Cultural Exchange in Nineteenth-Century Western Africa* (Cambridge: Cambridge U. Press, 2012), 29–30.

11. The consensus is that Dia, Diagha, Diakha, and Zāgha are variations of the same town, but for a dissenting view, see Claude Meillassoux, "L'itinéraire d'Ibn Battuta de Walata à Mali," *Journal of African History* (13) 1972: 389–95.

12. Ibid, 47–48; Téréba Togola, *Archaeological Investigations of Iron Age Sites in the Mema Region, Mali (West Africa)* (Oxford: Hadrian Books, 2008); Sam Nixon, "Excavating Es-Souk-Tadmakka (Mali): New Archaeological Investigations of Early Islamic Trans-Saharan Trade," *Azania: Archaeological Research in Africa* 44 (2009): 217–55. The Late Stone Age in West Africa is from 40,000 BCE to the first millennium CE.

13. R. McIntosh, *Peoples of the Middle Niger*, 57–61.

14. Ibid, 113–14, 257–65; Noemie Arazi, "An Archaeological Survey in the Songhay Heartland of Mali," *Nyame Akuma* 52 (1999): 25–43; ___, "Tracing History in Dia, in the Inland Niger Delta of Mali—Archaeology, Oral Traditions and Written Sources." (PhD Thesis, University College London, 2005).

15. R. McIntosh, *Ancient Middle Niger*, 168–70.

16. S. McIntosh, ed., *Excavations at Jenne-jeno, Hambarketolo, and Kaniana*, 375–76.

17. R. McIntosh, *Ancient Middle Niger*, 152–53.

18. S. McIntosh, ed., *Excavations at Jenne-jeno, Hambarketolo, and Kaniana*, 386.

19. According to Pliny the Elder's 19 CE report, a Garamatian capital of "Garama" was in the Fezzan. Timothy Insoll, *The Archaeology of Islam in Sub-Saharan Africa* (Cambridge: Cambridge U. Press, 2003), 211.

20. R. McIntosh, *Ancient Middle Niger*, 175–76.

21. R. McIntosh, *Peoples of the Middle Niger*, 194–99; D.P. Park, "Prehistoric Timbuktu and Its Hinterland," *Antiquity* 84 (2010): 1076–88.

22. Mamadou Cissé, Susan Keech McIntosh, Laure Dussubieux, Thomas Fenn, Daphne Gallagher, and Abigail Chipps Smith, eds., "Excavations at Gao Saney: New Evidence for Settlement Growth, Trade, and Interaction on the Niger Bend in the First Millennium CE," *Journal of African Archaeology* 11 (2013): 9–27; Timothy Insoll, "Iron Age Gao: An Archaeological Contribution," *Journal of African History* 38 (1997), 1–30: ____, ed., *Urbanism, Archaeology and Trade, Further Observations on the Gao Region (Mali): The 1996 Field Season Results* (Oxford: Archaeopress, 2000); Shoichiro Takezawa and Mamadou Cissé, "Discovery of the Earliest Royal Palace in Gao and Its Implications for the History of West Africa," *Cahiers d'études africaines* 208 (2012): 813–44; R.H. MacDonald and K.C. MacDonald, "A Preliminary report on the Faunal Remains Recovered from Gao Ancien and Gao Saney (1993 Season)," in Insoll, *Islam, Archaeology and History*, 124–26; Laure Dussubieux, C.M. Kusimba, V. Gogte, S.B. Kusimba, B. Gratuze, and R. Oka, "The Trading of Ancient Glass Beads: New Analytical Data from South Asian and East African Soda-Alumina Glass Beads," *Archaeometry* 50 (2008): 797–821; Mamadou Cissé, "Archaeological Investigations of Early Trade and Urbanism at Gao Saney (Mali)." PhD Thesis, Rice University, 2011; C. Flight, "The Medieval Cemetery at Sane: A History of the Site from 1939 to 1950," in Jean Devisse, ed., *Le sol, la parole, et l'écrit: 2000 ans d'histoire africaine: mélanges en homage à Raymond Mauny* (Paris: Bibliothèque d'Histoire d'Outre-mer, 1981), 91–107; Raymond Mauny, *Tableau géographique de l'Ouest africain au moyen âge, d'après les sources écrites, la tradition et l'archéologie* (Dakar : IFAN, 1961); ____, "Découverte à Gao d'un fragment de poterie émaillé du moyen âge musulman," *Hespéris* 39 (1952): 514–16.

23. R. McIntosh, *Peoples of the Middle Niger*, 200–203.

24. R. McIntosh, *Ancient Middle Niger*, 177.

25. Ibid, 177–79.

Chapter 2: Early Gao

1. The seminal work is Nehemiah Levtzion's *Ancient Ghana and Mali* (New York and London: Africana Publishing Co., 1973). Publications since include Anne Haour's *Rulers, Warriors, Traders, Clerics: The Central Sahel and the North Sea, 800–1500* (New York: Oxford U. Press, 2007), a comparison by category of developments in the central Sudan with those in Europe's North Sea.

2. See 'Abd al-Rahmān b. 'Abd Allāh b. 'Imrān al-Sa'dī, *Ta'rīkh as-sūdān* (henceforth *TS*), ed. and trans. O. Houdas (Paris: Librairie d'Amérique et d'Orient Adrien-Maisonneuve, 1900); Maḥmūd Ka'ti and Ibn al-Mukhtār, *Ta'rīkh al-fattāsh* (henceforth *TF*), ed. and trans. O. Houdas and M. Delafosse (Paris: Librairie d'Amérique et d'Orient Adrien-Maisonneuve, 1913). For an English translation of *Ta'rīkh as-sūdān*, see John O. Hunwick, *Timbuktu and the Songhay Empire. Al-Sa'dī's Ta'rīkh al-sūdān down to 1613 and other Contemporary Documents* (Leiden: E.J. Brill, 1999). See also the anonymous, untitled work written between 1067/1657 and 1079/1669 and published as second appendix to French translation of *TF* in Houdas and Delafosse, taken from introductory material and enfolding significant material from *TF*, called "*Notice historique*" by Hunwick, henceforth *NH*.

3. Paulo F. de Moraes Farias, in his *Arabic Medieval Inscriptions from the Republic of Mali: Epigraphy, Chronicles, and Songhay-Tuāreg History* (Oxford: Oxford U. Press, 2003), and in "Intellectual Innovation and Reinvention of the Sahel: The Seventeenth-Century Timbuktu Chronicles," in Shamil Jeppie and Souleymane B. Diagne, eds., *The Meanings of Timbuktu* (Cape Town: HSTC Press, 2008), 95–107, also argues the authors carefully crafted the chronicles, but to achieve ideological effect.

4. "All these are assigned," states al-Ya'qūbī, "to the kingdom of Kawkaw." J.F.P. Hopkins and Nehemia Levtzion, *Corpus of Early Arabic Sources for West African History* (Cambridge: Cambridge U. Press, 1981), 21 (hereafter, *Corpus*). See also Joseph M. Cuoq, *Recueil des sources arabes concernant l'Afrique occidentale du XIIIe au XVIe siècle (Bilad al-Sudan)* (Paris: Éditions du Centre National de la Recherche Scientifique, 1985), 52 (hereafter, *Recueil*). Of Ghana, al-Ya'qūbī wrote: "Then there is the kingdom of Ghana, whose king is also very powerful."

5. *Corpus*, 113.

6. Ibid, in Yāqūt, 174.

7. The evidence certainly qualifies Gao as a "state," defined as a "centralised political organization that consists of a territory, a population and a system of institutional power with well-established social divisions." Michal Tymowski, *The Origins and Structures of Political Institutions in Pre-Colonial Black Africa: Dynastic Monarchy, Taxes and Tributes, War and Slavery, Kinship and Territory* (Lewiston, NY: Edwin Mellen Press, 2009), 6, 10–11.

8. Mamadou Cissé, Susan Keech McIntosh, Laure Dussubieux, Thomas Fenn, Daphne Gallagher, and Abigail Chipps Smith, eds., "Excavations at Gao Saney: New Evidence for Settlement Growth, Trade, and Interaction on the Niger Bend in the First Millennium CE," *Journal of African Archaeology* 11 (2013): 9–27; Timothy Insoll, "Iron Age Gao: An Archaeological Contribution." *Journal of African History* 38 (1997): 4–11; Roderick J. McIntosh, *Ancient Middle Niger: Urbanism and the Self-Organizing Landscape* (New York: Cambridge U. Press, 2005), 148–49; ____, *The Peoples of the Middle Niger: The Island of Gold* (Oxford: Blackwell Publishers, Inc., 1988, 1998), 88–150; Zakari Dramani-Issifou, "Les Songhay: dimension historique," in Jean Devisse, ed., *Vallée du Niger* (Paris: Éditions de la Réunion des musées nationaux, 1993), 151–61; Boubou Hama, *Histoire des Songhay* (Paris: Présence Africaine, 1968); _____, *Histoire traditionelle d'un people: les Zarma-Songhay* (Paris: Présence africaine, 1967); Jean Gallais, *Hommes du Sahel: Espaces-Temps et Pouvoir. La Delta intérieur du Niger, 1960–1980* (Paris: Flammarion, 1984); Jean Rouch, *Les*

Songhay (Paris: Presses Universitaires de France, 1954); Jean Rouch, "Les Sorkawa, pecheurs itinerants du Moyen Niger," *Africa* 20 (1950): 5–21; ____, "Contribution à l'histoire des Songhay," *Mémoires de l'IFAN* 29 (1953): 137–259; P. G. Harris, "Notes on Yauri (Sokoto Province, Nigeria)," *Journal of the Royal Anthropological Institute*, 60 (1930): 283–334. One tradition derives "Gao" from the fruit (*gā'u*) of a local tree (*hanam*), while another maintains Kukiya is as old as Pharaonic Egypt. *NH*, 329–30; *TS* 3/6–7.

9. On the Sorko and other fisherfolk such as the Somono (a Bambara/Bamana or Mande term, more a caste than an ethnicity), Sorogo (or Bozo, the designation of outsiders), and Fono, see Dierk Lange, "From Mande to Songhay: Towards a Political and Ethnic History of Medieval Gao," *Journal of African History* 35 (1994): 275–301, specifically 295–99.

10. See N.A. Bako, "La Question du peuplement dendi dans la partie septentrionale de la République populaire du Bénin: le cas du Borgou" (Mémoire de maîtrise d'historique ronéoté, Université nationale du Bénin, Cotonou, 1988–89), in Dramani-Issifou, "Les Songhay," 20, 34–37, where a Muslim hailing from Gao reports (in Benin) that the Songhay originated in Yemen, reaching West Africa in stages. The claim was also made by *Askia al-ḥājj* Muḥammad Ture.

11. Placing a Greek astronomical system that divided the world into seven long latitudinal strips or "climes" (*iqlīm* in Arabic, extending from east to west) into conversation with the Persian *kishwar* system featuring regions (also seven in number), Arabic-writing geographers transitioned from viewing the earth as flat to spherical, conceptualizing landmass as a patch on the surface of water, with 180 degrees its maximum angular extent. The regions/climes were designated Bābil (at the center), Ḥijāz (Arabia), Miṣr (Egypt), Rūm (Europe), Hind (India), Ṣīn (China), and Ya'jūj wa Ma'jūj (Gog and Magog). See Hopkins and Levtzion, "The Climes," in *Corpus*, xv-xx.

12. Ibid, 27–28.

13. See John O. Hunwick, "Gao and the Almoravids Revisited: Ethnicity, Political Change and the Limits of Interpretation," *Journal of African History* 35 (1994): 271–72; ____, "Gao and the Almoravids: a hypothesis," in B. Swartz and R.A. Dumett, eds., *West African Cultural Dynamics: Archaeological and Historical Perspectives* (The Hague: Walter de Gruyter, 1979), 413–30; Dierk Lange, "From Mande to Songhay"; ____, "Les rois de Gao-Sané et les Almoravides," *Journal of African History* 32 (1991): 251–75. With Insoll, "Iron Age Gao," we have resolution to some of these issues. Also see Jean Sauvaget, "Notes préliminaires sur les épitaphs royales de Gao," *Revue des Études Islamiques 16* (1948), 7–8; ____, "Les épitaphs royales de Gao," *Bulletin de l'Institut Français* (later *Fondamental*) *d'Afrique Noire (IFAN)* 12 (1950): 418–40; Madeleine Viré, "Notes sur trois épitaphs royales de Gao," *Bulletin de l'Institut Français* (later *Fondamental*) *d'Afrique Noire (IFAN)* 20 (1958): 375, n. 2; P.F. de Moraes Farias, "Du nouveau sur les stèles de Gao: les épitaphs du prince Yāmā Kūrī et du roi F.n.dā (XIIIe siècle)," *Bulletin de l'Institut Français* (later *Fondamental*) *d'Afrique Noire (IFAN)* 26 (1974): 516–17; Farias, *Arabic Medieval Inscriptions*.

14. Independent of archaeological studies is the tradition that fourth/tenth-century Gao was originally located on the *gurma* side. *NH*, 329–30.

15. Shoichiro Takezawa and Mamadou Cissé, "Discovery of the Earliest Royal Palace in Gao and Its Implications for the History of West Africa," *Cahiers d'études*

africaines 208 (2012): 813–44. Gao-Saney's proximity to the Wādī Gangaber suggests arguments over whether the sources refer to the (Niger) river or the wādī as Gao's precise location are not worth the investment, as the distance from Gadei to Gao-Saney is less than seven kilometers. The debate is actually as old as al-Idrisī, who records "many of the Sūdān say that the town of Kawkaw is on the bank of the [*sic*] canal while others say that it is on a river which flows into the Nīl [the Niger]." *Corpus*, 113.

16. Takezawa and Cissé, "Discovery of the Earliest Royal Palace in Gao and Its Implications for the History of West Africa." The authors claim the residence in Gao Ancien is the first "'medieval' royal palace in West Africa" (835).

17. Insoll, "Iron Age Gao," 19–22; Cissé et al, "Excavations at Gao Saney," 9–27.

18. *Corpus*, 45. See also T. Lewicki, "L'état nord-africain de Tāhert et ses relations avec le Soudan occidentale à la fin du VIIIe au IXe siècle," *Cahiers d'études africaines* 8 (1962): 513–35; ____, "À propos du nom de l'oasis de Koufra chez les géographes arabes du XIe et du XIIe siècle,' *Journal of African History* 6 (1965): 295–306; ____, "Les origines et l'islamisation de la ville de Tādmakka d'après les sources arabes," in *2,000 ans d'histoire africaine: le sol, la parole at l'écrit. Mélanges en homage à Raymond Mauny* (Paris: Société française d'histoire d'outre-mer, 1981), 1: 439–44.

19. *Corpus*, 97.

20. Insoll, "Iron Age Gao," 23–29; Insoll, *The Archaeology of Islam in Sub-Saharan Africa*, 241–45. Insoll speculates the Arabic sources rarely mention ivory because the animals did not undergo ritual slaughter.

21. Al-Bakrī says the salt came from "an underground mine at Tūtak, in Berber country." *Corpus*, 87, 174.

22. Al-Muhallabī is quoted in Yāqūt b. 'Abd Allāh al-Hamawī al-Rūmī's *Mu'jam al-buldān* ("Dictionary of Nations"), published in 609/1212. *Corpus*, 174.

23. Abū 'Ubayd 'Abd Allāh b. 'Abd al-'Azīz al-Bakrī, *Kitāb al-masālik wa-'l-mamālik*, as *Kitāb al-mughrib fī dhikr bilād ifrīqiya wa-'l-maghrib*, with French title *Description de l'Afrique septentrionale*, ed. Baron William MacGuckin de Slane (Algiers, 1857); *Corpus*, 87; *Recueil*, 77–78, 182–84.

24. Lange ("From Mande to Songhay," 283–84) invokes al-Zuhrī's claim that Kawkaw was located on an island, but al-Zuhrī conflates Kawkaw with territory contiguous with contemporary Ethiopia.

25. Reformist Islam in West Africa usually refers to post-eighteenth century efforts to promote broader conversion and stricter adherence to Islam, often under the political leadership of clerics. By employing the concept here, I call attention to resonances between earlier and subsequent periods.

26. In one tradition (in the *Notice historique*) he travels with three other men and arrives in Kukiya, with the others eventually settling in Bornu, Baghana, and Walata/Biru; and in another account (also in *NH*), he is a giant apparently traveling alone, arriving in Gao and siring a child with an enslaved girl, who goes on to become ruler. In yet a third report (in *TS*) al-Ayaman arrives in Kukiya with a brother and is exalted after killing an oppressive, demonic "fish-king." Altogether, the *ta'rīkhs* provide a line of descent to a land of renown, the effect of Islam's subsequent influence, but also maybe a gesture toward long and extensive interaction between Sahara and Sahel. *NH*, 326–32; *TS*, 3–5/5–9. On West African connections to the Middle East,

see Michael A. Gomez, *Black Crescent: The Experience and Legacy of African Muslims in the Americas* (Cambridge: Cambridge U. Press, 2005).

27. H.T. Norris, *Saharan Myth and Saga* (Oxford: Oxford U. Press, 1972), 26–36, describes "the Himyarite myth" as "ancient" in North Africa, especially in Mauritania and among the Ṣanhāja, noting that Ibn Khaldūn dismissed it as "silly."

28. This could be read as a response to North Africa's Arabization, beginning with the fifth/eleventh-migration of the Banū Hilāl and Banū Sulaym from upper Egypt into North Africa, possibly in response to a stressed environment, possibly the Fāṭimid's way of punishing the Zīrids for abandoning Shī'a principles. The Banū Sulaym would concentrate in Libya's Cyrenaica, then later move to Tunisia, but the Banū Hilāl are said to have migrated well into Morocco. As the Banū Hilāl and Banū Sulaym purportedly hail from the Arabian Peninsula's Ḥijāz and Najd regions, the emphasis on Yemen may have been a sort of one-upmanship. Perhaps also in the fifth/eleventh century, but certainly by the ninth/fifteenth century, the Banū Ḥassān, who claim descent from the Ma'qil of the Arabian Peninsula, also moved into what is now Morocco and Mauritania, the Yemeni claim possibly a response to them as well. See Jamil Abun-Nasr, *A History of the Maghrib in the Islamic Period* (Cambridge: Cambridge U. Press, 1975), 85–86; H.T. Norris, *The Arab Conquest of the Western Sahara: Studies of the Historical Events, Religious Beliefs and Social Customs Which Made the Remotest Sahara a Part of the Arab World* (London: Longman, 1986), 26–27; Bruce S. Hall, *A History of Race in Muslim West Africa, 1600–1960* (Cambridge: Cambridge U. Press, 2011), 59.

29. *Ta'rīkh as-sūdān* appears to do the same. *TS* 2–3/4–5; Hunwick, *Timbuktu and the Songhay Empire*, 3–4. *Ta'rīkh as-sūdān* lists thirteen rulers between al-Ayaman and Kusuy/Kotso-Muslim: Zakoi, Takoi, Akoi, Kū, 'Alī Fay, Biyai Kumai, Biyai, Kurai, Yama Kurwai, Yama, Yama Danka Kība'u, Kūkurai, and Kinkin; and sixteen after Kusuy/Kotso-Muslim: Kusuy/Kotso Dāriya, Hen Kuz Wanga Dam, Biyai Koi Kīmi, Nintā Sanai, Biyai Kaina Kinba, Kaina Shanyunbu, Tib, Yama Dād, Fadazu, 'Alī Kur, Bīr Falaku, Yāsiboi, Dūru, Zunku Bāru, Bisi Bāru, and Badā. *Notice historique* has the same number of initial rulers of Gao, 14, though the names do not always align with those in *TS*: al-Yemen, Wa'ai, Kaien, Takai, Mata-Kai, Māli Kai, Māli Biyai, Biyai Kīma, Bai, Kirai, Yama Kalawai, Yama Dumbu, Yama Janaa, and Jatakorai, "all infidels who worshiped idols." It then lists "Kosho/Kotso Muslim, who was the first Muslim," after whom reigned another 14 *Zā* rulers: Kotso Dāria, Hūnabonūa Kodam, Yama-Kitsi, Barai, Bibai Kayna, Simanbao, Fanda Diarua, Yama Dāa, Arkūr Jua, Barai, Yassi-Bo'o, Bāru, Dūru, and Bitsi Barū, "the last of the *Jā's*." *NH*, 329–34. However, the author of *Notice historique* apparently thought Kusuy/Kotso-Muslim ruled later than ca. 400/1009–10, contesting the claim he began the practice of circumcision in Gao by citing Maḥmūd Ka'ti's statement (that the people of Gao had become Muslims between 471/1079 and 475/1082) as evidence Islam had already "existed among them." *NH*, 332–33.

30. Farias, *Arabic Medieval Inscriptions*, 166–70.

31. Farias persuasively argues "the Timbuktu kinglists can contribute very little to the interpretation of the epigraphic evidence, which is much older than them." (*Arabic Medieval Inscriptions*, 170). In contrast, Lange attempts to reconcile the ruler-lists with the tombstone inscriptions, arguing the former were deliberately

rearranged in the seventeenth century (Lange, "From Mande to Songhay," 276–81, 288–99).

32. Farias' rather dim view of the *ta'rīkhs* allows little space for their useful engagement. For example, see *Arabic Medieval Inscriptions*, 34, 69–77, 169–70.

33. *TS*, 3/4–5. To be more precise, the Arabic actually says, "And the one who converted to Islam was *Zā* Kusuy," implying he was the first ruler to do so.

34. *Corpus*, 87.

35. In this schema, nudity represented the lowest level of human existence, followed by clothing of animal skins, then raiment from processed materials such as wool and silk, signifying the threshold of true civilization.

36. *NH*, 332–33. Mauro Nobili and Mohamed Shahid Mathee, "Towards a New Study of the So-Called Tārīkh al-fattāsh," *History in Africa* 42 (2015): 37–73, contest the authorship of Maḥmūd Ka'ti. I explain my divergent view in chapter 8.

37. Farias, *Arabic Medieval Inscriptions*, 33–35, 127–34, has produced a wonderful study of this type of evidence.

38. *Corpus*, 98–99.

39. Ibid, 85, 149–50; Farias, *Arabic Medieval Inscriptions*, 134–49; Levtzion, *Ancient Ghana and Mali*, 29. 'Ibāḍism, a branch of Kharijism (*al-khawārij*), emerged in the first/seventh century, and among its distinctive beliefs is its insistence that the Muslim ruler need not be a descendant of the Qurasyh, the tribal affiliation of the Prophet.

40. Paulo F. de Moraes Farias, "The Oldest Extant Writing of West Africa: Medieval epigraphs from Essuk, Saney, and Egef-n-Tawaqqast (Mali)," *Journal des africanistes* 60 (2) 1990: 65–113.

41. Hunwick, "Gao and the Almoravids"; ____, "Gao and the Almoravids Revisited"; Lange, "From Mande to Songhay"; Sauvaget, "Notes préliminaires sur les épitaphs royales de Gao"; ____, "Les épitaphs royales de Gao"; Viré, "Notes sur trois épitaphs royales de Gao"; E. Lévi-Provençal, *Inscriptions arabes d'Espagne*, 3 vols. (Leiden: E.J. Brill and Paris: Maisonneuve et Larose, 1931); C. Burckhalter, "Listening for Silences in Almoravid History," *History in Africa* 19 (1992): 103–31.

42. *Corpus*, 84, 98–99.

43. Farias advances this argument in "The Oldest Extant Writing in West Africa," 93. Ghana and Tadmekka may also have been contesting control over slaving activities. *Corpus*, 98–99.

44. This raises the question of Mande activity in the northern cap of the Middle Niger floodplain. See Farias, *Arabic Medieval Inscriptions*, 209–10; Hunwick, "Gao and the Almoravids Revisited," 257–58; Lange, "From Mande to Songhay," 284–93.

45. Farias, *Arabic Medieval Inscriptions*, 123–27.

46. Sauvaget, "Notes préliminaires sur les épitaphs royales de Gao"; ____, "Les épitaphs royales de Gao"; Farias, *Arabic Medieval Inscriptions*, 152–53; Hunwick, "Gao and the Almoravids Revisited," 268–71; Lange, "From Mande to Songhay," 276–81, 288–99. The names: *Malik* 'Abu 'Abd Allāh Muḥammad b. 'Abd Allāh b. Zāghī/Zāghay (d. 494/1100), *Malik* 'Abū Bakr b. 'Abū Quhāfa (d. 503/1110), and *Malik* Yāmā b. Kumā b. Zāghī/Zāghay (d. 514/1120), also known as 'Umar b. al-Khattāb. However, a similar pattern occurs, sans apocryphal hint, in imperial Songhay over four hundred years later, with *Askia* Muḥammad and *Farans* Abū Bakr, 'Uthmān, and *Kanfāri* 'Umar.

47. Sauvaget, "Notes préliminaires sur les épitaphs royales de Gao"; ____, "Les épitaphs royales de Gao"; Farias, *Arabic Medieval Inscriptions*, 152–53; Hunwick, "Gao and the Almoravids Revisited," 268–71; Lange, "From Mande to Songhay," 276–81, 288–99.

48. *Corpus*, 111.

49. Farias, "The Oldest Extant Writing of West Africa," 79–91.

50. Farias, *Arabic Medieval Inscriptions*, 164–70.

51. *Corpus*, 188–89, 353–54; *Recueil*, 239–40; Dierk Lange, *Le Dīwān des sultans du [Kanem-] Bornū: Chronologie et histoire d'un royaume africain* (Wiesbaden, 1977); ____, "Un texte de Maqrīzī sur 'les races des Sūdān," *Annales islamologiques* 15 (1979): 187–209; H.R. Palmer, *The Bornu, Sahara, and Sudan* (London: J. Murray, 1936); Abdullahi Smith, "The Early States of the Central Sudan," in in J.F. Ade Ajayi and Michael Crowder, eds., *History of West Africa*, 1st ed. (London: Longman, 1971), 1:1:58–201; Louis Brenner, *The Shehus of Kukawa* (Oxford: Clarendon Press, 1973); Dierk Lange, *Ancient Kingdoms of West Africa: Africa-Centered and Canaanite-Israelite Perspectives* (Dettelbach: Verlag J.H. Röll, 2004); ____, *Le Dīwān des sultans du Kanem-Bornu* (Wiesbaden: Franz Steiner Verlag, 1977); Yves Urvoy, *L'empire du Bornou* (Paris: Larose, 1949); Bawuro Barkindo, "The Early States of the Central Sudan: Kanem, Borno, and Some of Their Neighbours to c. 1500 AD," in J.F. Ade Ajayi and Michael Crowder, eds., *History of West Africa*, 3rd ed. (New York: Longman, 1985), 1:225–54.

52. *Corpus*, 188.

53. The name of the polity is often synonymous with the name of the group occupying it. *Corpus*, 6–7; *Recueil*, 44. These observations do not align with Hall's claim that slavery in the region was "exclusively borne by people defined as 'black'." Hall, *A History of Race in Muslim West Africa*, 30.

54. The dubious 46/666–7 expedition of Umayyad general 'Uqba b. Nāfi' into what is now southern Libya draws upon the reputation of this region. *Corpus*, 12–13.

55. Ibid, 22.

56. Ibid, 41.

57. Ibid, 138.

58. Ibid, 14, 22; *Recueil*, 41.

59. *Corpus*, 172. The other Zawila is Zawīlat al-Mahdiyya in Ifrīqiya (*Corpus*, 399, endnote 14).

60. Ibid, 64.

61. Ibid, 15.

62. The land of Kawar, between Kanem and the Fezzan also challenges conventional ideas about the "land of the blacks." See *Corpus*, 13, 22, 174, 180.

63. Lydon, *On Trans-Saharan Trails*, 29–30.

Chapter 3: The Kingdoms of Ghana: Reform along the Senegal River

1. *Corpus*, 6–8.

2. Ibid, 21, 29, 32.

3. P.J. Munson, "Archaeological Data on the Origin of Cultivation in the Southwestern Sahara and Their Implication for West Africa," in Jack Harlan, Jan M.J. de Wet, and Ann B. Stemler, eds., *Origins of African Plant Domestication* (The Hague: Mouton, 1976), 187–209; ___, "Archaeology and the Prehistoric origins of the Ghana Empire," *Journal of African History* 21 (1980): 457–66; Jean Maley, *Études palynologiques dans le bassin du Tchad et Paléclimatologie de l'Afrique Nord-tropicale de 30,000 ans l'époque actuelle* (Paris: ORSTOM, 1981), 129, 528; McIntosh and Keech McIntosh, "The Inland Niger Delta before the Empire of Mali"; Hall, "Background to the Ghanaian Empire," 75–109; B. Wai Andah, "West Africa before the Seventh Century," *General History of Africa* 2 (Paris: UNESCO, 1981): 593–619; Clyde Aḥmad Waters, "The Migration Routes of the Proto-Mande," *Mankind Quarterly* 27 (1986): 77–96. Waters, pushing the thesis that the Mande did not originate in the Savannah (per linguistic evidence), but rather in the Sahara highlands, extends their Saharan origins back some 8000 years. On the linguistics, see C. Ehret and M. Posnansky, *The Archaeological and Linguistic Reconstruction of African History* (Berkeley: U. of California Press, 1982).

4. Jean Devisse and Boubacar Diallo, "Le seuil du Wagadu," in Jean Devisse, ed., *Vallée du Niger*, 103–108; Susan Keech McIntosh, "Reconceptualizing Early Ghana," *Canadian Journal of African Studies* 42 (2008): 347–73, 599. On Walata/Biru, see Timothy Cleaveland, *Becoming Walāta: A History of Saharan Social Formation and Transformation* (Portsmouth, N.H.: Heinemann, 2002).

5. McIntosh, "Reconceptualizing Early Ghana," 367.

6. Boubacar Diallo, "Les Soninko," in Jean Devisse, ed., *Vallée du Niger*, 134–38. Diallo postulates the Wangāra (or "Gangari") as an antecedent core community who later mixed with Fulbe, Berbers, etc., contrasting with the earlier speculations of Delafosse, who posit the Soninke originating in Masina or Diaga and moving north to settle in Nema, Walata, and "perhaps" Ghana, having been impacted by North African 'Judéo-Syriens' in Masina in the second century CE. See Delafosse, *Haut-Sénégal-Niger*, 1:254–55.

7. *Corpus*, 79.

8. See Levtzion, *Ancient Ghana and Mali*, 16–28; *TS*, 9/18; Hunwick, *Timbuktu and the Songhay Empire*, 13–14; *TF*, 41–42/75–79.

9. *Corpus*, 82, 107–12, 116, 120, 128–29, 186, 287, 320; *TF*, 38/65.

10. David Conrad and Humphrey Fisher, "The Conquest that Never Was: Ghana and the Almoravids, 1076. II. The Local Oral Sources," *History in Africa* 10 (1983): 54. See Charles Monteil, "La légende du Ouagadou et l'origine des Soninké," *Mélanges Ethnologiques* (Dakar: IFAN, 1953), 397, where Monteil says Wagadu means "land of the *wago* (Soninke aristocracy); Abdoulaye Bathily, "A Discussion of the Traditions of Wagadu, with some reference to Ancient Ghana, including a review of oral accounts, Arabic sources and archaeological evidence," *Bulletin de l'Institut Français* (later *Fondamental*) *d'Afrique Noire (IFAN)* 37 (1975): 1–94.

11. Levtzion, *Ancient Ghana and Mali*, 16–18; Charles Monteil, "La légende du Ouagadou et l'origine des Soninkés," *Mélanges Ethnologique*; Maurice Delafosse, *Haut-Sénégal-Niger (Soudan française)*, 3 vols. (Paris: Larose, 1912); ___, "Traditions historiques et légendaries du Soudan occidental traduits d'un manuscrit arabe," *Bulletin du Comité de l'Afrique française: Reseignement coloniaux*, 1913: 293–306,

325–29. 355–68; R. Arnaud, "La singulière légende des Soninké," *Bulletin du Comité d'Afrique française* 1912: 144; J. Vidal, "Le mystère de Ghana," *Bulletin d'Études Historiques et Scientifiques de l'Afrique Occidentale Française* 6 (1923): 512–24; M. Adam, "Légendes historiques du pays de Nioro (Sahel)," *Revue coloniale* (1903): 81–98, 232–48, 354–72, 485–96, 602–20, 734–4; 1904: 117–24, 233–48; L. Tautain, "Légendes et traditions des Soninké relatives à l'empire de Ghana," *Bulletin de Géographie historique et descriptive* (1895): 472–80; Claude Meillassoux, "Histoire et institutions du kafo de Bamako d'aprés la tradition des Niaré," *Cahiers d'Études Africaines* 4 (1963): 188–92; P. Smith, "Les Diakhanké: histoire d'une dispersion," *Bulletin et Mémoire de la Societé d'Anthropologie de Paris* 4 (1965): 238. See also Djibril T. Niane, *Sundiata: An Epic of Old Mali*, trans. G.D. Pickett (Essex, England: Longman, 1960), 32, where the Sisses claim descent from Alexander the Great.

12. Hunwick, *Timbuktu and the Songhay Empire*, 13–14. Abdel Wedoud Ould Cheikh, "Nomadisme, Islam, et pouvoir dans la société maure précoloniale (XIème siècle—XIXème siècle): Essai sur quelques aspects du tribalisme," 3 vols. (Paris: Doctorat d'État, 1985), 1:161, also mentions (though somewhat inaccurately) the "more or less mythical" accounts of ruling dynasties in the Savannah and Sahel.

13. As opposed to a two-month journey between Sijilmasa and Awdaghust, al-Bakrī says fifteen days separated Awdaghust from Ghana. *Corpus*, 22, 36, 46–49, 67–68, 168.

14. Ibid, 68, 168.

15. Ibid, 68. Al-Bakrī has even more to say about the sexual virtues of these women.

16. As will be discussed, I take a somewhat divergent view from three important discussions on race in the Sahel: Hall, *A History of Race in Muslim West Africa*; Chouki El Hamel, *Black Morocco: A History of Slavery, Race, and Islam* (Cambridge: Cambridge U. Press, 2013); and James Webb, *Desert Frontier: Ecological and Economic Change along the Western Sahel, 1600–1850* (Madison: U. of Wisconsin Press, 1995). All three posit a strong sense of "race" that antedates (but is obviously impacted by) the coming of Islam into the region, while I place greater emphasis on Islamic discursive processes.

17. *Corpus*, 45, 65–66, 139. Midrār was either a black man or a smith.

18. Al-Bakrī: "When the women of Awghām saw his dead body they threw themselves into wells or committed suicide in other ways out of grief for him or being too proud to be possessed by white men." Ibid, 69.

19. McIntosh, *Ancient Middle Niger*, 13; Albert Bonnel de Mézières, "Note sur ses récentes découvertes, d'après un télégramme adressé par lui, le 23 mars 1914, à M. le gouverneur Clozel," *Comptes-rendus des séances de l'Académie des Inscriptions et Belles-Lettres* 58 (1917): 253–57; Raymond Mauny, *Tableau géographique*; ___, "The Question of Ghana," *Journal of the International African Institute* 24 (1954): 200–13; Raymond Mauny and Paul Thomassey, "Campagne de fouilles à Koumbi Saleh," *Bulletin de l'Institut Français* (later *Fondamental*) *d'Afrique Noire (IFAN)*13 (1951): 438–62; Sophie Berthier, *Recherches archéologiques sur la capitale de l'empire de Ghana: Étude d'un secteur, d'habitat à Koumbi Saleh, Mauritanie: Campagnes II-III-IV-V (1975–1976)-(1980–1981)* (Oxford: Archaeopress, 1997). One hypothesis suggests "large-scale storage facilities" at neighboring Awdaghust were sufficient to

supply both Awdaghust and Kumbi Saleh's estimated population of 15,000 to 20,000. Augustin Hall, "Background to the Ghana Empire: Archaeological Investigations on the Transition to Statehood in the Dhar Tichitt Region (Mauritania)," *Journal of Anthropological Archaeology* 4 (1985): 74–75; Insoll, *The Archaeology of Islam in Sub-Saharan Africa*, 228. The estimate is based on Mauny, *Tableau géographique*.

20. *Corpus*, 79–80. The aforementioned archeological literature questions a bifurcated capital, as does my own assessment.

21. Ibid, 80–81.

22. Ibid, 80.

23. Ibid, 79. Basī was the predecessor of then-ruler *Tunka* Manīn, ascending the throne in 460/1067–8.

24. Ibid, 80–81.

25. Ibid, 79. But see Nehemia Levtzion, "Was Royal Succession in Ancient Ghana Matrilineal?" *International Journal of African Historical Studies* 5 (1972): 91–93.

26. See, for example, Yves Hazemann, "Un outil de la conquête coloniale: l'école des otages de Saint-Louis," in Jean Boulègue, ed., *Contributions à l'histoire du Sénégal* (Paris, 1987), 135–60; Denise Bouche, "Les écoles françaises au Soudan à l'époque de la conquête. 1884–1900," *Cahiers d'études africaines* 22 (1966): 228–67; Louis Faidherbe, *Le Sénégal: la France dans l'Afrique occidentale* (Paris: Hachette, 1889); Benjamin N. Lawrence, Emily Lynn Osborn, and Richard Roberts, eds., *Intermediaries, Interpreters, and Clerks: African Employees in the Making of Colonial Africa* (Madison: U. of Wisconsin Press, 2006). Of possible tributary states, al-Bakrī says that "Safanqū," perhaps located near the Niger River at Ra's al-Mā', was "the farthest dependency of Ghana." *Corpus*, 81–85. See Delafosse, *Haut-Sénégal-Niger*, 2:14, who says Safanqū could be Issabongo, the Songhay rendering of Ra's al-Mā'. Lange makes much more of this, arguing imperial Mali was premised on the Ghanaian presence in the Niger valley. See Lange, *Ancient Kingdoms of West Africa*.

27. Ibid, 81.

28. Ibid.

29. Tymowski, *Origins and Structures of Political Institutions in Pre-Colonial Black Africa*, 77–85, provides a general picture of power structures in West Africa.

30. *Corpus*, 77.

31. Ibid, 70–73, 77; 'Umar al-Naqar, "Takrūr: The History of a Name," *Journal of African History* 10 (1969): 367.

32. The Hal Pulaaren go by various designations: Fulbe, Fulani, Fula, and Tukulor are some of them.

33. *Corpus*, 107–8.

34. Ibid, 73–74.

35. *Corpus*, 98. On the term *janāwa* or *gnāwa*, see El Hamel, *Black Morocco*.

36. See Levtzion, *Ancient Ghana and Mali*, 44–48; J.S. Trimingham, *A History of Islam in West Africa* (London: Oxford U. Press, 1962), 29–30; David Conrad and Humphrey J. Fisher, "The Conquest that Never Was: Ghana and the Almoravids, 1076. I: The External Arabic Sources," *History in Africa* 9 (1982): 21–59; ———, "The Conquest that Never Was: Ghana and the Almoravids, 1076. II. The Local Oral Sources," *History in Africa* 10 (1983): 53–78; Paulo F. de Moraes Farias, "The Almoravids: Some Questions concerning the Character of the Movement during Its Periods

of Closest Contact with the Western Sudan," *Bulletin de l'Institut Français* (later *Fondamental*) *d'Afrique Noire (IFAN)* 29 (1967): 794–878; Pekka Masonen and Humphrey J. Fisher, "Not Quite Venus from the Waves: The Almoravid Conquest of Ghana in the Modern Historiography of West Africa," *History in Africa* 23 (1996): 197–231. Yaḥyā b. Abī Bakr, or Abū Bakr b. 'Umar, was from the Lamtūna, not the Masūfa. Ibn Khaldūn comes closest to describing a military conquest. *Corpus*, 333.

37. Abdoulaye Bathily, *Les portes de l'or: le royaume de Galam, Sénégal, de l'ère musulmane aux temps négriers, VIIIe- XVIIIe siècle* (Paris: L'Harmattan, 1989); Levtzion, *Ancient Ghana and Mali*, 16–18; Monteil, "La légende du Ouagadou et l'origine des Soninkes"; Delafosse, *Haut-Sénégal-Niger (Soudan française)*; ___, "Traditions historiques et légendaries du Soudan occidental traduits d'un manuscript arabe"; Arnaud, "La singulière légende des Soninké"; Vidal, "Le mystère de Ghana"; Adam, "Légendes historiques"; Tautain, "Légendes et traditions des Soninké relatives à l'empire de Ghana"; Meillassoux, "Histoire et institutions du kafo de Bamako d'aprés la tradition des Niaré"; Smith, "Les Diakhanké: histoire d'une dispersion."

38. *Corpus*, 109.

39. Devisse and Diallo, "Le seuil du Wagadu," 108–11.

40. *Corpus*, 106–7, 110.

41. Ibid, 111–12.

42. Ibid, 84–85, 111, 208, 169–70; A. Bonnel de Mézières, "Découverte de l'emplacement de Tirekka," *Bulletin du Comité des Travaux Historiques et Scientifiques: Section de Géographie* 29 (1914): 132–35. Al-Bakrī refers to this area as "Ghiyāru" and Kugha, while Yāqūt goes on to describe the "silent trade." Ibid, 32, 35–36, 177–78.

43. *Corpus*, 109–10.

44. One *ratl* equals .99 lbs. See "Ratl," in *First Encyclopedia of Islam* (Leiden: E.J. Brill, 1993), 1129.

45. *Corpus*, 109–10.

46. Ibid, 372.

47. Ibid, 118. Archaeological evidence that the town "flourished" until the seventh/thirteenth century does not necessarily contradict al-Idrisī, as much of this is impressionistic and relative. See Denise S. Robert, "Les fouilles de Tegdaoust," *Journal of African History* 11 (1970): 471–93; Denise and Serge Robert and Jean Devisse, eds., *Tegdaoust. I. Recherches sur Aoudaghost* (Paris: Arts et Métiers graphiques, 1970); Raymond Mauny, *Les siècles obscurs de l'Afrique noire* (Paris: Fayard, 1970), 153.

48. Ibn Ḥawqal had remarked in the fourth/tenth century that Ghana was heavily reliant upon that salt (*Corpus*, 49).

49. Levtzion, *Ancient Ghana and Mali*, 147; Hunwick, *Timbuktu and the Songhay Empire*, 9, note 5. Writing some time after 658/1269, Ibn Sa'īd barely mentions Awdaghust, while its discussion in Abū 'l-Fidā' is wholly taken from al-Muhallabī's fourth/tenth century description (*Corpus*, 192, 196–99,168).

50. *Corpus*, 143–53. This is because the author of *Kitāb al-Istibṣār*, written shortly after 529/1135, relies almost entirely on al-Bakrī regarding Ghana.

51. Ibid, 179–80, 184–85.

52. Ibid, 261, 276. Both Abū 'l-Fidā' (d. 732/131) and al-Dimashqī (d. 727/1327) also discuss Ghana, but the former's account is derivative of al-Idrisī and Ibn Sa'īd, whereas

the latter employs al-Bakrī, al-Idrisī, Ibn Sa'īd, and Abu 'l-Fidā', often without attribution. Trimingham, *History of Islam in West Africa*, 41–42, advances the idea that Takrur's rise as a polity explains its wider application, while 'Umar al-Naqar, "Takrūr: The History of a Name," *Journal of African History* 10 (1969): 370–72, argues it was due to "Takruri" visitors to Egypt and the Ḥijāz. Also see Ould Cheikh, "Nomadisme, Islam, et pouvoir dans la société maure précoloniale," 1:168–69; John Hunwick, "Notes on a Late Fifteenth-Century Document Concerning 'al-Takrūr'," in Christopher Allen and R.W. Johnson, eds., *African Perspectives* (Cambridge: Cambridge U. Press, 1970), 7–34.

53. Ibid, 319–20.

54. Ibid, 333.

55. *TF*, 41–42/75–79.

Chapter 4: Slavery and Race Imagined in Bilād As-Sūdān

1. *Corpus*, 22. See also M.J. Tubiana, *Survivances préislamiques en pays Zaghāwa* (Paris: Institut d'Ethnologie, 1964), 14, 17, 26.

2. *Recueil*, 66, 69.

3. *Corpus*, 302.

4. Ibid, 346–48.

5. *NH*, 332; *TS*, 2–5/4–9; Hunwick, *Timbuktu and the Songhay Empire*, 3–6.

6. *Corpus*, 97, 113, 174.

7. Ibid, 68.

8. Ibid, 22.

9. Ibid, 98–99. That such behavior continued a previous pattern is highly suspect in light of testimony prior to al-Zuhrī, for whom slaving was a singular focus, and who was invested in refashioning Ghana's image as a reformist power at a time when Takrur, Sila, and Tadmekka were also engaged in slaving. Their activity may explain al-Dimashqī's cryptic reference to "Takrūr al-'Abīd," possibly "Takrur, the [source] of slaves," or even "Takrur, the Enslaved." Ibid, 208.

10. Al-Zuhrī confuses matters more in saying the Amīma are a "tribe of the Janāwa who live in the eastern part of the desert between Zāfūn and Kawkaw near the Nile of Egypt." Ibid, 99.

11. Ibid, 108–9, 111–12. Monteil speculates that Ghiyāra, Ghiyārū, or Ghiyār may have been the Gundiuru or Kunjūru mentioned in *Ta'rīkh al-fattāsh*, 179–80/314–15. Charles Monteil, "Le site de Goundiourou," *Bulletin d'Études Historiques et Scientifiques de l'Afrique Occidentale Française* 11 (1928): 647–53. Also see H.J. Fisher, "The Early Life and Pilgrimage of al-ḥājj Muḥammad al-Amīn the Soninke," *Journal of African History* 11 (1970): 51–69.

12. Ibid, 186.

13. Ibid, 320.

14. Ibid, 108–12, 184. To Ghana's west was the land of the Maqzāra (or Mafzāra, Maghzāwa); that is, the Fulbe and Wolof and other West Atlantic language speakers, with Bambuk to the east ("the land of the Wanqāra").

15. Devisse and Sidibé differentiate between these designations, arguing "Lam" means "something that does not exist at all"; that "Dam" refers to blood or a multitude; and "Nam" signifies sleep, by inference the ignorance of Islam.

Jean Devisse and Samuel Sidibé, "Mandinka et mandéphones," in Jean Devisse, ed., *Vallées du Niger*, 144; *Corpus*, 31, 36–37, where they are referred to as the "Damādim" and the "Damdam."

16. *Corpus*, 86, 151.

17. Ibid, 212, 255, 320.

18. Ibid, 13, 18; *Recueil*, 46. Such irregular features are discussed in Norris, *Saharan Myth and Saga*, 31–33.

19. *Corpus*, 42; *Recueil*, 65.

20. *Corpus*, 47.

21. Ibid, 68.

22. Ibid, 153.

23. Ibid, 89–90.

24. See, for example, Gwyn Campbell, ed., *Structure of Slavery in Indian Ocean Africa and Asia* (London: Frank Cass, 2003); Edward A. Alpers, Gwyn Campbell, and Michael Salman, eds., *Resisting Bondage in Indian Ocean Africa and Asia* (London: Routledge, 2005).

25. Sūra 30, *al-Rūm*, verse 23.

26. *Corpus*, 134.

27. Ibid, 169–70.

28. Norris, *Saharan Myth and Saga*, 31–33. Herodotus placed the Blemmyes in Nubia.

29. *Corpus*, 23. The translation reads "Noah."

30. Ibid, 15.

31. Ibid, 34–36.

32. Ibid, 20–21.

33. Ibid, 212.

34. Genesis 9: 24–27. See also David M. Goldenberg, *The Curse of Ham: Race and Slavery in Early Judaism, Christianity and Islam* (Princeton: Princeton U. Press, 2003); Stephen R. Haynes, *Noah's Curse: The Biblical Justification of American Slavery* (New York: Oxford U. Press, 2002).

35. Ibn Khaldūn, *The Muqaddimah: An Introduction to History*, trans. Franz Rosenthal (Princeton: Princeton U. Press, 1967), 59–60.

36. *Corpus*, 107.

37. Ibid, 40–41. This is repeated by Ibn Ḥawqal, Ibid, 44–45.

38. Ibid, 321–22.

39. Ibn Khaldūn, *Muqaddimah*, trans. Rosenthal, 63–64.

40. Ibid, 117.

41. Al-Jirārī, "The Questions of Sa'īd b. Ibrāhīm al-Jirārī of Tuwāt" and Aḥmad Bābā, "The Fatwā of Aḥmad Bābā al-Tinbuktī: *The Ladder of Ascent Toward Grasping the Law concerning Transported Blacks*," in John O. Hunwick and Fatima Harrak, eds., *Mi'rāj al-ṣu'ūd: Aḥmad Bābā's Replies on Slavery* (Rabat: Institut des Études Africaines, Université Mohamed V, 2000), 41–76/13–40. See also Ousmane Oumar Kane, *Beyond Timbuktu: An Intellectual History of Muslim West Africa* (Cambridge: Harvard University Press, 2016), 98–106.

42. Aḥmad Bābā, "The Fatwā of Aḥmad Bābā al-Tinbuktī: *The Ladder of Ascent*," 64–65/34–35.

43. See El Hamel's excellent discussion of Ibn Khaldūn and Aḥmad Bābā in *Black Morocco*, 73–88. In largely agreeing with him, I further explore Ibn Khaldūn's observations, while directing attention to the potential irony of Aḥmad Bābā's comments. Also see Mahmoud A. Zouber, *Aḥmad Baba de Tombouctou* (Paris: Maisonneuve et Larose, 1977). Timbuktu's Aḥmad Bābā Centre (CEDRAB) has at least one manuscript, *Īḍāḥ al-sabīl 'alā tawḍīḥ alfāẓ Khalīl*, written by "al-Imām al-Sūdānī," now identified as Aḥmad Bābā; the manuscript is found elsewhere in North Africa, where its author is identified as the same al-Imām al-Sūdānī. Ms. 629, CEDRAB; John O. Hunwick and Rex S. O'Fahey, *Arabic Literature of Africa, Volume 4: The Writings of Western Sudanic Africa* (Leiden: E.J. Brill, 2003), 35.

44. Abū 'l-Ḥasan 'Alī b. al-Ḥusayn al-Mas'ūdī, *Murūj al-dhahab wa ma'ādin al-jawhar*, ed., [edited by] *A.C. Barbier de Meynard and Pavet de Courteille* (Paris: Imprimerie Impériale, 1861), 1:163–64.

45. *Corpus*, 214.

46. Ibid, 205–14.

47. Ibid, 35.

48. Ibid, 79.

49. *Recueil*, 109–10.

50. *Corpus*, 132–33.

51. Ibid, 109–16.

52. Ibid, 119.

53. Ibn Khaldūn, *Muqaddimah*, trans. Rosenthal, 60–61.

54. Hall notes that "whites" were those "who claimed Arab pedigrees." *History of Race in Muslim West Africa*, 2, 30–35.

55. See Michael A. Gomez, *Reversing Sail: A History of the African Diaspora* (Cambridge: Cambridge U. Press, 2005), 1–28, for a discussion of these matters.

56. *Corpus*, 28, 481. Ibn al-Faqīh wrote "the whole world is 24,000 *farsakhs*, of which the Sūdān is 12,000 *farsakhs*."

57. Regarding Indian Ocean studies, some of the most illustrative examples of this approach are Gwyn Campbell, "Introduction: Slavery and Other Forms of Unfree Labour in the Indian Ocean World," in Campbell, ed., *Structure of Slavery in Indian Ocean Africa and Asia*; ____, "The African Diaspora in Asia," in Kiran Kamal Prasad, Jean-Pierre Angenot, and Fitzroy André Baptiste, eds., *TADIA: The African Diaspora in Asia, Explorations on a Less Known Fact* (Bangalore: Jana Jagrati Prakashana, 2008), 43–82; ____, "The Question of Slavery in Indian Ocean World History," Abdul Sheriff and Engseng Ho, eds., *The Indian Ocean: Oceanic Connections and the Creation of New Societies* (London: Hurst, 2014), 123–48; ____, "Africa, the Indian Ocean, and the 'Early Modern': Historiographical Conventions and Problems," Toyin Falola and Emily Brownell, eds., *Africa, Empire and Globalization: Essays in Honour of A.G. Hopkins* (Durham: Carolina Academic Press, 2011), 81–92; Indrani Chatterjee, "Renewed and Connected Histories: Slavery and the Historiography of South Asia," in Indrani Chatterjee and Richard M. Eaton, eds., *Slavery and South Asian History* (Bloomington and Indianapolis: Indiana U. Press, 2006), 17–43; Sugata Bose, *A Hundred Horizons: The Indian Ocean in the Age of Global Empire* (Cambridge: Harvard U. Press, 2006); K.N. Chaudhuri, *Trade and Civilization in the Indian Ocean: An Economic History from the Rise of Islam to 1750* (New York: Cambridge U. Press,

1985); Abdul Sheriff, *Dhow Cultures and the Indian Ocean: Cosmopolitanism, Commerce, and Islam* (Oxford: Oxford U. Press, 2010); ____, "Between Two Worlds: The Littoral Peoples of the Indian Ocean," in Roman Loimeier and Rudiger Seeseman, eds., *The Global World of the Swahili* (Berlin: Beiträge zur Afrikaforschung, 2006). Regarding East Africa, Jonathan Glassman's *War of Words, War of Stones: Racial Thought and Violence in Colonial Zanzibar* (Bloomington and Indianapolis: Indiana U. Press, 2011), in taking issue with Mahmood Mandani's path-breaking *When Victims Become Killers: Colonialism, Nativism, and the Genocide in Rwanda* (Princeton: Princeton U. Press, 2002) and in his effort to reduce the colonial footprint, provides a discussion of the permutations of comparative racial thought, emphasizing how racial concepts tracing to earlier periods were politicized by "indigenous intellectuals." Elisabeth McMahon's well-researched *Slavery and Emancipation in Islamic East Africa* (Cambridge: Cambridge U. Press, 2013) attends more to ethnicity than race. Eve M. Trout Powell's exquisite work, *Tell This in My Memory: Stories of Enslavement from Egypt, Sudan, and the Ottoman Empire* (Stanford: Stanford U. Press, 2012), makes the striking point that the reduction in the diversity of slave origins in 'Alī Pasha Mubārak's al-Khiṭaṭ "is almost Manichean in its simplicity: black slave (*'abid*) and while slave (*mamluk*)" (14). El Hamel's *Black Morocco*, Hall's *History of Race in Muslim West Africa* (which in making an impressive case for "African histories of race" also takes on Mamdani), and Webb's *Desert Frontier*, all exemplary, have already been cited. Carina Ray's *Crossing the Color Line: Race, Sex, and the Contested Politics of Colonialism in Ghana* (Columbus, Ohio: Ohio U. Press, 2015) impressively demonstrates how Atlantic and African worlds intersect, with the policing of transracial relationships a focal point of colonial policy.

58. *Corpus*, 94–100. This places El Hamel, *Black Morocco*, in conversation with Webb, *Desert Frontier*. An example of a similar term acquiring meaning over time is *kunlun*, as it is known "with absolute certainty that the term initially had nothing whatsoever to do with color, let alone blackness of skin," but was rather "fundamentally geographical in conception," conveying remoteness and foreignness. Don J. Wyatt, *The Blacks of Premodern China* (Philadelphia: U. of Pennsylvania Press, 2010), 18.

59. In "Bellah Histories of Decolonization, Iklan Paths to Freedom: The Meanings of Race and Slavery in the Late-Colonial Niger Bend (Mali), 1944–1960," *International Journal of African Historical Studies* 44 (2011): 61–87, Hall may allude to this process in observing ethnicity "gained a racial gloss" as a result of "very old Sahelian ideas about blacks and non-blacks expressed in the frequent dichotomy made in the Arabic writing of the area, over many centuries" (63). See also Baz Lecocq, "The Bellah Question: Slave Emancipation, Race, and Social Categories in Late Twentieth-Century Northern Mali," *Canadian Journal of African Studies* 39 (2005): 42–68; ____, *Disputed Desert: Decolonization, Competing Nationalisms, and Tuareg Rebellions in Northern Mali* (Boston: E.J. Brill, 2010). In *History of Race in Muslim West Africa*, 49, Hall observes that Ibn Khaldūn's history of the Berbers was "probably the most widely read text in North African history."

60. On Safavid claims, see Roger Savory, *Iran under the Safavids* (Cambridge: Cambridge U. Press, 2007); ___, "Ebn Bazzaz," *Encyclopaedia Iranica* 8 (1997): 8; M. M. Mazzoui, *The Origins of the Safavids: Shi'ism, Sufism, and the Gulat* (Wiesbaden: Franz Steiner, 1972).

61. Hall, *History of Race in Muslim West Africa*, 39–45, 211–23, sees race's emergence in the Sahel as a function of efforts to construct a usable genealogy—race as descent from the central Islamic lands. I assign slavery as important a role.

62. Hall embeds race within linguistic groupings (*History of Race in Muslim West Africa*, 29–30), with "color" not necessarily correlative with race, though less interrogated are relations between different "sorts" of "blacks." In "Bellah Histories of Decolonization," 63–64, he discusses the *bellah*, the Songhay equivalent of the Tamasheq term *iklan*, which conjoins blackness and servility.

63. Some Africans even concluded Europeans were not human, but spirits and wizards. There are many examples of this response, with examples in Luise White, *Speaking with Vampires: Rumor and History in Colonial Africa* (Berkeley: U. of California Press, 2000); Michael A. Gomez, *Exchanging Our Country Marks: The Transformation of African Identities in the Colonial and Antebellum South* (Chapel Hill: UNC Press, 1998).

64. In *History of Race in Muslim West Africa*, 6 and 10, Hall stresses such qualifications. Cleaveland, *Becoming Walāta*, xx, suggests how the models can coexist in observing that most "white" Mauritanians are "culturally Arab," but "of mixed Berber, Arab, and sub-Saharan héritage."

65. Hall, *History of Race in Muslim West Africa*, 11, offers a universal definition of "racism"; here I am more concerned with "race."

Chapter 5: The Meanings of Sunjata and the Dawn of Imperial Mali

1. Djibril Tamsir Niane, "Histoire et tradition historique du Manding," *Présence africaine* 89 (1974): 67, lists some themes, not others.

2. The versions of the Sunjata epic consulted for this study are as follows: L.J.B. Bérenger-Féraud, *Les peuplades de la Sénégambie* (Paris: Éditions Ernest Leroux, 1879); Captain F. Quiquandon, "Histoire de la puissance Mandingue," *Bulletin de la Société de géographie commerciale de Bordeaux* (1892): 305–18, 369–87, 400–29; Lieutenant de Vaisseau Jamie, *De Koulikoro à Tombouctou à bord du "Mage," 1889–1890* (Paris: Librairie de la Société des Gens de Letters, 1894); Lieutenant de Vaisseau Hourst, *Sur le Niger et au pays des Touaregs: La mission Hourst* (Paris: Plon, 1898); M.G. Adam, "Légendes historiques du pays de Nioro (Sahel)," *Revue coloniale* (1904): 81–98, 232–48; 354–66; Lieutenant Lanrezac, "Au Soudan: La legénde historique," *La revue indigene* (1907): 292–97; Robert Arnaud, *L'Islam et la politique musulmane française en Afrique occidentale française* (Paris: Comité de l'Afrique française, 1912); Leo Frobenius, *The Voice of Africa*, vol. 2 (London: Hutchinson and Co., 1913); Franz de Zeltner, *Contes du Sénégal et du Niger* (Paris: Éditions Ernest Leroux, 1913); Maurice Delafosse, *Historiques et légendaries du Soudan occidentale: Traduites d'un manuscript arab inédit* (Paris: Comité de l'Afrique française, 1913); Paul Vidal, "La légende officielle de Soundiata fondateur de l'empire Manding," *Bulletin du Comité d'études historiques et scientifiques de l'Afrique occidentale française* 7 (1924): 317–28; Mamadou Aïssa Kaba Diakité, "Livre renfermant la généalogie des diverses tribus noires du Soudan et l'histoire des rois

après Mahomet, suivant les renseignements fournis par certaines personnes et ceux recueillis dans les anciens livres," trans. Henri Labouret, *Annales d'académie sciences coloniales* 3 (1929): 189–225; Abdoulaye Sadji, "Ce que dit la musique africaine," *L'éducation africaine* 94 (April-June 1936): 140–154; Maximilien Quenum, "La légende de Fama-Soundiata (Soudan Français)," in Maximilien Quenum, ed., *Légendes Africaines, Côte d'Ivoire-Soudan-Dahomey (*Rochefort-sur-Mer: Imprimerie A. Thoyen-Theze, 1946), 44–72; Charles Monteil, "La légende du Ouagadou et l'histoire des Soninké," *Mélanges ethnologiques* (1953): 362–408; Mamby Sidibé, "Soundiata Keita, héros historique et légendaire, empereur du Manding," *Notes Africaines* 82 (1959): 41–51; Maurice Delafosse, "Histoire de la lutte entre les empires de Sosso at du Mandé," *Notes Africaines* 83 (1959): 76–79 (this is extracted from his 1913 publication, *Historiques et légendaries du Soudan occidentale*); Niane, *Sundiata*; Robert Pageard, "Soundiata Keita et la tradition orale," *Présence Africaine* 36 (1961): 51–70; Charles Monteil, "Fin de siècle à Médine (1898–1899)," *Bulletin de l'Institut Français* (later *Fondamental*) *d'Afrique Noire (IFAN)* 28 (1966): 82–172, 369–84; Lassana Doucoure and Mme. Marta, *Soundiata* (np, 1970); Dembo Kanoute, "Formation de l'empire Mandingue," in T. Sanogho and I. Diallo, trans., *L'histoire de l'Afrique authentique* (Dakar, 1972), 30–71; Sory Konake, *Le grand destin de Soundjata* (Paris: ORTF-DAEC, 1973); Gordon Innes, *Sunjata: Three Mandinka Versions* (London: SOAS, 1974); Harold Courlander, *A Treasury of African Folklore* (New York: Crown Publishers, 1975); Michael Jackson, "Prevented Successions: A Commentary upon a Kuranko Narrative," in R.H. Hook, ed., *Fantasy and Symbol: Studies in Anthropological Interpretation* (London: Academic Press, 1979); Donald R. Wright, *Oral Traditions from the Gambia*, 2 vols. (Athens, Ohio: Ohio U. Press, 1979, 1980); B.K. Sidibé, *Sunjata: The Story of Sunjata Keita, Founder of the Mali Empire* (Banjul: Oral History and Antiquities Division of the Vice-President's Office, 1980); Camara Laye, *The Guardian of the Word: Kouma Lafôlô Kouma*, trans. James Kirkup (New York: Vintage Books, 1984), translated from *Le maître de la parole: Kouma Lafôlô Kouma* (Paris: Plon, 1978); Massa Makan Diabaté, *Le lion à l'arc* (Paris: Éditions Hâtier, 1986); Madina Ly-Tall, Seydou Camara, and Bouna Dioura, *L'histoire du Mandé d'après Jeli Kanku Madi Jabaté de Kéla* (Paris: SCOA, 1987); Youssouf Tata Cissé and Wâ Kamissòko, *La grande geste du Mali: Des origines à la fondation de l'Empire (Traditions de Krina au colloques de Bamako* (Paris: Karthala, 1988); Boniface Keita, *Kita dans les années 1910* (Bamako: Éditions Jamana, 1988); Youssouf Tata Cissé and Wâ Kamissòko, *Soundjata, la gloire du Mali: La grande geste du Mali*, vol. 2 (Paris: Karthala, 1991); Jan Jansen, *Siramuri Diabaté et ses enfants: une étude sur deux generations des griots Malinké* (Utrecht and Bamako: ISOR, 1991); Fa-Digi Sisòkò, *The Epic of Son-Jara: A West African Tradition*, trans. John William Johnson (Bloomington: Indiana U. Press, 1992); Sory Camara, *Gens de la parole: Essai sur la condition et le role des griots dans la société malinké* (Paris: Karthala, 1992); David C. Conrad, *Epic Ancestors of the Sunjata Era: Oral Tradition from the Maninka of Guinea* (Madison: U. of Wisconsin, 1999); David C. Conrad and Djanka Tassey Condé, *A West African Epic of the Mande Peoples* (Indianapolis: Indiana U. Press, 2004). See Stephen Bulman, "A Checklist of English and French Versions of the Sunjata Epic published before the 21st Century," http://www.hum2.leidenuniv.nl/verba-africana/malinke-fr/griots

/Bulman.pdf, lists a total of 64 published versions of the Sunjata epic, and updates his earlier article, "A Checklist of Published Versions of the Sunjata Epic," *History in Africa* 24 (1997): 71–94.

Related sources inappropriate for this study include Roland Bertol, *Sundiata: The Epic of the Lion King* (London: Ty Crowell Co., 1970), and Werewere Liking, *L'amour-cent-vies* (Paris: Présence Africaine, 1988). Plays (unconsulted) include Laurent Koudou Gbagbo, *Soundiata: le lion du Manding* (Abidjan: Éditions CEDA, 1979); Ahmed-Tidjani Cissé, *Le tana de Soumangouro* (Paris: Karthala, 1988); René Guillot, *La brousse et la bête* (Paris: Delagrave, 1950); and Théatre Dahoméen, "La ruse de Diégué," *Présence Africa* 5 (1948): 796–809.

3. See Ralph A. Austen, "Editor's Introduction," in Ralph A. Austen, ed., *In Search of Sunjata: The Mande Epic as History, Literature, and Performance* (Bloomington and Indiana: Indiana U. Press, 1999), 3. On the epic representing "masks and mask dances," see Jan Jansen, "Masking Sunjata: A Hermeneutical Critique," *History in Africa* 27 (2000): 131–41.

4. This issues into "the art of myth analysis." See Jackson, "Prevented Successions."

5. The difference between Keyla and non-Keyla traditions in the roles of griot families is an example, for me not terribly significant. See Jansen, "Masking Sunjata," 138–40.

6. Conrad stakes out a reasonable position: "While the mythical quality of some elements in the text is obvious . . . historians cannot afford to ignore the possibility that there is some information worth distilling." David C. Conrad, "Oral Sources on Links between Great States: Sumanguru, Servile Lineage, the Jariso, and Kaniaga," *History in Africa* 11 (1984): 35. Also see Stephen Bulman, "Sunjata as Written Literature: The Role of the Literary Mediator in the Dissemination of the Sunjata Epic," in Austin, ed., *In Search of Sunjata*, 231–51. Otherwise, useful discussions include Lisa Maalki, *Purity and Exile: Violence, Memory, and National Cosmology among Hutu Refugees in Tanzania* (Chicago: U. of Chicago Press, 1995); Achille Mbembe, *On the Postcolony* (Berkeley: U. of California Press, 2001); Steve Feierman, *Peasant Intellectuals: Anthropology and History in Tanzania* (Madison: U. of Wisconsin Press, 1990); Luise White, Stephen Miescher and David Cohen, *African Words, African Voices: Critical Practices in Oral History* (Bloomington: Indiana U. Press, 2001); Elizabeth Tonkin, "Investigating Oral Tradition," *Journal of African History* 27 (l986); P. Stephens, Jr., "The Kisra Legend," *Journal of African History* l6 (l975); Jack Goody, *The Interface between the Written and the Oral* (Cambridge: Cambridge U. Press, 1987); Bonnie L. Wright, "The Power of Articulation," in W. Arens and Ivan Karp, eds., *Creativity and Power* (Washington and London: Smithsonian Institution Press, 1989).

7. The spiderweb analogy in Jan Assman's *The Mind of Egypt: History and Meaning in the Time of the Pharaohs* (Cambridge: Harvard U. Press, 2002) is useful. But also consider Certeau's analysis of the interplay between oral and written testimony in sixteenth-century Brazil and the "possessed" nuns of Loudun, France. Michel de Certeau, *The Writing of History* (New York: Columbia U. Press, 1988).

8. This is related to Peter R. Schmidt's argument in *Historical Archaeology in Africa* (New York: Altamira, 2006), 27, that "oral traditions . . . must be seen for what they reveal, say, of disputes over power claims and land claims—the contexts from which history is made."

9. This is consistent with Burbank and Cooper's definition of empires as "large units, expansionist or with a memory of power . . . that maintain distinction and hierarchy as they incorporate new people. . . . The concept of empire presumes that different peoples within the polity will be governed differently" (*Empires in World History*, 8).

10. Ivor Wilks, "The History of the *Sunjata* Epic: A Review of the Evidence," in Austen, ed., *In Search of Sunjata*, 9–20. I have taken a few liberties to extend the logic to the narration itself.

11. Similarly, an examination of orality's didactic role in ancient Greece, particularly between the eighth and fifth centuries, renders the Homeric poem as a "metered text book," its substance "not as creative fiction, but as a compilation of inherited lore." Eric A. Havelock, *Preface to Plato* (Cambridge, Mass.: Harvard U. Press, 1963), 36–96. See also William V. Harris, *Ancient Literacy* (Cambridge, Mass.: Harvard U. Press, 1991).

12. Karim Traoré, "Jeli and *Sere*: The Dialectic of the Word in the Manden," in Austen, ed., *In Search of Sunjata*, 176–77.

13. Wilks, "History of the *Sunjata* Epic," 38–40; David C. Conrad, "Searching for History in the Sunjata Epic: The Case of Fakoli," *History in Africa* 19 (1992): 150; Niane, "Histoire et tradition historique du Manding," 67.

14. *Corpus*, 293.

15. Ibid, 295. Mārī Jāṭa was actually *Mansā* Mūsā's uncle, as he was the brother of the latter's grandfather. Charles Monteil, "Les empires du Mali: étude d'histoire et de sociologie soudanaises," *Bulletin du Comité d'études historiques et scientifiques de l'Afrique occidentale française* 12 (1929): 349–50. Austen makes the point that from Ibn Baṭṭūṭa the story of Sunjata appears in panegyric rather than epic form. See Ralph A. Austen, "The Historical Transformation of Genres: Sunjata as Panegyric, Folktale, Epic, and Novel," in Austen, ed., *In Search of Sunjata*, 70.

16. Niane, "Histoire et tradition historique du Manding," 59–60; Niane, "Recherches sur l'empire du Mali," *Recherches africaines*, 35–37; Austen, "Historical Transformation of Genres," 70.

17. Ralph A. Austen, *Trans-Saharan Africa in World History* (Oxford: Oxford U. Press, 2010), 109–11. Austen explains that *maana* derives from the Arabic *ma'anā* ("meaning"), linking to the effort to explain "difficult texts in Islamic religious studies."

18. David C. Conrad, *Sunjata: A West African Epic of the Mande Peoples* (Indianapolis: Indiana U. Press, 2004), xix.

19. Seydou Camara, "The Epic of *Sunjata*: Structure, Preservation, and Transmission," in Austen, ed., *In Search of Sunjata*, 59–60. Vidal refers to the Keyla griots as the "officially recognized guardians . . . of the tradition of the former Manding sovereigns." Vidal, "La légende officielle de Soundiata," 317.

20. Stephen Belcher, "*Sinimogo*, 'Man for Tomorrow': Sunjata on the Fringes of the Mande World," in Austen, ed., *In Search of Sunjata*, 90–102; Traoré, "Jeli and *Sere*," 177–78.

21. Jan Jansen, "An Ethnography of the Epic of *Sunjata* in Kela," in Austen, ed., *In Search of Sunjata*, 297–309.

22. David C. Conrad, "Mooning Armies and Mothering Heroes: Female Power in Mande Epic Tradition," in Austen, ed., *In Search of Sunjata*, 189.

23. Seydou Camara, "La tradition orale en question: Conservation et transmission des traditions historiques au Manden: Le Centre de Kela et l'histoire du Mininjan" (Thèse de doctorat de l'E.H.E.S.S., Paris, 1990), 4–32. Seydou Camara, in "Epic of *Sunjata*: Structure, Preservation, and Transmission," in Austen, ed., *In Search of Sunjata*, 65, says Bala Jabate, also known as Siramori Balaba, the griot of *Mansā* Manbi Keita, wrote down the epic, dictating it to a person of *sherīfian* heritage, who recorded it in *ajami*.

24. Jan Jansen, "An Ethnography of the Epic of *Sunjata* in Kela," 308–9.

25. See Austen, "Historical Transformations of Genres," 70–81.

26. Ibid, 77–79. Austen refutes the argument that the French promoted Kangaba as Mali's historic capital for its own imperial purposes. See Kathryn Green, "'Mande Kaba,' the Capital of Mali: A Recent Invention?" *History in Africa* 18 (1991): 127–35.

27. George E. Brooks, *Landlords and Strangers: Ecology, Society, and Trade in Western Africa, 1000–1630* (Boulder: Westview Press, 1993), 4.

28. *Corpus*, 82, 108; *Recueil*, 102. Al-Idrisī locates Daw and Malal in the "land of the Lamlam," with four days separating them. While al-Bakrī characterizes Daw as a "great kingdom," al-Idrisī describes Daw and Malal as "two small village-like towns." Al-Ya'qūbī also mentions a kingdom of "Malal," but in the Lake Chad area. Al-Idrisī goes on to say: "Their inhabitants, according to the reports of the people of that part of the world, are Jews [but] infidelity and ignorance overcome them." Al-Zuhrī also claims the Amīma "profess Judaism." (Ibid, 99–100). On the Jewish presence in early and medieval West Africa, see John Hunwick, *Jews of a Saharan Oasis: Elimination of the Tamantit Community* (Princeton: Markus Wiener, 2006); Peter Mark and José da Silva Horta, *The Forgotten Diaspora: Jewish Communities in West Africa and the Making of the Atlantic World* (Cambridge: Cambridge U. Press, 2011); Raymond Mauny, "Le judaïsme, les juifs du Sahara," *Bulletin de l'Institut Français* (later *Fondamental*) *d'Afrique Noire (IFAN)* 11 (1949): 354–78; Ismaël Diadié Haïdara, *Les juifs à Tombouctou, Recueil de sources écrites relatives au commerce juif à Tombouctou au XIXe siècle* (Bamako: Éditions Donniya, 1999); J. Oliel, *Les Juifs au Sahara. Le Touat au moyen âge* (Paris : Éditions de CNRS, 1994); M. Abitbol, "Juifs maghrébins et commerce transsaharien du VIII au XVè siècle," in *Le sol, la parole, et l'écrit: Mélanges en hommage à Raymond Mauny*, ed. Jean Devisse (Paris: Société française d'histoire d'outre-mer, 1981), 561–77; Nehemia Levtzion, "The Jews of Sijilmasa and the Saharan Trade," in *Communautés juives des marges sahariennes du Maghreb*, ed. Michel Abitbol (Jerusalem: Institut Ben-Zvi, 1982), 253–63; Idrissa Bâ, "La problématique de la présence juive au Sahara et au Soudan d'après Jean Léon l'Africain," *Lagos Historical Review* 5 (2005): 146–76.

29. *Corpus*, 82.

30. Ibid, 368–69.

31. Delafosse, *Haut-Sénégal-Niger (Soudan française)*; Jean Devisse and Samuel Sidibé, "Mandinka et mandéphones," in Jean Devisse, ed., *Vallée du Niger*, 146; Madina Ly-Tall, *Contribution à l'histoire de l'empire du Mali (XIIIe—XVIe siècles)* (Dakar: Les Nouvelles Éditions Africaines, 1975). David Conrad, "From the Banan Tree of Kouroussa: Mapping the Landscape in Mande Traditional History," *Canadian Journal of African Studies* 42 (2008): 398–99, locates Susu north of Banamba,

Koulikoro. Associating Susu with Futa Jallon and Do/Sankara is less convincing. See Stephen Bühnen, "In Quest of Susu," *History in Africa* 21 (1994): 1–47.

32. *Corpus*, 333.

33. Djibril T. Niane, "Recherches sur l'empire du Mali au moyen âge," *Recherches africaines: Études Guinéennes* 1 (1959): 38.

34. Niane, *Sundiata*, 32–41.

35. John William Johnson notes Sumaoro is "not despised" in Mali, and that what transpired was not "a question of good versus evil." Sisòkò, *Epic of Son-Jara*, 7–8.

36. The earliest French collections support a debilitated Maninka at the hands of Sumaoro, recording in 1309–10/1892 that "Sou-Mangourou" began "ravaging" them and placing them to "fire and the sword." Early fourteenth/twentieth-century accounts also mention Sumaoro's incursions into Malian territory. An Arabic version translated into French agrees, stating Sumaoro raised an army "to fall upon the Mande." Keyla griots in 1342–43/1924 also maintain Sumaoro "ravaged the Manding." But none of these accounts specify slaving. Quiquandon, "Histoire de la puissance Mandingue," 310; Adam, "Légendes historiques," 357–58; Arnaud, *L'Islam et la politique musulmane française*, 168; Zeltner, *Contes du Sénégal et du Niger*, 7; Delafosse, *Historiques et légendaries*, 20 (the Arabic original is missing); Vidal, "La légende officielle de Soundiata," 317–18, 322. Adam ("Légendes historiques," 81) identified his source as "a young Soninke marabout," while Delafosse (*Historiques et légendaries*, 3–4) says an Arabic manuscript from Nioro written by Mamadi Aissa was his source, which was actually Adam's source. Delafosse relied upon a copy of Aissa's work made by Aissa's nephew, Mamadou Sallama.

37. Cissé and Kamissòko, *La grande geste du Mali*, 26–27.

38. For example, Kamissòko claims Sunjata established towns for ex-slaves, reminiscent of French *villages de liberté*, and that Sunjata proclaimed the "abolition" of "black slavery" upon assuming power. Cissé and Kamissòko, *Soundjata, la gloire du Mali*, 28. There are a number of other such correlations. On the Bamana/Bambara analogy, see Richard L. Roberts, *Warriors, Merchants, and Slaves: The State and the Economy in the Middle Niger Valley, 1700–1914* (Stanford: Stanford U. Press, 1974); Louis Tauxier, *Histoire des Bambara* (Paris: P. Geuthner, 1942); Charles Monteil, *Les Bambara du Ségou et du Kaarta: étude historique, ethnologique, et littéraire d'une people du Soudan français* (Paris: Larose, 1924).

39. *Corpus*, 295.

40. Ibid, 333.

41. Versions completed from the middle to the end of the fourteenth/twentieth century include Niane, *Sundiata*, 2–3; Ly-Tall, et al, *L'histoire du Mandé*, 12–20; Sanassy Kouyaté, "Village Issues and Mande Ancestors," in Conrad, ed., *Epic Ancestors of the Sunjata Era*, 25; Mamadi Condé, "Sogolon and Sunjata," in Conrad, ed., *Epic Ancestors of the Sunjata Era*, 99–101; Sisòkò, *Epic of Son-Jara*, 25. Sisòkò simply states that "Bilal, his child was Mamadu Kanu," and that the latter has three sons, not four. See also David Conrad, "Islam in the Oral Traditions of Mali: Bilali and Surakata," *Journal of African History* 26 (1985): 33–49. Those compiled from the end of the thirteenth/nineteenth century are Diakité, "Livre renfermant la généalogie," 209–10 (published in 1929, but collected by Colonel Archinard in Nioro in 1891);

Delafosse, "Histoire de la lutte entre les empires," 77; Arnaud, *L'Islam*, 168; Vidal, "La légende officielle de Soundiata," 317–20.

42. According to this tradition, the oldest of Bilāl's alleged seven sons, Lawalo, left Mecca and settled in Mali, at the time a "Bambara" land. Lahilatul Kalabi, Lawalo's grandson, first of the line born in Mali to perform *ḥajj*, returned seven years later and was "recognized" as king by a *jinn*. Divine blessing was conferred on Lahilatul's two sons, Kalabi Bomba and Kalabi Dauman, who would claim "royal power" and "fortune and wealth," respectively, recalling the Jula and suggesting a tight bond with rulers.

43. *Kondolon Ni Sané* inhabit the first of three supernatural tiers, with other divinities and noncorporeal beings required to have a successful hunt, while the remaining two levels consist of the *boli*, paraphernalia required to withstand malevolent forces; and the *nyama* or life force animating all things. See Youssouf Tata Cissé, *La confrérie des chasseurs Malinké at Bambara: mythes, rites et récits initiatiques* (Ivry-sur-Seine: Éditions Nouvelles du Sud, 1994), 78–88.

44. There is also the tradition that the *simbon* title is established with the second generation of descendants from Lahilatul Kalabi (Bilāl's great-grandson), and that the *mansā* title develops with the fifth generation. Vidal, "La légende officielle de Soundiata," 320.

45. Niane, *Sundiata*, 3; Laye, *Guardian of the Word*, 65. Maghan Kon Fatta is known by many names, a mixture of titles and personal nouns varying by idiom, region, and the orthographic signatures of individual accounts. Examples include Diadiba Maka, *Mansā* Farako Mankégné, *Mansā* Farako, Farako Maghan Kenyin, etc.

46. Niane, *Sundiata*, 3. Adam, "Légendes historiques," 354–55, says his first wife had eleven children, his second wife, two at this time. The second wife would have another child, raising this particular count to fourteen. Delafosse says he had twelve sons, including Sunjata, and mentions at least one daughter (*Historiques et légendaries*, 21; "Histoire de la lutte entre les empires," 77).

47. Zeltner, *Contes du Sénégal*, 1–3; Demba Kouyaté, "Sunjata," in Conrad, ed., *Epic Ancestors of the Sunjata Era*, 164–67; Frobenius, *Voice of Africa*, 2: 451–57; Ly-Tall, et al, *L'histoire du Mandé*, 26–32; Cissé and Kamissòko, *La grande geste du Mali*, 50–53; Sisòkò, *Epic of Son-Jara*, 32–35; Kouyaté, "Village Issues and Mande Ancestors," 25; Niane, *Sundiata*, 4–9; Pageard, "Soundiata Keita," 53–54; Sadji, "Ce que dit la musique africaine," 142; Liking, *L'amour-cent-vies*, 43; Doucoure and Marta, *Soundiata*, 42–268; Laye, *Guardian of the Word*, 35–64. Conrad, "From the Banan Tree of Kouroussa," 393–94, locates Dò ni Kiri, or Dò and Kiri, near contemporary Segu.

48. According to *jeli ngara* Djanka Tassey Condé of Fadama (northeastern Guinea), the hunters were the Arab youths (*kamalenw*) Abdu Karimi and Abdu Kassimu from Morocco. Conrad, *Sunjata: A West African Epic*, 21–51.

49. There are many variations for the Traore brothers Dan *Mansā* Wulani and Dan *Mansā* Wulan Tamba, including Damba Masowlomba and Damba Sowlandi, Dan *Massa* Woulani and Dan *Massa* Woulan Tamba, etc.

50. Paulo Fernando de Moraes Faris, "The *Gesere* of Borgu: A Neglected Type of Manding Diaspora," in Austen, ed., *In Search of Sunjata*, 141–43. In Sadji, "Ce que dit la musique africaine," 142–43; however, it is Tiramakan, one of Sunjata's generals, who kills the buffalo.

51. Frobenius, *Voice of Africa*, 2: 454.

52. Cissé and Kamissòko, *La grande geste du Mali*, 51; Kanoute, "Formation de l'empire Mandingue," 31–32. Do-Kamissa is called Dossigui in Kanoute's version, in which the discussion of the buffalo woman is absent—she is simply a woman.

53. Laye, *Guardian of the Word*, 36; Konake, *Le grand destin*, 19–20.

54. Wright, *Oral Traditions from the Gambia*, 1: 31–37, 73–76. Illustrative of this tendency is an account of Koli Tengela negotiating a succession process that rotates the *mansaya* between male descendants of Tengela (the Sonko) and Jammeh female rulers, until a dispute won by the Sonko ends the arrangement.

55. Frobenius, *Voice of Africa*, 2: 456.

56. Laye, *Guardian of the Word*, 58; Sidibé, *Sunjata*, 2.

57. Cissé and Kamissòko, *La grande geste du Mali*, 68–71; Diabaté, *Le lion à l'arc*, 62; Kanoute, "Formation de l'empire Mandingue," 33, makes no mention of Sogolon's physical appearance.

58. Quiquandon, "Histoire de la puissance Mandingue," 307. Quiquandon's source explains that "Koutouma" means "one who has humps."

59. Niane, *Sundiata*, 7; Courlander, *Treasury of African Folklore*, 72; Condé, "Sogolon and Sunjata," 102, 106.

60. Condé, "Sogolon and Sunjata,"101.

61. Zeltner, *Contes du Sénégal et du Niger*, 3; Kouyaté, "Sunjata," 167–68; Frobenius, *Voice of Africa*, 2: 456–57; Ly-Tall et al., *L'histoire du Mandé*, 32.

62. Zeltner, *Contes du Sénégal et du Niger*, 67; Niane, *Sundiata*, 4–11. Alternatively, Maghan Kon Fatta is advised by five *marabouts* or clerics from Timbuktu, an "Islamicization" of the process. Kanoute, "Formation de l'empire Mandingue," 32–33.

63. Conrad, "Mooning Armies and Mothering Heroes," 190–92.

64. Conrad, *Sunjata: A West African Epic*, 52–81.

65. Niane, *Sundiata*, 10–12.

66. Laye, *Guardian of the Word*, 90; Zeltner, *Contes du Sénégal*, 8; Doucoure and Marta, *Soundiata*, 268–342. According to one Keyla tradition, Sassuma Berete has at least one child by Maghan Kon Fatta before Sogolon Kedju's arrival, one Nakana Tiriba, already a "young girl" and cause of "the breasts of her mother who had no other infants to fall," indicating her declining desirability. Ly-Tall, et al, *L'histoire du Mandé*, 23.

67. Conrad, "Mooning Armies and Mothering Heroes," 202. See also Laye, *Guardian of the Word*, 77–106, for a lengthy discussion of what was a brief courtship.

68. Niane, *Sundiata*, 11–12; Konake, *Le grand destin*, 23–24; Frobenius, *Voice of Africa*, 457. The Keyla *jeli* Jabaté states both Sogolon and Sassuma became pregnant three months after the consummation with Sogolon. Ly-Tall et al., *L'histoire du Mandé*, 34–35.

69. Some versions suggest the length of Sogolon's pregnancy was fairly normal; Quiquandon, for example, says it lasted twelve months ("Histoire de la puissance Mandingue," 307). But others vary from seven or seventeen years to over four million, during which time Sunjata leaves the womb nightly to prey on lizards and other animals, an allusion to his hunting prowess if not his bestial qualities. See Innes, *Sunjata*, 39; Courlander, *Treasury of African Folklore*, 72; Sadji, "Ce que dit la musique africaine," 144; Kouyaté, "Village Issues and Mande Ancestors," 26; Cissé and

Kamissòko, *La grande geste du Mali*, 73–79; Kouyaté, "Sunjata," 170; Sidibé, *Sunjata*, 2; Jackson, "Prevented Successions," 101–2.

70. Niane, *Sundiata*, 13.

71. Zeltner, *Contes du Sénégal*, 8; Jackson, "Prevented Successions," 114.

72. The Qur'ān does not detail the life of Ismā'īl (Ishmael), son of Ibrāhīm, but commentaries, drawing upon the Hebrew Old Testament, essentially conform to this account of the rivalry between Ya'qūb and al-'Īsū. Sisòkò, *Epic of Son-Jara*, 126, also mentions the story of al-'Īsū /Esau as a possible model.

73. Quiquandon, "Histoire de la puissance mandingue," 307; Niane, "Histoire et tradition historique du Manding," 61–62, 69 (Niane adds, "and not Niani, as I wrote in 1958"). There is disagreement as to whether Sunjata was born in Dakadiala/Dakajalan, capital of Mali under Maghan Kon Fatta, or Niani, residence of subsequent *mansās*. Dakadiala/Dakajalan is current day Niagassola, a Pullo village, on the border with Mali, approximately 455 kilometers to the south of Kita. Niani, located between the Niger and the Bakhoy (or Semefe) Rivers and to the west of Kangaba, was also near the Bure goldfields. One source even ventures a date: Ramaḍān 598/January 1202 (Laye, *Guardian of the Word*, 119). As for the birth order, see Sisòkò, *Epic of Son-Jara*, 49–50; Diabaté, *Le lion à l'arc*, 64–66; Zeltner, *Contes du Sénégal*, 8–11; Quiquandon, "Histoire de la puissance Mandingue," 306–308; Sidibé, *Sunjata*, 3; Ly-Tall et al., *L'histoire du Mandé*, 34–36; Frobenius, *Voice of Africa*, 2: 458–59. Also see David Conrad, "A Town Called Dakajalan: The Sunjata Tradition and the Question of Ancient Mali's Capital," *Journal of African History* 35 (1994): 355–77; Wladyslaw Filipowiak, *Études archéologiques sur la capitale mediévale du Mali* (Szczecinie: Museum Narodwc, 1979).

74. Diabaté, *Le lion à l'arc*, 64–66; Sisòkò, *Epic of Son-Jara*, 51–52.

75. Niane, *Sundiata*, 14. Niane adds (*Sundiata*, 23) that at age 10, "The name Sogolon Djata in the rapid Mandingo language became Sundiata or Sondiata."

76. Zeltner, *Contes du Sénégal*, 13–14; Sidibé, *Sunjata*, 16–17. Such a designation does not necessarily correlate with the birth order: accounts claiming Dankaran Tuman as the firstborn associate the name Sunjata with "thief," but another with the same claim names Sunjata as firstborn. See Sisòkò, *Epic of Son-Jara*, 51–52; Zeltner, *Contes du Sénégal*, 13–14.

77. The non-ambulatory phase spans seven to thirty years, in one instance a response to his father's denial of paternity (as he was born an actual lion). Quiquandon, "Histoire de la puissance Mandingue," 307; Sidibé, *Sunjata*, 3–8; Innes, *Sunjata*, 40–41; Kanoute, "Formation de l'empire Mandingue," 35–36; Zeltner, *Contes du Sénégal et du Niger*, 9–11; Vidal, "La légende officielle," 320.

78. Jackson, "Prevented Successions," 122–23, underscores the "ambivalence" between a desire to remain a child and the need to realize one's full potential, resulting in a psychological "immobilization."

79. Hourst, *Sur le Niger*, 50; Diakité, "Livre renfermant la généalogie," 209–10; Vidal, "La légende officielle," 320; Adam, "Legendes historiques," 354–55. Sunjata's inability to walk conforms to the notion of "mythical children" who "display great precocity *and* various infantilisms." See Jackson, "Prevented Successions," 120.

80. Sisòkò, *Epic of Son-Jara*, 52. See also Konake, *Le grand destin*, 25–31. Sassuma Berete tries to kill Sunjata in the womb in another version, but the "foremost sorcerers of Mali . . . declared themselves incapable of tackling Sogolon." Niane, *Sundiata*, 13.

81. "He was afraid Sunjata would kill him or take over the rule of Manding. So he went to the jinn [and the] jinn said: 'I told you he would be a great ruler. . . . All I can do for you is to paralyze him.' The father asked the jinn to do it. And Sunjata was paralyzed for seven years." Courlander, *Treasury of African Folklore*, 72.

82. Sunjata "had nothing of the great beauty of the father." Niane, *Sundiata*,15; Zeltner, *Contes du Sénégal*, 10–11.

83. Sisòkò, *Epic of Son-Jara*, 9. In symbolically comparing Maghan Kon Fatta (the largest man in the land) to Sunjata, the latter grows 3 feet taller. Maghan's father's clothes are too large for Dankaran Tuman, as they were made for "some kind of giant," but the grandfather's pants only come to Sunjata's knees, and his head is too big for his hat. See Zeltner, *Contes du Sénégal*, 13–15; Quiquandon, "Histoire de la puissance Mandingue," 307–8.

84. Conrad, *Sunjata: A West African Epic*, xxi-xxii.

85. Cissé and Kamissòko, *La grande geste du Mali*, 98–99.

86. Ly-Tall, et al, *L'histoire du Mandé*, 37.

87. Also known as Sugulun Kulukan, Diegue, Dyigui Maniamba Suko, Kilidiumasorho, Kenin-Kuru-Juma-Suho, etc., she "had nothing of her father's beauty," resembling her mother instead. Sisòkò, *Epic of Son-Jara*, 64–65; Innes, *Sunjata*, 47–48; Diabaté, *Le lion à l'arc*, 82; Zeltner, *Contes du Sénégal*, 17; Quiquandon, "Histoire de la puissance Mandingue," 308–9; Delafosse, *Historiques et légendaries*, 25–26. According to Niane (*Sundiata*, 15–17), Maghan banishes Sogolon and her children for a period, foreshadowing the exile to come.

88. Diabaté, *Le lion à l'arc*, 69–72; Vidal, "La légende officielle," 320–21; Hourst, *Sur le Niger*, 50–52; Kouyaté, "Village Issues and Mande Ancestors," 26–27; Niane, *Sundiata*, 20–22; Quiquandon, "Histoire de la puissance Mandingue," 308. In the latter account, the process is immediate rather than lasting a year.

89. There are variations on when and how he gains the facility to walk. See Diakité, "Livre renfermant la généalogie," 209–10; Adam, "Légendes historiques," 355–56; Conrad, *Sunjata: A West African Epic*, 74–78; Kouyaté, "Village Issues and Mande Ancestors," 26–27; Kouyaté, "Sunjata," 178; Courlander, *Treasury of African Folklore*, 72–73; Condé, "Sogolon and Sunjata," 107–9; Vidal, "La légende officielle," 321; Zeltner, *Contes du Sénégal*, 13; Delafosse, "Histoire de la lutte entre les empires," 77; Delafosse, *Historiques et légendaries*, 21; Keita, *Kita*, 10; Sadji, "Ce que dit la musique africaine," 145; Diabaté, *Le lion à l'arc*, 73–75; Sidibé, "Soundiata Keita," 41; Sidibé, *Sunjata*, 3–8; Sisòkò, *Epic of Son-Jara*, 57–59; Innes, *Sunjata*, 42; Niane, *Sundiata*, 18; Frobenius, *Voice of Africa*, 2: 459, 461–62; Laye, *Guardian of the Word*, 125–32; Pageard, "Soundiata Keita," 54; Quiquandon, "Histoire de la puissance Mandingue," 307. Some assert his father's condition that he walk before he could be circumcised. See Zeltner, *Contes du Sénégal*, 14–15; Innes, *Sunjata*, 40–42. On the matter of succession, see Jackson, "Prevented Successions," 115–17. Traditions of the last quarter of the fourteenth/twentieth century combine indigenous supernatural agency with clerics and Qur'ānic verse to affect Sunjata's ability to walk, even calibrating the month as the same as the birth of Prophet Muḥammad (Rabi I or Rabī' al-Awwal) and Bilāl b. Rabāḥ. See Courlander, *Treasury of African Folklore*, 73; Sisòkò, *Epic of Son-Jara*, 54–55; Diabaté, *Le lion à l'arc*, 72.

90. Zeltner, *Contes du Sénégal*, 13; Condé, "Sogolon and Sunjata," 110–11; Niane, *Sundiata*, 22–23. Again, Niani is mistakenly given as the capital.

91. Hourst, *Sur le Niger*, 52; Courlander, *Treasury of African Folklore*, 73. This same source maintains Maghan caused Sunjata his disability.

92. Kouyaté, "Village Issues and Mande Ancestors," 28; James R. McGuire, "Butchering Heroism? Sunjata and the Negotiation of Postcolonial Mande Identity in Diabaté's *Le Boucher de Kouta*," in Austen, ed. *In Search of Sunjata*, 256–57; Jackson, "Prevented Successions," 100; Innes, *Sunjata*, 46–47; Adam, *Légendes historiques*, 356–57; Diakité, "Livre renfermant la généalogie," 209–10.

93. Ly-Tall et al., *L'histoire du Mandé*, 40; Kanoute, "Formation de l'empire Mandingue," 36–37; Pageard, "Soundiata Keita," 54; Cissé and Kamissòko, *La grande geste du Mali*, 106–09; Frobenius, *Voice of Africa*, 459–60; Quiquandon, "Histoire de la puissance Mandingue," 308; Sidibé, *Sunjata*, 19; Diabaté, *Le lion à l'arc*, 80–82.

94. Diabaté, *Le lion à l'arc*, 82; Kanoute, "Formation de l'empire Mandingue," 36–37; Sisòkò, *Epic of Son-Jara*, 65. All this talk of killing Sunjata finds figurative expression in an early version in which he turns into a bull and is dismembered at the hands of sorcerers "at the request of his relatives." Recalling the Egyptian tale of Osiris, a sorcerer recovers and pieces together the bull's parts, bringing Sunjata back to life. Frobenius, *Voice of Africa*, 2: 462–63. See also Sidibé, "Soundiata Keita," 43; Sidibé, *Sunjata*, 19–25. Unlike Osiris, Sunjata apparently reconnects with his penis.

95. *Corpus*, 334. Conrad, "Searching for History in the Sunjata Epic: The Case of Fakoli," 149, discusses the condensing properties of the Sunjata epic in which "several centuries of history have been telescoped into the period."

96. *Sūra Yūsuf*, Qur'ān 12.

97. John William Johnson, "The Dichotomy of Power and Authority in Mande Society and in the Epic of Sunjata," in Austin, ed., *In Search of Sunjata*, 14–20; Roderick James McIntosh, *The Peoples of the Middle Niger: The Island of Gold* (Oxford: Blackwell Publishers, Inc., 1988, 1998), 135–37; Conrad, "From the Banan Tree of Kouroussa," 386–89.

98. This relates in particular to Fakoli, whose paternal ancestors are said to have preceded those of Sunjata. See Conrad, "Searching for History in the Sunjata Epic," 169–70.

99. Bird, "Production and Reproduction of *Sunjata*," 286. The statement is from Seydou Camara, the famous hunter's "bard." As will be seen, there is an echo of this in the protest of *Mansā* Kara Kamara of Niani. Diabaté, *Le lion à l'arc*, 104; Cissé and Kamissòko, *La grande geste du Mali*, 27, 216–19; Vidal, "La légende officielle," 325–26.

100. Niane, *Sundiata*, 16, 23–24. Other accounts also mention Sunjata taking his mother, younger sister, and younger brother. Jeli Mori Kouyaté, "Ancestors, Sorcery, and Power," in Conrad, ed., *Epic Ancestors of the Sunjata Era*, 58–59; Frobenius, *Voice of Africa*, 2:463–66; Kouyaté, "Village Issues and Mande Ancestors," 28–29; Konake, *Le grand destin*, 53–63; Keita, *Kita*, 10.

101. Diabaté, *Le lion à l'arc*, 82, insists the sister Kolokon remained in the capital. The host allegedly includes Sogolon's youngest daughter (and Sunjata's other sister) Jamaru; the young slave "Jonfisico" or "Jufisigu"; the four marabouts Ture, Sisse, Baghayoro, and Silla; the smiths Bomu, Sambahe, Jombana, and Mangara; Sunjata's "fabulous three dogs" Buju, Dafin, and Kilikana; his two magical knives Muruni-Pempete and Muruni-Niamohojata; his two lances (that never missed their

targets) Tamba-Dale-Jokhe and Tamba-Dale-Bine; and his "terrible ax" Bobo-Sombe. Niane, *Sundiata*, 26–27. Other accounts mention Sunjata taking two or more of these persons. Sogolon Kedju and Manden Bukari are constants, but the "younger sister" is not. Frobenius, *Voice of Africa*, 2:463–66; Kouyaté, "Village Issues and Mande Ancestors," 21–22; Vidal, "La légende officielle," 32; Zeltner, *Contes du Sénégal*, 18–19; Quiquandon, "Histoire de la puissance Mandingue," 308–309.

102. His maternal uncle Sankara Danguina Kante (or Sangaran Danguinin Konto) is said to have been ruler of Do/Sangara. Diakité, "Livre renfermant la généalogie," 209; Adam, "Légendes historiques," 357; Delafosse, *Historiques et légendaries*, 21–22; Delafosse, "Histoire de la lutte entre les empires," 77.

103. Niane, *Sunjata*, 28; Diabaté, *Le lion à l'arc*, 84–85; Cissé and Kamissòko, *La grande geste du Mali*, 108–27; Conrad, *Sunjata: A West African Epic*, 82–94.

104. Niane, *Sundiata*, 28–34. In Jedeba he plays *wori* with the ruler, *Mansā* Konkon the "great sorcerer," from whom he wins a sword. *Wori* is a "Sudanic" or West African form of chess with local variations, involving placing seeds or pebbles into a checkered board until a certain number have been placed in a given hole. See A. Deledicq and A. Popova, *Wari et solo: Le jeu de calculs africain* (Paris: CEDIC, 1977); François Pingard, *L'awele, jeu de stratégie africain* (Paris: Éditions Chiron, 1993); Hunwick, *Timbuktu and the Songhay Empire*, 128, note 49.

105. Zeltner, *Contes du Sénégal*, 19–22; Frobenius, *Voice of Africa*, 2: 463–66. Delafosse, *Historiques et légendaries*, 22–23, mentions the province of Labe, in Futa Jallon, and that "Tâbo" was the name of the ancestor of the Bambara clan named "Dâbo." Adam, "Légendes historiques," 358, mentions "Lambé."

106. The Sisses are said to descend from Alexander the Great (often identified with the Qur'ānic figure of Dhū al-Qarnayn). In Ghana, Sunjata learns that the Soninke are now "great traders," a reference to the Jula (or Wangāra), and that "the Cissés were very religious" with many mosques in Ghana. Niane, *Sundiata*, 28–34.

107. "Tunkara" is actually the Soninke title *tunka* or "ruler," used in early Ghana and continuing into tenth/sixteenth-century Songhay.

108. Niane, *Sundiata*, 35–37; Diabaté, *Le lion à l'arc*, 88; Quiquandon, "Histoire de la puissance Mandingue," 309.

109. Niane, *Sundiata*, 35–37; Innes, *Sunjata*, 54.

110. Niane, *Sundiata*, 32.

111. This is repeated in Sisòkò, *Epic of Son-Jara*, 71, 131, where the annotations state "Kisi" means "to be spared." There is confusion here, as the Kisi belong to the West Atlantic family of languages that include Wolof, Sereer, etc. Niane's account largely concurs, stating that Dankaran fled "to the land of cola; and in those forested regions he founded the town of Kissidougou." Niane, *Sundiata*, 42.

112. Diabaté, *Le lion à l'arc*, 90–93; Sisòkò, *Epic of Son-Jara*, 69–71; Ly-Tall et al., *L'histoire du Mandé*, 49–52; Vidal, "La légende officielle," 321–23; Kanoute, "Formation de l'empire Mandingue," 38–39; Niane, *Sundiata*, 40; Cissé and Kamissòko, *La grande geste du Mali*, 126–27, 132–33, 162–67; Kanoute, "Formation de l'empire Mandingue," 38–39; Niane, *Sundiata*, 40; Diakité, "Livre renfermant la généalogie," 209; Sidibé, "Soundiata Keita," 41; Quiquandon, "Histoire de la puissance Mandingue," 310. The sources differ, but generally Dankaran Tuman sends either his eldest daughter Tasuma or oldest sister Nānā Triban, accompanied by the *jeli* Jakuma

Doka, alleged ancestor of the Kuyate *jeliw*, to Sumaoro in exchange for capturing and returning Sunjata to Dankaran. Sumaoro rejects the alliance but keeps the daughter or sister, along with the *jeli*, severing his tendons because he plays Sumaoro's *balafon* (a Mande xylophone) with such great skill, renaming him Balla Faseke Kuyate. As the *jeli* actually "belongs" to Sunjata, it adds a personal layer to their eventual conflict.

113. Vidal, "La légende officielle," 322; Quiquandon, "Histoire de la pusissance Mandingue," 310; Kouyaté, "Village Issues and Mande Ancestors," 31; Kouyaté, "Ancestors, Sorcery, and Power," 60; Niane, *Sundiata*, 42–45; Zeltner, *Contes du Sénégal*, 24–25; Adam, "Légendes historiques," 358; Diabaté, *Le lion à l'arc*, 94–95. The delegation consists of Singbin Mara Sisse (Karamangangwe Sonke), Siriman Ganda Maghan Ture, Fudi Jane, a woman named Magnuma, Sassuma's brother, and Tumbunjan Nakajan (Manjan) Berete, who speaks for the group. Singbin Mara Sisse, or Burgariba Sisse ("Bugari/Bukari the Great"), is considered the ancestor of the Sisses in Mali, the first of the Sisse marabouts from Wagadu. In one account the first two are seers, and in another all five are referred to as marabouts. I blend versions, assuming Bukari Kuma in Quiquandon's account is Magnuma in Niane's. In contrast, Innes identifies Sunjata's younger brother as the one who searches for him in Nema, reporting their other brothers had been killed by Sumaoro. Innes, *Sunjata*, 55–56.

114. Cissé and Kamissòko, *La grande geste du Mali*, 136–37; Sidibé, "Soundiata Keita," 43; Sidibé, *Sunjata*, 25. Kanoute, "Formation de l'empire Mandingue," 31, says the five families represented by these individuals were originally from Timbuktu.

115. Vidal, "La légende officielle," 324; Zeltner, *Contes du Sénégal*, 24–25; Quiquandon, "Histoire de la pusissance Mandingue," 310; Kouyaté, "Village Issues and Mande Ancestors," 32–33; Diabaté, *Le lion à l'arc*, 94–95; Cissé and Kamissòko, *La grande geste du Mali*, 140–43; Ly-Tall et al., *L'histoire du Mandé*, 52–56; Innes, *Sunjata*, 56. In Niane's version (*Sundiata*, 41) he prays to the east: "Almighty God, the time for action has come. If I must succeed in the reconquest of Mali, Almighty, grant that I may bury my mother in peace here."

116. Monteil, "Fin de siècle," 167; Conrad, *Sunjata: A West African Epic*, 140–45.

117. Cissé and Kamissòko, *La grande geste du Mali*, 106–9; Courlander, *History of African Folklore*, 74–75; Niane, *Sundiata*, 28.

118. Quiquandon, "Histoire de la puissance Mandingue," 310–11; Sidibé, "Soundiata Keita," 43; Diabaté, *Le lion à l'arc*, 97; Kouyaté, "Ancestors, Sorcery, and Power," 61; Cissé and Kamissòko, *La grande geste du Mali*, 142–50; Ly-Tall et al., *L'histoire du Mandé*, 56–57; Niane, *Sundiata*, 46–47; Kanoute, "Formation de l'empire Mandingue," 40. I have blended source details, but in a number of versions Tunkara not only heeds the warning, but also supplies Sunjata with an escort of eighty-eight persons under his two sons *Faran* Tunkara and *Faran* Birama, and "an army" of 10,000 archers.

119. Zeltner, *Contes du Sénégal*, 26; Arnaud, *L'Islam*, 168–71; Monteil, "Fin de siècle," 168; Vidal, "La légende officielle," 322; Innes, *Sunjata*, 56–58; Mamadi Diabaté, "Fakoli," in Conrad, ed., *Epic Ancestors of the Sunjata Era*, 81–82. Sunjata is said to sack fifty villages, slitting their leaders' throats and taking their eldest sons hostage, while another tradition says it was Sumaoro who defeats Mema, putting Mūsā Tunkara to flight while "ravaging" the country.

120. Niane, *Sundiata*, 38–42; Innes, *Sunjata*, 130; Sidibé, *Sunjata*, 9.

121. Ibid; Quiquandon, "Histoire de la puissance Mandingue," 310; Sidibé, "Soundiata Keita," 44; Innes, *Sunjata*, 73–77; Diakité, "Livre renfermant la généalogie," 210; Kanoute, "Formation de l'empire Mandingue," 36; Delafosse, "Histoire de la lutte entre les empires," 79.

122. Ibid; Cissé and Kamissòko, *La grande geste du Mali*, 126–29.

123. Diakité, "Livre renfermant la généalogie," 209; Adam, "Légendes historiques," 357; Cissé and Kamissòko, *La grande geste du Mali*, 26; Hourst, *Sur le Niger*, 52.

124. Sadji, "Ce que dit la musique africaine," 151.

125. Sumaoro's sister Kanguba Kante, journeying to help his struggling brother and impregnated by a *jinn*, returns to Sumaoro with a red copper firearm that summons a large army of male *jinn* when fired, explaining his rise to power. Diabaté, *Le lion à l'arc*, 90; Cissé and Kamissòko, *La grande geste du Mali*, 152–55. In Sidibé, *Sunjata*, 9–10, the gift is a magical *balafon*. Conrad, *Sunjata: A West African Epic*, xxvi. Ma Sira Condé was otherwise available to Sunjata through his uncle, ruler of Dò ni Kiri.

126. Hourst, *Sur le Niger*, 52; Arnaud, *L'Islam*, 165; Ly-Tall et al., *L'histoire du Mandé*, 93; Conrad, *Sunjata: A West African Epic*, 118–22. Because of the duration of his occupation, and revealing a far less antagonistic perspective, Sumaoro is considered by some *jeliw* as "the first king of the Manden," for whom a *janjon* was composed, in power for thirty years. Cissé and Kamissòko, *La grande geste du Mali*, 132–35, 181; Cissé and Kamissòko, *Soundjata, la gloire du Mali*, 121; Jansen, *Siramuri Diabaté*, 38, 36; Charles Bird, "The Production and Reproduction of *Sunjata*," in Austen, ed., *In Search of Sunjata*, 281. Jeli Fayala Kouyaté, "Kamanjan and Islam," in Conrad, ed., *Epic Ancestors of the Sunjata Era*, 47, says Sumaoro was the second *mansā* of Manden, the first being Kamanjan. It is not clear if Sumaoro's 30-year reign includes war with Sunjata.

127. Adam, "Légendes historiques," 358–59; Delafosse, *Historiques et légendaries*, 25.

128. Sunjata is said to have initially taken up residence in his village of birth, Dakadiala/Dakajalan. Cissé and Kamissòko, *Soundjata, la gloire du Mali*, 24–25, 50–51.

129. Quiquandon, "Histoire de la puissance Mandingue," 310–11; Niane, "Recherches sur l'empire du Mali," 20; Cissé and Kamissòko, *Soundjata, la gloire du Mali*, 14; Niane, *Sundiata*, 32, 47–50, 68. In other sources Mema's assistance consists of 10,000 archers, with the same number of archers from Damba Musa Wulandi Traore of Tukofo (married to one of Sunjata's sisters and connecting with the Traore brothers who accompany Sogolon Kedju to Mali).

130. Tymowski, *Origins and Structures of Political Institutions in Pre-Colonial Black Africa*, 37–47, discusses the coercive and contractual bases of power, and the instrumentality of key figures, all of which are applicable to Sunjata.

131. Robin Law, *The Horse in West African History: The Role of the Horse in the Societies of Pre-colonial Africa* (London: International African Institute, 1980); Brooks, *Landlords and Strangers*, 99–100; Keech McIntosh, "Reconceptualizing Early Ghana," 358. McIntosh's dating is based on recovery of horse bones and statuettes.

132. Conrad, "Searching for History in the Sunjata Epic," 150–54. A military figure conflated in the sources with the archetypical pilgrim "Fajigi" and known in Gambia as "Sora Musa" or "Sora the Pilgrim," he brings back secret rites and other traditions from Mecca. In turn, the character of Fajigi is based on the *ḥajj* of *Mansā* Mūsā.

133. Ibid. Though possibly literal, the wide mouth is probably representative of "Mande perceptions of the supreme power of speech," as he is said to "have been extremely convincing with his words."

134. Jansen, *Siramuri Diabaté*, 39, 82; Kouyaté, "Kamanjan and Islam," 49; Conrad, "Searching for History in the Sunjata Epic," 159. As for the "big head," Conrad says it may refer to Fakoli wearing the mask of the Komo blacksmiths, the "most important initiation fraternity of Mande society."

135. She is also referred to as Kenda Kala Naniuma Damba. Niane, "Histoire et tradition historique du Manding," 68; Sidibé, *Sunjata*, 24; Jansen, *Siramuri Diabaté*, 39; Cissé and Kamissòko, *La grande geste du Mali*, 174–79; Ly-Tall et al., *L'histoire du Mandé*, 51. Reference to *Mansā* Kara wearing chain mail may be anachronistic.

136. Mamadi Condé, "Fakoli and Sumaworo," in Conrad, ed. *Epic Ancestors of the Sunjata Era*, 140–45; Kouyaté, "Sunjata," 189–90; Innes, *Sunjata*, 272–83; Kanoute, "Formation de l'empire Mandingue," 39; Sidibé, "Soundiata Keita," 45; Diabaté, "Fakoli," 84–89; Cissé and Kamissòko, *La grande geste du Mali*, 174–79; Ly-Tall et al., *L'histoire du Mandé*, 58; Diabaté, *Le lion à l'arc*, 105–6; Cissé, *Le tana de Soumangouro*, 48–51; Niane, "Recherches sur l'empire du Mali," 19; Innes, *Sunjata*, 295; Laye, *Guardian of the Word*, 177; Conrad, "Searching for History in the Sunjata Epic: The Case of Fakoli," 162–64. The *jeli ngara* Djanka Tassey Condé maintains Sumaoro took her as wife, but only as a cook, as she and he were related (Conrad, *Sunjata: A West African Epic*, 167–68). Elsewhere, Niane ("Histoire et tradition historique du Manding," 68) states Fakoli and Sumaoro "fell out" during festivities celebrating their victory over Niani *Mansā* Kara, not necessarily at odds with the majority view.

137. I take liberties referring to Fakoli as "gator-mouthed"; of course, crocodiles are found in Africa, not alligators. Fakoli Da-Ba means "Wide-Mouthed Fakoli." Niane, *Sundiata*, 61.

138. Sunjata is at Dayala on the Niger River, near Krina, on the verge of the decisive battle with Sumaoro, when word reaches him of Fakoli's defection. Sunjata's lieutenants gather their troops to receive Fakoli in ceremonial formation, and after consulting his "war chiefs," Sunjata accepts Fakoli's allegiance: "I am Fakoli Koroma . . . I bring you my strong-armed smiths, I bring you sofas." Niane, *Sundiata*, 61; Sisòkò, *Epic of Son-Jara*, 93–96.

139. Diabaté, *Le lion à l'arc*, 104; Innes, *Sunjata*, 301–3.

140. Sisòkò, *Epic of Son-Jara*, 89–90; Vidal, "La légende officielle," 324. The crossing required the help of Samayana or "Sasagalo the Tall," leader of the Somono.

141. Some state Sunjata initially loses a number of battles, with early accounts concurring, claiming Sunjata tasted defeat in 9,000 skirmishes and three major battles in a war lasting 20 years. See Vidal, "La légende officielle," 324–25; Monteil, "Fin de siècle," 168; Innes, *Sunjata*, 70; Quenum, 'La légende de Fama-Soundiata," 53–54; Sisòkò, *Epic of Son-Jara*, 90–91; Quiquandon, "Histoire de la puissance Mandingue," 315; Arnaud, *L'Islam*, 170.

142. Niane, *Sundiata*, 26. Conrad ("Mooning Armies and Mothering Heroes," 193) points out the ambiguous position of women in these stories.

143. "Sunjata appears, not as the agent of his destiny, but as an instrument determined by fate. The women are the determining actors in the story." Bird, "The Production and Reproduction of *Sunjata*," 287. On the various angles to Kolokon

ruse, see Diabaté, *Le lion à l'arc*, 105–6; Arnaud, *L'Islam*, 170–71; Innes, *Sunjata*, 72; Zeltner, *Contes du Sénégal*, 27–28; Hourst, *Sur le Niger*, 52; Sidibé, "Soundiata Keita," 44; Adam, "Légendes historiques," 358; Monteil, "Fin de siècle," 168; Quiquandon, "Histoire de la puissance mandingue," 315; Delafosse, *Historiques et légendaries*, 25–26; Delafosse, "Histoire de la lutte entre les empires," 78; Kanoute, "Formation de l'empire Mandingue," 48–51. In the most popularized version of Sunjata's story, it is Nānā Triban, daughter of Sassuma and sister of Dankaran, who returns to Sunjata with the vital information. See Diabaté, *Le lion à l'arc*, 90–92; Sisòkò, *Epic of Son-Jara*, 68–69; Ly-Tall, et al, *L'histoire du Mandé*, 49–51; Niane, *Sundiata*, 56–58.

144. Vidal, "La légende officielle," 322–23; Innes, *Sunjata*, 72–77; Zeltner, *Contes du Sénégal*, 28–29; Delafosse, *Historiques et légendaries*, 26; Quiquandon, "Histoire de la puissance Mandingue," 315; Adam, "Légendes historiques," 359–61; Diakité, "Livre renfermant," 210; Diabaté, *Le lion à l'arc*, 106; Delafosse, *Historiques et légendaries*, 25–26; Delafosse, "Histoire de la lutte entre les empires," 78; Arnaud, *L'Islam*, 170–71.Niane, *Sundiata*, 57–58, 64–65; Sidibé, "Soundiata Keita," 40–45; Monteil, "Fin de siècle," 169–70; Kanoute, "Formation de l'empire Mandingue," 48–51; Diakité, "Livre renfermant," 210; Sisòkò, *Epic of Son-Jara*, 91–93; Hourst, *Sur le Niger*, 52–53. In Quenum, 'La légende de Fama-Soundiata," 59–65, it is a black-and-white arrow that has lethal power over Sumaoro, and Kolokon (Jyégué in the text) takes it after their interlude. In Kanoute, "Formation de l'empire Mandingue," 48–51, Sumaoro says the source of his power, in addition to the rooster spur, comes from 100 "pygmies" in the forest.

145. Cissé and Kamissòko, *La grande geste du Mali*, 11, 54, 358–59; Pageard, "Soundiata Keita," 55; Niane, *Sundiata*, 55–56, 63; Cissé, *La confrérie des chasseurs Malinké at Bambara*, 29–43; Cissé and Kamissòko, *Soundjata, la gloire du Mali*, 11–16, state that "night combat" began at Krina, "the first of its kind experienced by Sudanese armies."

146. Adam, "Légendes historiques," 360–61. See also Cissé and Kamissòko, *Soundjata, la gloire du Mali*, 13–14; Delafosse, *Historiques et légendaries*, 28; Delafosse, "Histoire de la lutte entre les empires," 78; Cissé and Kamissòko, *Soundjata, la gloire du Mali*, 14–17; Niane, *Sundiata*, 59–69; Zeltner, *Contes du Sénégal*, 30–31; Monteil, "Fin de siècle," 170; Innes, *Sunjata*, 78–79.

147. Vidal, "La légende officielle," 324–25; Sidibé, "Soundiata Keita," 45; Zeltner, *Contes du Sénégal*, 32; Hourst, *Sur le Niger*, 53; Sisòkò, *Epic of Son-Jara*, 94–96; Innes, *Sunjata*, 311; Diakité, "Livre renfermant," 210; Delafosse, *Historiques et légendaries*, 26, 28–29; Delafosse, "Histoire de la lutte entre les empires," 79; Adam, "Légendes historiques," 362; Kanoute, "Formation de l'empire Mandingue," 51–52; Quiquandon, "Histoire de la puissance Mandingue," 316; Cissé and Kamissòko, *Soundjata, la gloire du Mali*, 22, 27; Niane, *Sundiata*, 64–83; Quenum, 'La légende de Fama-Soundiata," 67–69. Sidibé, *Sunjata*, 44, says Sumaoro became a "great whirlwind." On the Battle of Ngeboriya, see Conrad, *Sunjata: A West African Epic*, 175–77.

148. Niane, *Sundiata*, 67–69, 78; Niane, "Recherches sur l'empire du Mali," 23–24; Cissé and Kamissòko, *Soundjata, la gloire du Mali*, 17–24, 30; Delafosse, *Historiques et légendaries*, 30.

149. One tradition tells of the Susu seeking refuge in Futa Jallon and becoming the ancestors of the Jallonke. See Arnaud, *L'Islam*, 171.

150. Niane, *Sundiata*, 76; Quiquandon, "Histoire de la puissance Mandingue," 316. Niani is described a "rich and prosperous town," in existence from at least 550 CE. Niane, "Histoire et tradition historique du Manding," 74; Vidal, "La légende officielle," 325–26.

151. Niani is described a "rich and prosperous town," in existence from at least 550 CE. Niane, "Histoire et tradition historique du Manding," 74; Vidal, "La légende officielle," 325–26. See also Diabaté, *Le lion à l'arc*, 104; Cissé and Kamissòko, *La grande geste du Mali*, 27, 216–19; Vidal, "La légende officielle," 325–26; Sisòkò, *Epic of Son-Jara*, 97.

152. Niane, "Histoire et tradition historique du Manding," 69; Vidal, "La légende officielle," 328; Cissé and Kamissòko, *Soundjata, la gloire du Mali*, 50–51. Niani is said to subsequently become the residence of Mali's rulers and renamed Nianiba or "Niani the Great," though it may have not have become Mali's capital until the tenth/sixteenth century. Conrad, "A Town Called Dakajalan"; Filipowiak, *Études archéologiques sur la capitale medièvale du Mali*.

153. Boubacar Barry, *Le royaume du Waalo: Le Sénégal avant le conquête* (Paris: François Maspéro, 1972), 46–52; Boubacar Barry, *Senegambia and the Atlantic Slave Trade* (Cambridge: Cambridge U. Press, 1998), 5–25; Belcher, "*Sinimogo*, 'Man for Tomorrow'," 92–96.

154. Zeltner, *Contes du Sénégal*, 33–36; Quiquandon, "Histoire de la puissance Mandingue," 316. In another account, the Jolof king kills all but one of Sunjata's delegation, relieving him of his arm and eyes and sending him back with the message: "Tell him [Sunjata] that he is a shoe-wearing king, not a horse-riding king" (Innes, *Sunjata*, 82–83). In yet another, the "Jolofin Mansa" sends Sunjata dogs and animal skins, as he is "only a common hunter" (Diabaté, *Le lion à l'arc*, 117–18). According to Kanoute ("Formation de l'empire Mandingue," 39–30), the ruler of Jolof had been an ally of Sumaoro.

155. Diabaté, *Le lion à l'arc*, 117–21; Sisòkò, *Epic of Son-Jara*, 98–101; Kanoute, "Formation de l'empire Mandingue," 52–57; Innes, *Sunjata*, 82–83; Jansen, *Siramuri Diabaté*, 40, 47; Zeltner, *Contes du Sénégal*, 35–36; Quiquandon, "Histoire de la puissance Mandingue," 316; Cissé and Kamissòko, *La grande geste du Mali*, 28; Ly-Tall et al., *L'histoire du Mandé*, 66–69; Cissé and Kamissòko, *Soundjata, la gloire du Mali*, 97; Conrad, *Sunjata: A West African Epic*, 187–95. Reacting to Sunjata's insistence on going himself, Tiramakan lays in a grave, vowing to die if not given the honor. Stunned, Sunjata relents, with Tiramakan given the praise name Su-Sare-Jon, "slave of the tomb."

156. Quiquandon, "Histoire de la puissance Mandingue," 316; Barry, *Senegambia and the Atlantic Slave Trade*, 6–7; Vidal, "La légende officielle," 326; Levtzion, *Ancient Ghana and Mali*, 95. Along the Gambia this would include Gadugu, Baniakadugu, Gangaran, Diaka on the Bafin, Tambaora, Dentillia, Badon, Wuli, Niani, Diakoto, Nyanina, Gabon, Sansanto, Dakao, Baku, Seydiu, Diola, and Salum.

157. Barry, *Senegambia and the Atlantic Slave Trade*, 6–7.

158. Many claim origins in *tilebo*, "the East," a reference to Manden, and the relatively large clans of the Jammeh and Manneh in Gambia claim descent from "Sora Musa" or Fakoli, and Tiramakan, respectively. Wright, *Oral Traditions from the Gambia*, vols. 1 and 2; Donald R. Wright, "Koli Tengela in Sonko Traditions of Origin: An

Example of the Process of Change in Mandinka Oral Tradition," *History in Africa* 5 (1978): 258–61; Donald R. Wright, "Beyond Migration and Conquest: Oral Traditions and Mandinka Ethnicity in Senegambia," *History in Africa* 12 (1985): 335–48; Stephen Belcher, "*Sinimogo*, 'Man for Tomorrow'," 94–102.

159. Quiquandon, "Histoire de la puissance Mandingue," 316–17. Walata/Biru would have been around by then. Timothy Cleaveland, *Becoming Walāta*.

160. Cissé and Kamissòko, *Soundjata, la gloire du Mali*, 46–47. Discussion of conflict with the Tuareg relates to claims that Jula activity, referred to as "Marakas" in Manden, picks up considerably under Sunjata. See Niane, "Recherches sur l'empire du Mali," 24; Niane, *Sundiata*, 82; Cissé and Kamissòko, *La grande geste du Mali*, 183–84, 190–91; Cissé and Kamissòko, *Soundjata, la gloire du Mali*, 46–49.

161. As stated in the Prologue, my definition of "empire" is consistent with Burbank and Cooper (*Empires in World History*, 8). This approach also resonates with Nehemia Levtzion, "The Early States of the Western Sudan to 1500," in Ajayi and Crowder, eds., *History of West Africa* 3rd ed., 1:153–63; and John Hunwick, "Songhay, Borno and the Hausa States, 1450–1600," in Ajayi and Crowder, eds., *History of West Africa* 3rd ed., 1:347—who explain why they view Mali and Songhay as empires. I therefore differ with Tymowski (*Origins and Structures of Political Institutions in Pre-Colonial Black Africa*, 87–90), who posits that the Ethiopian church's "separate identity" (curious claim given the ties to Egypt) qualifies the state as an empire, as opposed to Muslim West African states that are not "fully formed imperial systems" in that their "center" was Mecca and Medina. In failing to differentiate between spiritual and political centers, he further disqualifies their heterogeneity as not "identical" with what he has in mind (suggesting ideas regarding the divergent nature of African societies?). See also Michal Tymowski, "Use of the Term 'Empire' in Historical Research on Africa: A Comparative Approach," *Afrika Zamani*, 2006.

162. Niane, *Sundiata*, 70–72; Cissé and Kamissòko, *Soundjata, la gloire du Mali*, 24–41.

163. Niane, *Sundiata*, 71–72; Cissé and Kamissòko, *Soundjata, la gloire du Mali*, 48.

164. Vidal, "La légende officielle," 325, 318.

165. Such as a griot. Diabaté, *Le lion à l'arc*, 15–16.

166. Kamanjan's archery skills are rivaled only by those of Sunjata himself. Kouyaté, "Ancestors, Sorcery, and Power," 61; Niane, *Sundiata*, 75.

167. Levtzion, *Ancient Ghana and Mali*, 55, 102, 106.

168. Niane says it came to mean "emperor" ("Recherches sur l'empire du Mali," 37–38).

169. Niane, *Sundiata*, 75; Cissé and Kamissòko, *Soundjata, la gloire du Mali*, 27–28.

170. Niane, *Sundiata*, 78; Cissé and Kamissòko, *Soundjata, la gloire du Mali*, 46–47.

171. Cissé and Kamissòko, *Soundjata, la gloire du Mali*, 47.

172. Ibid, 30; Niane, "Recherches sur l'empire du Mali," 21–22. The notion of a "constitution" governing political relations, a new "charter" for hunting societies, and the rearticulation of social principles, mores, and protocols are also cited in the secondary literature and in late fourteenth/twentieth century traditions, all rather for-

ward-looking. See Cissé and Kamissòko, *Soundjata, la gloire du Mali*, 39–41; Niane, "Recherches sur l'empire du Mali," 23; Youssouf Tata Cissé, *La charte du Mandé et autres traditions du Mali* (Paris: Albin Michel, 2003).

173. Johnson, "The Dichotomy of Power," 11–13.

174. Niani (*Sundiata*, 81) says "each year long caravans carried the taxes in kind to Niani."

175. The literature on slavery in Africa is extensive, with some listed in chapter 13.

176. Diabaté, *Le lion à l'arc*, 23–24; Johnson, "The Dichotomy of Power," 11. The *nyamakala* were further divided into the *numu* (blacksmiths), *jeliw* (griots), *garanke* (leatherworkers), and *fune* (less-regarded griots of the Bambara and Soninke).

177. For example, only the *horon* would subsequently be able to hold the office of the *dugu-kolo-tigi*, or "earth-surface master" responsible for the village's ritual life and an alleged to descend from the first to occupy the land; or that of the *dugu-tigi*, the "earth or village master" who exercised political authority and usually descended from a family who either conquered the village or protected it from conquest.

178. *Corpus*, 333. Cissé and Kamissòko (*La grande geste du Mali*, 28, 122), in saying Sunjata was in power for 40 to 45 years, concur he died in 656/1258. Niane initially estimates Sunjata died in 1250, only to later change it to 1255, yielding 1230 for the Battle of Krina. Niane claims support for these dates in *Ta'rīkh al-fattāsh*, but I am unable to locate that information. Niane, *Recherches sur l'empire du Mali*, 39–43.

179. Ibid, 82–83; Vidal, "La légende officielle," 326–28; Diabaté, *Le lion à l'arc*, 124–25. According to Kanoute ("Formation de l'empire Mandingue," 69–71), like Sumaoro, Sunjata disappears mysteriously. Another tradition says he drowns while fleeing the Fulbe of Wassulu. Sidibé, "Soundiata Keita," 45–47.

180. Cissé and Kamissòko, *La grande geste du Mali*, 29; Cissé and Kamissòko, *Soundjata, la gloire du Mali*, 131–34; Johnson, "The Dichotomy of Power," 13; Conrad, "Searching for History in the Sunjata Epic," 159.

181. For example, see Vidal, "La légende officielle," 321; Zeltner, *Contes du Sénégal*, 18–19; Quiquandon, "Histoire de la puissance Mandingue," 310. See also Camara, *Gens de la parole*, who provides useful insight into Mande social structure, including such matters as the "joking relationships" between them.

182. As such, Sunjata is emblematic of the "union of Saharan mercantilism, deeply marked by Islam," while Sumaoro is a smith, "and the blacksmith ancestor is responsible for all Mande civilization." See Bird, "Production and Reproduction of *Sunjata*," 290–92. This is related to "status discourse" in which recent arrivals are "younger brothers," able to achieve prominence without "older" authorities, aptly describing Sunjata's trajectory. See Jan Jansen, "The Representation of Status in Mande: Did the Mali Empire Still Exist in the Nineteenth Century?" *History in Africa* 23 (1996): 87–109; Stephen Bühnen, "Brothers, Chiefdoms, and Empires: On Jan Jansen's 'The Reproduction of Status in Mande'," *History in Africa* 23 (1996): 111–20; L.E. Kubeel, "On the History of Social Relations in the West [*sic*] Sudan in the 8th to the 16th Centuries," *Africa in Soviet Studies Annual* (1968): 109–28.

183. Bird makes this point in referencing the Mamprusi and Zarma and other "horse warriors" akin to the Maninka. Bird, "Production and Reproduction of *Sunjata*," 292.

184. Diakité, "Livre renfermant la généalogie," 209; Conrad, "Oral Sources and Links," 40–41; Niane, *Sundiata*, 38.

185. However, in a very late collection, he is rejected by Manden because he is a smith, a possible anachronism. Cissé and Kamissòko, *La grande geste du Mali*, 26, 128–29. In another account, Sogolon Kolokon tells Sumaoro that "a princess of Manding, and a smith would not sleep together," yet in many versions that is precisely what happens. Innes, *Sunjata*, 72.

186. Niane, "Recherches sur l'empire du Mali," 23–24; Arnaud, *L'Islam*, 171; Cissé and Kamissòko, *Soundjata, la gloire du Mali*, 30–31.

187. Niane, *Sundiata*, 61.

188. The idea that the Sumaoro-Sunjata conflict pitted ancestral religion against Islam is therefore less productive. As an example, consider the statement: "The fortified town of Soso was the bulwark of fetishism against the word of Allah." Ibid, 41.

189. For example, see Niane, *Sundiata*, 51–52, 59–60, 63, 73, 80.

190. One source states unequivocally that Sunjata was not a Muslim. Cissé and Kamissòko, *Soundjata, la gloire du Mali*, 249; Johnson, "The Dichotomy of Power," 13; Conrad, "Searching for History in the Sunjata Epic," 159.

191. Levtzion, *Ancient Ghana and Mali*, 190, lists five maraboutic families: the Berte, Ture, Sisse, Saghanogho, and Jane. The Baghayoro and Saghanogho are the same.

Chapter 6: Mansā *Mūsā and Global Mali*

1. M. Adam, "Légendes historiques du pays de Nioro (Sahel)," *Revue coloniale* 1903: 362; Dembo Kanoute, "Formation de l'empire Mandingue," in T. Sanogho and I. Diallo, trans., *L'histoire de l'Afrique authentique*, 69–71; Niane, *Sundiata*; Cissé and Kamissòko, *Soundjata, la gloire du Mali*, 131–36, 158–205; Cissé and Kamissòko, *La grande geste du Mali*, 29.

2. Not unlike social imbalances introduced into early-twentieth-century Botswana by migrant labor. See Julie Livingston, *Debility and the Moral Imagination in Botswana* (Bloomington and Indianapolis: Indiana U. Press, 2005), especially 107–41.

3. *Corpus*, 333–34.

4. Niane, "Recherches sur l'empire du Mali au moyen âge," 40.

5. *Corpus*, 79.

6. Ibid, 285. He mentions only seeing this elsewhere "among the Indian infidels in the land of Mulaybār."

7. Cissé and Kamissòko, *Soundjata, la gloire du Mali*, 131–36. The alleged revolt had roots in the previous century, when rogue Mande leader Bintu Mari enslaved Filadugu-Bankassi. Survivors resettled in Wassulu, but those remaining in Filadugu-Bankassi marched on Manden to avenge Bintu Mari's exactions, and were met at Damagan-Farani, resonating with the claim Sunjata was killed by the Fulbe of Wassulu.

8. One scenario has Fakoli fleeing Sunjata, removed from governing Susu for being too independent. Adam, "Légendes historiques," 362; Kanoute, "Formation de l'empire Mandingue," 69–71; Niane, *Sundiata*, 81.

9. Kamanjan supposedly takes seven years to raise an army, but dies just before he staging his return, his two younger brothers settling for control of Narena village. As Kong's founding is attributed to the Jula, possibly in the tenth/

sixteenth century, this account may seek to associate Kamanjan with the Jula. See Robert Launay, "Warriors and Traders: The Political Organization of a West African Chiefdom," *Cahiers d'études africaines* 28 (1988): 355–73; Mahir Saul, "The War Horses of the Watara in West Africa," *International Journal of African Historical Studies* 31 (1998): 537–70; Victor Azarya, "Jihads and the Dyula State in West Africa," in S.N. Eisenstadt, Michel Abitbol, and Naomi Chazan, eds., *The Early State in African Perspective* (Leiden: E.J. Brill, 1988), 60–97. Cissé and Kamissòko, *Soundjata, la gloire du Mali*, 201–206. This account claims the Grand Council sought to bring back "the vomit of the entire country," Sunjata's brother Dankaran Tumane.

10. One source names Mamuru Koroba as successor, either Sunjata's brother or first cousin. Cissé and Kamissòko, *La grande geste du Mali*, 29, 286–87; Cissé and Kamissòko, *Soundjata, la gloire du Mali*, 158–205; Paul Vidal, "La légende officielle de Soundiata fondateur de l'empire Manding," *Bulletin du Comité d'études historiques et scientifiques de l'Afrique occidentale française* 7 (1924): 328; Niane, "Recherches sur l'empire du Mali," 1:22, 39.

11. Niane, "Recherches sur l'empire du Mali,", 2:22.

12. *Corpus*; Cissé and Kamissòko, *La grande geste du Mali*, 286–87.

13. *Corpus*, 333; Adam, "Légendes historiques," 362.

14. Johnson, "The Dichotomy of Power and Authority in Mande Society," 14–20; Roderick James McIntosh, *The Peoples of the Middle Niger: The Island of Gold* (Oxford: Blackwell Publishers, Inc., 1988, 1998), 135–37.

15. *Corpus*, 333.

16. Ibid, 333–34; Niane, "Recherches sur l'empire du Mali," 1:40.

17. *Corpus*, 334.

18. Vidal, "La légende officielle," 328; Seydou Camara, "La tradition orale en question: Conservation et transmission des traditions historiques au Manden: Le Centre de Kela et l'histoire du Mininjan" (Thèse de doctorat de l'E.H.E.S.S., Paris, 1990), 382–83.

19. *Corpus*, 334.

20. Ibid, 456.

21. Ibid, 334.

22. Ibid, 305, 334; Niane, "Recherches sur l'empire du Mali," 1:40–42. Niani confuses what Ibn Khaldūn actually states regarding Mūsā's relationship to Sunjata.

23. *Corpus*, 268–69.

24. Most famously, see Ivan Van Sertima's *They Came Before Columbus: The African Presence in Ancient America* (New York: Random House, 1976) for speculation concerning West African pre-Columbian voyages to the Americas.

25. E. Mittelstaedt, "The Ocean Boundary along the Northwest African Coast: Circulation and Oceanographic Properties at the Sea Surface," *Progress in Oceanography* 26 (1991), 307–55; M. Zhou, J.D. Paduan, P.P. Niiler, "Surface Currents in the Canary Basin from Drifter Observations," *Journal of Geophysical Research* 105 (2000): 21893–21911; Joanna Gyory, Arthur J. Mariano, Edward H. Ryan, "The Canary Current," http://oceancurrents.rsmas.miami.edu/atlantic/canary.html; John Thornton, *Africa and Africans in the Making of the Atlantic World, 1400–1680* (Cambridge: Cambridge U. Press, 1992); Raymond Mauny, *Les navigations médiévales sur*

les côtes sahariennes antérieures à la découverte portugaise (1434) (Lisbon: Centro de Estudos Históricos Ultramarinos, 1960).

26. *Corpus*, 261, 333.

27. Ibid, 190–91. Blown off course, the crew was initially stranded among the Judāla (or Gudāla) Berbers along the coast from southern Mauritania to the Senegal.

28. Ibid, 272–73.

29. Ibid, 106–7, 110.

30. Alvise da Ca da Mosto, *The Voyages of Cadamosto*, G.R. Crone, ed. (London: Hakluyt Society, 1937), 20, 34.

31. Ca da Mosto, *The Voyages of Cadamosto*, 57–58.

32. On West African canoes, see Robin Law, "West Africa's Discovery of the Atlantic," *International Journal of African Historical Studies* 44 (2011): 1–5; K. Nwachukwu-Ogedengbe, "Slavery in Nineteenth-Century Aboh," in Suzanne Miers and Igor Kopytoff, eds., *Slavery in Africa: Historical and Anthropological Perspectives* (Madison: U. of Wisconsin Press, 1977), 142–50.

33. *Corpus*, 305. The date of Mūsā's *ḥajj* is reiterated in the sources, including Ibn al-Dawādārī, Ibn Khaldūn, and al-Maqrīsī (*Corpus*, 249–50, 334, 351).

34. *Recueil*, 327.

35. *Corpus*, 340–41, 335.

36. Ibid, 295–96.

37. Ibid, 305.

38. *Recueil*, 326–27.

39. *Corpus*, 351.

40. *TS*, 6/12–13; Hunwick, *Timbuktu and the Songhay Empire*, 9–10; *TF*, 34–35/57–61.

41. The figure of 15,000 is simply an average of the external sources, easily supported by the internal written documents.

42. *Corpus*, 250, 269, 323, 351.

43. Mauny, *Tableau géographique*, 300. If the Lobi goldfields are added (.2 tons per annum), the amount increases to 47 tons.

44. *Corpus*, 271, 305, 351. Al-Maqrīzī is even more dramatic, asserting gold fell by six *dirhams* per dīnār.

45. Ibid, 335.

46. Ibid, 267–68.

47. See Roberts, *Warriors, Merchants, and Slaves*.

48. *Corpus*, 272.

49. However, Keech McIntosh speculates Lobi may have been in production early in West Africa's gold trade. See Susan Keech McIntosh, "A Reconsideration of Wangāra/Palolus, Island of Gold," *Journal of African History* 22 (1981): 145–58.

50. *Corpus*, 250. As Christianity in West Africa as this time is unverifiable, in contrast to ancestral practice, their equation may have been meant as a critique of the former.

51. Ibid, 262. I differ just a bit with the translation of Levtzion and Hopkins.

52. Ibid, 276.

53. This arrangement was hardly novel; as early as the fourth/tenth century, al-Mas'ūdī (d. 345/956) describes participants transacting business without seeing each

other, expanded on by *Akbār al-zamān* ("History of the Ages") and repeated in several external sources—the infamous "silent trade." Ibid, 35–36, 39, 96, 169–70, 177–78.

54. Ibid, 39, 83, 148–49, 260.

55. Ibid, 128, 169–70, 177–78. Al-Idrisī states "opulent, wealthy merchants" from Aghmat entered "the land of the Sūdān with numbers of camels bearing immense sums in red and coloured copper and garments," underscored in the following century by al-Qazwīnī and Yāqūt b. ʿAbd Allāh al-Ḥamawī al-Rūmī.

56. Ibid, 272.

57. Mauny, *Tableau géographique*, 310, locates the mine in the Nioro region of the Sahel.

58. *TF*, 33/56–57.

59. See *TF*, 56, note 2; S.M. Cissoko, "Quel est le nom de plus grand empereur du Mali: Kankan Moussa ou Kankou Moussa," *Notes africaines* 124 (1969): 113–14; Hunwick, *Timbuktu and the Songhay Empire*, 9, note 1.

60. *TF*, 32/56–57.

61. On *baraka*, see John O. Hunwick, "Religion and State in the Songhay Empire, 1464–1591," in I.M. Lewis, *Islam in Tropical Africa* (London: Oxford U. Press, 1966).

62. Louise Levathes, *When China Ruled the Seas: The Treasure Fleet of the Dragon Throne, 1405–1433* (Oxford: Oxford U. Press, 1997); Edward Dreyer, *Zheng He: China and the Oceans in the Early Ming, 1405-1433* (London: Pearson, 2006).

63. Malyn Newitt, *A History of Portuguese Overseas Expansion, 1400–1668* (New York and London: Routledge, 2005); A.J.R. Russell-Wood, *The Portuguese Empire, 1415–1808: A World on the Move* (Baltimore: Johns Hopkins U. Press, 1998).

64. Periodic famine also played a role. See M. Ly-Tall, "The Decline of the Mali Empire," *UNESCO General History of Africa* 4 (Berkeley: U. of California Press, 1984), 172–86; Sékéné Mody Cissoko, "Famines et épidémies à Tombouctou et dans le Boucle du Niger du XVIe au XVIIIe siècle," *Bulletin de l'Institut Français* (later *Fondamental*) *d'Afrique Noire (IFAN)* 30 (1966): 806–21; M. Tymowski, "Famines et épidémies au Soudan nigérien du XVIe au XIXe siècle—causes locales et influences extérieures," *Hemispheres* 5 (1988): 5–27; A.G. Hopkins, "The Western Sudan in the Middle Ages: Underdevelopment in the Empires of the Western Sudan," *Past and Present* 37 (1967): 149–56; Jack Goody, ed., *Literacy in Traditional Societies* (Cambridge: Cambridge U. Press, 1968).

65. And the Mongols once had a fleet, allegedly destroyed off Japan's coast in 672–3/1274 and 679–80/1281 by a "divine wind" or *kamikaze*. See Timothy May, *The Mongol Conquests in World History* (London: Reaktion Books, 2012); Morris Rossabi, *The Mongols and Global History* (New York and London: W.W. Norton and Co., 2011); Thomas T. Allsen, *Commodity and Exchange in the Mongol Empire* (Cambridge: Cambridge U. Press, 1997): ____, *Culture and Conquest in Mongol Eurasia* (Cambridge: Cambridge U. Press, 2001); Virgil Ciocîltan, *The Mongols and the Black Sea Trade in the Thirteenth and Fourteenth Centuries*, trans. Samuel Willcocks (Leiden and Boston: E.J. Brill, 2012).

66. Abun-Nasr, *A History of the Maghrib in the Islamic Period* , 119–58.

67. Marshall G.S. Hodgson, *The Venture of Islam: Conscience and History in a World Civilization* (Chicago: U. of Chicago Press, 1974), 2:255–419.

68. Al-Maqrīzī maintains it was the following day, while Ibn Ḥajar simply gives the month. *Corpus*, 250, 305, 323, 340, 351.355, 358; *Recueil*, 327. *TF* claims the *mansā* was instructed by his "teachers" (*mashā'ikh*) to wait until the Saturday that fell on the twelfth day of the month before embarking—which would have been another nine months—to ensure his safe travel and return, unlikely since he would have had to make preparations in a significantly telescoped period of time. *TF*, 33/57.

69. *TS*, 7/13; Hunwick, *Timbuktu and the Songhay Empire*, 9–10.

70. 'Alī al-Janaḥānī also wrote that the "ramparts of the city were of salt as also all its walls, pillars, and roofs." *Corpus*, 282.

71. *TF*, 33–37/56–64.

72. *Corpus*, 323.

73. Ibid, 323, 355.

74. Ibid, 323, 355.

75. *TS*, 8/15; Hunwick, *Timbuktu and the Songhay Empire*, 10–11; *Corpus*, 299.

76. On Birkat al-Ḥabash, see Taqī 'l-Dīn Aḥmad al-Maqrīzī, *al-Mawā'iẓ wa'l-i'tibār bi-dhikr al-khiṭaṭ wa'l-āthār* (Cairo, 1270/1853), ii, 152–55.

77. Virgil Ciocîltan, *The Mongols and the Black Sea Trade*, 193.

78. Tetsuya Ohtoshi, "The Manners, Customs, and Mentality of Pilgrims to the Egyptian City of the Dead, 110–1500 A.D." *Orient* 29 (1993): 19–44; ____, "A Note on the Disregarded Ottoman Cairene Ziyāra Book," *Mediterranean World* 15 (1998): 75–85; L. Massignon, "La cité des morts au Caire (Qarāfa-Darb al-Ahmar)," *Bulletin de l'Institut français d'archéologie orientale* 57 (1958): 25–79; Y. Raghib, "Essai d'inventaire chronologique des guides à l'usage des pèlerins du Caire," *REI* 16 (1973): 259–80; ____,"Sur deux monuments funéraires du cimetière d'al-Qarafa al-Kubra au Caire," *Annales Islamologiques*, 40 (1972): 189–195; May al-Ibrashy, "Death, Life and the Barzakh in Cairo's Cemeteries: The place of the cemetery in the sacred geography of late Medieval Cairo," *Jusūr*, http://www.international.ucla.edu/cnes/jusur/article.asp?parentid=15501.

79. *Corpus*, 266–68; Niane, "Recherches sur l'empire Mali," 2:35. Levtzion and Hopkins translate *shi'ār* as "blazon," maybe too suggestive.

80. *Corpus*, 292.

81. Ibid, 323.

82. Ibid, 355.

83. Ibid, 305.

84. Ibid, 351. The *mihmandār* was the official charged with greeting important guests and arranging for their meeting the sultan.

85. Ibid, 269–70.

86. Ibid, 250–51.

87. Ibid, 305, 270.

88. Ibid, 351, 270.

89. "His robe of honour consisted of an Alexandrian open-fronted cloak (*muftaraj*) embellished with *ṭard waḥsh* cloth containing much gold thread and miniver fur, bordered with beaver fur and embroidered with metallic thread, along with gold fastenings, a silken skull-cap with caliphal emblems, a gold-inlaid belt, a damascened sword, a kerchief [embroidered] with pure gold, standards, and two horses saddled and bridled and equipped with decorated mule[-type] saddles." Ibid, 270.

90. Ibid, 250, 305, 358. His dating is the same as that of Ibn Kathīr, while Ibn Ḥajar says only "Mūsā b. Abī Bakr Sālim al-Takrūrī, king of the Takrūr . . . came for the Pilgrimage in Rajab 724/July 1324."

91. Otherwise, his journey would have been the lesser *umrah*, or visit to Mecca at a time other than the one prescribed.

92. *Corpus*, 323, 334, 340.

93. Ibid, 351, 358.

94. Ibid, 351, 355. The *maḥmil* was the litter or covered couch carried by two shafts, representing the sovereign political claims of the ruler (in this case the Mamluks) over Mecca. See P.M. Holt, *The Age of the Crusades: The Near East from the Eleventh Century to 1517* (London: Routledge, 2014), 151.

95. *Corpus*, 271.

96. Ibid, 268.

97. Ibid, 358.

98. Ibid, 351.

99. Ibid, 323.

100. Ibid, 358.

101. Ibid, 270.

102. Ibid, 271.

103. Ibid, 250. A more straightforward translation of *al-Qāhira wa-Miṣrā* is simply "Cairo and Egypt."

104. Ibid.

105. Ibid, 269.

106. Ibid, 250.

107. Ibid, 323.

108. Ibn Ḥajar, al-ʿUmarī, and Ibn Baṭṭūṭa all claim the *mansā* repaid his debts in full, whereas Ibn al-Dawādārī and Ibn Khaldūn say he did not. Ibid, 250, 269, 299, 323, 358.

109. Ibid, 299.

110. Ibid, 358, 299.

111. Ibid, 271.

112. Ibid, 271.

113. Ibid, 257, 262, 267, 272.

114. Ibid, 298.

115. Assuming Mūsā returned to Mali around 726/1326, al-Dukkālī could not have spent thirty-five years in Mali, as al-ʿUmarī had completed part of *Masālik al-abṣār* by 738/1338, and was dead by 749/1349. See Levtzion and Hopkins' introduction to al-ʿUmarī in *Corpus*, 252.

116. Ibid, 28.

117. Ibid, 58–59, 272, 267.

118. The equivocation in the second part of his answer can also be seen in his response to the *Qāḍī* Fahkr al-Dīn's question about "the place where gold grows with you." Ibid, 250.

119. Ibid, 270–71. Perhaps he encouraged al-ʿUmarī to assert that gold is harvested as "a plant which resembles, but is not *najīl* [grass]. The gold is obtained from the stalks." Ibid, 276.

120. Ibid, 351, 355.

121. Ibid, 265.

122. Ibid, 261.

123. Ibid, 334.

124. Ibid, 299.

125. *TF*, 36–37/62–65.

126. *Corpus*, 334, 326. Levtzion and Hopkins (424, note 63) speculate that al-Muammar's activities represent an (ongoing) expectation that the anticipated *Mahdī* will be a descendant of ʿAlī and Fāṭima, the cousin and daughter of the Prophet, respectively. The *Madhī* is an eschatological figure whose appearance signals the end of the world as it is currently known.

127. Ibid, 334.

128. The estimate is from D.T. Niane, "Mali and the Second Mandingo Expansion," *UNESCO General History of Africa* 4 (1984): 156.

129. *TS*, 7/14; Hunwick, *Timbuktu and the Songhay Empire*, 10.

130. *Corpus*, 320. In this instance, he attributes this to neither Sākūra nor Mūsā.

131. Ibid, 335, 351. Ibn Ḥajar characterizes the *mansā*'s loss as a "great number," while al-Maqrīzī quantifies the reduction in the vicinity of one-third.

132. *TF*, 32/55–56, 34/58–59; *TS*, 7/14; Hunwick, *Timbuktu and the Songhay Empire*, 10.

133. *TF*, 35/64; TS 7–8/14–16; Hunwick, *Timbuktu and the Songhay Empire*, 10–11.

134. *TS*, 9/17, Hunwick, *Timbuktu and the Songhay Empire*, 12.

135. *Mādugu* or *ma'a dugu* in *NH*, 334–35, is rendered *ma'a dugu* and *ma'aduku* in *TS*, 7–8/14–16, 21/37, 56/91; Hunwick, *Timbuktu and the Songhay Empire*, 10n, 10–12, 10n, 30, 81; and as *ma'aduku* in chapters 30 through 38 of *TS*. I will use *ma'aduku* when referring to it.

136. *TS*, 21/37; Hunwick, *Timbuktu and the Songhay Empire*, 30.

137. *Corpus*, 262, 287. Both Ibn Baṭṭūṭa and al-ʿUmarī actually cite the town of Muli ("Mūlī") as the easternmost point of Mali, possibly near Yatenga or further southeast.

138. Ibid, 284.

139. *TF*, 34/59.

140. *Corpus*, 255, 261–62, 276, 334. Al-ʿUmarī also says (*Corpus*, 272) the *mansā* reported his kingdom took about a year through which to travel, but that he (al-ʿUmarī) preferred al-Dukkālī estimate, as the *mansā* may have been exaggerating.

141. *TS*, 9/18; *TF*, 39/68.

142. *Corpus*, 77.

143. Ibid, 261–62.

144. Ibid, 106–7, 261.

145. *TS*, 9–11/18–21; Hunwick, *Timbuktu and the Songhay Empire*, 13–16. Levtzion, *Ancient Ghana and Mali*, 20, explains that Baghana is the Malinke name for Wagadu, a Soninke term.

146. *Corpus*, 262.

147. Ibid, 267.

148. Ibid, 305.

149. *TF*, 39–40/67–68.

150. In his "Songhay: An Interpretive Essay," Hunwick suspects as much, but does not pursue the matter. See Hunwick, *Timbuktu and the Songhay Empire*, xxix.

151. *Corpus*, 299.

152. Ibid, 286, 296.

153. *TS*, 9–10/18–20, 120/193; Hunwick, *Timbuktu and the Songhay Empire*, 165–66;

154. *TS*, 10/19–20, 75/123–25; Hunwick, *Timbuktu and the Songhay Empire*, 108, note 39.

155. *TF*, 62/118; also, see 118, note 5; Levtzion, *Ancient Ghana and Mali*, 86; Hunwick, *Timbuktu and the Songhay Empire*, 115, note 84.

156. *TS*, 126/230–31. See also Hunwick, *Timbuktu and the Songhay Empire*, 111, note 52; Charles Monteil, "Notes sur le tarikh es-Soudan," *Bulletin de l'Institut Français* (later *Fondamental*) *d'Afrique Noire (IFAN)* 27 (1965): 498.

157. *TS*, 128/204; Hunwick, *Timbuktu and the Songhay Empire*, 175.

158. *TS*, 122/195–97; Hunwick, *Timbuktu and the Songhay Empire*, 169, note 5.

159. *TS*, 128/204; Hunwick, *Timbuktu and the Songhay Empire*, 175; Niane, "Recherches sur l'empire Mali," 2:36, lists additional Songhay offices inherited from Mali, whose continuity is not obvious to me: the *Babili-farma* ("minister of cultures"); the *Wanei-farma* (minister of "propriété"); the *Hari-farma* ("minister of the waters of the Niger" and concerned with both fishing and navigation); the *Sao-farma* ("minister of the forests"); and the *Khalissi-farma* ("treasurer").

160. *TS*, 10–11/20–21, 184/281; Hunwick, *Timbuktu and the Songhay Empire*, 15–16, 236.

161. *TS*, 93/154–55, 179–84/274–81; Hunwick, *Timbuktu and the Songhay Empire*, 134, 231, 234–36; Levtzion, *Ancient Ghana and Mali*, 47.

162. *Corpus*, 266.

163. Ibid, 353.

164. Secondary sources have little to say on the question of the Malian military. See Levtzion, *Ancient Ghana and Mali*, 112; Pathé Diagne, "Contribution à l'analyse des régimes et systèmes politiques traditionnels en Afrique de l'Ouest," *Bulletin de l'Institut Français* (later *Fondamental*) *d'Afrique Noire (IFAN)* 32 (1970): 845–87.

165. Examples of the perspective and the literature upon which it builds include See Bruce S. Hall, "Arguing sovereignty in Songhay/Plaider la souveraineté en pays songhaï," *Afriques: Débats, méthodes et terrains d'histoire* 4 (2013) http://afriques.revues.org/1121; Haour, *Rulers, Warriors, Traders, Clerics*; Aidan Southall, *Alur Society: A Study in Processes and Types of Domination* (Nairobi : Oxford U. Press, 1970) ; ___, "The Segmentary State in Africa and Asia," *Comparative Studies in Society and History* 30 (1988): 463–91; P. de Maret, "The Power of Symbols and the Symbols of Power through Time: Probing the Luba Past," in S.K. McIntosh, ed., *Beyond Chiefdoms: Pathways to Complexity in Africa* (Cambridge: Cambridge U. Press, 1999), 151–65; M. Fortes and E.E. Evans-Pritchard, *African Political Systems* (London: Oxford U. Press, 1940); David N. Edwards, "Meroë and the Sudanic Kingdoms," *Journal of African History* 39 (1998): 175–93; Neil Kodesh, *Beyond the Royal Gaze: Clanship and Public Healing in Buganda* (Charlottesville: U. of Virginia Press, 2010); Timothy Earle, *How Chiefs Come to Power: The Political Economy in Prehistory* (Stanford:

Stanford U. Press, 1997); S.K. McIntosh, "Pathways to Complexity: An African Perspective," in S.K. McIntosh, ed., *Beyond Chiefdoms*, 1–30.

166. This literature certainly draws from scholarship outside of Africa, such as P.S. Stern, "'A Polity of Civil & Military Power': Political Thought and the Late Seventeenth-Century Foundations of the East India Company-State," *Journal of British Studies* 47 (2008): 253–83; J.H. Elliot, "A Europe of Composite Monarchies," *Past and Present* 137 (1992): 48–71; H.G. Koenigsberger, "Composite States, Representative Institutions, and the American Revolution," *Historical Research* 62 (1989): 135–53. Though more recent scholarship offers new interpretations, phrases like "Sudanic statecraft" were first used by such pioneers as Maurice Delafosse and J. Spencer Trimingham.

167. This is in not unlike Certeau's argument (*The Writing of History*) that the state exploited religious authority to enhance its own power, as opposed to maintaining independent nodes of power.

168. There is apparently no requirement to demonstrate or even address how composite monarchies/symbolic authorities migrate through space and time.

169. *Corpus*, 261–62, 322, 336–37.

170. The basic unit of the medieval *barīd*, though varying, theoretically represents a distance that could be traversed before needing to stop and refresh animals. See R. Dozy, *Supplément aux dictionnaires arabes* (Leiden: E.J. Brill, 1881), under the root *b.r.d.*

171. *Corpus*, 281–304.

172. See Conrad, "A Town Called Dakajalan"; Filipowiak, *Études archéologiques sur la capitale mediévale du Mali*; J.O. Hunwick, "The Mid-Fourteenth Century Capital of Mali," *Journal of African History* 14 (1973): 195–208; W.D. Cooley, *The Negroland of the Arabs* (London: J. Arrowsmith, 1841), 79–82; L.G. Binger, *Du Niger au golfe de Guinée* (Paris: Hachette, 1892), I, 56–57; Delafosse, *Haut-Sénégal-Niger (Soudan française)*, 2:180–82; ___, "Le Ghana et le Mali et l'emplacement de leur capitale," *Bulletin du Comité d'études historiques et scientifiques de l'Afrique de l'Afrique occidentale française* (1924): 479–542; Paul Vidal, "Au sujet de l'emplacement de Mali," *Bulletin du Comité d'études historiques et scientifiques de l'Afrique occidentale française* (1923): 251–68; ___, "Le veritable emplacement de Mali," *Bulletin du Comité d'études historiques et scientifiques de l'Afrique occidentale française* (1923): 606–19; Claude Meillassoux, "L'itinéraire d'Ibn Battuta de Walata à Mali," *Journal of African History* 13 (1972): 389–95; Ivor Wilks, "The Mossi and Akan States 1500–1800," in Ajayi and Crowder, eds., *History of West Africa* 1st ed. (London: Longman, 1971), 1:355–57; Niane, "Recherches sur l'empire Mali," 4:41–45.

173. Possible sites include Diara, Bitu, and a location on the Niger's left bank between Segu and Bamako. That Ibn Baṭṭūṭa never actually names the town lends credence to the theory that "Bny" or "Byty" derives from the Mande *banbī*, the dais on which sat the *mansā*, extended to mean the "seat" of government, not unlike the multiple shadings of the Arabic *qā'ida*.

174. *Corpus*, 283–302.

175. *TS*, 11/21; Hunwick, *Timbuktu and the Songhay Empire*, 16.

176. *TS*, 14/26; Hunwick, *Timbuktu and the Songhay Empire*, 20.

177. *TS*, 14/26; Hunwick, *Timbuktu and the Songhay Empire*, 20.

178. *TF*, 37–38/65.

179. *TS*, 10/19–20; *TF*, 38/66; Hunwick, *Timbuktu and the Songhay Empire*, 14–15, 359; Monteil, "Notes sur le tarikh es-Soudan," 486. Though Hunwick's map (*Timbuktu and the Songhay Empire*, 359) confines Kala to the area between the Niger and Bani, *TS* states that it extended to the west of the Niger, something Hunwick clearly takes into account in "The Mid-Fourteenth Century Capital of Mali," 199–200.

180. *Corpus*, 290–91.

181. Ibid, 335. On what else al-Sāḥilī may or may not have built in Mali, see Suzan B. Aradeon, "Al-Sahili: The Historian's Myth of Architectural Technology Transfer from North Africa," *Journal des africanistes* 59 (1989): 99–131.

182. *Corpus*, 80.

183. Ibid.

184. Ibid, 266.

185. Ibid, 291–92.

186. Ibid, 294.

187. Ibid, 284, 294, 415. See Levtzion, *Ancient Ghana*, 148; Charles Monteil, "Les empires du Mali: étude d'histoire et de sociologie soudanaises," *Bulletin du Comité d'études historiques et scientifiques de l'Afrique occidentale française* 12 (1929): 312–13, 417.

188. *Corpus*, 265.

189. *TS*, 6/10–11; Hunwick, *Timbuktu and the Songhay Empire*, 7–8.

190. *Corpus*, 80.

191. Ibid, 271, 346.

192. Ibid, 267.

193. Valentim Fernandes, *Description de la Côte d'Afrique de Ceuta au Sénégal* (Paris: Larose, 1938), 84–85.

Chapter 7: Intrigue, Islam, and Ibn Baṭṭūṭa

1. *Corpus*, 335, 358.

2. Ibid, 268.

3. Djibril T. Niane, "Recherches sur l'empire du Mali," *Recherches africaines*, 2:31.

4. *Corpus*, 335. Ibn Khaldūn first identifies Sulaymān as Mūsā's brother, but subsequently as his son, while Ibn Ḥajar says Sulaymān was Mūsā's uncle (Ibid, 341, 358).

5. Ibid, 266.

6. Niane, "Recherches sur l'empire du Mali," 1:37, 2:31.

7. Frédéric Bauden, "The Sons of al-Nāṣir Muḥammad and the Politics of Puppets: Where Did It All Start," *Mamlūk Studies Review* 13 (2019): 53–81; Linda S. Northrup, "The Bahri Mamluk Sultanate," in Carl F. Petry, ed., *The Cambridge History of Egypt: Islamic Egypt, 640–1517* (Cambridge: Cambridge U. Press, 1998) 1: 242–89.

8. Charles-André Julien, *Histoire de l'Afrique du Nord: Tunisie, Algérie, Maroc* (Paris: Payot, 1961), 178–82.

9. *Corpus*, 340–41.

10. Ibid, 341. Ibn Khaldūn's account introduces uncertainty in stating that Mūsā's "son" and successor Sulaymān received the Marinid delegation. Sulaymān could have

served as regent for young Maghā, but it could also mean the delegation reached Mali after Maghā's death.

11. Ibid, 250–51.

12. Ibid, 292.

13. Ibid, 294.

14. Ibid, 289.

15. Ibid, 341–42.

16. Ibid, 289–90.

17. Ibid, 295.

18. Ibid, 294. Talking locusts would not have challenged Ibn Baṭṭūṭa's credulity, as he reported many unusual occurrences, including beguiling devils (*shaytān*).

19. Ibid, 294–95.

20. Ibid, 295.

21. Ibid, 266.

22. Ibid, 335, 341.

23. Ibid, 342; Niane, "Recherches sur l'empire Mali," 2:31–32.

24. *Corpus*, 335.

25. Ibid, 335–36.

26. Niane, "Recherches sur l'empire Mali," 2:31–32. On Jāṭil as a form of Jāṭa, see Levtzion and Hopkins, *Corpus*, 416, note 42.

27. Ralph A. Austen and Jan Jansen, "History, Oral Transmission and Structure in Ibn Khaldun's Chronology of Mali Rulers," *History in Africa* 23 (1996): 17–28.

28. *Corpus*, 335–36. His depravation is encapsulated in an alleged sale of a gold "boulder" weighing 20 *quintārs*. This continues the trope of the unusually large gold rock repeated by al-Bakrī, al-Idrisī, and *Kitāb al-Istibṣār*'s author (Ibid, 81, 110, 148).

29. Ibid, 342. Sulaymān had prepared the gifts, and they reached Walata/Biru when he died. Mārī Jāṭā ordered the caravan to proceed, and it arrived in Fez in 762/1360.

30. Ibid, 336; Niane, "Recherches sur l'empire Mali," 2:31–32.

31. Niane, "Recherches sur l'empire Mali," 2:32.

32. *Corpus*, 337.

33. Niane, "Recherches sur l'empire Mali," 2:32; Austen, *Trans-Saharan Africa in World History*, 57.

34. Barry, *Senegambia and the Atlantic Slave Trade*, 6–7.

35. "The Letter of Antoine Malfante," in G.R. Crone, ed., *The Voyages of Cadamosto* (London: Hakluyt Society, 1937), 87; Newitt, *A History of Portuguese Overseas Expansion*.

36. Gomes Eannes de Azurara, *The Chronicle of the Discovery and Conquest of Guinea*, (London: Hakluyt Society, 1899), 2: 233–34; Newitt, *A History of Portuguese Overseas Expansion*, 23–25.

37. Diogo Gomes de Sintra, *El descubrimiento de Guinea y de las islas occidentals* (Seville: Universidad de Sevilla, 1992), 9.

38. Ca da Mosto, *Voyages of Cadamosto*, 17.

39. Ibid, 21.

40. Ibid, 23–25.

41. Ibid, 67–71.

42. Diogo Gomes, *El descubrimiento de Guinea*, 27; Ca da Mosto, *Voyages of Cadamosto*, 29–39.

43. Diogo Gomes, *El descubrimiento de Guinea*, 39–43. It is also possible that "Sambagenii" and "Samanogu" refer to Sunjata and Sumaoro, and that Diogo Gomes was recording traditions.

44. Ibid, 45. Further evidence of this conflation is yet another reference to the infamous "boulder of gold."

45. Ibid, 49–51.

46. Duarte Pacheco Pereira, *Esmeraldo de Situ Orbis* (London: Hakluyt Society, 1937), trans. George Kimble; Fernandes, *Description de la Côte d'Afrique de Ceuta au Sénégal*; J.D. Fage, "A Commentary on Duarte Pacheco Pereira's Account of the Lower Guinea Coastlands in His *Esmeraldo de Situ Orbis*, and on Some Other Early Accounts," *History in Africa* 7 (1980): 47–80.

47. Pacheco Pereira, *Esmeraldo*, 1:79–80, 87–88.

48. Ibid, 1:80–81, 88–89.

49. Fernandes, *Description de la Côte d'Afrique*, 84–85.

50. Ibid, 86–87.

51. *Corpus*, 288.

52. Ibid, 267.

53. The *zāwīya* can be found in North and West Africa, and usually consists of the tomb of the saint and surrounding gardens. The living make special entreaty there.

54. *Corpus*, 288.

55. *TS*, 57/92; Hunwick, *Timbuktu and the Songhay Empire*, 81, 81, note 2, where Hunwick makes this connection.

56. *TS*, 47/78, 51/83–84; Hunwick, *Timbuktu and the Songhay Empire*, 68–69, 74. There are discrepancies within *TS* as to when he may have lived, with the ninth/fifteenth century initially offered, followed by the claim he accompanied Mūsā on the return from *hajj* over one hundred years prior. The former is more likely, as Mūsā would need time to fill Timbuktu with "Sudanese" scholars.

57. *TS*, 47–48; Hunwick, *Timbuktu and the Songhay Empire*, 68–70. See also Elias N. Saad, *Social History of Timbuktu: The Role of Muslim Scholars and Notables, 1400–1900* (Cambridge: Cambridge U. Press, 1983), 38–39.

58. *Corpus*, 261, 287.

59. Hunwick, *Timbuktu and the Songhay Empire*, 69, note 131 states that "people of the west" refers "to the area of the inland delta," not inconsistent with Masina.

60. Levtzion, *Ancient Ghana and Mali*, 190–91.

61. *Corpus*, 287.

62. See Michael A. Gomez, *Pragmatism in the Age of Jihad: The Precolonial State of Bundu* (Cambridge: Cambridge U. Press, 1992); Lamin Sanneh, *The Jakhanke* (London: International African Institute, 1979); Thomas Hunter, "The Development of an Islamic Tradition of Learning among the Jahanka of West Africa" (PhD Thesis, University of Chicago, 1977); Zachary Valentine Wright, "Embodied Knowledge in West African Islam: Continuity and Change in the Gnostic Community of Shaykh Ibrāhīm Niasse (PhD Thesis, Northwestern University, 2010), 84–87; ____, *Living Knowledge in West African Islam: The Sufi Community of Ibrāhīm* Niasse (Leiden and Boston: Brill Academic Publishers, 2015); Tal Tamari, "The Development of Caste Systems in West Africa," *Journal of African History* 32 (1991): 221–50.

63. *Corpus*, 287; Ivor Wilks, "The Transmission of Islamic Learning in the Western Sudan," in Jack Goody, ed., *Literacy in Traditional Societies*, 161–95; ____, "The Saghanughu and the Spread of Mālikī Law," *Research Bulletin* (Centre of Arabic Documentation, Ibadan) 2/ii (1966): 11–18.

64. *TS*, 179/314.

65. *TS*, 8/16, 21/37, 56/91; Hunwick, *Timbuktu and the Songhay Empire*, 11, 30, 81.

66. A sixth/twelfth-century work that includes exegesis, Sunna, and history, and therefore resists straightforward classification as *adab*, or literature. See Clément Huart, *A History of Arabic Literature* (New York: Appleton Language, 1903), 320.

67. *Corpus*, 296. On the religious discipline of children in West Africa, see Rudolph T. Ware, III, *The Walking Qur'an: Islamic Education, Embodied Knowledge, and History in West Africa* (Chapel Hill: UNC Press, 2014).

68. Ramon J. Pujades i Bataller, *Les cartes portolanes: la representació medieval d'una mar solcada* (Barcelona: Institut Cartogràfic de Catalunya, 2008); Presciuttini Paola, *Coste del mondo nella cartografia europea: 1500–1900* (Ivrea: Priuli and Verlucca, 2000); Cecil Roth, *The Jewish Contribution to Civilization* (New York: Harper and Brothers, 1940); http://www.cresquesproject.net.

69. *Corpus*, 268.

70. Ibid, 300.

71. Ibid, 301–2.

72. Ibid, 303, 300.

73. Ibid, 292–93.

74. Ibid, 296–97.

75. Ibid, 294–95.

76. Ibid, 298, 295.

77. Ibid, 287.

78. Ibid, 265–66, 290–91.

79. *TS*, 6/12–13.

80. *Corpus*, 302.

81. Ibid, 266.

82. *TF*, 55–58/106–12, 64/121–22, 71–74/136–41. Manuscript C will be discussed.

83. *Corpus*, 335; Fernandes, *Description de la Côte d'Afrique*, 86–87.

84. Monteil, "Les empires du Mali," 312–13, 417; Levtzion, *Ancient Ghana and Mali*, 112.

85. *Corpus*, 284–88.

86. Ibn Baṭṭūṭa, *Riḥla Ibn Baṭṭūṭa* (Beirut: Dār Ṣadīr, 1964), 257–58; Ibn Baṭṭūṭa, *Riḥla Ibn Baṭṭūṭa: Al-Musamāh tuḥfat al-nuẓẓār fī gharā'ib al-amṣār wa-'ajā'ib al-asfār* (Cairo: Al-Maktabah al-Tijārīyah al-Kubrā, 1967), 162–64; H.A.R. Gibb, *Ibn Battuta: Travels in Asia and Africa, 1325–1354* (New York: Augustus M. Kelley, 1969); C. Defrémery, B.R. Sanguinetti, and Stefanos Yeraimos, *Ibn Batoutah: Voyages*, 3 vols. (Paris: Maspero, 1982), 2:90–93; Ross E. Dunn, *The Adventures of Ibn Battuta: A Muslim Traveler if the 14th Century* (Berkeley: U. of California Press, 2005); Said Hamdun and Noel Quinton, *Ibn Battuta in Black Africa* (Princeton: Markus Wiener, 2005); C. Defrémery and B.R. Sanguinetti, *Voyages d'Ibn Batoutah: text arabe, accompagné d'une traduction* (Frankfurt: Institute for the Study of Arabic-Islamic

Science, 1994). Gibb leaves details (that he apparently felt were unimportant) out of his translation. "Janāda's" location is unspecified.

87. *Corpus*, 298.

88. Ibid, 288.

Chapter 8: Sunni *'Alī and the Reinvention of Songhay*

1. The same is true elsewhere in West Africa. See, for example, Luise White, et al., *African Words, African Voices*; Tonkin, "Investigating Oral Tradition"; Stephens Jr., "The Kisra Legend,"; Goody, *Interface between the Written and the Oral*; Wright, "The Power of Articulation"; Jan Vansina, *Oral Tradition as History* (Madison: U. of Wisconsin Press, 1985).

2. Such information can be found in Rouch, *Les Songhay*; Hama, *Histoire des Songhay*; Nouhou Malio, *The Epic of Askia Mohammed*, ed. and trans. Thomas A. Hale (Bloomington and Indianapolis: Indiana U. Press, 1996).

3. Farias, in his *Arabic Medieval Inscriptions from the Republic of Mali*, and in "Intellectual Innovation and Reinvention of the Sahel," 95–107, is the first to make the point that "the appearance of continuity achieved by the chroniclers in their reconstructions of the past . . . are in fact an artfully constructed ideological effect. It reflects a political project of the Timbuktu historians, rather than the availability to them of detailed historical records extending back over the centuries." (xxxviii) According to this view, the chronicles constitute "an exercise in catastrophe management" in response to the Moroccan invasion of 999/1591. (lxxii) While I clearly benefit from this recontextualization, I do not see the texts as pure propaganda, but more as projects animated by different agendas.

4. Mauro Nobili and Mohamed Shahid Mathee, "Towards a New Study of the So-Called *Tārīkh al-fattāsh*," *History in Africa* 42 (2015): 37–73, argue *Ta'rīkh al-fattāsh*, published in 1913 by Houdas and Delafosse, constitutes a 'literary pastiche" of chronicles separated by centuries. They attribute an eleventh/seventeenth-century untitled work, represented by manuscripts A and B, to Ibn al-Mukhtār (calling it "Tārīkh Ibn al-Mukhtār"), while arguing the infamous manuscript C was authored in the 1230s-40s/1820s by one *Alfa* Nūḥ b. al-Ṭāhir b. Mūsā al-Fulānī, and that it is this latter work that actually bears the title *Ta'rīkh al-fattāsh*. Manuscripts A and C have long been missing, but the authors claim to have found a copy of the former—designated as IHERI-AB 3927 in Timbuktu's Institut des Hautes Études et de Recherches Islamiques—Ahmed Baba. In comparing it to manuscript C of the 1913 Houdas and Delafosse publication (and several additional related manuscripts), they contend Nūḥ b. al-Ṭāhir so "substantially transformed" manuscript A that manuscript C constitutes a "new, original work." Nobili and Mathee's work is impressive, an important contribution consistent with the current approach, for which manuscripts A and B are central. But on the subject of authorship, the position here, fleshed out subsequently, is that manuscripts A and B clearly identify Maḥmūd Ka'ti as the originator of the chronicle finished by Ibn al-Mukhtār (in opposition to Levtzion), and that there was only one Maḥmūd Ka'ti (as opposed to two different persons, as ventured by Hunwick, Brun, and Ly). As for titles, it is imperative to avoid conflating matters, while critical to recall others. That only manuscript C has (thus far) been shown to employ

the title *Ta'rīkh al-fattāsh* does not mean the other manuscripts did not have the same appellation—we do not yet know, as manuscripts A and B lack a proper name. At the same tine, assigning A and B an alternative designation may have the (hopefully unintended) consequence of creating even greater divergence than the evidence would support, as manuscript C's entire purchase is derived from both its basis in the original manuscript, and in the original's high regard in the region. Manuscript C's strategy of masquerading as the original renders unclear how adopting a completely different name could facilitate that objective. Furthermore, information pertinent to this study, found only in manuscript C, suggests a more complex, dialogic quality between the manuscripts than is currently understood, and that more research into their interconnection and circumstances of production are warranted. In taking care to differentiate between the various manuscripts, this study also calls attention to their imbricated nature, and treats the *Ta'rīkh al-fattāsh*-associated manuscripts as a composite, mutually constitutive project. See Hunwick, *Timbuktu and the Songhay Empire*, lxiii, 49, 179, 260, 262; ___, "Studies in *Ta'rīkh al-fattāsh*, I: Its Authors and Textual History," *Research Bulletin Centre of Arabic Documentation* (5) 1969: 57–65; ___ "Studies in *Ta'rīkh al-fattāsh*, II: An Alleged Charter of Privilege Issued by Akiya al-ḥājj Muḥammad to the Descendants of Mori Hawgāro," *Sudanic Africa* 3 (1992): 133–46; ___, "Studies in *Ta'rīkh al-fattāsh*, III: Ka'ti Origins," http://www.smi.uib.no/sa/12/12TF3.pdf; ___, *The Writings of Western Sudanic Africa* (Leiden: E.J. Brill, 2003); ___, *Sharī'a in Songhay: The Replies of al-Maghīlī to the Questions of Askia al-ḥājj Muḥammad* (Oxford: Oxford U. Press, 1985); Joseph P. Brun, "Notes sur le *Tarikh el-Fettach*," *Anthropos* (9) 1914: 590–96; Madina Ly, "Quelques remarques sur le *Tarikh el-Fettâch*," *Bulletin de l'Institut Français* (later *Fondamental*) *d'Afrique Noire (IFAN)* 34 (1972): 471–93; Nehemiah Levtzion, "A Seventeenth-Century Chronicle by Ibn al-Mukhtār: A Critical Study of the *Ta'rīkh al-fattāsh*," *Bulletin of the School of Oriental and African Studies* 34 (1971): 571–93; ___, "Maḥmūd Ka'ti fut-il l'auteur du *Ta'rīkh al-fattāsh*," *Bulletin de l'Institut Français* (later *Fondamental*) *d'Afrique Noire (IFAN)* 33 (1974): 665–74; ___, "Was Maḥmūd Ka'ti the Author of the *Ta'rīkh al-Fattāsh*," *Research Bulletin Centre of Arabic Documentation, University of Ibadan* 6–1/2 (1970): 1–12; Zakari Dramani-Issifou, *L'Afrique noire dans le relations internationals au XVIe siècle. Analyse de la crise entre le Maroc et le Sonrhaï* (Paris: Karthala, 1982), 27.

5. *NH*; *TF*, 9/5; *TS*, 35/57, 131/209, 211/322, 213/325; Aḥmad Bābā, "The Fatwā of Aḥmad Bābā al-Tinbuktī: *The Ladder of Ascent Toward Grasping the Law concerning Transported Blacks*," in Hunwick and Harrak, eds., *Mi'rāj al-ṣu'ūd*; Aḥmad Bābā, *Kifāyat al-muḥtāj li-ma'rifat man laysa fī 'l-dībāj* in two critical editions, Muḥammad Muṭī', 2 vols. (Rabat: al-Mamlakah al-Maghribīyah, Wizārat al-Awqāf wa-al-Shu'ūn al-Islāmīyah, 2000) and Abū Yaḥyā 'Abd Allāh al-Kundarī (Beirut: Dār Ibn Ḥazm, 2002), some of whose information is also found in (al-Ṭālib) Muḥammad b. Abī Bakr al-Ṣiddīq al-Bartalī al-Walātī, *Fatḥ al-Shakūr fī ma'rifat a'yān 'ulamā' al-Takrūr*, 2 vols. (Cairo: Dār Najībawayh lil-Barmajah, 2010); Aḥmad Bābā, *Nayl al-ibtihāj bi-taṭrīz al-dībāj*, on the margins of Ibn Farhūn, *al-Dībāj al-mudhahhab fī a'yān 'ulamā' al-madhhab* (Cairo: Maktabāt al-Thaqāfah al-Dīnīyah, 1932–33); Robert Brown, ed., *The History and Description of West Africa*, trans. John Pory (London: Hakluyt Society, 1896); Leo Africanus, *Description*

of Africa, addendum in Hunwick, *Timbuktu and the Songhay Empire* in *Timbuktu and the Songhay Empire*, 272–91; Jean-Leon l'Africain, *Historiale Description de l'Afrique* trans. Jean Temporal (Lyon: Jean Temporal, 1556); Jean-Leon l'Africain, *Description de l'Afrique* trans. Alexis Epaulard (Paris: Maisonneuve, 1956 and 1980); Giovan Leoni Africano, *Della discrittione dell'Africa*, in G.B. Ramusio, *Delle navigationi e viaggi* (Venice: Giunti, 1550); D.T. Niane, "Mythes, legends, et sources orals dans l'oeuvre de Mahmoûd Kâti," *Recherches Africaines* (4) 1964: 36–42; Saad, *Social History of Timbuktu*, 21.

6. Aḥmad Bābā's *Kifāyat al-muḥtāj* or *al-Dhayl* ("The Border") is an abridgement of his *Nayl al-ibtihāj bi-taṭrīz al-dībāj*, found on the margins of Ibn Farhūn's *al-Dībāj al-mudhahhab fī a'yān 'ulamā' al-madhhab.*

7. *TS*, 1–2/2–3; Hunwick, *Timbuktu and the Songhay Empire*, 1–2. I follow Hunwick's translation here. Mention of "the Aḥmadī, Hāshimī, 'Abbāsī dynasty, [that of] the sultan of the Red City, Marrakesh," is a reference to Morocco's Sa'dian dynasty.

8. *TS*, 2–5/4–9; Hunwick, *Timbuktu and the Songhay Empire*, 3–4.

9. *TS*, 25–26/42–44. Again, Norris, *Saharan Myth and Saga*, 26–26, discusses the mythology of these claims.

10. *TS*, 25/42–43.

11. *TF*, 42/78.

12. Hunwick, *Timbuktu and the Songhay Empire*, 2n, 13n-14n, argues for such a cultural interpretation of al-Sa'dī's framing.

13. *TS*, 168–76/256–70; Hunwick, *Timbuktu and the Songhay Empire*, lxii, 224–27, 269.

14. *TS*, 71/110; Hunwick, *Timbuktu and the Songhay Empire*, 100.

15. *TS*, 10–11/20–21; Hunwick, *Timbuktu and the Songhay Empire*, 15.

16. Nobili and Mathee, "Towards a New Study," eliminate Maḥmūd Ka'ti as playing any significant role in writing *Ta'rīkh al-fattāsh*. But in manuscript A of that document (*TF*, 48/92), Ibn al-Mukhtār clearly states he consulted his grandfather's "book" (*kitāb*), its precise form unclear, which was transmitted to Ibn al-Mukhtār through Maḥmūd Ka'ti's students. That Maḥmūd Ka'ti began *Ta'rīkh al-fattāsh* is reiterated in *Notice historique*, 332.

17. *TS*, 35/57, 211/322; Hunwick, *Timbuktu and the Songhay Empire*, 49, 260.

18. Saad, *Social History of Timbuktu*, 50–51;

19. Ferran Iniesta Vernet, "Un aspect de la crise Songhay au XVè siècle: Les Askya et la fin de la royauté divine," in *Le Maroc et l'Afrique Subsaharienne aux débuts des temps modernes: Les Sa'diens et l'empire Songhay* (Rabat: Publications de l'Institut des Études Africaines [Série Colloques et Séminaires, 2] 1995), 56.

20. *TS*, 9–85/5–160.

21. *TF*, Houdas and Delafosse, 5, note 1.

22. John O. Hunwick, "Studies in *Ta'rīkh al-fattāsh*, III: Ka'ti Origins," *Sudanic Africa* (11) 2001: 111–14. A possibility is that al-Mutawakkil's mother was Soninke with the family name "Ka'ti," and it was decided to privilege the West African lineage. That "Ka'ti" may be a corruption of "al-Qūtī," however, is indicated by the following from the margins of unpublished documentation: "I am Maḥmūd b. 'Alī b. al-Mutawakkil billahi b. Ziyād; al-Wakkari on my mother's side, al- Qūtī on the paternal side originating in al-Andalūs. The reason they call me Ka'ti is

a deformation due to the local language." Ismaël Diadié Haïdara, ed., *Marginalia: Corpus des marginalia des Wizigoths islamisés d'Afrique.* "De Ali b. Ziyad al-Quti de Toledo à Alfa Ismaël b. Maḥmūd Kati III de Kirchamba" (unpublished document), mss. 02–41, in Susana Molins Lliteras, "From Toledo to Timbuktu: The Case for a Biography of the Ka'ti Archive, and Its Sources," *South African Historical Journal* 65 (2013): 117–18. Possibly in support, *TS* (121/209) renders the name as "al-Kūti."

23. See John Hunwick, *Jews of a Saharan Oasis*, for al-Maghīlī's activity against Jews.

24. *TF*, 62–65/119–24. This is manuscript C. Nobili and Mathee, "Towards a New Study," 60–64, mobilize conflicting accounts of Tendirma's founding to underscore the extent to which this manuscript diverges from manuscript A, and are less concerned with a putative Jewish connection.

25. Nobili and Mathee, "Towards a New Study"; Levtzion, "A Seventeenth Century Chronicle by Ibn al-Mukhtār"; ____, "Maḥmūd Ka'ti, fut-il l'auteur du *Ta'rīkh al-fattāsh*"; and Hunwick, "Studies in the *Ta'rīkh al-fattāsh* (I)".

26. *TF*, 17/27.

27. *TF*, 77–78/147.

28. *TF*, 82/153; Levtzion, "A Seventeenth Century Chronicle by Ibn al-Mukhtār," 571–80. Nobili and Mathee, "Towards a New Study," essentially dismiss Maḥmūd Ka'ti as a contributor to *Ta'rīkh al-fattāsh*, but the very same construction, *fī ayyām*, is used to record the death of the famous saint Ṣāliḥ Diawara "during the reign" of *Askia* Muḥammad (*TF*, 82/154).

29. *TS*, 35/57, 43/71, 170/260, 212/324; Levtzion, "A Seventeenth Century Chronicle by Ibn al-Mukhtār," 574–75. That Maḥmūd Ka'ti would have lived 125 years, had he actually been born in 872/1468, is generally seen as preposterous. But do not Nobili and Mathee, after mentioning the inconsistent dating of Ka'ti's life, go on to matter-of-factly write that *Alfa* Nūḥ b. al-Ṭāhir died in 1277/1860 at the age of 122 (though, if indeed born in 1151/1738—as these scholars also state—he was actually 126 when he died)? "Towards a New Study," 64–68.

30. Barry, *Senegambia and the Atlantic Slave Trade*, 7–8.

31. Ibid; *Notice Historique*, 333, lists only five, and as follows: Barai, Yassi-Bo'o, Bāru, Dūru, and Bitsi Barū, "the last of the *jā's*."

32. *TS*, 3–4/5–6; Hunwick, *Timbuktu and the Songhay Empire*, 5.

33. *TS*, 5–6/9–12; Hunwick, *Timbuktu and the Songhay Empire*, 5–8; Farias, *Arabic Medieval Inscriptions*, lxxxix-xcvi. According to al-Sa'dī, 'Alī Kulun and Silman Nāri were sons of full sisters, Ummā and Fatī, impregnated by Yāsiboi on the same night and giving birth on the same night. Placed unwashed in a dark room until the next day, 'Alī Kulun is considered the firstborn because he is bathed first. This also parallels Ibrāhīm and Sāra-Hājar, as Yāsiboi only marries Ummā at the request of Fatī, who after a series of miscarriages suggests Ummā as the solution. "Ummā" may relate to the Arabic *umm* ("mother") and *umma* ("nation"), conveying her role as mother of both 'Alī Kulun and a revitalized Songhay people.

34. *NH*, 334–35.

35. *TS*, 6/11–12; Hunwick, *Timbuktu and the Songhay Empire*, 7–8; *NH*, 334.

36. Farias, *Arabic Medieval Inscriptions*, cvii-cxii.

37. *NH*, 334–39. The Sunnis/Chīs are listed in *NH* as Ali Kulum, Silman Nāri, Ibrāhīm Kabayao, Usuman Guīfu, Mākara Komsū, Būbacar Katiya, Ankada Dukuru, Kimi Yankoi Mūsā, Bāru Dal Yumbu, Mādao (or Muḥammad Dao), Muḥammad Kūkiya, Muḥammad Fāri, Balam, Sulaymān Dāma, 'Alī, and Bāru. *TF*, 42–43/80–80, 52/100 provides a partial list: Bāru Dal Yunbu, Māda'o, Muḥammad Kūkiyā, Muḥammad Fāri, Balma, Silmān Dāma or Dāndi, 'Alī, Abū Bakr or Bāru. The list in *Ta'rīkh as-sūdān* is as follows: 'Ali Kulun, Silman Nār, Ibrāhīm Kabai, 'Uthmān Kanafa, Bār Kaina Ankaboi, Mūsā, Bakar Zunku, Bakar Dala Buyunbi, Mār Kirai, Muḥammad Dā'o, Muḥammad Kūkiyā, Muḥammad Fāri, Karbīfo, Mār Fai Kuli Jimu, Māru Ārkana, Mār Ārandan, Sulīman Dām, 'Alī, and Bāru or Bakar Dā'o. *TS*, 3–4/5–6; Hunwick, *Timbuktu and the Songhay Empire*, 5. The eleven rulers listed in *Notice historique* from Mākara Komsū to *Sunni* 'Alī span some 144 years, from 720/1321 to 869/1464 (the year *Sunni* 'Alī came to power), an average of 13 years per reign, not terribly dissimilar from the average of 10 years for the eight Malian *mansās* from Mūsā in 711/1312 to Māghā in 792/1390 cited by Ibn Khaldūn.

38. Consider Madina Ly, "A propos de la continuité des dynasties Za et des Sonnis dans l'empire Songhay," *Bulletin de l'Institut Français* (later *Fondamental*) *d'Afrique Noire (IFAN)* 37 (1975): 315–17. Sunni/Chī origins in the Zuwā/Juwā/Jā' are further supported by the *Juwā-ber-banda*, "descendants of the great Juwā," who are intimately associated with *Sunni* 'Alī under *Askia al-ḥajj* Muḥammad (discussed in chapter 10). *Notice historique*, 333–34, identifies them as descendants of the Zuwā/Juwā/Jā' dynasty.

39. *TS*, 22/37; Hunwick, *Timbuktu and the Songhay Empire*, 30.

40. *TF*, 45/85. This may be reflected in *Notice historique*'s contention that earlier "infidel" rulers lived in Gao, though opposite the side of the river where the Sunnis would later reside. *NH*, 329–30.

41. *TS*, 6/12; Hunwick, *Timbuktu and the Songhay Empire*, 8, translates this passage as "The authority [of the Sunnis] extended merely to Songhay and its constituent territories, and was enlarged only under the supreme oppressor Sunni 'Alī," in which he translates *ahwāz* as "constituent territories," a more expansive rendering. If correct, it may refer to Kukiya and territories to the south forming the Dendi region. *Notice historique* states the Zuwās/Juwās/Jā's controlled the land west of Gao to Kima and Na'na', presumably somewhere between Gao and Timbuktu. *NH*, 334, also notes.

42. *TF*, 43/81; *TS*, 64/103; *NH*, 337.

43. *Ta'rīkh al-fattāsh* usually spells the *sunni*'s as *'Āli* rather than *'Alī*. Though this could be a regional variation, it could be intentional, as the verb *'āla* conveys a sense of oppression, distress, or deviancy. The form *'Āli* is used when first associating him with a long list of despicable qualities. In one of the few instances *'Alī* is used, it is only found in manuscript B, in one instance added between the lines, suggesting A and C represent how the name was originally spelled. For example, see *TF*, 43, note 3, 45, note 3.

44. *NH*, 338; *TF*, 42/80; *TS*, 3/6; Hunwick, *Timbuktu and the Songhay Empire*, 5.

45. *TF*, 55/107.

46. Ibid, 42–43/80–81.

47. *TF*, 44/83; *TS*, 64/104, 71/116; Hunwick, *Timbuktu and the Songhay Empire*, 91, 100.

48. *NH*, 338; *TF*, 42/80; *TS*, 3/6; Hunwick, *Timbuktu and the Songhay Empire*, 5.

49. Al-Maghīlī, in John O. Hunwick, *Sharī'a in Songhay*, 14/70.

50. *TF*, 45–52/85–100; *TS*, 64–71/103–116; Hunwick, *Timbuktu and the Songhay Empire*, 91–101.

51. *TF*, 45/85.

52. *TF*, 45/85–86, 47–48/92–93; *TS*, 69/115; Hunwick, *Timbuktu and the Songhay Empire*, 99. *TS* maintains the battle with the Mossi actually took place at Jinki-Tu'uy, a village near the town of Kubi.

53. *TS* states Maḥmūd was 5 years old when his family fled from Timbuktu to Walata/Biru, while *TF* mistakenly observes 'Alī conquered Timbuktu in the same year Maḥmūd returned to Timbuktu from Walata/Biru. *TS*, 64–65/105–6; Hunwick, *Timbuktu and the Songhay Empire*, 93; *TF*, 48/93.

54. Hunwick, *Timbuktu and the Songhay Empire*, 31, note 14, writes that "adda" means "Allāh" in the Tamasheq of the region, and so refers to him as Muḥammad-n-Allāh.

55. *TS*, 64/105; Hunwick, *Timbuktu and the Songhay Empire*, 92. The text, *talaba minhu an lā yukhrija bālahu/bi-illhi ma'ahu*, is a challenge. I venture *bi-illhi* rather than *bālahu*, but the general sense is the same.

56. *TS*, 64–65/105; Hunwick, *Timbuktu and the Songhay Empire*, 92–93.

57. *TS*, 22/37, 25–26/42–44; Hunwick, *Timbuktu and the Songhay Empire*, 31, 35–37, 35, note 1. Al-Sa'dī identifies the Maghsharan Tuareg as the Masūfa branch of the Ṣanhāja, and was probably informed by Ibn Khaldūn, who locates the *Tārjā* or *Tārgā* in the region and categorizes them as a branch of the Ṣanhāja. *Corpus*, 327, 331.

58. *TS*, 23/39–40; Hunwick, *Timbuktu and the Songhay Empire*, 32–33.

59. The *quṭb* or "spiritual axis" is an extremely pious individual, of whom there are a number, though it was originally believed there could only be one in the world. See "Kutb," *Encyclopedia of Islam* (Leiden: E.J. Brill, 1913–42), (2), v, 543; Hunwick, *Timbuktu and the Songhay Empire*, 32n.

60. Hunwick, *Timbuktu and the Songhay Empire*, 33, note 22, points out that the primary meaning of *qayn* is "blacksmith" or "artisan," but that it could also mean "slave," and that in the region, castes (blacksmiths, woodworkers, weavers, potters, griots, etc.), though not technically enslaved, are regarded as servile.

61. *TS*, 66/108; Hunwick, *Timbuktu and the Songhay Empire*, 94.

62. *TF*, 48–49/94–95.

63. *TF*, 50/97; *TS*, 13–16/24–28; Hunwick, *Timbuktu and the Songhay Empire*, 19–22.

64. *TS*, 13–16/24–28; Hunwick, *Timbuktu and the Songhay Empire*, 20–22.

65. *TF*, 50–51/96–98.

66. An anonymous scholar told al-Sa'dī that 'Alī stayed in Jenne for a year and one month, though it is unclear if this was at the conclusion of the siege or at another time; al-Sa'dī later states the *sunni* was in Jenne for thirteen months. *TS*, 16/28, 64/104; Hunwick, *Timbuktu and the Songhay Empire*, 22, 91.

67. This leg of the western strategy began with the village of Kutti', opposite Jenne on the right bank of the Bani, followed by a return to Kuna, upstream from what is now Mopti on the right bank of Bani (and to the southwest of Bandiagara), after which 'Alī killed the ruler named "Bisma," and then on to Tamsa'a.

68. *TS*, 109/177–78. See *TF*, trans. 88, note 1, and Hunwick, *Timbuktu and the Songhay Empire*, 153, note 69 for this location. Between Da' and Sura Bantanba the *sunni* campaigned in to Fakiri, presumably in the area of Da', then back to Tamsa'a, then to Kikiri (presumably northeast of Douentza), where he took captive one al-Mukhtār before fighting the people of Tundi (perhaps near the Hombori mountains and consistent with a northeasterly trajectory).

69. Thus, he observed the end of Ramaḍān in Kutti', then in Tamsa'a the following year, then again at Tamsa'a the next year, and then finally at Gao. *TF* 47–48/90–92.

70. Fulbe "whiteness" resonates with early anthropology and the idea that the "Ballāwīyūn," apparently Fulbe, were once Arabs who became acculturated among the "Bāfūr," possibly non-Muslim blacks. Norris, *Saharan Myth and Saga*, 153.

71. *TF*, 44/83–84.

72. Or Guma, southeast of Sarafere. *TF*, 47/90–91, 91n.

73. *TS*, 35–36/58; Hunwick, *Timbuktu and the Songhay Empire*, 49–50.

74. *TS*, 67/109–110; Hunwick, *Timbuktu and the Songhay Empire*, 95–96.

75. *TF*, 45–46/87–89; *TS*, 68/112; Hunwick, *Timbuktu and the Songhay Empire*, 97. In *TF*, there are two spellings (*Tusku* and *Tasgu*) etymologically similar and, given the context and in conjunction *TS*, seem to refer to the same place. Monteil identifies Tusku or Tusuku with Tassakant, near Timbuktu. Charles Monteil, "Notes sur le tarikh es-Soudan," *Bulletin de l'Institut Français* (later *Fondamental*) *d'Afrique Noire (IFAN)* 27 (1965): 459–61.

76. See Dierk Lange, "From Mande to Songhay: Towards a Political and Ethnic History of Medieval Gao," *Journal of African History* 35 (1994): 275–301, specifically 295–99, for a spirited reappraisal of Sorko involvement in Gao.

77. *TS*, 68/112; Hunwick, *Timbuktu and the Songhay Empire*, 97.

78. *TF*, 46–47/90–91.

79. *Corpus*, 262, 287; *TS*, 69/112–13; Hunwick, *Timbuktu and the Songhay Empire*, 97–98. Presumably the same "Mūlī" Ibn Baṭṭūṭa and al-'Umarī cite as the easternmost point of Mali, either near Yatenga or further southeast.

80. *TS*, 69–70/112–15; Hunwick, *Timbuktu and the Songhay Empire*, 97–99.

81. *TF*, 47–48/91–93.

82. Hunwick, *Timbuktu and the Songhay Empire*, 99n.

83. *TS*, 70/114–15; Hunwick, *Timbuktu and the Songhay Empire*, 99. See also G. Palausi, "Un projet d'hydraulique fluviale soudanaise au XVe siècle, le canal de Sonni Ali," *Note africaines* 78 (1958): 47–49; A. Konaré Ba, *Sonni Ali Ber* (Niamey: Études Nigériennes, 1977), 103–7.

84. *TS* states the battle actually took place at a village near Kubi called Jinki-Tu'y. *TS*, 70/114–15; Hunwick, *Timbuktu and the Songhay Empire*, 99.

85. *TF*, 48/92–93; *TS*, 70/114–15; Hunwick, *Timbuktu and the Songhay Empire*, 99.

86. *TS*, 70/114–15; Hunwick, *Timbuktu and the Songhay Empire*, 99–100, 99–100, note 50. Regarding "the mountains," Hunwick prefers Bandiagara, and believes "Gurma" in this instance probably refers to the area between Timbuktu and the lakes.

Chapter 9: The Sunni *and the Scholars: A Tale of Revenge*

1. *TS*, 65/105–6; Hunwick, *Timbuktu and the Songhay Empire*, 93–94.

2. *TS*, 65–66/106–7; Hunwick, *Timbuktu and the Songhay Empire*, 94.

3. *TS*, 66/107; Hunwick, *Timbuktu and the Songhay Empire*, 94. A more literal translation is "the space of the fate of the virgins."

4. *TS*, 27/45–46, 66–67/108–9; Hunwick, *Timbuktu and the Songhay Empire*, 33–34, 94–95. *TS* states 'Umar advised al-Mukhtār to tell 'Alī he had not seen 'Umar, that he may have fled, and that if successful, the *sunni* might appoint al-Mukhtār as Timbuktu-*koi*, putting him in position to protect their family interests in Timbuktu. The ploy apparently worked, but the account may have been invented to explain why Muḥammad Naḍḍa's family continued to prosper in Timbuktu under 'Alī. Locating Alfa Gungu is elusive, but presuming it was close to Timbuktu makes sense. As for Tagidda, a sultanate in the eighth/fourteenth and still around in some form, see Hunwick, *Timbuktu and the Songhay Empire*, 95n; J.O. Hunwick, "Takidda," *Encyclopedia of Islam Encyclopedia of Islam* (Leiden: E.J. Brill, 1913–42), (2), x, 133–34.

5. A *badal* is a Ṣūfī category referring to one of only seven figures who watch over the seven divisions (*aqālīm*) of the world. I. Goldziher, "Abdāl," in *Encyclopedia of Islam* (2), 95–96.

6. *TS*, 66–67/108–9; Hunwick, *Timbuktu and the Songhay Empire*, 95.

7. *TS*, 66/107–8; Hunwick, *Timbuktu and the Songhay Empire*, 94.

8. *TS*, 69/113–14; Hunwick, *Timbuktu and the Songhay Empire*, 98–99.

9. Ibid. His other reasons: the Sankore community "severs kinship ties" (obscure in this context), and wet-nurses spread "slanderous gossip among their masters" (an intriguing comment on the influence of the enslaved).

10. *TS*, 67/109–10; Hunwick, *Timbuktu and the Songhay Empire*, 95–96.

11. Ibid.

12. *TS*, 70/115; Hunwick, *Timbuktu and the Songhay Empire*, 100.

13. *TS*, 70/115; Hunwick, *Timbuktu and the Songhay Empire*, 100.

14. *TF*, 51/98–99.

15. *TS*, 67/110; Hunwick, *Timbuktu and the Songhay Empire*, 96.

16. *TF*, 43/82. My last sentence differs from Houdas and Delafosse's translation: "et qu'il parlât comme quelqu'un de trés verse dans la chose de la religion." The Arabic reads: *wa man lahu quwwa fī al-'ilm wa anẓara fī af'ālihi kufrihi*.

17. Al-Maghīlī, in Hunwick, *Replies*, 14–15/70–71.

18. Al-Maghīlī, in Hunwick, *Replies*, 15–16/71.

19. *TF*, 44/84. The text goes on to say that *dāli* was no longer in use, except by the Kūma-*koi* and Jenne-*koi*—its meaning may have changed. The allegations are tempered by their source, Muḥammad Wānkara b. 'Abd 'Allah b. Sanjūka al-Fulānī, who because of his Fulbe background may have had an axe to grind.

20. Al-Maghīlī, in Hunwick, *Replies*, 14–15/69–70. For the location of Fār, see 69n.

21. Al-Maghīlī, in Hunwick, *Replies*, 22–23/76–78.

22. Hunwick, *Replies*, 77n; M. Griaule and G. Dieterlen, *Le renard pale* (Paris: Institut d'Ethnologie, 1965); Marcel Griaule, *Conversations with Ogotemmêli: An Introduction to Dogon Religious Ideas* (Oxford: Oxford U. Press, 1965).

23. *TS*, 16–17/30–33; Hunwick, *Timbuktu and the Songhay Empire*, 24–26.

24. *TF*, 50–51/96–98.

25. Keeping in mind the "historical operation" as discussed by Certeau (*The Writing of History*). The critical work of Jean Rouch is an important source for this matter. See Rouch, *Les Songhay*; ____, *La religion et la magie songhay* (Paris : Presses Universitaires de France, 1960); ____, "Les Sorkawa, pecheurs itinerants du Moyen Niger," *Africa* 20 (1950), 5–21; ____, "Contribution à l'histoire des Songhay," *Mémoires de l'IFAN* 29 (1953): 137–259.

26. Rouch, *Les Songhay*, 48–61; Hammadou Soumalia, Moussa Hamidou, and Diouldé Laya, *Traditions des Songhay de Tera (Niger)* (Paris : Karthala, 1998), 23–25/171–73.

27. I borrow from Edward Kamau Brathwaite's brilliant *The Arrivants: A New World Trilogy* (Oxford: Oxford U. Press, 1988).

28. On *bori*, see Janice P. Boddy, *Wombs and Alien Spirits* (Madison: U. of Wisconsin Press, 1989); Nicole Echard, "Gender Relationships and Religion: Woman in the Hausa *Bori* of Ader, Niger," in Catherine Coles and Beverly Mack, eds., *Hausa Women in the Twentieth Century* (Madison: U. of Wisconsin Press, 1991); Ivan Karp, "Power and Capacity in Rituals of Possession," in Arens and Ivan Karp, eds., *Creativity of Power*; Adeline Masquelier, "Narratives of Power, Images of Wealth: The Ritual Economy of Bori in the Market," in Jean Comaroff and John Comaroff, eds., *Modernity and Its Malcontents: Ritual and Power in Postcolonial Africa* (Chicago: U. of Chicago Press, 1993); Michael Onwuejeogwu, "The Cult of the *Bori* Spirits among the Hausa," in Mary Douglas and Phyllis M. Kaberry, eds., *Man in Africa* (London: Tavistock, 1969); Paul Stoller, *Embodying Colonial Memories: Spirit Possession, Power, and the Hausa in West Africa* (New York: Routledge, 1995); I.M. Lewis and S. al-Safi Hurreiz, eds., *Women's Medicine, the Zar-Bori Cult in Africa and Beyond* (Edinburgh: Edinburgh U. Press, 1991); A.J.N. Tremearne, *The Ban of the Bori: Demons and Demon-Dancing in West and North Africa* (London: Heath, Cranton, and Ouseley, Ltd., 1919).

29. I agree with Ware that engendered, racialized notions of "African Islam" and "Islam in Africa" require debilitation, as "embodied practices" are everywhere. Even so, "accommodation" can be illuminating. Ware, *The Walking Qur'an*.

30. E.M. Sartain, "Jalāl ad-Dīn as-Suyūtī's Relations with the People of Takrūr," *Journal of Semitic Studies* 16 (1971): 193–98; ____, *Jalāl ad-Dīn as-Suyūtī: Biography and Background*, 2 vols. (Cambridge: Cambridge U. Press, 1975); Hunwick, *Replies*, 71n; *TS*, 64/103–4; Hunwick, *Timbuktu and the Songhay Empire*, 91. Timūr Lang or Tamerlane (d. 807/1405) was the Turko-Mongol ruler who conquered much of what is now Iraq, Iran, and parts of Asia, founding the Timurid dynasty.

31. *TF*, 43–44/81–84; *TS*, 6/12; Hunwick, *Timbuktu and the Songhay Empire*, 8; Hunwick, *Replies*, 23n; Sékéné Mody Cissoko, *Tombouctou et l'empire Songhay* (Dakar-Abidjan: Les Nouvelles Éditions Africaines, 1975), 183–84; J.O. Hunwick, "Religion and State in the Songhay Empire, 1464–1591," in Lewis, ed., *Islam in Tropical Africa*, 299–304; Pierre Philippe Rey, "La joncion entre réseau Ibadite Berbère et réseau Ibadite Dioula du commerce de l'or de l'Air à Kano et Katsina, au milieu du XVe siècle et la construction de l'empire Songhay par Sonni Ali Ber," in Laurent Bridel, Alain Morel, and Issa Ouseini, eds., *Au contact Sahara-Sahel: milieux et sociétés du Niger*

(Grenoble: Revue de géographie alpine, 1994), 111–36; E.W. Lane, *An Arabic-English Lexicon* (London: Williams and Norgate, 1863–85), s.v. *kh-r-j*.

32. *TS*, 37/60–61, 70/115–16; Hunwick, *Timbuktu and the Songhay Empire*, 52–53,100. Hunwick's translation of the latter passage states it was Umar b. Muḥammad Aqīt who made the *ḥajj*, but the text actually says it was his son Aḥmad. Hunwick also provides a date of 889, with the text stating 890.

33. *TF*, 48–49/94–96. Tichit or Tishīt in this context refers to the western town of Tichit in the Adrar of Mauritania (see Hunwick, *Timbuktu and the Songhay Empire*, 86n, 409). Lansiné Kaba, "The Pen, the Sword and the Crown: Islam and Revolution in Songhay Reconsidered," *Journal of African History* 25 (1984), says Hawki is Hawikit, 5 miles south of Kabara. The location of Fututi is speculative. If this attack occurred in 876/1472, the probable year of the siege of Jenne, it would have been an extension of a third wave of violence led by the Timbuktu-*koi* al-Mukhtār b. Muḥammad Naḍḍa, rather than a fifth.

34. *TF*, 46/89; *TS*, 130/208; Hunwick, *Timbuktu and the Songhay Empire*, 178, 344.

35. *TF*, 45–46/86–90.

36. *TS*, 68/110–11; Hunwick, *Timbuktu and the Songhay Empire*, 96–97.

37. Or Zoghrānī or Joghorānī, the Soninke term for the Diawambe, clients of the Middle Niger Fulbe against whom 'Alī had also fought.

38. *TF*, 52/100; *Notice historique*, 338; *TS*, 70/116; Hunwick, *Timbuktu and the Songhay Empire*, 100, 100n; H. Gaden, *Proverbes et maxims peuls et toucouleurs* (Paris: Institut d'Ethnologie, 1931), 319–20; Louis Tauxier, *Moeurs et histoire des Peuls* (Paris: Payot, 1937), 143–51; Jean-Pierre Olivier de Sardan, *Concepts et conceptions Songhay-Zarma* (Paris: Nubia, 1982), 425; Tal Tamari, *Les castes de l'Afrique occidentale: artisans et musiciens endogames* (Nanterre: Société d'Ethnologie, 1997), 102–106; Jean Rouch, *Contribution à l'histoire des songhay* (Dakar: IFAN, 1953), 185–89. Other traditions maintain the *sunni* died from illness at Tendirma. Soumalia, Hamidou, and Laya, *Traditions des Songhay*, 30–31/178–79.

39. *TS*, 68/116; Hunwick, *Timbuktu and the Songhay Empire*, 96. Kaba, "The Pen, the Sword and the Crown: Islam and Revolution in Songhay Reconsidered," *Journal of African History* 25 (1984), lays the critical foundation for such a conspiracy. Julde Layya, *Traditions historiques de l'Anzuru* (Niamey: Centre Régional de Documentation pour la Tradition Orale, Centre Nigérien de Recherches en Sciences Humanies, 1969), 32–33, records "Lorsque Mahammadu Asiciya [Muḥammad Ture]—Maamar, vous entendez de Maamar—a tué Sii Koraa [*Sunni* 'Alī], les fils de ce dernier ont puis la fuite."

40. *TS*, 68/111; Hunwick, *Timbuktu and the Songhay Empire*, 97.

41. Hunwick, *Timbuktu and the Songhay Empire*, 108.

42. *TF*, 45/86, 46/89–90; *Notice historique*, 337. In using Kurmina-*fari* and *Askia*, the *Ta'rīkh* looks ahead to the offices the brothers would assume. Interestingly, four of these five names correspond to the Prophet and the first three caliphs, but nothing here appears apocryphal.

43. *TF*, 46–47/88–91; *TS* 64/104; Hunwick, *Timbuktu and the Songhay Empire*, 92. The lofty statuses of the Dirma-*koi* and the Dendi-*fari* are also supported in manuscripts A and C of *TF*, 11/13–14. Locating the *hi-koi* at Gao is based on the discussion

of *Hi-koi* Bukar ʻAlī Dūdu/Dādu under Dāwūd, who remained with the *askia* in Gao until the latter appointed him Dendi-*fari*. *TS*, 101–2/165–67, 106/173, 108/176; Hunwick, *Timbuktu and the Songhay Empire*, 145–46, 150, 152.

44. *TF*, 45–46/88.

45. Farias, *Arabic Medieval Inscriptions*, xxxiv.

46. *TS*, 10/19–20, 75/123–25; Hunwick, *Timbuktu and the Songhay Empire*, 108, note 39.

47. *TF*, 62/118, 126/230–3; also, see 118, note 5; Levtzion, *Ancient Ghana and Mali*, 86; Hunwick, *Timbuktu and the Songhay Empire*, 111, note 52; 115, note 84; Charles Monteil, "Notes sur le tarikh es-Soudan," *Bulletin de l'Institut Français* (later *Fondamental*) *d'Afrique Noire (IFAN)* 27 (1965): 498.

48. *TS*, 72/118; Hunwick, *Timbuktu and the Songhay Empire*, 103.

49. *TF*, 43/82–83; *Notice historique*, 337; *TS* 65/105; Hunwick, *Timbuktu and the Songhay Empire*, 93; Hunwick, *Replies of al-Maghīlī*, 15–16/71.

50. *TF*, 43/82.

51. Ibid, 55–58/106–12, 64/121–22, 71–74/136–41.

52. Ibid, 57–58/11–12. Phrases such as "Jam Wali" and "Jam Tene" sound very much like greetings in Pulaar.

53. Ibid, 73–74/140–41.

54. Ibid, 57/110. The wording and syntax are a bit obscure.

55. Rouch, *Les Songhay*, 45–46.

56. *TF*, 73–74/140–41.

57. Ibid, 46/89; Rouch, *Les Songhay*, 22. Rouch uses the term "pirogue."

58. Ibid, 14/21, 27/46, 32/54.

59. Al-Maghīlī, in Hunwick, *Replies*, 22/76.

60. Ibid, 15/70–71.

61. *TF*, 44/84. Other groups claiming to be Muslims and enslaved by the *sunni* were found to be unbelievers. Al-Maghīlī, in Hunwick, *Replies*, 16/71, 22–25/76–79.

62. *TF*, 44/83–84, 45/87, 47/90–91; *TS*, 71/116; Hunwick, *Timbuktu and the Songhay Empire*, 100.

63. Rouch, *Les Songhay*, 4; Jean-Pierre Olivier de Sardan, *Les voleurs d'hommes (notes sur l'histoire des Kurtey)* (Paris: CNRS, 1969). They may also hail from Fulbe settled along the Sirba River to the west of Dendi.

64. *TS*, 51/83; Hunwick, *Timbuktu and the Songhay Empire*, 73. I assume the author meant *huwārī*, from which we get the image of the *houri*, rather than *juwārī*.

65. Rouch, *Les Songhay*, 32; Hunwick, *Timbuktu and the Songhay Empire*, lv. According to Zouber's sources, the name "Morikoyra" was coined by the Mossi and Bambara to refer to the "Cité-des-Marabouts." Mahmoud Abdou Zouber, *Traditions historiques Songhoy (Tindirma, Morikoyra, Arham)* (Niamey: Centre d'Études Linguistiques et Historiques pour la Tradition Orale, 1983), 23–30.

66. *TF*, 48/93–94. The text goes on to state, however, that an interrogation of persons from Diafunu and Kaniaga did not confirm this assertion.

67. *TF*, 51/99.

68. *TF*, 62/119. Zouber, *Traditions historiques Songhoy*, records a tradition claiming *Mōri* Hawgāru and *Askia* Muḥammad were first cousins by way of sisters,

and that the latter was the former's disciple, though this seems to confuse Hawgāru with *Mōri* Ṣāliḥ Diawara.

69. Few knew the tomb's location by the time of *Ta'rīkh al-fattāsh*'s revisions (as Yara was by then "in ruins"); Yara may refer to Diara of Kaniaga, or to a village nearby in Guidimakha. *TF*, 91–92/172; 94n in the French translation.

70. *TS*, 16/29–30; Hunwick, *Timbuktu and the Songhay Empire*, 23–24.

71. Between Bighu and Kokiri, the latter in the province of Kala, south of Masina and on the western border of Dia/Diagha. Hunwick, *Timbuktu and the Songhay Empire*, 23, note 3.

72. *TF*, 75/142–43; *TS* 84–85/140–41; Hunwick, *Timbuktu and the Songhay Empire*, 122.

73. *TS*, 16/29–30, 84–85/140–41; Hunwick, *Timbuktu and the Songhay Empire*, 23–24, 122.

74. *TS*, 16–17/30–33; Hunwick, *Timbuktu and the Songhay Empire*, 24–26.

75. *TS* maintains there were many *bayḍān* scholars from Timbuktu who also settled in Jenne, but provides no details. *TS* 19–20/33–35; Hunwick, *Timbuktu and the Songhay Empire*, 26–28.

76. *TS*, 47/78, 51/83–84; Hunwick, *Timbuktu and the Songhay Empire*, 68–69, 74.

77. *TS*, 57–58/91–93; Hunwick, *Timbuktu and the Songhay Empire*, 81–82; Saad, *Social History of Timbuktu*, 38–40.

78. *TS*, 47–48; Hunwick, *Timbuktu and the Songhay Empire*, 68–70; Saad, *Social History of Timbuktu*, 64–67.

79. Hunwick, *Timbuktu and the Songhay Empire*, 69, note 131 states that "people of the west" refers "to the area of the inland delta," consistent with Masina (which he makes clear on lvii).

80. *TS*, 27/45–46; Hunwick, *Timbuktu and the Songhay Empire*, 38–39, 38, note 2.

81. *TS*, 47–49/77–81; Hunwick, *Timbuktu and the Songhay Empire*, 69–72.

82. *TS*, 23/39, 50–51/81–84; Hunwick, *Timbuktu and the Songhay Empire*, 32–33, 73–74. The French translation erroneously gives the date of al-Tādalisī's death as 868.

83. *TS*, 35–36/58; Hunwick, *Timbuktu and the Songhay Empire*, 49–50; Hunwick, *Replies*, 19; H.T. Norris, "Sanhaja Scholars of Timbuctoo," *Bulletin of the School of Oriental and African Studies* 30 (1967): 634–40; Saad, *Social History of Timbuktu*, 41.

84. *TS*, 21/37; Hunwick, *Timbuktu and the Songhay Empire*, 30.

85. *TS*, 28/47–48; Hunwick, *Timbuktu and the Songhay Empire*, 40.

86. *TS*, 28/47–48; Hunwick, *Timbuktu and the Songhay Empire*, xxvi, 40.

87. *TS*, 27–63/45–103; Hunwick, *Timbuktu and the Songhay Empire*, 38–90.

88. *TS*, 37/61; Hunwick, *Timbuktu and the Songhay Empire*, 52.

89. *TS*, 29–31/48–52; Hunwick, *Timbuktu and the Songhay Empire*, 40–43. What is meant by *muftī* in this context is unclear, as the *qāḍī* adjudicated legal matters. The term rarely appears in the sources.

90. *TS*, 28/48, 30/51, 47/78, 65/106; Hunwick, *Timbuktu and the Songhay Empire*, 40, 43, 69, 93.

91. *TS*, 50/82–83; Hunwick, *Timbuktu and the Songhay Empire*, 72–73.

92. *Corpus*, 143–51; Lydon, *On Trans-Saharan Trails*, 11–12; Charles Stewart, *Islam and Social Order in Mauritania* (Oxford: Clarendon Press, 1973); Yahya ould el-Bara, "The Life of Shaykh Sidi al-Mukhtar al-Kunti," in Jeppie and Diagne, eds., *The Meanings of Timbuktu*; Hall, *History of Race in Muslim West Africa*, 61–62.

Chapter 10: Renaissance: The Age of Askia Al-Ḥājj *Muḥammad*

1. Hunwick, *Timbuktu and the Songhay Empire*, xlix; S.M. Cissoko, "The Songhay from the 12th to the 16th Century," *UNESCO General History of Africa* 4 (1984): 206.

2. *TF*, 52–53/100–3; *Notice historique*, 338; *TS*, 71/116–17; Hunwick, *Timbuktu and the Songhay Empire*, 100–2.

3. *TF*, 52/100. The precise sequence is unclear, however, as *TF* says the army elevated him to the throne, whereas *TS* maintains Bāru assumed power in the town of Danagha, without specifying the army had ever moved from Ba'aniyya. If the army did not move from Ba'aniyya, it would suggest that Bāru did not enjoy unanimous support. *TF* also rejects the unrecovered *Durar al-hisān*'s assertion that Bāru took power in Diagha/Diakha/Dia.

4. *TS*, 71/116–17; Hunwick, *Timbuktu and the Songhay Empire*, 100.

5. *TF*, 53/101–2; *Notice historique*, 338; *TS*, 71–72/117; Hunwick, *Timbuktu and the Songhay Empire*, 102–3.

6. Hunwick, *Timbuktu and the Songhay Empire*, 102–3n, says that in this instance *TS* copies the account of *TF*.

7. Soumalia, Hamidou, and Laya, *Traditions des Songhay*, 31–40/179–88.

8. *TF*, 53/102; *Notice historique*, 338–39.

9. *TF*, 53/102.

10. The phrase is *shaykh kabīr*, which could alternatively be read as "eminent teacher," but there is no context to support this.

11. *TF* makes explicit what *TS* implies, as the latter asserts Muḥammad Ture "attended to his ambition in many details . . . bringing together the various strands of his scheme," while the former records he sought conspirators throughout Songhay and "Takrur," a category that may have included Mema, Diafunu, even Mali.

12. *TS*, 72/118; Hunwick, *Timbuktu and the Songhay Empire*, 103.

13. *TF*, 61–65/118–24; *TS*, 72/118–19, 75/125; Hunwick, *Timbuktu and the Songhay Empire*, 103, 109.

14. *TS*, 68/111; Hunwick, *Timbuktu and the Songhay Empire*, 97, 97, note 31.

15. Reference to "Tendi" is also in manuscripts A and B (*TF*, 63/121). Zouber, *Traditions historiques Songhoy*, 9–22, also discusses Tendirma's origins.

16. *TS*, 72/117–18; Hunwick, *Timbuktu and the Songhay Empire*, 103.

17. *TF*, 45–46/88; Farias, *Arabic Medieval Inscriptions*, xxxiv.

18. Farias, *Arabic Medieval Inscriptions*, c-cxii; Thomas A. Hale and Nouhou Malio, *Scribe, Griot and Novelist: Narrative Interpreters of the Songhay Empire* (Gainesville: U. of Florida Press, 1990); Jean Paul Lebeuf, *Carte archeologique des*

abords du lac Tchad (Cameroun, Nigeria, Tchad), (Paris: CNRS, 1969); 56–61; Robert Smith, "Peace and Palaver: International Relations in Pre-Colonial West Africa," *Journal of African History* 14 (1973): 599–621; Paul Stoller, *Fusion of the Worlds: An Ethnography of Songhay Possession* (Chicago; U. of Chicago Press, 1989); Olivier de Sardan, *Concepts et conceptions*; ___, *Les sociétés Songhay-Zarma (Niger-Mali): chefs, guerriers, esclaves, paysans* (Paris: Karthala, 1984); Soumalia, Hamidou, and Laya, *Traditions des Songhay de Tera*, 27–30/175–78; Malio and Hale, *The Epic of Askia Muḥammad.*

19. Malio and Hale, *The Epic of Askia Muḥammad*, 17–23.

20. Ibid, 3–6; Hunwick, *Timbuktu and the Songhay Empire*, xxviii.

21. *TS*, 1–2/2–3; Hunwick, *Timbuktu and the Songhay Empire*, 1–2. I follow Hunwick's fine translation here.

22. *TS*, 1–2/2–3; Hunwick, *Timbuktu and the Songhay Empire*, 1–2.

23. Futa Toro is usually viewed as the land of the Fulbe or Hal Pulaaren, rather than the Soninke, though elements of the latter were certainly there. The Anṣār were residents of Medina who aided and sided with Prophet Muḥammad when he made *hijra* in 1/622. Interestingly, manuscript C of *TF* traces the alleged Anṣārī lineage of Kasay through Yemen, comporting with other regional traditions. *TF*, 114n of the French translation.

24. *TF*, 10/9, 48/93–94; 59/114; *TS*, 71/117; 134/212; Hunwick, *Timbuktu and the Songhay Empire*, 102/181, 181, note 52.

25. *TF*, 61/117.

26. Ibid, 53–55/102–6.

27. Al-Maghīlī, in Hunwick, *Sharī'a in Songhay*, 17–18/72–73, 23/77; 40–42 of Chapter One; *TF*, 69/132. Houdas and Delafosse assert that al-Maghīlī visited Gao in 1502, but provide no basis for that assertion (*TF*, 15, note 2).

28. *TF*, 33/56–57.

29. *TS*, 72–73/119; Hunwick, *Timbuktu and the Songhay Empire*, 103–5.

30. *TF*, 64, note 1, where is provided a condensed passage from manuscripts A and B. The same information is found in manuscript C, 65/123–24, another instance in which the latter conforms to A and B. Manuscript C provides the date of the *askia*'s departure for Mecca as Safar of the following year, 903 (September through October of 1497).

31. The office of *Bār-koi* may relate to commerce, or horses or cavalry. See Houdas and Delafosse, *TF*, 124n.

32. *TF*, 186/325.

33. *TS*, 73/119; Hunwick, *Timbuktu and the Songhay Empire*, 105. That other funds had been deposited in the palace suggests the latter was at least one location of the "state" treasury. Manuscript C of *TF*, 65/124–25, records the *askia* was accompanied by 800 soldiers, that "good-natured" *Khaṭīb* 'Umar was the source of the 300,000 *mithqāls* of gold, and that the palace money had been hidden underground and in containers or chests, and was "an enormous sum" (*kathīr*).

34. On the role of *baraka* in the transition to the Askia dynasty, see Hunwick, "Religion and State in the Songhay Empire, 1464–1591."

35. *TF*, 64, note 2, 125, note 3. Houdas and Delafosse identify the term "kuray" (or *korey*) as a Songhay term meaning "white."

36. *TF*, 9/5, manuscript C only; Saad, *Social History of Timbuktu*, 50–51.

37. *TF*, 65/125–26; *TS*, 73/119; Hunwick, *Timbuktu and the Songhay Empire*, 104–5, 104, note 18. *Mansā* Kūra is said to have been awarded the "land of "Far" or "Fay" for helping defeat *Sunni* Bāru. The citation in *TF* is from manuscript C, in which ʿAlī Fulan is spelled ʿAlī Fulān, suggesting that it is a *nisba* for al-Fulānī.

38. *TF*, 65/125–26; *TS*, 72/119; Hunwick, *Timbuktu and the Songhay Empire*, 103–4.

39. *TS*, 72/119; Hunwick, *Timbuktu and the Songhay Empire*, 103–4. Hunwick's translation, "in the company of notables *chosen* [emphasis added] from every group," underscores the *askia*'s intentionality.

40. *TS*, 73/120; Hunwick, *Timbuktu and the Songhay Empire*, 105.

41. *TF*, 65–68/126–32; *TS*, 72–73/119; Hunwick, *Timbuktu and the Songhay Empire*, 103–4.

42. *TF*, 69/132. But see Hunwick, *Replies*, 42–44.

43. Following Baghdad's fall to the Mongols in 656/1258, the Abbasids relocated to Cairo, but were a nominal force, as the Mamluks were the real power. *TF*, 68–70/131–35; *TS*, 37/60–61, 73/120–21; Hunwick, *Timbuktu and the Songhay Empire*, 52, 105–106; J.O. Hunwick, "Askiya al-Ḥājj Muḥammad and His Successors: The Account of al-Imām al-Takrūrī," *Sudanic Africa: A Journal of Historical Sources* 1 (1990): 85–90; ___, "A Note of Askiya Muḥammad's Meeting with al-Suyūṭī," *Sudanic Africa: A Journal of Historical Sources* 2 (1991): 175–76; E.M. Sartain, "Jalāl ad-Dīn as-Suyūtī's Relations with the People of Takrūr," *Journal of Semitic Studies* 16 (1971): 193–98; ___, *Jalāl ad-Dīn as-Suyūtī*.

44. *TF*, 86–87/161–63.

45. The traditions agree he spent two years "in Mecca." Julde Layya, *Traditions historiques des ethnies de la region de Dooso (Dosso)* (Niamey: Centre Régional de Recherche et Documentation pour la Tradition Orale, 1970), 70–71.

46. *TF*, 69/132.

47. *TF*, 153/274; Michal Tymowski, "Légitimation du pouvoir de la dynastie Askia au Songhay du XVè siècle: Islam et culture locale," *Hemispheres* 7 (1990): 189–98.

48. *TF*, 70/135; *TS*, 38, 74–75/62–63, 121–23; Hunwick, *Timbuktu and the Songhay Empire*, 54, 107–8.

49. *TF*, 70/134–35; *TS*, 74/121–23; Hunwick, *Timbuktu and the Songhay Empire*, 106–107; Ivor Wilks, "The Mossi and the Akan States," in Ajayi and Crowder, eds., *History of West Africa*, 3rd ed, 1: 465–502; Michel Izard, "The Peoples and Kingdoms of the Niger Bend and the Volta Basin from the 12th to the 16th Century," *UNESCO General History of Africa* 4 (1984): 211–27.

50. *TS*, 69/112–13; Hunwick, *Timbuktu and the Songhay Empire*, 97–98. The traditions appear to refer to this *jihād* in discussing the *askia*'s command to "Alhazi Mamuudu" to fight "les Gurmance," having asked the holy man, "Where is there a powerful chief in this region who does not follow God?" Layya, *Traditions historiques*, 66–67.

51. *TF*, 70/135–36; *TS*, 75/124–25, 134/212; Hunwick, *Timbuktu and the Songhay Empire*, 108–109, 182; H.T. Norris, *The Tuaregs, Their Islamic Legacy and Its Diffusion in the Sahel* (Warminster: Aris and Phillips, 1975), 89–91.

52. *TF*, 71/137; *TS*, 76/125–26; Hunwick, *Timbuktu and the Songhay Empire*, 109–10, 109, note 47; *Notice historique*, 333–34; Rouch, *Contribution á l'histoire des*

songhay, 196. *Notice historique* notes that the *Juwā-ber-banda* were descendants of the earlier Zuwā/Juwā/Jā' dynasty at Gao, and not *Sunni* 'Alī. Hunwick seems to agree with Rouch that these elites were in fact the *sunni's* descendants, but given the year of this battle they could not have been, as they were contemporaries. As *Notice historique* establishes they antedate the Sunnis, a tangible memory of the Zuwā/Juwā/Jā' dynasty continued during the time of the Sunnis.

53. *TF*, 69–70/133–34.

54. *TS*, 134/212; Hunwick, *Timbuktu and the Songhay Empire*, 182. Zāra Kabirun-*koi*'s name is variously spelled Zāra Kunban-*koi* and Zāraku Banki. Presumably "Busu-*koi*" refers the ruler of Busa, as the cognates are spelled differently in the Arabic.

55. Djibo Hamani, "Le Hausa entre le Maroc et le Songhay à la fin du XVIè siècle," *Le Maroc et l'Afrique Subsaharienne aux débuts des temps modernes*, 72.

56. *TF*, 77/147; *TS*, 78/129–30; Hunwick, *Timbuktu and the Songhay Empire*, 113–14. Scholars questioning or qualifying Songhay's campaigning in Hausaland include H.J. Fisher, "Leo Africanus and the Songhay Conquest of Hausaland," *International Journal of African Historical Studies* 11 (1978): 86–112; Murray Last, "Beyond Kano, before Katsina: Friend and Foe on the Western Frontier," in Bawuro M. Barkindo, ed., *Kano and Some of Her Neighbours* (Zaria: Ahmadu Bello U. Press Ltd., 1989): 125–46.

57. *TF*, 75–76/143–45; *TS*, 76–78/126–30; Hunwick, *Timbuktu and the Songhay Empire*, 110–11, 111, note 53, 114. Houdas and Delafosse speculate that Kilanbut/Kilanbuti/Kalanbut may have been Galam, that is, Gajaga on the Upper Faleme. But given *TF*'s stress on the distances involved in the *kanfāri*'s travel to Kaniaga to fight against Tengela, this is less likely, as Gajaga is even farther from the Middle Niger. *TF*, 143, note 3.

58. See Oumar Kane, *La première hégémonie peule: le Fuuta Tooro de Koli Tengella à Almaami Abdul* (Dakar: Karthala, 2004); Claude Halle, "Notes sur Koly Tenguella, Olivier de Sanderval et les ruines de Gueme-Sangan," *Recherches Africaines* 1 (1960): 37; D.T. Niane, "A propos de Koly Tenguella," *Recherches africaines* [*Études Guinéenes*] 4 (1960): 33–36; Donald R. Wright, "Koli Tengela in Sonko Traditions of Origin: An Example of the Process of Change in Mandinka Oral Tradition," *History in Africa* 5 (1978): 257–71.

59. See El Hamel, *Black Morocco*.

60. The literature on all of this is extensive, but one could begin with the following: Michael A. Gomez, *Pragmatism in the Age of Jihad*; ____, "The Problem with Malik Sy and the Foundation of Bundu," *Cahiers d'études africaines* 25 (1985): 537–53; Boubacar Barry, "La guerre des marabouts dans la region du fleuve Sénégal de 1673 à 1677," *Bulletin de l'Institut Français* (later *Fondamental*) *d'Afrique Noire (IFAN)* 22 (1971): 564–89; ____, *Le Royaume de Waalo* (Paris: François Maspéro, 1972); Philip D. Curtin, "Jihad in West Africa: Early Phases and Interrelations in Mauritania and Senegal," *Journal of African History* 12 (1971): 11–24; H.T. Norris, "Znāga Islam during the Seventeenth and Eighteenth Centuries," *Bulletin of the School of Oriental and African Studies* 32 (1969): 496–98; ____, *The Tuaregs: Their Islamic Legacy and Its Diffusion in the Sahel* (Warminster, Wilts: Aris and Phillips, 1975); Charles C. Stewart, "Southern Saharan Scholarship and the Bilad al-Sudan," *Journal*

of African History 17 (1976): 90–91; ___, "Political Authority and Social Stratification in Mauritania," in Ernest Gellner and Charles Micaud, eds., *Arabs and Berbers* (London: Duckworth, 1973), 375–93; Ould Cheikh, "Nomadisme, Islam et pouvoir politique dans la société Maure précoloniale (XIème siècle—XIXème siècle)"; Paul Marty, *L'emirat des Trarzas* (Paris: Éditions Ernest Leroux, 1919); Nehemia Levtzion, "North-West Africa," in *Cambridge History of Africa* vol. 4 (Cambridge: Cambridge U. Press, 1975); Oumar Kane, "Chronologie des Satigis de XVIIIème siècle," *Bulletin de l'Institut Français* (later *Fondamental*) *d'Afrique Noire (IFAN)* 32 (1970): 755–65; Sire Abbas Soh, *Chroniques du Fouta sénégalaises*, trans. Maurice Delafosse and Henri Gaden (Paris: Éditions Ernest Leroux, 1913); Jean Suret-Canale and Boubacar Barry, "Western Atlantic Coast to 1800," in J.F.A. Ayaji and Michael Crowder, eds., *History of West Africa* 2nd ed. (New York: Columbia U. Press, 1976); David Robinson, *Chiefs and Clerics: Abdul Bokar Kan and Futa Toro (1853–1891)* (Oxford: Clarendon Press, 1975).

61. *TF*, 76/145.

62. *TS*, 77/127–28; Hunwick, *Timbuktu and the Songhay Empire*, 111–12. *TS* records that Koli Tengela fled to Futa Toro after his father's defeat and defeated the ruler of Jolof, becoming "a formidable sultan who wielded great power." He was succeeded by his son Yoro Yim (who could be the much later ruler Yero Diam Koli), followed by Galājo (or "Kalāyī/Kalāya" in the Arabic), described as "virtuous, benevolent, and honest . . . such that he has no equal in all of the Maghrib save the *sulṭān* of Mali, *Kankan* Mūsā, may God Most High have mercy on them." Also see David Robinson, Philip Curtin, and James Johnson, "A Tentative Chronology of Futa Toro from the Sixteenth through the Nineteenth Centuries," *Cahiers d'études africaines* 12 (1972): 555–92; Charles Monteil, "Notes sur le Tarikh as-Soudan," *Bulletin de l'Institut Français* (later *Fondamental*) *d'Afrique Noire (IFAN)* 27 (1965): 479–530; A. Texeira da Mota, "Un document nouveau pour l'histoire des Peuls au Sénégal pendant les XVème et XVIème siècles," *Boletim Cultural da Guiné Portuguesaé* 24 (1960): 781–860.

63. *TF*, 76–78/145–47; *TS*, 77–78/127–29; Hunwick, *Timbuktu and the Songhay Empire*, xxvi-xxvii, 111–13.

64. *TF*, 77/145–47.

65. *TS*, 73–74/121; Hunwick, *Timbuktu and the Songhay Empire*, 14, note 7, 106; Monteil, "Notes sur le Tarikh as-Soudan," 486.

66. *TS*, 99/163; Hunwick, *Timbuktu and the Songhay Empire*, 142, 142, note 21.

67. *TS*, 78129–30/163; Hunwick, *Timbuktu and the Songhay Empire*, 113–14.

68. *TS*, 78/129–30; Hunwick, *Timbuktu and the Songhay Empire*, 113–14.

69. Leo Africanus, *Description of Africa*, addendum in Hunwick, *Timbuktu and the Songhay Empire* in *Timbuktu and the Songhay Empire*, 284–89, 285n; H.J. Fisher, "Leo Africanus and the Songhay Conquest of Hausaland," *International Journal of African Historical Studies* 11 (1978): 86–112; Djibo M. Hamani, *Au carrefour du Soudan et de Berbérie: le sultanate Touareg de l'Ayar* (Niamey: Institut de Recherche en Sciences Humaines, 1989); D.M. Last, "Beyond Kano, Before Katsina: Friend and Foe on the Western Frontier," in Bawuro M. Barkindo, ed., *Kano and Some of Her Neighbours*, 125–46.

70. *The Kano Chronicle*, in H.R. Palmer, ed. and trans., *Sudanese Memoirs: Being Mainly Translations of a Number of Arabic Manuscripts relating to the Western and*

Central Sudan 3 vols. (Lagos: Government Printer, 1928; and London: Cass, 1967); John O. Hunwick, "Not Yet the Kano Chronicle: King-Lists with and without Narrative Elaboration from Nineteenth-Century Kano," *Sudanic Africa* 4 (1993): 95–130; D.M. Last, "Historical Metaphors in the Intellectual History of Kano before 1800," *History in Africa* 7 (1980) 177; M.G. Smith, "The Kano Chronicle as History," in Bawuro M. Barkindo, *Studies in the History of Kano* (Kano: Bayero University, 1983), 31–56,

71. Al-Maghīlī, *Replies*, 25–31/79–83. I substitute *ṣāliḥ* for *islāh* in the text, rendering "lacking in virtue." Otherwise, see Hunwick's translation.

72. For example, see subsequent references to the Baghana-*fari* in *TS*, 117/188, 124/198–99; Hunwick, *Timbuktu and the Songhay Empire*, 162–63, 171.

73. *TF*, 55/105, 58–59/114; *TS*, 11/21, 18/32, 22/38, 58/94, 72/117, 74/122; Hunwick, *Timbuktu and the Songhay Empire*, 15, 26, 31, 83, 103, 106. See Hunwick, *Timbuktu and the Songhay Empire*, xlii; Fred Donner, *The Early Islamic Conquests* (Princeton: Princeton U. Press, 2014); H.A.R. Gibb, "amīr al-mu'minīn," in *The Encyclopaedia of Islam* (Leiden: E.J. Brill, 1982), 5: 628; H.A.R. Gibb and J.H. Kramers, "amīr al-mu'minīn," in *Shorter Encyclopaedia of Islam* (Ithaca, NY: Cornell U. Press, 1953).

74. J.O. Hunwick, "West African Manuscript Colophons, I: Askia Muḥammad Bāni's Copy of the *Risāla* of Ibn Abī Zayd," *Bulletin d'Information* (Fontes Historiae Africanae) 7/8 (1982–83): 51–58; _____, *Timbuktu and the Songhay Empire*, 351.

75. Hunwick, *Timbuktu and the Songhay Empire*, xliii-xliv, note 66.

76. Ibid, in Yāqūt, 174.

77. *TS*, 101–3/165–69; Hunwick, *Timbuktu and the Songhay Empire*, 145–47. Hunwick may agree with this conclusion, though his position is not clear as he does not directly address this question. The Songhay suffix *ije*, like the Arabic *walad*, refers to the mother (Hunwick, *Timbuktu and the Songhay Empire*, 147, note 25).

78. *TS*, 101–3/166–69; Hunwick, *Timbuktu and the Songhay Empire*, 145–47.

79. *TS*, 124/199; Hunwick, *Timbuktu and the Songhay Empire*, 171, and Hunwick's discussion, xliii-xliv.

80. *TS*, 80/132; Hunwick, *Timbuktu and the Songhay Empire*, 116.

81. *TF*, 11/13–14.

82. Malio and Hale, *The Epic of Askia Muḥammad*, 32.

83. *TF*, 79/149; *TS*, 133–34/211–12; Hunwick, *Timbuktu and the Songhay Empire*, 180, 182. Al-Sa'dī states: "The *amīr Askīa al-ḥājj* Muḥammad b. Abī Bakr had many children, male and female, and some of them shared the same name, among them *Askīa* Mūsā, Mūsā Yanbalu, and Kiray-*farma* Mūsā." *TF* also distinguishes among the three.

84. *TS*, 79/130–31; Hunwick, *Timbuktu and the Songhay Empire*, 115–16; *TF*, 82 or *TS*, 94. Based upon *fari-mondio*'s meaning as "chief of fields," Hunwick suggests the office may have "overseen the royal estates and more generally the taxation of crops," an office of expansive purview. Houdas and Delafosse, *TF*, 164n, provide an explanation of the office as the "inspector of agriculture" ("inspecteur des cultures"), but they similarly translate as "minister of agriculture" ("chef des cultures," "minister de l'agriculture") the *Bābali-farma*, held by a son of far less importance, Fāma. *TF*, 150n. If indeed the *Bābali-farma* oversaw agriculture, it would make sense for the *Fari-mondio* Mūsā to have held a more prestigious title and set of responsibilities.

85. *TF*, 78–82/147–53; *TS*, 133–35/211–15; Hunwick, *Timbuktu and the Songhay Empire*, 180–85; *Appendix*, 338–44.

86. *TS*, 133–35/211–15; Hunwick, *Timbuktu and the Songhay Empire*, 180–85.

87. *TS*, 79–80/129–30; Hunwick, *Timbuktu and the Songhay Empire*, 115–16.

88. *TF*, 11/13.

89. Africanus, *Description of Africa*, addendum in Hunwick, *Timbuktu and the Songhay Empire*, 283, 272.

90. Africanus, *Description of Africa*, addendum in Hunwick, *Timbuktu and the Songhay Empire*, 281.

91. *TF*, 11/13–14.

92. *TS*, 79/131; Hunwick, *Timbuktu and the Songhay Empire*, 115–16.

93. *TF*, 114/209.

94. *TF*, 11/14; *TS*, 101/167, 127/203, 129/206; Hunwick, *Timbuktu and the Songhay Empire*, 145, 174, 176. Hunwick writes (*Timbuktu and the Songhay Empire*, xx-viii) that *jèsérè* or *gesere* is Soninke, while Tamari, *Les castes de l'Afrique occidentale*, 84, opines *dunka* may simply be *tunka*, or "ruler," which would make the entire construction Soninke. Hale has argued there was an influx of *geseru* (plural of *gesere*) into Gao when Muḥammad Ture became *askia*. Malio and Hale, *The Epic of Askia Muḥammad*, 4; Thomas A. Hale, *Scribe, Griot, and Novelist: Narrative Interpreters of the Songhay Empire* (Gainesville: U. of Florida Press, 1990). The anthropological literature also maintains Songhay's royal griots were all of Soninke descent. Olivier de Sardan, *Concepts et conceptions Songhay-Zarma*, 52–73.

95. Houdas and Delafosse, *TF*, 14, note 5.

96. *TF*, 179/313–14.

97. *TS*, 29/49–50; Hunwick, *Timbuktu and the Songhay Empire*, 42.

98. Africanus, *Description of Africa*, addendum in Hunwick, *Timbuktu and the Songhay Empire*, 278, 285.

99. Africanus, *Description of Africa*, addendum in Hunwick, *Timbuktu and the Songhay Empire*, 281.

100. *TF*, 54/104.

101. Africanus, *Description of Africa*, addendum in Hunwick, *Timbuktu and the Songhay Empire*, 281, 281n, 283. Hunwick says the reference to wild fennel refers to wood that "resembles the giant fennel."

102. *TS*, 72/118; Hunwick, *Timbuktu and the Songhay Empire*, 103.

103. *TF*, 77/146.

104. Hunwick, *Timbuktu and the Songhay Empire*, xlvi-xlvii, conjectures that the "rank and file of the central army was composed mainly of such servile people," which may have been the case.

105. *TS*, 124/199; Hunwick, *Timbuktu and the Songhay Empire*, 171.

106. Al-Maghīlī, in Hunwick, *Replies*, 13–25/69–79. Aboubakr Ismaïl Maïga, en collaboration avec Laya Diouldé, trans. by Mahibou Sidi Mohammed, *La culture et l'enseignement islamiques au Soudan Occidental de 400 à 1000h sous les empires du Ghana, du Mali et du Songhay* (Niamey: Nouvelle Impr. du Niger, 2003), also discusses the replies.

107. Al-Maghīlī, in Hunwick, *Replies*, 35–39/85–89.

108. Ibid, 31–34/83–85.

109. Qur'ān 9:60. The eight categories: those in abject poverty; those unable to meet basic needs; the collectors of *kharāj* or *zakāt*; non-Muslims either interested in or wanting to convert; those seeking manumission from slavery; homeless children and sojourners; the overly indebted seeking to meet basic needs; those working "in the way of God."

110. *TF*, 73–74/140–41; 57/110–11.

111. Africanus, *Description of Africa*, addendum in Hunwick, *Timbuktu and the Songhay Empire*, 277, 280, 283–84.

112. On *kharāj* and *zakāt*, see Usuman dan Fodio, "Kitāb al-Farq," trans, Mervyn Hiskett, *Bulletin of the School of Oriental and African Studies* 23 (1960): 558–79; *Encyclopedia of Islam* 2nd ed. (Leiden and London: E.J. Brill, 1955), s.v. Kharāj; *Encyclopedia of Islam* 1st ed. (Leiden and London: E.J. Brill, 1913–35), s.v. Zakāt; Nicolas P. Aghnides, *Mohammedan Theories of Finance* (Lahore: Premier Book House, 1961), 341–74.

113. Africanus, *Description of Africa*, addendum in Hunwick, *Timbuktu and the Songhay Empire*, 286. Hunwick (286n) equates 150,000 *mithqāls* with 637 kilograms, and avers the gold reached Agades from the Akan auriferous zone through Hausaland. My calculations render 546 kilograms, or 1,204 pounds.

114. Aghnides, *Mohammedan Theories of Finance*, 401, 406, 444 ff; R. Levy, *The Social Structure of Islam* (Cambridge: Cambridge U. Press, 1957), 308 ff.

115. Africanus, *Description of Africa*, addendum in Hunwick, *Timbuktu and the Songhay Empire*, 277–84.

116. *TS*, 73–74/121; Hunwick, *Timbuktu and the Songhay Empire*, 106.

117. M. Malowist, "The Social and Economic Stability of the Western Sudan in the Middle Ages," *Past and Present* 33 (1966), 14.

118. For example, see *TF*, 110/202; *TS*, 105/171–72, 111/180, 122/196; Hunwick, *Timbuktu and the Songhay Empire*, 149, 155–56, 168–69; Hunwick, *Replies*, 107–8.

119. *TF*, 100/202–3; *TS*, 106/174; Hunwick, *Timbuktu and the Songhay Empire*, 150–51.

Chapter 11: Of Clerics and Concubines

1. *TF*, 59/114, 79/148; *TS*, 134/212; Hunwick, *Timbuktu and the Songhay Empire*, 181.

2. *TS*, 128/204; Hunwick, *Timbuktu and the Songhay Empire*, 175.

3. Malio and Hale, *The Epic of Askia Muḥammad*, 4; Hale, *Scribe, Griot, and Novelist*; Olivier de Sardan, *Concepts et conceptions Songhay-Zarma*, 52–73.

4. However, there is a reference to the late tenth/sixteenth century *Mōri* Ag-Samba, *imām* of Kabara, whose name appears to be a Tamasheq construction. *TF*, 130/237.

5. *TS*, 192/293; Hunwick, *Timbuktu and the Songhay Empire*, 247; *TF*, 141–42/255–57, much of which is only in manuscript C.

6. Houdas and Delafosse speculated that it was a section or quartier of Gao. *TF*, 15, note 5.

7. *TS*, 16/29–30, 84–85/140–41; Hunwick, *Timbuktu and the Songhay Empire*, 23–24, 122. Al-Sa'dī says *Mōri* Magha Kankoi went to Jenne in the mid-ninth/fif-

teenth century, and told *Askia* Mūsā he had been living in Jinjo since the time of *Sunni* 'Alī, so he must have been advanced in age when he met Mūsā after 936/1529–30.

8. *TS*, 61/99; Hunwick, *Timbuktu and the Songhay Empire*, 86–87.

9. *TF*, 82/154; 53/103; *TS*, 72/119; Hunwick, *Timbuktu and the Songhay Empire*, 104. *Ta'rīkh al-fattāsh* uses the title *Alfā* instead of *Mōri*.

10. *TF*, 82/154.

11. *TF*, 62–65/119–24. *Mōri* al-Sādiq's lineage is as follows: *Mōri* al-Sādiq b. *Mōri* Māma b. *Mōri* Māmaka b. *Mōri* Hawgāru.

12. *TF*, 12/15, 15/22, 71–74/137–41. The first two citations are from manuscript C, and maintain the Mori Koyra were free to marry anyone in the realm, whereas the last citation qualifies that freedom. Michal Tymowski, "Dispute au sujet du caractère de la propriété au Songhay au XVIè siècle," in *Le Maroc et l'Afrique Subsaharienne aux débuts des temps modernes*, 59–63, uses this account to briefly explore notions of individual and communal property.

13. The children would be free should this happen. However, if the husband dies or repudiates a Sorko/Arbi wife, she again becomes the *askia*'s property (*mulk*).

14. Per Hunwick, *Timbuktu and the Songhay Empire*, 338–44, the functions of the Kalisi-*farma* and Wanay-*farma* have been discussed, while the Shā'-*farma* was "probably" head of the town of Sa/Sah on the Niger, north of Debo. The Hari-*farma*'s responsibilities are unknown, though the title means "chief of water."

15. *TF*, 87/163–64; *Notice historique*, 323; *TS*, 83–86/137–44; Hunwick, *Timbuktu and the Songhay Empire*, 120–23.

16. *TF*, 79/149–50; *TS*, 133/211; Hunwick, *Timbuktu and the Songhay Empire*, 180.

17. *TF*, 36/62–63. Anecdotally, forty mules carried the *mansā*'s gold to Mecca.

18. *TF*, 9/5, Manuscript C only; *TS*, 131/209; Hunwick, *Timbuktu and the Songhay Empire*, 179; Saad, *Social History of Timbuktu*, 50–51.

19. Al-Maghīlī, in Hunwick, *Replies*, 2–3/60–61.

20. Zouber, *Traditions historiques Songhoy*, 29–20.

21. Saad, *Social History of Timbuktu*, 11. See also 94–108, 147–57, especially 153–54 for a more detailed argument regarding Timbuktu's autonomy.

22. Nehemiah Levtzion, "The Western Maghrib and Sudan," in *Cambridge History of Africa*, (Cambridge: Cambridge U. Press, 1977), 3: 429.

23. Sékéné Cissoko, *Tombouctou et l'empire Songhay*, 107–8.

24. Hunwick, *Replies*, 20–21.

25. *TF*, 179/314.

26. Michael A. Gomez, "Timbuktu under Imperial Songhay: A reconsideration of Autonomy," *Journal of African History* 31 (1990): 5–24, for the thesis's early version. For the response, see J.O. Hunwick, "Secular Power and Religious Authority in Islam: The Case of Songhay," *Journal of African History* 37 (1996): 175–94.

27. *TF*, 35/60 (and 60, note 2), 109–10/202–3, 122/223; Cissoko, *Tombouctou*, 107–8; Hunwick, *Replies*, 107–8; ____, *Timbuktu and the Songhay Empire*, 338–44; Lansiné Kaba, "The Pen, the Sword and the Crown: Islam and Revolution in Songhay Reconsidered," *Journal of African History* 25 (1984), 242–51. There is some disagreement over whether the Timbuktu-*mondio* office was separate from the Timbuktu-*koi*, as Hunwick suggests, or if they were the same, per Saad. The

position here is they were separate posts, but neither should be confused with the Tasara- or Tusur-*mondio*, a different official in Timbuktu. See *TF*, 131/239; Saad, *Social History of Timbuktu*, 16, 55, 99; Hunwick, "Songhay, Borno and the Hausa states, 1450–1600," in Ajayi and Crowder, eds., *History of West Africa* 3rd ed., 1: 324–26.

28. *TF*, 126/130–31; Saad, *Social History of Timbuktu*, 103–4, note 58.

29. *TF*, 35/60; *TS*, 105/171–72, 158–59/243–45; Hunwick, *Timbuktu and the Songhay Empire*, 149, 207–9.

30. Saad, *Social History of Timbuktu*, 94–99.

31. See J.O. Hunwick, "Religion and State in the Songhay Empire, 1464–1591," in Lewis, ed., *Islam in Tropical Africa*.

32. *TF*, 65/107–8.

33. Sékéné Cissoko, "L'intélligentsia de Tombouctou aux XVe et XVIe siècles," *Presence Africaine* 72 (1969): 61.

34. See Saad, *Social History of Timbuktu*, 102–3, where he interprets these events very differently.

35. *TF*, 109–10/202–3. See Saad, *Social History of Timbuktu*, 52, for a different interpretation. Because *TF* records the visit of Dāwūd to Timbuktu after returning from Mali, Saad views the episode as singular and unique. However, *TF* employs the term *'āda* ("habit" or "custom") in characterizing Dāwūd's itinerary to Timbuktu, leaving little doubt such trips were a predictable pattern. Later in his study, Saad seems to concede this point (*Social History of Timbuktu*, 153–55).

36. Houdas and Delafosse, *TF*, 202, note 2.

37. *TF*, 126/230–31; *Encyclopedia of Islam*, 1st ed. (Leiden and London, 1913–35), s.v. "Zakāt"; Hunwick, *Replies*, 107; note 45; Saad, *Social History of Timbuktu*, 55, 99, 103–4, note 58. Saad avers that *zakāt* was probably collected at Kabara, that the Tusur-*mondio* was a tax collector, and that part of the revenues he collected went to the *qāḍī*, partly based on the following passage in *TF* (131/238–39) describing the rebellion of Sādiq against his brother Muḥammad Bani (995/1586–996/1588), and his killing of a second brother, Ṣāliḥ: "And the people of Timbuktu, their merchants and some of the *'ulamā'*, agreed with [Ṣāliḥ's men] on [their proclamation of Sādiq], as did the *askia*'s representatives who resided in Timbuktu, including the *mondio* and the Tusur-*mondio*."

38. *Encyclopedia of Islam*, 2nd ed., s.v. "Maks."

39. Hunwick, "Songhay, Borno and the Hausa States, 1450–1600," 341–42.

40. *TF*, 60–61/115–17.

41. *TS*, 34, 40–41/66–67; Hunwick, *Timbuktu and the Songhay Empire*, 47, 57–58; Aḥmad Bābā, *Nayl al-ibtihāj bi-taṭrīz al-dībāj*, on the margins of Ibn Farhūn, *al-Dībāj al-mudhahhab fī a'yān 'ulamā' al-madhhab*, henceforth *Nayl*, 218; Aḥmad Bābā, *Kifāyat al-muḥtāj li-ma'rifat man laysa fī 'l-dībāj*, 2 vols, ed. Muḥammad Muṭī' (Rabat, 2000), henceforth *Kifāyat* (Muṭī'), 1:377/no. 393; and Aḥmad Bābā, *Kifāyat al-muḥtāj li-ma'rifat man laysa fī 'l-dībāj*, ed. Abū Yaḥyā 'Abd Allāh al-Kundarī (Beirut, 2002), henceforth *Kifāyat* (Abū Yaḥyā), 273/no. 388.

42. *TS*, 32–33/53–54; Hunwick, *Timbuktu and the Songhay Empire*, 46–47, 60–62; *Nayl*, 93–94; *Kifāyat* (Muṭī'), 1:137–39/no. 94; *Kifāyat* (Abū Yaḥyā), 79–80/no. 93.

43. B. G. Martin, "A Muslim Political Tract from Northern Nigeria: Muḥammad Bello's *Usūl al-Siyāsa*', in Daniel F. McCall and Norman R. Bennett, eds., *Aspects of West African Islam* (Boston: Boston U. African Studies Center, 1971), 82.

44. *TF*, 75–76/143–45; *TS*, 62–63/101–2, 76/126–27; Hunwick, *Timbuktu and the Songhay Empire*, 88, 110. Al-Sa'dī claims 'Abd al-Raḥmān remained in the post for ten years, not two, dying in 943/1536 (*TS*, 91/151; Hunwick, *Timbuktu and the Songhay Empire*, 132).

45. Aḥmad Bābā, *Nayl al-Ibtihāj*, in M. A. Cherbonneau's "Essai sur la littérature arabe au Soudan d'aprés le Tekmilat ed-Dibadje d'Ahmed Baba, le Tombouctien," *Société Archéologique de la Province de Constantine* (Paris, 1854), 15.

46. *TF*, 75/123; cf. Saad, *Social History of Timbuktu*, 49: both Abū Bakr and al-Mukhtār appear to have been candidates for the post themselves.

47. Saad, *Social History of Timbuktu*, 41.

48. *TS*, 63/102–3; Hunwick, *Timbuktu and the Songhay Empire*, 89.

49. *TS*, 100/164; Hunwick, *Timbuktu and the Songhay Empire*, 142–43. This Maḥmūd Yāza, though called *khadīm*, was of caste background (*qayn*, literally "blacksmith").

50. *TS*, 98/162, 117–18/188–90; Hunwick, *Timbuktu and the Songhay Empire*, 140, 163.

51. *TF*, 109/201–2.

52. Aḥmad Bābā, *Nayl al-Ibtihāj*, in M. A. Cherbonneau's "Essai sur la littérature arabe au Soudan d'aprés le Tekmilat ed-Dibadje d'Ahmed Baba, le Tombouctien," 15.

53. *TF*, 88–90/167–69. See Andreas W. Massing, "Baghayogho: A Soninke Muslim Diaspora in the Mande World," *Cahiers d'études africaines* 4 (2004): 887–922, for an attempt to follow the dispersal of the Baghayughu family through time.

54. *TS*, 27–28/46–47; Hunwick, *Timbuktu and the Songhay Empire*, 39–40.

55. *TF*, 113–15/207–10.

56. Felix Dubois, *Timbuctoo the Mysterious*, trans. Diana White (New York: Longmans, Green, and Co., 1896), 298.

57. Horace Miner, *The Primitive City of Timbuctoo* (Princeton: Princeton U. Press, 1953), 6; Kaba, "The Pen, the Sword, and the Crown," 249, 253; Eugenia Herbert, "Timbuktu: A Case Study of the Role of Legend in History," in Swartz and Dumett, eds., *West African Cultural Dynamics*, 431–54; Nehemiah Levtzion, "The Western Maghrib and Sudan," 3:417; Saad, *Social History of Timbuktu*, 54–56.

58. Saad, *Social History of Timbuktu*, 54–56.

59. Aḥmad Bābā, *Nayl al-Ibtihāj*, in M. A. Cherbonneau's "Essai sur la littérature arabe au Soudan d'aprés le Tekmilat ed-Dibadje d'Ahmed Baba, le Tombouctien," 15.

60. Hunwick, *Replies*, 60–69; *TF*, 59/118.

61. Zouber, *Aḥmad Baba de Tombouctou*, 18.

62. *TS*, 82–84/136–40; Hunwick, *Timbuktu and the Songhay Empire*, 118–22.

63. *TS*, 88–89/146–48; Hunwick, *Timbuktu and the Songhay Empire*, 127–28. Hunwick's "wag their tongues" phrasing is incorporated here.

64. Levtzion, "The Western Maghrib and Sudan," 3: 420–24.

65. *TF*, 178–79/312–13. I think *fitna*, found in manuscripts B and C, makes more sense than *maḥalla* (unless the latter is construed to mean "occupation" in this instance).

66. Africanus, *Description of Africa*, addendum in Hunwick, *Timbuktu and the Songhay Empire*, 281.

67. *TF*, 180–81/315–16. Saad, *Social History of Timbuktu*, 89–90, arrives at 200 students.

68. Saad and Cissoko are comfortable with the lower 7,500 estimate. Saad, *Social History of Timbuktu*, 89–90; Cissoko, *Tombouctou*, 160.

69. See Kane, *Beyond Timbuktu*; Jeppie and Diagne, eds., *The Meanings of Timbuktu*. The former refreshingly articulates West Africa's past contributions with contemporary developments, whereas the second, though occasionally venturing beyond Timbuktu, largely brings into greater relief the city's accomplishments in celebratory fashion.

70. Ware, *Walking Qur'an*.

71. These include Saad, *Social History of Timbuktu*; Sékéné Cissoko, "L'intélligentsia de Tombouctou aux XVe et XVIe siècles," *Presence Africaine* 72 (1969); ____, *Tombouctou*; John O. Hunwick, "Studies in *Ta'rīkh al-fattāsh*, III: Ka'ti Origins," *Sudanic Africa* (11) 2001: 111–14; ____, "Religion and State in the Songhay Empire, 1464–1591," in Lewis, ed., *Islam in Tropical Africa*, 299–304; ____, "Songhay, Borno and the Hausa states, 1450–1600," in Ajayi and Crowder, eds., *History of West Africa* 3rd ed. ; ____, *Replies*; ____, *Timbuktu and the Songhay Empire*; Zouber, *Aḥmad Baba de Tombouctou*.

72. See Dubois, *Timbuctoo the Mysterious*; Cissoko, "L'intélligentsia de Tombouctou aux XVe et XVIe siècles."

73. Hunwick makes the first part of this point regarding the Islamic world context in Hunwick, *Timbuktu and the Songhay Empire*, lviii.

74. *TS*, 110/179, 214/326–27; 215/328; Hunwick, *Timbuktu and the Songhay Empire*, 155, 263. Presumably the mosque of the Tuwātīs was something other than Sīdī Yaḥyā mosque, where so many Tuwātīs were buried.

75. *TS*, 7–8/14–16, 21/37, 56–62/91–101; Hunwick, *Timbuktu and the Songhay Empire*, 10–12, 10, note 11, 30, 81–88.

76. But before *'aṣr*, the afternoon prayer, replacing for that day the *ẓuhr* prayer, after midday.

77. *TS*, 47/78, 51/83–84; Hunwick, *Timbuktu and the Songhay Empire*, 68–69, 74.

78. *TS*, 57–58/91–93; Hunwick, *Timbuktu and the Songhay Empire*, 81–82; Saad, *Social History of Timbuktu*, 38–40.

79. There is some confusion in al-Sa'dī's account. *Imām* Aḥmad is here presented as succeeding *Sīdī* Abū 'l-Qāsim al-Tuwātī, when earlier al-Sa'dī states *Sīdī* Abū 'l-Qāsim al-Tuwātī was succeeded by *Sayyid* Mansūr al-Fazzānī.

80. *TS*, 112/182, 213/326; Hunwick, *Timbuktu and the Songhay Empire*, 157, 262.

81. *TS*, 57–58/91–93; Hunwick, *Timbuktu and the Songhay Empire*, 81–82; Saad, *Social History of Timbuktu*, 38–40, 237 for a list of the *imāms* of Jingereber mosque.

82. *TS*, 58/93–94; Hunwick, *Timbuktu and the Songhay Empire*, 82–83.

83. *TS*, 23/39, 50–51/81–84; Hunwick, *Timbuktu and the Songhay Empire*, 32–33, 72–74.

84. *TF*, 124–25/227–28

85. *TS*, 62/101; Hunwick, *Timbuktu and the Songhay Empire*, lviii, 88.

86. *TS*, 27/45–46; Hunwick, *Timbuktu and the Songhay Empire*, 38–39, 38–39, note 5.

87. *TS*, 47–49/77–81; Hunwick, *Timbuktu and the Songhay Empire*, 32, 32, note 18, 69–72. While Abū 'Abd Allāh Anda ag-Muḥammad the Elder was in Timbuktu around this time and also of Ṣanhāja origin, the sources do not specify he immigrated from Walata/Biru. Meanwhile, the *nisba* "al-Tādalisī" suggests an origin in the town of Dellys, between Algiers and Bougie. See Hunwick, *Timbuktu and the Songhay Empire*, xxvi.

88. *TS*, 27/45; Hunwick, *Timbuktu and the Songhay Empire*, 38. Hunwick, *Timbuktu and the Songhay Empire*, lix, note 125, actually places al-Kāborī at Sīdī Yaḥyā mosque, the evidence for which I cannot locate.

89. That is, 'Iyāḍ b. Mūsā al-Yahsubī al-Sabtī, d. 544/1149. For examples of the literature involved, see *TS*, 29–56/48–91; Hunwick, *Timbuktu and the Songhay Empire*, 41–80, lx-lxiii; Saad, *Social History of Timbuktu*, 74–81.

90. By the time of my last visit to northern Mali in 2009, there were some twenty-two private libraries in Timbuktu alone, in addition to the Aḥmad Bābā Centre for Documentation and Research (CEDRAB), which at the time housed over 30,000 manuscripts. The Mama Haïdara Commemorative Library itself held some 22,000 manuscripts, and at Abdel Kader Haïdara's personal residence I saw thousands of manuscripts that had yet to undergo processing, with some 5,000 in *'ajamī* script. Haïdara had brought part of the region under the umbrella organization of SAVAMA (Safeguarding and Valorization of Manuscripts) for the purpose of collecting family manuscripts, and at Jenne a central library was nearing completion that would house the city's various manuscript collections, consisting of at least 10,600 volumes from nineteen family libraries (though the *imām*'s library would be separate), a plan confirmed by the city's Chef de la Mission Culturel at the time, M. Yamoussa Fané. Plans were also underway to gather family manuscript collections in one library in Gao, and Segu also had thousands of manuscripts. The foregoing relates to large urban areas, but the smaller towns have manuscripts as well, and in visits to the homes of leading individuals, such as Kabara's *imām*, I saw containers filled with unprocessed manuscripts. In addition to the many works on *fiqh*, *ḥadīth*, and other categories normally associated with the "Islamic sciences," these libraries contain many works on astronomy/astrology (*'ilm al-falak* and *'ilm al-nujūm*), medicine (*al-ṭibb*), arithmetic (*'ilm al-ḥisāb*), divination (*ḍarb al-raml*), and so forth. London's Al-Furqān Islamic Heritage Foundation began cataloguing materials in the 1990s.

91. *TS*, 34–35/56–57; Hunwick, *Timbuktu and the Songhay Empire*, 48–49, 48, note 48; *Nayl*, 95, where he is referred to as Aḥmad b. Sa'īd; *Kifāyat* (Muṭī'), 1:139/no. 95; *Kifāyat* (Abū Yaḥyā), 80/no. 94, where he is called Aḥmad b. Muḥammad.

92. *TS*, 54–55/87–90; Hunwick, *Timbuktu and the Songhay Empire*, 77–79.

93. *TS*, 47/78; Hunwick, *Timbuktu and the Songhay Empire*, 69.

94. *TS*, 43/70, 118/189; Hunwick, *Timbuktu and the Songhay Empire*, 61–62, 163; *Nayl*, 93–94; *Kifāyat* (Muṭī'), 1:137–39/no. 94; *Kifāyat* (Abū Yaḥyā), 79–80/no. 93. This Aḥmad b. *al-ḥājj* Aḥmad would appear to be the same person as Abū 'l-Abbās Aḥmad b. *al-ḥājj* Aḥmad mentioned later in *TS*, although two slightly separate dates are given for his death—17 or 27 Sha'bān 991/5 or 14 September 1583.

95. *TS*, 39–41/63–67; Hunwick, *Timbuktu and the Songhay Empire*, 56–58; *Nayl*, 93–94, 218, 335; *Kifāyat* (Muṭī'), 1:377/no. 393 and 2:222/no. 630; *Kifāyat* (Abū Yaḥyā), 273/no. 388 and 474/no. 626.

96. *TS*, 45–46/74–76; Hunwick, *Timbuktu and the Songhay Empire*, 65–66; *Nayl*, 341–42; *Kifāyat* (Muṭī'), 2:237–40/no. 646; *Kifāyat* (Abū Yaḥyā), 476–79/no. 641.

97. Saad, *Social History of Timbuktu*, 59–73, 247–49; Hunwick, *Timbuktu and the Songhay Empire*, lviii-lix.

98. See, for example, Louis Brenner, *West African Sufi: The Religious Heritage and Spiritual Search of Cerno Bokar Saalif Taal* (Berkeley and Los Angeles: U. of California Press, 1984); Amadou Hampâté Bâ, *A Spirit of Tolerance: The Inspiring Life of Tierno Bokar* (Bloomington: World Wisdom Books, 2008): Khadim Mbacke, *Sufism and Religious Brotherhoods in Senegal* (Princeton: Markus Wiener, 2005). However, the caution that the experiential is not confined to Sufism is correct. See Ware, *The Walking Qur'an*.

99. *TF*, 68/131, 91/171; *TS*, 18/32; Hunwick, *Timbuktu and the Songhay Empire*, 26.

100. *TS*, 56–63/91–103, 73–74/120–21; Hunwick, *Timbuktu and the Songhay Empire*, 81–90, 105–106.

101. *TS*, 47/78; Hunwick, *Timbuktu and the Songhay Empire*, 68–69.

102. *TF*, 32/53, 53/103, 108–9/199–201; *TF*, 65–67/125–29 (manuscript C); *TS* 73–74/120–21; Hunwick, *Timbuktu and the Songhay Empire*, 105–106.

103. *TF*, 48/93–94; 72–73/139.

104. *TS*, 16/29; Hunwick, *Timbuktu and the Songhay Empire*, 23.

105. *TF*, 54/105, 72/138–39.

106. *TS*, 69/113; Hunwick, *Timbuktu and the Songhay Empire*, 98.

107. *TF*, 180–81/315–16. Saad, *Social History of Timbuktu*, 89–90, arrives at 200 students.

108. Saad, *Social History of Timbuktu*, 85–88; Auguste Dupuis-Yacouba, *Industries et principales professions des habitants de la région de Tombouctou* (Paris: Larose, 1921); ____, "Note sur la population de Tombouctou, castes et associations," *Revue ethnographique* 8–9 (1910): 233–36; A. Hacquard, *Monographie de Tombouctou* (Paris: Société des Études Coloniales et Martimes, 1900), 40–44.

109. *TS*, 60–61/97–99; Hunwick, *Timbuktu and the Songhay Empire*, 86. They did, collecting 700 *mithqāls*. On the concept of the "religious estate," see Hunwick, *Timbuktu and the Songhay Empire*, liv-lxiii.

110. *TS*, 38/62–63; Hunwick, *Timbuktu and the Songhay Empire*, 53–54.

111. *TF*, 91–92/172.

112. *TS*, 74/122; Hunwick, *Timbuktu and the Songhay Empire*, 106–107.

113. *TF*, /213; *TS*, 72/119, 78/130; Hunwick, *Timbuktu and the Songhay Empire*, 104, 114.

114. *TS*, 16/29–30, 84–85/140–41; Hunwick, *Timbuktu and the Songhay Empire*, 23–24, 122.

115. *TS*, 16–17/30–33; Hunwick, *Timbuktu and the Songhay Empire*, 24–26.

116. Tetsuya Ohtoshi, "The Manners, Customs, and Mentality of Pilgrims to the Egyptian City of the Dead, 110–1500 A.D." *Orient* 29 (1993): 19–44; ____, "A Note

on the Disregarded Ottoman Cairene Ziyāra Book," *Mediterranean World* 15 (1998): 75–85; L. Massignon, "La cité des morts au Caire (Qarāfa-Darb al-Ahmar)," *Bulletin de l'Institut français d'archéologie orientale* 57 (1958): 25–79; Y. Raghib, "Essai d'inventaire chronologique des guides a l'usage des pèlerins du Caire," *REI* 16 (1973): 259–80; ____, "Sur deux monuments funéraires du cimetière d'al-Qarafa al-Kubra au Caire," *Annales Islamologiques*, 40 (1972): 189–95; May al-Ibrashy, "Death, Life and the Barzakh in Cairo's Cemeteries: The place of the cemetery in the sacred geography of late Medieval Cairo," *Jusūr*, http://www.international.ucla.edu/cnes/jusur/article.asp?parentid=15501.

117. *TS*, 38/62–63, 74–75/123, 76/126, 82/136; Hunwick, *Timbuktu and the Songhay Empire*, 53–54, 54, note 14, 107, 110, 119; *Kifāyat* (Muṭī'), 2:245–46/no. 655; *Kifāyat* (Abū Yaḥyā), 483–84/no. 650.

118. *TS*, 38/62–63; Hunwick, *Timbuktu and the Songhay Empire*, 53–55, 54, notes 17–19; *Kifāyat* (Muṭī'), 2:245/no. 655; *Kifāyat* (Abū Yaḥyā), 483–84/no. 650. Three of the five books he usually taught were the *Mukhtaṣar* of Khalīl b. Isḥāq, the *Risāla* of Ibn Abī Zayd, and the *Mudawwana* of Saḥnūn.

119. *TS*, 31/51–52; Hunwick, *Timbuktu and the Songhay Empire*, 43–44, 43, note 43.

120. *TS*, 37/61; Hunwick, *Timbuktu and the Songhay Empire*, 52; *TS*, 30/54; Hunwick, *Timbuktu and the Songhay Empire*, 43. That is, 'Abd Allāh's significance should not be overlooked simply because he lived in a small village. *Sīdī* Muḥammad al-Bakrī, or Abū 'l-Makārim Shams al-Dīn Muḥammad b. Abī 'l-Ḥaṣan 'Alī al-Bakrī al-Shāfi'ī (d. 994/1586), was an important Egyptian scholar and Ṣūfī. Hunwick, *Timbuktu and the Songhay Empire*, 45, note 40.

121. *TS*, 33/55; Hunwick, *Timbuktu and the Songhay Empire*, 47. Masire Bēr appears to be the same person as Masire Būbu al-Zughrānī, mentioned later in *TS* as the "friend of the jurist Maḥmūd b. 'Umar," and an associate of Maḥmūd's son, the ascetic 'Abd al-Raḥmān. *TS*, 51–52/84; Hunwick, *Timbuktu and the Songhay Empire*, 74.

122. *TS*, 33–34/55; Hunwick, *Timbuktu and the Songhay Empire*, 47.

123. *TS*, 38–40, 98, 107–8/63–66, 162, 175–76; Hunwick, *Timbuktu and the Songhay Empire*, 54–55, 57, 140, 152.

124. *TS*, 34, 40–41/66–67; Hunwick, *Timbuktu and the Songhay Empire*, 47, 57–58; *Nayl*, 218; *Kifāyat* (Muṭī'), 1:377–78/no. 393; *Kifāyat* (Abū Yaḥyā), 273/no. 388.

125. *TS*, 34, 117–18/55–56, 189–90; Hunwick, *Timbuktu and the Songhay Empire*, 47–48, 163–64.

126. Hunwick, *Timbuktu and the Songhay Empire*, 47, translates *tawārīkh wa ayyām al-nās* as "the history and battles of the Muslims."

127. *TS*, 34/55–56; Hunwick, *Timbuktu and the Songhay Empire*, 47–48.

128. *TS*, 31/54, 37/60–61, 70/115–16; Hunwick, *Timbuktu and the Songhay Empire*, 43, 52–53,100.

129. *TS*, 31–32, 169–70/52–53, 258–60; Hunwick, *Timbuktu and the Songhay Empire*, 44–45, 219–20.

130. *TS*, 32, 41–42/52–53, 67–68; Hunwick, *Timbuktu and the Songhay Empire*, 45–46, 59–60; *Nayl*, 102; *Kifāyat* (Muṭī'), 1:181/no. 137; *Kifāyat* (Abū Yaḥyā), 112–13/no. 135.

131. *TS*, 32–33/53–54; Hunwick, *Timbuktu and the Songhay Empire*, 46–47, 60–62; *Nayl*, 93; *Kifāyat* (Muṭī'), 1:137–39/no. 94; *Kifāyat* (Abū Yaḥyā), 79–80/no. 93.

132. *TS*, 30–31/50–51, 38/62, 69/113–14; Hunwick, *Timbuktu and the Songhay Empire*, 43, 53, 98–99.

133. *TS*, 30–31/50–51, 39/64; Hunwick, *Timbuktu and the Songhay Empire*, 43, 55–56.

134. Except for one who did not eat the meal. *TS*, 27–28/45–47, 48/79–80; Hunwick, *Timbuktu and the Songhay Empire*, 38–40, 39, note 7, 70.

135. *TS*, 57–59/93–96; Hunwick, *Timbuktu and the Songhay Empire*, 82–84.

136. *TS*, 53–54/86–87; Hunwick, *Timbuktu and the Songhay Empire*, 76–77.

137. *TS*, 60/96–97; Hunwick, *Timbuktu and the Songhay Empire*, 85.

138. *TF*, 91/171; *TS*, 177/271, 213–14/325–27, 218/333; Hunwick, *Timbuktu and the Songhay Empire*, 229, 262–63, 268. *Qa'id* Manṣūr's son would later return his father's remains to Marrakesh.

139. *TS*, 27/ 45, 47–48/78; Hunwick, *Timbuktu and the Songhay Empire*, 38, 69.

140. *TF*, 91–92/171–74, 81/159–60; *TS*, 91–92/151–52; Hunwick, *Timbuktu and the Songhay Empire*, 132.

141. For example, see Muḥammad Bello, *Infāq al-maysūr fī ta'rīkh bilād al-takrūr* (Rabat: Institute of African Studies, 1996); Usuman dan Fodio, *Bayān al-wujūb al-hijra 'alā 'l-ibād*, ed. and trans. F.H. El Masri (Khartoum: Oxford U. Press, 1978); Hall, *A History of Race in Muslim West Africa*. As an example of a quibble, Muḥammad Bello was not in complete agreement with Aḥmad Bābā as to which communities qualified as Muslim.

142. *TS*, 28/48, 30/51, 47/78, 65/106; Hunwick, *Timbuktu and the Songhay Empire*, 40, 43, 69, 93.

143. *TS*, 28/47–48; Hunwick, *Timbuktu and the Songhay Empire*, 40.

144. *TS*, 27–63/45–103; Hunwick, *Timbuktu and the Songhay Empire*, 38–90.

145. *TS*, 37/61; Hunwick, *Timbuktu and the Songhay Empire*, 52.

146. *TS*, 34–35, 43/57, 71; Hunwick, *Timbuktu and the Songhay Empire*, 48–49, 62; *Nayl*, 95; *Kifāyat* (Muṭī'), 1:139/no. 95; *Kifāyat* (Abū Yaḥyā), 80/no. 94.

147. *TS*, 29–30/48–50, 63/101–2; Hunwick, *Timbuktu and the Songhay Empire*, 41–42, 88–89.

148. *TS*, 57–58/91–93; Hunwick, *Timbuktu and the Songhay Empire*, 81–82; Saad, *Social History of Timbuktu*, 38–40.

149. *TS*, 70/115; Hunwick, *Timbuktu and the Songhay Empire*, 100.

150. *TS*, 63/102; Hunwick, *Timbuktu and the Songhay Empire*, 89.

151. *TS*, 219/334; Hunwick, *Timbuktu and the Songhay Empire*, 269.

152. *TF*, 79–80/150–51; *TS*, 94/156, 134/212; Hunwick, *Timbuktu and the Songhay Empire*, 135, 181.

153. *TS*, 105–8/173–76; Hunwick, *Timbuktu and the Songhay Empire*, 150–52.

154. *TF*, 118/216–17; *TS*, 109/178, 136/214; Hunwick, *Timbuktu and the Songhay Empire*, 154, 184.

155. Muhammad Bello, *Infaku'l Maisuri* trans. E.J. Arnett in *The Rise of the Sokoto Fulani* (Kano, 1922); *The Kano Chronicle*, in H.R. Palmer, *Sudanese Memoirs* (Lagos, 1928), vol. 3.

156. The literature includes Edna G. Bay, *Wives of the Leopard: Gender, Politics, and Culture in the Kingdom of Dahomey* (Charlottesville and London: U. of Virginia Press, 1998); Jean Marie Allman, *The Quills of the Porcupine: Asante Nationalism in*

an Emergent Ghana (Madison: U. of Wisconsin Press, 1993); Cathy Skidmore-Hess, "Queen Njinga, 1582–1663: Ritual, Power and Gender in the Life of a Precolonial African Ruler" (PhD Thesis, U. of Wisconsin-Madison, 1995); Adriano Parreira, *Economia e sociedade em Angola na época da Rainha Jinga (século XVII)* (Lisbon: Editorial Estampa, 1997); Emily Lynn Osborn, *Our New Husbands Are Here: Households, Gender, and Politics in a West African State from the Slave Trade to Colonial Rule* (Athens, OH: Ohio U. Press, 2011); Lisa Lindsay, *Working with Gender: Wage Labor and Social Change in Southwestern Nigeria* (Portsmouth, NH: Heinemann, 2003).

157. John Thornton, *The Kongolese Saint Anthony: Dona Beatriz Kimpa Vita and the Antonian Movement, 1684–1706* (Cambridge: Cambridge U. Press, 1998). This resonates with female Nyabingi healers operating at the level of political opposition. See Steven Feierman, "Colonizers, Scholars, and the Creation of Invisible Histories," in Victoria E. Bonnell and Lynn Hunt, eds., *Beyond the Cultural Turn: New Directions in the Study of Society and Culture* (Berkeley: U. of California Press, 1999), 182–211.

158. *TS*, 64/104; Hunwick, *Timbuktu and the Songhay Empire*, 92, 92, note 7. Monteil observes that "Bīkun Kābi" could be a phrase referring to a *kado* or non-Fulbe woman, and not necessarily a personal name. See Charles Monteil, "Notes sur le tarikh es-Soudan," *Bulletin de l'Institut Français* (later *Fondamental*) *d'Afrique Noire (IFAN)* 27 (1965): 495.

159. *TF*, 140–42/254–57. Embedded in the story is an isolet found only in manuscript C that discusses the "Zanjī." There are several other issues with this passage, beginning with difficulties in determining the locations. The year for 'Alī's defeat of Yānū, 997/1588, is almost 100 years after his death. Buyo is spelled "Bunio" in the French translation. Finally, the account is unclear in following the outcome of the friendship between 'Umar and Jata, either suggesting it resulted in the actual transfer of authority over Buyo to Tendirma, or that the latter developed a sort of "joking relationship" with the former and claimed sovereignty over Buyo.

160. *TF*, 81/151–52, 152, notes 1–6, 94/177; *TS*, 110/179, 134–35/212–13; Hunwick, *Timbuktu and the Songhay Empire*, 155, 182. The others are Āmina (or Mina) Kiraw, mother of *Askia* Muḥammad Bonkana; Mina Kay or Āmina Wāy Bardā, mother of *Askia* al-Ḥājj b. Dāwūd; Amisi Kāru or Kāra, mother of *Askia* Muḥammad Bāni; Fāṭima Buṣu al-Joghranīa, mother of *Askia* Isḥāq Joghranī; Zābēr-banada, mother of al-Hādī; Kamsa Mīman-*koi*, mother of *Kanfāri* 'Uthmān Yawbābo; Tāti Za'ankoi, mother of 'Uthmān Tinfarin; and Aryū (Aryaw) bt. *Askia al-ḥājj* Muḥammad, mother of *Kanfāri* Ḥammād. Aryū is actually listed here as *Askia al-ḥājj* Muḥammad's sister, but see *TF*, 87/163; *TS*, 94/156; Hunwick, *Timbuktu and the Songhay Empire*, 135, where she is identified as his daughter. Hunwick points out the similarity between Zābēr-banada and *Zuwā-bēr-banda*, or descendant of the "great Zuwā," so this woman may have traced her ancestry over 200 years to the Zuwā/Juwā/Jā' dynasty, may have been related to *Sunni* 'Alī, and this may not be her personal name.

161. *TF*, 81/151–52.

162. *TF*, 78/149; *TS*, 94/156; Hunwick, *Timbuktu and the Songhay Empire*, 135–36. Manuscript C of *TF* (58/113) says he was 50 years old in 898/1493, so the accounts are fairly consistent.

163. *TF*, 78–79/149, 117–18/215; *TS*, 133/211, 136/214; Hunwick, *Timbuktu and the Songhay Empire*, 180. 184. Hunwick, *Timbuktu and the Songhay Empire*, 180,

note 40, 184, note 68, reports that in the margins of a manuscript he consulted, Muḥammad and Dāwūd are said to have had 471 and 333 children each, respectively.

164. See Claire Robertson, "We Must Overcome: Genealogy and Evolution of Female Slavery in West Africa," *Journal of West African History* 1 (2015): 68–69; M. Gaudefroy-Demombynes, *Muslim Institutions* (London: Allen and Unwin, 1950), 136–37; Humphrey J. Fisher, *Slavery in the History of Muslim Black Africa* (New York: New York U. Press, 2001), 194.

165. Olivier de Sardan, *Les sociétés Songhay-Zarma*, 33–40, 121; ____, "The Songhay-Zarma Female Slave: Relations of Production and Ideological Status," in Claire C. Robertson and Martin A. Klein, eds., *Women and Slavery in Africa* (Madison: U. of Wisconsin, 1983), 141–42; ____, "Captifs ruraux et esclaves impériaux du Songhay," in Claude Meillassoux, ed., *L'esclavage en Afrique précoloniale* (Paris: François Maspéro, 1975), 99–134.

166. On the recognition of matrilineality, see Olivier de Sardan, *Les sociétés Songhay-Zarma*, 32–33; ____, "The Songhay-Zarma Female Slave," 140.

167. *TS*, 134–36/212–14; Hunwick, *Timbuktu and the Songhay Empire*, 182–83. I follow Hunwick on the name 'Alī Bindi-Kanyiya, though in the text it is "'Alā K-n-d N-k-n-ī." Also, Hunwick explains the Ajur (or Ājur/Azer/Azayr) are a "Soninke creole heavily influenced by Znaga," so this woman's "ethnicity" stems from her language; Kīsu could be Kissou, between Goundam and the Niger River (Hunwick, *Timbuktu and the Songhay Empire*, 183n).

168. *TS*, 57–58/91–93; Hunwick, *Timbuktu and the Songhay Empire*, 81–82; Saad, *Social History of Timbuktu*, 38–40.

169. *TS*, 52/84; Hunwick, *Timbuktu and the Songhay Empire*, 74.

170. *TS*, 67/109–10, 192/293; Hunwick, *Timbuktu and the Songhay Empire*, 95–96, 247; *TF*, 141–42/255–57, much of which is only in manuscript C.

171. *TS*, 38/62–63; Hunwick, *Timbuktu and the Songhay Empire*, 53–54.

172. *TF*, 59/114–15.

173. *Askia* Muḥammad's pluralization policy differs from the experience in Morocco, where the sultans *Mawlāy* Ismā'īl (d. 1140/1727), *Mawlāy* 'Abd al-Raḥmān (d. 1276/1859), and *Mawlāy* al-Ḥasan (d. 1311/1894) were all sons of "black" concubines, but their "Arab" paternity was emphasized to the exclusion (if not denial) of their West African maternal heritage. See El Hamel, *Black Morocco*, 94–98.

174. Africanus, *Description of Africa*, addendum in Hunwick, *Timbuktu and the Songhay Empire*, 283, 272.

175. On the Ottoman harem, see Leslie Peirce, *The Imperial Harem: Women and Sovereignty in the Ottoman Empire* (Oxford: Oxford U. Press, 1993); Suraiya Faroqhi, *Subjects of the Sultan: Culture and Daily Life in the Ottoman Empire* (New York: I.B. Tauris, 1995); Dror Ze'evi, *Producing Desire: Changing Sexual Discourse in the Ottoman Middle East, 1500–1900* (Berkeley: U. of California Press, 2006); Alev Lytle Croutier, *Harem: The World Behind the Veil* (New York: Abbeville Press, 1991); John Freely, *Inside the Seraglio: Private Lives of the Sultans in Istanbul* (New York: Viking, 1999) Caroline Finkel, *Osman's Dream: The History of the Ottoman Empire* (New York: Basic Books, 2007).

176. Makhlūf al-Balbālī, "Fatwā on the Slaves of the Sūdān," in Hunwick and Harrak, *Mi'rāj al-ṣu'ūd: Aḥmad Bābā's Replies on Slavery*, 95/11–12.

177. Ibid.

178. Aḥmad Bābā explains his response was to a query "from the land of Tuwāt" submitted three years earlier, followed by a second request in 1023/1614–15. Al-Jirārī, "The Questions of Sa'id b. Ibrāhīm al-Jirārī of "Tuwāt" and Aḥmad Bābā, "The Fatwā of Aḥmad Bābā al-Tinbuktī: *The Ladder of Ascent Toward Grasping the Law concerning Transported Blacks*," in Hunwick and Harrak, *Mi'rāj al-ṣu'ūd*, 51/21. Concerning *Mi'rāj al-ṣu'ūd*, there is another version and translation into English (regarded by Hunwick as "amateurish") in Bernard Barbour and Michelle Jacobs, "The Mi'raj: A Legal Treatise on Slavery by Ahmad Baba, in J.R. Willis, *Slaves and Slavery in Muslim Africa* (London: Frank Cass, 1985), 2:125–59. See also Zouber, *Ahmad Bābā de Tombouctou*; E. Zeys, "Esclavage et guerre sainte: consultation juridique adressé aux gens de Touat par un érudit nègre, câdi de Tombouctoo au dix-septième siècle," *Bulletin de la Réunion d'études Algériennes* 2 (1900): 125–51, 166–89; M.A. Cherbonneau, "Essai sur la littérature arabe au Soudan d'après le Tekmilet ed-Dibadje d'Ahmed Baba le Tombouctien," *Annales de la Société archéologique de Constantine* 2 (1854–55): 1–42; ____, "Notice sur Ahmed Baba, écrivain berbère e Tombouctou," *Revue Orientale* (1955): 306–14. A very useful discussion can also be found in Marta García Novo, "Islamic Law and Slavery in Premodern West Africa," *Entremons: UPF Journal of World History* 2 (2011): 1–20.

179. Aḥmad Bābā's dates of exile in Morocco are provided in *TS*, 174/265–66, 218/333; Hunwick, *Timbuktu and the Songhay Empire*, 225, 269.

180. Aḥmad Bābā, "The Fatwā of Aḥmad Bābā al-Tinbuktī: *The Ladder of Ascent*," 53–54/23.

181. Al-Jirārī, "The Questions of Sa'id b. Ibrāhīm al-Jirārī," 44/14.

182. Aḥmad Bābā, "The Fatwā of Aḥmad Bābā al-Tinbuktī: *The Ladder of Ascent*," 54–56/24–27.

183. Ibid, 57/27, 70/39–40. Aḥmad Bābā slightly qualifies al-Balbālī's ruling by including "most" of the Fulbe rather than "all." See Hunwick and Harrak, *Mi'rāj al-ṣu'ud*, 39–40, for identifications of these groups. Aḥmad Bābā may simply confuse Borgu (*kurma*), whom he lists first, with Krmu (*krmu*), listed last. As for the Yoruba, Hunwick and Harrak venture the term "no doubt" refers to "the northern Yoruba centered round Old Oyo . . . just to the south of Borgu."

184. Al-Īsī and Aḥmad Bābā, "The Questions of al-Īsī and the Replies of Aḥmad Bābā," in Hunwick and Harrak, *Mi'rāj al-ṣu'ud*, 79–91, 96–97/41–53. Regarding the "Irbā," Aḥmad Bābā corrects or changes the spelling to "yurbā," similar to the "yurba" he uses in *Mi'rāj al-ṣu'ūd.*

185. Hall, *History of Race in Muslim Africa*, 82–87, questions the idea that a person's status derived from the land of origin. Yet Aḥmad Bābā fully engaged the premise.

186. *Corpus*, in Yāqūt, 174.

187. *TF*, 114/208–9.

188. *TS*, 124/199; Hunwick, *Timbuktu and the Songhay Empire*, 171.

189. *TF*, 76/144–45; *TS*, 77/127; Hunwick, *Timbuktu and the Songhay Empire*, 111.

190. Hunwick, *Timbuktu and the Songhay Empire*, xlvi-xlvii, conjectures that the "rank and file of the central army was composed mainly of such servile people."

191. *TF*, 126/231.

192. Ibid, 55–58/106–12, 64/121–22, 71–74/136–41. Houdas and Delafosse, *TF*, 21, note 5, and Hunwick, *Timbuktu and the Songhay Empire*, xxxii, note 36, translate the term Arbi to mean "black man," and say it refers to an ancient aboriginal population. The question becomes, at what point does this term come into use, and/or acquire this meaning?

193. *TF*, 78/147–48. I am interpreting *ahl* as "leaders" because it renders the entire statement more sensible, as the *askia* would not have received advice from the general public. Hunwick similarly understands that in *Ta'rīkh as-sūdān* the phrase *ahl Sughay*, or "people of Songhay," refers to its ruling elite. In this instance *ahl* is used instead of *ahl Sughay*, but it seems to mean the same. I am not prepared to say that every use of *ahl* or *ahl Sughay* refers to elites, but certainly many do. See Hunwick, *Timbuktu and the Songhay Empire*, xlv. In this same passage in *TF*, the notion that Yaḥyā was the brother of Muḥammad and 'Uthmān is challenged, and he is described as either Muḥammad's step-son, his step-brother, or his nephew (the son of his mother's brother).

194. *TS*, 79–81/130–34; Hunwick, *Timbuktu and the Songhay Empire*, 115–17.

195. For example, see *TF*, 82 or *TS*, 94.

196. *TF*, 78/148. In labeling the brothers "rebellious," the text uses *khārijūn*, the same term employed by al-Sa'dī and al-Suyūṭī to denounce *Sunni* 'Alī as a *khārijī*.

197. *TS* (81/134) says he was in office 36 years and six months, and *TF* says 39 years (78/149). See Hunwick, *Timbuktu and the Songhay Empire*, 117n, whose corrected estimate is adopted here.

198. *TF*, 83/155–57, states that Mūsā kicked his father out of the palace, but allowed him to continue living in Gao.

199. *TS*, 72/117; Hunwick, *Timbuktu and the Songhay Empire*, 103.

Chapter 12: Of Fitnas *and Fratricide: The Nadir of Imperial Songhay*

1. *TS*, 81/134; Hunwick, *Timbuktu and the Songhay Empire*, 118.

2. *TS*, 79/131, 82/137; Hunwick, *Timbuktu and the Songhay Empire*, 115, 119.

3. If indeed Yaḥyā was the brother of Muḥammad and 'Umar.

4. *TS*, 92–83/155. Regarding David and Absalom, see 2 Samuel 12:11–12, 16:15–23.

5. *TS*, 81/134; Hunwick, *Timbuktu and the Songhay Empire*, 118. Kirin-kirin may mean "very black" in Soninke. Charles Monteil, "Notes sur le tarikh es-Soudan," *Bulletin de l'Institut Français* (later *Fondamental*) *d'Afrique Noire (IFAN)* 27 (1965): 502.

6. *TS*, 81–83/134–39; Hunwick, *Timbuktu and the Songhay Empire*, 118–21. Kamsa Mīman-*koi*'s name, like that of *Askia* Mūsā's mother Zāra Kabirun-*koi*, suggests she had been the wife or concubine of a ruler, the Mīman-*koi*, a possible reference to Mema. Cf. *TS*, 10 and 135.

7. In going to war, the griot's role was to "challenge, flatter, sing praises, give courage." Olivier de Sardan, *Les sociétés Songhay-Zarma*, 76.

8. On Toya's location see Monteil, "Notes sur le tarikh es-Soudan," 497, 528; Hunwick, *Timbuktu and the Songhay Empire*, 108, note 38.

9. Hunwick, *Timbuktu and the Songhay Empire*, 120, note 11, explains "the losers" is a phrase repeated a number of times in the Qur'ān and refers to losing out on "eternal bliss."

10. *TS*, 86/142–43, 135/213; Hunwick, *Timbuktu and the Songhay Empire*, 124, 183. On the location of Mansur/a, see Houdas and Delafosse, *TF*, 88, note 4.

11. *TF*, 83/156; *TS*, 83–84/139–40; Hunwick, *Timbuktu and the Songhay Empire*, 120–22.

12. *TF*, 118/216–17.

13. *TS*, 9/17, 20–24/35–42, 36/58–59, 65/105–6; Hunwick, *Timbuktu and the Songhay Empire*, 12, 29–33, 50, 93. Hunwick suggests the term "Maghsharan" may derive from the Tamasheq term for "noble" (*imoshagh*). Hunwick, *Timbuktu and the Songhay Empire*, 12n. This episode also underscores that Walata/Biru, having represented the northernmost point of imperial Mali, was never incorporated into imperial Songhay, explaining why it continued as a city of refuge from its rulers.

14. *TS*, 83–84/139–40; Hunwick, *Timbuktu and the Songhay Empire*, 121–22.

15. See also *TS*, 134/139–40; Hunwick, *Timbuktu and the Songhay Empire*, 181. Balla and Alfaqi Dunku were also related through their Fulbe mothers who were sisters.

16. *TS*, 84–85/140–42; Hunwick, *Timbuktu and the Songhay Empire*, 122–23.

17. *TF*, 83/156; *TS*, 85–86/142–43; Hunwick, *Timbuktu and the Songhay Empire*, 123–24.

18. See Hunwick, *Timbuktu and the Songhay Empire*, 123–24, note 31, 343.

19. *TF*, 85/159 says that it was Muḥammad Bonkana who led the fight against Mūsā in 937/1531 (the year is inferred by Houdas and Delafosse), and does not mention of ʿAlī. Also, *TF*, 82/155 gives the length of Mūsā's rule as one year and nine months, while *TS*, 86/143 (Hunwick, *Timbuktu and the Songhay Empire*, 124), says it was two years, eight months and fourteen days.

20. *TS*, 88/146; Hunwick, *Timbuktu and the Songhay Empire*, 126–27.

21. *TS*, 87/144–45; Hunwick, *Timbuktu and the Songhay Empire*, 125–26. The office of Kūma-*koi* is obscure, possibly the same as the Goima-*koi* in *TF* (150/270), apparently the official in charge of Gao's harbor. See Hunwick, *Timbuktu and the Songhay Empire*, 125, note 36. Muḥammad Bonkana's response to the Kūma-*koi* recalls that of King David in the Hebrew Old Testament, who killed the messenger claiming to have killed King Saul (2 Samuel 1).

22. *TF*, 83–84/157–58; *TS*, 87/145; Hunwick, *Timbuktu and the Songhay Empire*, 126.

23. *TS*, 89/148; Hunwick, *Timbuktu and the Songhay Empire*, 129.

24. *TF*, 83–84/157–58.

25. *TF*, 84/158.

26. *TS*, 87–88/145–46; Hunwick, *Timbuktu and the Songhay Empire*, 126–27.

27. *TS*, 88, 92–93/153; Hunwick, *Timbuktu and the Songhay Empire*, 127, 133.

28. *TS*, 87–88/145–46; Hunwick, *Timbuktu and the Songhay Empire*, 126–27.

29. *TF*, 84–85/158–59 says ʿUthmān Tinfarin could have been the son of either *Askia* Muḥammad or *Kanfāri* ʿUmar, and provides a very different version of his relations with Muḥammad Bonkana.

30. *TS*, 87/145; Hunwick, *Timbuktu and the Songhay Empire*, 126.

31. Rouch, *Les Songhay*, 4; *TF*, 186/325. According to Olivier de Sardan (*Les sociétés Songhay-Zarma*, 20–21, 42–43, 75), descendants of the Sunnis would be chased south by the Askias, who in turn were chased south by the Arma, but clearly not all of the Sunnis' family fled the Askias.

32. *TF*, 87/163–64; *TS*, 94/156; Hunwick, *Timbuktu and the Songhay Empire*, 135.

33. *TF*, 80/151.

34. *TF*, 84–85/159. This battle supposedly took place between Timbuktu's river port of Kabara and either Aljefe or Jenne. It is a challenge to understand why such a significant battle is not mentioned by al-Sa'dī, even mystifying, as it is presented as a struggle between Muḥammad Bonkana and *Kanfāri* 'Uthmān Tinfarin.

35. *TS*, 124/199; Hunwick, *Timbuktu and the Songhay Empire*, 126.

36. *TF*, 114/208–9; *TS*, 124/199; Hunwick, *Timbuktu and the Songhay Empire*, 171.

37. For example, see *TS*, 90/149; Hunwick, *Timbuktu and the Songhay Empire*, 130. Hunwick prefers the phrase "the Songhay folk."

38. On eunuchs and gelding, see Ehud Toledano, *The Ottoman Slave Trade and Its Suppression: 1840- 1890* (Princeton: Princeton U. Press, 1982); John O. Hunwick and Eve Troutt Powell, eds. *The African Diaspora in the Mediterranean Lands of Islam* (Princeton: Markus Wiener, 2001); Ralph A. Austen, "The Trans-Saharan Slave Trade: A Tentative Census," in H. Gemery and J. S. Hogendorn, eds., *The Uncommon Market: Essays in the Economic History of the Atlantic Slave Trade* (New York: Academic Press, 1979), 23–76; Heinrich Barth, *Travels and Discoveries in North and Central Africa* (London: Frank Cass, 1965); Dennis D. Cordell, "Warlords and Enslavement: A Sample of Slave Raiders from Eastern Ubangi-Shari, 1878–1920," in *Africans in Bondage: Studies in Slavery and the Slave Trade*, ed. Paul E. Lovejoy (Madison: U. of Wisconsin Press, 1986); ____, *Dar al-Kuti and the Last Years of the Trans- Saharan Slave Trade* (Madison: U. of Wisconsin Press, 1985); Fisher, *Slavery in the History of Muslim Black Africa*; Elizabeth Savage, *The Human Commodity: Perspectives on the Trans-Saharan Slave Trade* (London: Frank Cass, 1992).

39. *TS*, 88/146; Hunwick, *Timbuktu and the Songhay Empire*, 127.

40. *TF*, 85/159.

41. *TS*, 89/147–48; Hunwick, *Timbuktu and the Songhay Empire*, 128–29. On Sudanic chess, see page 137, note 104.

42. *TS*, 78/129–30; Hunwick, *Timbuktu and the Songhay Empire*, 113–14.

43. *TS*, 88–89/146–47; Hunwick, *Timbuktu and the Songhay Empire*, 127–28.

44. *TS*, 90–91/149–51; Hunwick, *Timbuktu and the Songhay Empire*, 130–31.

45. *TF*, 85–86/159–61, initially says the date was the following year, 2 Dhū 'l-Qa'da 944/2 April 1538, but then corrects the year to 943/1537.

46. *TF*, 81/160.

47. *TS*, 89–90/148–49; Hunwick, *Timbuktu and the Songhay Empire*, 129–30. Parts of this passage are obscure.

48. *TS*, 95/157; Hunwick, *Timbuktu and the Songhay Empire*, 136–37. *TF*, 87/164, gives the length of his reign as two years, seven months, and six days.

49. *TF*, 87/164, 92–93/174; *TS*, 91–92/151; Hunwick, *Timbuktu and the Songhay Empire*, 132.

50. *TF*, 85/160; *TS*, 92–94/152–55; Hunwick, *Timbuktu and the Songhay Empire*, 132–35.

51. The *Sanqara-zūma'a* was a military official in charge of Mali's southern hemisphere. *TS*, 10–11/20–21, 184/281; Hunwick, *Timbuktu and the Songhay Empire*, 15–16, 236.

52. While al-Sa'dī hints at a split between these two (*TS*, 87/145; Hunwick, *Timbuktu and the Songhay Empire*, 126), *TF*, 84–85/158–59, asserts there was a bloody struggle. Equivocating on whether 'Uthmān Tinfarin was the son of *Askia al-ḥājj* Muḥammad or *Kanfāri* 'Umar, the text identifies the fifteen brothers felled in the battle as "sons of *Askia* [*al-ḥājj*] Muḥammad."

53. Kala was located between the Niger and Bani Rivers, south of Masina and west of Diagha/Diakha/Dia.

54. *TS*, 94/156; Hunwick, *Timbuktu and the Songhay Empire*, 135. I infer that *al-ṭulū' inqaṭa'a qalbuhu*, "the rising in his heart was blocked," refers to a heart attack, or even a stroke. Regarding *al-mughanī*, presumably *al-mughannin* was meant.

55. *TF*, 68–70/131–35, 86–87/161–63; *TS*, 37/60–61, 73/120–21; Hunwick, *Timbuktu and the Songhay Empire*, 52, 105–6; J.O. Hunwick, "Askiya al-Ḥājj Muḥammad and His Successors: The Account of al-Imām al-Takrūrī, *Sudanic Africa: A Journal of Historical Sources* 1 (1990): 85–90; ___, "A Note of Askiya Muḥammad's Meeting with al-Suyūṭī," *Sudanic Africa: A Journal of Historical Sources* 2 (1991): 175–76. As mentioned, Hunwick argues it was the Abbasid caliph of Cairo, not the Meccan *sharīf*, who appointed Muḥammad as his deputy for the "land of Songhay," to which the later passage in *TF* certainly alludes. Also, the turban changes colors from blue to green in *TF*. Finally, *TF* records that despite Songhay lore that Muḥammad had found the sword in the plain of Badr to the accompaniment of celestial drums, suggesting it had been used on behalf of the Prophet in his tremendous victory over the Quraysh in Ramadan 2/March 624, the sword was in fact a gift. What happened to it remains a mystery, with three possibilities: Isḥāq II ("the Zughrānī") took it to "Gurma" when fleeing from Muḥammad Gao in 1000/1592, where it was confiscated by the ruler there; it was confiscated from Muḥammad Gao when he was arrested by the Moroccans near Kukiya that same year; or *Askia* Nūḥ took it with him to Dendi in 1001–2/1592–93 in the process of resisting the Moroccans.

56. *TF*, 87/164 *TS*, 94/156; Hunwick, *Timbuktu and the Songhay Empire*, 136. It is unclear how Hunwick arrives at 31 January/1 February 1538 (136, note 20).

57. *TF*, 87/163–64; *TS*, 94–95/156–57; Hunwick, *Timbuktu and the Songhay Empire*, 135–36. Based on the *balma'a* succession list found in *TS*, 135/213; Hunwick, *Timbuktu and the Songhay Empire*, 183. Ḥammād may have even been *balma'a* before his promotion to *kanfāri*, replacing Muḥammad Dundumiya b. *Askia al-ḥājj* Muḥammad (appointed by Muḥammad Bonkana Kirya).

58. Africanus, *Description of Africa*, addendum in Hunwick, *Timbuktu and the Songhay Empire*, 283–84, says one horse sold for 40 to 50 *mithqāls*, which Hunwick says would be the cost of 7 or 8 prime slaves, or roughly 6 *mithqāls* per slave (284, note 66). He also calculates a general rate of 3000 cowries to 1 *mithqāl* for the Middle Niger from the sixteenth to the nineteenth century (282n), which yields the result that 300 cowries were equivalent to .1 *mithqāls*, one-sixtieth the general rate.

59. *TF*, 87/164; *TS*, 95/157; Hunwick, *Timbuktu and the Songhay Empire*, 136.

60. *TS*, 86/142–43, 95/157; Hunwick, *Timbuktu and the Songhay Empire*, 124, 137. It is not clear who was *balma'a* at the time. Muḥammad Dundumiya had been appointed to the office by Muḥammad Bonkana, and there is no record of when he was replaced, but the *balma'a* succession list (found in *TS*, 135/213; Hunwick, *Timbuktu and the Songhay Empire*, 183) names Muḥammad Dundumiya followed by Hammād w. Aryu, followed by 'Alī Kusira.

61. *TF*, 81/152, 92–93/174–75; *TS*, 100/164, 135/212; Hunwick, *Timbuktu and the Songhay Empire*, 143, 182.

62. *TF*, 87–88/165–66.

63. *TS*, 95–96/157–58; Hunwick, *Timbuktu and the Songhay Empire*, 136–37.

64. *TS*, 96/158–59; Hunwick, *Timbuktu and the Songhay Empire*, 138.

65. *TS*, 100/164; Hunwick, *Timbuktu and the Songhay Empire*, 142–43.

66. *TF*, 88/166; *TS*, 96/159, 104/170–71; Hunwick, *Timbuktu and the Songhay Empire*, 138, 148–49. As for the discrepancy between Kala and Bendugu, it is of little consequence as it reflects imprecise borders and that they were contiguous, with Kala representing the land between Niger and Bani Rivers south of Masina and west of Diagha/Diakha/Dia, and Bendugu consisting of a string villages along the Bani River's right bank, from Jenne to beyond Segu. Indicative of the threat Muḥammad Bonkana Kirya posed, Dāwūd would tell his sons or grandsons Maḥmūd and Sa'īd upon arriving in Sama: "My eyes have not had any sleep since your father and mother joined to plot against me." (Hunwick, *Timbuktu and the Songhay Empire*, 148, note 34, points out that the phrase "two sons of daughters" of Muhammad Bonkana Kirya appears in manuscript C of *TS*, introducing uncertainty as to whether Maḥmūd and Sa'īd were Muhammad Bonkana Kirya's sons or grandsons.)

67. The trope of death-by-well is first mentioned with the Awghām women flinging themselves down a well to avoid capture in 350/961–2, in connection with Dankara, who chose not to throw Sunjata down a well, and also Sumaoro, who allegedly flung Sunjata's father and brothers down a well.

68. *TS*, 97–98/160–61; Hunwick, *Timbuktu and the Songhay Empire*, 139–40.

69. *TS*, 98/161–62; Hunwick, *Timbuktu and the Songhay Empire*, 140.

70. *TS*, 99–100/163–64; Hunwick, *Timbuktu and the Songhay Empire*, 142. See Leo Africanus, 1956, ii, 423, who says "Beni Sabih" was the leading town in the Dar'a.

71. *TF*, 92–93/174–75; *TS*, 98/162, 100/164; Hunwick, *Timbuktu and the Songhay Empire*, 140–41, 143. *Qāḍī* Muḥammad would remain in office for 17 years and 3 months, until Safar 973/September 1565, expiring at the age of 63.

Chapter 13: Surfeit and Stability: The Era of Askia *Dāwūd*

1. *TS*, 100/164–65, 113/182–83; Hunwick, *Timbuktu and the Songhay Empire*, 143–44, 158. *TF*, 93/176, 119/217 states Dāwūd came to power in 955/1548, a mistake given its own account that Isḥāq Bēr's reign ended in 956/1549, though it maintains he was in power until 991/1583.

2. *TS*, 102–3/168, 110/178, 113/182; Hunwick, *Timbuktu and the Songhay Empire*, 147, 154, 157. Hunwick (*Timbuktu and the Songhay Empire*, 154, note 76) explains *masar* is the Songhay term for syphilis.

3. *TF*, 93/175; *TS*, 99/163; Hunwick, *Timbuktu and the Songhay Empire*, 141–42.

4. Or Bunkānū Fāriyu. *TF*, 81/151–52, 94/177; *TS*, 110/179, 134–35/212–13; Hunwick, *Timbuktu and the Songhay Empire*, 155, 182.

5. *TF*, 93/176.

6. Ibid, 94/177–78. *Askia* Muḥammad's prophecy is repeated in the traditions. Soumalia, Hamidou, and Laya, *Traditions des Songhay*, 40–41/188–89.

7. Houdas and Delafosse, *TF*, 149, note 3, describe this office as the "minister of the whites," as the Songhay term *korey* signifies "white." Hunwick, *Timbuktu and the Songhay Empire*, 144, note 2, reiterates this point. Al-Ḥājj's actual name was *Askia al-ḥājj* Muḥammad b. *Askia* Dāwūd, or *Askia al-ḥājj* Muḥammad II.

8. *TF*, 79/149.

9. Africanus, *Description of Africa*, addendum in Hunwick, *Timbuktu and the Songhay Empire*, 283.

10. *TF*, 110/202–3.

11. *TS*, 111/181, 114–21/184–95; Hunwick, *Timbuktu and the Songhay Empire*, 156, 160–67, 347.

12. *TS*, 100/165, 106/173, 135/213; Hunwick, *Timbuktu and the Songhay Empire*, 144, 150, 182. This asserts Kashiya/ā was the son of 'Uthmān Tinfarin b. 'Umar, not 'Uthmān Yawbābo b. *Askia* Muḥammad. The sources are not clear on this. Both 'Uthmāns had served as *kanfāri*.

13. *TS*, 99/163; Hunwick, *Timbuktu and the Songhay Empire*, 141.

14. Muḥammad was probably the same person as Muḥammad Dalla-ije ("son of Dalla"), demonstrating close ties between the royal branches, as his father 'Alū Zalīl was also the son of *Kanfāri* 'Umar. *TS*, 103/169; Hunwick, *Timbuktu and the Songhay Empire*, 147.

15. *TS*, 103/169; Hunwick, *Timbuktu and the Songhay Empire*, 147. He was the brother of Muḥammad Bonkana Kūma, son of *Faran* 'Umar Komadikha, which must be a reference to *Kanfāri* 'Umar. Muḥammad Bonkana Kūma may therefore be the same person as the deposed *Askia* Muḥammad Bonkana Kirya. 'Alī Dādu means 'Alī son of Dado," a Soninke woman's name, so he was better known as the son of his mother. Monteil, "Notes sur le tarikh es-Soudan," 505; Hunwick, *Timbuktu and the Songhay Empire*, 145n.

16. *TS*, 102/168, 106/173, 110/179; Hunwick, *Timbuktu and the Songhay Empire*, 146, 150, 154–55. Dāwūd retreated in the second campaign, and between 978/1570 and 985/1577–78 would again march to the Mossi border, but without actually fighting them.

17. Given Katsina's distance from Gao, al-Sa'dī may have meant Kebbi. *TS*, 103/168–69; Hunwick, *Timbuktu and the Songhay Empire*, 147. "Quilted armor" is from the Arabic *ahl Libti*, with *Libti* the Hausa word *lifidi*, from the Arabic *lubbāda* for "saddle blanket." 'Alī Dādu's brother Muḥammad Bonkana Kūma also died.

18. At this juncture Bukar 'Alī Dūdu/ Bukar Shili-ije is referred to as 'Alī Fulan's son. He is not mentioned at all in *Ta'rīkh al-fattāsh*. *TS*, 100–1/163–64; Hunwick, *Timbuktu and the Songhay Empire*, 144–45.

19. *TS*, 101–2/165–67, 106/173, 108/176; Hunwick, *Timbuktu and the Songhay Empire*, 145–46, 150, 152.

20. *TS*, 103/169, 107/175; Hunwick, *Timbuktu and the Songhay Empire*, 148, 151–52. Hunwick, 151 notes, based on Kuba, suggests Barka is Borgu, and the mountain is in the Atakora range.

21. *TS*, 102/168; Hunwick, *Timbuktu and the Songhay Empire*, 146, 146, note 18. Toya, or the territories of "Tirmissi" (Termes) and Kuma. Hunwick speculates these Fulbe decided to remain in Baghana and not migrate to Masina with other Fulbe groups.

22. *TS*, 103–4/169–70; Hunwick, *Timbuktu and the Songhay Empire*, 148.

23. Al-Sa'dī identifies the Maghsharan Tuareg as the Masūfa branch of the Ṣanhāja, revealing a view of the Tuareg as a distillation of the Masūfa and the Kel Tamasheq. *TS*, 22/37, 25–26/42–44; Hunwick, *Timbuktu and the Songhay Empire*, 31, 35–37, 35, note 1.

24. *TS*, 109–10/177–78; Hunwick, *Timbuktu and the Songhay Empire*, 153–54.

25. *TS*, 102/168; Hunwick, *Timbuktu and the Songhay Empire*, 147; Olivier de Sardan, *Concepts et conceptions Songhay-Zarma*, 282–83; Hunwick, *Timbuktu and the Songhay Empire*, 147, note 20.

26. *TS*, 104/170; Hunwick, *Timbuktu and the Songhay Empire*, 148. I am following Hunwick's translation of *qullāt* as "water vessels."

27. *TS*, 103/169; Hunwick, *Timbuktu and the Songhay Empire*, 147. Hunwick (*Timbuktu and the Songhay Empire*, 147, note 26, 150, note 45) initially locates "Borno" or "Barno" as a hilly location on the Niger's left bank near Gao, but as al-Sa'dī uses the term again concerning the Mossi, Hunwick proposes another "Borno" on the Niger's other side. It makes sense that al-Sa'dī means the latter location in both uses of the term.

28. *TS*, 105/171–72; Hunwick, *Timbuktu and the Songhay Empire*, 149–50.

29. *TS*, 112/181–82; Hunwick, *Timbuktu and the Songhay Empire*, 156–57.

30. *TS*, 110/179; Hunwick, *Timbuktu and the Songhay Empire*, 154–55. Dāwūd seized, then released the Da'a-*koi*'s children in response to the Uma-*koi*, who also headed a community in Bendugu.

31. *TS*, 105–8/173–76; Hunwick, *Timbuktu and the Songhay Empire*, 150–52.

32. *TF*, 118/216–17; *TS*, 109/178, 136/214; Hunwick, *Timbuktu and the Songhay Empire*, 154, 184.

33. *TF*, 117–18/215–17; *TS*, 109–12/177–81; Hunwick, *Timbuktu and the Songhay Empire*, 154–56, 184. Hunwick (*Timbuktu and the Songhay Empire*, 184, note 68) states that in the margins of one of his consulted manuscripts, Dāwūd is said to have had 333 children. Regarding enslaved soldiers bringing their wives, see Martin Klein, "Women and Slavery in the Western Sudan," in Robertson and Klein, eds., *Women and Slavery in Africa*, 81.

34. *TF*, 95–101/179–189. Houdas and Delafosse on the meaning of Misakul Allāh: "God is the one who foreordained and created all that was or is, whether in this world or the next." Is "Abdā" derived from the Arabic for "eternal," or does it refer to the "place of slaves?"

35. *TF*, 100/188, 104/194. Each sack has a capacity of approximately 210 pounds U.S., (with the conversion of 100 *mudde* or liters into ounces resulting in over 3,381, or 211 lbs. U.S.). Houdas and Delafosse arrive at 240 liters per sack by a process I cannot follow.

36. Heinrich Barth, *Travels and Discoveries in North and Central Africa; Being a Journal of an Expedition Undertaken under the Auspices of H.B.M.'s Government, in the Years 1849–1855* (London: Longmans and Roberts, 1859), 3:363.

37. Al-ʿUmarī mentions fiefs (*iqṭāʿā*) in imperial Mali, though not on this scale. *Corpus*, 266.

38. There is some confusion over 1,700 to 2,700 slaves alleged to have worked at "Faran-Taka" plantation. Paul E. Lovejoy, *Transformations in Slavery: A History of Slavery in Africa* (Cambridge: Cambridge U. Press, 1983), 32. But see N.G. Kodjo, "Contribution à l'étude des tribus dites serviles du Songhai," *Bulletin de l'IFAN* 38 (1976): 809.

39. *TF*, 94/178–79.

40. Ibid, 94–95/179.

41. Ibid, 97/183.

42. Ibid, 101/188.

43. *TS*, 111–12/180–81; Hunwick, *Timbuktu and the Songhay Empire*, 155–57.

44. *TS*, 112/181; Hunwick, *Timbuktu and the Songhay Empire*, 157. I suggest there is more innuendo here than Hunwick allows. Muḥammad Bonkana refers to Yāsī as *yā hāthā al-ʿabd al-dāsir*, which can mean "pushy" (as Hunwick translates), but also has the connotation of sexual penetration or violation when applied to women, and as Yāsī was likely a eunuch, an angered Muḥammad Bonkana was insulting him on this basis. Interpreting *al-sūʾ* in Yāsī's response (*akhṭātu fī al-khiṭāb qul lī yā hāthā al-ʿabd al-sūʾ*) to mean "unfortunate" rather than "evil" is consistent with this reading.

45. *TF*, 101–107/189–99.

46. This is not necessarily so, as the *khadīm* Maḥmūd Yāza under *Askia* Isḥāq Bēr was of caste background (*qayn*, literally "blacksmith").

47. *TF*, 102/190–91.

48. Though not as productive as Abda, where approximately 5 *ṣunūn* of grain were allegedly harvested for every slave, compared with 3 *ṣunūn* under Mūsā Sagansāru.

49. Olivier de Sardan, *Les sociétés Songhay-Zarma*, 52; Roberta Ann Dunbar, "Slavery and the Evolution of Nineteenth Century Damagaran," in Miers and Kopytoff, eds., *Slavery in Africa*, 165; Mohammed Bashir Salau, *The West African Plantation: A Case Study* (New York: Palgrave Macmillan, 2011). Such conventions were also found as far south as the Igbo in the nineteenth century, among whom a slave's property "was, in law, held at the pleasure of his master. In practice, however, the slave's right to property was accepted." K. Nwachukwu-Ogedengbe, "Slavery in Nineteenth-Century Aboh," in Miers and Kopytoff, eds., *Slavery in Africa*, 150.

50. *TF*, 97/183.

51. Ibid, 103–4/191–93.

52. Ibid, 104/193–94.

53. Ibid, 104/194, 134/245; *TS*, 125/201; Hunwick, *Timbuktu and the Songhay Empire*, 173.

54. *TF*, 106–8/196–99

55. Ibid, 107/197.

56. Olivier de Sardan, *Les sociétés Songhay-Zarma*, 23–76; ___, "The Songhay-Zarma Female Slave," 130–43. See also the discussion of amelioration with re-

spect to *captifs de case* and *captifs de traite* in Martin A. Klein's *Slavery and Colonial Rule in French West Africa* (Cambridge: Cambridge U. Press, 1998), 5–9.

57. *TF*, 108–9/199–201.

58. See Hunwick, *Timbuktu and the Songhay Empire*, lxi.

59. Yuna's location is provided by Houdas and Delafosse, *TF*, 201, note 1.

60. Another account only in manuscript C of *TF* is consistent with the foregoing, but the specifics are highly suspect, alleging that after Dāwūd "accidentally" kills a *sherīfian*, he gives the deceased's brother three different, specific properties on which were the *Zanj*, a seeming example of incorporating the claims of *Shehu* Amadu Lobbo. *TF*, 116–17/212–15.

61. Fisher, *Slavery in the History of Muslim Black Africa*, 316–21, discusses "slaves as currency," or payment for goods and services. In building on the concept, I am talking about the use of slaves in quest of the supernal, a settling of celestial accounts.

62. But, of course there are limits to this analysis, as the conversion of slaves, incumbent upon slaveholders, did not require their manumission.

63. Patrick Manning, *Slavery and African Life: Occidental, Oriental, and African Slave Trades* (Cambridge: Cambridge U. Press, 1990), 116; Suzanne Miers, "Slavery: A Question of Definition," *Slavery and Abolition* 24 (2003): 5. Dunbar ("Slavery and the Evolution of Nineteenth Century Damagaran," 170–71), in delineating the roles of slaves as titled officials, also comments the "employment of slaves as soldiers is an ancient practice in the Central Sudan and elsewhere." This was also true in Muslim-influenced societies as well as others. See Robin Law, *The Oyo Empire, c. 1600-c. 1836* (Oxford: Clarendon Press, 1977), 68–70; James H. Vaughan, "Mafakur: A Limbic Institution of the Margi," in Miers and Kopytoff, eds., *Slavery in Africa*, 93–94.

64. Claude Meillassoux, "Female Slavery," in Robertson and Klein, eds., *Women and Slavery in Africa*, 54–66; Miers, "Slavery: A Question of Definition," 8–11.

65. *TS*, 106/174; Hunwick, *Timbuktu and the Songhay Empire*, 151.

66. *TF*, 126–35/231–45; *TS*, 122–23/196–97; Hunwick, *Timbuktu and the Songhay Empire*, 169.

67. *TF*, 116/211. *TF* hastens to add the arrogation did not include soldiers' daughters, subject to sexual assault by divine right going back to at least *Sunni* 'Alī.

68. These categories are even more complex in the thirteenth/nineteenth century among the Songhay-Zarma, with smithing performed by both slaves and by groups originally from elsewhere, such as "les boisseliers *Saace* (woodworkers), forgerons *zem cire* ("red smiths") et les griots *Sillincé*" who were essentially castes. Griots were also divided between the more mundane, who were slaves, and the descendants of court griots, alternatively considered slaves or nobles. Olivier de Sardan, *Les sociétés Songhay-Zarma*, 51–53.

69. This vast literature includes Barry, *Senegambia and the Atlantic Slave Trade*; Mariana P. Candido, *An African Slaving Port and the Atlantic World* (Cambridge: Cambridge U. Press, 2013); Robert Harms, *The Diligent: A Voyage through the Worlds of the Slave Trade* (New York: Basic Books, 2003); Joseph E. Inikori, ed., *Forced Migration: The Impact of the Export Slave Trade on African Societies* (New York: Oxford U. Press, 1982); Joseph E. Inikori and Stanley L. Engerman, eds., *The Atlantic Slave Trade: Effect on Economies, Societies, and Peoples in Africa, the Americas, and Europe*

(Durham and London, 1992); David Eltis, *Economic Growth and the Ending of the Transatlantic Slave Trade* (New York: Oxford U. Press, 1987); James A. Rawley, *The Transatlantic Slave Trade: A History* (New York: W.W. Norton and Co., 1981); Jean Mettas, *Répertoire des expéditions négrières françaises au XVIIIe siècle*, 2 vols. (Paris: Société française d'histoire d'outre-mer, 1978, 1984); Colin Palmer, *Human Cargoes: A History of the Atlantic Slave Trade, 1518–1865* (Chicago: U. of Illinois Press, 1981); Serge Daget, *Répertoire des expéditions négrières françaises à la traite illegale (1814–1850)* (Nantes: Centre de Recherche sur l'Histoire du Monde Atlantique, Université de Nantes, 1988); David Richardson, "Slave Exports from West and West-Central Africa, 1700–1810: New Estimates of Volume and Distribution," *Journal of African History* 30 (1989): 1–22; Suzanne Miers and Richard Roberts, eds., *The End of Slavery in Africa* (Madison: U. of Wisconsin Press, 1988); Joseph E. Inikori, "Slaves or Serfs? A Comparative Study of Slavery and Serfdom in Europe and Africa," in Isidore Okpewho, Carole Boyce Davies, and Ali Al-Amin Mazrui, eds., *The African Diaspora: African Origins and New World Identities* (Bloomington: Indiana U. Press, 1999), 49–75; Paul Lovejoy, "The Impact of the Atlantic Slave Trade on Africa," *Journal of African History* 30 (l989): 365–94; George Metcalf, "A Microcosm of Why Africans Sold Slaves," *Journal of African History* 28 (l987): 377–94; Ojo Olatunji and Nadine Hunt, eds., *Slavery in Africa and the Caribbean: A History of Enslavement and Identity since the 18th Century* (New York: I.B. Tauris, 2012).

70. In partial response to Suzanne Miers and Igor Kopytoff's "'Slavery' as an Institution of Marginality" in Miers and Kopytoff, eds., *Slavery in Africa* is Frederick Cooper's incisive case for slavery's proprietary basis in "The Problem of Slavery in African Studies," *Journal of African History* 20 (l979): 103–25. Both Claude Meillassoux, *The Anthropology of Slavery* (Chicago: U. of Chicago Press, 1991), and Lovejoy (with his own definition of slavery in *Transformations*, 2–3) emphasize slavery's violent nature, as do Paul E. Lovejoy and Jan S. Hogendorn, eds., *Slow Death for Slavery: The Course of Abolition in Northern Nigeria, 1897–1936* (Cambridge: Cambridge U. Press, 1993); Paul E. Lovejoy, "Plantations in the Economy of the Sokoto Caliphate," *Journal of African History* 19 (1978): 341–68; Jan S. Hogendorn, "The Economics of Slave Use on Two 'Plantations' in the Zaria Emirate of the Sokoto Caliphate," *International Journal of African Historical Studies* 10 (1977): 369–83. Orlando Patterson's *Slavery and Social Death: A Comparative Study* (Cambridge, Harvard U. Press, 1985) is insightful but often misrepresented. As Klein's *Slavery and Colonial Rule in French West Africa*, 5–10, makes apparent, most models envision servility as "coerced." Miers complicates servitude, and I follow her suggestion in focusing on the local and offering my own definition (Miers, "Slavery: A Question of Definition," 2–14).

71. This is not unlike Nwachukwu-Ogedengbe's definition in "Slavery in Nineteenth-Century Aboh," 139–40, underscoring a slave's "unquestioned obedience to the wishes of another."

72. See Nwachukwu-Ogedengbe, "Slavery in Nineteenth-Century Aboh," 147, for a similar assessment.

73. Lineage building was one reason for slavery, as there were others, including the acquisition of slaves as "prestige items"; such reasons should not be confused with slavery itself. See Barbara Isaacman and Allen Isaacman, "Slavery and Social Stratifi-

cation among the Sena of Mozambique"; Joseph C. Miller, "Imbangala Lineage Slavery"; and Wyatt MacGaffey, "Economic and Social Dimensions of Kongo Slavery" in Miers and Kopytoff, eds., *Slavery in Africa*, 105–20, 205–33, 235–57.

74. Manning underscores this point in warning the "upward mobility and the power of individual slaves should not be distorted" (*Slavery and African Life*, 116).

75. *TF*, 113–15/207–10; *TS*, 34–35/55–56, 43–45/70–75, 108/176–77; Hunwick, *Timbuktu and the Songhay Empire*, 48, 62–65, 152–53. He also taught Muḥammad Kibi b. Jābir Kibi, who in 974/1566 became Gao's *khaṭīb*.

76. *TF*, 119/217; *TS*, 107–8/176, 113/183, 117–18/189; Hunwick, *Timbuktu and the Songhay Empire*, 152, 158, 163; *Nayl*, 219. *TF* maintains Dāwūd passed in Rajab 991/August 1583, the same month and year given for al-ʿĀqib's death in *TS*; whereas *TS* provides Rajab 990/August 1582 as the year of Dāwūd's passing.

77. *TF*, 121–24/221–27. He mispronounced *al-wabl* ("rain") as *al-wail* ("woe"), altering the passage's meaning.

78. *TF*, 121–22/221–23; *TS*, 108–9/177, 110/179; Hunwick, *Timbuktu and the Songhay Empire*, 153, 155. There is confusion in the sources between the mosques of *Sīdī* Yaḥyā and the market. Houdas and Delafosse suggest they were the same (*TF*, 223n), but al-Sa'dī and *TF* make temporal distinctions between the two.

79. *TF*, 122–23/223–24. The passage refers to "al-Ḥājj al-Amīn," but as Jingereber's renovation was finished before *Askia* al-Ḥājj, this may be a veiled reference to Dāwūd.

80. *TF*, 109/201.

81. *TS*, 110/178; Hunwick, *Timbuktu and the Songhay Empire*, 154.

82. *TF*, 109–10/202–4.

83. Ibid, 109/202.

84. Ibid, 110–11/203–4; TS, 110/178–79; Hunwick, *Timbuktu and the Songhay Empire*, 154.

85. *TS*, 106/174–75; Hunwick, *Timbuktu and the Songhay Empire*, 151; Ann McDougall, "The Question of Tegaza and the Conquest of Songhay: Some Saharan Considerations," in *Le Maroc et l'Afrique Subsaharienne aux débuts des temps moderne*, 251–82. As Muḥammad Ikumā was Taghaza-*mondio*, how the nephew would have "led" Taghaza is unclear; the text simply says Dāwūd "appointed him as administrator of Taghaza's affairs" (*wallāhu amr Taghāza*). Loyal Tuareg surviving al-Filālī's attack began operations later that year at Taghaza al-ghizlān ("Taghaza of the gazelles").

86. Abun-Nasr, *A History of the Maghrib in the Islamic Period*. On Sa'dian and Ottoman perspectives, see Louis Mougin, "Les premiers sultans sa'dides et le Sahara," *Revue de l'Occident Musulmane et de la Méditerranée* 19 (1975): 169–87; Ahmed Boucharb, "La présence européenne sur la côte ouest africaine et la politique soudanaise de la dynasties Sa'adienne," and Abderrahman Moudden, "Tasā'ulāt ḥaula mauqif al-ʿuthmānīīn min al-gazw as-sa'adī li as-sūdān," in *Le Maroc et l'Afrique Subsaharienne aux débuts des temps modernes*, 23–24, 11–19 (Arabic section).

87. *TS*, 111/180; Hunwick, *Timbuktu and the Songhay Empire*, 155.

88. *TF*, 116/212, 118–19/215–17; *TS*, 113/182–83; Hunwick, *Timbuktu and the Songhay Empire*, 157–58.

Chapter 14: The Rending Asunder: Dominion's End

1. Al-Sa'dī lists him first among the sons of Dāwūd named Muḥammad, consistent with al-Hādī's comments to al-Ḥājj upon the latter's succession as *askia*: "Only following the rule of seniority, concerning which if Muḥammad Bonkana had been present here today [at the death of Dāwūd], the *askiyate* (*hāthā al-amr*) would not have come to you." *TS*, 114/185, 136/214; Hunwick, *Timbuktu and the Songhay Empire*, 160, 184.

2. *TF*, 119–20/219.

3. *TS*, 113/183; Hunwick, *Timbuktu and the Songhay Empire*, 158.

4. Muḥammad Bonkana's own sons—'Umar Bēr, 'Umar Katu, and Yimba Koyra-ije—went into hiding, reappearing just before the reign of Isḥāq b. *Askia* Dāwūd to avenge their father upon Amar who, becoming aware of the plot, joined the *sūmā*, a group responsible for preparing the *askia* for the succession.

5. *TF*, 120/219; *TS*, 114/184, 134/213; Hunwick, *Timbuktu and the Songhay Empire*, 160, 182. I arrive at "Āmina Gāy Bardā" by associating the variants most proximate.

6. *TS*, 115/185; Hunwick, *Timbuktu and the Songhay Empire*, 161. I venture al-Sa'dī is signaling the enslaved in using *al-'ibād*. Hunwick: "allegiance was paid to him by the commanders and the soldiers, and by the populace at large." Houdas: "les généraux, les troupes, la population tout entière at les dévôts personnages prêtèrent serment d'obéissance à El-Hâdj." The passage: *bāya'ahu al-qiyād wa 'l-ajnād wa sā'ir al-khalq wa 'l-'ibād.*

7. *TF*, 120–21/219–21.

8. Ibid, 119/218, 126/230; *TS*, 114–15/184–85; Hunwick, *Timbuktu and the Songhay Empire*, 160–61.

9. Bukar, learning of al-Ḥājj's succession, returned with son Marbā to Gao from exile in Kala, and was rewarded with the post of Baghana-*fari*. *TS*, 116–17/188–89; Hunwick, *Timbuktu and the Songhay Empire*, 162–63.

10. *TF*, 121/221; *TS*, 117–18/189; Hunwick, *Timbuktu and the Songhay Empire*, 163. According to *TF*, he was born in 913/1507–8.

11. *TS*, 31–32/52–53, 34/55–56, 117–18/189–90, 169–70/258–60; Hunwick, *Timbuktu and the Songhay Empire*, 44–45, 47–48, 163–64, 219–20.

12. *TS* claims Abū Ḥafṣ 'Umar declined the *askia*'s invitation on at least three occasions, while *TF* cites an unspecified "incident" (*waq'*) as the reason the *askia* refused to issue an invitation in the first place. *TF*, 119–25/219–29; *TS*, 117–18/189–90. Hunwick, *Timbuktu and the Songhay Empire*, 163–64.

13. Regarding the fate of Aḥmad Mu'yā (or Mughyā), see *TF*, 174/305–6; *TS*, 168–70/256–60; Hunwick, *Timbuktu and the Songhay Empire*, 218–20.

14. *TF*, 186/324; *TS*, 118–19/190–93; Hunwick, *Timbuktu and the Songhay Empire*, 164–65.

15. Chantal de la Véronne and Joseph de León, *Vie de Moulay Isma'il, roi de Fès et de Maroc: d'après Joseph de León, 1708–1728: étude et édition* (Paris: P. Geuthner, 1974); Mercedes García-Arenal, *Ahmad al-Mansur: The Beginnings of Modern Morocco* (Oxford: Oneworld, 2009); El Hamel, *Black Morocco*; 'Abd ar-Raḥmān b, Zaydān, *al-Manza' al-Latīf fī mafākhir al-Mawlā Ismā'īl ash-Sharīf*, ed. 'Abd al-Hadi al-Tazi (Casablanca: Dār al-Bayḍā' 1993); Richard L. Smith, *Ahmad al-Mansur:*

Islamic Visionary (New York: Pearson Longman, 2006); Nabil Mouline, *Le califat imaginaire d'Ahmad al-Mansūr* (Paris: Presses Universitaires de France, 2009).

16. *TS*, 120–21/193–94; Hunwick, *Timbuktu and the Songhay Empire*, 166–67. Hunwick translates *sanānīr al-ġāliya* as "civet cats" rather than ivory, which I concede is speculative, as the normal term for ivory is *'āj*.

17. Hunwick, "Songhay, Borno and the Hausa States, 1450–1600," in Ajayi and Crowder, eds., *History of West Africa* 3rd ed., 1: 361, locates this mine at Tin-Wadar, "perhaps" in the Taoudeni area.

18. *TF*, 125–26/230; *TS*, 121/194; Hunwick, *Timbuktu and the Songhay Empire*, 167.

19. *TF*, 125–26/230; *TS*, 121–22/195; Hunwick, *Timbuktu and the Songhay Empire*, 168.

20. *TF*, 126/230–31.

21. *TS*, 114–21/184–95; Hunwick, *Timbuktu and the Songhay Empire*, 160–68. *TF*, 186/324, maintains al-Ḥājj executed al-Hādī, interring him without a proper Muslim burial, his feet still shackled.

22. Written by Muḥammad al-Amīn b. Bābā Gānū. *TF*, 126–29/231–35; *TS*, 122–23/196–97; Hunwick, *Timbuktu and the Songhay Empire*, 169–70.

23. *Khādam* (pl. *khadam*) could also refer to a eunuch, or to a female slave. The phrase *'abd al-khaṣī* or "castrated slave" is far less ambiguous.

24. *TF*, 130–31/237–38. Embedded in this account is an intriguing discussion of amulets, suggesting their instrumentality in causing this death. In discussing imperial Songhay's demise, the traditions begin with this episode. Soumalia, Hamidou, and Laya, *Traditions des Songhay*, 41–58/189–206.

25. *Ta'rīkh al-fattāsh* suggests the insurgency was an afterthought, but al-Sa'dī reports the *balma'a* told one Māranfa *al-ḥājj* prior to the incident: "You have seen the situation here as it relates to us. I want you to join us," to which Māranfa *al-ḥājj* replied, "O *Balma'a*, by God I swear that I will not follow anyone as long as one finger of *Askia* Muḥammad Bāni moves." *TF*, 126–29/231–35; *TS*, 122–23/196–97; Hunwick, *Timbuktu and the Songhay Empire*, 169–70.

26. Houdas and Delafosse, *TF*, 233–34n, on the location of Amadia; and Charles Monteil, "Notes sur le tarikh es-Soudan," *Bulletin de l'Institut Français* (later *Fondamental*) *d'Afrique Noire (IFAN)* 27 (1965): 497, 528, on the location of Toya or Toy. See also Hunwick, *Timbuktu and the Songhay Empire*, 108n.

27. *TF*, 128–30/234–37; *TS*, 122–23/196–97; Hunwick, *Timbuktu and the Songhay Empire*, 169–70.

28. *TF*, 129/236, says *Kanfāri* Ṣāliḥ died the evening of 25 Rabī' al-Ākhir 996/24 March 1588. *TS* maintains Muḥammad Koi-ije first struck the *kanfāri*, while *TF* insists it was the *balma'a*, discounting a competing claim that a slave of Muḥammad Koi-ije did it.

29. Benga-*farma* Muḥammad Haïga (*Askia* Muḥammad's grandson through the *Hari-farma* 'Abd Allāh) instead fled to Gao upon hearing the *balma'a*'s "criminal plans" (*jāniyāt*). *TF*, 131–32/239–40; *TS*, 124/199; Hunwick, *Timbuktu and the Songhay Empire*, 170–71.

30. Hunwick, "Songhay, Borno and the Hausa States, 1450–1600," in Ajayi and Crowder, eds., *History of West Africa* 3rd ed., 1: 361 cites the cause of death as a heart attack, or "possibly an epileptic fit."

31. On the *bārai-koi*, see Hunwick, *Timbuktu and the Songhay Empire*, 197, note 61.

32. *TF*, 132–33/240–42.

33. Though not the entire army, as al-Sa'dī says the *huku-kuru-koi* separated from them with his 4,000-eunuch cavalry. *TF*, 134–35/244–45; *TS*, 124–25/199–200; Hunwick, *Timbuktu and the Songhay Empire*, 171–72.

34. *TF*, 131/238–39.

35. This parallels *Balma'a* Muḥammad Kiray's concern with 'Uthmān Sīdī and Bukar Kirin-kirin, that war turned on the character and exploits of individuals.

36. *TF*, 137/249–50; *TS*, 125–28/200–5; Hunwick, *Timbuktu and the Songhay Empire*, 172–74. The duties of the *ḥaṣal-farma* (and the *latina-farma*) are not provided; the *arya-farma* may relate to flooding issues. For the latter, see Houdas and Delafosse, *TF*, 216, note 11.

37. *TF*, 138/251–52; *TS*, 128/204–5; Hunwick, *Timbuktu and the Songhay Empire*, 175.

38. *TF*, 138–42/251–57.

39. *TS*, 128/204–5; Hunwick, *Timbuktu and the Songhay Empire*, 175. The *bana-farma* seems to have been concerned with paying salaries. Houdas and Delafosse, *TF*, 216, note 5.

40. *TF*, 142–43/258; *TS*, 128–31/205–9; Hunwick, *Timbuktu and the Songhay Empire*, 175–79. Al-Sa'dī mentions others who received sentences or pardons, including Ya'qūb w. Arbanda (nearly flogged to death), the Azawa-*farma* Bukar b. Ya'qūb (imprisoned and later released under the Moroccans); Bukar b. al-Faqqi Dunku (advanced in age and therefore verbally humiliated); Kurka-*mondio* Surku w. Kalasha' (also elderly and released after being disgraced); and Sa'īd Māra (eventually pardoned). The function of the office of *Yāyī-farma* is not provided. Of Yāsī Buru-Bēr, al-Sa'dī says he was one of Dāwūd's "best sons . . . with the most excellent character and greatest virtue, having never committed any reprehensible act, which could not be said for the rest of them!"

41. "An Account of the Sa'dian Conquest of Songhay by an Anonymous Spaniard," in Hunwick, *Timbuktu and the Songhay Empire*, 326. This is translated from Henri de Castries, "La conquête du Soudan par el-Mansour," *Hespéris* 3 (1923): 433–88. This in turn is based upon an appendix in Marcos Jiménez de la Espada, *Libro del conosçiemento de todos los reynos y tierras y señorios que son por el mundo* (Madrid: Imprenta de Fortanet, 1877). The original account is dated 1003–04/1595 and is entitled *Relación de la jornada que el rey de Marruecos he hecho a la conquista del reyno de Gago, primero de la Guinea hacia la parte de la provincia de Quitehoa, y lo que ha sucedido en ella hasta agora.*

42. *TF*, 143/258–59, 145–46/261–62. Here I enter a debate over whether Gao, Kano or Timbuktu was the greatest and most important urban center.

43. *TF*, 145/261; *TS*, 131/208–9; Hunwick, *Timbuktu and the Songhay Empire*, 178–79. Muḥammad Hayku and his brother the Tunṭī-/Tunki-*farma* Tiliti were reportedly so handsome they were followed all around Timbuktu. Isḥāq b. *Askia* Dāwūd named Yimba w. Sāy Wulli/Walu as *fari-mondio*, al-Ḥasan as Timbuktu-*koi*, and Ag-Maẓul as Maghsharan-*koi*. Al- Ḥasan would defect to the Moroccans ("the Arabs"); interestingly, Ag-Maẓul did not.

44. *TF*, 146/262; *TS*, 131–33/209–11; Hunwick, *Timbuktu and the Songhay Empire*, 179–80.

45. *TF*, 146/263; *TS*, 137–38/215–17; Hunwick, *Timbuktu and the Songhay Empire*, 186–88; R. Dozy, *Supplément aux dictionnaires arabes*, ii, 159; Th. Monod, "A propos d'un document concernant la conquête du Soudan par le Pasha Djouder (1591)," *Académie Royale des Sciences d'Outre-Mer, Bulletin des Séances* 4 (1964): 770–91; Ismaël Diadie Haïdara, "La conquête sa'dienne du Songhay: Les questions logistiques," in *Le Maroc et l'Afrique Subsaharienne aux débuts des temps modernes*, 89–118, provides a detailed analysis of Moroccan forces. See also his *El Bajá Yawdar y la conquista saadí del Songhay (1591–1599)* (Almeria: Instituto des Estudios Almerienses, 1993). Houdas and Delafosse and Hunwick translate *al-ʿiljī* as "le renégat" or "the Renegade," with the understanding that the term refers to Christian converts to Islam. As the Anonymous Spaniard also calls them "renegades" ("Account of the Sa'dian Conquest of Songhay by an Anonymous Spaniard," in Hunwick, *Timbuktu and the Songhay Empire*, 319, 330), the term better reflects how Christian Europe viewed them.

46. "Account of the Sa'dian Conquest of Songhay by an Anonymous Spaniard," in Hunwick, *Timbuktu and the Songhay Empire*, 319, 330. As for the term *spahi*, it is transliterated in *TF* 146/263 as *ṣbāḥīa*.

47. *TS*, 137–38/215–16; Hunwick, *Timbuktu and the Songhay Empire*, 186–87, 186, note 5. I believe *bi-ikhbāj* should be *bi-ikhbār*, and translate it as such. According to al-Fishtālī, it was *Askia* Isḥāq's brother, ʿAlī b. *Askia* Dāwūd, who came to Marrakesh, and Hunwick speculates Wuld Kirinfil may have represented himself as such. See Abū Fāris ʿAbd al-ʿAzīz al-Fishtālī, *Manāhil al-Ṣafā' fi ma'āthir mawālīnā al-shurafā'*, ed. ʿAbd al-Karīm Kurayyim (Rabat, Manshūrāt Kulliyat al-ādāb wa'l-ʿulūm al-insāniyya, Jāmi'at Muḥammad al-Khāmis, 1964).

48. *TS*, 137–38/215–17; Hunwick, *Timbuktu and the Songhay Empire*, 186–88; "Letter from *Mūlāy* Aḥmad al-Manṣur to *Askiya* Isḥāq II, dated Ṣafar 998/December 1589," in Hunwick, *Timbuktu and the Songhay Empire*, 294–96.

49. See Hunwick, *Timbuktu and the Songhay Empire*, 187–88, note 11.

50. What follows can be found in *TF*, 146–84/263–321; *TS*, 138–52/215–17; Hunwick, *Timbuktu and the Songhay Empire*, 188–203; "Account of the Sa'dian Conquest of Songhay by an Anonymous Spaniard," in Hunwick, *Timbuktu and the Songhay Empire*, 322–23.

51. The Anonymous Spaniard says the battle lasted two hours. "Account of the Sa'dian Conquest of Songhay by an Anonymous Spaniard," in Hunwick, *Timbuktu and the Songhay Empire*, 323. Regarding tactics and other aspects, see Thierno Mouctar Bah, "La bataille de Tondibi," in *Le Maroc et l'Afrique Subsaharienne aux débuts des temps modernes*, 161–87; R. Rainero, "La bataille de Tondibi (1591) et la conquête marocaine de l'empire songhay," *Genève-Afrique* 5 (1966): 217–47.

52. The authoritative work on the Arma period remains Michel Abitbol, *Tombouctou et les Arma. De la conquête marocaine du Soudan nigérien en 1591 à l'hégémonie de l'empire peul du Maçina en 1853* (Paris: Maisonneuve et Larose, 1979).

53. *TF*, 152/272.

54. This is a point stressed by Thomas A. Hale, "La chute de l'empire Songhay en 1591: Une interpretation comparative à partir des *Tārīkhs* et l'*Epopée d'Askia*

Muḥammad," in *Le Maroc et l'Afrique Subsaharienne aux débuts des temps modernes*, 305–12.

55. Vernet, "Un aspect de la crise Songhay au XVe siècle," 48. Michal Tymowski, "L'économie et la société dans le basin du moyen Niger. Fin du XVIè à XVIIè siècles," *Africana Bulletin* 18 (1973): 9–64, argues for subsequent economic decline.

SELECT BIBLIOGRAPHY

Oral Primary Sources

Adam, M. G. "Légendes historiques du pays de Nioro (Sahel)." *Revue coloniale* 1903: 81–98, 232–48, 354–72, 485–96, 602–20, 734–4; 1904: 117–24, 233–48.

Arnaud, Robert. *L'Islam et la politique musulmane française en Afrique occidentale française.* Paris: Comité de l'Afrique française, 1912.

Bérenger-Féraud, L.J.B. *Les peuplades de la Sénégambie.* Paris: Éditions Ernest Leroux, 1879.

Cissé, Youssouf Tata and Wâ Kamissòko. *La grande geste du Mali: Des origines à la fondation de l'Empire (Traditions de Krina au colloques de Bamako).* Paris: Karthala, 1988.

Cissé, Youssouf Tata and Wâ Kamissòko. *Soundjata, la gloire du Mali: La grande geste du Mali.* Vol. 2. Paris: Karthala, 1991.

Conrad, David C. *Epic Ancestors of the Sunjata Era: Oral Tradition from the Maninka of Guinea.* Madison: U. of Wisconsin Press, 1999.

Conrad, David C. and Djanka Tassey Condé. *A West African Epic of the Mande Peoples.* Indianapolis: Indiana U. Press, 2004.

Courlander, Harold. *A Treasury of African Folklore.* New York: Crown Publishers, 1975.

Delafosse, Maurice. *Historiques et légendaries du Soudan occidentale: Traduites d'un manuscrit arab inédit.* Paris: Comité de l'Afrique française, 1913.

Diakité, Mamadou Aïssa Kaba. "Livre renfermant la généalogie des diverses tribus noires du Soudan et l'histoire des rois après Mahomet, suivant les renseignements fournis par certaines personnes et ceux recueillis dans les anciens livres." Henri Labouret, trans. *Annales d'académie sciences coloniales* 3 (1929): 189–225.

Frobenius, Leo. *The Voice of Africa.* Vol. 2. London: Hutchinson and Co., 1913.

Innes, Gordon. *Sunjata: Three Mandinka Versions.* London: SOAS, 1974.

Keita, Boniface. *Kita dans les années 1910.* Bamako: Éditions Jamana 1988.

Laye, Camara. *The Guardian of the Word: Kouma Lafôlô Kouma.* James Kirkup. trans. New York: Vintage Books, 1984.

Ly-Tall, Madina, Seydou Camara, and Bouna Dioura, *L'histoire du Mandé d'après Jeli Kanku Madi Jabaté de Kéla.* Paris: SCOA, 1987.

Malio, Nouhou. *The Epic of Askia Mohammed.* Thomas A. Hale, ed. and trans. Bloomington and Indianapolis: Indiana U. Press, 1996.

Monteil, Charles. "La légende du Ouagadou et l'histoire des Soninké." *Mélanges ethnologiques* (1953): 362–408.

Niane, Djibril T. *Sundiata: An Epic of Old Mali.* G.D. Pickett, trans. Essex, England: Longman, 1960.

Quiquandon, Captain F. "Histoire de la puissance Mandingue." *Bulletin de la Société de géographie commerciale de Bordeaux* (1892): 305–18, 369–87, 400–29.

Sidibé, B.K. *Sunjata: The Story of Sunjata Keita, Founder of the Mali Empire.* Banjul: Oral History and Antiquities Division of the Vice-President's Office, 1980.

Sisòkò, Fa-Digi. *The Epic of Son-Jara: A West African Tradition.* John William Johnson, trans. Bloomington: Indiana U. Press, 1992.

Vaisseau Hourst, Lieutenant de. *Sur le Niger et au pays des Touaregs: La mission Hourst.* Paris: Plon, 1898.

Vidal, J. "Le mystère de Ghana." *Bulletin d'Études Historiques et Scientifiques de l'Afrique Occidentale Française* 6 (1923): 512–24.

Vidal, Paul. "La légende officielle de Soundiata fondateur de l'empire Manding." *Bulletin du Comité d'études historiques et scientifiques de l'Afrique occidentale française* 7 (1924): 317–28.

Zeltner, Franz de. *Contes du Sénégal et du Niger.* Paris: Éditions Ernest Leroux, 1913.

Written Primary Sources

Abd al-Rahmān b. 'Abd Allāh al-Sa'dī. *Ta'rīkh as-sūdān.* O. Houdas, ed. and trans. Paris: Librairie d'Amérique et d'Orient Adrien-Maisonneuve, 1900.

Africanus, Leo. *Description of Africa.* Addendum in John O. Hunwick, *Timbuktu and the Songhay Empire. Al-Sa'dī's Ta'rīkh al-sūdān down to 1613 and other Contemporary Documents.* Leiden: E.J. Brill, 1999.

Aḥmad Bābā. "The Fatwā of Aḥmad Bābā al-Tinbuktī: *The Ladder of Ascent Toward Grasping the Law concerning Transported Blacks.*" John O. Hunwick and Fatima Harrak, eds. *Mi'rāj al-ṣu'ūd: Aḥmad Bābā's Replies on Slavery.* Rabat: Institut des Études Africaines, Université Mohamed V, 2000.

Aḥmad Bābā. *Kifāyat al-muḥtāj li-ma'rifat man laysa fī 'l-dībāj.* 2 vols. Edition Muḥammad Muṭī'. Rabat:, al-Mamlakah al-Maghribīyah, Wizārat al-Awqāf wa-al-Shu'ūn al-Islāmīyah, 2000.

Aḥmad Bābā. *Kifāyat al-muḥtāj li-ma'rifat man laysa fī 'l-dībāj.* 2 vols. Edition Abū Yaḥyā 'Abd Allāh al-Kundarī. Beirut: Dār Ibn Ḥazm, 2002.

Aḥmad Bābā. *Nayl al-ibtihāj bi-taṭrīz al-dībāj.* On the margins of Ibn Farhūn. *Al-Dībāj al-mudhahhab fī a'yān 'ulamā' al-madhhab.* Cairo: Maktabāt al-Thaqāfah al-Dīnīyah, 1932–33.

Al-Jirārī. "The Questions of Sa'īd b. Ibrāhīm al-Jirārī of Tuwāt." John O. Hunwick and Fatima Harrak, eds. *Mi'rāj al-ṣu'ūd: Aḥmad Bābā's Replies on Slavery.* Rabat: Institut des Études Africaines, Université Mohamed V, 2000.

Al-Maghīlī. *Sharī'a in Songhay: The Replies of al-Maghīlī to the Questions of Askia al-ḥājj Muḥammad.* John O. Hunwick, trans. Oxford: Oxford U. Press, 1985.

Al-Ṭālib Muḥammad b. Abī Bakr al-Ṣiddīq al-Bartalī al-Walātī. *Fatḥ al-Shakūr fī ma'rifat a'yān 'ulamā' al-Takrūr.* 2 vols. Cairo: Dār Najībawayh lil-Barmajah, 2010.

Azurara, Gomes Eannes de. *The Chronicle of the Discovery and Conquest of Guinea.* London: Hakluyt Society, 1899.

Ca da Mosto, Alvise da. *The Voyages of Cadamosto.* G.R. Crone, ed. London: Hakluyt Society, 1937.

Cherbonneau, M.A. "Essai sur la littérature arabe au Soudan d'aprés le Tekmilat ed-Dibadje d'Ahmed Baba, le Tombouctien," 1–42. *Société Archéologique de la Province de Constantine* (Paris, 1854).

Cuoq, Joseph M. *Recueil des sources arabes concernant l'Afrique occidentale du XIIIe au XVIe siècle (Bilad al-Sudan)*. Paris: Éditions du Centre National de la Recherche Scientifique, 1985.

Fernandes, Valentim. *Description de la Côte d'Afrique de Ceuta au Sénégal*. Paris: Larose, 1938.

Hopkins, J.F.P. and Nehemia Levtzion. *Corpus of Early Arabic Sources for West African History*. Cambridge: Cambridge U. Press, 1981.

Hunwick, John O. *Timbuktu and the Songhay Empire. Al-Sa'dī's Ta'rīkh al-sūdān down to 1613 and other Contemporary Documents*. Leiden: E.J. Brill, 1999.

Ibn Baṭṭūṭa. *Riḥla Ibn Baṭṭūṭa*. Beirut: Dār Ṣadīr,1964.

Ibn Baṭṭūṭa. *Riḥla Ibn Baṭṭūṭa: Al-Musamāh tuḥfat al-nuẓẓār fī gharā'ib al-amṣār wa-'ajā'ib al-asfār*. Cairo: Al-Maktabah al-Tijārīyah al-Kubrā, 1967.

Ibn Khaldūn. *The Muqaddimah: An Introduction to History*. Franz Rosenthal, trans. Princeton: Princeton U. Press, 1967.

Maḥmūd Ka'ti and Ibn al-Mukhtār. *Ta'rīkh al-fattāsh*. O. Houdas and M. Delafosse, eds. and trans. Paris: Librairie d'Amérique et d'Orient Adrien-Maisonneuve, 1913.

Makhlūf al-Balbālī. "Fatwā on the Slaves of the Sūdān." John O. Hunwick and Fatima Harrak, eds. and trans. *Mi'rāj al-ṣu'ūd: Aḥmad Bābā's Replies on Slavery*. Rabat: Institut des Études Africaines, Université Mohamed V, 2000.

Monteil, Charles. "Notes sur le tarikh es-Soudan." *Bulletin de l'Institut Français* (later *Fondamental*) *d'Afrique Noire (IFAN)* 27 (1965): 459–61.

Moraes Farias, Paulo F. de. *Arabic Medieval Inscriptions from the Republic of Mali: Epigraphy, Chronicles, and Songhay-Tuāreg History*. Oxford: Oxford U. Press, 2003.

Muḥammad Bello. *Infāq al-maysūr fī ta'rīkh bilād al-takrūr*. Rabat: Institute of African Studies, 1996.

Palmer, H.R., ed. and trans. *The Kano Chronicle*, in *Sudanese Memoirs: Being Mainly Translations of a Number of Arabic Manuscripts relating to the Western and Central Sudan*. 3 vols. Lagos: Government Printer, 1928; and London: Cass, 1967.

Pereira, Duarte Pacheco. *Esmeraldo de Situ Orbis*. London: Hakluyt Society, 1937.

Sintra, Diogo Gomes de. *El descubrimiento de Guinea y de las islas occidentals*. Seville: Universidad de Sevilla, 1992.

Usuman dan Fodio. *Bayān al-wujūb al-hijra 'alā 'l-ibād*. F.H. El Masri, ed. and trans. Khartoum: Oxford U. Press, 1978.

Usuman dan Fodio. "Kitāb al-Farq." Mervyn Hiskett, trans. *Bulletin of the School of Oriental and African Studies* 23 (1960): 558–79.

Secondary Scholarship

Abitbol, Michel. *Tombouctou et les Arma. De la conquête marocaine du Soudan nigérien en 1591 à l'hégémonie de l'empire peul du Maçina en 1853*. Paris: Maisonneuve et Larose, 1979.

Aghnides, Nicolas P. *Mohammedan Theories of Finance*. Lahore: Premier Book House, 1961.

Ajayi, J.F. Ade and Michael Crowder, eds. *History of West Africa*. 3rd ed. London: Longman, 1985.

Austen, Ralph A. and Jan Jansen. "History, Oral Transmission and Structure in Ibn Khaldun's Chronology of Mali Rulers." *History in Africa* 23 (1996): 17–28.

Austen, Ralph A., ed. *In Search of Sunjata: The Mande Epic as History, Literature, and Performance*. Bloomington and Indiana: Indiana U. Press, 1999.

Ba, A. Konaré. *Sonni Ali Ber*. Niamey: Études Nigériennes, 1977.

Barry, Boubacar. *Le royaume du Waalo: Le Sénégal avant le conquête*. Paris: François Maspéro, 1972.

Barry, Boubacar. *Senegambia and the Atlantic Slave Trade*. Cambridge: Cambridge U. Press 1998.

Bathily, Abdoulaye. *Les portes de l'or: le royaume de Galam, Sénégal, de l'ère musulmane aux temps négriers, VIIIe- XVIIIe siècle*. Paris: L'Harmattan, 1989.

Bulman, Stephen. "A Checklist of Published Versions of the Sunjata Epic." *History in Africa* 24 (1997): 71–94.

Burbank, Jane and Frederick Cooper. *Empires in World History: Power and the Politics of Difference* (Princeton: Princeton U. Press, 2010).

Brun, Joseph P. "Notes sur le Tarikh el-Fettach." *Anthropos* (9) 1914: 590–96.

Cherbonneau, M.A. "Notice sur Ahmed Baba, écrivain berbère e Tombouctou." *Revue Orientale* (1955): 306–14.

Cissé, Youssouf Tata. *La confrérie des chasseurs Malinké at Bambara: mythes, rites et récits initiatiques*. Ivry-sur-Seine: Éditions Nouvelles du Sud, 1994.

Cissoko, Sékéné Mody. *Tombouctou et l'empire Songhay*. Dakar-Abidjan: Les Nouvelles Éditions Africaines, 1975.

Cleaveland, Timothy. *Becoming Walāta: A History of Saharan Social Formation and Transformation*. Portsmouth, N.H.: Heinemann, 2002.

Conrad, David. "From the Banan Tree of Kouroussa: Mapping the Landscape in Mande Traditional History." *Canadian Journal of African Studies* 42 (2008): 384–408.

Conrad, David C. "Oral Sources on Links between Great States: Sumanguru, Servile Lineage, the Jariso, and Kaniaga." *History in Africa* 11 (1984): 35–55.

Conrad, David C. "Searching for History in the Sunjata Epic: The Case of Fakoli." *History in Africa* 19 (1992): 147–200.

Conrad, David C. *Sunjata: A West African Epic of the Mande Peoples*. Indianapolis: Indiana U. Press, 2004.

Conrad, David. "A Town Called Dakajalan: the Sunjata Tradition and the Question of Ancient Mali's Capital." *Journal of African History* 35 (1994): 355–77.

Conrad, David and Humphrey Fisher. "The Conquest that Never Was: Ghana and the Almoravids, 1076." *History in Africa* 9 (1982): 21–59 and 10 (1983): 53–78.

Delafosse, Maurice. *Haut-Sénégal-Niger (Soudan française)*. 3 vols. Paris: Larose, 1912.

Devisse, Jean, ed., *Vallée du Niger*. Paris: Éditions de la Réunion des musées nationaux, 1993.

Dramani-Issifou, Zakari. *L'Afrique noire dans le relations internationals au XVIe siècle. Analyse de la crise entre le Maroc et le Sonrhaï*. Paris: Karthala, 1982.

Dubois, Felix. *Timbuctoo the Mysterious*. London: Longmans, Green, and Co., 1897.

Dupuis-Yacouba, Auguste. *Industries et principales professions des habitants de la région de Tombouctou*. Paris: Larose 1921.

El Hamel, Chouki. *Black Morocco: A History of Slavery, Race, and Islam*. Cambridge: Cambridge U. Press, 2013.

Fisher, H.J. "Leo Africanus and the Songhay Conquest of Hausaland." *International Journal of African Historical Studies* 11 (1978): 86–112.

Gallais, Jean. *Hommes du Sahel: Espaces-Temps et Pouvoir. La Delta intérieur du Niger, 1960–1980*. Paris: Flammarion, 1984.

Gomez, Michael A. *Black Crescent: The Experience and Legacy of African Muslims in the Americas*. Cambridge: Cambridge U. Press, 2005.

Gomez, Michael A. *Pragmatism in the Age of Jihad: The Precolonial State of Bundu*. Cambridge: Cambridge U. Press, 1992.

Gomez, Michael A. "Timbuktu under Imperial Songhay: A reconsideration of Autonomy." *Journal of African History* 31 (1990): 5–24.

Hacquard, A. *Monographie de Tombouctou*. Paris: Société des Études Coloniales et Martimes, 1900.

Hale, Thomas A. and Nouhou Malio. *Scribe, Griot and Novelist: Narrative Interpreters of the Songhay Empire*. Gainesville: U. of Florida Press, 1990.

Hall, Bruce S. *A History of Race in Muslim West Africa, 1600–1960*. Cambridge: Cambridge U. Press, 2011.

Halle, Claude. "Notes sur Koly Tenguella, Olivier de Sanderval et les ruines de Gueme-Sangan." *Recherches Africaines* 1 (1960): 37–41.

Hama, Boubou. *Histoire des Songhay*. Paris: Présence Africaine, 1968.

Herbert, Eugenia. "Timbuktu: A Case Study of the Role of Legend in History," 431–54. In B. Swartz and R.A. Dumett, eds. *West African Cultural Dynamics: Archaeological and Historical Perspectives*. The Hague: Mouton, 1980.

Hunwick, John O. "Askiya al-Ḥājj Muḥammad and His Successors: The Account of al-Imām al-Takrūrī." *Sudanic Africa: A Journal of Historical Sources* 1 (1990): 85–90.

Hunwick, John O. "A Contribution to the Study of Islamic Teaching Traditions in West Africa: The Career of Muḥammad Baghayogho, 930/1523–4—1001/1594." *Islam et societies au sud du Sahara* 4 (1990): 149–63.

Hunwick, John O. "Gao and the Almoravids Revisited: Ethnicity, Political Change and the Limits of Interpretation." *Journal of African History* 35 (1994): 271–72.

Hunwick, John O. "Gao and the Almoravids: a hypothesis," 413–30. In B. Swartz and R.A. Dumett, eds. *West African Cultural Dynamics: Archaeological and Historical Perspectives*. The Hague: Walter de Gruyter, 1979.

Hunwick, John O. *Jews of a Saharan Oasis: Elimination of the Tamantit Community*. Princeton: Markus Wiener, 2006.

Hunwick, John O. "The Mid-Fourteenth Century Capital of Mali." *Journal of African History* 14 (1973): 195–208.

Hunwick, John O. "A Note on Askiya Muḥammad's Meeting with al-Suyūṭī." *Sudanic Africa: A Journal of Historical Sources* 2 (1991): 175–76.

Hunwick, John O. "Not Yet the Kano Chronicle: King-Lists with and without Narrative Elaboration from Nineteenth-Century Kano." *Sudanic Africa* 4 (1993): 95–130.

Hunwick, John O. "Notes on a Late Fifteenth-Century Document Concerning 'al-Takrūr'," 7–34. In Christopher Allen and R.W. Johnson, eds. *African Perspectives*. Cambridge: Cambridge U. Press 1970.

Hunwick, John O. "Religion and State in the Songhay Empire, 1464–1591." In I.M. Lewis, ed. *Islam in Tropical Africa*. London: Oxford U. Press, 1966.

Hunwick, John O. "Secular Power and Religious Authority in Islam: The Case of Songhay." *Journal of African History* 37 (1996): 175–94.

Hunwick, John O. "Songhay, Borno and the Hausa States, 1450–1600," 1: 323–71. In J.F. Ade Ajayi and Michael Crowder, eds. History of West Africa. 3rd ed. London: Longman, 1985.

Hunwick, John O. "Studies in Ta'rīkh al-fattāsh, I: Its Authors and Textual History." *Research Bulletin Centre of Arabic Documentation* 5 (1969): 57–65.

Hunwick, John O. "Studies in Ta'rīkh al-fattāsh, II: An Alleged Charter of Privilege Issued by Akiya al-ḥājj Muḥammad to the Descendants of Mori Hawgāro." *Sudanic Africa* 3 (1992): 133–46.

Hunwick, John O. "Studies in Ta'rīkh al-fattāsh, III: Ka'ti Origins." http://www.smi.uib.no/sa/12/12TF3.pdf.

Hunwick, John O. and Eve Troutt Powell, eds. *The African Diaspora in the Mediterranean Lands of Islam*. Princeton: Markus Wiener, 2001.

Insoll, Timothy. "Iron Age Gao: An Archaeological Contribution." *Journal of African History* 38 (1997): 1–30.

Jansen, Jan. "Masking Sunjata: A Hermeneutical Critique." *History in Africa* 27 (2000): 131–41.

Jeppie, Shamil and Souleymane B. Diagne, eds. *The Meanings of Timbuktu*. Cape Town: HSTC Press, 2008.

Julien, Charles-André. *Histoire de l'Afrique du Nord: Tunisie, Algérie, Maroc*. Paris: Payot, 1961.

Kaba, Lansiné. "The Pen, the Sword and the Crown: Islam and Revolution in Songhay Reconsidered." *Journal of African History* 25 (1984): 242–51.

Kane, Ousmane Oumar. *Beyond Timbuktu: An Intellectual History of Muslim West Africa*. Cambridge: Harvard University Press, 2016.

Kane, Oumar. *La première hégémonie peule: le Fuuta Tooro de Koli Tengella à Almaami Abdul*. Dakar: Karthala, 2004.

Lange, Dierk. "Les rois de Gao-Sané et les Almoravides." *Journal of African History* 32 (1991): 251–75.

Lange, Dierk. "From Mande to Songhay: Towards a Political and Ethnic History of Medieval Gao." *Journal of African History* 35 (1994): 275–301.

Layya, Julde. *Traditions historiques de l'Anzuru*. Niamey: Centre Régional de Documentation pour la Tradition Orale, Centre Nigérien de Recherches en Sciences Humanities, 1969.

Layya, Julde. *Traditions historiques des ethnies de la region de Dooso (Dosso)*. Niamey: Centre Régional de Recherche et Documentation pour la Tradition Orale, 1970.

Levtzion, Nehemiah. *Ancient Ghana and Mali*. New York and London: Africana Publishing Co., 1973.

Levtzion, Nehemiah. "Maḥmūd Ka'ti fut-il l'auteur du Ta'rīkh al-fattāsh." *Bulletin de l'Institut Français* (later *Fondamental*) *d'Afrique Noire (IFAN)* 33 (1974): 665–74.

Levtzion, Nehemiah. "A Seventeenth-Century Chronicle by Ibn al-Mukhtār: A Critical Study of the Ta'rīkh al-fattāsh." *Bulletin of the School of Oriental and African Studies* 34 (1971): 571–93.

Levtzion, Nehemiah. "Was Maḥmūd Ka'ti the Author of the Ta'rīkh al-Fattāsh." Research Bulletin Centre of Arabic Documentation, University of Ibadan 6–1/2 (1970): 1–12.

Ly, Madina. "A propos de la continuité des dynasties Za et des Sonnis dans l'empire Songhay." *Bulletin de l'Institut Français* (later *Fondamental*) *d'Afrique Noire (IFAN)* 37 (1975): 315–17.

Ly, Madina. "Quelques remarques sur le Tarikh el-Fettâch." *Bulletin de l'Institut Français* (later *Fondamental*) *d'Afrique Noire (IFAN)* 34 (1972): 471–93.

Ly-Tall, Madina. *Contribution à l'histoire de l'empire du Mali (XIIIe—XVIe siècles).* Dakar: Nouvelles Éditions Africaines, 1975.

Lydon, Ghislaine. *On Trans-Saharan Trails: Islamic Law, Trade Networks, and Cross-Cultural Exchange in Nineteenth-Century Western Africa.* Cambridge: Cambridge U. Press, 2012.

Maïga, Aboubakr Ismaïl. *La culture et l'enseignement islamiques au Soudan Occidental de 400 à 1000h sous les empires du Ghana, du Mali et du Songhay.* Niamey: Édition, 2003.

Manning, Patrick. *Slavery and African Life: Occidental, Oriental, and African Slave Trades.* Cambridge: Cambridge U. Press, 1990.

Le Maroc et l'Afrique Subsaharienne aux débuts des temps modernes: Les Sa'diens et l'empire Songhay. Actes du Colloque International organisé par l'Institut des Études Africaines [Université Mohammed V, Rabat], Marrakech, 23–25 octubre 1992. Rabat: Publications de l'Institut des Études Africaines (Série Colloques et Séminaires, 2), 1995.

Massing, Andreas W. "Baghayogho: A Soninke Muslim Diaspora in the Mande World." *Cahiers d'études africaines* 4 (2004): 887–922.

Mauny, Raymond. *Tableau géographique de l'ouest africain au moyen âge, d'après les sources écrites, la tradition et l'archéologie.* Dakar: IFAN, 1961.

McCall, Daniel F. and Norman R. Bennett, eds. *Aspects of West African Islam.* Boston: Boston U. African Studies Center, 1971.

McIntosh, Roderick J. *Ancient Middle Niger: Urbanism and the Self-Organizing Landscape.* Cambridge: Cambridge U. Press, 2005.

McIntosh, Roderick J. *The Peoples of the Middle Niger: The Island of Gold.* Oxford: Blackwell Publishers, Inc., 1988, 1998.

McIntosh, Susan Keech, ed. *Excavations at Jenne-jeno, Hambarketolo, and Kaniana (Inland Niger Delta, Mali): The 1981 Season.* Berkeley: U. of California Press, 1995.

McIntosh, Susan Keech. "A Reconsideration of Wangāra/Palolus, Island of Gold." *Journal of African History* 22 (1981): 145–58.

McIntosh, Susan Keech. "Recent Archaeological Research and Dates from West Africa." *Journal of African History* 27 (1986): 413–42.

McIntosh, Roderick J. and Susan Keech McIntosh. "The Inland Niger Delta before the Empire of Mali: Evidence from Jenne-jeno." *Journal of African History* 21 (1981): 1–22.

Miner, Horace. *The Primitive City of Timbuctoo.* Princeton: Princeton U. Press, 1953.

Monod, Théodore. "A propos d'un document concernant la conquête du Soudan par le Pasha Djouder (1591)." *Académie Royale des Sciences d'Outre-Mer, Bulletin des Séances* 4 (1964): 770–91.

Monteil, Charles. *Les Bambara du Ségou et du Kaarta: étude historique, ethnologique, et littéraire d'une people du Soudan français*. Paris: Larose, 1924.

Monteil, Charles Monteil. "Les empires du Mali: étude d'histoire et de sociologie soudanaises." *Bulletin du Comité d'études historiques et scientifiques de l'Afrique occidentale française* 12 (1929): 349–50.

Moraes Farias, Paulo F. de. "The Oldest Extant Writing of West Africa: Medieval epigraphs from Essuk, Saney, and Egef-n-Tawaqqast (Mali)." *Journal des africanistes* 60: 2 (1990): 65–113.

Mougin, Louis. "Les premiers sultans sa'dides et le Sahara." *Revue de l'Occident Musulmane et de la Méditerranée* 19 (1975): 169–87.

Niane, Djibril T. "A propos de Koly Tenguella." *Recherches africaines [Études Guinéenes]* 4 (1960): 33–36.

Niane, Djibril T. "Mythes, legends, et sources orals dans l'oeuvre de Mahmoûd Kâti." *Recherches africaines* (4) 1964: 36–42.

Niane, Djibril T. "Recherches sur l'empire du Mali au moyen âge." *Recherches africaine [Études Guinéennes]* 1 (1959): 6–56.

Nobili, Mauro and Mohamed Shahid Mathee. "Towards a New Study of the So-Called Tārīkh al-fattāsh." *History in Africa* 42 (2015): 37–73.

Norris, H.T. "Sanhaja Scholars of Timbuctoo." *Bulletin of the School of Oriental and African Studies* 30 (1967): 634–40.

Norris, H.T. *Saharan Myth and Saga*. Oxford: Oxford U. Press, 1972.

Norris, H.T. *The Tuaregs, Their Islamic Legacy and Its Diffusion in the Sahel*. Warminster: Aris and Phillips, 1975.

Novo, Marta García. "Islamic Law and Slavery in Premodern West Africa." *Entremons: UPF Journal of World History* 2 (2011): 1–20.

Rainero, R. "La bataille de Tondibi (1591) et la conquête marocaine de l'empire songhay." *Genève-Afrique* 5 (1966): 217–47.

Ray, Carina. *Crossing the Color Line: Race, Sex, and the Contested Politics of Colonialism in Ghana*. Columbus, Ohio: Ohio U. Press, 2015.

Roberts, Richard L. *Warriors, Merchants, and Slaves: The State and the Economy in the Middle Niger Valley, 1700–1914*. Stanford: Stanford U. Press, 1974.

Robinson, David. *Chiefs and Clerics: Abdul Bokar Kan and Futa Toro (1853–1891)*. Oxford: Clarendon Press, 1975.

Rouch, Jean. "Contribution à l'histoire des Songhay." *Mémoires de l'IFAN* 29 (1953):137–259.

Rouch, Jean. *Contribution à l'histoire des songhay*. Dakar: IFAN, 1953.

Rouch, Jean. *La religion et la magie songhay*. Paris: Presses Universitaires de France, 1960.

Rouch, Jean. *Les Songhay*. Paris: Presses Universitaires de France, 1954.

Saad, Elias N. *Social History of Timbuktu: The Role of Muslim Scholars and Notables, 1400–1900*. Cambridge: Cambridge U. Press, 1983.

Sardan, Jean-Pierre Olivier de. "Captifs ruraux et esclaves impériaux du Songhay," 99–134. In Claude Meillassoux, ed. *L'esclavage en Afrique précoloniale*. Paris: François Maspéro, 1975.

Sardan, Jean-Pierre Olivier de. *Concepts et conceptions songhay-zarma*. Paris: Nubia, 1982.

Sardan, Jean-Pierre Olivier de. *Les sociétés Songhay-Zarma (Niger-Mali): chefs, guerriers, esclaves, paysans*. Paris: Karthala, 1984.

Sardan, Jean-Pierre Olivier de. "The Songhay-Zarma Female Slave: Relations of Production and Ideological Status," 141–42. In Claire C. Robertson and Martin A. Klein, eds. *Women and Slavery in Africa*. Madison: U. of Wisconsin Press, 1983.

Sardan, Jean-Pierre Olivier de. *Les voleurs d'hommes (notes sur l'histoire des Kurtey)*. Paris: CNRS, 1969.

Sartain, E.M. *Jalāl ad-Dīn as-Suyūtī: Biography and Background*. Cambridge: Cambridge U. Press, 1975.

Sartain, E.M. "Jalāl ad-Dīn as-Suyūtī's Relations with the People of Takrūr." *Journal of Semitic Studies* 16 (1971): 193–98

Sauvaget, Jean. "Les épitaphs royales de Gao." *Bulletin de l'Institut Français* (later *Fondamental) d'Afrique Noire (IFAN)* 12 (1950): 418–40.

Sauvaget, Jean. "Notes préliminaires sur les épitaphs royales de Gao," *Revue des Études Islamiques* (1948): 7–8.

Soumalia, Hammadou, Moussa Hamidou, and Diouldé Laya. *Traditions des Songhay de Tera (Niger)*. Paris: Karthala, 1998.

Stewart, Charles. *Islam and Social Order in Mauritania*. Oxford: Clarendon Press, 1973.

Tauxier, Louis. *Histoire des Bambara*. Paris: P. Geuthner, 1942.

Tauxier, Louis. *Moeurs et histoire des Peuls*. Paris: Payot, 1937.

Trout Powell, Eve M. *Tell This in My Memory: Stories of Enslavement from Egypt, Sudan, and the Ottoman Empire*. Stanford: Stanford U. Press, 2012.

Tymowski, Michal. "Légitimation du pouvoir de la dynastie Askia au Songhay du XVè siècle: Islam et culture locale." *Hemispheres* 7 (1990): 189–98.

Tymowski, Michal. *The Origins and Structures of Political Institutions in Pre-Colonial Black Africa: Dynastic Monarchy, Taxes and Tributes, War and Slavery, Kinship and Territory*. Lewiston, NY: Edwin Mellen Press, 2009.

Ware III, Rudolph T. *The Walking Qur'an: Islamic Education, Embodied Knowledge, and History in West Africa*. Chapel Hill: UNC Press, 2014.

Webb, James. *Desert Frontier: Ecological and Economic Change along the Western Sahel, 1600–1850*. Madison: U. of Wisconsin Press, 1995.

Wright, Donald R. "Koli Tengela in Sonko Traditions of Origin: An Example of the Process of Change in Mandinka Oral Tradition." *History in Africa* 5 (1978): 257–71.

Zouber, Mahmoud Abdou. *Aḥmad Baba de Tombouctou (1556–1627): sa vie et son œuvre*. Paris: Maisonneuve et Larose,, 1977.

Zouber, Mahmoud Abdou. *Traditions historiques Songhoy (Tindirma, Morikoyra, Arham)*. Niamey: Centre d'Études Linguistiques et Historiques pour la Tradition Orale, 1983.

INDEX

Abbasid *sharīf*, 328
Abbasids, 39, 235, 245, 328
'Abd 'Allāh b. ("son of") Yāsīn, 36–37. *See also* Almoravids
'Abd al-Jabbar (*faqīh*), 198
'Abd al-Malik (son of *Askia* Isḥāq Bēr), 335
'Abd al-Raḥmān (*qāḍī* of Mali), 155, 164
'Abd al-Raḥmān al-Tamīmī, 196
'Abd al-Raḥmān b. ("son of") 'Abd Allāh b. 'Imrān al-Sa'dī, 92, 171–77, 181, 186–91, 194–99, 204–9, 214–17, 221, 228–29, 232–36, 241–47, 256, 281–90, 296–302, 309–11, 316–30, 336–39, 355–67. See also *Ta'rīkh as-sūdān*
'Abd al-Raḥmān b. ("son of") Abū 'Abd Allāh Anda ag-Muḥammad the Elder, 216, 291; daughters, 217
'Abd al-Raḥmān b. ("son of") Abī Bakr (temporary *qāḍī* of Timbuktu), 271–72
'Abd al-Wāsi'a al-Masrātī (merchant), 345–46
"Abdā" (or Abda, name of a plantation), 340–51, 353–54. *See also* plantation
Abdelhamid Abu Zayd, 369–72
'abīd ("slaves," s. *'abd*), 136, 139, 161, 261, 302, 338, 340–51, 353–54. *See also* slavery
Abū 'l-Abbās Aḥmad b. ("son of") *al-faqīh* Muḥammad al-Sa'īd (grandson of *Qāḍī* Maḥmūd b. 'Umar), 179, 285–86, 295, 351
Abū 'l-Abbās Aḥmad b. ("son of") al-Ḥāk (Mamluk official), 116–19. See also *mihmandār*
Abū 'l-'Abbas Aḥmad Buryu ("the Handsome") b. ("son of") Aḥmad (*faqīh*), 216–17
Abū 'Abd Allāh Anda ag-Muḥammad the Elder (*qāḍī* of Timbuktu), 193–97, 215–17, 250, 271, 281–83, 290–91, 295–96, 339
Abū 'Abd Allāh Anda ag-Muḥammad b. ("son of") al-Mukhtār al-Naḥwī (*imām* of Sankore mosque), 216
Abū 'Abd Allāh *Modibo* Muḥammad al-Kāborī (a *walī*), 156, 214–17, 259, 283–88, 293–95
Abū 'Abd Allāh Muḥammad (*qāḍī* from Sijilmasa), 155
Abū 'Abd Allāh Muḥammad b. ("son of") Wāsūl, 134
Abū Bakar/Muḥammad b. ("son of") Abī Bakr al-Tūrī (father of *Askia al-ḥājj* Muḥammad), 229
Abū Bakr/Bata Manden Bori/Abubakar II, 94–95, 98
Abū Bakr b. ("son of") Aḥmad Bēr, 272, 292, 296
Abū Bakr b. ("son of") *al-ḥājj* Aḥmad b. 'Umar b. Muḥammad Aqīt, 284, 292
Abū Bakr b. ("son of") *al-Qāḍī* al-Ḥājj, 198–99, 272
Abū Ḥafṣ 'Umar *al-ḥājj* Aḥmad b. ("son of") 'Umar b. Muḥammad Aqīt (*faqīh*), 291–92
Abū Ḥāmid, 48, 53
Abū 'l-Ḥasan (Marinid sultan), 104, 145–47
Abū 'l-Ḥasan 'Alī b. ("son of") Amīr Ḥājib (governor of Old Cairo), 100, 107, 115, 119, 159
Abū 'Inān (Marinid sultan), 148
Abū Muḥammad 'Abd Allāh (*muftī* and grandson of *al-ḥājj* Aḥmad b. ("son of") 'Umar b. Muḥammad Aqīt), 217
Abū 'l-Rūḥ 'Īsā al-Zawāwī (*faqīh*), 108–9, 121
Abū Tāshfīn (Tlemcen ruler), 104, 117
Abū Zayd 'Abd al-Raḥmān b. ("son of") *Qāḍī* Maḥmūd b. 'Umar (Timbuktu), 217, 291, 294
al-'Adāla (sultan of Agades), 239
Adelāsegh and Aligurran (oral tradition), 227–28
Adiki-*farma* (unspecified office), 309
Agades, 7, 22, 95, 223, 236–39, 243, 248, 255–56, 310, 366. *See also* Air
Agadir, 353
age of jihad (in West Africa), 19

A NOTE ON THE TYPE

THIS BOOK has been composed in Miller, a Scotch Roman typeface designed by Matthew Carter and first released by Font Bureau in 1997. It resembles Monticello, the typeface developed for The Papers of Thomas Jefferson in the 1940s by C. H. Griffith and P. J. Conkwright and reinterpreted in digital form by Carter in 2003.

Pleasant Jefferson ("P. J.") Conkwright (1905–1986) was Typographer at Princeton University Press from 1939 to 1970. He was an acclaimed book designer and AIGA Medalist.

The ornament used throughout this book was designed by Pierre Simon Fournier (1712–1768) and was a favorite of Conkwright's, used in his design of the *Princeton University Library Chronicle.*